Contents

KT-467-769

Festivals of Taiwan
colour section following
p.264

**Taiwan's National
Parks** colour section
following p.392

◀◀ Dragon dance during Keelung Ghost Festival ◀ Taipei, Baoan Temple door god

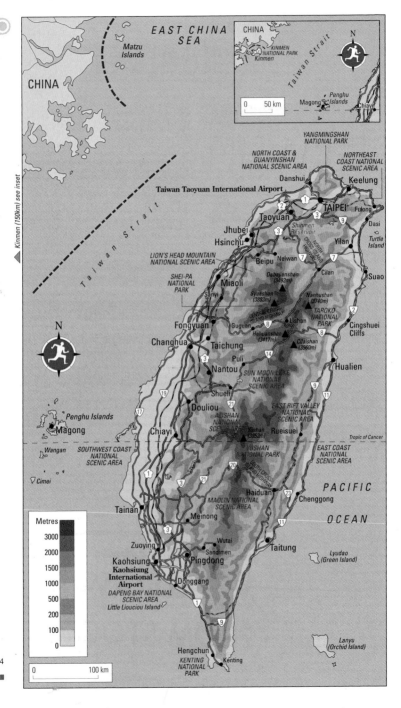

EAST CHINA
SEA

*Matzu
Islands*

CHINA

CHINA

KINMEN
NATIONAL PARK
Kinmen

Taiwan Strait

0   50 km

*Penghu
Islands*
Magong   Chiayi

YANGMINGSHAN
NATIONAL PARK

NORTH COAST &
GUANYINSHAN
NATIONAL SCENIC AREA

NORTHEAST
COAST NATIONAL
SCENIC AREA

Danshui

Keelung

Taiwan Taoyuan International Airport

TAIPEI   Fulong

Taoyuan

Shihmen
Reservoir

Jhubei

Dasi

Hsinchu

Yilan

Turtle
Island

LION'S HEAD MOUNTAIN
NATIONAL SCENIC AREA

Beipu   Neiwan

Cilan

Suao

SHEI-PA
NATIONAL
PARK

Miaoli

*Dabajianshan
(3492m)*

Sanyi

*Syueshan
(3883m)*

*Nanhushan
(3740m)*

TAROKO
NATIONAL
PARK

Fongyuan   Guguan   Lishan

*Hehuanshan
(3417m)*

*Cilaishan
(3560m)*

Cingshuei
Cliffs

Changhua

Taichung

Puli

Nantou

SUN MOON LAKE
NATIONAL
SCENIC AREA

Hualien

Shuei

Douliou

ALISHAN
NATIONAL
SCENIC AREA

EAST RIFT VALLEY
NATIONAL
SCENIC AREA

Chiayi

*Yushan
(3952m)*

Rueisuei

Tropic of Cancer

Wangan

SOUTHWEST COAST
NATIONAL
SCENIC AREA

YUSHAN
NATIONAL PARK

EAST COAST
NATIONAL
SCENIC AREA

Cimei

Haiduan

Chenggong

PACIFIC

Tainan

MAOLIN NATIONAL
SCENIC AREA

Meinong

OCEAN

Zuoying

Wutai

Kaohsiung

Sandimen

Taitung

*Lyudao
(Green Island)*

**Kaohsiung
International
Airport**

Pingdong

DAPENG BAY NATIONAL
SCENIC AREA
Little Liouciou Island

Donggang

*Lanyu
(Orchid Island)*

Metres

3000
2000
1500
1000
500
200
100
0

Penghu Islands

Magong

N

Taiwan Strait

Hengchun

KENTING
NATIONAL
PARK

Kenting

0   100 km

Introduction to
Taiwan

Taiwan is the most underrated tourist destination in Asia. It's hard to understand why – it has some of the most captivating scenery anywhere on the planet, sensational cuisine and a fascinating cultural mix. In the 1990s Taiwan became the first true Chinese democracy, developing a sense of civil society bewildering to its giant neighbour across the Taiwan Strait. Since then popular culture has blossomed on the island, an eclectic mix of Chinese, Western, Japanese and indigenous influences.

But Taiwan is also an intensely traditional place, with Chinese and aboriginal festivals, performing arts and religious belief preserving a legacy that goes back millennia. Taiwan's hinterland offers more surprises: towering mountains, including Northeast Asia's tallest, six national parks, a selection of alluring offshore islands and, thanks to its volcanic past, numerous hot-spring resorts.

Taiwan's perception problem stems in part from its astonishing economic success. The **Taiwan Miracle**, the island's transformation into one of the world's richest countries in less than fifty years, created images of endless manufacturing plants, a pile of overcrowded cities and factories somewhere off China's southeast coast. The country's long struggle to establish a distinct political and cultural identity in the shadow of its big brother on the mainland hasn't helped – for years its rulers insisted that Taiwan was the "real China". Not any more: Taiwan has preserved much of the civilization and many

Fact file

- Lying just 130km off the southeast coast of China at its closest point, the island of Taiwan is slightly larger than Belgium, and bisected by the Tropic of Cancer.

- The population of 23 million is ethnically 98 percent Han Chinese, with the remaining two percent made up by the Austronesian indigenous population.

- Known as Formosa in the West until the 1950s, Taiwan's official name has been the Republic of China (ROC) since 1949.

- Almost half of Taiwan is covered by mountains, with 258 peaks over 3000m: the tallest is Yushan (3952m). The Jhuoshuei River is the island's longest (186km).

- Taiwan is a democracy with the president directly elected by universal suffrage every four years, and empowered to appoint the premier who assembles a cabinet comprising the heads of all ministries, known as the Executive Yuan. The Legislative Yuan acts as Taiwan's parliament, its members also elected every four years.

- Taiwan's main exports are electronics (including 75 percent of the world's laptop computers and 40 percent of its LCD screens), mechanical appliances and plastics. Taiwan's per-capita GDP is around US$25,000 (PPP basis).

of the traditions lost on the mainland, but while its political future remains uncertain, Taiwan is fast developing a dynamic culture all of its own.

One of the most endearing things about the island is the overwhelming **friendliness** of its people – Taiwan is one of the most welcoming countries in the world, and you are bound to encounter numerous acts of generosity or kindness throughout your travels, whether it's a taxi driver rounding down a fare, a stranger offering to buy a ticket or help with directions, or a family providing a lift or even a bed for the night. **Eating** in Taiwan comes a close second, a vast array of Chinese food and local delicacies on offer in every town and locale. Travelling around the island is relatively straightforward, though the lack of English can make things a challenge at times, particularly as most timetables tend to be displayed solely in Chinese. Taiwan is a relatively rich country compared to

▲ Matzu, Chiang Kai-shek statue on Nangan

Hot springs

With over 150 locations scattered all over the island, Taiwan has the world's second highest concentration of hot springs after Japan – many were developed commercially during the Japanese occupation and offer the same quality, scenery and therapeutic effects at a fraction of the cost. Many of the most famous springs are piped directly into hotel rooms and spa pools, where you can sample the waters via public baths or private tubs, but there are still places, usually in the mountains, where springs gush naturally from rocks or rivers and can be experienced for free. It's important to acquaint yourself with hot-spring etiquette before having a dip: unless the pools are mixed sex, you're expected to be naked, and you should shower before getting in. It's best to wait at least an hour after eating before bathing, and to avoid hot springs altogether if you've been drinking alcohol.

China or southeast Asia, but prices are generally lower than in most other developed nations, and the willingness of almost every one you meet to help means it's almost impossible to get stuck.

Where to go

Most visits to Taiwan begin in **Taipei**, the capital and largest city, home to Taipei 101, the National Palace Museum and some of the island's best restaurants, bars and night markets. It's also surrounded by a host of worthy day-trips including the hot springs at **Beitou** and the volcanic peaks of **Yangmingshan National**

Taiwanese food

Taiwan is celebrated for its **"little eats"** (*xiaochi*), tasty snack food typically served in small portions at **night markets** all over Taiwan. **Taiwanese cuisine** has its foundation in Fujianese cooking, but has been influenced by almost every other region of China, each town and village special-izing in a particular dish: beef

▲ Night markets

noodles in Taipei, *danzi* noodles in Tainan, meatballs in Changhua, rice noodles in Hsinchu, and fish balls and milkfish in Kaohsiung – all washed down by large quantities of *Taiwan Beer* or *Kaoliang* liquor, the specialty of Kinmen. Taiwan's wet, tropical climate also makes it ideal for a vast range of **tropical fruits**, from the relatively humble banana, to bright pink dragonfruit. For more on food in Taiwan see Basics p.37.

Park. The north coast is also just a short bus ride away, its storm-battered shore encompassed by the **North Coast and Guanyinshan National Scenic Area**. Inland from the forts and wonderful night market in **Kee-lung** lies the **Pingsi Branch Line Railway** and picturesque Shihfen Falls, while the old mining towns of **Jinguashi** and **Jiufen** are deservedly popular for their historic streets and teahouses, and the **Northeast Coast National Scenic Area** contains some of the most rugged coastline on the island. Southwest of Taipei, the **Northern Cross-Island Highway** is a winding, scenic route that connects the historic town of Dasi with the Atayal village

◄ Taipei, Changing of the guard at CKS Memorial

of Baling, high in the mountains. Further south along the coastal plain, **Hsinchu** makes an excellent base for trips to **Hakka country**, while the rustic temples and giant Buddha statue in **Lion's Head Mountain Scenic Area** border the **Shei-Pa National Park**, providing an opportunity to tackle some of Taiwan's largest and most memorable peaks. Nearby **Taian Hot Springs** is perhaps the island's most alluring hot-spring resort.

Central Taiwan is home to some spectacular scenery, though it pays to spend a couple of days in vibrant **Taichung**, Taiwan's third largest city, renowned for its teahouses and lively nightlife. Not far from the city, **Dajia**'s annual Mazu Pilgrimage is Taiwan's largest religious festival, while **Changhua** is noted principally for its Great Buddha Statue, one of Asia's biggest, and atmospheric **Lugang** is a historic town celebrated for its craftsmen and classical architecture. East of Taichung, picture-perfect **Sun Moon Lake** makes a fitting introduction to Taiwan's mighty central ranges, a place for languid lakeside walks and gorgeous views. Just outside Puli, to the north of the lake, **Chung Tai Chan Monastery** is a man-made wonder, a remarkable blend of modern architecture and Zen Buddhism. Heading south, **Chiayi** provides a staging post for the great Mazu temple

> While its political future remains uncertain, Taiwan is fast developing a dynamic culture all its own.

at **Beigang**, as well as the Alishan Forest Railway, an engineering marvel that links the tropical plains with the cool valleys and Tsou villages of the **Alishan National Scenic Area**. Beyond this lies **Yushan National Park** and the scintillating hike up Taiwan's highest mountain, commanding awe-inspiring, cloud-capped vistas.

9

Betel nut

Betel nut, the seed of the Betel Palm (*Areca catechu*), has almost iconic status in Taiwan, where chewing it is viewed as stereotypically Hoklo or Taiwanese behaviour. It's also big business: some estimates claim the industry nets annual revenue of around NT$100bn. In Taiwan it's particularly popular with truck drivers, who prefer its stimulating effects to coffee: the nut is wrapped in *areca* leaf, topped with slaked lime paste and chewed without swallowing. Its most celebrated by-product is the **betel nut beauty** (*binlang xishi*), scantily clad girls hired to sell the nuts from glass-encased booths on roadsides all over the island. In 2002 excessive nudity was banned within Taipei, but elsewhere the girls are as prolific as ever, and their outfits just as revealing: their images have become as iconic as the nut itself. More ominously, betel nut is a known **carcinogen**: Taiwan now has one of the highest rates of mouth and throat cancer in Asia, a statistic most doctors link with chewing the nut.

South Taiwan is the most traditional part of the island and the area first colonized by the Chinese, with **Tainan,** Taiwan's first capital, making the obvious introduction to the region, a modern city crammed with historic sights and particularly temples, complemented by superb food. To the north, the **Southwest Coast National Scenic Area** brings together salt mountains and impressive religious sites, while the dramatic **Southern Cross-Island Highway** heads east across the mountains to Taitung, slicing through the northern end of **Maolin National Scenic Area**, rich in Paiwan and Rukai culture. **Kaohsiung** is Taiwan's second city and an earthy counterweight to Taipei, its smattering of sights enhanced by a growing number of parks, outdoor cafés and bars. Nearby is the elegant monastery at **Foguangshan** while **Donggang**, Taiwan's tuna-fish capital, lies on the coast to the south, opposite the attractive coral island of **Little Liouciou**. The southern tip of Taiwan is dominated by **Kenting National Park**, with its popular beaches and surf spots.

The **east coast** is a world apart, isolated from the rest of Taiwan until very recently and still home to the greatest concentration of its indigenous tribes. Most visitors make for **Taroko National Park**, with spectacular Taroko Gorge at its heart, in parts an incredibly narrow gap between lofty walls of stone. **Hualien** is the largest settlement on the east coast and makes the ideal gateway to Taroko, with plenty of opportunities to buy its famous

marble, tasty dumplings and sweet-filled rice cakes. From here there are two routes south: the East Rift Valley is noted for its hot springs and rafting on the Siouguluan River, while the coastal road twists past isolated beaches and Ami villages. Both end up at the laid-back town of **Taitung**, location of the National Museum of Prehistory and base for trips to **Lyudao** (Green Island) with its exceptional outdoor springs. Further offshore is **Lanyu** (Orchid Island), the enchanting ocean home of the Tao tribe.

Taiwan's offshore islands, with their own distinctive cultures and histories, are less visited but equally rewarding destinations. **Penghu**, in the middle of the Taiwan Strait, is an archipelago of magnificent beaches, old temples and crumbling fishing villages, a haven for windsurfing and other water sports. Just off the coast of China's Fujian province, the **Matzu Islands** provide a rare taster of traditional northern Fujian culture, as well as Taiwan's recent military history. The theme is continued on **Kinmen**, literally within sight of the now booming mainland city of Xiamen and rapidly remodelling itself as an open-air museum.

When to go

Taiwan has a subtropical monsoon **climate**, with wet, humid summers and short, relatively mild winters (though it often snows on the highest peaks). The north tends to be several degrees colder, and a lot wetter than the tropical south. The island is affected by two separate monsoons: the **northeast monsoon** lasts about six months from October to late March and brings wet weather to Keelung and the northeast side

▲ Mazu at Kaiji Tianhou Temple in Tainan

of the island, while central and southern regions stay relatively dry. The **southwest monsoon** starts in May and ends in late September, primarily affecting the south. The latter part of this monsoon season is associated with **typhoons** that batter the east coast and central mountain range, with an average two to three direct hits a year. That's not the end of the rain, however – the annual "**plum rain**" season can bring two months of rain any time between early spring and early summer, affecting the whole island.

Temples

Taiwan is a land of temples, monasteries and shrines, home to a vast pantheon of Taoist gods and one of the world's great centres of Buddhism. Taiwanese temples are incredibly opulent, gaudy affairs: most traditional, classical-style temples feature gable-and-hip roofs with double eaves, embellished with ornate, multicoloured dragons. Outside, lions and colourfully painted door gods protect the gates, while the main halls are atmospheric, incense-filled shrines, often busy with worshippers and crammed with intricate carvings, paintings and dragon pillars. The chief deities are represented by numerous images in the heart of the temple, often the scene of fortune-telling, chanting and other religious rituals. See Contexts p.532, for more on temples.

▼ Taipei, Longshan Temple entrance

In winter, the average monthly **temperature** ranges from 15 to 20°C across the island, while mid-30s are common in the summer. Temperatures in the high mountains can be substantially lower than on the plains. In general, autumn and winter are the best times to visit, though early summer (May to July) can also be pleasant at higher elevations and in the north, and the high temperatures in midsummer make water sports and beaches far more tempting.

Domestic tourism is big business in Taiwan, which means travelling at the **weekends** can be a frustrating experience, shared with vast hordes of local tourists – it also pays to be aware of **local holidays**, when all the major sights (and forms of transport) will be packed (see Basics p.50).

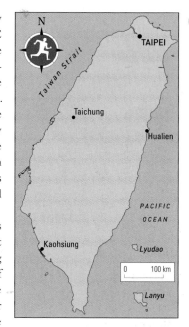

Average daily temperatures and monthly rainfall

	Jan	Feb	Mar	Apr	May	Jun	Jul	Aug	Sep	Oct	Nov	Dec
Taipei												
max (°C)	19	19	22	26	29	32	34	34	31	28	24	21
min (°C)	13	14	15	19	22	24	26	26	24	22	19	15
rainfall (mm)	87	166	180	183	259	319	248	305	275	139	86	79
Taichung												
max (°C)	22	22	25	28	30	32	33	32	32	30	27	24
min (°C)	12	13	16	19	22	24	25	25	24	21	18	14
rainfall (mm)	36	88	94	135	225	343	246	317	98	16	18	26
Kaohsiung												
max (°C)	23	24	27	28	30	32	32	32	31	30	27	25
min (°C)	15	16	19	22	24	26	26	26	25	24	20	17
rainfall (mm)	20	24	39	73	177	398	371	426	187	46	13	12
Hualien												
max (°C)	21	21	23	26	28	30	32	32	30	28	25	22
min (°C)	15	16	17	20	22	24	25	25	24	22	19	17
rainfall (mm)	72	100	87	96	195	220	1	1	344	367	171	68

things not to miss

It's not possible to see everything Taiwan has to offer in a single trip – and we don't suggest you try. What follows is a selective taste of the island's highlights: vibrant temples and monasteries, exuberant festivals, mouthwatering cuisine and spectacular landscapes. They're arranged in five colour-coded categories with a page reference to take you straight into the guide, where you can find out more.

01 National Palace Museum Page **112** • View the former contents of Beijing's Forbidden City in this world-famous museum, an extraordinary collection of Chinese art and historical artefacts.

02 Climbing Yushan Page **301** • At 3952m, Yushan (Jade Mountain) is far and away northeast Asia's highest peak, but a spectacular and well-trodden trail to the summit makes it surprisingly accessible.

03 Taipei 101 Page **116** • At 509m, the world's tallest building dominates central Taipei, providing mind-blowing views of the surrounding area.

04 Festivals Page **50** • Taiwan's festivals are often loud, boisterous affairs associated with the vast pantheon of Chinese gods, involving floating lanterns, exuberant parades and tons of fireworks. See also the *Festivals of Taiwan* colour section.

05 Taichung teahouses Page **245** • Taiwan is littered with teahouses, but the greatest variety can be found in Taichung, the home of "bubble-tea", where they range from classical Chinese to hip contemporary cafés.

07 Kinmen Page **463** • This island is the frontline between Taiwan and China - the latter is literally a stone's throw away - and now an absorbing blend of former battlefields and well-preserved imperial Chinese monuments.

06 Chung Tai Chan Monastery Page **273** • Nothing else quite looks like this enormous Buddhist monastery, packed with artistic gems, elegant shrines and innovative architecture.

08 Alishan Forest Railway Page **297** • The crown jewel of Taiwan's narrow-gauge rail lines, this historic train takes passengers on an amazing climb from lowland rice paddies into age-old alpine forests.

09 Northeast Coast National Scenic Area Page **183** • The magnificent stretch of coastline east of Keelung is riddled with sandy beaches, ample surf and fantastic cliff-top trails with spectacular views of enigmatic Turtle Island.

10 Night markets Page **175** • Taiwan's night markets are the best and cheapest places to try a selection of the island's famous "little eats".

11 Big Buddhas Page **256** • Taiwan is littered with huge statues of Buddha, from the 72m giant at Emei Lake to the tranquil image in Changhua, in addition to numerous oversized gods from the Taoist pantheon.

13 Matzu Islands Page **497** • Scattered just off the coast of mainland China, these seldom visited – and heavily militarized – islands are bastions of northern Fujianese architecture, culture and food.

12 East Coast National Scenic Area Page **408** • From the north's towering cliffs to the south's expansive beaches, the east coast is a feast for the eyes and is a hotbed of aboriginal cultures.

14 Surfing Page **60** • The island's lengthy stretch of Pacific coastline has vastly underrated surfing, with countless breaks – and plenty of typhoon swell – to challenge both beginners and serious shredders.

15 **Sun Moon Lake** Page **275** • One of the island's most relaxing retreats, with nature walks, cool breezes, calming views and a shoreline brimming with cultural interest.

16 **Adventure sport** Page **54** • With some of Asia's most rugged wilderness, the island's mountains, rivers and sea offer an adventure-sport paradise of trekking, mountain biking, white-water rafting, windsurfing and paragliding.

17 **Dajia Mazu pilgrimage** Page **250** • One of the world's biggest festivals
involves thousands of pilgrims on an animated seven-day parade circuit between the
revered Mazu temples in Dajia and Singang.

19 **Hakka culture** Page **204**
• Hakka culture, characterized
by delicate arts and crafts and delicious
cuisine, is undergoing a revival in Taiwan,
most evident in regional centres such as
Beipu and Meinong.

18 **Lugang** Page **257** • Taiwan's most
attractive old town, with traditional
architecture, beautiful temples, tasty snack food
and shops stocked with the work of the island's
most accomplished craftsmen.

20 Lanyu (Orchid Island) Page
432 • Inhabited almost solely by the seafaring Tao tribe, whose traditional ways of life give this lush Pacific island an almost Polynesian flavour.

22 Taroko National Park
Page **395** • Taiwan's most visited national park is sliced in half by narrow, deep-cut Taroko Gorge, one of Asia's top natural wonders and an absolute must-see.

21 Aboriginal culture Page 518 •
Taiwan's indigenous peoples, divided into thirteen officially recognized tribes and several other distinct groups, have their own vibrant cultures quite separate from the Chinese majority.

23 Tainan
Page **313** • The old capital of Taiwan remains an important stronghold of Taiwanese culture, its myriad temples the perfect places to absorb its complex religious traditions.

24 **Lishan** Page **226** • Cradled in the heart of the Central Cordillera, this idyllic tea-picking community has magically sculpted hillside terraces and is on the road to Taiwan's second-highest peak, 3886m Syueshan.

25 **Cross-island highways** Page **334** • Three rough-hewn highways wind over the island's mountainous spine in the north, centre and south, making for heart-stopping, white-knuckle rides with spectacular views.

26 **Hot springs** Page **212** • Taiwan has over 150 hot springs, most set among mountainous landscapes and piped into hotel resorts, ranging from the ultra-hip to the cheap and cheerful.

27 **Chaotian Temple, Beigang** Page **289** • Taiwan's temples are opulent, frenetic places of worship, and this one lays claim to some of the most fervent crowds of devotees each and every weekend.

28 **Kenting National Park** Page **371** • Studded with fine-sand beaches and rolling surf, this resort-fringed national park covers Taiwan's southern tip and is a haven of snorkelling and diving.

29 **Lyudao (Green Island)** Page **425** • This tiny volcanic island boasts dramatic coastal scenery and is flanked by thriving coral, home to abundant marine life and some exciting snorkelling.

30 **Penghu Islands** Page **454** • This windswept archipelago in the middle of the Taiwan Strait is a treasure-trove of historic sights, curious geological formations, white-sand beaches and year-round windsurfing.

Basics

Basics

Getting there

Taiwan's main international gateway is Taiwan Taoyuan International Airport, located near the city of Taoyuan, about 50km southwest of the capital Taipei – it handles almost all long-haul flights as well as dozens of daily flights from within Asia. The only other international airport is Kaohsiung International Airport, serving the country's second-largest city. Nearly all of the international traffic into this airport is from Southeast Asia, especially Hong Kong.

Although there are several direct flights to Taipei from North America every day, if you're coming from anywhere else in the world you'll likely have to first stop somewhere else in Asia – and **Hong Kong** is without question the closest and most convenient place, with dozens of regional carriers flying into Taipei and Kaohsiung on a daily basis. Note that there are no direct flights to Taiwan from elsewhere in China.

Fares to Taipei from most places are fairly consistent throughout the year, but during the fortnight just before the Lunar New Year (see p.51) – the biggest holiday of the year for most Chinese people – ticket prices tend to soar for most Asian destinations, and finding available flights can be a real nightmare. Even then, however, you're still likely to find a ticket from Hong Kong to Taipei, but be advised that the high level of domestic travel in Taiwan during this holiday can make it hard for foreigners to get round the country.

From the US and Canada

There are several daily nonstop flights to Taiwan from North American cities on both the east and west coasts. From the **US**, direct flights leave from Honolulu, Los Angeles, New York and San Francisco, with the average return fare hovering between US$600–700. Return flights from west-coast cities, booked online, often come in well under the US$600 mark. Most flights from **Canada** transit through Vancouver.

From the UK and Ireland

There has long been a dearth of direct air connections between the **UK** and Taiwan, and the same is true when flying from

Ireland or continental Europe. Almost all travellers coming from Europe will need to make at least one stop, with the closest and most convenient being **Hong Kong**, followed by Bangkok.

At the time of writing, the only airline with direct flights from **London** to Taipei was one of Taiwan's two national carriers, EVA Air, which flies 6 days a week via Bangkok (15hr) for about £700 return. The same airline also offered direct flights from **Paris** (thrice weekly; 12hr 50min) and services via Hong Kong from Amsterdam (four weekly; 15hr) and Vienna (thrice weekly, 15hr). Taiwan's other national airline, China Airlines, had a direct flight from **Amsterdam via Bangkok** to Taipei for around £570 return. In addition, KLM offers a regular service from Amsterdam to Taipei (with a stopover in Hong Kong) for about £1000 return.

From Australia and New Zealand

Almost all flights between **Australia** and Taiwan have a stopover somewhere else in Asia, with **Hong Kong** again being the closest and most well-connected. Some of the cheapest fares to Hong Kong from Sydney are with Cathay Pacific, China Airlines and EVA Air. Coming from Sydney, it's also possible to transit in Bangkok or Singapore. The only nonstop flight between **Sydney** and Taipei (9hr) is via China Airlines, for about A$1450 return.

Flights from **New Zealand** are limited, but EVA Air offers a nonstop service from **Auckland** to Taipei (11hr). Other carriers such as Air New Zealand, Cathay Pacific and Singapore Airlines fly from Auckland to Taipei, but they first stop in Hong Kong.

Fly less – stay longer! Travel and climate change

Climate change is the single biggest issue facing our planet. It is caused by a build-up in the atmosphere of carbon dioxide and other greenhouse gases, which are emitted by many sources – including planes. Already, flights account for around 3–4% of human-induced global warming: that figure may sound small, but it is rising year on year and threatens to counteract the progress made by reducing greenhouse emissions in other areas.

Rough Guides regard travel, overall, as a global benefit, and feel strongly that the advantages to developing economies are important, as are the opportunities for greater contact and awareness among peoples. But we all have a responsibility to limit our personal "carbon footprint". That means giving thought to how often we fly and what we can do to redress the harm that our trips create.

Flying and climate change

Pretty much every form of motorized travel generates CO_2, but planes are particularly bad offenders, releasing large volumes of greenhouse gases at altitudes where their impact is far more harmful. Flying also allows us to travel much further than we would contemplate doing by road or rail, so the emissions attributable to each passenger become truly shocking. For example, one person taking a return flight between Europe and California produces the equivalent impact of 2.5 tonnes of CO_2 – similar to the yearly output of the average UK car.

Less harmful planes may evolve but it will be decades before they replace the current fleet – which could be too late for avoiding climate chaos. In the meantime, there are limited options for concerned travellers: to reduce the amount we travel by air (take fewer trips, stay longer!), to avoid night flights (when plane contrails trap heat from Earth but can't reflect sunlight back to space), and to make the trips we do take "climate neutral" via a carbon offset scheme.

Carbon offset schemes

Offset schemes run by **climatecare.org, carbonneutral.com** and others allow you to "neutralize" the greenhouse gases that you are responsible for releasing. Their websites have simple calculators that let you work out the impact of any flight. Once that's done, you can pay to fund projects that will reduce future carbon emissions by an equivalent amount (such as the distribution of low-energy light bulbs and cooking stoves in developing countries). Please take the time to visit our website and make your trip climate neutral.

ⓦ **www.roughguides.com/climatechange**

From South Africa

The closest entry point to Taiwan from **South Africa** is Hong Kong, and South African Airways has direct service from Johannesburg to Hong Kong.

Airlines, agents and operators

Airlines

US and Canada

Air Canada ☎1-888/247-2262, ⓦwww
.aircanada.com.

All Nippon Airways (ANA) ☎1-800/235-9262,
ⓦwww.anaskyweb.com.
American Airlines ☎1-800/433-7300, ⓦwww
.aa.com.
Asiana Airlines US ☎1-800/227-4262, ⓦwww
.flyasiana.com.
Cathay Pacific ☎1-800/233-2742, ⓦwww
.cathay-usa.com.
China Airlines ☎917/368-2000, ⓦwww.china
-airlines.com.
Continental Airlines International ☎1-800/231-
0856, ⓦwww.continental.com.
Delta International ☎1-800/241-4141, ⓦwww
.delta.com.
EVA Air ☎1-800/695-1188, ⓦwww.evaair.com.

JAL (Japan Air Lines) ☎1-800/525-3663, ⓦwww
.japanair.com.
Korean Air ☎1-800/438-5000, ⓦwww.koreanair
.com.
Singapore Airlines US ☎1-800/742-3333,
Canada ☎1-800/387-8039 or 663-3046, ⓦwww
.singaporeair.com.
Thai Airways US ☎1-800/426-5204, Canada
☎1-800/668-8103, ⓦwww.thaiair.com.
United Airlines International ☎1-800/538-2929,
ⓦwww.united.com.
US Airways International ☎1-800/622-1015,
ⓦwww.usair.com.

UK and Ireland

British Airways UK ☎0870/850 9850, Republic
of Ireland ☎1800/626 747, ⓦwww.ba.com.
Cathay Pacific UK ☎020/8834 8888, ⓦwww
.cathaypacific.com/uk.
China Airlines UK ☎020/7436 9001, ⓦwww
.china-airlines.com.
EVA Air UK ☎020/7380 8300, ⓦwww.evaair.com.
Finnair UK ☎0870/241 4411, Republic of Ireland
☎01/844 6565, ⓦwww.finnair.com.
KLM (Royal Dutch Airlines) UK ☎0870/507
4074, ⓦwww.klm.com.
Lufthansa UK ☎0845/773 7747, Republic of
Ireland ☎01/844 5544, ⓦwww.lufthansa.com.
Malaysia Airlines UK ☎0870/607 9090, Republic
of Ireland ☎01/676 2131, ⓦwww.malaysia
-airlines.com.
Singapore Airlines UK ☎0870/608 8886,
Republic of Ireland ☎01/671 0722, ⓦwww
.singaporeair.com.
Thai Airways UK ☎0870/606 0911, ⓦwww
.thaiair.com.
Virgin Atlantic Airways UK ☎01293/747 747,
ⓦwww.virgin.com/atlantic.

Australia and New Zealand

Air New Zealand Australia ☎13 2476, New
Zealand ☎0800 247 764; ⓦwww.airnewzealand
.com.
Cathay Pacific Australia ☎13 1747, New Zealand
☎09/379 0861; ⓦwww.cathaypacific.com.
China Airlines Australia ☎02/9244 2121, New
Zealand ☎09/308 3371, ⓦwww.china-airlines
.com.
EVA Air Australia ☎02/8338 0419, New Zealand
☎09/358 8300, ⓦwww.evaair.com.
Malaysia Airlines Australia ☎13 2627, New
Zealand ☎0800/777 747 or 649/379 3743;
ⓦwww.malaysiaairlines.com.

Qantas Australia ☎13 1313, New Zealand
☎09/357 8900 or 0800/808 767; ⓦwww.qantas
.com.
Royal Brunei Australia ☎07/3017 5000, New
Zealand ☎09/977 2240, ⓦwww.bruneiair.com.
Singapore Airlines Australia ☎13 1011 or
☎02/ 9350 0262, New Zealand ☎09/379 3209;
ⓦwww.singaporeair.com.
Thai Airways Australia ☎1300 651 960, New
Zealand ☎09/377 3886; ⓦwww.thaiair.com.

South Africa

South African Airways ☎ 0861/359 722,
ⓦwww.flysaa.com.

Booking flights online

UK and Ireland

ⓦwww.ebookers.com
ⓦwww.expedia.co.uk
ⓦwww.lastminute.com
ⓦwww.opodo.co.uk
ⓦwww.travelocity.co.uk

US and Canada

ⓦwww.expedia.com
ⓦwww.expedia.ca
ⓦwww.orbitz.com
ⓦwww.travelocity.com
ⓦwww.travelocity.ca

Australia and New Zealand

ⓦwww.zuji.com.au
ⓦwww.zuji.co.nz

Specialist tour operators

Absolute Asia ☎1-800/736-8187, ⓦwww
.absoluteasia.com. Feature several country-wide
luxury tours ranging from four to nine days.
Adventures Abroad ☎1-800/665-3998,
ⓦwww.adventures-abroad.com. Offer a general
six-day tour covering major destinations throughout
Taiwan.
Goway Travel Experiences ☎1-800/387-8850
or 416/322-1034, ⓦwww.goway.com. Three-day
city tours of Taipei.
Wings ☎1-888/293-6443 or 520/320-9868,
ⓦwww.wingsbirds.com. Specialists in bird-watching
tours that cover most of Taiwan.

Getting around

Getting around in Taiwan can be ultra-convenient or infinitely frustrating, depending on where you are and what the weather is like. After spending time along the heavily populated western corridor, with its efficient rail links and high-speed superhighways, it's difficult to reconcile it with the spotty connections of the mountainous interior and the barren simplicity of the east coast. Still, all of the major offshore islands are easily accessible by sea and air in good weather, and if you need to quickly get from one side of Taiwan to the other, then flying over the mountains is almost always an option.

While the rugged mountains that bisect the island make for some convoluted travel logistics, which can be further complicated by oft-heavy rains, for most travellers the biggest challenge to getting around comes down to **language**. Though signs in English – or at least in romanized script – are becoming more common and some train and bus station attendants can understand carefully enunciated fragments of English, it still takes some planning to make your connections if you don't speak or read Chinese. One of the best ways around this is to ask someone (such as a tourist information centre worker) to **write down** the name of your destination in Chinese so that you can show it to clerks in bus and train stations. Likewise, it can pay to have the name of your hotel and/or the sites you wish to visit written in Chinese so you can show them to taxi drivers or people on the street if you get lost.

Those hoping to travel further afield, particularly into the **mountains** or over one of Taiwan's three major **cross-island routes**, should allow ample time for their journeys and be prepared for landslips, rockslides and road closures during inclement weather. In some cases, it's altogether quicker to head back to the nearest train station and start making your way around the island by train.

By rail

Taiwan's **train network** is the cornerstone of its transport system, moving as many as a half million people per day. The efficient Taiwan Railway Administration (TRA) runs trains on the main Western and Eastern rail lines, with a shorter southern link connecting the two. The most heavily used trunk system is the **Western Line**, with regular connections between Keelung in the north and the island's second-largest city, Kaohsiung, in the south. The major stops along this line are, from north to south: Taipei, Taoyuan, Jhongli, Hsinchu, Taichung, Changhua, Chiayi and Tainan. The less developed **Eastern Line** runs from Shulin through Taipei to Yilan and Suao, then hugs the coastline until Hualien before cutting inland through the East Rift Valley on the way to the southeastern city of Taitung. Diesel engines traditionally ran along this line, but in recent years it has been electrified and expanded to two tracks. The scenic **South-link Line**, completed in 1991, begins in Taitung and heads south along the coast, turning west after Dawu to cross the island before heading north to Pingdong and Kaohsiung.

In addition to these important passenger lines, the TRA also maintains four slower, narrow-gauge **branch lines** that mostly transport tourists inland to Alishan (see p.297), Jiji (see p.263), Neiwan (see p.284) and Pingsi (see p.180). These tourist trains have become immensely popular and have helped the TRA offset losses in passenger numbers due to increased competition from bus companies and airlines.

Updated **timetable** and fare information is listed on the *Taiwan Railway Passenger Train Timetable*, which can be found at train station information centres, as well as some convenience stores and kiosks. To check schedules online or make bookings 24 hours in advance, check the TRA's website at Ⓦwww.railway.gov.tw.

Buying tickets

Train stations usually have separate **queues** for advance and same-day departures, as well as for cash and credit card purchases – this is usually labelled in English on the cashier's window. For shuttle journeys from main stations it's faster to use the **ticket machines** which are labelled in English. It's imperative that you **retain your ticket** when you get off the train, as you're still required to return it at the gate to exit the train station – if you lose it, you'll have to pay a fine.

There are four classes of train, from express to shuttle services (see below). For the three fastest classes, it's often a good idea to buy your ticket **in advance** (either online or at the station), especially if you plan to travel on a weekend or public holiday, when all seats are commonly full. When no seats are available, you'll usually still be sold a ticket, but you'll have to either pay full price (for Tze-Chiang) or settle for a twenty percent discount (for Chu-Kuang and Fu-Hsing) for **standing-room only**. If you do have a standing-room only ticket but manage to find a free seat, it's acceptable to sit there until the valid ticket holder turns up and politely asks you to vacate.

If you're rushing to catch a certain train, in many stations you can buy a **platform ticket** from the machines for NT$5, which will allow you onto the platform so you can board your desired train. After boarding, you'll need to find the conductor and pay for a ticket upgrade.

On the whole, **food** served on trains is overpriced and not recommended; if you're going on a long train journey, you'll be better off buying food and drinks ahead of time, even if only from a convenience store such as the 7-Elevens that are outside every train station.

Train classes and fares

Tze-Chiang The fastest and most expensive, with assigned seating, air conditioning and, in some cases, a dining car.
Chu-Kuang The second-fastest, also with assigned seating and air conditioning.
Fu-Hsing The third-fastest, also with assigned seating. Has air conditioning but is not as comfortable as the two higher classes.
EMU (Electric Multiple Unit) Short- to medium-distance commuter train which stops at all stations. There is no assigned seating.

Sample train fares

Taipei–Kaohsiung Tze-Chiang (NT$845), Fu-Hsing (NT$544).
Taipei–Taichung Tze-Chiang (NT$375), Fu-Hsing (NT$241).

The High Speed Rail system

Taiwan's long-anticipated **High Speed Rail** system is set to radically alter the island's traditional concept of train travel, with a bullet train that will cut the travelling time from Taipei to Kaohsiung by two thirds, to about an hour and a half. The train, which will be one of the world's fastest, will initially stop at eight stations along the 345-kilometre length of track, dramatically reducing the travel time between all major west coast cities and opening up a convenient and exciting alternative to tourists. Modelled after Japan's extraordinary Shinkansen, the twelve-carriage train will travel at an average speed of about 300kph and will seat 989 passengers. However, while the transit time between cities will be markedly reduced, it's worth noting that some of the stations are well outside of city centres and will mean an additional shuttle leg for travellers looking to stay in the heart of major cities. With budget hotels still clustered near the regular train stations of west-coast cities, the old trains should still hold their appeal for tourists, as accommodation is always just a short walk from the exit. The first eight high-speed rail stations to open will be: Taipei, Banciao, Taoyuan, Hsinchu, Taichung, Chiayi, Tainan and Zuoying (Kaohsiung). At a later stage, four more stations will be added: Nangang, Miaoli, Changhua and Yunlin. In the works for well over a decade, the massive project was delayed repeatedly, both in the early financing stages as well as in the construction phase. It opened in January 2007 (ⓦwww.thsrc.com.tw). A one-way Taipei-Kaohsiung ticket will cost NT$1490.

Taipei–Tainan Tze-Chiang (NT$741); Fu-Hsing (NT$476).
Taipei–Hualien Tze-Chiang (NT$445); Chu-Kuang (NT$343).
Taipei–Taitung Tze-Chiang (NT$800); Chu-Kuang (NT$616).
Kaohsiung–Taitung Tze-Chiang (NT$364); Chu-Kuang (NT$280).

By bus

Buses are cheaper than trains, and in some cases can actually be much faster – provided you travel when traffic is light and there are no road accidents (see p.67). On long-distance routes between the big west-coast cities, which are linked by multi-lane freeways, buses can cut travel time dramatically. In addition, the best bus companies have extremely comfortable air-conditioned coaches, with big cozy **armchair-style seats**, movies and an on-board toilet (though these can be exceedingly small). Bear in mind the air conditioning is never turned off, so it can get quite chilly on board – best to take a jumper with you for long trips.

But while there are many bus services on well-travelled routes, those in **rural areas** are being dropped each year, as more Taiwanese tourists take to the roads in their own cars or book guided package tours. For independent travellers, this is indeed a shame, as it is making already hard-to-reach mountain areas even more difficult to get to without your own transport. In years past, it was possible to bus-hop your way over some of the cross-island highways, but this is getting much harder as bus companies abandon these unprofitable routes.

Buying tickets

Buying bus **tickets** is relatively easy, once you find the office of the bus company dealing with your route. In most cities, the main private companies have ticket offices clustered around the train station, and their buses usually stop right outside the office. Be sure to save your ticket until you get off the bus, as you are often required to return it to the driver before you are allowed off – if you lose it you might be asked to pay for another ticket. For more information on bus routes and recommended companies, see the relevant chapter of the guide.

Bus companies and fares

Aloha Bus ☎ 02/25508488
Dragon Bus ☎ 02/25710166
Evervoyage Transport Corp ☎ 03/3570498
Free Go Express ☎ 02/25863065
Kuo Kuang ☎ 0800/010138; ☎ 03/3834004
Taoyuan Bus Corp ☎ 03/3753711
Ubus ☎ 02/29957799; 03/3834779

Sample bus fares

Taipei–Kaohsiung NT$500
Taipei–Taichung NT$260
Taipei–Tainan NT$450
Taipei–Sun Moon Lake NT$300

By car

In more remote areas such as the cross-island highway routes and segments of the east coast, **hiring a car** can be the most convenient way to get around. However, driving in major cities can be extremely stressful – and dangerous for inexperienced drivers – though anyone used to driving in big European and North American cities should find it manageable. Note that Taiwanese drive on the right-hand side of the road.

Most of Taiwan's cities have car rental shops, but it's often preferable to hire a vehicle at the airport when you arrive, as they're usually located away from heavier traffic areas. In addition, rental agencies at the country's main airports (Taipei and Kaohsiung, as well as those in Hualien and Taitung) usually have English-speaking staff who are used to dealing with foreigners.

Foreign tourists renting a car in Taiwan will need to produce an **international driver's licence** and their **passport**; longer-term foreign residents who possess an **ARC** (Alien Resident Certificate) can often drive legally with their home-country licences, but this varies among countries and some foreign nationals might be required to obtain a Taiwanese driver's licence. **Prices** vary depending upon location, time of the week and the type of vehicle, but in general full-day rental ranges from NT$1500 to NT$2500, and discounts of ten to fifteen percent are usually given for multi-day rentals (although they're often not given during public holiday periods). Deposits are typically about NT$10,000 for

Taiwanese cars and NT$20,000 for imported models, and this can almost always be charged to your credit card.

By scooter

Foreigners spending any length of time in Taiwan will quickly find that a **scooter** is often an indispensable item, whether for wheeling around traffic-clogged cities or travelling in far-flung areas with little or no public transport – especially the offshore islands of the Pacific and the Taiwan Strait. In most such places, there is no shortage of scooter rental outlets, invariably offering a good choice of 50cc, 100cc and 125cc machines (the last two recommended for hilly areas).

However, while renting a scooter is easy for Taiwanese, the requirements for **foreigners** vary wildly. In some areas all foreigners have to do is pay up front (an average daily scooter fare is about NT$400) and they'll be given the machine of their choice and a **helmet** (helmets are required by law and highly recommended although there are places in Taiwan where this is not enforced). But, an increasing number of rental shops are refusing to rent scooters to foreigners unless they have a valid **ARC (Alien Resident Certificate)** and can show proof of their permanent address in Taiwan (many shop owners have been stuck with hefty fines resulting from traffic violations unwittingly committed by tourists who are long-since gone by the time the ticket arrives). In practice, it helps if you have an **international driver's licence**: even though such a permit only allows tourists to legally drive a 50cc scooter, some rental shops – especially those on the offshore islands – seem satisfied with this. However, this is becoming increasingly unlikely in most major cities, and you might find yourself wandering from one shop to another in search of an amenable outlet.

Another crucial thing to remember is that most rental shops will give you a scooter with only a small amount of fuel – often just enough to get you to the nearest petrol station – so be sure to check your fuel gauge when you start and make haste to the nearest station if you're running low.

Cycling

The use of **bicycles** for short rides and day-trips is becoming increasingly common in many tourist destinations, with new designated cycle paths cropping up all over the country. Most such routes are well designed and easy to follow, with bicycle-only lanes running alongside main roads, many of them marked with signposts outlining the main sights. In places with such paths, bicycles – ranging from basic three-speeds (usually costing NT$50–100 per day) to multi-speed mountain bikes and even tandems (typically NT$150 per day) – can easily be **rented**. While these rental bicycles are generally well maintained and fine for short rides on paved paths, they're not suited to longer-distance touring, and those planning on covering longer distances should arrive with their own or buy a higher-quality bike from a shop in a major city. While **cycle touring** is gaining popularity, this is largely (and wisely) contained to the quieter areas of the east coast as well as the more challenging cross-island highway routes over the mountains (see p.57).

By boat

There are regular **passenger ferries** to Taiwan's **outlying islands**, although in winter many services are scaled back. The Pacific Islands of Lyudao (Green Island) and Lanyu (Orchid Island) are easily reached by ferry in good weather, while the Taiwan Strait islands of Little Liouciou, Kinmen, the Matzu Archipelago and the Penghu Archipelago are accessible by ferry for much of the year. Although flying to these islands has become a more popular option among Taiwanese tourists, travelling by ferry is cheaper and can really add perspective to your journey despite the occasionally rough seas. All ferry routes to outlying islands are covered in greater detail in the relevant chapters.

By air

In Taiwan's fast-paced society, **air transport** is growing in popularity, not just for business travel between major cities, but also for holidaymakers looking to cut down on their travel times. In particular, flights to Taiwan's **outlying islands** have become popular with domestic tourists, largely due to the widespread fear of motion sickness on the choppy seas that surround the island.

Taipei's **Songshan Airport**, just to the north of central Taipei operates services to many outlying islands, as well as daily flights to most major cities, including Chiayi, Hualien, Kaohsiung, Pingdong, Taichung, Tainan and Taitung. In addition, the **domestic airports** in Chiayi, Kaohsiung, Taichung and Tainan also have several domestic routes. Prices are usually set wholesale by the airlines, so there's little point in going to

an agent. Taiwan's competitive domestic market might appear a bit over-serviced, but this helps keep prices down.

Domestic airlines

Daily Air Corp ☎02/27123995, ⊛www.dailyair .com.tw
Far Eastern Air Transport ☎02/33935388, ⊛www.fat.com.tw
Mandarin Airlines ☎02/27171230 ⊛www.mandarin-airlines.com
TransAsia Airways ☎02/29724599, ⊛www .tna.com.tw
Uni Air ☎02/23583131, ⊛www.uniair.com.tw

Accommodation

Taiwan offers travellers a wide range of accommodation, from spartan dormitories and weathered white-tile hotels to quaint, family-run homestays and plush five-star resorts. Given the domestic tourism boom of recent years, most accommodation caters to the growing numbers of Taiwanese who evacuate the island's crowded west-coast cities on weekends and public holidays. Note that many terms commonly used in the West take on altogether different meanings in Taiwan, so it's important to keep this in mind when choosing your lodgings.

Few Taiwanese travel alone, so there is a severe shortage of true single rooms with one single bed. In most cases, the Taiwanese equivalent is a room with a **queen-sized bed** suitable for most couples – and priced accordingly. A **double room** usually has a king-sized bed and is more expensive still, while a **twin room** – also a rarity – comes with two single beds. Though lone travellers are sometimes shown into twins, they are rarely given sizeable discounts for sleeping on a single bed. Given the popularity of family travel in Taiwan, most hotels have plenty of **triples** (one king-sized bed and a queen or single) and **quadruples** (usually with two king-sized beds), convenient for foreign families and groups of friends.

Room **prices** vary considerably, depending on location, the season or time of week. While rack rates can be alarmingly high, they are only charged during **peak times**, such

as weekends, public holidays and during the summer school break (and even then mostly just at beach resorts and the most famous attractions). Travellers on a **budget** should plan their schedules around this, visiting non-urban attractions during the week and then retreating to the cities on weekends and holidays. In the off-season and mid-week, as well as during adverse weather such as typhoons, significant **discounts** can be expected. The price quoted to you usually has the discount factored in, and this can be checked against hotel leaflets (typically called "DMs" in Taiwan), which are available at most reception desks. Discounts of thirty percent are common, but in low season it's often possible to pay only half the rack rate. By far the most expensive time to travel in Taiwan is during **Chinese New Year**, when prices can be double the rack rates. Hotels also are often full at this time, so if you plan

Accommodation price codes

The accommodation listed in this book has been assigned one of the following **price codes**, which represent the price of a **standard double room** (ie those with queen-sized beds, but typically not the top doubles with scenic views). Our listed prices in most cases reflect the discounts normally offered at hotels, so they are often lower than listed rack rates. Note, however, that room rates on weekends and public holidays may be higher than those listed in the guide.

❶ Under NT$500
❷ NT$501–1000
❸ NT$1001–1500
❹ NT$1501–2000
❺ NT$2001–2500
❻ NT$2501–3000
❼ NT$3001–5000
❽ NT$5001–7000
❾ Over NT$7000

to travel during this holiday you should try to make bookings in advance.

If you're arriving at Taiwan Taoyuan International Airport and haven't already arranged your accommodation in Taipei, there are **tourist information** booths in both terminals that can make bookings and arrange transport for you. Likewise, there is a tourist office in Kaohsiung's International Airport which offers the same services.

Hotels

Most cities and tourist destinations have a variety of hotels covering the gamut of price ranges. Basic **budget hotel** rooms can be had for as little as NT$600 per night at off-peak times. At this price, rooms are likely to be a bit tatty and damp, probably with cigarette burns on the furniture and a smell of stale smoke. Still, most of them will have an attached bathroom with shower, TV and phone and will offer complimentary toiletry packages. The majority of patrons to these hotels are working-class Taiwanese, so often little if any English is spoken. And with many Taiwanese preferring to bathe at night, you're usually only guaranteed hot water in the evening.

Mid-range hotels usually cost NT$1000–3000, and standards generally vary in accordance with price. At the lower end, rooms are likely to resemble cleaner versions of budget hotels, often with the only difference being that they offer hot water and packets of tea and coffee in addition to cable TV. At the higher end, rooms can be quite clean and comfortable, with big bathtubs and/or shower cubicles, and breakfast is often included in the price. You're also more likely to encounter staff that can speak a few words of English.

All of the biggest cities, but especially Taipei, have international **five-star hotels** that feature everything you'd expect from such chains, including giant beds with fine linen, high-speed Internet connections in the rooms, business centres, fitness rooms, spa and massage services and luxury restaurants. Though discounts are sometimes offered, these hotels generally charge a minimum of NT$4000 for a standard room and prices are often twice that. Staff at these usually speak English.

Hot-spring hotels

Hot-spring hotels are all the rage in Taiwan, but standards vary wildly according to location. Those in resorts close to big cities can be expensive, often charging at least NT$6000 for rooms with **en-suite Jacuzzis**, while those further afield can offer the same amenities for less than half of that price. Almost all offer **public pools**, which are free to paying guests and can be used by non-guests for what is usually a nominal fee. Many hot-spring hotels also rent rooms for shorter periods for those wishing to bathe in private without paying for overnight accommodation. Note that the quality of the spring water varies between resorts, and even between hotels at the same resort. In general, the older-looking hotels tend to be disappointing, often only having small bathtubs into which the "spring water" is piped through the tap. Meanwhile, newer – and considerably more expensive – hotels have been designed with a keener eye for aesthetics, with larger tubs made of marble or with Japanese-style wooden designs.

Homestays

So-called **"homestays"** are sprouting up all over Taiwan, particularly in rural scenic areas, where private families are increasingly setting up bed-and-breakfast style businesses to take advantage of mounting tourist numbers. However, the nature of these homestays varies dramatically, and many are nothing more than tiny, family-run hotels. Rooms are usually in wings that adjoin the owners' houses and breakfast, though provided, is typically not eaten with the family. However, places advertising themselves as homestays (*minsu*) are nearly always clean, friendly, and good value as well as exuding more character than most hotels. There are many homestays listed in the guide, but new ones are constantly opening in places such as hill resorts, so keep a lookout when you arrive. Although many aren't directly accessible by public transport, most offer **pick-up** services from the nearest train or bus station if you ring them in advance. In **aboriginal villages**, especially those in national scenic areas such as Alishan and Maolin, overnighting in homestays can give fascinating glimpses into the island's indigenous cultures.

Hostels

These days **hostels** are just about the only accommodation in Taiwan that could accurately be described as budget, though some of the nicest of these can actually be more expensive than dingy old-school hotels. The attraction of hostels to students and the budget-conscious are their **dormitories**, the most basic of which offer beds for as little as NT$250–300 per night, with discounts often doled out for long-term stays. Many hostels also have a few **private rooms**; though invariably small, they can be good value, with some going for as low as NT$500 a night, even in big cities – these tend to be the preferred haunts of newly arrived English teachers, who often rent them on a weekly or monthly basis, so sometimes they can be hard to find.

A few hostels in Taiwan have affiliation with Hostelling International (ⓦwww.hihostels .com) and will provide discounts to card holders, but many of those outside of the cities cater mostly to Taiwanese students and do not recognize international student credentials. Many hostels have laundry facilities and common cable TV rooms, while some offer shared use of their Internet connections for free. Kitchens can still be found in some.

Camping

Camping is becoming increasingly popular in Taiwan, especially in national scenic and forest recreation areas. If you have your own transport, bringing camping equipment will open a whole new window of possibilities, allowing you to explore the island's wilder side at your own pace. In many coastal areas and on some offshore islands, large-scale **campsites** have been built, with some offering spots on the grass and others featuring elevated wooden platforms that make camping in rainy weather more bearable. If you have your own gear, grass spots generally go for about NT$200, while those with raised platforms usually cost about NT$300. Some campsites also offer **rentals** with eight-person tents and sleeping bags and pads provided for around NT$800 – which for groups is undoubtedly some of Taiwan's cheapest accommodation. Almost all of these types of camping areas have adjoining barbecue pits and public showers and toilets.

In **national parks** and other remote areas, camping is often your only option, though there are few designated sites and low-impact methods are recommended – **campfires** should be forsaken in favour of cooking stoves, for example. As landslips occur on mountain trails with frightening regularity, care should be taken when choosing where to pitch your tent, especially in rainy weather. Due to the extremely high precipitation levels in Taiwan's mountains – including ample snow in winter – three- or **four-season tents** are advisable, especially if you plan to sleep at altitude, where nights can be remarkably chilly even in the summer. The intensity of the island's rain can test the waterproofing of even the most high-end tents, so make sure yours has been fully **seam-sealed**, particularly if you'll be camping on bare earth (in which case a ground sheet is highly recommended).

Food and drink

Taiwan offers a huge variety of cuisines, from Chinese and Taiwanese food to Japanese and aboriginal dishes. Choices range from super-cheap night markets and street stalls, to wallet-draining restaurants featuring some of Asia's best chefs. In the major cities there's also plenty of Western food, from smart Italian eateries to all the familiar fast-food chains.

Taiwanese food

Taiwanese cuisine is difficult to define, and best thought of as an umbrella term for a huge variety of dishes and styles, most of which can be summarized as *xiaochi*, or "**little eats**". Though these are primarily served in simple canteens or night markets, there are also plenty of restaurants specializing in Taiwanese food. In general, Taiwanese dishes utilize relatively simple ingredients and cooking techniques, reflecting the humble rural origins of the island's early Chinese settlers. Although Taiwanese cuisine is rooted in **Fujianese** cooking, since 1949 many dishes have evolved from specialties originating in other parts of China. In addition, much of what's considered Taiwanese food, particularly cakes and desserts, was influenced by the **Japanese** during the occupation period. Being an island, Taiwan is particularly renowned for its **seafood**: **shellfish, squid** and **crab** are extremely popular, with local **mullet, sea bream** and **milkfish** (a favourite in the south) common local fish. **Bluefin tuna**, caught in August off Donggang, is highly prized, and there's a large **freshwater fish** and **shrimp** industry.

One of the classic dishes found all over Taiwan is known as *sanbei*, "**three cups**", a sumptuous blend of soy sauce, rice wine and sesame oil, seasoned with various spices, added to meat or tofu and usually served in a clay pot. Other national staples are *lu rou fan* (**braised pork rice**) and **oyster omelette** (*e-a jian*). In addition, there are numerous styles and types of **noodles** cooked up on almost every street corner in the country. **Shaved ice stalls** (*tsua bing*) are another national institution and best in the hot summer months, mounds of ice topped with fruits or traditional sweets such as red bean and sweet taro. *Douhua*, **soybean pudding**, is another popular dessert, and Taiwan's excellent tropical **fruits** are sold everywhere as nutritious snacks, peeled and chopped into bite-sized chunks.

Local specialties

One of the most appealing aspects of any visit to Taiwan is discovering local favourites: each region, town and even village has a speciality, eagerly dished out by local vendors. Taipei undoubtedly has the greatest variety of food, Taichung is noted for its teahouses, Tainan for its more traditional Taiwanese dishes and Kaohsiung for its seafood. Tainan's signature dish is *danzi mian*, a mixture of pork, noodles and usually egg or shrimp. **Fish balls** (*yuwan*) are popular all over the island but best associated with Danshui, Kaohsiung (marlin), Tainan (milkfish) and Nanfangao (*mahi-mahi*). **Rice noodles** (*mifen*) are noted in Hsinchu, while thick **Shilin sausages** (*da xiangchang*), named after Shilin Night Market in Taipei, are now a juicy island-wide snack. **Sichuan beef noodles** (*niu rou mian*) is another dish primarily associated with Taipei, while steamed or deep-fried **meatballs** (*gong-wan or ba wan*) are best in Changhua and Hsinchu. **Turkey rice** (*ji rou fan*) is a Chiayi innovation while Shenkeng is Taiwan's **tofu** capital. The most infamous tofu dish is *chou doufu*, or **stinky tofu,** the smell of which sickens most foreigners but tastes delicious. In fact Taiwan offers plenty of dishes most Westerners find revolting: good examples are pig intestines and *lu wei*, a mix of tofu and various internal organs of cows or pigs, simmered in a tasty broth, and often eaten cold. Try them and you're bound to win the respect of the incredulous Taiwanese sitting next to you. **Cakes** and **sweets**, usually produced in historic and atmospheric bakeries, are just as diverse: examples are suncakes (*taiyang bing*) in Taichung, phoenix-eye cakes in Lugang, *mashu* or *muaji* in Hualien, brown-sugar cake in Penghu and taro balls in Jiufen.

Hakka food

Hakka food has become very popular in Taiwan, with restaurants dishing up classic favourites in all the major cities. Hakka cuisine is noted for its strong, rich flavours and salty, fatty ingredients, particularly **pork**, traditionally designed to fill hungry agricultural labourers. Favourites include *ban tiao* (tasty fried noodles), bamboo shoots, braised stuffed tofu, *kejia mashu* (glutinous rice cakes rolled in peanuts) and fried pork intestines with ginger – this tastes a lot better than it sounds. One of the major fads sweeping Hakka tourists spots across the island is *lei cha* (cereal tea), a tasty, thick blend of nuts and tea leaves, best experienced in Beipu.

Aboriginal food

Aboriginal food differs slightly between tribes, but the main ingredients tend to be the same. **Ginger** is a frequent ingredient in soups and tea, while the most celebrated dish is undoubtedly "**mountain pig**" (*shan zhu*) or wild boar, which is usually roasted. **Millet wine** is mildly alcoholic and served at all times of the day, and **freshwater fish** is also a regular feature of aboriginal meals, served with mountain vegetables such as sweet potato. **Bamboo rice** (*zhu tong*), or rice cooked in bamboo tubes, is tasty but not really traditional food – rice arrived with Chinese immigrants in the seventeenth century.

Breakfast

Traditional **breakfasts** in Taiwan, particularly in the north and in the cities, follow a modified northern-Chinese style, with common items including *dou jiang* (soybean milk), *you tiao* (foot-long dough fritters), *dan bing* (egg pancake), *mantou* (steamed bread) and a variety of steamed buns (*baozi*) and stuffed baked buns (*shao bing*). You can usually find small hole-in-the-wall type places or stalls serving these snacks in every neighbourhood, and while the formica tables and greasy-spoon atmosphere might be off-putting, the food is well worth a try. In south Taiwan, particularly in smaller towns, rice-based dishes are more common, and in Tainan it's not unusual to see people eat

Vegetarian food

Vegetarian food has a long history in Chinese culture, and as in China, vegetarianism in Taiwan is primarily associated with Buddhism. At the cheaper end of the scale, vegetarians will find plenty of food at **night markets**: roast corn-on-the-cob and sweet potatoes, tofu, and a huge range of fruits and nuts. Almost every city and town will have cheap **vegetarian buffets** where you can pile as many vegetables on your plate as you like – the price is calculated by weight but is rarely more than NT$100 for a large serving. The larger, more formal **restaurants** tend to be Buddhist inspired (identified by images of Buddha, Guanyin or lotus flowers on the walls). **Chinese vegetarian food** ranges from simple, fresh dishes of green vegetables to more elaborate combinations of herbs, roots and even flowers. One aspect of this might confuse foreign vegetarians however: tofu and gluten are often cooked to reproduce the textures and flavours of meat, transformed into remarkably good imitations of classics such as roast pork. Taiwanese vegetarians, including many Buddhist monks, applaud these culinary skills – eating food that tastes like meat is perfectly acceptable if it doesn't involve killing animals. Non-Buddhist vegetarians are still quite rare in Taiwan, but most Taiwanese understand the concept, at least in the cities, though it can be hard to find decent non-meat options in rural areas, where rice and local vegetables will have to suffice: note that many sauces, even on vegetables, contain shrimp or fish.

large meals of seafood and milkfish to start the day.

Starbucks has a major presence in Taiwan, and has spawned a large number of local **coffeeshop chains** such as *Barista Coffee*, *Dante*, *Mr Brown* and *IS Coffee*, though for many Taiwanese a "Western" breakfast comprises fried egg sandwiches loaded with mayonnaise and spam, sold at an increasing number of cheap roadside stalls, especially in the cities.

Regional Chinese cuisine

Chinese food is incredibly varied, and China's **regional cuisine** is well represented in restaurants all over Taiwan. The most respected northern school is **Beijing**, with its emphasis on bread, noodles, dumplings and **Beijing duck**, its most famous dish. It's rare to find places specializing in other northern styles: the handful of Shaanxi and Xinjiang restaurants are not very authentic, though **Mongolian barbecues**, where you roast your own meat and vegetables on griddles placed in the middle of the table, are deservedly popular.

Eastern-style cuisine such as **Shanghainese** food is best known for *xiaolong bao* or pork dumplings, and is big business in Taiwan; the craze for 1930s-style Shanghai restaurants and food has also made its way to the island, with favourites including eel, freshwater fish with corn and pine nuts (*songren yumi*), pomfret (*changyu*), yellow croaker (*huangyu*) and drunken chicken (*zuji*). Cuisine based on Zhejiang and Jiangsu specialties including **Huangzhou** food, which also features delicately flavoured freshwater fish, is fairly easy to find.

Southern cuisine is best epitomized by **Cantonese** food, a global favourite with colourful and varied ingredients, but fewer spices than other schools. Often associated with lavish banquet food such as shark's fin soup, **dim sum** (*dianxin*) and the ubiquitous **roast meat** stalls make a more affordable meal. **Fujianese** food is closely related to Taiwanese; "Buddha Jumps over the Wall" is probably its most lauded (and expensive) dish, a rich stew of rare seafood and meats, but the most authentic seafood dishes are found on Matzu and Kinmen.

Sichuanese food is part of the Western school, the spiciest of all Chinese cuisines, with fiery chilli and black peppercorns added to dishes such as *mapo doufu*, and chicken with peanuts (*gongbao jiding*). Two Taiwanese obsessions are derivatives of Sichuan dishes: **beef noodles** and **hotpot** (*huoguo*). The latter has blossomed into a major fad on the island, with Japanese (*shabu-shabu*) Cantonese, Mongolian, and spicy hotpot variations; the main difference is the sauces and stock used to flavour the water. Once you've chosen the sauce, you select your raw ingredients, and boil them in a gas-fired cauldron. **Hunan** food, as spicy as Sichuan food but more oily and featuring dishes such as honey ham and minced pork, is not so common and found primarily in the capital.

Japanese food

Japanese food is extremely common in Taiwan, ranging from traditional, highly expensive restaurants in hotels, to cheap, local derivatives with a decidedly Taiwanese flavour – you'll also see plenty of Japanese snacks such as *onigiri* (sticky rice wrapped in seaweed) in local convenience stores. Japanese food traditionally revolved around **rice**, but today is associated with richer fare, usually involving **seafood**: the most well-known is *sashimi* or raw fish, typically served on rice to create *sushi*, which in Taiwan can be very affordable and also sold in most supermarkets. Numerous restaurants specialize in *shabu shabu* (hotpot), Japanese curry rice, *ramen*, *soba* or *udon* noodles, *yakitori* (chicken kebabs), *tempura* (battered and deep-fried seafood and vegetables) and *teppanyaki* (stir-fried meat and vegetables).

Western and other international food

The choice of Western food, especially in the big cities, continues to improve in Taiwan, but quality varies and many restaurants produce highly localized versions of the original cuisine. Bars and pubs often serve decent staples such as burgers, sandwiches and basic Tex-Mex favourites, while hotels offer more upmarket options. In cities like Taipei and Taichung, the choice of **French**, **Italian** and **American-style** food isn't bad, with plenty of expat chefs and talented locals opening restaurants all the time – prices tend to be higher than local food however. **Korean food** is gaining popularity on the island, and tends to be a lot more authentic than Southeast Asian cuisine such as **Thai**, which is usually adapted to local tastes and blander than what you'd get in Bangkok. South Asian and **Indian** food, buoyed primarily by a small but growing Pakistani and Bangladeshi expat population, is becoming more available in Taiwan, while major **fast-food chains** such as *Burger King*, *Domino's Pizza*, *KFC*, *McDonald's* and *Pizza Hut* can be found all over the country.

Where to eat

Night markets are the best places to sample local food at budget prices (typically NT$20–40 per dish), usually located along streets lined with both permanent shops and temporary stalls, though in cities such as Taipei and Tainan, a few markets have specially built premises. Some stalls open for lunch, but in general things only really get going after 5pm and start to wind down after 11pm, though many stay open till the early hours, especially at weekends. Language is not a problem – just point and get stuck in. The crowds can be suffocating at the weekends, but that's all part of the experience and probably the reason why most also feature foot massage centres. It's not just about food – most markets are intensely commercial affairs, with everything from cheap T-shirts to wooden toys on sale. Cheap local **diners** and **buffets** (*zizhu can*) offer similar fare, the latter an especially good idea if you want to avoid having to order in Chinese. Hygiene standards are better than they seem at these places, and it's generally safe to drink water or tea served for free on your arrival (which will have been boiled or purified).

If you fancy a stronger tipple with your food, **beerhouses** (*pijiu wu*) are atmospheric locations to try Taiwanese snacks such as squid, steamed peanuts with small fish, fried oysters, fresh clams and fried prawns. **Teahouses** also serve delicious food (see below).

Restaurants

Restaurants in Taiwan, as in China, tend to be set up for groups: diners sit at large,

round tables in order to share the sizeable plates of food on the menu. It's quite acceptable to dine alone anywhere on the island, but with more people the more dishes you'll be able to try. All the major hotels operate expensive but top-notch restaurants, their lavish buffets the best value if you want to splurge. Restaurants get going early in Taiwan, opening for lunch well before midday. Most close in the afternoons and open again at 5pm for dinner – only a handful of places do a brisk trade later in the evenings, though most will stay open to 10pm. Prices vary according to the quality of the establishment, but it's rare to pay less than NT$100 per dish, or NT$400 at smarter places.

Ordering can be difficult if there's no English menu or English-speaking staff, but unless it's exceptionally busy someone will usually be able to help. Often there will be an English menu somewhere on the premises if you ask for one, and at street stalls pointing is usually sufficient. Chopsticks are *de rigueur* in all Chinese-style restaurants, but larger places will have knives, forks and definitely spoons if you ask. Most restaurants will serve filtered or bottled **water** for no extra charge (other places will serve tea). Tap water is treated in Taiwan and nominally safe to drink (see p.43).

Tea and teahouses

Taiwan produces some of the world's finest **tea**, and as a result is a good place to drink and buy various strains, particularly *oolong*. **Dongding oolong** is often considered the best tea in Taiwan, produced around the town of Lugu in the heart of the country. Relatively mild, the tea is dried for a brief period over a charcoal fire, giving it a subtle smoky flavour. Taiwan's other famous strain is **Oriental Beauty**, grown in Hsinchu and Miaoli counties and deriving its rich flavour from insect eggs that get brewed with the leaves. Taiwan's most expensive tea is **Lishan oolong**, grown at heights above 2200m near the town of Lishan, and regarded as a rare, fine strain.

Teahouses are an important part of contemporary Taiwanese culture, ranging from the traditional to the ultra chic, but only became popular in the late 1970s. In fact, the only "traditional" places are known as **old man teahouses** (*laoren chaguan*), found in the back streets of districts such as Wanhua in Taipei, and patronized by Taiwan's senior citizens. The teahouses most frequented by locals today are generally known as "**tea art houses**" (*chayiguan*), first appearing in the 1980s and 1990s. These days Taiwan is regarded as a global leader in tea innovation: its modern teashops were responsible for Asia-wide fads such as **bubble tea** (*paomo hongcha*) and its upscale establishments have added modern twists to ancient tea ceremonies. It's the latter, featuring contemporary interpretations of classical Chinese or Asian architecture, which visitors tend to find most interesting.

Visiting a teahouse

At traditional-style teahouses, after choosing your tea type, you'll be given a tea pot, a flask or kettle of hot water, several smaller pots and a bag of dried tea leaves, enough for several rounds. When it comes to making tea the traditional way, Taiwan is far less rigid than Japan, but although methods do vary around the country the basic principles remain the same. The first brew washes the leaves and is poured away, while the second is drunk after a few seconds, the tea poured out of the pot into a separate container before being served into small drinking cups (get the wait-staff to help if you get confused). These days you can order a wide range of meals and snacks with the tea – tea-flavoured ice cream, cakes, buns and dumplings brewed in tea are often available.

Note that particularly in Taipei you'll see places advertising "**afternoon tea**", a new fad loosely based on the English tradition, with hotels and even local chains serving up black tea with cups and saucers, milk and plenty of scones.

Alcohol

Taiwan's tipple of choice is **beer** (*pijiu),* and the number one bestseller by far is **Taiwan Beer**, the brand produced by state-owned Taiwan Tobacco and Liquor Corp – Taiwanese are immensely proud of the brew (though it's fairly average by international standards) and you'll gain much kudos by drinking it, especially in rural areas. It's sold in cheap cans (NT$35) or bottles (NT$55) in convenience stores and at food stalls, though it's rarely served in bars in the cities (especially in Taipei). Western mass-produced brands such as Budweiser, Carlsberg, San Miguel and Heineken are available in most bars and stores (along with all major Japanese brews) but a more diverse range of Irish, German, Belgian or British beers and ales is limited to a few pubs in the big cities. **Microbrews** (Deluxe Beer, Taiwan Micro Brew Co and Le blé d'or) are slowly gaining a foothold in Taiwan, though most of the beer is sold through shops and regular bars rather than in special pubs.

Taiwan's national spirit is known as *gaoliang*, made from sorghum. **Kinmen Kaoliang Liquor** is its most celebrated incarnation, available at 38 or 58 percent proof (NT$500 per bottle). **Tunnel 88** is a slightly cheaper version (38 to 42 percent proof) made in Matzu. **Rice wines**, such as the **Shaoxing** variety made in Puli, tend to be too sour or sweet for Western tastes, and grape wines are slowly becoming more popular, particularly in Taipei, where the annual release of *Beaujolais Nouveau* has become the latest fad for the fashion conscious. It's expensive, thanks to heavy taxation, and you'll only get a good selection in the larger or Western-oriented supermarkets and specialty stores – Australian wines are best value in regular supermarkets (NT$400–500). Other spirits are easily available in Taiwan, and cocktails are also popular in the cities.

Soft drinks

Canned juices are sold throughout the island, and there are numerous fresh fruit stalls. Be warned, however, that it's common to add milk, syrup and often sugar to juice drinks in Taiwan, so check before you order. Freshly pressed **sugar cane juice** is a delicious, sweet drink served by street vendors all over the country, while **papaya milk** is especially associated with Kaohsiung. Most supermarkets and convenience stores stock all the usual soft drinks, as well as fresh **milk** and a bewildering range of **soy** and **yoghurt drinks**; low-fat (or skimmed) and non-sugar versions of all of these are slowly becoming available.

Health

As one of Asia's most highly developed destinations, Taiwan on the whole doesn't present many significant health risks for foreign travellers and residents – most visitors will find that using the same precautions they exercise in their home countries will be more than enough to keep them healthy during their stays. Given the high stress and crowded conditions of Taiwan's major west-coast cities, minor ailments such as colds and flu are common, as is the occasional stomach upset. By far the biggest health threat to foreigners is road traffic accidents, and the utmost care should be taken when navigating hectic city streets, especially by scooter. Medical facilities in the big cities are of a high standard, although English-language abilities vary so if you don't speak Chinese you may need the help of someone who does.

Before you go

The only **vaccinations** required for Taiwan are for **yellow fever** and **cholera**, but only if you're entering Taiwan within six days of leaving an area where these diseases are endemic. If you're travelling to Taiwan from affected parts of Africa or South America, vaccination certificates for these might be required for entry. However, you should first ask a knowledgeable health-care professional whether these precautions are suitable for you.

There isn't a long list of jabs recommended for travellers to Taiwan, especially if the duration of your stay is short and you're not planning to leave Taipei. If you'll be staying longer and plan to travel to more remote areas, including agricultural zones, mountainous regions or the outlying islands, you might want to review your entire vaccination record, but the only vaccines recommended for all travellers to Taiwan are for hepatitis A and typhoid.

Hepatitis A is a viral infection spread by contaminated food and water which causes an inflammation of the liver, and is present throughout Taiwan. The main symptoms are jaundice – yellowing of the skin and eyes – and nausea, sometimes accompanied by sustained periods of lethargy. There is no specific treatment for hepatitis A, other than to eliminate consumption of alcohol and other substances that are harmful to the liver while it heals.

Typhoid is a serious bacterial infection spread by contaminated food and water,

generally in localized epidemics. Symptoms include headaches and high fever that slowly intensify, often accompanied by acute stomach pain and constipation that can give way to diarrhoea in the later stages. Immediate medical treatment is required if infected, though blood tests are necessary for positive diagnosis. Treatment is with antibiotics. The vaccination isn't totally effective, so the usual discretion is advised when eating and drinking.

Optional vaccinations

Though the risks of contracting the rare mosquito-borne viral disease **Japanese B encephalitis** are extremely low in Taiwan, vaccination is sometimes advised for travellers who plan to spend more than one month outside of major population centres. The transmission season is when mosquitoes are most prevalent, usually from June to October, and there are slight risks everywhere except the cooler climes of the central mountain range.

The **hepatitis B** series of vaccines, fairly standard for most travellers, might also be worth considering before coming to Taiwan. Hepatitis B is spread by body fluids, usually through sexual contact but also from blood transfusions and unsterilized needles. Symptoms include gradual yellowing of the skin and eyes, preceded by bouts of lethargy, fever and pains in the upper right abdomen.

While it is rare for travellers, Taiwan has a high infection rate of **tuberculosis** (TB), and medical or aid workers and long-term residents expecting to have significant contact with locals should take precautionary measures. This serious airborne respiratory disease is transmitted by inhalation, and spread by coughing and spitting, so those travelling in the betel-nut-chewing hotbeds of central and southern Taiwan could be at slight risk.

Influenza is common in Taiwan and is typically transmitted during the winter months, usually from November to April. If you'll be travelling at this time you may want to consider a flu vaccination, especially if you're over age 65 or have underlying medical conditions such as diabetes, heart disease or lung disease. One injection usually lasts for about two months.

If you think you need any of these vaccinations, visit a doctor as far ahead of your trip as possible to ensure that you have enough time to complete the necessary courses before your departure. You should have all your jabs **recorded** on an International Certificate of Vaccination, as much to keep track of your vaccination record as to show immigration authorities when necessary.

Prescription medications should be kept in their original, labelled containers and you should carry photocopies of the prescription notes with the date and signature visible – not only will this help customs officials

verify the legitimacy of your medication, but it also could come in handy if you need to get a prescription filled in Taiwan.

Drinking water

The water in Taiwan is a potential cause of minor stomach ailments, especially for first-time visitors. Though **tap water** is considered potable in most places, it's not a good idea for travellers to drink it unless it has first been boiled – many hotels provide an electric kettle for this purpose. It's best to buy **bottled water**, but be wary of generic-looking bottles sold in smaller shops – some of these might contain unboiled tap water. Some people avoid **ice** in outdoor markets, where at times unboiled or contaminated water has been used. However, the ice used at dessert and iced teashops is almost always safe.

Water purification

When hiking in the national parks and recreation areas, try to carry all the water you'll need with you. However, for multi-day trekking or climbing trips, you'll need to rely partially on source water and you should choose these carefully. Avoid water which is in the vicinity of animals, particularly grazing mammals such as water buffalo, cows, sheep or goats, and especially if they have

Suggested first-aid kit

It's worth bringing your own **first-aid kit**, especially if you'll be spending time in rural or remote areas – such as the mountains – where there is limited or no access to medical care. At the bare minimum, include the following:

• Plasters (band-aids) of various sizes
• Sterile bandages in sealed packets
• Medical tape
• Painkillers and anti-inflammatories
• Antiseptic spray and/or cream
• Insect repellent (preferably DEET-based)
• Calamine lotion and/or aloe vera
• High-factor sunscreen and hat
• Rehydration salts or tablets
• Course of multi-purpose antibiotics
• Water sterilization tablets or purification filter
• Emergency diarrhoeal suppressant
• Multi-vitamin supplements

left droppings in the area. In general, the higher you go the less chance there is of contamination, but caution should be taken even with high-altitude spring water. Water should typically be **boiled** for at least ten minutes to kill microorganisms, but at higher altitudes the boiling temperature might not be sufficient to destroy them and so it's best to filter or chemically treat it. The most widely used chemical purifier is **iodine**, which these days is most commonly found in tablet form, but this gives the water a foul taste and in any case should not be used for more than a few consecutive days. Iodine also should never be used for pregnant women, babies or those with thyroid conditions. If done properly, hand-pump **filtering** is generally a safe and effective method of purifying water and is worth considering if you plan to spend several days in remote areas where you'll definitely need to rely on source water. Many hand-pump filters are extremely lightweight and compact, but the smallest ones can be time-consuming to use and are easily clogged. Most modern hand pumps funnel water over carbon or ceramic – both are effective, and which to choose is a matter of preference. Whichever you choose, if you're planning to be in remote areas for several weeks, carry a replacement filter for your pump. Buy these from specialist outdoor equipment outlets before you leave. Such equipment also can be found at a handful of outdoor shops in Taipei and Taichung.

Food hygiene

Food hygiene in Taiwan is generally quite high, though standards can vary considerably. Eat at places that look clean and are busy; apart from having the locals' confidence, busier venues are more likely to have a steady supply of freshly prepared food. Likewise, be wary of spartan self-serve buffets where the food may have been sitting out for too long, particularly in the heat of summer and when insects such as flies are present. Stick to thoroughly cooked food, and when sampling street food in outdoor markets remember that deep-fried dishes are usually safest. Lovers of raw fish can in general be confident in the freshness of most **sashimi** and **sushi**, particularly in coastal towns with renowned fish markets such as

Donggang and Chenggong, but the usual caution should be exercised when choosing trays from the revolving conveyor-belt sushi bars. Be selective when eating shellfish, especially on hot summer days – while they can comprise some of the most delightful dishes in Taiwan, there is a potential hepatitis A risk with many types, particularly if they have been left in the sun for too long.

Fresh **fruit** is safer if you peel it or wash it in clean water and dry before eating, while raw **vegetables** could be dirty or might have been washed in unclean water. Eating **utensils** are usually clean, but you might want to avoid reusable chopsticks if they are wooden – most restaurants will provide disposable chopsticks if you ask.

Intestinal problems

Diarrhoea is the most common affliction for travellers to Taiwan, though most bouts are likely to be mild and short-lived, brought about by changes in diet as your stomach adjusts to new bacteria. In most cases, it will pass in a day or two, but in the meantime it's important to rest and stay well hydrated, especially in a humid climate such as Taiwan, where constant sweating will only hasten your water loss. In serious cases of diarrhoea, when you're also vomiting or unable to eat, you should replace lost salt and minerals with an **oral rehydration solution**; this is critical for young children. If you don't have any packets with you, make your own by mixing half a teaspoon of salt and three of sugar into a litre of clean water (see p.46 for more on staying hydrated). Until the diarrhoea has subsided, stick to bland items such as white rice, plain rice porridge, simple soups and biscuits. Yoghurt is also particularly helpful in balancing stomach acids. Caffeinated drinks such as coffee, tea and colas can irritate the intestine and are diuretics that precipitate water loss, so they should be avoided, as should alcohol.

Emergency **diarrhoeal suppressants** such as those which contain Loperamide are only temporary blockers and don't solve the underlying problems; as such, they should only be used if you're in a remote area and must walk long distances or undergo an extended bus or train journey. Once you reach a place where you can rest you should discontinue use of these and allow your body to flush out the causes of your diarrhoea. Don't use such stoppers if you have a fever or if there is blood or mucus in your faeces. Most general-purpose **antibiotics** will quickly wipe out the bacteria that usually cause travellers' diarrhoea, but at the same time they can strip away much of your natural immunity and many doctors maintain that their use should be limited to emergencies.

If you have diarrhoea for more than five consecutive days, or if there is blood or mucus in your faeces, you could have a more severe problem such as dysentery or giardiasis and should seek immediate medical help. While it is uncommon in Taiwan and is not likely to affect the casual traveller, **giardiasis** is a legitimate risk if you're drinking from streams and rivers, particularly those in proximity to animals. The telltale symptoms are burps and excess gas that smell of rotten eggs, along with nausea, painful stomach bloating, profound fatigue and intermittent bouts of watery, discoloured diarrhoea (though without blood or mucus). If you're planning a multi-day traverse of a national park, where you'll need to drink from mountain streams, you should filter all water with a hand pump or purify it with iodine tablets (see p.44). If you'll be in remote areas for weeks, it's a good idea to carry a course of the effective antibiotic Metronidazole (marketed under the brand name Flagyl).

Dengue fever

There is no malaria in Taiwan, but **dengue fever** – a mosquito-borne viral disease whose symptoms are similar to malaria – has been a resurgent problem in recent years, in both rural areas and cities. There is no vaccine, nor are there any prophylactics against the disease, so the only way to prevent it is to avoid being bitten by mosquitoes. The *aedes aegypti* mosquitoes that transmit dengue bite day and night, so you should use insect-avoidance measures at all times. Also known as "break bone fever", the onset of the disease is characterized by severe joint pain that gives way to high fever, sweating and pounding headaches. Some people may also develop a rash over their torso and limbs. There's no cure, but bed rest is recommended while the symptoms run their course,

and paracetamol can help the headache. The symptoms usually subside after several days of rest, but they can return intermittently over the next several weeks. Although dengue is not life-threatening to adults, a more virulent strain called **dengue haemorrhagic fever** primarily affects young children and can be dangerous for infants. There have been cases of dengue all over Taiwan, but over the past two decades it has been more common in the south, particularly in Kaohsiung and Pingtung counties. Outbreaks tend to occur after summer rains, when pools of standing water stagnate, creating breeding grounds for the *aedes aegypti*.

Avoiding bites

To avoid being bitten, cover exposed skin with **insect repellent**, the most effective of which contains DEET (diethyltoluamide). However, the chemical is toxic and prolonged use can cause side effects. It's not recommended for young children and should be kept away from eyes and open wounds. Rub-on or spray repellent is widely available in larger shops, but some of the sprays sold in convenience stores are not very effective. As mosquitoes are usually more active at dusk and dawn, you might want to wear long sleeves and trousers at these times and avoid dark colours. If you'll be staying in rustic dwellings with cracks and open windows, sleeping under a **mosquito net** is a good idea, but make sure the mesh is not torn and tuck the edges in under the mattress. Few places provide mosquito nets, so you should bring your own or buy one in a major city. **Mosquito coils** also are effective deterrents and are more widely used by the Taiwanese than nets. At many outdoor restaurants, the staff will burn these coils under tables in the evenings – if you're being bitten, just ask for one.

SARS and avian influenza

In the spring of 2003, the outbreak of the potentially lethal **SARS** (Severe Acute Respiratory Syndrome) virus spread to Taiwan, causing considerable panic. The earliest cases were thought to have been contracted in neighbouring China and Hong Kong and brought to the island, but by the time the outbreak had been brought under control in mid-June, Taiwan had the world's third-highest number of confirmed cases, at 346, and the fourth-highest number of deaths, at 37, according to World Health Organisation figures. Still, the vast majority of the 8096 cases and 774 deaths reported worldwide were in China and Hong Kong, and in Taiwan many of the infected were hospital workers. The flu-like virus had the same symptoms as many other respiratory illnesses – high fever and cough – and those suspected of being infected were immediately quarantined. There have been no confirmed cases of SARS in Taiwan since June 2003.

Since the outbreak, the practice of wearing **surgical masks** when suffering from colds and flu has become much more common in Taiwan, and there is a heightened awareness of the health risks of coughing and spitting in public.

Avian influenza ("bird flu")

A mounting concern of public health officials are the continuing outbreaks of **avian influenza**, an infectious disease of birds caused by type A flu strains, that is increasingly being transmitted from birds to humans. Although the so-called "bird flu" usually only infects birds and pigs, the number of humans being infected with a mutated form of the virus has been rising, especially in countries such as China and Vietnam, and there also have been cases in Taiwan. Most travellers aren't at much risk of bird flu, unless they visit commercial or backyard poultry farms or markets selling live birds such as chickens, geese, ducks, pigeons and wild waterfowl.

Sexually transmitted diseases

Public awareness of the risks of **sexually transmitted diseases** (STDs) is high and transmission rates are generally lower than most other Asian countries, especially China. Still, despite the widespread availability of condoms, there are extremely low usage rates between couples of university age or lower, and officials are concerned that this could reverse the declining trend.

The most common STDs in Taiwan are chlamydia, genital warts (HPV), gonorrhoea, herpes and syphilis, and condoms can help prevent all but genital warts and herpes. **Chlamydia** is common in teenagers and young adults, and is of concern to health officials because carriers often have no symptoms, although if you have watery or milky discharge or experience pain while urinating you should get checked out. If left untreated in women chlamydia can lead to infertility. It can be cured with antibiotics if detected early. **Gonorrhoea** and **syphilis** also are risks, and are identifiable by rashes around the genitals and painful discharge. If diagnosed early, both can be cured with antibiotics. Of the more than seven thousand confirmed **HIV/AIDS** cases in Taiwan, more than eighty percent are believed to have been contracted through **unprotected sex**. Foreigners who are tested for HIV in Taiwan and are found to be positive will be deported.

A wide variety of **condoms**, including some imported brands, are sold in most convenience stores.

Environmental hazards

With Taiwan roughly divided between the subtropical north and the tropical south, temperatures can remain very high for much of the year, and the **heat** is compounded by high levels of **humidity** that take many foreign travellers by surprise. If you're not accustomed to this type of climate, allow yourself a week or two to acclimatize before you undertake any significant physical challenges, and avoid exerting energy during the hottest parts of the day – in summer, the comparatively cooler periods around dawn and dusk are ideal times for sightseeing.

Dehydration and heat stroke

If you'll be engaged in strenuous activity or exposed to the sun for extended periods, it's essential to stay hydrated, and that means drinking plenty of **mineral water**: a minimum of four litres in a 24-hour period, or enough to ensure that you're urinating regularly and that your urine is clear in colour. Be sure to drink mineral water rather than the **distilled** variety, which doesn't contain the minerals you need to stay hydrated. Most of the bottled water sold in convenience stores such as 7-Eleven is mineral water, but you should first check to be sure. On days when you're sweating considerably, it's a good idea to supplement your water intake with **rehydration solution** to replenish the salt and minerals you're losing. "**Ion-supply drinks**" such as Gatorade and Pocari Sweat, both high in sodium and sugar, are very useful to this end, and if you drink these at intervals throughout the day they also can help ensure that your body will absorb the water you drink. If you do get dehydrated – signified by infrequent urination and dark-coloured urine – drink an ion-supply beverage or a salt-and-sugar solution (see p.44). In extreme cases, dehydration can give way to **heat stroke**, which can become serious if ignored and could even require hospital treatment. The main symptoms are high body temperature, an inability to sweat, a racing pulse and flushed skin. In such cases, reducing your body temperature is pivotal, whether it means just finding some shade or even taking a lukewarm shower. This should be followed by rehydration efforts.

Sunburn and skin problems

During the hottest parts of the day, **sunburn** happens rapidly and can be severe, so it's important to stay covered and to protect all exposed skin with high-factor sunscreen, which is sold in most convenience stores and pharmacies.

The high humidity can cause all manner of **skin problems**, from **heat rashes** and prickly heat to **fungal infections** of the groin and feet. The best way to prevent these is to wear loose-fitting clothes made of natural fibres, to wash regularly and dry off thoroughly. Anti-fungal powders or ointments, or a combination of both, will be needed by most foreigners during the warmer months. **Prickly heat** is caused by excessive sweating, which can block your pores and cause inflammation of the skin, resulting in painful red "pinpricks". It usually goes away after a shower with warm water and soap.

Hypothermia

The **cold** can also be a big problem in Taiwan, especially in the mountains, which can get decidedly chilly even in summer and pose a significant risk of **hypothermia**. The abundant **rain** that douses the mountains most summer days in some ways poses a greater risk of hypothermia than the snow that covers them in winter, as the rain can leave your clothes completely soaked and this will cause your body temperature to plummet, especially if there are strong winds. Warning signs for hypothermia include disorientation, numbness, slurred speech and sluggishness, and the onset is marked by a weak pulse. Victims often lose all sense of their body temperatures and begin to engage in irrational behaviour such as removing much-needed clothing. To treat hypothermia, get the victim away from the elements and into shelter and give them hot drinks and easily digestible food to help raise the body temperature. All wet garments should be removed and replaced with dry ones.

Altitude sickness

Taiwan's mountains are the tallest in northeast Asia, and there are dozens of peaks higher than 3500 metres, the elevation at which many people start to feel the effects of **high altitude**. However, as most peak-baggers in Taiwan descend shortly after reaching the summit, few experience prolonged symptoms of **acute mountain sickness** (AMS) and this is not a major worry for most reasonably fit climbers. Still, it's possible for those overnighting near the summits to develop symptoms such as headaches, shortness of breath, exhaustion, nausea and difficulty sleeping; in such cases the best course of action is to move immediately to lower elevation.

Women's health

Feminine hygiene products are widely available in all of Taiwan's cities and towns, and **tampons** and sanitary towels are sold in 24-hour convenience stores everywhere. Some Western brands are available, and there is usually a greater selection in chain pharmacies such as Watson's. In some places, **birth-control** options can be very limited, so bring plenty of your own contraceptives.

Due to the heat and humidity in Taiwan, many women travellers suffer from **vaginal yeast infections** (thrush). Although the conventional treatment is with antibiotics, some prefer over-the-counter remedies, and an increasing number of women are starting to employ do-it-yourself cures. For more information on these, visit ⓦ www.msu.edu /user/eisthen/yeast.

Getting medical help

There are **pharmacies** in all Taiwanese towns, and most of them are of a high standard and offer a similar range of products to those in Western countries. Near the prescription windows there are sometimes counters offering treatment advice for a variety of ailments, but usually little if any English is spoken at these. In emergencies, you may wind up having to play a slightly embarrassing game of charades, acting out your ailment and pointing to the affected area – in such cases, the Taiwanese are invariably earnest and will try to help you without showing the faintest trace of amusement. Most pharmacies have a wide range of antibiotics.

There are **public health clinics** in most towns, and they generally are of a reasonable standard and can offer diagnoses and provide medication for most non-emergency conditions. Services of these are not expensive, especially in comparison with most Western countries, but you'll be expected to pay first and then make the claim to your insurance company later.

For emergencies and serious illnesses, you should go to a **hospital** – all major towns have them, although if you have time, you should try to get to a major city as their hospitals are usually of a higher quality and there is a greater likelihood that English will be spoken. The best hospitals are in **Taipei**, but Kaohsiung, Taichung, Tainan, Taitung,

Chiayi and Hualien all have adequate hospitals. At these, you'll also be expected to pay on the spot for treatment and make your own insurance claim later.

Travel health resources

Besides consulting the resources and clinics listed below, you can get practical information on staying healthy during your trip from the *Rough Guide to Travel Health*.

Medical resources for travellers

US and Canada

CDC ☏ 1-877-394-8747, ⓦ www.cdc.gov/travel. Official US government travel health site.
International Society for Travel Medicine ☏ 1-770-736-7060, ⓦ www.istm.org. Has a full list of travel health clinics.
Canadian Society for International Health ⓦ www.csih.org. Extensive list of travel health centres.

Australia, New Zealand and South Africa

Travellers' Medical and Vaccination Centre ☏ 1300/658 844, ⓦ www.tmvc.com.au. Lists travel clinics in Australia, New Zealand and South Africa.

UK and Ireland

British Airways Travel Clinics ☏ 0845/600 2236, ⓦ www.britishairways.com/travel /healthclinintro.
Hospital for Tropical Diseases Travel Clinic ☏ 0845/155 5000 or ☏ 020/7387 4411, ⓦ www .thehtd.org.
MASTA (Medical Advisory Service for Travellers Abroad) ☏ 0113/238 7575, ⓦ www .masta.org
Travel Medicine Services ☏ 028/9031 5220.
Tropical Medical Bureau Republic of Ireland ☏ 1850/487 674, ⓦ www.tmb.ie.

The media

As the only true democracy in the Chinese-speaking world, the Taiwan of today safeguards freedom of expression, and its media – print, radio, television and Internet – consistently exhibit a level of openness that is almost unheard of in Asia's other Chinese societies, including Hong Kong and Singapore. Since the end of martial law in 1987, when the ban on new newspapers was lifted, there has been a rapid proliferation in print media, with the number of papers rising from a few dozen to well over two hundred. Few topics are taboo, as evidenced by the gory full-page photos of bloody accidents that dominate the front pages and the racy escort-girl ads plastered inside. As all of this is in Chinese, however, it will be only a passing curiosity for most Westerners, who must rely on a handful of English-language newspapers, magazines and websites for news and information.

Newspapers and magazines

For English-language news on Taiwan and the rest of the world, there are three **daily newspapers**, all of which have online editions: The *China Post* (ⓦwww.chinapost.com.tw), the *Taipei Times* (ⓦwww.taipeitimes.com) and *Taiwan News* (ⓦwww.etaiwannews.com). The writing and editing standards of these papers are fairly high, and some of the domestic coverage can be quite incisive; however, international news is largely restricted to wire copy. All three have weekend **entertainment listings** and can be bought at bookshops, convenience stores, kiosks and business-class hotels. Adding to the island's daily domestic coverage is the online-only newspaper *Taiwan Sun* (ⓦwww.taiwansun.com). For deeper international news and business coverage, newspapers such as the *Asian Wall Street Journal*, the *Financial Times* and the *International Herald Tribune* can be found in five-star hotels and some news kiosks in Taipei.

For a more academic view of Taiwan, the monthly **magazine** *Sinorama* (ⓦwww.sinorama.com.tw) has well-researched, in-depth articles on a wide range of topics, including art, culture, finance, history, language, law, politics, sport and travel – many translated into English. For localized **listings** and coverage of nightlife, food and entertainment in Taiwan's major cities, the Compass Group publishes three free monthlies: *Taiwan Fun* (Taipei and Hsinchu), *Compass* (Taichung) and *FYI South* (Tainan, Kaohsiung and Chiayi).

All are available in Western bars and restaurants in the respective cities, or online "flip-book" versions can be downloaded at their website: ⓦwww.taiwanfun.com.

Radio and television

There are more than 150 radio broadcasting companies in Taiwan, with regular domestic programming by medium-wave AM and VHF FM stations in Mandarin and other Chinese dialects, chiefly Taiwanese and Hakka. The only predominantly English-language **radio station**, International Community Radio Taipei (**ICRT**; ⓦwww.icrt.com.tw), broadcasts 24 hours a day at 576MHz (AM) and 100MHz (FM). Its FM broadcasts include a mix of Western pop music, news headlines, talk shows and community service segments. Although it broadcasts nationally, it's difficult to get reception outside of the major cities.

Taiwanese **television** can offer travellers some interesting insights into nuances of the island's popular culture, with a host of variety and game shows, sitcoms, soap operas and films in Mandarin, Taiwanese and Hakka. Even if you don't speak Chinese, it's worth channel-surfing in your hotel room at least once, just to get a feel for what the locals watch. In terms of English-language programming, **cable TV** is available in most urban areas, offering the usual assortment of international news, movie and theme channels. When travelling in remote areas such as the mountains or some offshore islands, you're unlikely to get cable reception in your hotel room.

Festivals and public holidays

One of Taiwan's greatest novelties is the sheer range and depth of festivals, all celebrated with a passion and fervour unique to the island. While the biggest ones are the traditional Chinese festivals – which double as public holidays – there is also an eclectic collection of religious festivals (many commemorating the "birthdays" of gods and goddesses in the general Chinese pantheon) as well as an amazing array of time-honoured aboriginal celebrations, many paying tribute to the summer harvest or other tribal rites of passage. With so many festivals held throughout the year, it's likely that your visit will coincide with one or more, giving you the opportunity to see them first-hand – most are colourful affairs that give fascinating glimpses into the island's mysterious undercurrent of superstition and should simply not be missed.

The majority of cultural and religious festivals follow the **Chinese calendar**, which is mostly **lunar** in the sense that the first day of each month is that on which the moon is least visible, with the full moon marking the middle of each month. As such, the actual Gregorian calendar dates on which they are celebrated tend to fluctuate significantly each year – in our **festival calendar** (below), we have listed them under the Gregorian calendar month in which they are usually celebrated, with a note of their actual Chinese lunar calendar dates. We also specify which are **public holidays** (P) during which banks and government and private offices are closed, though many shops and restaurants remain open and indeed do a brisk business.

Travellers should note that during the major festivals – particularly **Chinese New Year** – the island's **public transport** groans under the pressure from domestic holiday-makers. Traffic backs up for miles on all major roads, while tickets for trains, buses, boats and planes are usually sold out weeks in advance, making travel during this time impossible or at best decidedly uncomfortable. Furthermore, businesses, shops and even some tourist attractions close during Chinese New Year, making travelling even more difficult, and **hotels** tend to raise their rates by at least four times during this period. Also, international **air tickets** from places with sizeable Taiwanese populations – from Los Angeles to New York to Vancouver – can

be harder to buy, while the many daily flights from Hong Kong are usually booked solid.

Aboriginal festivals

Though Chinese traditional and religious festivals are routinely well-publicized, many **aboriginal celebrations** remain closely guarded **secrets**, and even local tourism officials are often confused about or unaware of the actual dates on which they are observed. Villages typically stage their own celebrations, and **tribal elders** usually set the dates for these in accordance with a variety of factors. Further complicating this, established dates can be changed at the last minute in the face of inauspicious omens such as the sudden illness or death of a village elder. Finally, the truly authentic aboriginal celebrations are taken very seriously, with ancient rituals performed with pinpoint precision. As such, most tribes don't want their traditions to become a spectacle for busloads of camera-toting Taiwanese tourists, so many – especially those along the east coast – make a concerted effort to hide their celebration dates from tourism officials. However, individual **foreign travellers** or those in small groups are generally welcomed to events such as **harvest festivals** with open arms, often being invited to drink **local spirits** with the tribesmen. Those fortunate enough to experience these thriving cultures will learn about a side of Taiwan that most foreigners – and many Taiwanese – know precious little about, and it's well worth the effort to seek them out.

For the many **summer celebrations** along the east coast, travellers armed with scooters and strong Chinese skills are likely to be the most successful in finding them (see east coast p.438).

Festivals calendar

January

Foundation Day/New Year's Day Jan 1 (P). Marks the founding of the Republic of China in 1911, but also gives a nod to the beginning of the Gregorian calendar year. Offices and schools are shut, with many remaining closed on Jan 2 & 3.

January/February

Chinese New Year Lunar Jan 1–3 (P). Taiwan's most important festival, marking the start of the Chinese year. Celebrations centre mostly on family gatherings with lavish meals, usually including fish; "lucky" money in small red envelopes is exchanged; fairs and public parades are held.
Qingshui Zushi's Birthday Lunar Jan 6. Commemorates the quasi-historic figure from Fujian, revered for his wisdom and munificence (see Contexts p.530). Main ceremonies at Zushih Temple in Sansia, outside Taipei, including the ritual slaying of "God Pigs".
Jade Emperor's Birthday Lunar Jan 9. Pays tribute to the chief Taoist deity, the head of celestial government thought to mirror that of Imperial China (see Contexts p.531). Main ceremonies at temples in Dasi, Taichung and Tainan.
Lantern Festival Lunar Jan 15. Marks the end of Chinese New Year festivities, but itself often lasts several days in big cities such as Taipei and Kaohsiung; main activities are the public distribution and display of paper lanterns; in some cities, paper lanterns are launched into the sky, most famously during the Heavenly Lantern Festival in Pingsi; another popular event is the Beehive Rockets Festival in Yanshuei near Tainan, where an almost 200-year tradition of setting off fireworks has transformed into an annual free-for-all. Prayers for sons are popular at this time.

February

Peace Memorial Day Feb 28 (P). Instituted in 1997, and also known as "2-28 Memorial Day", it commemorates the 2-28 Incident, in which massive public protests which started on February 28, 1947 sparked a military crackdown that claimed at least 28,000 lives and ushered in forty years of martial law (see Contexts p.513).

February/March

Wenchang Dijun's Birthday Lunar Feb 3. Pays respect to the God of Literature or Culture, revered by students and their parents ahead of exams. Offerings of incense and wishes are written on colourful paper placed in glass jars.
Mayasvi Festival Tsou tribe celebration of warriors returning from battle, with rituals giving thanks to the God of War and the God of Heaven. Hosted annually in rotation between Dabang and Tefuye villages.

March

Guanyin's Birthday Lunar Feb 19. The Goddess of Mercy's birthday is celebrated at Buddhist temples throughout the country, but the main place to mark the occasion is Taipei's Longshan Temple. The event is also marked at the Tzuchu Temple (or the "Purple Bamboo" Temple) in Neimen, which holds a festival celebrating its 300-plus-year history as one of the most sacred sites for Taiwanese Buddhists. The festival features the island's most important annual performances of the Song Jiang Battle Array, ritualised martial performing arts depicting symbolic battles with a variety of traditional weapons, including farm tools.
Youth Day March 29 (P). Pays tribute to the more than one hundred of Sun Yat-sen's revolutionaries who were killed in the failed Canton Uprising against the imperial Qing government on March 29, 1911. Taiwan's President officiates at a public service at the National Revolutionary Martyrs' Shrine in Taipei, and local governments hold similar ceremonies.

March/April

Queen Mother of the West's Birthday Lunar March 3. Honours the highest-ranking female deity, often portrayed as the Jade Emperor's wife (see Contexts p.531). Main festivities in Hualien (where it is celebrated on Lunar 18/7), the centre of her cult in Taiwan.
Supreme Emperor of the Dark Heaven's Birthday Lunar March 3. Pays respect to the controller of the elements, particularly fire (see Contexts p.531). Worshipped at some four hundred temples throughout Taiwan.

April

Tomb Sweeping Day April 5 (P). Families visit cemeteries to clean graves of relatives and pay respect to their ancestors. In Taiwan, it's celebrated on the anniversary of Chiang Kai-shek's death; "Grave cakes" are offered and paper money is burnt.
Baosheng Dadi's Birthday Lunar March 15. Marks the birthday of Baosheng Dadi, the "Great

Emperor who Preserves Life". Biggest celebration is held in Syuejia, north of Tainan.

April/May

Bunun Ear-shooting Festival Most important celebration of the Bunun tribe, traditionally a test of archery skills to mark the coming of age of the tribe's males.

Dajia Mazu Pilgrimage This eight-day, seven-night pilgrimage comprises one of the world's biggest religious festivals, with worshippers parading a caravan containing one of the island's most revered Mazu deities around a circuit before returning it to its mother temple in Dajia (see p.250). Always preceding Mazu's birthday celebration, the pilgrimage is part of the month-long Dajia Mazu Culture Festival.

Mazu's Birthday Lunar March 23. One of Taiwan's most important folk festivals, celebrating the birthday of Mazu, Goddess of the Sea, the island's most popular folk deity. Mazu deities are returned to their "mother temples" on this day to be blessed and increase their spiritual powers. The liveliest celebrations are held at Dajia's Jhenlan Temple (see p.249), Beigang's Chaotian Temple (see p.289) and Lugang's Tianhou Temple (see p.260).

May

Labour Day May 1 (P). Celebrates workers' rights and the eight-hour workday in line with international convention.

Donggang Bluefin Tuna Festival Taiwanese flock to this fishing town to feast on fresh Pacific Bluefin Tuna, revered by the Japanese (see South Taiwan p.363).

May/June

Cleansing Buddha Festival Lunar April 8. Celebrates the birth of Buddha in accordance with the Mahayana School. Worshippers flock to Buddhist temples island-wide, with monasteries such as Chung Tai Chan, Foguangshan and Dharma Drum hosting legions of devotees.

Tainan City God Birthday Lunar April 20. Main festivities are held at the venerated Tainan City God Temple (see p.326).

Dragon Boat Festival Lunar May 5 (P). One of the three major Chinese holidays, featuring dragon boat races held in honour of the poet Qu Yuan who, according to legend, drowned himself in protest after being slandered by envious officials on this date in 280 BC. Races are held in most major cities with waterways – including international races in Taipei and Keelung – but the most distinctly Taiwanese are

the aboriginal-style races held in Erlong (see p.190), near the east coast hot-springs resort of Jiaosi.

June

Taipei City God Birthday Lunar May 13. Includes fireworks, elaborate dances by temple guardians and a lavish parade in which the deity is carried around the streets surrounding Taipei's City God Temple (see p.105).

July/August

Guan Di's Birthday Lunar June 24. Honours one of Taiwan's most admired deities, the red-faced patron of chivalrous warriors, misleadingly known as the God of War (see Contexts p.529). Ceremonies held island-wide, but Taipei's Xingtian Temple hosts the biggest.

Yimin Festival Lunar July. The most important annual observance of the Hakka people honours groups of Hakka militia from the late eighteenth century. The main celebration is held at the Yimin Temple in Fangliao, near Hsinchu, and is marked by offerings to ancestors, music and the ritual slaying of several dozen force-fed "God Pigs" – an increasingly controversial ceremony that is seldom witnessed by foreigners (see North Taiwan p.205).

August

Austronesian Culture Festival International festival of aboriginal cultures in Taitung, designed to instil pride and preserve traditions, using the example of indigenous peoples such as the Maori of New Zealand.

Ami Harvest Festival One of the most colourful aboriginal celebrations, centred on dancing, singing and coming-of-age rituals for young men. Although dates vary from year to year, the most important festival of the Ami tribe is generally held in late summer, often in August. Ask at villages north of Taitung (see p.410).

August/September

Ghost Month Begins Lunar July 1. The time when the gates of hell are opened and spirits of "hungry ghosts" haunt the living (see Contexts p.525). Daily rituals include burning of incense and paper money, while major festivals are held in Keelung, Toucheng and Hengchun at the middle and end of the month.

Ghost Festival Lunar July 15. Appeasement ceremonies held at temples across the island. Families offer flowers, fruit and three sacrificial offerings: chicken (or duck), pig and fish. Taiwan's most famous is the Keelung Ghost Festival, a unique version of Zhongyuan Pudu, where an elaborate night parade is held before thousands of glowing "water lanterns" are released onto the Keelung River to appease the ghosts of those killed by drowning (see North Taiwan p.173).

Dizang Wang's Birthday Lunar July 30. Marks the birthday of this Buddhist deity, misleadingly known as the King of Hell (see Contexts p.532). Main offerings at Chiayi's Beiyu (North Hell) Temple (see Central Taiwan p.287).

Ghost Month Ends Midnight Lunar July 30. On the last day of Ghost Month, the gates of hell close and hungry ghosts return to the underworld. In the month's last hour, contests called *ciang gu* – in which men race to climb tall bamboo towers to collect meat and rice dumplings – are held; the most famous is in Toucheng near Yilan, while a similar event also is staged in Hengchun in the southwest.

Thao Pestle Music Festival Held during the seventh lunar month in Itashao Village on Sun Moon Lake, members of the Thao tribe – Taiwan's smallest aboriginal group (see Contexts p.523) – pound grain into a stone mortar with bamboo pestles, creating a traditional harmony.

September

Armed Forces Day Sept 3. Honours all branches of Taiwan's military while also marking the end of China's eight-year War of Resistance against Japan. Big ceremonies at martyrs' shrines around Taiwan and military parades in the big cities.

Chiayi City God Birthday Lunar Aug 2. Held at Chiayi's City God Temple (see p.286).

Teachers' Day/Confucius's Birthday Sept 28. Pays tribute to teachers on the birthday of China's best-known educator and scholar, Confucius. Unique dawn ceremonies are held at Confucius temples nationwide, with the biggest at Taipei's Confucius Temple (see Taipei p.109).

September/October

Mid-Autumn Festival Lunar Aug 15 (P). Also known as the "Moon Festival" – families gather in parks and scenic spots to admire what is regarded as the year's most luminous moon and to share moon cakes and pomeloes. Since the festival coincides with the fall harvest, the Taiwanese also mark it by making offerings to the Earth God – or Tudi Gong in Mandarin – for a bountiful harvest. Small, often almost makeshift shrines to the Earth God are found all over the island.

Double Ninth Day Lunar Aug 9. Nine is a number associated with yang, or male energy, and on the ninth day of the ninth lunar month certain qualities such as male strength are celebrated through a variety of activities, including hill walking and drinking

chrysanthemum wine. In Taiwan, kite-flying also has become popular. In 1966, the day also was designated as "Senior Citizens' Day", and since then it has been viewed as a time to pay respect to the elderly.

October

Hualien Stone Sculpture Festival Highlights the work of local and international stone sculptors (see p.392).

Sanyi Woodcarving Festival Held in Taiwan's woodcarving capital to celebrate the craft. Includes ice sculpting and carving contests (see p.211).

National Day Oct 10 (P). Also known as "Double Tenth Day", it commemorates the Wuchang Uprising that led to the overthrow of the Qing dynasty in 1911 by revolutionaries led by Sun Yat-sen. Military and public parades and fireworks displays are held in front of the Presidential Building in Taipei.

Retrocession Day Oct 25. Marks the official end of fifty years of Japanese colonial rule over Taiwan on October 25, 1945. The national flag is flown everywhere.

November

Rukai Black Rice Festival The Rukai tribe's major festival, named in honour of what was once their staple diet but is rarely seen today. Offerings are made for abundant harvests, and it's a traditional time for marriage proposals and weddings. The biggest ceremony is held at Duona, usually in late November, in Maolin National Scenic Area (see p.360).

Ritual of the Short Black People The most poignant expression of Saisiyat ("true people") identity, meant to appease spirits of a people the tribe is believed to have exterminated (see Contexts p.522). Major festival held every ten years, with a smaller one every other year.

Birth of Bodhidharma Lunar Oct 5. Honours the legendary Buddhist monk, also known as the Tripitaka Dharma Master, traditionally credited as the founder of the meditative Chan – or Zen as it's known in Japan and the West – school of Buddhism (see Contexts p.527). Rites performed at the Chung Tai Chan Monastery near Puli (see p.273).

Sun Yat-sen's Birthday Nov 12 (P). Marks the birthday of Sun Yat-sen, founder of the Republic of China and the Chinese Nationalist Party who is commonly known as the father of modern China.

Qingshan's Birthday Lunar Oct 22. Celebrates the birthday of the King of Qingshan (Green Mountain), who is believed to ward off pestilence and dispense justice in the underworld. Ceremonies held at Taipei's ornate Qingshan Temple (see Taipei p.103).

December

Puyuma Ear-shooting Festival Celebration of the Puyuma tribe, traditionally a test of archery skills. Rituals held near Jhihben, to the south of Taitung.
Tsou Fona Festival Celebration of the "fona", Tsou language for the hyacinth bean, symbol of the longevity of the Tsou nation. Festivities include a modified Tsou wedding ceremony which takes place at the 47.5-kilometre marker of Highway 18.
Constitution Day Dec 25. Commemorates the passage of the Constitution of the Republic of China on 25 December 1946. The national flag is flown throughout the country, but these days Christmas is also giving cause for celebration.

Outdoor activities and adventure sports

One look at a relief map of Taiwan shows you its huge adventure sports potential; bisected by northeast Asia's highest mountains and with the rushing rivers and sheer cliffs of the east coast spilling into an emerald sea, this hidden paradise of outdoor pursuits is starting to attract more and more adventurous travellers from Asia and the rest of the world. As well as a haven for trekkers and mountaineers, the island also offers excellent conditions for a range of activities, from mountain biking and kayaking to paragliding and surfing, with many grassroots operators springing up to meet the needs of travellers.

Hiking and trekking

Contrary to the widely held assumption that Taiwan is one giant industrial wasteland, most of the island is, in fact, rugged wilderness that offers some of Asia's most amazing **hiking** and **trekking** possibilities. With an extensive network of national parks, scenic areas and forest reserves – all of which are laced with trails – the hardest part for most hikers is deciding where to start. For those just looking for a stroll in the fresh air, there are scores of low-elevation **nature walks** and **historic trails** throughout the island that give walkers a glimpse of its rugged beauty without the need for much advance preparation. With Taiwan's three biggest cities – Taipei, Kaohsiung and Taichung – either surrounded by mountains or just a stone's throw away, many of these trails can even be accessed by public transport, making them ideal day-trip destinations. Whether it's in the lushly vegetated mountains of Yangmingshan National Park that envelope Taipei or the Shoushan Nature Reserve within the Kaohsiung city limits, there's little excuse for nature lovers not to escape from the urban congestion. Those seeking some more **intermediate hikes** a bit further afield have no shortage of options, with dozens of national scenic areas featuring a variety of trails that showcase the island's diverse scenery. For experienced outdoor enthusiasts in search of multi-day, **unsupported treks** through remote mountain ranges, the often arduous trails (variously built by aboriginal hunters, Qing-dynasty soldiers or Japanese loggers) that cut through otherwise untouched preserves such as Shei-Pa National Park or the vast Yushan National Park represent true wilderness challenges. However, for most of these you must first obtain a **Class A mountain permit**, and some will also require the hiring of an experienced guide (see p.56 for more on permits).

There also are seventeen **forest recreation areas** in Taiwan, with two more being planned. While the trails in some of them have suffered extensive typhoon damage and are in a perpetual state of disrepair, others boast well-marked paths, some of which have English signage. For more

Hiking/mountain climbing equipment

When hiking you should carry plenty of warm, dry clothing, dress in **layers** and wear a hat and breathable waterproofs on top and bottom, even in summer. Pack your spare clothes and sleeping bag in dry bags or waterproof ziplocs to keep them from getting wet. The same rules apply in winter, and although the colder temperatures often make for a dryer **snow**, at times the sun can melt it very quickly and walking through the high-altitude bamboo stalks can leave you drenched and miserable. The following **check list** should prepare you for most hiking conditions.

- Sturdy, lightweight boots or trainers
- Spare socks
- Blister tape
- Waterproofs (preferably jacket and rain trousers)
- Lightweight, breathable clothing
- Dry bags/large-size ziploc bags for keeping clothes/food dry
- Headlamp and spare batteries
- Hats (one that shields from the sun and one warm winter hat)
- Sunglasses with UV protection
- Sleeping bag
- Inflatable air mattress or foam pad
- High-energy food and snacks
- Water containers (bladders or canteens)
- Waterproof, durable rucksack
- Sunscreen
- Basic first-aid kit (see p.43)
- Gloves
- Fleece (thin pullover or thick fleece for colder weather)
- Water filter (carbon or ceramic) or iodine tablets (not for extended use)

For longer, multi-day treks in remote areas or climbing high peaks during winter:
- Warm, waterproof gloves and/or mittens
- Crampons (from late December to early February the highest peaks are often covered in snow/ice)

on these areas, visit the Forestry Bureau's website: ⒲recreate.forest.gov.tw.

A monumental effort is under way to link up many of Taiwan's major trails into an island-wide, north-to-south interlocking network known as the **National Trail System** – which could someday make it possible for hikers to traverse the entire length of Taiwan. However, the series of typhoons that strikes the island each summer inevitably wipes out various sections of trail, often taking years to rebuild, so the prospect of a completely unified network is perhaps an overly optimistic undertaking. For more detail on the trails that will comprise the system, visit ⒲trail .forest.gov.tw.

Mountaineering

With 258 mountains over 3000m and the **highest peaks** in northeast Asia (excluding some of the volcanoes on northeastern Russia's Kamchatka peninsula), you'd think Taiwan would be a mountaineering mecca, but some of its most stunning peaks are only summitted by a few climbers each year. While mountain-worshipping Japanese and Korean climbers have long recognized, and coveted, the stark beauty of its mountains, Westerners – and indeed non-aboriginal Taiwanese themselves – have only in recent years begun to scale the best-known peaks. Many of the trails are cut straight into the mountainsides and are thus extremely prone to dangerous **landslips** – especially during spring and summer rain – but apart from this most of the main routes up major peaks pose few technical challenges. Despite this, a **Class A mountain permit** is required for almost all of them (see box below).

By far the most famous is **Yushan** (Jade Mountain), which at 3952m is Northeast Asia's tallest. Ironically, it's one of the most accessible, thanks to a well-built, scrupulously maintained trail and one of Taiwan's most often-used mountain shelters. In good weather, reasonably fit climbers can ascend Yushan and its surrounding peaks without much difficulty (see Central Taiwan, p.306).

Taiwan's second-tallest peak, the 3886-metre **Syueshan** (Snow Mountain), makes for a beautiful climb that often yields awe-inspiring vistas of the mountains of Shei-Pa National Park and nearby Taroko National Park. During winter, Syueshan and the surrounding mountains that make up the so-called Holy Ridge live up to its name, often remaining covered in snow for months. The main trail to the summit is usually in excellent nick, and though the climb is steeper than that for Yushan, there are two mountain shelters that can help break up the journey (see North Taiwan p.221). Also in Shei-Pa National Park, and only a long day's walk from Syueshan, is the rocky, pyramid-shaped peak of **Dabajianshan**, which stands at 3492m. Although typhoon damage has temporarily caused the main trail from the northwestern side of the park to be closed, it's still possible to reach Dabajianshan via the backdoor route from Syueshan, provided you can convince park police to issue you a permit (see North Taiwan p.221).

One of Taiwan's most notoriously hair-raising climbs is the 3605-metre Cilai North Peak, located along the jagged Cilai Ridge, the site of dozens of fatal accidents. While the climb presents no real technical issues, the weather in this part of Taroko National Park is prone to sudden changes; at times leaving climbers lost in a sea of storm clouds (see East Coast p.402). However, the favourite of almost every serious Taiwanese climber

Class A mountain permits

One of the main reasons why relatively few foreigners get to climb Taiwan's tallest peaks – and as a result miss out on one of the island's most extraordinary features – is the astounding level of misinformation regarding **Class A mountain permits**. Taiwanese and foreign expats alike talk about them as if they're next to impossible to obtain, and even some official sources insist the only way foreigners can climb major peaks is to join one of the regular weekend climbing excursions arranged by **outdoor shops** in major cities, especially Taipei (the ones along Zhongshan North Rd are the most reputable). While these shops will take care of the permit paperwork and can cut out most of the logistical planning – attractive options for non-Chinese speakers with limited time – the downside is that you'll be shunted into a twelve-person **group** of complete strangers of varying experience and abilities, and you won't be allowed to stray from them for the entire journey. In addition, most foreigners will find that the group pace is ridiculously slow, and the noise levels are so high that you're almost guaranteed not to spot any wildlife.

It's therefore well worth **arranging your own permit**, the process for which is continually being simplified for travellers. No longer is it necessary to hire a local **guide** for walks up the main mountains, although it's still advised for peaks that require technical climbing skills, as well as for multi-day treks across remote stretches of the parks. The minimum-person rule also has been abolished, and it's possible for individual climbers to obtain **solo permits**, although park officials might be reluctant to issue these for more dangerous mountains, or during periods of heavy rain or snow. Note that if you're caught in a restricted area without a mountain permit the **fine** is a steep NT$15,000. However, of greater importance than this is the safety factor: by applying and submitting your contact information you're letting officials know where you'll be and how to contact you in the event of an emergency.

is **Nanhushan**, also known as "Nanhu Dashan". Tucked away in the far northwest corner of Taroko National Park, this gorgeous 3742m peak has been climbed by precious few foreigners (see East Coast p.406).

If you don't want to plan your own climb, a reputable outdoor adventure company is the Taipei-based **FreshTreks** (Ⓦwww.freshtreks .com), which usually organizes several climbs of the most famous peaks each year. The company, run by an energetic Frenchman, can arrange individual or group outings, and also specializes in activities such as rock climbing, river tracing and whitewater rafting.

Mountain biking

Given its hilly terrain and extensive trail network, Taiwan has some of the world's top **mountain biking**, rivaling the best of North America and Southern Europe. Heart-stopping downhill courses, technical rock gardens, jumps, berms and super-fast single track: the island has it all, and much is easily accessible from cities such as Taipei and Taichung. If you're an avid trail rider and

plan to visit Taiwan for any length of time, it's worth bringing your bike with you (rental bikes tend not to be suitable for mountain biking, see p.33). And, as Taiwan is one of the world's leading producers of high-end mountain-bike frames and components, you won't have much trouble finding service or replacement parts in major cities, whether you ride a hard-tail or full-suspension bike. Plus, there's an organized group of experienced and affable riders known as the **Formosan Fat Tire Association** whose members will take you out on the trails if you contact them in advance. Their website has a superb archive of photos, trail reviews, contact details and a forum which will help you hook up with local riders: Ⓦwww .formosanfattire.com.

Cycle touring

Another two-wheeled activity for which Taiwan is well suited is **bicycle touring**, as the dramatic "cross-island" roads that wind their way across the central mountain ranges offer remarkable alpine scenery

In all cases, the easiest way to apply is **in person** at the headquarters of the relevant park, as this allows you to thoroughly explain your plan to conservation section officials. It also enables them to suss out your prior experience and climbing ability as well as inspect your kit. And while they're under no obligation to do so, park officials will sometimes prepare your permit more quickly if you apply in person.

Application forms

If you aren't able to apply in person, for the time being the only other way for foreigners to apply is by completing the **English application form** and **posting** it to the relevant park's conservation section (Shei-Pa, Taroko and Yushan national parks all have an online application process for Chinese readers, but it's not yet available in English). The form, which must be received by the park one week (but not more than a month) before the planned start of your climb, is standard for all three parks and can be downloaded on the Yushan National Park **website** (Ⓦwww.ysnp.gov.tw). For group trips, the maximum number of hikers that can be covered under a single permit is twelve.

In addition to providing your personal details, you'll need to submit a photocopy of your passport photo page and list an **emergency contact** as well as your mobile phone number (although you'll rarely get a signal in the mountains). You'll also need to briefly outline your proposed **itinerary**, including the expected date and time of your start and where you plan to spend each night: for **mountain cabins**, the park will reserve spaces for you, though you must bring your own sleeping bag and foam or air mattress.

Once approved, officials will either fax or post two copies of the permit to you (specify which method you prefer and add your contact details to the application form).

and an honest cycling challenge to boot. The **Southern Cross-Island Highway**, which at its highest point cuts through part of Yushan National Park, is highly recommended, though during heavy rains there can be dangerous rockslides and caution is essential on the road's many blind curves. The **Northern Cross-Island Highway** is also an extremely rewarding route, as are the amazingly scenic **central cross-island routes**. Although the highway that runs along the east coast from Taipei to Taitung is a tempting option, the road is choked with giant gravel trucks and runs through several long, dark tunnels, making for a very harrowing ride. To see much of the island's best mountain and coastal scenery in one long ride, try a route that combines one of the central cross-island routes with the southern one: start at Sun Moon Lake or Puli and head north past Wushe until you reach Dayuling, then turn east and ride through the Taroko Gorge until you come out at Highway 9; go south to Hualien and follow Highway 9 through the East Rift Valley to just before Haiduan, then head west over the Southern Cross-Island Highway (see p.334). When the road finally spills out at Laonong, you could carry on cycling south into the Maolin National Scenic Area.

White-water rafting and kayaking

Taiwan's steep mountains combined with typically heavy spring and summer rains often make for solid white-water rafting and kayaking conditions. Though many streams are too steep and technical for all but the most experienced kayakers, a few of the island's rivers are well-known for **white-water rafting**. By far the most popular – and one of the safest – is the **Siouguluan River**, which at 104km is eastern Taiwan's longest. The main 24-kilometre run begins in Rueisuei, about midway between Hualien and Taitung on the East Rift Valley's Highway 9, and cuts through a gorge in the Coastal Mountain Range to finish at the Changhong Bridge just before the Pacific estuary at Dagangkou. (see East Coast p.414).

The second most popular white-water rafting spot is an eighteen-kilometre stretch of the **Laonong River** between the hot-springs resort of Baolai and the Sinfa Bridge on the Southern Cross-Island Highway. Several rafting companies based in Baolai offer reasonably priced trips from June to September, with mid-summer usually the best time to go (see South Taiwan p.362). Bear in mind that if you have rafted on more challenging rivers such as those in North America, you might find the Taiwanese approach is overcautious with operators on both rivers using support rafts and speedboats, leading to a less exciting experience.

If you prefer to negotiate your white water in a **kayak**, there are several other less-commercialized rivers. Some kayakers put in at the headwaters of Taipei County's **Nanshih River** at Fushan and paddle all the way down to Wulai, an elevation loss of about 200m. Another appealing option is the **Beigang River** in Nantou County's Huisun Forest, which has a fast-but-short stretch of rapids.

Paragliding

The exhilarating sport of **paragliding** is gaining enormous popularity in Taiwan, with a steady stream of fledgling pilots joining a dedicated community of die-hard expats and Taiwanese. There are over a half-dozen well-known flying sites scattered across the island, each with its own prime season, making it possible for local pilots to pretty much fly year round – and regularly attracting paragliders from neighbouring Hong Kong, Japan and Korea. Two places vie for honours as Taiwan's top paragliding spot: Luye High Terrace, in the East Rift Valley near Taitung, and the Saijia Aviation Park in Pingdong County, not far from Kaohsiung. The **Saijia Aviation Park**, which is popular in winter, was the first in Taiwan to open to paragliding and has the largest landing and best thermalling potential (see South Taiwan p.361). **Luye High Terrace**, which generally has better conditions in summer, has two specialized take-off sites with rubber running-track surfaces and is the site of an international competition that attracts some of the world's most talented pilots (see East Coast p.416). Although **Tiger Head Mountain** near Puli was once a very well-known spot, much of the surrounding terrain was destroyed in the 921 earthquake and its popularity has since waned. Along the northeast coast are some popular paragliding sites, such as **Feicueiwan** (Green Bay) near Keelung, as well as **Yilan** and **Hualien**. Taiwan's best English-language website on paragliding is at Ⓦwww.wingstaiwan.com.

Diving and snorkelling

Taiwan's **scuba diving** and **snorkelling** spots are not nearly as famous as those of Thailand, Indonesia, Malaysia and the Philippines, but a few of them easily rival or surpass those of their Southeast Asian counterparts. While most Taiwanese are very aware of the splendid diversity of **marine life** that flourishes along bits of the coast and several outlying islands, the widespread fear of ocean swimming (see Culture and Etiquette p.65) coupled with stringent rules for such activities has enabled much of the island's **coral reefs** to survive – especially those of some offshore islands. For the Western traveller, this is both a blessing and a curse, as it means there is plenty of exotic sea life to enjoy, but much of it takes considerable effort to reach and in most places there is little infrastructure to support serious scuba diving. The top spots are **Kenting National Park**, Little Liouciou Island, the Penghu Islands, and the superb Pacific islands of **Lyudao** and **Lanyu**. However, while the Kenting area has numerous dive shops that offer scuba trips, most of the other spots have less reliable operators, and if you want to undertake serious dives in these areas it's best to arrange them in advance through one of the many scuba companies in major cities such as Taipei.

Some operators offer reasonably priced **scuba courses**, with basic open water certification available for as little as NT$5000. Otherwise, if you're content with **snorkelling**, short excursions can easily be arranged on the spot at all the offshore islands, although you should be aware that many companies insist that you wear a wet suit, a life vest, and, in some cases, that you go tethered to a chain of Taiwanese tourists. If you know you'll be travelling to one or more of these islands, it's a good idea to bring your own **mask** and **snorkel** to avoid this hassle; fins are not essential, but in some places **neoprene booties** are necessary to keep from cutting your feet on the coral as you wade out. If you don't have your own kit with you, it's worth asking snorkelling shop owners if you can rent just the mask, snorkel and booties for a discounted rate and make your own way to the reef. In summer, there is little need for a wet suit in Taiwan's warm tropical waters, and, though some shop owners may tell you that the wet suit is needed to protect you from jellyfish, in most cases this is not necessary.

As for marine **wildlife**, the Pacific islands of Lyudao and Lanyu are veritable treasure troves of tropical fish, and sightings of sea turtles and magnificent striped sea snakes are possible even while snorkelling (see East Coast pp.425–39). Advanced scuba divers can see giant schools of **hammerhead sharks** off the southern tip of Lyudao from January to March of each year. For more information, visit Ⓦwww.greenislanddiving.com.

Windsurfing

Taiwan is well known for its **windsurfing**, and the **Penghu Islands** of the Taiwan Strait are widely considered one of the world's top windsurfing spots. Given the islands' unique flatness, the northeast monsoon winds that whip across the strait are especially powerful here with wind speeds of up to 50 and sometimes even 60 knots possible in winter. And the horseshoe-like shape of the Penghu Archipelago generates a venturi effect that squeezes every bit of the wind pressure, making it a spectacular place for slalom sailing, chop hopping and just pure speed.

While Penghu is packed with Taiwanese tourists in summer, due to the fierce winter winds it's practically deserted from October through March, save for the growing number of world-class windsurfers who are making the islands part of their annual circuit. Indeed, for the past several years Penghu has been one of the main stops on the annual **Asian Windsurfing Tour** (Ⓦwww.asianwindsurfingtour.com), and some years contestants have claimed it had the best overall conditions. The event, known as the **Penghu ProAm**, is usually held in November, and the local government has heavily supported it, investing in a windsurfing facility near the Guanyin Pavilion in Magong (see Taiwan Strait Islands p.453). Apart from Penghu, there are several other popular windsurfing venues, including

Baishawan near mainland Taiwan's northern tip (see North Taiwan p.166).

Surfing

Although Taiwan's **surf** is not of the same calibre and consistency as the likes of Hawaii, Indonesia or Sri Lanka, anyone who has surfed the island on its day will tell you that it can be nothing short of inspiring. Rideable waves can be found from tip to toe of Taiwan, but in general those that travel across the Pacific to crash against the eastern coastline are the ones to look out for – especially in the days preceding a **typhoon**. There are spots suited to all levels, from sandy beach breaks swarmed with beginners to reef breaks that only the experienced should attempt. For advanced surfers, crowds aren't a major problem, as the only really big waves are at the vanguard of typhoons or during the winter when you'll need a wetsuit, especially in the north.

While there are some **surf shops** near the higher-use beaches, these rent mostly longboards and only sell basics such as baggies, rash vests and wax, so bring your own board and back-up supplies if you're planning any serious surfing. The beaches best kitted out for travellers looking to surf are **Dasi** on the northeast coast (see North Taiwan p.186) and Nanwan and Jialeshuei near the island's southern tip (see South Taiwan p.378), as both **board rental** and **accommodation** are possible. But most of the best breaks are near the tiny farming hamlets north of Taitung, where the local scene is of farmers in straw hats rather than surfers in flip-flops. To surf these, you'll need your own board, private transport, loads of time to scout out the coastline, and plenty of experience navigating reef. One of the easiest to find is the **Donghe River mouth** – if you can catch it when there is solid grounds-well from a typhoon you'll be smoking some heavy river mouth barrels (see East Coast p.412). The best homegrown surfing **website** on Taiwan is at Ⓦwww.bluebirdboarding .com/gazza.htm, where there are photos, tips on some of the hotspots and a forum for local and visiting surfers.

Culture and etiquette

Mainstream Taiwanese culture is a curious combination of traditional Chinese practices, modern commercialism and technological ingenuity, capped off with a palpable Japanese flavour left over from decades of colonial rule. This mixture, together with an overwhelming desire for recognition by the rest of the world, makes the country an endlessly fascinating place to visit. Those expecting stereotypical "Chinese" experiences akin to what can be had in mainland China or even Hong Kong are likely to be surprised and enchanted by the striking behavioural differences between the Taiwanese and their fellow Chinese neighbours.

For starters, Taiwan people are unquestionably some of the friendliest in Asia, if not the entire world, and most foreign visitors are impressed by the oftenstaggering level of **hospitality** from the moment they arrive. It's quite common for foreigners to be approached by complete strangers – of all ages – typically offering to help them find their way or just striking up casual conversation in Chinese or English. While such random acts of friendliness can take some foreigners off guard, these encounters are invariably free of ulterior motives. Many Westerners who have spent considerable time in the Chinese-speaking world sense that the Taiwanese generally don't regard them with the same suspicion that often can be felt in places such as mainland China, Hong Kong and Singapore.

Curiosity and questions

What the Taiwanese lack in suspicion of foreigners they certainly make up for in **curiosity**, and visitors can expect the friendly third-degree numerous times during their stays. These innocuous interrogations usually begin with the well-established Chinese canon of **questions** regarding nationality, age, marital status, children and occupation. Unlike in mainland China, however, where foreigners are routinely asked how much money they make per month, most urban Taiwanese refrain from prying into personal financial matters – or are at least more circumspect in their approaches. If you're asked about your **salary level**, remember that many Chinese don't consider this to be private information and are unaware that Westerners usually find such questions to be downright nosy. Try not to be offended.

Like most Asian countries, Taiwan has a very family-orientated social structure, and the Taiwanese will be thrilled to hear about your family, whether you're rattling off a list of siblings or describing your spouse and children. **Photographs** of your loved ones can be particular crowd-pleasers, and they often wind up being passed around restaurant tables, train and bus station waiting rooms and hotel lobbies.

Depending on your disposition, and often on your level of Chinese, encounters with strangers can be limited to brief conversations or can lead to invitations to lunch, dinner or even to be a guest at one's home. Being open to such entreaties can give an insight into Taiwanese customs that might well be missed if you shy away from such interaction. Even if you're not an outgoing person, allow yourself to join a local for a meal out or even to share a home-cooked dinner with a Taiwanese family – in addition to sampling some authentic local dishes, you might well find yourself making lasting friendships.

Visiting a Taiwanese home

If you're invited to someone's home, it's generally expected that you should bring a **gift**, usually something simple such as flowers, a tin of biscuits or cookies, or a box of chocolates. As a rule of thumb, gifts should be items that are easily reciprocated, as Taiwanese are likely to offer you a gift as well. Don't be surprised if at first your host politely refuses your gift, exclaiming that it's not necessary and that you're being too thoughtful – this is an essential step to the time-tested ritual of gift-giving and receiving, and you are expected to gently insist that they accept it, stating that you would be honoured. Once a gift has been accepted, the recipient is unlikely to open it in front of you, for such action is viewed as crude or even greedy. Likewise, if you're presented with a gift it's a nice gesture to gently refuse at first, and once you've accepted it's best to put it aside to open later.

When visiting families, greeting the eldest member first is regarded as a sign of respect, although it's fine to first greet the family member whom you know the best. Before entering someone's home, always remember to first remove your **shoes**, even if your host at first says it's not necessary. Most Taiwanese don't wear their street shoes inside the home, and if your hosts take their shoes off at the door it means you should too. Usually shoes are left on racks in the entranceway or just outside the door – if the latter, rest assured that your footwear will still be there when you leave. Slippers are usually provided to wear indoors, and if you're wearing socks it's best to leave them on. Usually there will be a second pair of slippers to don before entering the washroom, as the floors are often wet. This "no-shoes" protocol often applies to hotel rooms, particularly Japanese-style quarters with elevated wooden floors. Even when viewing such rooms you're expected to remove your shoes before entering.

Eating out

As elsewhere in Asia, **restaurant bills** in Taiwan are rarely, if ever, divided up between parties, and attempts to do so can cause considerable embarrassment. Instead, guests will typically go to elaborate lengths to claim the honour of paying the entire bill, and this grappling between parties can often become animated and even comical. Despite the dramatics, the person perceived as the most senior at the table will generally emerge with the bill. The main exception to this rule is when someone less senior has specifically invited the others to dine with the explicit intention of paying for the meal. Still, as a foreigner, you should also offer to pick up the tab, but unless you're much older than your company or are dining with close friends, someone else will generally pip you at the post.

Facing up to face

As in many parts of Asia, the concept of "**face**", the grey area between politeness and public pride, is an omnipresent reality in Taiwan, and foreigners who are by nature thoughtful and sensitive to others are not likely to encounter serious problems. Unlike most mainland Chinese, many Taiwanese have travelled, studied or worked overseas and are somewhat accustomed to behaviour that could be categorised as "Western". As such, many Taiwanese, particularly in urban areas, are extremely accommodating of foreigners and often grant them general amnesty from the Taiwanese nuances of face. The best working rule is to avoid behaving in a way that causes someone to be embarrassed in front of others, or in front of you. Pointing out other people's mistakes or shortcomings, especially in public, is rarely appreciated and will usually precipitate the proverbial "loss of face". Losing one's **temper** in public and openly expressing anger is a sure-fire way to lose face, both for yourself, the recipients of your outburst, and sometimes even for those in the near vicinity. Not only are such public displays of emotion likely to cause profound embarrassment, they often will convince others that you are uncivilised and undeserving of further attention or assistance. This doesn't mean that Taiwanese people don't get angry, but rather that there is a general belief in the virtue of self-control when dealing with others.

When Taiwanese are embarrassed or upset, they often will **smile** or giggle nervously, which can be confusing or even annoying for the uninitiated foreigner. Understand that such smiles or laughter are in fact expressions of apology rather than amusement, and try to respond with a smile of your own.

The art of flattery

In Taiwan, a little **flattery** goes a long way, and newcomers are often taken aback at the astounding number of compliments they can receive on a daily basis. Often the use of a few basic Chinese greetings by a tourist can elicit howls of approval from onlookers, who might then offer profuse praises of your speaking proficiency. While this can be alarming for some, particularly those who can't speak Chinese, the best response is to very humbly accept the praise and then come back with some **compliments** of your own. At times, both men and women might be told publicly that they look "handsome" or "beautiful"; such comments are rarely intended as come-ons or pick-up lines, nor are they intended to embarrass, objectify or degrade the recipient. On the contrary, they almost always are intended to put one at ease, and it's usually best to modestly accept the compliment and return it if you feel inclined.

Physical gestures and greetings

Visitors to Taiwan and many other Asian countries will notice that most people beckon to each other with their palms facing down, waving towards the ground, and travellers are well advised to emulate this – calling people towards you by rolling your fingers back with your palms up is widely considered to be crudely suggestive, particularly when a man is motioning towards a woman.

Although in Chinese tradition **shaking hands** was not the usual manner of greeting, Taiwanese men now commonly practise this custom, particularly in business circles. However, powerful or overly enthusiastic handshakes are considered aggressive and can cause considerable bewilderment. Men and women generally don't shake hands upon meeting, opting instead for slight nods of deference, although this is changing and urban businesswomen are increasingly likely to offer their hands when meeting foreigners.

Business cards

Exchanging **business cards** is a Taiwanese obsession, even between people with no business intentions, and name cards with contact details can be very useful for any foreigner planning to spend time in Taiwan. Printing of business cards in Taiwan is cheap and quick; sophistication and detail are not essential, with your telephone, email address, and preferably your **name in Chinese characters** being sufficient.

When exchanging business cards, gifts or tokens of esteem, presenting them with **both hands** tells your counterpart that you are offering them unreservedly, as a wholehearted expression of yourself. To the contrary, passing business cards with one hand or flipping them across tables is uniformly viewed as uncultivated, flippant and even disrespectful. When receiving another's business card it's considered respectful to read their name and title and, when appropriate, to praise them for their position on the career ladder. Avoid immediately putting cards in your wallet or pockets – even if you're only trying to secure them, such action is likely to be interpreted as a sign of disinterest. Also, **writing** on business cards – especially in red ink, which is typically reserved for letters of protest or angry remarks – is still a major faux pas in Taiwan. This should only be done when you need to jot down essential information, such as a mobile phone or hotel room number, and have nothing else to write on. Even then it's best to first apologize and ask permission.

Clothing and appearance

Taiwan is a developed country with a fairly high degree of affluence, especially in cities, and people generally make an effort to look neat and presentable. As most foreigners are perceived to be people of means, Taiwanese have relatively high expectations for their standard of attire and dirty, tatty or **torn clothing** can at times be frowned upon. And while Taiwanese men can be seen riding around on scooters wearing nothing but shorts and flip-flops, bare bellies to the wind, foreign males who mimic this behaviour are likely to draw curious stares from both men and women. Although in most cases such displays are unlikely to offend, it's to be expected that the sight of bare skin and the often hairy flesh of foreign men will attract a considerable amount of attention. The same holds true for foreign men attempting to

replicate the common Chinese male practice of lifting one's shirt to expose the midriff while eating or drinking in outdoor markets.

As in most countries, upscale restaurants, bars, nightclubs and theatres in Taiwan often have **dress codes**, and if you turn up to these in shorts and sandals you might well be refused entry. However, this is more likely to happen at a posh Taipei establishment than elsewhere in the country, and venues with dress codes will often exempt foreigners as an expression of hospitality. There is some resentment of this double standard, especially in cities such as Taichung, where legions of sloppily dressed British and North American English teachers habitually abuse this goodwill.

In recent years, **skimpy attire** for Taiwanese women has become much more common, especially during the blistering summer heat. Mini-skirts and skin-tight tank tops are fairly popular, although they are more commonly worn at night, when there is no risk of getting tanned by the sun. While many of Taiwan's aboriginal women have no fear of flaunting heavily pigmented skin, the majority of Chinese women prefer to hide themselves under wide-brimmed hats and umbrellas during hot summer days; in fact, you'll often find Taiwanese beaches deserted until the cooler early-evening hours.

It's for this reason as much as any other that **bikinis** and other forms of revealing swimwear are uncommon in Taiwan. Although they are entirely acceptable for foreign women, wearing them can cause curious stares from both Taiwanese men and women at beaches, public pools and even communal hot springs. Women going topless and **nudity** – male or female – is almost unheard of, except at some segregated hot-springs baths.

Most Chinese men have little facial hair, and it is generally quite thin, so beards are an extremely uncommon sight. Even for foreign men, long **facial hair** is widely viewed as slovenly, although closely cropped beards and goatees are still on the whole acceptable.

Staring and spitting

Most foreigners will attract a fair few **stares** while travelling around Taiwan, and these are likely to increase in both number and intensity the further you get from the major cities. Those travelling to remote agricultural or mountain areas where foreigners are seldom seen can expect to receive considerable attention, although people still tend to keep a respectful distance and it will rarely seem invasive. In fact, those who have already cut their teeth travelling round mainland China, where point-blank stares and seemingly endless shouts of *laowai* ("foreigner") are the norm, might even find themselves feeling relatively ignored in Taiwan.

The unhygienic habit of **spitting** in public still exists in Taiwan, though at nowhere near the same scale as in mainland China. Although this is more common in rural areas where standards of public hygiene are lower, Taiwan's main spitting problem stems from the popular practice of **betel nut** chewing. Reviled as it is by urban sophisticates in Taipei and surrounding northern areas, betel nut chewing is nonetheless a national obsession, and it only gets more commonplace the further one ventures south into the island's Hoklo heartland. Here, virtually every other male can be seen with one or both cheeks crammed full of the flavourful nuts, the dark maroon juice staining their lips and teeth. Most veteran betel nut chewers aim to swallow the bulk of the juice, which contains a powerful stimulant, though in practice many spit out the bittersweet fluid that flows just after they crack open the nut – this is the source of the reddish-purple streaks that line sidewalks throughout central and southern Taiwan. These days, and especially since the spring 2003 outbreak of SARS spread to Taiwan, betel nut chewers are making a more concerted effort to confine their colourful saliva to plastic cups.

Superstition

One of the most fascinating features of Taiwan, and one that never ceases to amaze even the longest-term of foreign expatriates, is how some of the most ancient of Chinese **superstition** has survived – and even thrives – in one of the world's most technologically advanced societies. This seeming paradox pervades everyday life in Taiwan and is visible through countless actions, from the hip young computer salesman making elaborate

offerings at a makeshift shrine in front of his trendy downtown Taipei shop to the practising female geneticist praying fervently to a fertility god for the blessing of a son.

While most of the places of ancient lore are in mainland China, many of the traditional practices no longer exist there, stamped out during decades of Maoist revisionism and replaced primarily with conspicuous consumerism. And though traditional southern Chinese beliefs such as those of the Cantonese have survived in places such as Hong Kong and Macau, nowhere are age-old Chinese superstitions – mostly Fujianese – more a part of everyday life than in Taiwan (see Contexts p.525 for more on Taiwanese belief).

Bad omens

For the visitor, one of the most obvious aspects of this is the widespread belief in **bad omens**, and the lengths to which many Taiwanese will go to avoid them. Comments or jokes that imply **death** or disaster are almost certain to elicit visible cringes from those within earshot and can make some people decidedly edgy. For example, a seemingly innocuous statement such as "she's going to get herself killed walking in front of all that traffic," can imply that this will actually happen in the minds of many Taiwanese. This is not to say that warning people to be careful is taboo, but rather to not follow up a warning with a statement of what could happen if it's not heeded.

Actions that are implicit on the notion that something untoward could happen are also widely avoided in Taiwan, which helps to explain why so many Taiwanese refuse to write **last wills** out of fear that such action could precipitate their own demise. Giving someone a **handkerchief** as a gift, for example, is not recommended as it implies that the recipient may soon have reason to cry. Likewise, things that are symbolic of death, such as **white flowers** – requisite at funerals – are to be avoided. If you want to give someone flowers, it's best to choose other colours.

Even words or phrases that remind people of death can cause offence, with the most obvious of these being mispronunciations of the Chinese word for **"four,"** which said in the wrong tone can mean "death". Giving **clocks** as gifts also is unthinkable, as the Mandarin phrase "to give a clock" can remind people of that for "to attend a funeral".

Swimming

Another fairly common Taiwanese fear that in part can be chalked up to superstition is that of **deep water**. Many Taiwanese are unwilling to venture into water that is deeper than their heads, and most public swimming pools are no more than chest deep. Although this can be partially attributed to poor Taiwanese swimming standards – generally much lower than those of most Western countries – for some it has more to do with the fear that discontented ghosts lurking beneath the surface could possess them, as their bodies are believed to be particularly vulnerable while submerged in water. During the seventh lunar month, which usually lands in August, many Taiwanese – especially older ones – will avoid the sea altogether. However, this belief is far less common among the young and is quickly dying out.

Women travellers

Taiwan is an extremely safe country, and most **women travellers** here are unlikely to attract any special attention other than that usually paid to most foreign visitors. Still, it's always a good idea to be cautious when walking at night or through unlit areas such as underground tunnels, and, if possible, to take a friend with you. Some women travellers and residents have complained of occasionally being groped on crowded buses and Taipei's MRT, but the vast majority of foreign women never experience this. In recent years, there have been a few reports of late-night assaults on women by their **taxi drivers**, and though the police take this very seriously, you should be attentive if you take a taxi at night by yourself. You'll minimize the possibility of being harassed if the driver knows he is accountable – calling for a cab and taking down the vehicle number is good practice, or if you hail one on the street you might visibly jot down the driver's name and vehicle number. Having a friend hail the taxi and take down the vehicle number is even

better. Also, if you are carrying a mobile phone, make sure it's visible to the driver.

Racial issues

Although Taiwanese are generally extraordinarily tolerant of others and exhibit far less racial chauvinism than their counterparts in mainland China, some travellers and residents of African and Middle Eastern origin have complained of instances of subtle **discrimination** when applying for English-teaching jobs or dealing with officialdom, such as when seeking visa extensions. Most foreigners with excellent Chinese-language skills will attest that the Taiwanese can be very race-specific when referring to foreigners.

On the domestic front, and despite the official veneer of racial harmony in Taiwan, there is still a considerable level of antagonism between various **ethnic groups**, such as that between the Hakka and the Taiwanese-speaking Hoklo. In the years since the rise to power of the DDP, which is widely viewed as favouring the Hoklo, there also has been growing animosity between native Taiwanese speakers and the native Mandarin speakers who are often perceived as the offspring of Kuomintang invaders (see Contexts p.513 for more on this history). But by far the most derogatory racial comments are typically those directed at various "aboriginal" groups by those considering themselves to be largely Chinese.

Gay and lesbian travellers

Despite the traditional underpinnings of Taiwanese society, **homosexuality** is no longer considered taboo and the general public view of gays and lesbians is far more progressive than that of most of its Asian neighbours. Though pockets of prejudice remain, public acceptance of homosexuality has grown markedly since the lifting of martial law in 1987, and there are now thriving gay communities in big cities such as Taipei, Kaohsiung and Taichung. The country's **legal stance** towards homosexuals is widely considered the most advanced in Asia, with gays and lesbians enjoying most of the same freedoms as heterosexuals: there is no law against sodomy, and homosexual behaviour between consenting adults over age 16 in private is legal. In 2003, the government proposed legislation that would legalize same-sex marriages and allow homosexual couples to adopt children – if passed, it would make Taiwan the first country in Asia to afford gays this safeguard.

Much of this public enlightenment has been the result of a concerted drive by Taiwan's homosexual community, which boasts more than thirty gay and lesbian organizations. The country's first **gay pride festival** was held in 1997 at the 2-28 Peace Park, a popular nighttime cruising spot for gay men, and what was hailed as the first gay rights parade in the Chinese-speaking world was held in Taipei in 2003. However, less than five hundred activists joined the march, and many wore masks. Despite the progress, there has been considerable antagonism between some municipal police forces and the gay male community, with certain saunas being targeted for raids.

While Taipei undoubtedly has the most sophisticated **gay scene**, with numerous bars, clubs and saunas specifically catering to gays and lesbians, such venues are springing up in other major cities and same-sex couples are commonly seen in mainstream social establishments as well. Given this openness, gay and lesbian travellers should easily find places to hang out: some of the best-known venues in Taipei (see p.130) have information on gay clubs in other cities and often can provide you with their business cards. For current information on gay life in Taiwan check out ⓦwww .utopia-asia.com/tipstaiw.htm.

Tipping

On the whole, **tipping** at restaurants, bars and in taxis is not expected, although this is changing slowly in big-city districts that are populated with Western English teachers and students. When you're travelling round the country you'll rarely be expected to tip, except perhaps in the occasional Western-orientated establishment, particularly those run by North American expats. Even then, many of these will levy a ten-percent **service charge** onto your bill, obviating the need for any further gratuity. In some areas, such as Taipei's university district, you may receive a bill pointing out that a ten-percent service charge is not included, indicating that some sort of tip is expected.

Crime and personal safety

For the vast majority of foreign travellers and residents, Taiwan is an exceptionally safe place, and foreigners are seldom witnesses – much less victims – of crime. Though there are incidences of random street crime, it's not a major problem and foreigners who exercise the usual basic precautions are unlikely to be affected. By far the biggest threat to personal safety in Taiwan is traffic accidents, especially those involving scooters and motorcycles, and foreigners should employ extreme caution while out on the roads.

Crime

Even though foreigners are very rarely **mugged** in Taiwan, those walking home from bars or nightclubs late at night are advised to do so in groups. If you are robbed, try to stay calm and don't resist – it's better to lose your spare cash than risk injury. Though **pickpockets** are not as common in Taiwan as in many other Asian countries, they do exist, and travellers should be careful to conceal their valuables, especially on crowded buses or trains and in busy markets. When withdrawing money using debit or credit cards, only use **ATMs** in banks, convenience stores or post offices, as there have been cases of fake ATMs that download card information; however, most of these have been targeted at domestic bank account holders.

All **drugs** including marijuana are strictly illegal, and simple possession can lead to jail time and almost certain expulsion from the country. Police **raids** on clubs are common, especially in Taipei and Taichung, and in a few cases the police have taken all revellers to the station for urine tests. Dealing drugs is an even riskier affair, as it can be punishable by death; some foreigners convicted of drug dealing are now doing time in Taiwanese prisons.

Theft of personal items is not a major worry, but if you're staying in a business-class hotel with a safe it's best to lock up any valuables you're not carrying with you. Though hotel rooms are almost invariably secure, it's unwise to tempt cleaning staff by leaving valuables in visible places. Those sharing space with others in youth hostels, homestays and **dormitories** are most at risk of having something stolen, and fellow travellers are typically the culprits – don't leave money or expensive items such as camera equipment unattended in shared rooms. Unfortunately, **burglaries** are common in most Taiwanese cities, which explains the prevalence of bars on most apartment windows. Foreign expats leaving for extended holidays are advised to appoint a friend to either house-sit or to collect mail and check regularly on their flats.

Prostitution is big business in Taiwan, but it is almost exclusively geared towards the domestic market and hidden in **karaoke lounges** and **saunas**. With most of the trade controlled by organized crime syndicates, street prostitution is much less common than in many other Asian countries, and single foreign men are less likely to be solicited. As is the case in mainland China, in some parts of Taiwan seeming "hairdresser" salons are simply fronts for prostitution and are best avoided.

Taking **taxis** late at night can be a risk for unescorted foreign women; many Taiwanese cab drivers have criminal records, and there have been a few cases in which solitary **female passengers** have been assaulted (see p.65 for precautions).

Police and emergencies

In general, Taiwanese are reluctant to involve the **police** in all but the direst of emergencies thanks to their reputation for corruption. However travellers shouldn't hesitate to approach them. While cases of petty theft are likely to elicit only a perfunctory response, violent incidents such as unprovoked attacks on foreigners are usually taken more seriously (although bar fights involving foreign males might well be ignored). Police departments in most big cities have **foreign affairs sections** that are normally staffed with English-speaking officers. The national number for police is ☎110, while the island-wide number for **general emergencies** such as fire or ambulance services is ☎119. Police **contact numbers** for major cities are: Taipei ☎02/25566007; Kaohsiung ☎07/215 4342; Taichung ☎04/23273875; Tainan ☎06/2229704; and Taitung ☎089/322034 ext 2122.

Traffic hazards

Traffic accidents – especially those involving scooters – are the leading cause of death and injury to foreigners. The dangers of the country's roads are apparent from the moment you arrive: vehicles of all sizes, from giant buses to cars to scooters, all aggressively jockeying for position with reckless disregard for road rules. Indeed, it's fair to say that **road rules** are almost universally ignored in Taiwan, and it's debatable whether most Taiwanese have even a rudimentary understanding of traffic laws or even general safety rules.

In fact, the only practice that seems to be universally accepted is that drivers are only responsible for **what lies ahead**, and monitoring what is happening behind or to one's side is almost completely unheard of. This comes as a shock to most first-time foreign drivers in Taiwan, who are invariably forced into brake-screeching halts by scooter-driving grandmothers who pull straight out onto busy streets without so much as glancing at oncoming traffic. The dangers are compounded by the sheer number of **scooters** and motorcycles on the roads: there are more than ten million in Taiwan, giving it the world's largest per-capita ownership level. Perhaps the greatest problem with scooters is the rampant disparity of speeds between them and other vehicles – in major cities such as Taipei and Taichung, rush-hour traffic resembles formations of kamikaze pilots bearing down on the next red light.

Given all this, it's imperative for foreigners to **drive defensively**, employing tactics such as the "two-second rule" to allow space between yourself and any vehicles in front of you. Liberal use of **horns** is recommended, especially to alert those pulling out in front of you of your incoming presence. Those on scooters should wear **helmets** at all times, making sure they fit well and are properly fastened. The national number for **reporting traffic accidents** is ℡110.

Living in Taiwan

Taiwan has long attracted foreigners to work or study. The island is a haven for English-language teachers, offering decent pay and ample job opportunities, while for those wishing to study Mandarin, Taipei is widely acknowledged to be one of the best places in the world to master the language, and in recent years universities in other major cities also have begun to attract foreign students.

Teaching English

Despite the growing numbers of foreign **English teachers** in most major Taiwanese cities, there seems to be a continual demand for their services, and few qualified teachers come away empty-handed. In fact many travellers make a side trip to Taiwan to teach English while backpacking around Asia, attracted by its reputation as on easy place to live, work and save money.

Unlike places such as Hong Kong and Singapore, where teachers with English accents are preferred, in Taiwan it is the **North American accent** that is almost universally desired, so Americans and Canadians comprise the majority of teachers. However, the number of teachers from countries such as the UK, Ireland, Australia, New Zealand and South Africa is growing rapidly, and if English is your first language it shouldn't be too hard to land a job.

Finding teaching jobs

Although it's possible to source jobs from your home country before you leave, it can be difficult to determine the legitimacy of your company from overseas and most teachers recommend that you simply pick the place where you most want to live and turn up to look for work. The **highest-paying jobs** are typically in the biggest cities, especially Taipei, Taichung and Kaohsiung, but positions abound in other large cities such as Tainan, Hsinchu, Taoyuan, Keelung, Jhongli, Changhua, Chiayi, Hualien and Taitung. In fact, most larger cities have English-teacher populations that are sizeable enough to support a host of **expat-orientated** businesses such as Western-style restaurants, pizza parlours and pubs. If you would prefer a less insulated, more authentically **Taiwanese experience**, then smaller places – perhaps east coast towns such as Hualien, Yilan or Taitung – would be more suitable. In general, the best times to look are towards the end of summer and just after the Lunar New Year.

It's possible to teach a wide variety of **age groups** in Taiwan, from kindergarteners singing English songs to businessmen looking to refine their formal English skills. However, probably the most plentiful job opportunities are with the ubiquitous **bushiban** (after-hours cram schools, mostly for teenagers). While these night-time language centres are a major employer of English teachers, many foreigners have found teaching overworked and exhausted high school kids to be depressing.

Qualifications, work visas and pay

To teach legally, you must have a **bachelor's degree** or the equivalent from an accredited university in an English-speaking country. It's not imperative to have **TESL** (Teaching English as a Second Language) or **TEFL** (Teaching English as a Foreign Language) certification, but it will bolster your credentials and make your job easier and more rewarding – in some cases it might also put you into a higher pay bracket.

Once you've found work and signed a contract, your school will apply for your **work visa**, which will qualify you for an **Alien Resident Certificate** (ARC) and basic health insurance.

Many schools pay on a monthly basis, so you may have to wait for your first payment and should come with enough money to live on for at least one month (at least NT$40,000). Though **salaries** depend largely upon your experience and where you live, new teachers generally earn a minimum of about NT$600 an hour. Many teachers supplement their incomes – and try to dodge taxes – by taking side jobs that pay cash under the table, such as **private tutoring**. However, in the unlikely event that you are caught doing this, you are almost certain to be kicked out of the country.

Useful websites

The following **websites** have job listings, flats for rent, and regularly updated information on issues affecting English teachers in Taiwan: Ⓦwww.tealit.com; Ⓦwww.forumosa.com. Another useful site with information for English teachers around the world, including Taiwan job postings, is Ⓦwww.daveseslcafe.com.

Office work

While the overwhelming majority of foreigners working in Taiwan are English teachers, there are some **white-collar job** opportunities, though these invariably require proficiency in spoken Mandarin, and some call for Chinese-reading abilities as well. There is considerable demand for freelance **journalists** to write for English-language magazines and websites,

but the pay for these can be spotty, and full-time jobs for the main English-language newspapers usually require prior experience and strong language skills. Some white-collar professionals keen on working in Taiwan simply turn up and teach English while they look for jobs in their chosen fields. Another route that some expats take is opening their own businesses, particularly bars and restaurants catering to the overseas crowd.

Studying Chinese

Foreigners have been coming to Taiwan to learn Chinese for decades, with many claiming that Taipei is the best place in the world to study **Mandarin** as the version spoken here is far more intelligible than the heavily accented drawls of the Beijing dialect, for example. Be aware, however, that if you study in central or southern Taiwan – places where the Taiwanese dialect is commonly spoken – you are likely to hear highly corrupted forms of Mandarin in your daily activities, and this can seriously complicate the learning process.

In Taipei, serious students attend formal courses at the **Center for Chinese Language & Culture Studies** on Heping Rd (℡02/23218457, Ⓦwww.ntnu.edu.tw/mtc /index.htm), but there are seven other universities which run programmes. There also are many **language schools** in Taipei offering classes on a more casual basis, providing a useful way of obtaining extendable visas: CLI (ex-Flag Language Institute), Rm 1, 3/F, 61 Yenping S Rd (℡02/23313000); Pioneer Language Institute, 6/F, 200 Heping E Rd Sec 1 (℡02/23633535, Ⓦwww.chinese .org.tw); Taipei Language Institute, 4/F, Taipei Roosevelt Center, 50 Roosevelt Rd Sec 3 (℡02/23678228, Ⓦwww.tli.com.tw).

Taichung also is a popular place to study Mandarin, with classes in Taiwanese available as well. The **Taipei Language Institute Taichung Center** on Taiping Road (℡04/22254681, Ⓦwww.tli.com.tw) is a reputable private school with a variety of classes and prices. The more established schools are attached to the major universities: the city's largest public university is **National Chunghsing University** (℡04/22873181, Ⓦwww .nchu.edu.tw); apply six weeks in advance for courses at Fengchia University's Language

Center (℡04/24517250, ⓦwww.fcu.edu.tw); the Chinese Language Center at Donghai University also comes highly recommended (℡04/23590259, ⓦwww.thu.edu.tw).

Flat hunting

Finding a place to live in Taiwan is exceedingly easy, with a range of options suited to most budgets. Many foreigners choose to live in a **youth hostel** or budget hotel for the first few weeks, while they search for jobs and get established. The next step is often to move into a shared flat with other expats or to find a cheap studio apartment. The cost of a room in a pre-furnished **shared flat** varies widely, but in general they range from NT\$5000–10,000 per month in the big cities, althogh you can expect to pay around NT\$20,000 per month in Taipei.

Small **studio** or one-bedroom apartments tend to cost NT\$8000–12,000 a month, depending upon location and level of comfort. Even if you don't speak Chinese, it's entirely possible to find a flat without paying for the services of a property agent – there are listings in all local **expat magazines** and newspapers, see also "useful websites" p.49.

Travel essentials

Costs

Taiwan is one of Asia's most developed countries, and, as such, is a more expensive place to travel than say Thailand or Vietnam. Still, you'll find it considerably cheaper than Hong Kong, Japan or South Korea, and there are plenty of ways for inventive travellers to keep their costs to a manageable level.

While staying in Taipei can be challenging for backpackers on a tight budget, once you get outside the capital you'll find that prices typically run the gamut of budgets, from backpacker to mid-range to luxury traveller. **Accommodation** ranges from as little as NT\$300 (US\$9/£5/€7) for a hostel dorm bed to NT\$8000 (US\$240/£130/€190) for a standard double in a business-class hotel, while **food** can cost as little as NT\$30 (US\$1/£0.5/€0.7) for basic street food such as noodles to easily more than NT\$1000 (US\$30/£16/€23) for a meal in a semi-posh sit-down restaurant. By staying in basic doubles and keeping mostly to ordinary, working-class Chinese eateries, most budget-conscious travellers should be able to keep their costs to around NT\$1500 (US\$45/£24/€35) per day, perhaps a bit more when undertaking long train, bus or boat journeys.

Admission prices to most museums and tourist sights are usually quite reasonable; government-run venues are typically very cheap, while the cost of privately operated attractions varies wildly. Though discounts to museums and public performances are usually given to seniors and students, most travellers are unlikely to fit in the second category as foreign student cards are generally not recognized. However, foreigners who are genuinely in Taiwan to study Mandarin on a full-time basis can qualify for **student cards** that will be honoured throughout the country.

Bargaining is becoming less common in Taiwan as the country grows more affluent, but it's still an acceptable practice at most **souvenir shops** and many markets, especially if you're buying multiple items. Unlike in mainland China, where overcharging foreigners is often considered one's civic duty, this seldom happens in Taiwan, and in fact young foreigners might at times be quoted prices that are well below the standard rate. Given these factors, frequent haggling is unlikely to be appreciated and will probably not reduce your overall costs by much. However, **rack**

rates for accommodation are generally not observed and discounts are routinely given (see Accommodation p.34).

Disabled travellers

Though Taiwan's major cities are slowly trying to develop some basic infrastructure to make them more navigable for the disabled, overall the country is woefully unequipped to accommodate travellers with **disabilities**. Most city streets and sidewalks pose formidable challenges, with consistently uneven pavements, steep inclines, steps and few access ramps to be found. While some public buildings in the main cities have **access ramps**, and new structures in Taipei must be designed for the disabled in accordance with revamped construction codes, most buildings remain frustratingly inaccessible for those with walking disabilities. The heavy traffic in most cities also can make getting around dangerous, especially given that sidewalks are usually completely blocked off by rows of parked scooters, relegating pedestrians to the streets themselves. A further complication in big cities is the many pedestrian overpasses and underpasses filled with steps, few of which have access ramps. In addition, most forms of public transport are not equipped with disabled access. However, **reserved parking** for the disabled is becoming more common and is normally respected. Some public museums and tourist sites offer discounted tickets for disabled people.

Entry requirements

Nationals of the UK, Ireland, US, Canada, Australia, New Zealand and South Africa do not require a visa for stays of up to thirty days. This **visa-free period** is for travel only – working is not permitted – and it cannot be extended under any circumstances. Citizens of these countries must have a passport valid for at least six months from the date of entry, a return or onward air ticket and no criminal record. US passport holders with less than six months' validity remaining can apply for a thirty-day non-extendable **landing visa** upon arrival, provided that they have a return air ticket and no criminal record. For the landing visa application, two passport-sized photos are required, as is a NT$1200

visa fee and a NT$800 handling fee. Note, however, that the landing visa application procedure is only straightforward if you're arriving at Taiwan Taoyuan Airport, where the Bureau of Consular Affairs (BoCA) has a **visa office** just before the immigration counters. If you're entering the country at Kaohsiung International, you'll need to apply for a "temporary entry permit" at the Kaohsiung Aviation Police Station in the airport and then have it changed to a visa at one of the four BoCA offices (Mon–Fri 8.30am–5pm) within three days. Other foreign nationals can get information on various visa requirements at the Taiwanese legation in their home country, or on the BoCA **website:** ⊛www.boca.gov .tw. The site also outlines the procedures for changes of visa status, such as from student to resident.

If you plan to stay longer than three months and work in Taiwan, you'll need to obtain an **Alien Resident Certificate** (see p.69). However, Australians and New Zealanders aged eighteen to thirty are eligible to apply for a **working holiday visa** which allows them to engage in part-time work while they travel for up to one year.

BoCA offices

Taipei headquarters 3-5/F, 2-2 Jinan Rd Sec 1 ☏02/23432888
Hualien 6/F, 371 Jhongshan Rd ☏03/833 1041
Kaohsiung 2/F, 436 Chenggong First Rd ☏07/211 0605
Taichung 1/F, 503 Liming Rd Sec 2 ☏04/22510799

Embassies and consulates

Due to the pressures of the **"One China Policy"** only 24 states have full diplomatic relations with Taiwan under its official name Republic of China (see Contexts p.516 for the full list). These states have proper embassies in Taipei, and likewise Taiwan has full missions in their capitals under the ROC name. Most other states are represented in Taipei by a "trade and cultural" or "commerce and industry" office. Despite such names, however, these offices provide the same services as all other embassies and consulates.

Similarly, Taiwan is represented in most countries by **consular, information and**

trade offices, but adding to the confusion is the fact that most don't have "Taiwan" or "Republic of China" in their names – caving in to pressure from the PRC, most countries insist that something such as "Taipei" is used instead.

Taiwanese foreign legations

Australia Taipei Economic & Cultural Office Ⓦwww.teco.org.au. Unit 8, 40 Blackall St, Barton, ACT 2600, Canberra ☎02/6120 2000; Level 46, 80 Collins St, Melbourne, VIC 3000 ☎03/9650 8611; Suite 1902, Level 19, MLC Centre, King St, Sydney, NSW 2000 ☎02/9223 3233

Canada Taipei Economic & Cultural Office. 45 O'Connor St, Suite 1960, World Exchange Plaza, Ottawa, Ontario K1P 1A4 ☎613/231 5080; 151 Yonge St, Suite 1202, Toronto, Ontario M5C 2W7 ☎416/369 9030; 2008, Cathedral Place, 925 West Georgia St, Vancouver, BC V6C 3L2 ☎604/689 4111

Hong Kong Chung Hwa Travel Service, 40/F, Tower 1, Lippo Centre, 89 Queensway ☎852/2525 8315

Ireland Taipei Representative Office, 8 Lower Hatch St, Dublin 2 ☎01/678 5413

New Zealand Taipei Economic & Cultural Office. Level 21, 105 The Terrace, Wellington ☎04/473 6474; Level 18, 120 Albert St, Auckland ☎09/303 3903

Singapore Taipei Representative Office, 460 Alexandra Rd, 23-00 PSA Bldg 119963 ☎65/6278 6511

South Africa Taipei Liaison Office. 1147 Schoeman St, Hatfield, Pretoria ☎012/430 6071; 1004, 10/F, Main Tower, Standard Bank Centre, Foreshore, Cape Town ☎021/418 1188; 10/F, Rennies House, 19 Ameshoffn St, Braamfontein, Johannesburg 2001 ☎011/403 3281

Thailand Taipei Economic & Cultural Office, 20/F, Empire Tower, 195 South Sathorn Rd, Yannawa, Bangkok 10120 ☎02/670 0200

UK Taipei Representative Office. 50 Grosvenor Gardens, London SW1W OEB, England ☎020/7881 2650; 1 Melville St, Edinburgh EH3 7PE, Scotland ☎0131/220 6886

USA Taipei Economic & Cultural Representative Office Ⓦwww.teco-us.org. 4201 Wisconsin Ave, NW, Washington DC 20016 ☎202/895 1800; Two Prudential Plaza, 180 North Stetson Ave, Suite 5701, Chicago, IL 60601 ☎312/616 0100; 2746 Pali Hwy, Honolulu, Hawaii 96817 ☎808/595 6347; 3731 Wilshire Blvd, Suite 780, Los Angeles, CA 90010 ☎213/389 1158; 1 East 42nd St, 4/F, New York, NY 10017 ☎212/486 0088; 555 Montgomery St, Suite 200, San Francisco, CA 94111 ☎415/362 7680

Customs

You're allowed to **import** into Taiwan up to two hundred cigarettes, 25 cigars or 454g of tobacco and a one-litre bottle of liquor. Adults can bring in goods valued up to NT$20,000, and the duty-free allowance is up to NT$6000. It's prohibited to import gambling articles, non-canned meat products and toy pistols, and **drug trafficking** can be punishable by death. Publications promoting communism are prohibited on paper, although in practice this is rarely enforced.

Insurance

It's essential to take out an insurance policy before travelling to Taiwan, as much to cover against theft and loss or damage to property as for illness and accidental injury. A typical **travel insurance policy** usually provides cover for the loss of baggage, tickets and – up to a certain limit – cash or cheques, as well as cancellation or curtailment of your journey. Most of them exclude injuries caused by so-called **dangerous sports** unless an extra premium is paid, and it's crucial to ensure that any borderline activities you're likely to engage in are covered. In Taiwan, this can mean cycling, mountain biking (trail riding), paragliding, river tracing, rock climbing, scuba-diving, surfing (especially during storms), whitewater rafting, windsurfing and even trekking. Given the likelihood that you'll find yourself driving or riding on the back of a motorcycle or **scooter** while travelling round Taiwan – especially if you plan to visit any offshore islands – you should make sure this activity is covered as well. If you need to **make a claim**, you should keep receipts for medicines and medical treatment, including copies of signed medical reports clearly stating the diagnosis and prescribed treatment, in English if possible. In the event you have anything stolen, you'll need to visit the nearest police station and file a report for **stolen property**. Although this can be complicated in small towns where little English is spoken, police stations in the biggest cities usually have somebody on hand who can speak some English.

Finally, if your trip to Taiwan is part of a longer, multi-country journey, make sure that your policy covers Taiwan in the first place: some insurers will not provide coverage for Taiwan due to perceptions of military-political risk.

Rough Guides has teamed up with Columbus Direct to offer you **travel insurance** that can be tailored to suit your needs. Products include a low-cost **backpacker** option for long stays; a **short break** option for city getaways; a typical **holiday package** option; and others. There are also annual **multi-trip** policies for those who travel regularly. Different sports and activities (trekking, skiing, etc) can usually be covered if required.

See our website (Ⓦ www.roughguides insurance.com) for eligibility and purchasing options. Alternatively, UK residents should call ☎ 0870/033 9988; Australians should call ☎ 1300/669 999 and New Zealanders should call ☎ 0800/55 9911. All other nationalities should call ☎ +44 870/890 2843.

Internet

Taiwan is one of the world's biggest users of the **Internet** although most surfing is done via home PCs and laptops, so Internet cafés are not as common as might be expected. If you're travelling with your laptop and have cash to splash out on mid-range to business-class hotels, then getting a high-speed connection in your room shouldn't be a problem, although five-star hotels can charge formidable amounts for this service. If you don't have a laptop with you, top-end hotels usually offer Internet access in their business centres, although the charges for this can also be exorbitant.

In the more touristy bits of Taiwan, there are usually **Internet cafés**. However, in most places – even in the big cities – you may be forced to enter the grisly world of the Taiwanese **computer game centre**. At these, you are likely to find a high-speed Internet connection but you'll have to endure the background noises of automatic gunfire and the maniacal screeches of Taiwanese kids, and enough secondhand cigarette smoke to make the Marlboro Man suffocate. **Prices** vary among computer game centres, but in general most charge about NT$25–30 per hour (double this in Taipei) and usually offer discounts for multiple-hour use. At some of these, you might be provided with a plastic

cup for unlimited refills of **iced tea** although others require you to buy a tea or coffee (usually about NT$40–50), which will entitle you to use a computer for one hour (be sure to ask first). Some centres might have a computer with **English-language software** such as Microsoft Word, so if you need to draft a document you should ask first in order to be seated at the proper terminal.

Another option, though one that takes some planning, is to visit a **local library**. Internet access at these is usually free for a specified period of time (typically about an hour), but you might have to queue up for a terminal so if you know you'll need one it's best to turn up early in the day to put your name on the waiting list.

Mail

Taiwan's **postal service**, the state-owned **Chunghwa Post**, is speedy and reliable, offering a range of services that are user-friendly even if you don't speak Chinese. **Post offices** are located in all cities, towns and most villages, though **opening hours** vary in accordance with their size – expect most to be open from about 8am until 5pm Monday to Friday and about 8.30am to 12pm on Saturday. In small villages, offices are usually open from about 8am to 3.30pm on weekdays, closed on weekends, while main branches in the biggest cities have much longer hours, often from 8am to 8pm on weekdays and 8.30am to 4.30pm on Saturday.

Domestic mail is generally delivered to most places on the island within two days, sometimes a bit longer for remote areas and the offshore islands. **International post** usually takes about six or seven days to reach most destinations in North America or Western Europe, and only four to five days to Hong Kong, Japan and South Korea. Note that it's essential to write "**airmail**" on the envelope – and if buying stamps at the post office to also remind the teller to send by air – as letters that don't specify this are at times sent by sea instead. **Stamps** can be bought at post offices, convenience stores, and even online at Ⓦ www.post.gov .tw, where you also can find a list of prices, branch addresses and opening hours. In addition, the website allows for tracking of international letters and parcels, as well as for items sent via the post office's own **Express Mail Service**, which costs considerably more than airmail but is much quicker and ensures registered delivery. Just as secure but not as fast is **registered mail**, which is only slightly more expensive than regular airmail. Most of the big post offices also offer a useful **packing service**, boxing and sealing parcels for a nominal fee – it's worth using this to ensure that your parcel is properly packed; otherwise, it may need to be opened and repacked.

Mailboxes come in two colours: the red box is where you post overseas mail (in the left-hand slot) and Taiwan express mail (in the right-hand slot). Green boxes are for domestic surface mail (left) and local city mail (right).

Poste restante services are available at the main post offices of the large cities. Letters should be addressed to GPO Poste Restante, together with the city name – be sure to use the romanisation for city names that is used in this book.

Money

Taiwan's currency is the **New Taiwan Dollar** (NT$) although it's usually referred to by the generic Mandarin terms **yuan** or **kuai**. Notes come in denominations of NT$ 100, 200, 500, 1000 and 2000, while coins come in units of 1, 5, 10, 20 and 50 cents; in reality, however, cents are not used and prices are quoted in dollar amounts. At the time of writing, the **exchange rate** was around NT$32 to the US dollar, NT$65 to the pound and NT$42 to the euro; you can check current exchange rates at Ⓦwww.xe.com. Note that foreign currencies will almost never be accepted in Taiwan.

Almost all cities and towns have **ATMs** from which travellers can withdraw funds using bank **debit** or **credit cards** – this is by far the most convenient and safe method of obtaining cash for daily expenses. Though some ATMs are only for domestic bank account holders, many of them support international systems such as Accel, Cirrus, Interlink, Plus and Star (always check for the correct logo). The most common ATMs – and the most useful to foreigners – are those of **Chinatrust Commercial Bank**, which

allow cash advances from major credit cards and can be found in **7-Eleven convenience stores** throughout the country. Though these can be found in most cities and towns, if you're planning to spend time in rural or remote areas make sure you take out enough to get you to the next major town. Most mid-range travellers should be able to get by on NT$10,000–15,000 a week, so making one such withdrawal per week should allow you ample cash for travelling while minimizing the risk of carrying larger sums. Other banks with ATMs that recognize international debit or credit cards are **Bank of Taiwan** and **International Commercial Bank of China** (ICBC). Citibank and HSBC also have branches in Taiwan's five biggest cities.

Only use ATMs in banks, convenience stores or post offices, as there have been cases of fake ATMs that download card information; however, most of these have been targeted at domestic bank account holders.

While it's important to ensure that you're carrying enough cash, you can reduce the need to carry large sums by balancing your payments with a credit card, especially when paying for accommodation in most cities and towns. Most **hotels** accept credit card payment, with Visa and MasterCard the most widely accepted. American Express and Diners Club also are fairly commonly recognized, though this is more the case in the big cities. Stores in most cities will accept credit card payment, although in many rural areas this is not possible.

Private money changers are rare in Taiwan, and if you need to exchange foreign currency you'll probably have to do so in a bank – in most towns, Bank of Taiwan will have a **foreign exchange counter**, and these are usually centrally located. The most widely accepted currency for exchange in Taiwan is **US dollars**, followed by **British pounds** and **Hong Kong dollars**.

Traveller's cheques are becoming increasingly outmoded in Taiwan and are probably more trouble than they're worth if the island is your only destination. However, if you're visiting Taiwan as part of an extended journey that includes countries in which traveller's cheques are useful, you can still cash them in most towns. Those cut in US dollars are the easiest to cash.

Phones

Domestic calls are easily made from private and public telephones, the latter of which come in two types: coin and card. Though there are still a few **coin booths** around, most of them only take NT$1 coins, and with local calls costing NT$2 for up to two minutes (NT$6 for two-minute calls to mobile phones) you need a stack of coins to make it worth your while. Far more common these days are **card phones**, and the ones marked with yellow can be used for both domestic and international calls.

Phone cards

There are two types of prepaid **phone cards**: magnetic strip stored value and IC stored value, and both can be bought in convenience stores and some bus and train stations. The IC stored value cards typically cost about NT$300, and all are enabled for short **overseas calls**. However, some cards are designed to offer discounts to certain destinations, so ask the cashier for a look at the cards on offer before you buy one – those with flags of the country you wish to call prominently displayed will offer better value. To use these, you must first dial the toll-free number listed, then enter the code printed on the card. At the prompt, dial the country code, area code and phone number.

You also can make an overseas direct-dial call by first keying in ☎009 or ☎002, followed by the country code, area code and number. It's possible to call via an **international operator** on ☎100, but this is very expensive. English **directory assistance** is on ☎106 and costs NT$3 per call.

For domestic calls, there is no need to dial the area code when making calls within the same area code.

Taiwan phone codes

Country code ☎886
Taipei ☎02
Kaohsiung ☎07
Kinmen ☎0823
Matzu Islands ☎0836
Miaoli ☎037
Nantou ☎049
Pingdong, Little Lioucio Island ☎08
Taichung, Changhua ☎04
Tainan, Penghu Islands ☎06
Taitung, Lyudao, Lanyu ☎089
Taoyuan, Hsinchu, Yilan, Hualien ☎03
Wuciou Island ☎0826
Yunlin, Chiayi ☎05

Mobile phones

Your **mobile phone** may already be compatible with the Taiwanese network, which is GSM 900MHz/1800MHz (visitors from North America should ensure their phones are GSM/Triband and have the appropriate MHz capabilities), though note that if you are using your home provider you will pay a premium for roaming charges and that callers within Taiwan will have to make an international call to reach your phone. For more information, check the manual that came with your phone, or with the manufacturer and/or your telephone service provider.

A much more economical option would be to buy a GSM-standard **SIM card** from a cellular phone shop or convenience store, which gives you a new number for use within Taiwan. In **convenience stores** such as 7-Eleven, these SIM cards can be bought for as little as NT$600. You must fill out a form and

Calling home from abroad

Note that the initial zero is omitted from the area code when dialling the UK, Ireland, Australia and New Zealand from abroad.

Australia 00 + 61 + city code
Ireland 00 + 353 + city code
New Zealand 00 + 64 + city code
UK 00 + 44 + city code
US and Canada 00 + 1 + area code

provide a photocopy of your passport, and in some cases you will need to fax the information to the service provider – in 7-Eleven most clerks seem happy to fax it for you from the machine in the store. The number is usually activated within 24 hours. Most of these SIM cards allow you to receive incoming calls for free; you're only charged for the calls you make. Once you've used up the initial phone credit, you'll still be able to receive calls, but before you can make any more calls you'll need to return to a convenience store and top up your minutes: you'll be given a card that resembles a calling card, and you'll need to follow the instructions to reactivate your account. The three main cellular providers in Taiwan are Chunghwa Telecom, FarEasTone and Taiwan Cellular.

Time

Taiwan is eight hours ahead of GMT throughout the year, the same as Beijing, Hong Kong, Macau and Singapore. Daylight-saving time is not observed. GMT is five hours ahead of US Eastern Standard Time and ten hours behind Australian Eastern Standard Time.

Tourist information

Taiwan's Tourism Bureau has made a concerted effort in recent years to promote itself internationally as a destination for Western travellers, particularly those from English-speaking countries. But despite all the well-funded media blitzes and the glitzy promotional materials, there's an underlying lack of substance to most of the information that can be found at tourism offices in Taiwan and abroad. The reasons for this mostly come down to numbers: the domestic tourism market is enormous enough already, and the biggest body of foreign tourists – the Japanese – merit considerable attention given the tourism revenue they represent.

Still, the tourism bureau operates a number of **overseas branches** (see below), with offices in Australia and the US offering colourful materials on Taiwan's best-known attractions. There also are tourism offices scattered across Asia, with those in Hong Kong and Singapore offering the best range of English-language materials.

In Taiwan itself, reliable English information is a pretty mixed bag, especially considering the formidable number of **tourist information centres** around the island. Most of the material is simply translated directly from the original Chinese version, with literal interpretations that are more likely to leave tourists revelling in their literary merit than their usefulness. Similarly, most of the English pages on domestic websites add more confusion, with rampant inaccuracies and discrepancies between municipal, regional and national sites.

The most useful information sources are the **visitor centres** of the national parks and scenic areas, which often have educational overviews with English labelling and free pamphlets. Some of these, especially the national parks, offer the most functional and detailed **maps** in the country.

Other useful resources for independent travellers are the **tourist information booths** just outside many of the country's train stations. Although their opening hours are sporadic, if you arrive in a given town during the day you're likely to encounter an English-speaking volunteer, often a student wishing to speak to native speakers. While you're gleaning information, you might ask them to write down a few of your destinations in Chinese characters – useful if you need to ask someone on the street for directions.

Published under the auspices of the tourism bureau, the glossy bi-monthly *Travel in Taiwan* (ⓦ www.sinica.edu.tw/tit) contains features on a variety of travel destinations and is worth seeking out. The free publication, which has **calendars of events** throughout the country, is available in many tourist information centres.

Useful phone numbers

English-language directory assistance ⓣ 106
Weather information ⓣ 166
Time ⓣ 117
Tourist information hotline ⓣ 02/2717 3737
24-hour toll-free travel information
ⓣ 0800/011 765

Taiwanese tourist offices abroad

Australia Travel Section, Taipei Economic & Cultural Office, Suite 1904, Level 19, MLC Centre,

19-29 Martin Place, Sydney, NSW 2000 ⊕02/9231 6942 ⊚www.taiwantourism.org.
Hong Kong Taiwan Visitors Association, Room 904, 9/F, Nan Fung Tower, 173 Des Voeux Rd, Central, Hong Kong ⊕852/2581 0933.
Singapore Taiwan Visitors Association, 5 Shenton Way, 31-11 UIC Building, Singapore 068808 ⊕65/6223 6546.
USA Taiwan Visitors Association ⊚www.go2taiwan .net. The Wilshire Colonnade Building, Suite 780, 3731 Wilshire Boulevard, Los Angeles, CA 90010 ⊕213/389 1158; 1 East 42nd St, 9/F, New York, NY 10017 ⊕212/867 1632; 555 Montgomery St, Suite 505, San Francisco, CA 94111 ⊕415/989 8677.

Travel advisories

Australian Department of Foreign Affairs ⊚www.smartraveller.gov.au.
British Foreign & Commonwealth Office ⊚www.fco.gov.uk.
Canadian Department of Foreign Affairs ⊚www.voyage.gc.ca.
Irish Department of Foreign Affairs ⊚foreignaffairs.gov.ie.
New Zealand Ministry of Foreign Affairs ⊚www.mfat.govt.nz.
South Africa Department of Foreign Affairs ⊚www.dfa.gov.za.
US Department of State ⊚travel.state.gov.

Guide

Guide

① Taipei and around

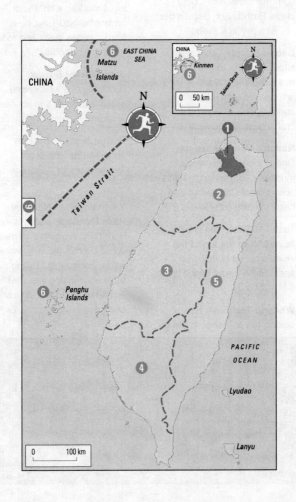

CHAPTER 1 # Highlights

✳ **Festivals** Witness the raucous birthday celebrations for the City God or attend the world's most famous commemoration of Confucius's Birthday on September 28. **See p.105 & p.109**

✳ **Baoan Temple** Other religious sites get more tourists, but this temple is a work of art, packed with intricate carvings and exceptional craftsmanship. **See p.110**

✳ **National Palace Museum** One of the world's greatest museums with an extraordinary collection of Chinese art and historical artefacts. **See p.112**

✳ **Taipei 101** Take the world's fastest lift to the top of the world's tallest building for spectacular views of the city. **See p.116**

✳ **Wistaria Teahouse** Sip oolong tea and absorb the historical ambience at Taipei's oldest teahouse. **See p.123**

✳ **Shilin Night Market** Taipei's largest and most popular night market, with a vast array of cheap Taiwanese food, clothes stalls and foot massage parlours. **See p.128**

✳ **Jade Market** Browse hundreds of jewellery and antique stalls at this absorbing weekend market. **See p.136**

✳ **Beitou** Soak up the hot-spring baths in one of Taiwan's oldest Japanese spas. **See p.138**

✳ **Yangmingshan National Park** This accessible National Park brings together dormant volcanoes ringed with steam vents, hot springs, hiking trails and Chiang Kai-shek's last summer house, all a short bus ride from downtown. **See p.141**

△ Baoan Temple

Taipei and around

T aiwan's political and financial heart, **TAIPEI** is one of the most densely inhabited cities on earth. Surrounded by mountains at the northern tip of the island, the capital is a bustling melee of motor scooters, markets, skyscrapers and temples, with almost three million people packed into the Taipei Basin. Despite being crammed with world-class attractions and some of the best Chinese food on the planet, the city is vastly underrated as a tourist destination. Don't be put off by first impressions: much of its architecture is shabby and unattractive, the result of slapdash construction in the early years of Kuomintang (KMT) rule, primarily to accommodate almost one million new arrivals from China in 1949. The KMT government (and many residents) regarded Taipei as a temporary home, a base from which to launch the recovery of the mainland. Not anymore – Taipei's newest buildings are smart, stylish and built to last, and it's the most international place on the island. English is widely spoken and there are numerous Western chains, restaurants and pubs, but it's by no means "Westernized". What you'll find instead is a modern, high-tech and innovative city (the first to offer wireless Internet on a large scale), with a distinct local character.

Though you could spend months here and still not absorb all the city has to offer, a week is usually enough to get a decent taster. Many tourists come solely to visit the mind-blowing **National Palace Museum**, but they risk missing out on a host of other attractions. West Taipei is the historic core of the city and where many of its best sights are located: tour the **Presidential Building**, **National Taiwan Museum** and **Chiang Kai-shek Memorial Hall** to grapple with Taiwan's complex history, while **Longshan Temple** is the best introduction to its religious traditions. Further north, **Dihua Street** is packed with traditional stores, while **Baoan Temple** is one of the country's most elegant shrines and the **Shunyi Museum of Formosan Aborigines** is an excellent introduction to Taiwan's indigenous peoples. East Taipei offers a change of pace and scenery, with **Xinyi** district a showcase of gleaming office towers and glitzy shopping malls, all of them overshadowed by cloud-scraping **Taipei 101**, the world's tallest building. Eating in Taipei is always memorable, with a huge choice of exceptional **restaurants**, **teahouses** and some of Taiwan's best **night markets**, while a vast range of department stores, specialist shops and antique stalls makes **shopping** in the city just as rewarding. To the north, **Yangmingshan National Park** and **Beitou** are where the best hikes and hot springs are located, while **Wulai** to the south provides a taster of Taiwan's wilder hinterland.

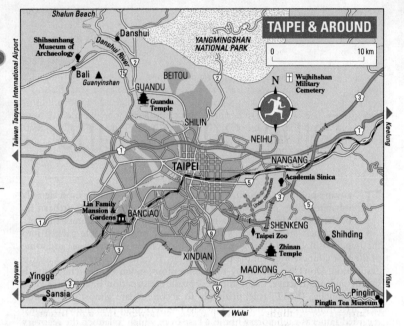

Some history

People have lived in the Taipei Basin for thousands of years, but the modern city is an amalgamation of several villages brought together little over a century ago. The region's original inhabitants were the indigenous people known as the **Ketagalan** (see p.519), but the Qing government in Beijing, having assumed control of Taiwan in 1683, granted farmer **Chen Lai-zhang** (from Quanzhou in Fujian), the first official licence to settle the Taipei area in 1709. More immigrants followed, leading to the creation of **Bangka**, Taipei's first Chinese settlement and today's Wanhua district. In 1853, new arrivals from Tongan in Fujian clashed with more established settlers from Zhangzhou in what's known as the **Ding-Xia Feud**. The fight left 38 dead and led to the establishment of **Dadaocheng** (today's Datong) by the aggrieved Tongans – the latter had the last laugh because the new village, situated down river and therefore closer to the sea and the port at **Danshui**, soon prospered.

Taipei (literally "North Taiwan") Prefecture was created in 1875, one of several measures designed to better defend the island in the wake of the Japanese expedition to Taiwan the year before (see p.509). The location of the city was carefully chosen midway between Bangka and Dadaocheng so as not to provoke the rival clans. Construction of the city walls began in 1879, but hampered by lack of funds they weren't complete until 1884, marking the official **founding of the city**. When Taiwan was upgraded to a province of China in 1885, first governor **Liu Mingzhuan** was already living in Taipei, but Dadun (modern Taichung), was chosen as the provincial capital. Liu started to develop Taipei regardless, building schools, establishing Taiwan's first railway, electric street lighting and postal service, and commissioning a British architect to construct the first bridge over the Danshui River in 1888. Taipei was finally made **provincial capital** of Taiwan in 1894, on the eve of the

Japanese occupation a few months later. The Japanese era (1895–1945) saw the emergence of modern Taipei – many of the capital's finest buildings were constructed in the first half of the twentieth century, and with the destruction of the city walls between 1900 and 1904, Bangka and Dadaocheng were gradually absorbed.

In February 1947, the **2-28 Incident** began here (see Contexts p.513) and in 1949 Taipei became the **capital of the Republic of China**, its population swollen by an influx of mainland Chinese – by 1967 it had topped 1.5 million. These days being Taipei mayor is one of the nation's top jobs; President **Chen Shui-bian** and former president Lee Tung-hui both held the post, and popular KMT chairman **Ma Ying-jeou**, whose second term ended in 2006, may stand for the presidency in 2008.

Arrival and information

Most visitors' first experience of Taipei is the traffic-choked ride along the expressway from the **airport**, a distant 50km from the city centre. Unfortunately there's no alternative to this and journey times vary according to the traffic – it's best to allow at least an hour. From elsewhere in Taiwan, arriving at the domestic airport or train station is far more convenient.

By air

All **international flights** to Taipei arrive at **Taiwan Taoyuan Internatonal Airport** (formerly Chiang Kai-shek International Airport Ⓦwww .cksairport.gov.tw), near Taoyuan, southwest of the capital. Terminal one's **Tourist Service Center** (daily 6.30am–11.30pm) and hotel reservations desk (daily 9am–9.30pm) is on the right as you exit immigration. In terminal two the Tourist Service Center (daily 6.15am–10.55pm) is located in the middle of the arrivals area, while ATMs and exchange counters are available in both terminals.

Several **bus** companies offer services into the city from both terminals, with bus stations clearly signposted in each arrival hall. Airbus is the most comfortable and offers two popular loop routes: the West Line (daily 6am–11pm; every 20 min; NT$100) covers all the major hotels in West Taipei between the *Grand Hotel* and *Sheraton* (two minutes from the *Taipei Hostel*), while the East Line (daily 5.50am–12.50am; every 20 min; NT$145) ends up at the *Grand Hyatt* in Xinyi. Both routes pass a couple of MRT stations – just tell the ticket seller where you want to go and they will identify the closest stop. Kuo Kuang operates a service to Taipei Main Station (daily 6am–12.50am; every 15 min; NT$125) and Songshan Airport (daily 6.10am–midnight; every 20 min; NT$125). You can also take buses to **Hsinchu** and **Taichung** – buy tickets at the same counters. Note that shuttle buses will eventually connect the airport

Taipei arrival

Taiwan Taoyuan International Airport	臺灣桃園國際航空站	táiwān táoyuán guójì hángkōngzhàn
Songshan Airport	台北松山機場	táiběi sōngshān jī chǎng
Taipei Main Station	台北車站	táiběi chēzhàn
West Bus Station	國光西車站	guóguáng xīchēzhàn
East Bus Station	國光東車站	guóguáng dōngchēzhàn

to the new **Taoyuan High-Speed Rail Station**, just 6km away, providing a fast service to all points south. **Taxis** are available at both terminals twenty-four hours a day. All taxis use the meter but heading into the city a fifty-percent surcharge is incurred – expect to pay NT$1100–1300.

Domestic flights arrive at **Songshan Airport** (Ⓦwww.tsa.gov.tw), conveniently located at the top of Dunhua Road on the edge of downtown Taipei. Facilities include a post office, bank, 24hr lockers, ATM machines and **visitor information center** (daily 8am–8pm). Buses leave from outside the terminal to all corners of the city: #5 and #262 will get you to the main train station, but it's less than NT$200 by taxi to most destinations in central Taipei from here.

By train and bus

All **trains** stop at **Taipei Main Station**, though none terminate here; services from the south usually end up at **Songshan** in the eastern part of the city,

Moving on from Taipei

Taipei has connections to just about everywhere in Taiwan, though it's best to buy tickets in advance if you're planning to travel at the weekend, when transportation is jammed with locals pouring out of the city.

By air

Buses to the **international airport** are plentiful (see p.85). Taxi drivers rarely use the meter – if you negotiate you should get them to take you for NT$1200 or less. You can buy tickets for **domestic flights** by simply rolling up to one of the airline desks at **Songshan Airport** an hour before departure, though it's obviously safer to reserve a seat in advance. From Taipei there are regular flights to every major destination in Taiwan – see Listings (p.137) for airline numbers.

By train

Taipei Main Station is at the heart of Taiwan's rail system with services to all major cities: southbound trains follow the **Western Line** to Taichung (NT$375) and Kaohsiung (NT$845) while "northbound" services go to Keelung (NT$43) or travel the **Eastern Line** to Hualien (NT$445) and Taitung (NT$800). Taiwan High Speed Rail services also depart from here (see Basics p.31). The station is relatively easy to navigate for non-Chinese speakers: there are separate windows for advance and same-day departures, though for shorter journeys it's faster to use the ticket machines which are labelled in English. If you're travelling to the station by metro you can beat the queues by following signs to the "TRA Transfer Area" before you exit the MRT station.

By bus

Most buses operate from the **Taipei Inter City Bus Terminal** on the corner of Yanping Road and Civic Boulevard, not far from the train station: private companies such as Ubus run frequent 24hr services to all the major cities, and buses several times a day to destinations such as **Beigang**, **Budai** and **Lugang**. Kuo Kuang buses to **Jinshan** and the north coast, **Miaoli** and **Yilan/Luodong** depart from here. Kuo Kuang also operates frequent services to Taichung, Tainan and Kaohsiung from the **West Bus Station**, a short walk west of the train station or exit 8 from the Station Front Metro Mall which connects to the MRT station. The smaller **East Bus Station** is next door with frequent services to Keelung (6am–midnight; NT$50) and Taiwan Taoyuan Airport (5am–11.30pm; NT$125). Several bus routes start in **East Taipei** near Zhongxiao Fuxing MRT station: Green Transit's useful hourly service to **Puli** and **Sun Moon Lake** (6am–10pm; NT$350) runs from the south side of Zhongxiao Road – take exit 4 from the MRT station.

while those from the east coast head for the southwestern suburb of **Shulin**. It's best to get off at the main station since several hostels and hotels are within walking distance and it's easy to transfer to the MRT network – save time by following the signs on the platform to the special MRT transfer exits rather than walking up to the main concourse. Taxis line up at the station entrance and there's a **visitor information center** (daily 8am–8pm) on the northeast side of the main ticket hall. Most **buses** arrive at the new bus terminal near the train station (see box p.86).

Information

Taipei's main **Travel Information Service Center** (daily 8am–7pm, ☎02/27173737) is at 240 Dunhua North Road, close to Songshan Airport. The English-language material here is limited, though some of the staff speak English and can help with basic enquiries. There's also a small **visitor information center** (daily 10am–6pm), located beneath Zhongxiao Road in East Metro Mall between Zhongxiao Fuxing and Dunhua MRT stations, while a range of English publications on Taipei can be purchased at Taipei's **Department of Information** (ⓦwww.taipei.gov.tw) gift shop at City Hall on Shifu Road. Taipei City Government also produces free magazines *Discover Taipei* (bimonthly) and *My Taipei* (quarterly) which have useful features – copies are available at all visitor centres. The pocket-size *Culture Express* (ⓦexpress .culture.gov.tw) is published monthly and provides a comprehensive listing of every artistic event and exhibition in the city: it's available in bars, restaurants and many MRT stations. The quickest way to get a feel for what's going on is to scan ⓦwww.urbanpeople.net, which lists upcoming events and club nights, or grab the Friday editions of Taiwan's three English-language daily newspapers, which have a definite Taipei bias (see Basics p.49 for a full list of national publications).

Tours

The Tourism Bureau's "Taiwan Tour Bus" programme offers several Taipei **guided tours**: a NT$800 half-day guided tour of the city's principal sights (8am–noon), and an evening tour which takes in Huaxi Night Market for NT$1200 (6–10pm). There are also half-day tours to Sansia and Yingge, Yangmingshan National Park and Wulai. Visitor information centres and most hotels can arrange bookings – English-speaking guides are usually available.

Orientation

Taipei lies within a basin formed by the Danshui River, with the main suburbs following river valleys through the mountains north, south and east. The best way to get your bearings is to use the metro lines, which divide central Taipei north–south and east–west. **Taipei Main Station** lies at the centre of West Taipei, a hub for all train, MRT and bus services. The Danshui Line (red) north of here slices between **Datong** and **Zhongshan** towards **Shilin** and the National Palace Museum, while lines south serve **Wanhua** and **Zhongzheng**. The Bannan Line (blue) and Muzha (brown) lines divide **East Taipei**, with **Zhongxiao Fuxing Station** the centre point.

The **road layout** of the city is fairly logical once you understand the rules. An elaborate grid, the central point is the junction of Zhongxiao and Zhongshan roads just east of the main station. Major roads leading east or west off

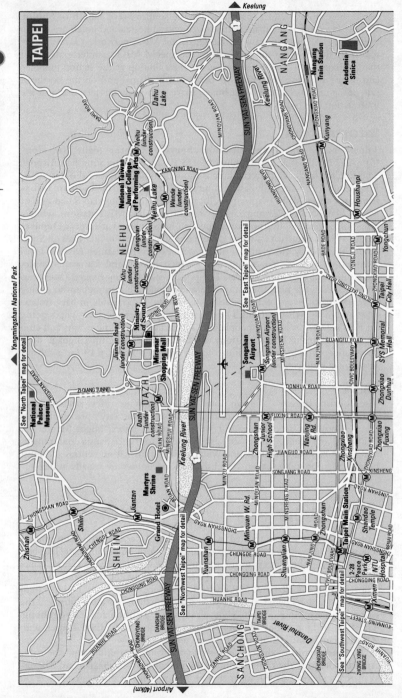

TAIPEI

▲ *Keelung*

▲ *Yangmingshan National Park*

NANGANG

Nangang
Train Station

Academia
Sinica

Junyang

Houshanpi

Yongchun

Taipei
City Hall

SYS Memorial
Hall

Zhongxiao
Dunhua

Zhongxiao
Fuxing

Zhongxiao
Xinsheng

Kinsheng

Shandao
Temple

Taipei Main Station

NTU
Hospital

Ximen

See "East Taipei" map for detail

See "Southwest Taipei" map for detail

NEIHU

National Taiwan
Junior College
of Performing Arts

Neihu
(under
construction)

Wende
(under
construction)

Gangqian
(under
construction)

Xihu
(under
construction)

Dahu Lake

KANGNING ROAD

Neihu Lake

DAHU ROAD

MINQUAN ROAD

MINQUAN ROAD

SUN YAT-SEN FREEWAY

Keelung River

ZHONGYANG ROAD

NANGANG ROAD

BADE ROAD

YONGJI ROAD

NANJING ROAD

GUANGFU ROAD

CIVIC BOULEVARD

DONHUA ROAD

Fuxing Road

Nanjing
E. Rd.

Songshan Airport

Songshan Airport
(under construction)

MINSHENG ROAD

MINQUAN ROAD

Ministry
of Sound

Jianan Road
(under construction)

Miramar
Shopping Mall

Dazhi
(under
construction)

DAZHI

BINHE BLVD

JIHE ROAD

BINHE ROAD

National
Palace
Museum

See "North Taipei" map for detail

ZI-QIANG TUNNEL

Dahu Lake

JIANAN ROAD

MINGSHUI ROAD

BEIAN ROAD

Martyrs'
Shrine

Keelung River

Zhongshan
Junior
High School

JIANGUO ROAD

SONGJIANG ROAD

MINSHENG ROAD

MINZU ROAD

Grand
Hotel

Jiantan

Shilin

Zhishan

ZHONGSHAN ROAD

CHENGDE ROAD

ZHONGSHAN N. ROAD

SHILIN

Yuanshan

CHENGDE ROAD

CHONGQING ROAD

Minquan W. Rd.

Shuanglian

ZHONGSHAN ROAD

Zhongshan

NANJING ROAD

CIVIC BOULEVARD

KINSHENG ROAD

RENAI ROAD

CHONGQING ROAD

2-28
Peace
Park

KUNMING STREET

HUANHE ROAD

SANHE BRIDGE

TAIPEI BRIDGE

Danshui River

DANSHUI BRIDGE

CHONGYONG BRIDGE

HUANHE ROAD

CHINGAN RD

ZHONGXIAO BRIDGE

ZHONG XING BRIDGE

SANCHONG

CHONGQING ROAD

HUANHE ROAD

See "Northwest Taipei" map for detail

Keelung River

SUN YAT-SEN FREEWAY

SUN YAT-SEN FREEWAY

▼ *Airport (40km)*

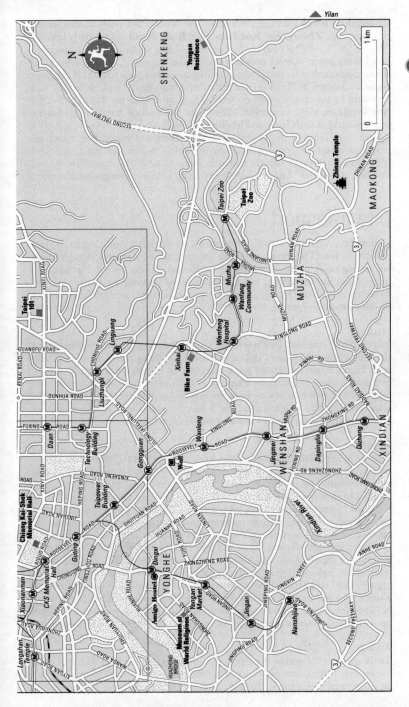

▲ *Yilan*

N

SHENKENG

Yongan
Residence

SECOND FREEWAY

3

Zhinan Temple

ZHINAN ROAD

MAOKONG

Taipei Zoo

Taipei
Zoo

XINGUANG ROAD

MUZHA ROAD

Muzha

MUZHA

Wanfang
Community

Wanfang Hospital

XINGLONG ROAD

MUZHA ROAD

XINHAI RD

SECOND FREEWAY

BAODAO ROAD

GUANGFU ROAD

Taipei
101

XINYI ROAD

Linguang

CHONGDE ROAD

Xinhai

Bike Farm

JILONG (KEELUNG) ROAD

RENAI ROAD

DUNHUA ROAD

Liuzhangli

Daan

FUXING ROAD

Technology
Building

Gongguan

Wanlong

XINGLONG ROAD

Jingmei

FUHE ROAD

ZHONGZHENG RD

Dapinglin

ZHONGYANG ROAD

WENSHAN

Zhongxing

ZHONGXING RD

Dizhang

XINDIAN

Wall

ROOSEVELT ROAD

Chiang Kai-Shek
Memorial Hall

XINYI ROAD

HEPING ROAD

Taipower
Building

XINSHENG SOUTH ROAD

ROOSEVELT ROAD

SHUIYUAN ROAD

Xindian River

Guting

JINSHAN ROAD

JINSHAN ROAD

HEPING ROAD

Xiaonanmen

AIGUO ROAD

CKS Memorial
Hall

CHONGQING ROAD

TINGZHOU ROAD

HUANHE ROAD

HUANHE ROAD

ZHONGZHENG ROAD

JINGPING ROAD

ANHE ROAD

JINGMEI ROAD

Longshan
Temple

Amigo Hostel

Dingxi

YONGHE

Yongan
Market

Museum of
World Religions

HUAZHONG
BRIDGE

ZHONGSHAN ROAD

JINAN ROAD

Jingan

JINGPING ROAD

JUNGSING ROAD

JUNGSING ROAD

SECOND FREEWAY

Nanshijiao

YUANSING STREET

3

XIYUAN ROAD

WANDA ROAD

HUAJIANG
BRIDGE

0   1 km

Zhongshan Road have the suffix "East" or "West" while roads heading north or south from **Zhongxiao Road** and later **Bade Road** are similarly labelled "North" or "South". Roads are further divided into **sections**, with Zhongxiao East having seven – street numbers reset at the beginning of each section, so the section number is crucial when finding an address. Side streets off the main roads are known as "lanes": Lane 180, Zhongxiao East Road, Section 4, can be found by locating no. 180 on section four of Zhongxiao East Road – the lane should be right next to it. "Alleys" are the smallest units in the system, interconnecting with lanes and labelled similarly.

Note that Taipei City Government uses **Hanyu Pinyin** (see Language p.548) as its official romanization system, which includes all street signs and MRT stations, though suburbs falling in Taipei County (Xindian, Banciao and Yonghe) and in the "Around Taipei" section (p.138), use **Tongyong Pinyin**.

City transport

Getting around Taipei is fairly straightforward though it's too big to explore entirely on foot. The most convenient way to travel is by **metro**, though **buses** are getting easier to use for non-Chinese speakers. **Taxis** are not expensive for journeys within the centre, and it's best to avoid **driving** yourself unless you have nerves of steel. During the week, try to avoid the peak rush hour periods (8–9am and 5.30–7pm).

Buses

Taipei has an extensive **bus network**, with destinations marked in English on the front of most buses, and electronic screens displaying the name of each stop once inside. English-language route maps can be obtained from MRT stations or visitor centres and fares are cheap at NT$15 per sector, which covers most journeys within the city. Note, however, that bus stops have maps and timetables solely in Chinese, which means you'll have to plan ahead and look for bus numbers (usually displayed as Western numerals).

Metro

The opening of Taipei's metro system, known as the **MRT** ("Mass Rapid Transit"), revolutionized travel around the city in the 1990s and is by far the best way to get around. The system comprises three colour-coded main lines; Bannan (blue), Danshui (red) and Muzha (brown). The Danshui Line south of Chiang Kai-shek Memorial Hall station splits into the Zhonghe (orange) and Xindian (green) lines – it's easy to pick up **maps** from stations. Further extensions are expected in 2009. Services operate at short intervals from 6am to midnight every day and are efficient, clean and fast. Tickets cost NT$20–65 depending on distance travelled and can be purchased from ticket offices or machines in the stations: you can buy a one-day, unlimited travel card for NT$200 (including a NT$50 refundable deposit), though if you're planning to stay longer than a week it's a good idea to buy an **EasyCard**. This costs NT$500 (including a NT$100 refundable deposit) and can also be used on buses – it's easy to top it up with coins, notes or credit cards via machines located in all MRT stations.

Taxis

Taxis are plentiful within the city centre: the initial fare is NT$70 and is good for the first 1.5km, after which it's NT$5 for each additional 300m. After 11pm, an extra twenty percent is charged automatically and carrying luggage incurs another NT$10 fee. The meter is always used, the only exception being trips to the airport which are often negotiated in advance.

Accommodation

Taipei has a plentiful supply of mid-range and luxury **hotels** scattered all over the city, with hefty discounts available year round (see Basics p.34) – beware of major trade shows such as Computex (May/June) however, which can lead to a shortage of rooms. It's also worth remembering that the bigger hotels tend to be a focus for banquets and weddings at the weekends, and at these times the lobby might feel more like a metro station in rush hour. Budget accommodation is also easy to find, with Taipei the only city in Taiwan that offers a decent choice of **hostels**. Most of the cheap accommodation is concentrated in the old city centre close to the train station, in the lower parts of **Zhongshan** district or **Zhongzheng**.

Where you stay will largely depend on your priorities: the area around the train station is the best base for getting around and convenient if arriving by bus or train, but Zhongshan is where you'll find most of the mid-range hotels and several five-stars. This district is not quite as convenient for transport but there's

Taipei accommodation

Ambience Hotel	喜瑞飯店	*xǐruì fàndiàn*
Charming City Hotel	香城大飯店	*xiāngchéng dàfàndiàn*
Chun Shai Han She Hotel	君帥函舍商務旅店	*jūnshuài hánshèshāngwù lǚdiàn*
City Suites	城市商旅	*chéngshì shānglǚ*
Delight Hotel	大來飯店	*dàlái fàndiàn*
Evergreen Laurel Hotel	長榮桂冠酒店	*chángróngguìguàn jiǔdiàn*
Far Eastern Plaza Hotel	遠東國際大飯店	*yuǎndōng guójì dàfàndiàn*
Ferrary Hotel	華麗大飯店	*huálì dàfàndiàn*
Friends Spring Hotel	友春大飯店	*yǒuchūn dàfàndiàn*
Friends Star Hotel	友星大飯店	*yǒuxīng dàfàndiàn*
Grand Formosa Regent	晶華酒店	*jīnghuá jiǔdiàn*
Grand Hotel	圓山大飯店	*yuánshān dàfàndiàn*
Grand Hyatt Taipei	台北君悦大飯店	*táiběi jūnyuè dàfàndiàn*
Hsuan Mei Hotel	宣美商務飯店	*xuānměi shāngwù fàndiàn*
K Hotel III	柯達大飯店台北三店	*kēdá dàfàndiàn táiběi sāndiàn*
Keyman's Hotel	懷寧旅店	*huáiníng lǚdiàn*
Landis Taipei Hotel	台北亞都麗緻大飯店	*táiběi yàdūlìzhì dàfàndiàn*
Le Petit Sherwood	台北小西華飯店	*táiběi xiǎoxīhuá fàndiàn*
Leofoo Hotel	六福客棧	*liùfú kèzhàn*
Les Suites Taipei (Qingcheng)	台北商旅 (慶城)	*táiběi shānglǚ (qìngchéng)*
Royal Castle Hotel	成都大飯店	*chéngdū dàfàndiàn*
Sheraton Taipei Hotel	台北喜來登大飯店	*táiběi xǐláidēng dàfàndiàn*
Taipei Fullerton 41 Hotel	台北馥敦飯店 復南館	*táiběi fùdūnfàndiàn fùnánguǎn*
Taipei House Hostel	台北之家	*táiběizhījiā*
Taipei YMCA International Guest House	台北市中國基督教青年會	*táiběishì zhōngguó jīdūjiào qīngniánhuì*
Taipei Youth Hostel	台北YH國基青年會館	*táiběiYH guójī qīngniánhuìguǎn*
United Hotel	國聯大飯店	*guólián dàfàndiàn*

plenty to eat and Zhongshan Road is one of the city's more leafy (and upmarket) thoroughfares. **Wanhua** and **Datong** are historic neighbourhoods, good for temples and traditional food, but with less choice when it comes to hotels and a long way from the nearest nightlife. **East Taipei**, which includes Songshan, Xinyi and most of Daan district is where the majority of luxury hotels are located – this is the modern financial and commercial heart of the city as well as the location of its trendier restaurants and bars, and beds are priced accordingly. Note that all the hotels listed have ADSL (broadband) connections in rooms unless otherwise stated.

Zhongzheng

See map p.98

Friends Star Hotel 11 Heping W Rd Sec 1 ⊕02/23943121, ⊛www.ffh.com.tw. Convenient location close to Guting MRT station (exit 8), featuring modern rooms with raised wooden floors and brightly tiled bathrooms. Extras include free shuttle bus to Xinyi (8am–8pm) and cheap DIY laundry. ⑤

Keyman's Hotel 1 Huaining St ⊕02/23114811, ⊛www.keymans.com.tw. Close to the junction with Zhongxiao Road and convenient for the main station, this is popular with travellers and a great budget option with decent discounts. Recently renovated rooms with a pleasant inner atrium – a real contrast to the bustle outside. ④

Sheraton Taipei 12 Zhongxiao E Rd Sec 1 ⊕02/23215511, ⊛www.sheraton-taipei.com. Re-opened in 2005 after a comprehensive facelift, this five-star is now a showcase for contemporary Asian design; standard rooms are a little small however. Highlights include the soaring inner atrium with the *Kitchen 12* buffet at its base, outdoor eighteenth-floor pool and hip lobby lounge bar. ⑧

Taipei Hostel 6/F, 11, Lane 5, Linsen N Rd ⊕02/23952950, ⊛www.taipeihostel.com. This hostel opened in 1975 making it the oldest in town; rooms and common areas are a little shabby, though the small balcony on the roof is a decent place to chill out. Dorm beds NT$300, singles NT$500 and doubles NT$550.

Taipei Train Station Hostel 4/F, 16 Beiping W Rd ⊕02/23753443. Established by the owner of *Happy Family Hostel* (see Zhongshan section), with a/c, kitchen, laundry, cable TV, free Internet and a laid-back roof area. Take exit E3 from the main station, cross the road in front of you and walk 100m on the right side of the street: the hostel is in the white building ahead. Dorm beds NT$300, singles NT$400 and doubles NT$700.

Taipei YMCA International Guest House 19 Xuchang St ⊕02/23113201, ⊛www.ymcataipei .org.tw. Located just behind the Caesar Park Hotel in a convenient central location, this remains popular with travellers though it's certainly not the cheapest or the most comfortable option in town. Rooms are

adequate but simple, there's no breakfast and it's NT$100 per day to use the Internet. ⑤

Taipei Youth Hostel 13/F, 50 Zhongxiao W Rd Sec 1 ⊕02/23880885, ⊛www .yhtaiwan.com. Smart hostel with spotless dorms and family rooms, free Internet, lockers and a/c, coin laundry and 24hr front desk. You have to be a member of the IYHF to stay: temporary membership is NT$100 or NT$400 for one year (free for ISIC card holders). Conveniently located opposite the station, in the K Mall building next to Shin Kong Tower – take the elevator from the main entrance. Dorm beds NT$540-650.

Wanhua

See map p.98

Chun Shai Han She Hotel 4/F, 68 Chengdu Rd ⊕02/23718812. One of Taipei's most appealing hotels, a short walk from Ximen MRT station. Rooms are tastefully decorated in classical Chinese style with wooden furniture and gold-painted carvings on the walls. The entrance is actually on Lane 76 off Chengdu Road: look for the "Hotel" sign in between Taipei Milk King and the Olympia Bakery. ⑤

Ferrary Hotel 41 Kangding Rd ⊕02/23818111, ⊛www.f-hotel.com.tw. Pleasant hotel offering excellent value for money in the heart of Wanhua, with clean, modern rooms and a host of amenities: breakfast in an attractive restaurant overlooking the street, free Internet access and DIY laundry, plus a small gym. ④

Royal Castle Hotel 115 Chengdu Rd ⊕02/23831123. Cosy hotel, a short walk from busy Ximending and renovated in 2004. Rooms have smart new beds and dark wood furnishings – it's worth paying slightly more for the bigger rooms though. Free Internet. ④

Datong

See map p.106

City Suites 69 Nanjing W Rd ⊕02/25507722, ⊛www.citysuites.com.tw. Set in one of Taipei's oldest neighbourhoods, this five-star boutique is excellent value; rooms feature a blend of wood,

marble and soothing beige tones, topped off with flat-screen TVs, DVD players and wireless Internet. **7**
Dongwu Hotel 238 Yanping N Rd Sec 2 ⓣ02/25571261, ⓦwww.dongwu-hotel.com. Business hotel situated in an interesting part of Datong opposite the Ci Sheng Temple, providing useful maps and information on local attractions and cheap eats. Rooms are modern and comfortable, with free wireless Internet access. **5**

Southern districts
See map p.88

Amigo Hostel 14, Lane 157, Yonghe Rd Sec 2, Yonghe ⓣ02/29297583, ⓦ0808.net/hostel. Friendly hostel, 15min from downtown by MRT and comprising two separate properties. Check in at homely *Amigo 1* on Lane 157, opposite Dingxi MRT station's exit 1, which has basic dorm beds (NT$245–350) and private rooms (NT$350–420) with free internet. *Amigo 2* is at 302 Yonghe Rd Sec 2 – the comfortable en-suite singles here are a real bargain and the most sought after in the city, so book ahead (NT$525–700).

Zhongshan
See map p.107

🏃 **Ambience Hotel** 64 Changan E Rd Sec 1, ⓣ02/25410077, ⓦwww.ambiencehotel .com.tw. One of Taipei's newest designer hotels, with rooms decked out with sleek Philippe Starck and Ferruccio Laviani furniture, flat-screen TVs and a striking all-white colour scheme. **7**
Evergreen Laurel Hotel 63 Songjiang Rd ⓣ02/25019988, ⓦwww.evergreen-hotels.com. You wouldn't guess it from the lime green tiles out front, but this is one of the city's most opulent hotels. Superior rooms feature 37-inch plasma TVs and rather gaudy gold-plated bathroom fittings, but the high-tech soundproofing makes them the most tranquil corners of downtown Taipei. **8**
Friends Spring Hotel 55 Minquan W Rd ⓣ02/25972588, ⓦwww.ffh.com.tw. Cosy option just off Zhongshan Road, offering clean Japanese-style rooms with raised wooden floors and screen windows. It's handy for the MRT and regular 25 percent discounts make this great value. **5**
Grand Formosa Regent Taipei 3, Lane 39, Zhongshan N Rd Sec 2 ⓣ02/25238000, ⓦwww .grandformosa-taipei.com.tw. Taipei institution, serving as a frenetic hub for banquets, weddings and family get-togethers. Rooms are comfortable if standard five-star fare, but the views are impressive and the rooftop pool is a good place to escape the crowds. **8**
Grand Hotel 1 Zhongshan N Rd Sec 4 ⓣ02/28868888, ⓦwww.grand-hotel.org. The

Imperial-style architecture and Chinese decor definitely have character, though the spacious rooms are a little worn for a five-star and the spectacular views are only available from deluxe rooms and above. The historic *Yuan Yuan Teahouse*, still serving Madam Chiang's favourite red-bean cake, adds ambience, but Internet is a hefty NT$500 per day. The inconvenient location is mitigated somewhat by free shuttle bus to Yuanshan MRT station. **7**
Guest House Taiwanmex 2/F, 18-1, Lane 18, Nanjing W Rd ⓣ02/55529798, ⓔtaiwanmex@hotmail .com. Convenient location right next to Zhongshan MRT station (exit 1), with tiny but relatively new, spotlessly clean rooms managed by an extremely friendly Mexican/Taiwanese couple. Extras include free a/c, Internet access and laundry. Dorm beds are NT$300 with private rooms from NT$400.
Happy Family Hostel 2/F, 2, Lane 56, Zhongshan N Rd Sec 1 ⓣ02/25810716, ⓦhappyfamily.tripod .com. Backpacker institution, with clean, if rather aging, rooms close to the main station. The local owner is a font of information and there's a small balcony and washing machine on the top floor. Dorm beds NT$300, singles NT$450 (NT$50 extra for a/c).

🏃 **Hsuan Mei Hotel** 52 Jianguo N Rd Sec 1 ⓣ02/87713066 ⓦwww.hsuanmeihotel .com. Stylish hotel with a mix of contemporary and Asian design; standard rooms come with DVD player, shower, spa and wireless Internet. Discounts make this one of Taipei's best bargains but though the central location is handy for buses and taxis, it's a bit of a hike to the MRT. **7**
K Hotel III 15, Lane 83, Zhongshan N Rd Sec 1 ⓣ02/25319999. One of Taipei's most stylish hotels, with a goldfish pond at the entrance and Hokusai's iconic wave painting on tiles in the lobby. Comfortable rooms have flat-screen TVs and spa bathtubs. Located on Lane 83 just off Linsen Road. **7**
Landis Taipei Hotel 41 Minquan E Rd Sec 2 ⓣ02/25971234, ⓦwww.landistpe.com.tw. Taipei's classiest hotel, its elegant Art Deco theme reflected in the lobby and deluxe rooms, all upgraded in 2004. The posh French restaurants are a nice bonus: try *La Brasserie* for an aperitif and *Paris 1930* for dinner. There's a gym but no pool. 8
Leofoo Hotel 168 Changchun Rd ⓣ02/25073211, ⓦwww.leofoo.com.tw. Mid-range stalwart in standard drab Taipei building, a long way from the MRT, saved somewhat by traditional Chinese theme inside. Singles are small and a little worn – the twin rooms are slightly bigger. Free Internet. **5**
Taipei House Hostel Rm 1101 293 Songjiang Rd ⓣ02/25035819 or 0918865102, ⓦwww .hosteltaipei.com.tw. One of Taipei's cleanest and most comfortable hostels, with washing machine,

dryer and Internet. IYHF members pay NT$490, otherwise it's NT$550 for dorm beds and NT$1280-1650 for private rooms – you can join the IYHF on arrival (NT$600). The local owner is a Christian and though the hostel attracts plenty of like-minded backpackers, everyone is welcome. Call in advance to make sure she's around.

World Scholar House 8/F, 2, Lane 38, Songjiang Rd ⊕02/25418113, ⊛www.worldscholarhouse .com. Friendly hostel, popular with long-stay guests, with cable TV, laundry and microwave. Rooms are basic but adequate and have electric fans, but you'll pay extra to use the a/c. It's not marked from the street – just find no. 2 and take the lift up. Dorm beds NT$350-400, singles NT$550 and doubles NT$800.

East Taipei

See map p.117

Charming City Hotel 295 Xinyi Rd Sec 4 ⊕02/25621962 or 0800/021112 ext 205, ⊛www .city-hotel.com.tw. This friendly hotel is the best deal in Xinyi, with a vast array of rooms and prices. Ignore the garish lobby with its mix of Asian and baroque decor – rooms are extremely stylish, with flat-screen TVs, DVD players and designer furniture. Pay a little more for the spa and Jacuzzi tubs. ⑤

Delight Hotel 432 Changchun Rd ⊕02/27160011, ⊛www.delighthotel.com.tw. Smart business hotel and one of the best bargains in the city, all a short walk from Nanjing E Rd MRT station. Chinese art lines the corridors and rooms have been decorated in a swish, contemporary style. ⑥

Far Eastern Plaza Hotel 201 Dunhua S Rd Sec 2 ⊕02/23788888, ⊛www.feph.com.tw. Taipei's tallest and one of its most luxurious hotels, close to the bars on Anhe Road. Rooms have the best views in the city though the real highlight is the fabulous 43rd-floor pool. ⑨

🏃 **Fortuna Hostel** 3/F, 310 Songlong Rd ⊕0930494498, ⊛www.fullgass.net. The best budget option in town, with a new location 10min

walk from Yongchun MRT station. Features two spotlessly clean bathrooms, washing machine and dryer, TV, DVD player, free Internet and decent kitchen. There's one dorm room with 6 beds (NT$300), 3 doubles and one twin (NT$800 each).

Grand Hyatt Taipei 2 Songshou Rd ⊕02/27201234, ⊛www.taipei.hyatt.com. Gargantuan five-star with vast, marble-clad lobby and 800 luxurious rooms in the heart of Xinyi's business district. Taipei's biggest outdoor pool area and a spread of upmarket, trendy restaurants make nice extras, but you'll pay NT$692 per day to use the Net. ⑧

🏃 **Le Petit Sherwood** 370 Dunhua S Rd Sec 1 ⊕02/27541166 ⓔlps@sherwood.com .tw. This stylish boutique hotel is a real treat, with a contemporary European theme and tranquil lobby where free coffee, tea and cookies are served on Versace-designed china. Rooms are a little compact, but equipped with flat-screen TVs, wireless Internet and chic, white marble bathrooms. ⑦

🏃 **Les Suites Taipei** 12 Qingcheng St ⊕02/87127688, ⊛www.suitetpe.com. Taipei's top boutique hotel, close to the MRT, with a sleek, contemporary Asian design and plenty of clever touches; a lounge offering free hot drinks and biscuits throughout the day, a 24hr computer room and a bamboo-fringed garden for breakfast. Rooms feature modern Chinese art and canopy beds, with Japanese baths in superiors. ⑧

🏃 **Taipei Fullerton 41** 41 Fuxing S Rd Sec 2 ⊕02/27031234, ⊛www.taipeifullerton.com .tw. Worthy rival to other boutique hotels in this part of town, with attractive inner atrium and chic, comfortable rooms. The main difference is price; hefty discounts make this exceptionally good value. ⑦

United Hotel 200 Guangfu S Rd ⊕02/27731515, ⊛www.unitedhotel.com.tw. Chic, contemporary minimalist design with elegant slate and marble fittings, attracting rock stars and business visitors alike. Rooms are a little overpriced, but feature vintage clawfoot tubs in glass-walled bathrooms – there are blinds for the modest. ⑧

The City

Taipei is modern Taiwan at its most dynamic, the fusion of ancient Chinese tradition, state-of-the-art technology and contemporary pop culture more pronounced here than anywhere else on the island. The frenetic energy of the streets is part of the attraction, but there's a surprising array of fascinating sights tucked away between the concrete and neon.

Taipei sights

Academia Sinica	中央研究院	*zhōngyāng yánjiūyuàn*
Baoan Temple	保安宮	*bǎoān gōng*
Chiang Kai-shek Memorial Hall	中正紀念堂	*zhōngzhèng jìniàntáng*
Chang Foundation Museum	鴻禧美術館	*hóngxǐ měishùguǎn*
Cisheng Temple	慈聖宮	*císhènggōng*
Ciyou Temple	慈祐宮	*cíyòugōng*
Confucius Temple	孔廟	*kǒngmiào*
Dihua Street	迪化街	*díhuà jiē*
Discovery Center of Taipei	台北探索館	*táiběi tànsuǒguǎn*
Lin An Tai Historical Home	林安泰古厝	*línāntài gǔcuò*
Lin Family Mansion and Garden	林本源園邸	*línběnyúanyúandǐ*
Longshan Temple	龍山寺	*lóngshān sì*
Museum of Contemporary Art	台北當代藝術館	*táiběi dàngdài yìshùguǎn*
Museum of World Religions	世界宗教博物館	*shìjiè zōngjiào bówùguǎn*
National Dr. Sun Yat-sen Memorial Hall	國立國父紀念館	*guólì guófù jìniànguǎn*
National Museum of History	國立歷史博物館	*guólì lìshǐ bówùguǎn*
National Palace Museum	國立故宮博物院	*guólì gùgōng bówùyuàn*
National Revolutionary Martyrs' Shrine	忠烈祠	*zhōngliècí*
National Taiwan Museum	國立臺灣博物館	*guólì táiwān bówùguǎn*
North Gate	北門	*běimén*
Presidential Building	總統府	*zǒng tǒng fǔ*
Qingshan Temple	青山宮	*qīngshāngōng*
Qingshui Temple	清水巖	*qīngshuǐyán*
Shilin Official Residence	士林官邸	*shìlín gūandǐ*
Shunyi Museum of Formosan Aborigines	順益台灣原住民博物館	*shūnyì táiwān yuánzhùmín bówùguǎn*
Taipei Fine Arts Museum	台北美術館	*táiběi měishùguǎn*
Taipei 101	台北一零一	*táiběi yīlíngyī*
Taipei Zoo	臺北市立動物園	*táiběishìlì dòngwùyuán*
Lin Liu-Hsin Puppet Theatre Museum	林柳新紀念偶戲博物館	*línliǔ xìn jìniàn ǒuxì bówùguǎn*
2-28 Peace Park	二二八和平公園	*èrèrbā hépínggōngyuán*
2-28 Memorial Museum	二二八紀念館	*èrèrbā jìniànguǎn*
Xiahai City God Temple	霞海城隍廟	*xiáhǎi chénghuáng miào*
Ximending	西門町	*xīméndīng*
Xingtian Temple	行天宮	*xíngtiān gōng*

Start exploring in West Taipei; the southern half contains **Zhongzheng** district, the city's historic and political core and where the influence of colonial Japan is most pronounced, especially in the old walled city. **Gongguan** and **Shida** further south are lively student areas, containing plenty of cheap bars and restaurants. To the west and sandwiched against the Danshui River, the districts of **Wanhua** and **Datong** are the city's oldest neighbourhoods, home to Taipei's dwindling stock of ramshackle wooden houses and early twentieth-century facades. The streets are narrower here, crammed with traditional stores, temples and restaurants – best explored on foot. **Zhongshan** is a more affluent district with a smattering of sights, while **East Taipei**, including Songshan, Xinyi and parts of Daan district, is the city's modern business centre, chiefly noted for its department stores and restaurants as well the world's tallest building, Taipei 101. **Nangang** lies further east, while **Shilin**, which contains the National Palace Museum, lies north of the Keelung River. The **southern districts** include the appealing teahouses and temples of Maokong in Wenshan, while the city's other southern suburbs fall under Taipei County administration, based in **Banciao**, and include **Yonghe** and **Xindian**.

Zhongzheng

Renamed to commemorate Chiang Kai-shek in 1990, **Zhongzheng** district is where Taipei was born in the 1880s. Today the old walled city lies just south of Taipei Main Station and still contains most of Taiwan's government offices. Further south are the National Museum of History and Chiang Kai-shek Memorial Hall, one of Taipei's most famous landmarks. The area is easily accessed by MRT, though distances are not great and it's possible to walk between the main sites.

The old walled city

Little remains of Liu Mingzhuan's **old walled city** today, as the walls and most of the early buildings were demolished by the Japanese after 1895 and only the gates survive. In fact, it's the Japanese period that gives the area much of its historic character, most evident in its numerous government offices and the particularly distinctive **Presidential Building** southwest of **2-28 Peace Park**, another colonial legacy. Today's Zhongxiao, Zhongshan, Aiguo and Zhonghua roads follow the line of the old walls.

Taiwan Storyland

Just south of the main train station on Zhongxiao Road is the K Mall, worth a quick visit for **Taiwan Storyland** (daily 10.30am–11pm; NT$250), a slightly kitsch but absorbing reconstruction of a Taiwanese neighbourhood, circa 1965. It's located in the basement, and includes several restaurants and snack stalls.

National Taiwan Museum

The building you'll see heading south along Guanqian Road from K Mall and lofty Shin Kong Tower, is the beautifully restored **National Taiwan Museum**

The city gates

The old city originally had five gates but only four remain today, the West Gate being destroyed by the Japanese. Five minutes walk west of Taipei Main Station along Zhongxiao Road stands Taipei's modest **North Gate**, once known as "Chengen Gate" meaning "to receive beneficence", an allusion to the emperor far to the north in Beijing. Today it's the only example of the original south-Fujian style of the gates, and one of the few surviving Qing dynasty structures in the centre of Taipei, though its location in the middle of a traffic circle overshadowed by a concrete overpass is hardly picturesque. The **Zhongxi Gate** (Little South Gate), **Lizheng Gate** (South Gate) and **Jingfu Gate** (East Gate) were substantially altered in 1966 as part of a restoration programme and now reflect Chiang Kai-shek's penchant for Northern Chinese architecture.

(Tues–Sun 10am–5pm, last entry 4.30pm; NT$20; ⓦ www.ntm.gov.tw). The museum was completed in 1915 to house artefacts dug up by Japanese archeologists and was dedicated to Governor-General Kodama Gentaro. The city's most important Mazu temple was demolished to build it, but the original golden-faced Mazu deity was saved and now stands in Fucheng Temple in Sanjhih on the north coast (it's brought back to Taipei each year for Mazu's birthday). Today, the museum is one of Taipei's finest colonial buildings, with a Neoclassical facade and 32 Corinthian columns flanking a magnificent white-washed lobby.

Despite containing four floors of exhibition rooms, only a small part of its huge collection of artefacts can be displayed at one time, mostly through temporary exhibits on the first and third floors. The only permanent displays are on the second floor, with a marginally interesting area dedicated to Taiwan's animals and plants, and the far more absorbing original collection of **aboriginal artefacts**. Highlights include some rare *pingpu* finds, such as tools and wood carvings, as well as a small **prehistoric area** containing a remarkable ensemble of Neolithic pottery and tools, many from the Peinan site (see p.422), and a replica of the skull of **Tsochen Man**, unearthed in Tainan County and estimated to be between 20,000 and 30,000 years old. The basement has a history section partly designed to mimic the bowels of a seventeenth-century Dutch ship, primarily targeted at local school children. At the time of writing the museum had only basic labelling in English.

2-28 Peace Park and Museum

Behind the museum, **2-28 Peace Park** (daily 10am–5pm; free) was created by the Japanese in 1899 and known as Taipei Park or New Park until 1997. It was renamed by former Taipei mayor Chen Shui-bian to commemorate the tragic massacre that began on 28 February 1947 and led to forty years of "White Terror" (see Contexts p.513). The park featured heavily in Pai Hsien-yung's groundbreaking novel *Crystal Boys* which highlights the struggles of Taipei's gay community in the 1960s, but today it's a popular place for locals to stroll, have lunch and take photos. It contains several Qing dynasty and Japanese-era relics, though many of the latter have been torn down over the years, most notably Kodama's statue, destroyed to make way for the spire-like **2-28 Monument** in the centre of the park. The memorial towers over a pool of water and a marble globe; inscribed onto this is a 642-character long explanation of the massacre written by a committee of six scholars – they met nearly thirty times before the final version of the text was agreed.

In the southeast corner of the park, the former home of Japan's colonial Taipei Broadcasting Bureau has been converted into the **2-28 Memorial Museum** (Tues–Sun 10am–5pm; NT$20; free on Wed), a fascinating if sobering place to learn about the 2-28 Incident and subsequent struggle for democracy in Taiwan. Apart from an informative video with English subtitles, the rest of the museum's extensive displays are frustratingly labelled in Chinese only so it's best to visit midweek, when there are fewer visitors, and ask for an English-speaking guide (free). The first-floor exhibits provide the historical context of the incident, starting with the Japanese occupation, while the second floor recounts the major events of the massacre and subsequent "White Terror".

The Presidential Building

Leave the park at the southern entrance, then turn right on Ketagalan Boulevard and walk towards the imposing redbrick facade of the **Presidential Building** (Mon–Fri 9am–12pm; free), its 60-metre tower for years the highest point in

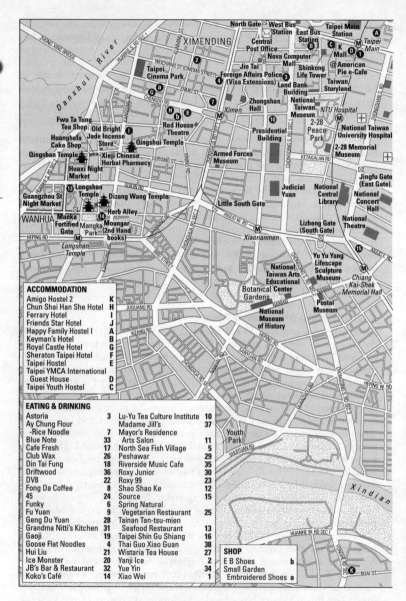

ACCOMMODATION
Amigo Hostel 2	K
Chun Shai Han She Hotel	H
Ferrary Hotel	I
Friends Star Hotel	J
Happy Family Hostel I	A
Keyman's Hotel	B
Royal Castle Hotel	G
Sheraton Taipei Hotel	F
Taipei Hostel	E
Taipei YMCA International Guest House	D
Taipei Youth Hostel	C

EATING & DRINKING
Astoria	3	Lu-Yu Tea Culture Institute	10
Ay Chung Flour -Rice Noodle	7	Madame Jill's	37
Blue Note	33	Mayor's Residence Arts Salon	11
Cafe Fresh	17	North Sea Fish Village	5
Club Wax	26	Peshawar	29
Din Tai Fung	18	Riverside Music Cafe	35
Driftwood	36	Roxy Junior	30
DV8	22	Roxy 99	23
Fong Da Coffee	8	Shao Shao Ke	12
45	24	Source	15
Funky	6	Spring Natural Vegetarian Restaurant	25
Fu Yuan	9		
Geng Du Yuan	28	Tainan Tan-tsu-mien Seafood Restaurant	13
Grandma Nitti's Kitchen	31		
Gaoji	19	Taipei Shin Gu Shiang	16
Goose Flat Noodles	4	Thai Guo Xiao Guan	38
Hui Liu	21	Wistaria Tea House	27
Ice Monster	20	Yanji Ice	2
JB's Bar & Restaurant	32	Yue Yin	34
Koko's Café	14	Xiao Wei	1

SHOP
E B Shoes	b
Small Garden Embroidered Shoes	a

the city. The public areas of the building contain a curious but edifying mix of contemporary and historical exhibitions. The president and vice-president still work here and security is understandably tight: the weekday entrance is at the back of the building on Boai Road where you must show some form of photo ID (passport preferably), and be "properly dressed," which in practice means no open-toe sandals (shorts and T-shirts seem to be OK). English-speaking guides

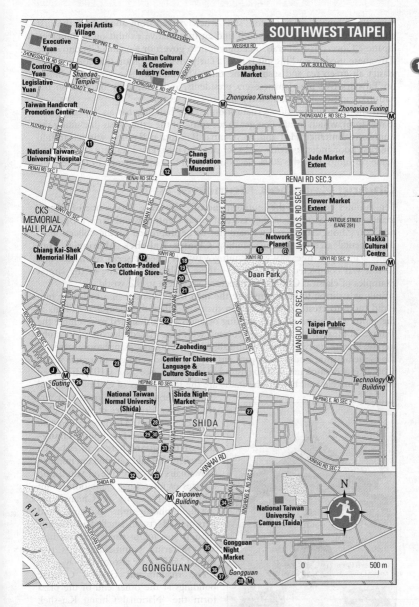

SOUTHWEST TAIPEI

Taipei Artists Village

Executive Yuan

Control Yuan

Legislative Yuan

Shandao Temple

Huashan Cultural & Creative Industry Centre

Guanghua Market

Taiwan Handicraft Promotion Center

Zhongxiao Xinsheng

Zhongxiao Fuxing

National Taiwan University Hospital

Chang Foundation Museum

Jade Market Extent

RENAI RD SEC.3

CKS MEMORIAL HALL PLAZA

Flower Market Extent

ANTIQUE STREET (LANE 291)

Hakka Cultural Centre

Chiang Kai-Shek Memorial Hall

Lee Yao Cotton-Padded Clothing Store

Network Planet @

Daan Park

Daan

Zaoheding

Center for Chinese Language & Culture Studies

Taipei Public Library

Technology Building

Guting

National Taiwan Normal University (Shida)

Shida Night Market

SHIDA

HEPING E. RD SEC.2

Taipower Building

Gongguan Night Market

National Taiwan University Campus (Taida)

N

0   500 m

GONGGUAN

Gongguan

River

are provided free of charge – it's not possible to tour the place without one and many exhibits have Chinese-only captions.

Constructed between 1912 and 1919 by the Japanese to mimic British imperial architecture, the building served as the office of Japanese Governor-Generals until 1945, assuming the function of Taiwan's presidential office from 1949. The first-floor rooms are arranged around two inner gardens that form the Chinese character for "sun" when viewed from above (also the first character for "Japan"). Here you'll find an informative exhibit on all nineteen Japanese Governor-Generals, including fourth governor Kodama Gentaro – the Taiwanese used to say "his spit is law," a fairly vivid indication that colonial rule wasn't all green tea and sushi at the time. The building also contains exhibits on Taiwan's five post-Japanese-era presidents, and temporary displays on the nation's traditional crafts, industry and tourism sectors.

On the first Sunday of alternate months, the building has an "open house" (8am–4pm), which means you get to see some of the other areas (including the impressive Entrance Hall and Presidential Reception Room), wander around the first floor independently and take photographs. The President's Office was made off limits after the 2004 election, though this may change in future.

Chiang Kai-shek Memorial Hall

Ten minutes walk from the southern end of 2-28 Peace Park is one of Taipei's grandest sights. Standing at the "Gate of Great Centrality and Perfect Uprightness" on Zhongshan Road, it's hard not to be impressed by the collection of monumental architecture surrounding **Chiang Kai-shek Memorial Hall** (daily 9am–5pm; free; Ⓦwww.cksmh.gov.tw). It doesn't seem to matter that all this was completed in the 1980s – these buildings are some of the largest examples of classical Chinese architecture anywhere in the world.

Built as a shrine to commemorate the man that – admire him or loathe him – did more to create modern Taiwan than any other, the memorial hall sits at the centre of a grand plaza, its striking octagonal roof designed to resemble the Temple of Heaven in Beijing and covered with blue glazed tiles. Start by climbing the granite stairway to the main hall, which contains a giant bronze statue of the Generalissimo under an elegant red cypress wood ceiling – though it seems a bit like a mausoleum, Chiang isn't buried inside (see box p.101). Inscribed onto the marble wall behind the statue are the three pillars of Chiang's political

thought, loosely adapted from Sun Yat-sen's "Three Principles of the People": Science (*ke xue*), Democracy *(minzu)* and Ethics *(lun li)*. The hourly **changing of the guard** here is an elaborate ceremony that takes around ten minutes. Downstairs on ground level you'll find a series of interesting exhibition rooms which tell the story of Chiang's life through photographs, paintings and personal effects, all labelled in English, though you might tire of the predictably flattering commentary. His two shiny Cadillacs are also on display.

The magnificent classical Chinese buildings at the other end of the plaza form the "National Chiang Kai-shek Cultural Center" (daily noon–8pm; Ⓣ02/33939831, Ⓦwww.ntch.edu.tw), Taiwan's premier performing arts venue, and comprise the **National Theater** (closest to the MRT station exit) and the **National Concert Hall**.

△ Chiang Kai-shek Memorial Hall

Chiang's final resting place

Chiang Kai-shek was Taiwan's official president from 1950 until his death in 1975. His last wish was to be buried in China near his mother, in the small village of Xikou in Zhejiang province where he grew up. This was impossible at the time, so he was instead placed in a temporary mausoleum in Cihhu, south of Taoyuan (see p.195) with the somewhat optimistic belief that China and Taiwan would be peacefully reunited under a post-Communist regime soon after. Thirty years later that was still looking highly unlikely and sometime in 2007, after repeated delays, the Generalissimo should finally be laid to rest in the country he always regarded as a short-term home. You can visit his relatively modest tomb, embossed with a giant Kuomintang star and given the quasi-Imperial title *Chiang Ling*, in **Wujhihshan Military Cemetery**, on the slopes of Yangmingshan northeast of Taipei – take a taxi from Kunyang MRT station (NT$300). His son, former president Chiang Ching-kuo (who died in 1988 and was buried near his father), will be reburied here at the same time. The cemetery also contains the tombs of Chiang Wei-kuo, Chiang Kai-shek's adopted son, and former president Yen Chia-kan.

National Museum of History and around

A fifteen-minute walk west along Nanhai Road from the CKS Memorial MRT station, the **National Museum of History** (Tues–Sun 10am–6pm; NT$20; ⓦ www.nmh.gov.tw) was founded in 1955, the third in a series of aging Ming and Qing dynasty replica buildings along this stretch of road. The bulk of its collection, largely comprising artefacts from central China, was transferred from the Henan Museum back on the mainland in 1949. If you've already been to the National Palace Museum, you might feel it's a waste of time coming here, but it's much smaller and easier to absorb – the extensive collection of **Shang and Zhou dynasty bronzes** is particularly impressive and the temporary exhibits usually have a Taiwanese focus, with a bias towards painting and calligraphy. If you're still not impressed, grab a coffee at the second-floor Pavilion of Tranquillity, which commands a picture-perfect location overlooking the lily pond in the Botanical Gardens.

The classical Chinese building just before the museum is the **National Taiwan Arts Educational Center** (daily 9am–5pm; free), which organizes mildly interesting art exhibitions, while just beyond the small lily pond behind the centre (to the left) you'll find the entrance to the **Botanical Gardens** (daily 4am–10pm; free), one of Taipei's most tranquil open spaces. Another park built by the Japanese, this time in 1921, its undoubted highlight is the expansive lotus pond with giant Amazonian water lilies that flower in June.

Head back towards Chiang Kai-shek Memorial Plaza and at the junction of Chongqing and Nanhai Roads you'll find the **Chinese Postal Museum** (Tues–Sun 9am–5pm; NT$5) which has English labelling and an illuminating account of China's postal history, but only worthwhile for die-hard philatelists. Opposite is the tiny **Yu Yu Yang Lifescape Sculpture Museum** (Mon–Sat 11am–5pm; free), dedicated to the work of sculptor Yu Yu Yang (1926–1997), one of Taiwan's most famous modern artists. Born in Taiwan, his family moved to Beijing to work in the film business and he later studied in Japan, finally returning home in the 1970s to set up a studio on the east coast and teaching other talented sculptors such as Ju Ming (see p.168). The museum's small collection of cast steel and bronze pieces is particularly striking, but labelling is in Chinese only.

Chang Foundation Museum

Located in the eastern corner of Zhongzheng, the **Chang Foundation Museum** (Tues–Sun 10.30am–4.30pm; NT$100) has an exquisite collection of classical Chinese art and historical artefacts that makes it another mini version of the Palace Museum, but more easily digested. Highlights include its Jingdezhen **porcelain** and **ceramics** of the Song, Ming and Qing dynasties, its gilt metal Buddhist images and scholars' seals. The museum is twenty minutes' walk south of Zhongxiao Xinsheng MRT station at 63 Renai Road Section 2.

Wanhua

Wanhua district, bounded by Zhongzheng to the east and the Danshui River to the west, is the oldest part of the city. Founded by immigrants from China in the early eighteenth century, the village was gradually absorbed by newly created Taipei in the 1890s. Originally known as **Bangka** or Manka in Taiwanese (from the Ketagalan word for "canoe"), the Japanese changed the name in 1920: the new characters read "Manka" in Japanese but "Wanhua" in Chinese.

It's a place best explored on foot – some of the city's most famous temples and markets remain squashed between modern apartment blocks and to the north, **Ximending** is one of Taipei's funkier neighbourhoods. Before you start exploring, take a look at **Bird Street,** just east of Longshan Temple MRT station. This exotic market is marked by red bird-shaped signs and lined with shops selling parrots, cockatoos and macaws – it's the stretch of Heping West Road between Nanning Road and Bangka Boulevard.

Longshan Temple and around

The most important of Wanhua's "big three" temples (the others being Qingshui and Qingshan), and arguably Taipei's most famous, **Longshan Temple** (daily 6am–10pm) is the ideal place to soak up Taiwan's vibrant religious traditions. Located a block north of Longshan Temple MRT station across Mangka Park, the temple was established in 1738 (making it Taipei's oldest), renovated 1919–1924 and partially rebuilt after US bombing destroyed much of the complex during World War II. It's principally a Buddhist temple dedicated to the bodhisattva **Guanyin**, but there are more than a hundred deities worshipped here, mostly from the Taoist pantheon.

The main entrance on Guangzhou Street borders a pleasant courtyard, replete with artificial waterfall on the right-hand side. Before entering the temple proper, take a look at the two dragon pillars outside the **Front Hall**, the only bronze pair in Taiwan. Once inside you'll see prayer tables and worshippers facing the **Main Hall** in the centre where Guanyin is enshrined – the principal image of the goddess has proved virtually indestructible over the years, surviving local conflicts, earthquakes and even the US bombing. Note the two gold censers in front of the hall, with their vivid cast images of "silly barbarians lifting a corner of the temple", supposedly eighteenth-century depictions of the Dutch. This is the busiest part of the temple, but the deity-packed **Rear Hall** also receives a steady stream of visitors. The goddess Mazu is worshipped in the centre and fringed by *guangming* lights, each representing a donation made in the hope of attracting good fortune. To the far right is a separate shrine dedicated to the gods of literature, primarily Wenchang Dijun in the middle, patronized by students and anxious parents at examination time. Guan Di occupies the shrine on the far left and in front of this in a side hall is a newer altar dedicated to the Matchmaker, a sort of Chinese cupid (see p.532). Black-robed devotees chant prayers in front of the Main Hall several times a day, and the best time to see them is from 6 to 9am and 5 to 6pm when the temple tends to get more crowded with worshippers making offerings and tossing *zhi jiao* or "throwing blocks" to communicate with the gods. The principle **festival** here is Guanyin's birthday on Lunar February 19 but almost every other major Taoist festival is celebrated, and the temple is also busy over Chinese New Year when elephant-size lanterns occupy the courtyard.

Turn left on exiting the temple and you'll see the entrance to Lane 224 or **Herb Alley**, a narrow, L-shaped street crammed with 100-year-old stalls selling aloe vera, sweet basil and a variety of Chinese herbs and roots including "white-horse dung" – you'll probably smell it before you see it. At the end of the alley, walk across Xichang Street to **Dizang Wang Temple** (daily 6am–10.30pm), which looks like a dilapidated garage but is, in fact, an important part of the district's religious life, established in 1760 and rebuilt in 1838. Known in English as the "King of Hell" the name is misleading – the main deity is not the Chinese Satan but a bodhisattva known as Ksitigarbha (Dizang in Chinese). The main shrine contains an image of the deity, and is where locals make offerings to reduce the time relatives spend in hell, or to help end suffering associated with terminal diseases – you can even reduce your own future punishment in the afterlife by praying here (the Chinese concept of hell is quite different to that held in the West; see Contexts p.532 for more on this and Dizang Wang).

Retrace your steps and pass Longshan Temple in the other direction to Xiyuan Road: beyond this point **Guangzhou Street Night Market** gets going from around 5pm and connects to the venerable **Huaxi Tourist Night Market**, also known as Snake Alley (see p.128). Keep going for another 25m and you should see narrow Lane 223 on the right. Sitting astride the entrance is the grandly titled **Manka Fortified Gate**, a tiny remnant of what were once common local defences in the early nineteenth century against bandits and other Chinese clans – today it seems pitifully inadequate. Head back to Xiyuan Road and turn left: the row of shops here sell colourful Buddhist paraphernalia such as carvings, statues, CDs, lamps and incense.

Qingshan and Qingshui Temples

Keep walking a couple of blocks north on Xiyuan Road and you'll reach Guiyang Street, lined with many of Wanhua's early twentieth-century buildings and traditional stores – the clapboard shophouses near here date from the Japanese Taisho period (1912-1925). Turn left, and you should see the narrow facade of **Qingshan Temple** (daily 5.30am–9.30pm) ahead on the left. Established in 1854 by immigrants from Quanzhou, it's dedicated to General Zhang, a quasi-historical figure from China's Three Kingdoms period, also known as "King of Qingshan" and a popular administrator. Admirers began to worship him after his death, and in time he was credited with special powers of protection – he was also the deity favoured by tea merchants in the area. The temple and the whole of Wanhua comes alive to celebrate his birthday (Lunar October 22, usually November or December) with fireworks and three days of parades. Qingshan is enshrined amidst an elaborate gold altar in the **Main Hall**; beyond here the **Rear Hall** houses various deities, but don't miss the temple's gold-painted **carvings**, particularly on the beams and third-floor ceiling which are incredibly ornate.

Turn right on leaving the temple and walk along Guiyang Street, past some of the area's **oldest stores**. Just beyond the Xiyuan Road junction at no. 200 is the **Huanghefa Cake Shop** established in 1909, but now a specialist producer of bright-red cakes used as temple offerings. The **Fwu Ta Tung Teashop** at no. 196 sells ancient Pu Er tea from China, while the **Xieji Chinese Herbal Pharmacy** at no. 186 was established over eighty years ago. On the other side of the road at no. 153, the **Old Bright Jade Incense Store** is another atmospheric shop, founded in 1897. After a couple of blocks you'll reach Kangding Road; on the other side is a traditional gate leading to **Qingshui Temple** (daily 6am–9pm) at the end of a narrow lane bordered by a row of cheap food stalls. The temple was built in 1787 by immigrants from Anxi County in Fujian and is dedicated to Chinese hero Chen Zhao-ying, another historical figure that was later deified (see Contexts p.530). The temple was burned to the ground during the "Ding-Xia" Feud in 1853, but rebuilt by 1867 – the **Main Hall** has survived more or less intact since then and contains the seven original images of the deity brought from China. The most powerful is known as the "Penglai Divine Progenitor", whose nose is said to fall off in times of danger, only to miraculously reattach itself when the coast is clear. He's shared with the Qingshui Temple in Danshui, spending six months in each place. Note the intricate artwork inside, particularly on the roof beams. It's a short walk from here to Zhonghua Road and Ximen MRT station along Changsha Street, north of the temple.

Ximending

Forming the northern section of Wanhua, **Ximending** is a grid of narrow streets squashed into a triangle formed by Chengdu and Zhonghua Roads with the Danshui River. Named after the long-gone West Gate and now a trendy shopping district accessible from Ximen MRT station, this is where Taipei's teenagers come to have fun – at weekends it's packed with Mandopop fans checking out wannabe performers and wearing the latest fads. It's also famous for its cinemas – **Wuchang Street** is packed with them, with **Taipei Cinema Park** at its western end containing an open-air space for showing films and

△ Ximending

a small exhibition hall about the area (daily 9am–5pm). Just south of the main Ximen plaza is the **Red House Theatre** (see p.132) while the **Armed Forces Museum** (Mon–Sat 9am–4pm; NT$20) is just off Zhonghua Road on Guiyang Street, providing an enlightening, if slightly biased, account of the nation's military history, comprehensively labelled in English. It's also a reminder of Taiwan's confusing official status as Republic of China – it covers the period from the founding of the Republic in 1911 through to the present day.

Datong

Taipei's second oldest neighbourhood after Wanhua, **Datong** lines the Danshui River north of Ximending and Taipei Main Station. The district evolved from two villages; north of Minquan Road, **Dalongdong** was established in the early eighteenth century while to the south **Dadaocheng**, meaning "big rice drying yard", was created in 1853 by refugees from Wanhua. The latter flourished in the 1870s as tea exports boomed and foreign companies established bases on the wharf. Today it's a fascinating place to wander, its narrow lanes littered with historic buildings, traditional shops and temples.

Dihua Street

Historic **Dihua Street** cuts through the southern half of Datong, crammed with photogenic shophouses built in Chinese Baroque style, many dating from the 1920s; at Chinese New Year the street expands into an open-air emporium for traditional gifts and snacks. Start exploring at the Nanjing Road end, thirty minutes' walk east of Zhongshan MRT station. North of here, the road is lined with silk and cloth stores, followed by Traditional Chinese Medicine, herbs and dried-food sellers. Just beyond Yun-Lo Market on the right, the **Xiahai City God Temple** (daily 6am–8pm) at no. 61 may be small but it's one of Taipei's most venerated places of worship. The temple was completed in 1859 by Tongan migrants to replace the one destroyed in Wanhua six years earlier – the main City God statue had been brought to Taiwan from its hometown in China in 1821. The main shrine contains the revered City God image and his officials, but it's also the most popular place in Taipei to make offerings to the Old Man Under the Moon, also known as the "**Matchmaker**", represented by a small image of an old man with a long beard in front of the main altar to the left. Praying to this Chinese cupid is believed to result in finding your ideal partner in less than six months – about two hundred worshippers claim success each year. The side hall to the right of the main shrine contains Guanyin (nearest the entrance), the City God's wife next door and at the end, an altar commemorating the 38 men (the *Yi Yong Gong*) killed saving the City God in the Ding-Xia Feud of 1853. The City God's birthday on Lunar May 13 (usually in June) is one of Taipei's biggest religious **festivals** involving fireworks, parades and traditional performances over several days.

Just north of the temple is the traditional **Qianyuan Medicine Shop** at no.71, established in the nineteenth century and renowned for its powerful remedies. At Minsheng Road turn left and walk a block to Guide Street; it's the narrow lane on the left just before Huanhe Road and **Dadaocheng Wharf**, the place to catch ferries upriver on the **Blue Highway** (see box p.108). Guide Street ran along the quayside in the nineteenth century, facing the Danshui River and home to Taipei's affluent tea merchants – you can still see the raised foundations that protected them from flooding. The best preserved house is tea

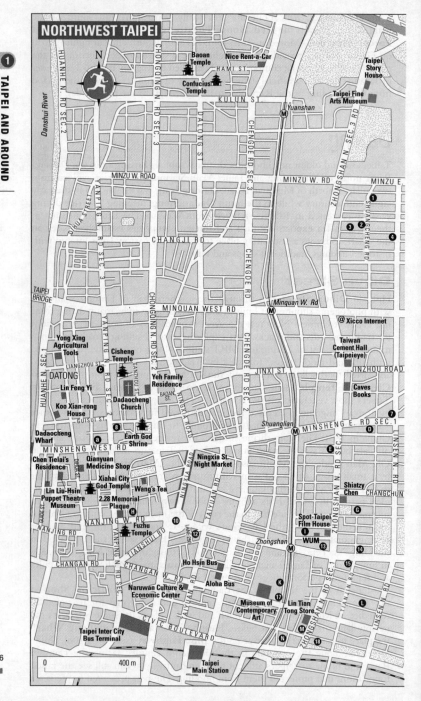

NORTHWEST TAIPEI

N

Danshui River

HUANHE N RD SEC. 2

CHONGQING N RD SEC. 3

Baoan Temple

Nice Rent-a-Car

HAMI ST

Confucius Temple

KULUN ST.

DATONG ST.

CHENGDE RD SEC. 3

ⓂYuanshan

Taipei Story House

Taipei Fine Arts Museum

MINZU W. ROAD

YANPING N RD SEC. 3

MINZU W. RD

ZHONGSHAN N SEC. 3 RD

MINZU E.

SHUANGCHENG RD

❶
❸ ❷
❹

DIHUA STREET

CHANGJI RD

CHENGDE RD

TAIPEI BRIDGE

MINQUAN WEST RD

CHONGQING N RD SEC. 2

ⓂMinquan W. Rd

@ Xicco Internet

YANPING N RD SEC. 3

Yong Xing Agricultural Tools

Cisheng Temple

Taiwan Cement Hall (Taipeieye)

HUANHE N SEC. 2

LIANGZHOU ST.

DATONG

Ⓒ

GANZHOU ST.

Yeh Family Residence

JINXI ST.

Caves Books

JINZHOU ROAD

Lin Feng Yi

Koo Xian-rong House

Dadaocheng Church

BAOAN ST.

NINGXIA ROAD

CHENGDE RD SEC. 2

❼

ZHONGSHAN N RD SEC. 2

GUTSUT ST.

Ⓑ

Earth God Shrine

Ⓜ Shuanglian

MINSHENG E. RD SEC. 1

Ⓓ

LINSEN N. RD

Dadaocheng Wharf

ⓐ

MINSHENG WEST RD

Chen Tielai's Residence

Qianyuan Medicine Shop

Ningxia St. Night Market

Ⓔ

DIHUA ST.

NINGXIA ROAD

Xiahai City God Temple

Wang's Tea

TAIYUAN RD

Shiatzy Chen

CHANGCHUN

Lin Liu-Hsin Puppet Theatre Museum

2.28 Memorial Plaque

Ⓗ

Ⓖ

GUIDE ST.

Fuzhu Temple

NANJING W RD

YANPING N RD SEC. 2

❿

Spot-Taipei Film House

Ⓘ

ZHONGSHAN N RD SEC. 1

NANJING RD

⓬

LANE 250

Zhongshan

WUM

⓭

⓮

TIANSHUI RD

CHANGAN RD

CHANGAN W. RD

Ho Hsin Bus

ⓀＭ

⓯

TIANJIN RD

LINSEN N. RD

Aloha Bus

Ⓛ

Naruwan Culture & Economic Center

TAIYUAN RD

ZHONGSHAN N RD SEC. 1

⓱

Lin Tian Tong Store

Museum of Contemporary Art

ⓝ

Ⓜ

⓲

CIVIC BOULEVARD

Taipei Inter City Bus Terminal

Taipei Main Station

0 ———— 400 m

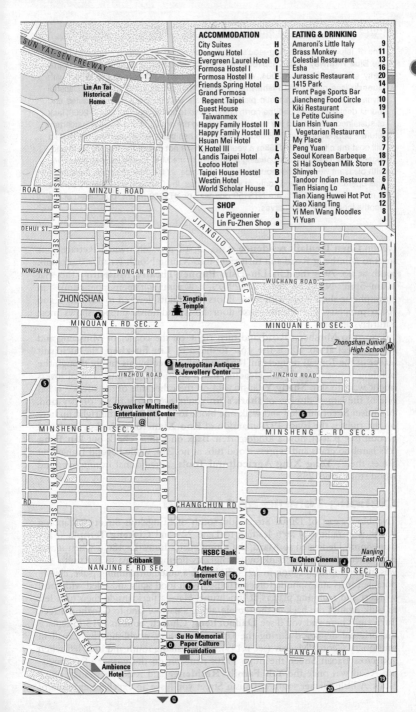

ACCOMMODATION

City Suites	H
Dongwu Hotel	C
Evergreen Laurel Hotel	O
Formosa Hostel I	I
Formosa Hostel II	E
Friends Spring Hotel	D
Grand Formosa Regent Taipei	G
Guest House Taiwanmex	K
Happy Family Hostel II	N
Happy Family Hostel III	M
Hsuan Mei Hotel	P
K Hotel III	L
Landis Taipei Hotel	A
Leofoo Hotel	F
Taipei House Hostel	B
Westin Hotel	J
World Scholar House	Q

SHOP

| Le Pigeonnier | b |
| Lin Fu-Zhen Shop | a |

EATING & DRINKING

Amaroni's Little Italy	9
Brass Monkey	11
Celestial Restaurant	13
Esha	16
Jurassic Restaurant	20
1415 Park	14
Front Page Sports Bar	4
Jiancheng Food Circle	10
Kiki Restaurant	19
Le Petite Cuisine	1
Lian Hsin Yuan Vegetarian Restaurant	5
My Place	7
Peng Yuan	3
Seoul Korean Barbeque	18
Si Hai Soybean Milk Store	17
Shinyeh	2
Tandoor Indian Restaurant	6
Tien Hsiang Lo	A
Tian Xiang Huwei Hot Pot	15
Xiao Xiang Ting	12
Yi Men Wang Noodles	8
Yi Yuan	J

TAIPEI AND AROUND

107

Blue Highway – white elephant?

One of Taipei Mayor Ma Ying-jeou's ambitious schemes to develop tourism in Taipei, the **Blue Highway** (☎02/25531368 or 02/28059022), has become mired in controversy since it opened in 2004. A ferry route connecting **Dadaocheng Wharf** with **Guandu** (see p.151) and **Fisherman's Wharf** (see p.150) lower down the Danshui River, it's part of an optimistic plan to integrate ferry services, bicycle routes and tourist destinations around the north coast. Despite some improvement in 2006, lack of sustained interest and the cost of maintaining the boats means it has an uncertain future – opposition from DPP council members has been fierce, claiming the project will cost the city at least NT$8m a year. Though it's not one of the world's most photogenic boat rides, it's an appealing alternative to the MRT for the journey downriver, with pleasant views of the mountains on either side. At the time of writing the service was operating at weekends only, at irregular times: the Dadaocheng–Guandu service is most frequent. Tickets are NT$150 one-way or NT$300 return, purchased at the booths located by the wharves.

tycoon **Chen Tienlai's residence** at no. 73, still privately owned. Retrace your steps to Minsheng Road and turn right into Xining North Road: a short walk south at no. 79 is the **Lin Liu-Hsin Puppet Theatre Museum** (Tues–Sat 10am–5pm; NT$120; ☎02/25529079, ✉admin@taipeipuppet.com), an atmospheric shophouse with three floors of exhibits devoted to Taiwanese and Asian puppetry. The theatre next door hosts traditional puppet shows most Saturdays at 3pm.

Return to Minsheng Road and turn right: on the corner of Minsheng and Dihua Street at no. 105 is the store founded by **Lin Fu-zhen**, the merchant leader of the Tongan refugees in 1853 and still owned by his family, though the building is not the original. Heading north again along Dihua, animal lovers might want to skip **Sheng Yi** at no. 144 on the other side of the street – it has one of the largest displays of **shark's fin** you're ever likely to see on dry land. At Guisui Street turn left and walk one block to Lane 303 on the right: up here on the right is the lavish 1920 mansion of **Koo Xian-rong**, the Lugang-based tycoon (see p.262), now a kindergarten. Back on Dihua, check out **Lin Feng Yi**'s bamboo crafts and cypress wood tubs at no. 214, while beyond Liangzhou Street, there's **Yong Xing Agricultural Tools**, a traditional ironmonger and wood store at no. 288.

Cisheng Temple and around

Two blocks east of Dihua Street, just south of Liangzhou Street on Yanping Road, is a traditional arch leading to Lane 225 and **Cisheng Temple** (daily 6am–8pm). Dedicated to Mazu, the temple dates from the 1860s when it was established on the river bank by immigrants fleeing Wanhua to the south – it was moved to this location in 1914. Today it's a quiet, unassuming place, chiefly notable for its atmospheric forecourt lined with food stalls and filled with local workers and mahjong players at lunchtime. Have a peek inside then turn left to walk around the back of the temple, along a narrow lane to Ganzhou Street. Turn right here and you'll see **Dadaocheng Church**, built in 1915 to replace the original destroyed during the Japanese invasion, established by Canadian missionary George Mackay (see p.149). Keep walking south and look left when you cross Baoan Street: the huge 1920s mansion on the corner of Chongqing Road was once the **Yeh Family Residence** and is now a swanky office block. A little further south at Guisui Street you'll see an excellent example of a neighbourhood **Earth God shrine,** or *Tudi Gong Miao* (see Contexts p.529). Completed in 1914, this one is usually quite active – in addition to a steady stream of worshippers you'll see a motley collection of old boys playing dominoes or sipping beer outside most afternoons. Turn right here and walk along Guisui Street to Yanping Road. Continue south on Yanping to Lane 61 and turn left: keep bearing straight ahead beyond a small junction (it's now Lane 64) and less than 50m on the right is **Wang's Tea** at no. 26. Housed in a beautifully restored building, this teashop was first established in Fujian, China, in the 1880s and opened here after the family fled the mainland in 1949 – you can sample quality Taiwanese tea inside. If you've still got some energy left, walk south along Chongqing Road, turn right along Nanjing West Road and after a block you'll see a small memorial commemorating the shot that triggered the **2-28 Incident,** in front of the traditional Sheng Yuan Drug Store at no. 181.

Museum of Contemporary Art

The **Museum of Contemporary Art** (Tues–Sun 10am–6pm; NT$50; Ⓦ www.mocataipei.org.tw) at 39 Changan West Rd is an innovative modern art gallery, housed in one of the most attractive Japanese-era buildings in the city. Constructed in the 1920s and 1930s, it served as an elementary school and Taipei's City Hall before opening in 2001. The thought-provoking temporary exhibitions here feature international but primarily Taiwanese artists and include contemporary painting, installation art, sculpture, photography, video and film. Be warned, however, MOCA sometimes closes for up to two weeks in between exhibitions. The museum is a short walk from Zhongshan MRT station.

Dalongdong

The northwest corner of Datong occupies the site of the eighteenth-century village of **Dalongdong,** once famed as the home of scholars, though little remains of it today apart from two of the city's most alluring temples. Both are a short walk from Yuanshan MRT station.

Confucius Temple

Taipei's **Confucius Temple** (Tues–Sat 8.30am–9pm, Sun 8.30am–5pm; Ⓦ www.ct.taipei.gov.tw) is best known for hosting the world's most authentic annual celebration of Confucius's **birthday** on September 28 (see Festivals section p.53). Though the great teacher is still revered in Taiwan, he's not associated with any of the daily rituals that make other temples so colourful, and on other days it's relatively peaceful. Built in South Fujianese style but laid out according to the original Confucius temple in Qufu (in China's Shandong province), the oldest buildings were constructed between 1927 and 1939.

Enter via the **Hong Gate** on Dalong Street, which leads into a garden with Minglun Hall on your left and the **Li Gate** just ahead; walk through this to get to the front of the main temple complex. The first building on your left is the ceremonial **Ling Xing Gate,** while beyond this the **Yi Gate** fronts the central stone courtyard and **Dacheng Hall,** the most important part of the temple. Note the decorated cylinders on the hall's roof, symbolising the bamboo containers used to hide Confucian classics during the Qin Emperor's fanatical "Burning of the Books" in 213 BC. The hall is typically bare inside: it contains a single tablet commemorating Confucius in the centre, and sixteen others for the Four Sages (including Mencius) and the Twelve Wise Men, all Confucian disciples, as well as various musical instruments used in ceremonies.

The black tablet hanging from the beams above the shrine was written by Chiang Kai-shek and says "Education for All". The courtyard is ringed by the **East and West Rooms**, containing the memorial tablets of 154 other Confucian disciples and scholars, and a small office (daily 8.30am–5.30pm) on the right where you can pick up English leaflets, while the **Chong Sheng Shrine** at the back of the complex houses tablets venerating the first five generations of Confucius' ancestors. The temple hosts calligraphy classes every Wednesday (2–4pm), poetry recitals on Saturday (2–4pm) and sessions of *nanguan* music every third Sunday (10am–noon).

Baoan Temple

Baoan Temple (daily 6am–10pm; Ⓦ www.paoan.org.tw), a few metres north of the Confucius Temple on Hami Street, is Taipei's most beautiful shrine. Though there are many deities enshrined here, the principal figure is Baosheng Dadi, regarded as a god of medicine or healing (see Contexts p.530). Tradition maintains that immigrants from Tongan began worshipping here in 1742 and a simple shrine was completed in 1760, but the first official temple was constructed between 1805 and 1830. The temple won a UNESCO conservation award in 2003 in recognition of the incredible restoration work completed in the 1990s.

Before you go in, check out the painted wall carving inside the East Gate to the right of the Entrance Hall – it features Chinese hero Yue Fei having the words "Serve Your Country" being carved onto his back by his patriotic mother. Once inside you'll see the **Main Hall** across the courtyard, packed with numerous images of Baosheng and surrounded by statues of the **36 celestial officials**, carved between 1829 and 1834 and exceptionally rare pieces of temple art. Hard to spot, but there are slight differences between the left and right sides of the hall, a result of the rivalry between the two master craftsmen hired for the restoration of 1917. You won't miss the seven eye-catching **murals** that adorn the outer walls of the hall however – they depict various Chinese legends and were completed in 1973. The **Drum Tower** on the left (west) side of the courtyard houses a shrine to the Birth Goddess, while the **Bell Tower** on the opposite side is a shrine to Mazu. Shennong Dadi, the god of agriculture, is worshipped in the **Rear Hall**. The **Baosheng Cultural Festival** is usually held April–May and comprises several weeks of traditional performances to celebrate **Baosheng's birthday** (Lunar March 15), including an extensive programme of Chinese opera and music in the evenings. The birthday is marked by a solemn ceremony in the temple, while a boisterous parade usually takes place the day before.

Zhongshan

Bounded by Fuxing Road in the east and maple-lined **Zhongshan Road** in the wet, one of the city's more pleasant throughfares, Zhongshan is a lively modern district covering much of the northern part of central Taipei. Though there's plenty to see, especially in its northern half, Zhongshan is primarily a collection of residential neighbourhoods, shopping streets and offices with no discernable centre, its sights spread out and often best combined with attractions in other areas; Taipei's excellent **Fine Arts Museum** is close to Yuanshan MRT station and the temples in Dalongdong (see p.109), while the **Su Ho Paper Culture Foundation** lies much further south, best approached from Zhongxiao Xinsheng MRT station.

Taipei Fine Arts Museum

If you only have time for one art gallery in Taipei, make it the **Taipei Fine Arts Museum** (Tues–Sun 9.30am–5.30pm, Sat closes 9.30pm; NT$30; Ⓦ www .tfam.gov.tw) on Zhongshan North Road Section 3, a short walk across the park from Yuanshan MRT station. Its four floors primarily showcase modern Taiwanese art – though exhibitions change every few months, they usually include pieces from the museum's extensive and important permanent collection. This includes Chen Cheng-po's nostalgic *Street Scene on a Summer Day* and Liao Chi-chun's colourful oil painting *Courtyard with Banana Trees*, as well as work by Li Chi-mao, Lee Chun-shan and Yu Cheng-yao (see Contexts p.535). There's a bookstore and coffeeshop in the basement. Next door, the **Taipei Story House** (Tues–Sun 10am–6pm; NT$30; Ⓦ www.storyhouse .com.tw) was built in 1914 as an opulent private mansion, and is now a venue for art exhibitions and performances of *nanguan* music, as well as containing an elegant **teahouse**.

Lin An Tai Historical Home

Set on the northern edge of Xinsheng Park, around 750m east of the Fine Arts Museum, the **Lin An Tai Historical Home** (Tues–Sat 9am–9pm, Sun 9am–5pm; free) is Taipei's oldest residential building. It was built by wealthy merchant Lin Hui-gong in 1783–85, and moved here from its original location in Daan district in 1983, to avoid destruction during a road-building project. The house is a pristine example of southern Fujian-style architecture from the Qing dynasty, though apart from a few pieces of furniture there's not much to see inside – the historic atmosphere is reduced further by the roar of jets coming into land at Songshan Airport, and the highway overpass at the back. You can walk here from the Fine Arts Museum, but it can be dangerous crossing Xinsheng Road and it's best to take a taxi.

Xingtian Temple

Set on the corner of Minquan and Songjiang Roads, **Xingtian Temple** (daily 3.30am–11pm) was built in classical Chinese style in 1968, and is a fascinating place to observe **traditional rituals**. Dedicated to Guan Di, represented by a large statue in the **Main Hall,** the main attraction for locals is the smorgasbord of spiritual services on offer; these include *ping an dai* (a charm worn around the neck), *shou hun* (spiritual healing) and *chou qian* (fortune telling by drawing lots). Most temples offer the latter, but here believers have a choice of 100 readings dating back over eight hundred years, compared to the usual 64 (for more on this and Guan Di see Contexts p.529). Volunteers, often English-speaking and wearing blue robes (*dao yi*), are on hand to answer questions. The temple is a long walk from any MRT station and best approached by taxi or bus.

Su Ho Memorial Paper Culture Foundation

Twenty minutes' walk north of Zhongxiao Xinsheng MRT Station, the **Su Ho Memorial Paper Culture Foundation** (Mon–Sat 9.30am–4.30pm; NT$100; Ⓦ www.suhopaper.org.tw), at 68 Changan East Road, is one of Taipei's few craft-based museums, offering a welcome break between temples and department stores, and the chance to make your own traditional Chinese paper.

Crammed into this four-storey shophouse are tastefully presented displays on **paper making** and Taiwan's paper industry, a mini paper mill and a decent gift shop – though most of the labels are in Chinese, there's an informative English audio-guide included in the entry price. The paper-making sessions can be a lot of fun; they start at 2pm on Saturdays (NT$180), though if your visit coincides with private tour groups on other days you're welcome to join in.

National Palace Museum and around

The district of Shilin, north of the Keelung River, is noted principally for being the home of Taipei's biggest **night market** (see p.128) and the **National Palace Museum**, one of the world's finest collections of Chinese art and historical artefacts. It's obviously one of the city's highlights and needs several hours to do it justice, though there are a couple of other sights near Shilin MRT station to keep you occupied for a day or so. The northern part of Shilin contains **Tianmu**, an affluent suburb favoured by many expat residents and packed with shops and restaurants, but with nothing much to see for visitors.

National Palace Museum

The **National Palace Museum** (daily 9am–5pm; NT$100; ⑭www.npm.gov .tw) is the most famous attraction in Taiwan, pulling in over two million visitors a year with its unparalleled collection of **Chinese art**, a priceless treasure trove going back five thousand years. The museum also owns hundreds of documents, pieces of furniture, rare books and official decrees issued by the Imperial Chinese government, as well as masses of everyday items that provide a fascinating insight

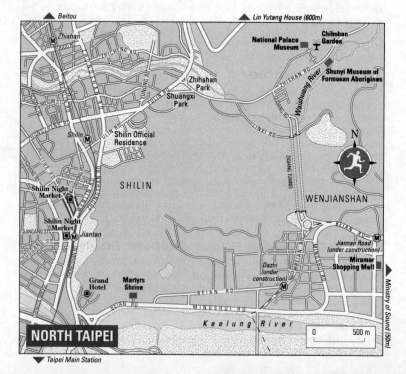

into life at court. Very little of this has to do with Taiwan of course – the contents are a legacy of Chiang Kai-shek's retreat from China in 1949, when the former Imperial art collection was shipped, crate by crate, across the Taiwan Straits. While the Forbidden City in Beijing (also known as the Palace Museum) has more items, the finest pieces ended up in Taipei, becoming a contentious and often heated political issue between the two countries.

To get here, take the MRT to Shilin station and look for the Zhongzheng Road exit: at the end of the plaza bus #304, #255, Red #30 and minibuses 18 and 19 pass the museum in around ten minutes (NT$15). Next door to the museum, the **Chihshan Garden** (Tues–Sun 7am–7pm; NT$10) is a pleasant and fairly authentic reproduction of a classical Song dynasty garden, best enjoyed in spring when the flowers are in bloom.

Some history

While the museum continues to expand (mostly from donations), at its core remains the priceless collection of art and artefacts once owned by the Chinese emperors. The **Imperial collection** was formally established in the reign of the first Song dynasty emperor, Taizu (960–975), who seized the artwork owned by rulers he had defeated in battle – his brother and successor, Taizong (976–997), expanded the hoard considerably, commissioning new pieces and collecting ceramics, artwork and statuary from all over China. This very private collection ended up in Beijing's Forbidden City, and it wasn't until the last emperor **Pu Yi** was forced to leave in 1924 that it was opened to the public: it became the **National Palace Museum** one year later. After the Japanese invaded Manchuria, its precious contents were carted around the country by the Nationalist government, on and off, for almost sixteen years, but by 1949 defeat at the hands of the Communists looked certain. During one, tense night in February of that year, most of the collection was packed into crates and shipped from Nanjing to Taiwan, just weeks before the city fell. It's worth noting, however, that although the most valuable pieces were spirited across the Taiwan Strait, much was left behind. The retreat was meant to be temporary, and it took another fifteen years before the authorities, resigned to the status quo, decided to unpack the boxes and build a museum in 1965.

China, where many see the removal of the collection as looting, would love to see it returned to the mainland. The museum has also stirred controversy within Taiwan: in the 1970s the KMT used it to support its claim that the Republic of China was the sole legitimate government of China, and in the 1990s Taiwan independence supporters responded by suggesting it should be returned. There's little chance of that happening any time soon: most Taiwanese point to the destruction of artwork during China's **Cultural Revolution** in the late 1960s and claim that they have worked hard to protect important treasures that might otherwise have been lost, something that transcends nationalism. Their case certainly seems stronger than that of Western institutions such as the British Museum, which has used similar arguments to successfully hold onto its Greek Parthenon friezes. Meanwhile, as Taiwan gradually sees itself as part of a wider East Asian community, with ties to Japan as well as China, a new branch of the museum, to be opened near Chiayi in 2008, will centre on **Asian art**, and emphasize the foreign traditions that have influenced Chinese culture.

The collection

The museum's collection of over 654,500 pieces is still too large to be displayed at the same time, but thanks to the completion of a major renovation project in 2006, more can be exhibited than ever before. The museum is arranged chronologically: start on the third floor and work down. The daily tours in English (free) at 10am and 3pm offer a more digestible introduction to the main exhibits, while the *San Hsi Tang Tea Room* on the fourth floor is the best place to regroup.

Early China: the third floor

The third floor charts the beginnings of Chinese civilization in the Neolithic period, through to the end of the Han dynasty in 220 AD. The museum's remarkable ensemble of Neolithic artefacts (galleries 303 and 304) primarily comprises early pottery and exquisite **jade** pieces – at this time jade was believed to be a medium for spirits, and as such was given special reverence. Don't miss the impressive **Jade Tablet** and mysterious **Ts'ung Tube**, engraved with seventeen small eyes. The real highlights, however, are the collection of stunning **bronzes** from the Shang and Zhou dynasties (1600–221 BC; gallery 305), principally ritual vessels owned by the wealthy. Typical pieces include the cauldron-like *ting*, and sets of cast bronze bells, which had a ceremonial function. The most celebrated exhibit is the **San P'an basin** dating from the late Western Zhou dynasty (700–900 BC), a ritual water vessel with an invaluable 350-character inscription inside. The innovative, multimedia **Mystery of Bronze** exhibition (gallery 300) is an enlightening introduction to the relatively advanced technologies of the era.

The **Qin and Han dynasties** (221 BC–220 AD; gallery 307) were the last to use ritual jades and bronzes, represented by the highly ornate *tsun*, or wine vessel. The gallery also contains some rare glazed ware, used by the rich, and "grey pottery", often used by commoners to store burial goods. The third floor also contains a gallery of **Imperial Seals** (306), and the **Special Permanent Exhibition** (308) which features a selection of the museum's most important pieces: the most popular item here is the exceptional *Jadeite Cabbage with Insects*, a Qing dynasty jade carving made to look like *bok-choy*.

Han to Qing dynasty: the second floor

The second floor covers the flowering of Chinese civilization from the end of the Han to the Qing dynasty (221–1911). Here the range of artwork, mediums and materials expands dramatically from porcelain and ceramics, to fine art, jewellery and sculpture. The museum's rare collection of silk-screen **painting** and **calligraphy** (West Wing galleries) is truly magnificent, beginning with masterpieces from the **Song dynasty** (960–1279), when landscape watercolour painting was reaching its zenith: highlights include Fan K'uan's *Travellers Among Mountains and Streams*, the lyrical *Storied Mountains and Dense Forests* by Chu-jan, and *Early Spring* by Kuo Hsi (note that paintings are usually on display for no longer than three months at a time to prevent light damage). The museum also has an extensive collection of Ming and Qing dynasty artwork.

China's golden age, the **Tang dynasty** (618–907) is represented in gallery 201. The era is one of the few in Chinese history when plump women were considered attractive: the earthenware figures of suitably curvaceous court ladies are indicative of the period. Porcelain and ceramics also flourished in the Song period. Don't miss the rare *Ju Ware Narcissus Planter in Blue Glaze*, a striking container dating from Northern Song dynasty, in the Prototypes of Modern Styles gallery (203), which also covers the **Yuan dynasty** (1279-1368).

The **Ming dynasty** (1368–1644) galleries (205 & 207) feature the best of China's porcelain and ceramics, much of it from the famous kilns at Jingdezhen. The intricate *Tou-ts'ai Cup with Chickens* and *Blue-and-white Flat Vase with Figures* are considered the most accomplished pieces from the early part of the era (205), while the *Bright Yellow Ting with Animal-mask Patterns* is a striking piece from the later period (207). The **Qing dynasty** (1644–1911) collections (rooms 209 and 211) contain a staggering number of artworks from elaborate *cloisonné* and high-quality porcelain to ornate jade and stone carvings. Notable items include *The Nine Elders of Mount Hsiang* (209), an intricate sculpture carved from a single piece of aloeswood.

The first floor
The first floor has galleries dedicated to **Qing dynasty furniture** (108), a vast array of **religious sculptural art** (101) and **rare books** (103-104): the Gems in the Rare Books Collection contains the *Erh-ya*, one of the most famous ancient texts, a Song dynasty imprint of a far older book on the study of language.

Shunyi Museum of Formosan Aborigines

The **Shunyi Museum of Formosan Aborigines** (Tues–Sun 9am–5pm, closed Jan 20–Feb 20; NT$150; ⓦwww.museum.org.tw), 100m up Zhishan Road from the Palace Museum, is one of Taipei's most appealing museums, providing a thorough introduction to Taiwan's indigenous population (see also p.518). As of January 2007 there were thirteen formally recognized tribes, though the museum focuses on the nine most prominent: the Ami, Atayal, Bunun, Paiwan, Puyuma, Rukai, Saisiyat, Tao and the Tsou. The collection isn't particularly large, but it's well presented in English and Chinese, and videos covering the origins and current social situation of the various tribes on the **first floor** are excellent – just make sure you avoid school parties and tour groups because you'll miss most of the commentary. The **basement** is the most intriguing part of the museum, highlighting festivals, myths and rituals, with a special area dedicated to head-hunting and a selection of ceremonial weapons.

Shilin Official Residence

Just to the east of Shilin MRT station, a short walk along Fulin Road, the **Shilin Official Residence** (Mon–Fri 8.30am–5pm, Sat–Sun 8.30am–7pm; free) was the most important of **Chiang Kai-shek**'s fifteen former estates. The problem is that the actual "main official residence" isn't open to the public – all you can see are the gardens, which are admittedly attractive and often full of flowers, and a brief glimpse of the main house through iron gates and drooping palms. There are plans to open the house in the future: if so, it's likely to become one of Taipei's most popular attractions.

National Revolutionary Martyrs' Shrine

Just over 1km east of Jiantan MRT station, not far from the Keelung River, the **National Revolutionary Martyrs' Shrine** (daily 9am–5pm; free) is the largest of similar memorials all over Taiwan, dedicated to more than 300,000 civilians and soldiers killed in struggles with the Qing dynasty, the Japanese and the Communists. It's also another reminder of Taiwan's official status as Republic of China – most of the people honoured here died on the mainland. The main gate sits on Beian Road, but you have to trudge across a vast plaza from here to get to the grand collection of buildings known as the Sanctuary. Completed in 1969 to resemble the Taihedian in Beijing's Forbidden City, the **Main Shrine** contains a central tablet which commemorates all those who died – Taiwanese visitors usually bow here. Note the painting of Sun Yat-sen to the left. Individual tablets are enshrined in the **Civilian Martyrs' Shrine** on the right side of the complex, or the **Military Martyrs' Shrine** on the left, the whole thing encircled by a walkway lined with paintings and boards describing every military campaign fought by the Nationalists. The **colour guard ceremonies** (daily 8.50am & 5pm) or failing that, the hourly **changing of the guard**, are extremely elaborate affairs, lasting more than fifteen minutes and highly photogenic. It's a bit awkward to get here – Red Bus #5 from Yuanshan MRT station is one of several services that stop outside, or it's a ten-minute walk from the *Grand Hotel*.

East Taipei

East Taipei, comprising Songshan, Xinyi, most of Daan and the suburban district of Nangang, is the modern commercial heart of the city. Best known for Taipei's premier **shopping malls** and its most hip **restaurants** and **nightlife**, there are also a handful of worthwhile sights tucked in between the office towers.

Xinyi

Central **Xinyi** is sandwiched between Zhongxiao and Xinyi roads, bounded to the west by Keelung Road and to the east by mountains. It's a former wasteland that as little as twenty years ago was covered in sugar cane. Today it's plastered with **shopping malls**, modern residential blocks and office towers including the world's tallest, **Taipei 101**, and the **International Convention Center**, venue for some of Asia's biggest trade shows.

A short walk from Taipei City Hall MRT station, the **Discovery Center of Taipei** (Tues–Sun 9am–5pm; free) is a good place to start a tour of the area. It's located within **City Hall** and contains several floors of high-tech displays focusing on Taipei's history and culture. For the **Puppetry Art Center of Taipei,** see p.132.

Taipei 101

Looming over Xinyi, and indeed the whole of Taipei, **Taipei 101** became the world's tallest building on completion in 2003. Designed by Taiwanese architect C.Y. Lee to resemble a stalk of bamboo, at 508m (and 101 floors) it's 56m higher than the Petronas Twin Towers in Malaysia, and likely to hold the title until at least 2008. The entrance is on the fifth floor of the shopping mall (see p.134), where the world's fastest elevators shoot to the top in just 37 seconds. Up on the eighty-ninth floor, the indoor **observatory** (Tues–Sun 10am–10pm, last entry 9pm; NT$350) provides unparalleled views of the city and the surrounding mountains. A free audio-guide provides commentary on the views, but don't miss the massive steel-plated **damper** in the centre which at 660 tons is the world's largest and helps stabilize the building in case of typhoons. Shuttle buses travel between 101 and Taipei City Hall MRT throughout the day.

National Dr Sun Yat-sen Memorial Hall

Grandly located in a small park on the western edge of Xinyi, a short walk from City Hall, the **National Dr Sun Yat-sen Memorial Hall** (daily 9am–5pm; free; ⓦ www.yatsen.gov.tw), is a striking postmodern recreation of a classical Chinese palace, with concrete pillars and bright yellow roof. It was completed

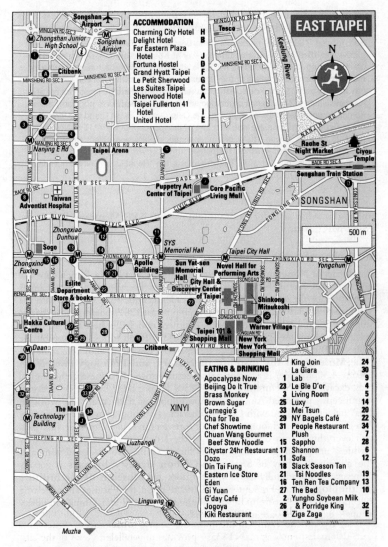

ACCOMMODATION
Charming City Hotel H
Delight Hotel B
Far Eastern Plaza
  Hotel J
Fortuna Hostel D
Grand Hyatt Taipei F
Le Petit Sherwood G
Les Suites Taipei C
Sherwood Hotel A
Taipei Fullerton 41
  Hotel I
United Hotel E

EATING & DRINKING
Apocalypse Now   1
Beijing Do It True   23
Brass Monkey   3
Brown Sugar   25
Carnegie's   33
Cha for Tea   29
Chef Showtime   31
Chuan Wang Gourmet
  Beef Stew Noodle   15
Citystar 24hr Restaurant 17
Dozo   11
Din Tai Fung   18
Eastern Ice Store   21
Eden   16
Gi Yuan   27
G'day Café   2
Jogoya   26
Kiki Restaurant   8

King Join   24
La Giara   30
Lab   9
Le Ble D'or   4
Living Room   5
Luxy   14
Mei Tsun   20
NY Bagels Café   22
People Restaurant   34
Plush   7
Sappho   28
Shannon   6
Sofa   12
Slack Season Tan
  Tsi Noodles   19
Ten Ren Tea Company   13
The Bed   10
Yungho Soybean Milk
  & Porridge King   32
Ziga Zaga   E

in 1972 to preserve the memory of the founder of the Republic of China, and what's now referred to, in all seriousness, as "Sunology" – in Chinese the hall is known as "Memorial to Father of the Nation."

A giant bronze statue of Sun Yat-sen guards the main entrance, and here you can witness another solemn **changing of the guard** ceremony (daily, on the hour). On either side of the statue are rooms documenting Sun's life and his relationship with Taiwan, though labelling is in Chinese only and you'll see scant mention of his influential wife, Soong Qing-ling, who sided with the Communists after his death and died in Shanghai in 1981. The rest of the building contains several **galleries** which showcase Taiwanese art, while the **History Room** on the third floor focuses on the history of the

> ## Sun Yat-sen: father of the nation?
>
> Sun Yat-sen (1866-1925) made just three brief visits to Taiwan: in 1900, 1913 (for a day) and 1918 (when he was turned away at Keelung harbour). Despite growing apathy among younger generations, he is still officially regarded as the **father of modern China** on both sides of the Taiwan Strait; every town in Taiwan (and China) has a "Zhongshan" Road or building, recalling Sun's preferred Chinese name, and his mausoleum in Nanjing is a pilgrimage site for all Chinese. Sun's popularity stems from his crucial role in the overthrow of the Qing dynasty in 1911, and the formation of the Republic of China. He was also one of the founders of the KMT or Nationalist party in 1912. In Taiwan, many pro-independence politicians object to his title as "founding father" (used in school textbooks) for the obvious reason that he had little to do with the island, but while Taiwan remains the "Republic of China", have little hope of changing his formal status.

building and has an informative English video. SYS Memorial Hall is the closest MRT station.

Academia Sinica

The district of **Nangang,** east of Xinyi, is home to **Academia Sinica** (Ⓦwww .sinica.edu.tw), one of Taipei's less-visited treasures. Founded in 1928 as China's foremost academic research institute, the Academia relocated to Taiwan with the Nationalists in 1949 and today the main campus is at 128 Academia Road, with a couple of fine museums clustered at the southern end. To get here take the MRT to Kunyang, look for exit 4 and cross Zhongxiao Road to the bus stop on the other side. Bus #212, #270, or Blue #25 pass the campus in about ten minutes.

The **Museum of the Institute of History and Philology** (Wed & Sat 9.30am–4.30pm; free) is a remarkable treasure-trove of Chinese archeological finds, excavated by the institute in the 1930s. It's not huge, but the collection is magnificently presented. Among the most important artefacts are the "**wooden slips**" (tablets inscribed with Chinese characters), dating from the Han dynasty (206 BC–220 AD) and found at frontier fortresses in Gansu Province. Inscribed with everything from official orders to the letters of ordinary soldiers, they provide a unique insight into everyday life in China two thousand years ago. The museum's display of **Shang and Zhou dynasty bronzes** is equally impressive and beautifully laid out. Next door, the **Museum of the Institute of Ethnology** (Mon–Fri 9am–5pm, Sat 9am–noon; free) houses an interesting collection of artefacts from Taiwan's indigenous tribes and China's minority groups – explanations are in Chinese only.

The southern districts

Taipei's southern districts require a little effort to explore, encompassing an eclectic but intriguing mix of museums, temples and teahouses. Densely packed **Yonghe** and **Banciao** in the southwest are beyond the city boundary and fall under Taipei County administration – the latter is home to the county government and the historic **Lin Family Mansion**, while Yonghe contains the **Museum of World Religions**, one of Taipei's most thought-provoking sights. In the southeast, **Taipei Zoo** lies in Wenshan district, just to the north of **Maokong**, a valley crammed with picturesque teahouses and temples.

Lin Family Mansion and Garden

Once the home of one of Taiwan's richest families, the **Lin Family Mansion and Garden** (Tues–Sun 9am–5pm, last tickets 4pm; NT$100), is tucked away in Banciao, at 9 Ximen Road, not far from Wenhua Road. Today it's the biggest and most extravagant example of a classical Chinese garden in Taiwan. Wealthy rice merchant Lin Ping-hou began construction on the current site in 1847, while the **Three-Courtyard House** was commissioned by his sons in 1851. The rest of the complex was built in the 1880s and 90s and donated to the city in 1976 after a long period of disuse. Most of the site has been authentically renovated and rebuilt since then – some of the materials used were modern brick and concrete however, and the piped folk music drifting across the gardens creates a slightly kitsch, theme-park feel. The most attractive parts of the complex are the **Banyan Shade Pond** and the Three-Courtyard House – the latter still serves as the Lin ancestral hall and can only be visited as part of a guided tour, leaving from the entrance roughly every half hour (Chinese only). The site is a short walk from Fuzhong MRT Station.

Museum of World Religions

Located in the heart of Yonghe, the **Museum of World Religions** (7/F, 236 Zhongshan Rd Sec 1; Tues–Sun 10am–5pm; NT$150, students NT$80; Ⓦwww.mwr.org.tw) is one of Taipei's more unusual attractions, a stimulating mix of innovative exhibits and Buddhist philosophy. It was founded by Master Hsin Tao in 2001, a monk born in Myanmar to Chinese parents, and though the museum ostensibly promotes understanding of all religions the overall ethos is unmistakeably Buddhist. The **Great Hall of World Religions** provides a nicely condensed summary of all the major faiths, but it's the thought-provoking **Meditation Gallery** and **Hall of Life's Journey**, dedicated to a high-tech portrayal of birth, death and the afterlife, that will leave a stronger impression. The museum is a twenty-minute walk from Dingxi MRT station, or five to ten minutes on bus #706, #297, #51 and #243.

Taipei Zoo

The last stop on the Muzha MRT line, around fifteen minutes from Zhongxiao Fuxing station, **Taipei Zoo** (daily 9am–5pm; NT$60; Ⓦwww.zoo.gov.tw) is set into a lush hillside in Wenshan district, southeast of the city centre. Home to a

---

Yonghe – the home of soybean milk

The suburb of Yonghe has become synonymous with delicious soybean (soya bean) milk and associated breakfast snacks not just in Taiwan but throughout the Chinese-speaking world. In fact so many soybean shops in Taiwan and Asia use the word "Yungho" in their name that even many Chinese don't know it's actually a place near Taipei. Soybean milk originated in China in the nineteenth century, becoming popular as a drink in the 1930s and imported to Taiwan when the Nationalists fled the mainland in 1949; Donghai ("East Ocean") was the original store, established in Yonghe in 1955. It became so successful that today, even in China, thousands of stores call themselves "Taiwan Yungho Soybean Milk" in deference and it's become one of the country's most successful examples of what the Taiwanese call "selling back" to China. Donghai was renamed "World Soybean Milk Magnate" in 1968 and can be found a short walk north of Dingxi MRT station at 284 Yonghe Rd Sec 2.

vast range of wildlife, the overall layout is fairly creative, though there are still plenty of disturbingly small cages around, and the only unique section is the **Formosan Animal Area** – this is probably the closest you're likely to get to much of Taiwan's indigenous species since many are now very rare in the wild. Highlights include the beautiful Formosan Clouded Leopard, which is regarded by the Rukai tribe as their spiritual ancestor. Elsewhere, the African Animal Area is where you'll find the elephants, gorillas, giraffes and lions and the Asian Tropical Rainforests Area has the monkeys, tigers and leopards. The most popular section of the zoo is the Koala House, while creepy crawlies abound in the Insectarium, the newest attraction.

Maokong

The valley south of Taipei Zoo is known as **MAOKONG**, one of Taiwan's oldest tea-growing areas and famous for its teahouses, temples and romantic night views of the city. Production of **Tieguanyin** (a high-quality, semi-fermented oolong tea), began here in the 1880s, though **Baozhong** (another type of oolong) is just as prevalent. In both cases production is relatively small and it's "tea tourism" which brings in the cash today – by early 2007 a four-kilometre **cable car** is expected to link Maokong and Zhinan Temple to Taipei Zoo.

The alternative way to tour the valley is to take **Minibus S10** (daily 6am–10pm; NT$15) from Wanfang Community MRT station, which departs at hourly intervals and follows an anti-clockwise route around the valley as far as the Maokong stop, approximately halfway around. The first main bus stop is Zhinan Elementary School on Lane 34, off Zhinan Road Section 3. Get off here if you want to walk up the valley, as signposted trails lead to Sanxuan Temple and **Zhangshan Temple**, both connecting with the bus route further up the hill. The latter is a Buddhist shrine dedicated to Guanyin with a breathtaking view of Taipei – to avoid a steep climb get off at Zhangshan Temple stop #2 and walk down the lane on the right. Maokong's **teahouses** are predominantly scattered on this south side of the valley; pots of tea usually start at NT$200–250 and can last most of the afternoon depending on how many people are in your group – expect to pay a cover charge or "water fee" of around NT$60 per person at the better places. *Yuanxuyuan* at no. 16 on Lane 38, has a cosy, classical Chinese interior – its wooden booths overlook the valley and are set around an indoor fishpond bridged by stepping stones. Get off the bus at the **Sanxuan Temple** stop and take the left-hand fork at the junction here – the teahouse is 50m on the right, marked by a "moongate" or round entrance. The bus continues along Lane 38 in the other direction, passing several teahouses with superb views of Taipei and Zhinan Temple across the valley, especially at night: the *PLC*

Maokong		
Maokong	貓空	*māo kōng*
Dachahuyiguan	大茶壺藝館	*dàcháhú yì guǎn*
Sanxuan Temple	三玄宮	*sanxúan gōng*
Taipei Tea Promotion Center	台北市茶推廣中心	*táiběishì chá tuī guǎng zhōng xīn*
Tian En Temple	天恩宮	*tiānēn gōng*
Yaoyue Teahouse	邀月茶坊	*yāoyùe cháfāng*
Yuanxuyuan	緣續緣	*yúanxùyúan*
Zhangshan Temple	樟山寺	*zhāngshān sì*
Zhinan Temple	指南宮	*zhǐnán gōng*

Tea Tavern at no. 33 offers a veranda with classical Chinese furniture, as well as a large selection of outdoor tables, while *Dachahuyiguan* at no. 37, a short walk further on, offers tea upstairs and a popular restaurant on the first floor.

Beyond here the bus passes **Tian En Temple**, a good example of an I-kuan Tao shrine (see Contexts p.525), and the red-brick **Taipei Tea Promotion Center** (daily 9am–4.30pm; free) at 8, Lane 40, which houses a small but informative exhibition – the bus stops right outside. Continue walking for around 400m (turn right on exiting the centre) to reach *Yaoyue Teahouse* at 6, Lane 40 (daily 24hr), one of the best teahouses in Maokong with rustic wooden pavilions and a series of outdoor terraces overlooking tea and bamboo plantations. The entrance is marked by a Chinese gate flanked by lanterns on the left.

Zhinan Temple

The main attraction on the north side of the valley is **Zhinan Temple** (daily 4am–8.30pm), one of Taiwan's most important religious centres. Established in 1891 and expanded in 1904, it blends Confucian, Taoist and Buddhist practices featuring five main halls dedicated to a mixture of gods. The chief deity, and the biggest draw for pilgrims, is **Lu Dong-bin**, one of the "Eight Immortals" and a patron of barbers, though like many gods he's supposed to grant good health and general prosperity to all his believers. There's one exception: legend has it that Lu was rejected by the only female member of the Eight Immortals, Ho Hsien-ku, and driven by jealousy, he's been an incorrigible flirt ever since making it bad luck for couples to visit the temple.

The most important part of Zhinan, the **Original Hall**, contains an image of Lu Dong-bin and is often packed with praying devotees. The biggest shrine, and the one you can see all over the valley, is **Daxiong Hall**, a short walk to the right (facing the Original Hall). This is a Buddhist temple, with gold statues of Sakyamuni Buddha, Amitabha, and the Medicine Buddha in the main hall.

Before the cable car, the traditional way down (and up) from Zhinan was via the stone stairs in front of the Original Hall: the first section ends a short way down the mountain at a small Earth God shrine – turn right and follow the stone pathway, lined with Japanese stone lanterns, 900m to Lane 33, a short walk from Zhinan Road and the bus stop on the edge of Muzha. There are supposed to be 1185 or 1192 steps, depending on where you start counting. Alternatively, bear right just below the Original Hall, passing a row of antique and snack stalls, to reach the temple bus station, where bus #530 (5.30am–10pm; every 15–20min; NT$15) will take you to Wanfang Hospital MRT station.

Eating

Taipei is one of the world's greatest showcases for **Chinese cuisine**. Be adventurous; many places have English menus or at least photographs of food, and where one dish is the main feature, pointing will usually suffice. In addition to a vast array of **restaurants** (see p.124), the city's **teahouses** are atmospheric places to eat light meals and sip Chinese-style tea. For a cheaper, more local experience try the ubiquitous **soybean milk stores** with their associated snacks, or Taipei's vibrant **night markets** which offer a bewildering range of dishes and excellent value for money. Another budget favourite are the "**Taiwan Buffets**" (*zizhu can*) you'll see in every neighbourhood – these canteen-style places allow you to pile up as much food on your tray as you like, with each dish incurring a small charge (it's rarely more than NT$120 for a huge plateful). In the summer

Taipei coffeeshops, teahouses and night markets

Breakfast and Coffeeshops

Astoria	明星咖啡廳	míngxīng kāfēitīng
Fong Da Coffee	蜂大珈琲	fēngdà kāfēi
Koko's Café	穀鳥軒	gǔ niǎo xuān
Si Hai Soybean Milk Store	四海豆漿店	sìhǎi dòujiāngdiàn
Yungho Soybean Milk & Porridge King	永和豆漿大王	yǒnghé dòujiāng dàwáng

Teahouses

Cha for Tea	喫茶趣	chī chá qù
Geng Du Yuan	耕讀園	gēngdúyuán
Hui Liu	回留素食	huíliú sùshí
Lu-Yu Tea Culture Institute	陸羽茶藝中心	lùyǔ cháyì zhōngxīn
Ten Ren Tea	天仁集團	tiānrén jítúan
Wistaria Teahouse	紫藤廬	zǐténglú
Yue Yin	月飲	yùe yǐn

Night markets

Gongguan Night Market	公館夜市	gōngguǎn yèshì
Guangzhou Street Night Market	廣州街夜市	guǎngzhōjiē yèshì
Huaxi Street Night Market	華西街夜市	huáxījiē yèshì
Raohe Street Night Market	饒河街夜市	ráohéjiē yèshì
Shida Night Market	師大路夜市	shīdàlù yèshì
Shilin Night Market	士林夜市	shìlín yèshì

make for a **shaved ice** (*tsua bing*) stall – the sweet, tasty toppings make sumptuous desserts. If it's too hot, almost every department store has an air-conditioned **food court** in the basement, with the biggest under Taipei 101.

Breakfast and coffeeshops

You can usually find hole-in-the-wall type places serving soybean milk and traditional **breakfast** snacks (see Basics p.38), all over Taipei. Western food is just as popular with locals these days, however, with a host of Taiwanese coffeeshop chains such as *Dante* and *IS Coffee* competing with *Starbucks* for those lattes and croissants. Only a few of the city's historic **coffeeshops** remain, but they are particularly atmospheric.

Astoria 2/F, 5 Wuchang Street Sec 1 (Zhong-zheng). Charming western-style café established by émigré Russians in 1949 with decent coffee, cakes and light meals (NT$280–350 per dish). It's the closest thing Taipei had to a literary salon in the 1950s – some of the famous regulars that once dined here include writers Huang Chun-ming and Pai Hsien-yung. Daily 10am–9.30pm.
Fong Da Coffee 42 Chengdu Rd. Cosy coffeeshop close to Ximen MRT, established in 1956 and always busy. Antiquated machinery grinds and roasts fresh coffee near the entrance (NT$85 per cup). Daily 8am–10.30pm.
Koko's Café 150 Guangzhou Road. Historic café set inside an old Wanhua building, not far from

Longshan Temple. It's been given a facelift recently but still features simple bamboo decor, wooden tables and black-and-white photos on the walls. Coffee is NT$70. Daily 11am–10pm.
NY Bagels Café 147 Renai Rd Sec 4 (Daan). The best place to satisfy cravings for a traditional NYC breakfast. Bagels start at NT$50 but there are also sandwiches (NT$100 up) and decent cooked breakfasts (NT$200). Even better, it's open 24hrs.
Si Hai Soybean Milk Store 29 Changan W Rd. Part of a chain created in 1968 by one of the owners of the original soybean store in Yonghe (see p.119), "Four Seas" still knocks out excellent soybean and traditional snacks (NT$25–50), with seating area at the back. Daily 5.30am–10pm.

Yungho Soybean Milk & Porridge King 132–138 Fuxing S Rd Sec 2. A 10min walk south of Daan MRT station, this no-nonsense local diner has been in business for over forty years, selling a variety of buns, spring rolls, egg pancakes, noodles and soybean milk. Open 24hrs.

Teahouses

Taipei's numerous **teahouses** are ideal places to sample Taiwan's celebrated infusions. **Wenzhou Street**, north of Gongguan MRT station, has the most variety, but there are plenty of decent alternatives scattered all over the city.

Cha for Tea 331 Dunhua S Rd Sec 1. One of Taiwan's most popular teahouse chains, this is an easy introduction to the island's fine teas – a pot here will cost from NT$100–300, with an incredible spread of snacks and dishes on the English menu (from NT$50). Daily 11am–11.30pm.

Geng Du Yuan 12–14, Lane 68, Shida Rd. This is a branch of the well-known Taichung chain, tastefully decorated in classical Chinese style. Range of quality teas from around NT$300 for a pot. Daily 10am–2am.

Hui Liu 9, Lane 31, Yongkang St ☎02/23926707. Tranquil and elegant teahouse located on the corner of Yongkang Park, with wooden tables and beautiful handicrafts. Organic specialties include Tieguanyin tea (NT$100–120), and there's an excellent vegetarian menu – avoid meal times if you just want to drink (minimum charge NT$250).

Lu-Yu Tea Culture Institute 3/F, 62/64 Hengyang Road ☎02/23316636; @ luyutea@ms59.hinet.net. Best place to see tea ceremonies and tea masters at work, with classes held 9.30–11.30am and 7–9pm a couple of times a week, though it's best to call ahead (Chinese only). In the same building is a branch of *Cha for Tea* (2/F) and *Ten Ren Tea* (G/F). Daily 9am–10pm.

Ten Ren Tea 174 Zhongxiao E Rd Sec 3. Founded in Taiwan in 1953, this is one of the largest and most respected tea manufacturers in Asia, with stores all over the island. This branch, just off Dunhua Road, also doubles as a simple café with a take-away counter and a few chairs and tables inside to sample the formidable range of teas (NT$60 a cup). Daily 9am–10.30pm.

🏃 **Wistaria Teahouse** 1, Lane 16, Xinsheng S Road Sec 3. Taipei's most historic Japanese-era teahouse, best known for being the meeting place of artists and political dissidents post-1949, and where much of the movie *Eat Drink Man Woman* was shot. Sip tea (NT$200–300) in the main room with simple wooden tables and chairs, or try the Japanese rooms with tatami mats further back. Daily 10am–11.30pm.

Yue Yin 80 Wenzhou St. Atmospheric, classical-style teahouse with cosy wooden booths and tables, some arranged around goldfish tanks. Pots of tea from NT$200 (no English menu). Daily 10am–2am.

Shaved ice stores

Taipei's scorching, humid summers make its **shaved ice** (*tsua bing*) stores essential pit stops. 🏃 *Ice Monster* at 15 Yongkang Street is a Taipei institution, with massive plates of mango ice, kiwi, strawberry milk and other exotic fruits, topped with delicious homemade ice cream for NT$120–150 (daily 10.30am–midnight). The *Eastern Ice Store* (*Dong Qu Feng Yuan*) at 38, Lane 216, Zhongxiao East Road Section 4 is the best place in East Taipei, with a small seating area and a choice of three toppings for NT$45 (daily 11am–11pm), while *Yanji Ice* at 38–40 Hankou Road Section 2 is a more traditional, no-nonsense shop in Ximending serving ice with delicious, authentic toppings such as thick taro, peanuts and corn: huge bowls cost NT$40–60 (daily noon–10pm).

△ Wistaria teahouse

Restaurants

The capital's **Chinese restaurants** run the gamut of almost every regional cuisine from Beijing duck and spicy Sichuan dishes to Cantonese *dim sum*, and of course Taiwanese specialties (see p.37). Taipei also has more **Japanese** restaurants than any city outside Japan, while **Western** options, though still a bit hit-and-miss, have mushroomed in recent years – all the major fast food chains from *McDonalds* to *Pizza Hut* are well represented if you get really desperate. Luxury hotels are the best places to splurge, and usually cater to all tastes

Taipei restaurants

Restaurants

Ay Chung Flour-Rice Noodle	阿宗麵線	ā zōng miànxiàn
Beijing Do It True	北京都一處	běijīng dūyīchù
Celestial Restaurant	天廚菜館	tiānchú càiguǎn
Chef Showtime	阿正廚坊	āzhèng chúfǎng
Citystar 24hr Restaurant	京星港式飲茶	jīngxīng gǎngshì yǐnchá
Din Tai Fung	鼎泰豐	dǐngtàifēng
Eastern Ice Store	東區粉圓	dōngqūfěnyuán
Goose Flat Noodles	鴨肉扁土鵝專賣店	yāròu biǎntǔé zhuānmàidiàn
1415 Park	三橋會官	sān qiáo huìguǎn
Fu Yuan	馥園	fùyúan
Gaoji	高季	gāojì
Gi Yuan	驥園	jì yúan
Ice Monster	冰館	bīngguǎn
Jogoya	上閣屋	shànggéwū
Kiki Restaurant	Kiki餐廳	kiki cāntīng
King Join	京兆尹	jīngzhàoyī
Lian Hsin Yuan Vegetarian Restaurant	蓮心園素食餐廳	liánxīnyuán sùshí cāntīng
Madame Jill's	翠薪越南餐廳	cuìxīn yuènán cāntīng
Mayor's Residence Arts Salon	官邸藝文沙龍	guāndī yìwén shālóng
Mei Tsun	梅村	méicūn
North Sea Fish Village	北海漁村	běihǎiyúcūn
Peng Yuan	彭園	péngyúan
People Restaurant	人間	rénjiān
Seoul Korean Barbeque	漢城餐廳	hànchéng cāntīng
Shao Shao Ke	勺勺客	sháoshàokè
Shinyeh	欣葉台菜本店	xīnyè táicài běndiàn
Slack Season Tan Tsi Noodles	度小月擔仔麵	dùxiǎoyùe dānzǎimiàn
Spring Natural Vegetarian Restaurant	春天素食餐廳	chūntiān sùshí cāntīng
Tainan Tan-tsu-mien Seafood Restaurant	台南擔仔麵	táinàn dànzǎimiàn
Taipei Shin Gu Shiang	臺北新故鄉	táiběi xīngùxiáng
Thai Guo Xiao Guan	泰國小館	tàiguó xiǎoguǎn
Tian Xiang Huwei Hot Pot	天香回味	tiānxiāng huíwèi
Xiao Wei	小魏	xiǎowèi
Xiao Xiang Ting	小巷亭	xiǎoxiàngtíng
Yanji Ice	楊記冰店	yángjì bīngdiàn
Yi Men Wang Noodles	意麵王	yìmiànwáng

– **buffets** here are incredibly elaborate affairs, with gargantuan piles of food and correspondingly high prices.

All the restaurants listed below have English menus and are open 11.30am–2.30pm, and around 5–10pm, unless stated otherwise. It's rarely worth making a reservation unless you're eating on a Friday or Saturday night in one of the more upmarket places.

Zhongzheng

see map pp.98–99

Fu Yuan 17 Linyi St ☎02/23210279. One of Taipei's best restaurants, the food is a mixture of high-quality Chinese, Italian and Japanese cuisine. It's worth the high prices (set lunch from NT$800, dinner NT$1800) for innovative dishes that include "foie gras with herbal tea sauce", and for the building itself, which is an elegant reproduction of a Ming dynasty teahouse.

Madame Jill's 11, Lane 24, Tingzhou Rd Sec 3. Taipei's best Vietnamese restaurant, tucked away in the heart of Gongguan and knocking out cheap but mouthwatering favourites such as spring rolls (NT$95), curry chicken (NT$95) and spicy coconut beef with French bread (NT$100).

Mayor's Residence Arts Salon 46 Xuzhou Rd. This gallery and café has one of the most atmospheric settings in the city: a beautifully restored Japanese-style wooden house, once the home of Taipei's mayors. Try the coffee or smoothies (NT$180), light pasta dishes (NT$220) and tasty sandwiches (NT$120). Daily 9am–11pm.

North Sea Fish Village 8 Hangzhou S Rd Sec 1. One of the best-value seafood restaurants in town, with fish, shellfish and prawns flown in daily from Penghu and prices reasonable at NT$200–300 per dish.

Shao Shao Ke 15, Lane 41, Renai Rd Sec 2. Laid-back Shanxi-style restaurant with succulent lamb kebabs, and soup with unleavened bread (*pauh moh*, NT$160): break the bread into chunks before the soup is served. The graffiti-covered stucco walls are supposed to resemble a cave dwelling, but it's more like a student diner.

Thai Guo Xiao Guan 219 Tingzhou St Sec 3. There are many Thai restaurants in Taipei, but few are as authentic or cheap as this student hangout in Gongguan. Most dishes are NT$100–200, but with no English menu you'll have to point at the photos.

Xiao Wei 3/F, 13 Gongyuan Rd. Venerable Sichuan restaurant with a reputation for quality despite the very plain decor inside. Favourite orders include fiery *mapo doufu* and the stir-fried chilli shrimp (NT$100–300 per dish). There are no English signs – just take the lift up to the third floor.

Wanhua

see map pp.98–99

Ay Chung Flour-Rice Noodle 8 Ermei St. A Taipei institution, this stall has been serving sumptuous rice noodles in delicious soup (NT$35–50) for over thirty years –the added slices of pig intestine may not be to everyone's taste but this is the best bowl of noodles in the city. Take away or eat standing up. Daily 11.30am–11pm.

Goose Flat Noodles 98-2 Zhonghua Rd Sec 1. Cheap, no-nonsense local diner serving delicious goose noodles in soup (NT$40) and plates of sliced goose meat (NT$60). Daily 9.30am–10.30pm.

Tainan Tan-tsu-mien Seafood Restaurant 31 Huaxi St. Taipei's seafood pioneer, this elegant but oddly incongruous baroque dining room is set in the heart of Snake Alley. Select which fresh fish, crab or prawns you want to eat, then grab a table inside – the signature *danzi mian* (minced pork noodles, NT$50) also makes a tasty snack. Daily 11.30am–10.30pm.

Datong

see map p.106

Xiao Xiang Ting 8, Lane 250, Nanjing W Rd. This is a fun, cheap place to eat: a collection of small Japanese sushi stalls and restaurants, clustered in an alley off Nanjing Road. Grab a tray and choose your food first, before heading to the outside tables to eat (NT$400). Daily from 5pm.

Yi Men Wang Noodles 204 Guisui St. This small local diner has been cooking up cheap beef noodles for over fifty years (NT$40-50) and makes a handy pit-stop in historic Datong. Daily 10.30am–9pm.

Zhongshan

see map pp.106–107

1415 Park 16, Lane 11, Zhongshan N Rd Sec 2. Shanghai food served in renovated 1920s building with bright, modern interior and lots of red brick. Tasty dishes such as eel (NT$280), steamed fish (NT$300) and dumplings (NT$80) are reasonably priced. Daily noon–11pm.

Amaroni's Little Italy 218–220 Changchun Rd. Bustling Italian-American eatery: pastas (NT$280), pizzas (NT$400–550) and mains (NT$400) come in individual or huge portions meant for sharing. Daily 11am–midnight.

Celestial Restaurant 3/F, 1 Nanjing W Rd. The best value Beijing duck in Taipei (NT$800), though the "duck cake" (duck wrapped in pancake) is cheaper (NT$360) for small groups and there's plenty of other dishes on the menu. Look for the Royal Inn Taipei entrance and take the lift up.

Kiki Restaurant 28 Fuxing Rd Sec 1. Trendy Sichuan restaurant with bright, contemporary decor and extensive menu providing spiciness ratings (1–5) for each dish (NT$180–300). Open till midnight.

Le Petite Cuisine 45 Shuangcheng St ☎02/25973838. Exquisite French food and five-star service mark this stylish basement restaurant owned by Justin Quek, the respected Singaporean chef. Lavish set menus from NT$1800, with *a la carte* mains from NT$1400 and foie gras NT$750. Closed Mondays.

Peng Yuan 2/F, 380 Linsen N Rd. Named after founder and celebrated chef, Peng Chang Gui, this banquet-style restaurant specializes in fiery Hunan cuisine. "Peng's Tofu" (NT$280), served with pork and chillies, is a must order but everything else is excellent.

Seoul Korean Barbeque 4, Lane 33, Zhongshan N Rd Sec 1. Aging but atmospheric Korean diner, specializing in succulent barbecued meat (*bulgogi*) and decorated in classical style. Prices are reasonable with dishes of meat from NT$150 and vegetables NT$90.

Shinyeh 34 Shuangcheng St ☎02/25963255; 2/F, 112 Zhongxiao E Rd Sec 4 ☎02/27529299. Celebrated Taiwanese restaurant chain, the Shuangcheng branch is the original while the outlet at Zhongxiao Road is newer and slightly more upmarket. The food is outstanding – expect to pay NT$100–200 for noodles or rice and NT$200–400 for a main dish. Specialties include fried oyster omelette, pumpkin congee and pork knuckle.

Tandoor Indian Restaurant 10, Lane 73, Hejiang St. Taipei's first Indian restaurant and still one of its best, serving North Indian food characterized by rich, thick gravies and subtle spices. Mains around NT$220–300, and there's a good-value weekend lunch buffet for NT$400.

Tian Xiang Huwei Hot Pot 2/F, 16 Nanjing E Rd Sec 1. Popular *mala* or spicy hotpot restaurant, Mongolian style. There's no English but the menu has pictures and it's basically a case of choosing which meat (NT$160–300) and vegetables (less than NT$100) to stick in the pot. Daily 11.30am–2am.

Tien Hsiang Lo B1, Landis Hotel, 41 Minquan E Rd Sec 2 ☎02/25971234. One of Taipei's most elegant restaurants, blending modern and classical design and offering an extensive menu of Hangzhou-style food including fried shrimps with Longjing tea leaves (NT$580), drunken chicken (NT$280) and West Lake-style steamed fish (NT$180).

Daan

🏃 **Chef Showtime** 20, Lane 81, Dunhua S Rd Sec 2 ☎02/27025277 (see map p.117). Low-key restaurant with European-themed decor and superb fusion cuisine, blending Taiwanese, French and Italian dishes. It's reasonably priced considering the quality: try the fried pork Taiwan style (NT$380) or duck with orange (NT$580).

🏃 **Chuan Wang Gourmet Beef Stew Noodle** 2/F, 94 Zhongxiao E Rd Sec 4 ☎02/27110388 (see map p.117). Voted Taipei's best beef noodle restaurant, the eponymous dish is simply delicious (NT$150-200). Daily 11am-10pm.

Citystar 24hr Restaurant 216 Zhongxiao E Rd Sec 4 (see map p.117). Respectable *dim sum* restaurant that stays fairly busy all night, with a convenient location on the corner of Dunhua and Zhongxiao roads. Good-value Cantonese food at NT$100–300 per dish.

Din Tai Fung 194 Xinyi Rd Sec 2 ☎02/23218928 (see map p.117). This Taiwan institution has been serving up sumptuous dumplings for thirty years, though its Shanghai-style food is a little over-hyped. It's still worth trying those legendary steamed pork dumplings (*xiao long bao*) – which at NT$150 for ten are not bad value. The original site is on Xinyi Rd and open all day but there's a smarter branch at 218 Zhongxiao E Rd Sec 4 (☎02/27217890): enter via Lane 216. Be prepared to wait at both venues.

Dozo 102 Guangfu S Rd, ⓦwww.dozo.com.tw (see map p.117). Hip Japanese *Izakaya* bar-restaurant with large, open-plan area, sunken tables and dark, minimalist decor. Variety of Japanese sushi, rice, noodles and meat dishes for NT$80–300, and giant two or four-litre towers of Orion draft beer for NT$780/NT$1480. Daily 6pm–3am.

Gaoji 5 Yongkang St (see map p.98). A worthy alternative to *Din Tai Fung* just around the corner, with wide selection of Shanghai-style food and steamed pork dumplings that are just as tasty (NT$150). Daily 9.30am–10.30pm.

Gi Yuan 324 Dunhua S Rd Sec 1 (see map p.117). Sichuan restaurant with signature stone-pot chicken soup, a delicious broth made from three chickens simmered for over 12 hours and added to various meats and vegetables: one pot is good for 4 people (NT$1760) while an individual portion is NT$500.

🏃 **Grandma Nitti's Kitchen** 8, Lane 93, Shida Rd (see map p.98). Great-value

Western diner attracting crowds of expats, students and young professionals. The all-day breakfast is first-rate, and the burritos, sandwiches and pasta dishes on offer make perfect brunch material (from NT$150). Check out the rooftop terrace. Daily 9am–11pm.

La Giara 2/F, 352 Fuxing S Rd Sec 1 (see map p.98). One of Taipei's most elegant Italian restaurants, with chic, modern decor and an extensive menu: the strong Sicilian element reflects the origin of the two owners. Set lunches are around NT$440, with home-made pastas and pizzas from NT$420 and mains NT$890.

Mei Tsun 6, Lane 216, Alley 32, Zhongxiao E Rd Sec 4 (see map p.117). If you fancy gorging on Japanese food, this is the place to do it: for NT$428 on weekdays and NT$468 on weekends you can order as much sushi and tempura as you can handle. No English menus – point to the photos instead. Located just off Guangfu Road.

 People Restaurant B1, 191 Anhe Rd Sec 2 (see map p.117). One of the capital's hippest restaurants, the shiny, sleek interior has a lounge-bar atmosphere while the menu comprises Chinese fusion cuisine and plenty of cocktails (NT$220). A light-sensor opens the huge bronze doors, activated by putting your hand into the stone lantern outside.

Slack Season Tan Tsi Noodles 26, Alley 5, Lane 170, Zhongxiao E Rd Sec 4 (see map p.117). This restaurant opened in 1999 but is a branch of the revered Tainan noodle maker established over one hundred years ago (see p.330). Deservedly popular, the *danzi* noodles (NT$50 for a bowl) are a must-order. The decor is sleek, contemporary Chinese; the chef cooks over charcoal-fired pots near the entrance.

Taipei Shin Gu Shiang 37 Xinyi Rd Sec 3 (see map p.98). The most atmospheric restaurant in downtown Taipei, located inside a rustic wooden hall just off Xinyi Road. There's no menu – the staff bring out a selection of dishes and as much delicious pork oil rice as you can eat for NT$200 per person. The decor recalls Taiwan of the 1950s and 60s and old pop songs play in the background.

East Taipei
see map p.117

Beijing Do It True 506 Renai Rd. Cheerful Beijing-style restaurant, best known for its Chinese sesame buns served with sliced pork, fried "jumbo" dumplings and Beijing Style Hotpot (NT$200–400). It's named after an old restaurant in Beijing, feted by Emperor Qianlong.

G'day Café 180 Xingan St. Small and homely diner with a decent selection of Western comfort food on the edge of Songshan district, popular with expats and locals alike. Mexican favourites like burritos, burgers, sandwiches, some basic Asian dishes and as much coffee as you can drink, all reasonably priced at NT$150–200.

Jogoya 3/F, 22 Songshou Rd ☎02/27205555. Hip modern restaurant with huge buffet of Japanese food including sushi, tempura and teppanyaki, with Chinese favourites such as dumplings thrown in. The free wine, draft beer and Haagen-Dazs ice cream are welcome extras. Buy a ticket and pay before you go inside: the price ranges NT$568–758 depending on the time of day. Daily 11.30am–3am.

Taipei 101 Shopping Mall 45 Shifu Rd. The fourth floor of Taipei's smartest mall is a cavernous atrium ringed by nine hip, contemporary restaurants: *iR China* offers a fusion of Yunnan and Sichuan cuisine and *Wasabi* is a stylish, modern Japanese diner. NT$250–400 per order.

Ziga Zaga 2/F Grand Hyatt Taipei, 2 Songshou Rd ☎02/27201200. Taipei's swankiest Italian restaurant serving pasta and pizza (NT$400–500), and main dishes from NT$800. Turns into a club and bar after 9.30pm with live music, DJs and cocktails (NT$330).

Mon–Sat 11.30am–2.30pm, 6pm–9.30pm (club till 2–3am).

Night markets and food streets

Night markets are a quintessential part of the Taipei food experience, offering a vast range of cheap *xiaochi* or "little eats" (see Basics p.37). You'll rarely pay more than NT$25-40 per order. It's also worth exploring some of Taipei's "food streets": **Yongkang Street** south of Xinyi Road has a huge range of restaurants, from Chinese dumpling stores to Vietnamese and German cafés, while **Huaxin Street** near Nanshijiao MRT station is the home of Taipei's Burmese-Chinese community and the best place to sample cheap Burmese, Yunnan and Thai dishes. The alleys between **Linsen** and **Tianjin roads**, north of Changan and south of Nanjing Road, are packed with authentic Japanese restaurants, about fifteen minutes' walk from Zhongshan MRT station.

Gongguan Night Market (Gongguan MRT station). Gongguan is a student area and especially lively at night: food stalls cram the lanes between Roosevelt and Tingzhou roads south and north of the MRT station. Note the queues at 93 Tingzhou Road Section 3 – this nameless stall, known as *Gongguan Red Bean Pastry*, serves sweet cakes stuffed with red bean paste (NT$20).

Guangzhou Street Night Market (near Longshan Temple). Traditional outdoor market with the best stalls on the junction with Wuzhou Street: *Memory Ay Yuh Ice* serves cooling "aiyu" jelly drinks (NT$30), made from the seeds of a fig-like fruit, while *Ding Ji Tempura* on the other side offers Taiwanese-style squid tempura (NT$35).

Huaxi Street Tourist Night Market (between Guangzhou Street and Guiyang Street). This covered pedestrian-only street is half food and half CDs, bags, foot massages and jewellery (try *Bishan Guohua Tang* at no. 39 for Chinese fans). It's famous for snake dishes (it's also known as "Snake Alley") and gruesome "snake shows" where the snakes are fed, toyed with and slit open – try no. 49 and 53.

Raohe Street Night Market (near Ciyou Temple in Songshan). This market is one of the city's liveliest – the specialty is pork and mutton stewed in fragrant Chinese herbs, and the delicious charcoal-baked Fuzhou beef pepper pies near the temple-end of the street. Don't miss the *Ju Zi Fang* antique store at no. 196; *Dongfa Restaurant* at no. 94 (for oyster noodles); and the street's oldest store, tiny *Hu's Sesame Oil* at no. 84, in business since 1859.

Shida Night Market (close to Taipower Building MRT station). An eclectic mix of fried chicken, crepes, burritos, Chinese, Indian and Thai influences, most of the stalls and restaurants line Longquan Street parallel to Shida Road from Lane 50 to Heping Road. *Wei Jue You Xi* at no. 52 is the place to try *lu wei*: select meat and vegetables first, then wait while they're boiled in a tasty broth.

Shilin Night Market (opposite Jiantan MRT station). If you have time for just one night market in Taipei, make it this one. It's the city's biggest and oldest (dating from 1910), and because the main "food square" is located in a large covered building it's generally weatherproof. Try the *da bing bao xiao bing* ("little pastry wrapped in big pastry") and Shilin sausage with raw garlic. The market also occupies the narrow lanes between Wenlin and Dadong roads just to the north, selling mostly clothes but peppered with snack stalls.

Drinking and nightlife

In recent years **nightlife** in Taipei has expanded from a small cluster of mainly expat pubs and local beerhouses to a variety of lounge bars and a decent selection of live music venues. Taipei's nightclubs have also taken off in a big way – though the situation is constantly changing, the scene here is as good as any in Asia, regularly attracting top DJs from Japan, North America and Europe.

Bars

Taipei's bars and clubs are scattered throughout the city in much the same way as everything else, but there are enough clusters to allow some stumbling around on foot. For years the area around **Shuangcheng Street** north of Minquan Road (in Zhongshan district), was considered the centre of Taipei nightlife, particularly for foreigners. US soldiers on R&R frequented the area until the late 1970s and it's still known as the "**Combat Zone**" today. Though it's packed with over twenty pubs it's decidedly tired compared to more hip parts of the city and tends to be frequented by an older crowd. The university districts of **Shida** and **Gongguan** in the southwestern half of the city are funkier hunting grounds for cheaper pubs and clubs, while upscale **East Taipei** is where you'll find many of Taipei's lounge bars. The main clusters are around the lanes both sides of **Zhongxiao Road** between Dunhua and Guangfu roads, around **Anhe Road** to the south, and in **Xinyi**, an upcoming nightlife area feted by Taiwan's rich and famous. Unless dinner is involved, most bars don't get going till late, especially at the weekends, with the action best between midnight and two or three in the morning when most of them close. The closest thing to a local pub is a **beerhouse** (*piju wu*): a cross between a beer hall and Chinese restaurant, the emphasis here is on drinking cheap, usually Taiwanese beer, and stuffing yourself with snack food.

Shida
see map pp.98–99

45 45 Heping E Rd Sec 1. North American-style bar, with two floors accessed via a narrow stairway from street level, close to Guting MRT station and popular with expats and students. Snack food and beers from NT$130 (pitchers NT$500), cocktails from NT$200. Daily 11.30am–4am.

Blue Note 4/F, 171 Roosevelt Rd Sec 3. This pioneer jazz club, established in 1974, is a little hard to find but well worth the effort for the cosy venue and quality live jazz (entry varies NT$250–300 and includes one drink). The entrance is on Shida Road: look for the first doorway on the left after Roosevelt Road and take the lift up. Daily 7pm–2am.

DV8 223 Jinhua St. Compact, unpretentious bar attracting a mixed crowd of locals and expats with loud music and a free pool table downstairs. Bottled beers from NT$150. Daily 7.30pm–3am.

JB's Bar & Restaurant 148 Shida Rd. English-style pub serving excellent food including fish and chips (NT$420) and a huge all-day breakfast for NT$399. The bar upstairs serves English draught beers (Abbot Ale and Ruddles from NT$180). Sun–Thurs 11.30am–1.30am, Fri–Sat 11.30am–3am.

Peshawar 3, Lane 80, Shida Rd. Chilled-out ethnic café and bar (not a South Asian restaurant), and a good place for a quiet drink or tasty European food: home-made quiche (NT$100), pasta (NT$180) and sandwiches, plus decent coffee, bottled beers and cocktails from NT$170. Daily noon–2am.

Roxy Junior 1, Lane 80, Shida Rd. Another popular pub with students and expats in the heart of busy Shida, with a selection of reasonably priced spirits and beers (NT$160) plus comfy sofas; there are pool tables in the basement. Daily 11am–4am.

Gongguan
see map pp.98–99

Driftwood 4, Alley 9, Lane 316, Roosevelt Rd Sec 3. This beerhouse has an aboriginal theme, with slate tables, plenty of Taiwan Beer, and karaoke in the corner. It's become a hangout for Taipei's indigenous community – make friends over a bottle of millet wine from the east coast (NT$100–300). Daily 5pm–2am.

Riverside Music Café 2, Lane 244, Roosevelt Rd Sec 3. Live music venue just off Roosevelt Road, shows start from 9.30pm most days (cover charge NT$250 or NT$300 at weekends with one drink), though it tends to be quiet at other times. Daily 7pm–2am.

The Wall B1, 200 Roosevelt Rd Sec 4 ⓦwww.the-wall.com.tw. Taipei's best live rock venue with acts playing most nights from 9.30pm, though it can close early once the music stops – check the website for times. Located just off the busy Roosevelt and Keelung Road junction, next to a cinema entrance. Admission NT$300–500.

Zhongshan
Brass Monkey 166 Fuxing N Rd (see map p.106). Popular pub close to Nanjing E Road MRT station

with quality beers on tap and large servings of Western food on the menu. Big-screen TV means it's a popular expat venue for major sports events. Daily 5pm–1am (2am weekends).

Front Page Sports Bar 600 Linsen N Rd (*Imperial Hotel*, see map p.106). Popular hotel bar with local businessmen and drinkers heading into the Zone: it feels a bit like a comfortable gentleman's club during the day, reverting to sports bar at night with giant TV screen. Taiwan Beer on tap for NT$90.

Jurassic Restaurant 196 Bade Rd Sec 2 (see map p.107). Classic beerhouse with a cave-like interior, complete with mock dinosaur skeletons. Live music, extensive menu of Chinese comfort food (*sanbei* from NT$450) and seven-litre beer kegs for NT$1000.

My Place 3-1, Lane 32, Shuangcheng St (see map p.106). Closest thing the Zone has to an institution, this smoky British-style pub is one of the oldest in the area, opening in 1975. Open till 4am at the weekends.

East Taipei
see map p.117

Apocalypse Now 323 Fuxing N Rd. One of the liveliest beerhouses in town with cheap beer (NT$780 for 4.5 litres) and long wooden tables. Has the usual menu of seafood and snacks (*sanbei* from NT$450). Daily 11am-3am.

The Bed 29, Alley 35, Lane 181, Zhongxiao E Rd Sec 4. Taipei's answer to the *Buddha Bar*, with dark corners, comfy sofas, divans and a couple of beds to lounge on amidst the vaguely Angkorian decor: if the cocktails (NT$200–300) and beers (NT$250) aren't enough, for NT$500 you can puff on a *shisha* (water pipe filled with fruit-flavoured tobacco). It's

not far from *Lab* and *Sofa*, on the corner of Lane 205. Daily 6pm–2am.

Brown Sugar 101 Songren Rd ⓦwww .brownsugar.com.tw. This jazz club and restaurant has a regular programme of international acts from 9.30pm, reverting to a trendy nightclub after 1am. Packed at weekends, with a big cocktails and drinks list, it's tucked away behind the Capital Center: walk down the alley at the end of Songshou Road. Daily noon–4am.

Carnegie's 100 Anhe Rd Sec 2. Big expat favourite (the original is in Hong Kong) and the place to come for dancing on tables and general drunken mayhem. It's also one of the best places for English pub food (NT$350–460), including Sunday roasts with Yorkshire pudding, plus alfresco dining in the summer. Daily 11.30am–2am (5am weekends).

Lab 19, Alley 35, Lane 181, Zhongxiao E Rd Sec 4. Hip-hop bar and club with decent selection of American food such as *Sloppy Joe* (NT$250), and happy hour 5–8pm. It's a bit hard to find: Alley 35 runs off Lane 181 parallel to Civic Blvd, just to the north. Daily 5pm–3am.

Le blé d'or 100 Dunhua Rd (courtyard of Asiaworld) ⓦwww.lebledor.com.tw. Enjoy the outdoor tables at Taipei's only microbrew pub – try the stout and pale ales, though the beer fruit slushies are thirst quenching in summer (NT$150). Daily 5pm–2am.

Living Room 3/F, 8 Nanjing E Rd Sec 5, ⓦwww .livingroomtaipei.com. Candles, bookshelves and sofas make this a cosy bar for drinks and home-made food, while the space next door acts as small venue for live acts from reggae and rock to poetry readings (Tues–Sat). Open from 6.30pm, with NT$300–400 minimum charge at weekends.

Gay nightlife

Taipei has come a long way since the dark old days depicted in Pai Hsien-yung's *Crystal Boys* (see p.542) and the city has a thriving gay community. *Funky* at B1, 10 Hangzhou South Road Section 1 (NT$300–450) is the oldest gay bar in town and open from 8pm–2am daily (4am weekends) with a mix of music and young, fashionable clientele; *Café Fresh* at 2/F, 7 Jinshan South Road Section 2 has two lounge bars, a cosy garden, and one club level which gets busy at the weekends: look for the red door leading to a narrow staircase (Tues–Thurs 9.30pm–3am; Fri–Sun 8pm–3am; NT$250). *The Source* (daily 7pm-5am), at 1 Roosevelt Road Section 1, is a nightclub and bar that tends to attract a mixed crowd these days, but remains gay-friendly with plenty of foreigners and locals ready to mingle. There are several **lesbian** bars in Taipei, though the scene keeps evolving: try *Sappho* at B1, 1, Lane 102, Anhe Road Section 1 (Tues–Sun 9pm–3am; ☏02/27005411) which is mixed but holds regular women-only parties, and *Esha* at B1, 156 Jianguo North Road Section 1 (Fri–Sat 10pm–5am; NT$250–500) which has a club feel and attracts plenty of straight women: gay men allowed inside accompanied by three women only.

Shannon 6 Dunhua N Rd. Taipei's best Irish pub offers live bands at weekends (NT$250 cover after 9pm) and Guinness on tap (NT$230 a pint), though the pub food (such as pies and Irish stews from NT$375) could be better. Happy hour (Mon–Sat 4–7pm) beers are NT$150. Daily 11.30am–1am (2am weekends).

Sofa 56, Lane 161, Dunhua S Rd Sec 1. Cool lounge bar with a late 1960s feel – patterned wallpaper and lots of comfy sofas. Cocktails are not bad at NT$220–250, but at the weekends tables tend to get booked in advance. The entrance is actually on Lane 205, north of Zhongxiao East Road Section 4. Daily 2pm– 3am.

Clubs

Taipei has a dynamic club scene, with its biggest **nightclubs** regularly hosting global DJ icons. Hardcore clubbers will appreciate the multi-room venues, but there are also several disco-type places more popular with students where a round of drinks won't break the bank.

Club Wax B1, 67 Roosevelt Rd Sec 2. Fun club popular with students and expats, packed most weekends and all you can drink for NT$500 – just hold on to your glass and they'll keep filling it up. Daily 9pm–2am or 6am weekends.

Eden 11/F, 98 Zhongxiao E Rd Sec 4. Stylish lounge bar that switches to club mode weekends with dance floor surrounded by plush sofas, and DJs playing funky house and hip-hop: drinks are reasonable (NT$180–300) and there's usually no cover. Daily 9pm–3am.

Luxy 5/F, 201 Zhongxiao E Rd Sec 4 ⓦwww .luxy-taipei.com. Current trendsetter in the heart of Daan with two separate dance floors and a big cocktail list. Resident DJs offer tough competition to the big names that fly in every weekend – check the website for details. NT$500 cover most nights.

Ministry of Sound 310 Lenqun Third Road ⓦwww.mos-taipei.com. Offshoot of the legendary

London club with the big sound system, its two dance floors and three floors provide an excellent venue for international DJs and hip-hop acts. The only downside is the location – in 2004 MoS had its own building specially constructed way out here in Neihu (NT$200 by taxi). Wed–Sat 9pm–5am, cover NT$200–700.

Plush Living Mall, 12/F, 138 Bade Rd Sec 4. Cool lounge bar and club with great views of the city, glass-walled dance area and popular ladies nights (Wednesday). The *Party Room* next door attracts a younger crowd with a hip-hop slant. Both open 9pm–4am.

Roxy 99 B1, 218 Jinshan Rd Sec 2. Place to come for unpretentious drinking and dancing, with a good mix of expats and locals. The drinks are cheap, and the music ranges from hip-hop and house to rock and pop. NT$300 cover with one free drink. Daily 9pm–4am.

Entertainment and the arts

Taipei has an incredibly vibrant **cultural life**, a quick glance through one of the city's English-language publications (see p.49) revealing a daily feast of exhibitions, shows, gigs, plays and traditional performances, competing with a massive appetite for movies. Performance groups such as **U-Theatre**, **Cloud Gate** and **Han-Tang Yuefu** (see Contexts p.536), all based in the city, are world class. The best way to buy **tickets** is to approach the venue directly or visit one of the ERA ticket offices located in Eslite or Kingstone bookstores. The comprehensive Culture Express website (ⓦexpress.culture.gov.tw) provides listings of upcoming events, while the Tourism Bureau or your hotel should also be able to help.

Chinese opera and traditional performing arts

Taipei is one of the world's best places to see **traditional Chinese performing arts** (such as acrobatics, puppetry and music) and various styles of **Chinese**

Huashan Cultural & Creative Industry Centre	華山創意文化園區	*huáshān chuàngyì wén huàyúanqū*
National Concert Hall	國家音樂廳	*guó jiā yīnyùetīng*
National Taiwan Junior College of Performing Arts	國立臺灣戲曲專科學校	*guólì táiwān xìqǔ zhuānkē xuéxiào*
Novel Hall for Performing Arts	新舞臺	*xīnwǔtái*
Red House Theatre	紅樓劇場	*hónglóu jùchǎng*
SPOT-Taipei Film House	光點台北電影主題館	*guāngdiǎn táiběi diànyǐng zhǔtíguǎn*
Taipei Arena	台北小巨蛋	*táiběi xiǎojùdàn*
Taipei Artists Village	台北國際藝術村	*táiběi guójìyìshùcūn*
TaipeiEYE	臺北戲棚	*táiběi xìpéng*
Warner Village	華納威秀影城	*huánà wēixiù yǐngchéng*
Zhongshan Hall	中山堂	*zhōng shāntáng*

opera – it's not unusual to have ten or more productions running each month in various locations. An easily digested taster is provided by **TaipeiEYE**, a weekly show held on the third floor of the Taiwan Cement Hall, at 113 Zhongshan North Road Section 2 (☎02/25682677, ⓦwww.taipeieye.com). Featuring various acts from aboriginal song and dance to Chinese puppetry and opera, it's firmly targeted at tourists but the standard is high – many of Taiwan's premier troupes play here (Fri–Sat 8–10pm; NT$880). The students at the **National Taiwan Junior College of Performing Arts** at 177 Neihu Road Section 2 (☎02/27962666, ⓦwww.ntjcpa.edu.tw) also perform from a varied repertoire Monday and Thursdays 10–11.45am (NT$400), comprising thirty minutes of acrobatics, a tour of the Chinese Opera Museum upstairs, a video and a 35-minute performance taken from a Beijing opera. The upstairs teahouse in the **Red House Theatre** at 10 Chengdu Road (☎02/23119380) in Ximending hosts Chinese opera and traditional dance performances on Sunday afternoons (1–5pm). The building was completed in 1908 to house a market and is open daily 11am–10pm. Traditional **puppet shows** are held every weekend at the **Lin Liu-Hsin Puppet Theatre Museum** in Datong (p.108) and the **Puppetry Art Center** (99 Civic Blvd Sec 5; Tues–Sun 10am–5pm; NT$100) next to the Living Mall, a lavish tribute to Chinese puppetry in Taiwan, though sadly there are no labels in English (this may be rectified in the future). Puppet shows (NT$300) are held on Saturdays and Sundays, usually performed by the **Pili Puppetry Troupe**, arguably Taiwan's most famous.

Concert venues

Western classical and Chinese music, especially *nanguan* (see Contexts p.536) is usually performed somewhere in Taipei year round and the standards are generally high – prices vary from show to show (see above for information about tickets). The **National Concert Hall** in Chiang Kai-shek Memorial Plaza on Zhongshan Road (☎02/23431587, ⓦwww.ntch.edu.tw) is where Taiwan's premier orchestra, the National Chinese Orchestra, regularly performs Chinese classical music. At other times expect to see a wide range of jazz or Western classical music. The **Novel Hall for Performing Arts** in Xinyi at 3 Songshou Road (☎02/27224302,

@www.novelhall.org.tw) is one of the city's newest and plushest venues, with a varied programme of Chinese opera, theatre, classical and choral music. It can be hard to find the entrance – look for the white China-trust building and walk round the back. In contrast, **Zhongshan Hall** near Ximending at 98 Yanping South Road (☎02/23813137, @www.csh .taipei.gov.tw) is Taipei's oldest concert hall, completed in 1936 (the Japanese in Taiwan surrendered here in 1945) and a venue for traditional Chinese or classical music. The futuristic **Taipei Arena** at 10 Nanjing East Road Section 4 hosts pop concerts and sporting events, also housing a skating rink.

Cinemas

Taipei is loaded with cinemas, most of them packed at the weekends. All the major Hollywood movies arrive in Taiwan soon after their US release dates and are rarely dubbed into Chinese: **Wuchang Street** (known as "movie street") in Ximending is where you'll find the older and larger screens – check times in local English newspapers. **Warner Village** (18 Songshou Rd @www .warnervillage.com.tw; tickets NT$270 or NT$290 booked over the Inter-net) is a huge multiplex cinema in Xinyi and one of the most popular places in town. **Ta Chien Cinema** in basement 2 of the *Westin Hotel* (133 Nanjing E Rd Sec 3 ☎02/87706565; NT$350 per movie) is Taipei's only luxury cinema, with comfy two-seater sofas from which you can order snacks and drinks from the hotel menu. For art films try the **SPOT-Taipei Film House** at 18 Zhongshan North Road Section 2 (☎02/25117786, @www .spot.org.tw; NT$220 per movie), which screens six movies daily (local and international) and is located within the tastefully restored former US consul-ate built in 1926. It also houses a bookstore, café and bar with terrace (daily 11am–10pm).

Art galleries

Contemporary and classical **art** is booming in Taipei, with numerous galleries, museums and shops displaying everything from traditional Chinese paintings to installation art and glass sculpture. The **Apollo Building** at 218-220 Zhongx-iao East Road Section 4 has five tower blocks packed with over twenty galleries displaying art for viewing and buying – B block contains the best taster. Most shops are open 10.30am to 6.30pm. To catch up on some of Taiwan's alterna-tive art trends, try the **Huashan Cultural & Creative Industry Centre** at 1 Bade Rd (daily 10am–11pm, some galleries close at 6pm; ☎02/23926180, @www.huashan-ccc.com), within the grounds of the old Taipei Winery and a ten-minute walk from Zhongxiao Xinsheng MRT station. The more inti-mate **Taipei Artists Village** at 7 Beiping Road (☎02/33937377, @www .artistvillage.org) is close to the main station: the first floor galleries are open to the public while artists in residence occupy the higher floors (daily 10am–6pm).

Festivals and events

Taipei has an extensive line-up of annual **festivals** – check the Tourism Bureau website for a full listing or Basics (p.50) for all the major national events. The **Lantern Festival** on the fifteenth day after Chinese New Year (January or Febru-ary) sees giant lantern installations located around Chiang Kai-shek Memorial

Plaza, City Hall or Sun Yat-sen Memorial Hall, while in April or May Baoan Temple hosts the energetic month-long **Baosheng Cultural Festival**. The **Taipei Mazu Culture Festival** kicks off in April or May the week before the birthday of the goddess, with Taipei's original Mazu statue (now in Sanjhih) paraded around the city and displayed at 2-28 Peace Park. The **Taipei Festival of Traditional Arts** usually opens in April at Zhongshan Hall, a comprehensive introduction to Taiwanese song, music, dance and drama, while the **International Taipei Dragon Boat Festival** normally falls in June and involves several days of races along the Keelung River at Dajia Riverside Park. One of Taipei's biggest religious festivals also takes place in June – the **birthday of the Xiahai City God** on Dihua Street (see p.105). The **Formoz Festival** (ⓦ www.formoz.com) is one of Taiwan's biggest international live rock and pop events, running over three days in July at the Children's Recreation Center near Yuanshan MRT station. The most prominent religious festival, **Confucius's Birthday Ceremony**, takes place on September 28 each year at the Confucius Temple (see p.109). Taipei holds the most important and lavish **National Day** celebrations on October 10 with spectacular fireworks outside the Presidential Building, while the annual **Taipei Arts Festival** usually takes place in October. Taiwan's premier film festival is the art-movie oriented **Taipei Golden Horse Film Festival** (ⓦ www.goldenhorse.org.tw) held in November and December. The **birthday of Qingshan** in November or December is the last of the year's major religious festivals (see p.103).

Shopping

Taipei is packed with huge **shopping malls**, most of them upmarket affairs located in East Taipei, while **traditional shops** tend to be in the older, western parts of the city. In addition to night markets (see p.128) and the shops listed below, **Ximending** (see p.104) is the place to check out Taipei street fashion. Elsewhere, the weekend **Jade Market** is a definite highlight, while **Guanghua Market** is computer geek heaven.

Department stores and shopping malls

Eslite 245 Dunhua S Rd Sec 1. Stylish department store packed with boutiques such as Xiao Yu (1/F) selling the work of local designers, including renowned Tian Bu handmade cloth shoes; Zhang Yi Fang (B1) sells Taiwanese puppets. *Eslite Bookstore* (2/F) has a decent English-language selection and is open 24hrs.

Core Pacific Living Mall 138 Bade Rd Sec 4. Try the eighth floor of this futuristic shopping mall for several upscale Chinese arts and crafts shops: there's a decent *National Palace Museum* gift shop here, and a branch of *Bamboola* (ⓦ www .bamboola.com.tw) selling exquisite bamboo boxes, tea sets and chopsticks. Shops open daily 11am–10.30pm. *Cinemark* (B1) shows films 24 hours.

The Mall 203 Dunhua S Rd Sec 2. This upmarket shopping centre next to the *Far Eastern Hotel* contains *Wuching Gold Creation* (gold sculptures, earrings and necklaces) on the first floor; the

Pei-Hao Wang Collection (jewellery and accessories) on the second floor; and *Tittot* glassware and the *Franz Collection*'s award-winning porcelain designs on the fifth floor. Daily 11am–9.30pm.

Miramar Entertainment Park 20 Jingye 3rd Rd. This new shopping centre in Dazhi, just north of the Keelung River, is home to Asia's largest IMAX cinema screen and its second largest Ferris wheel (NT$200 per ride), which helps justify the taxi fare. Daily 11am–10pm.

Sogo 45 Zhongxiao E Rd Sec 4. Posh Japanese department store selling just about anything, from designer clothes to steel woks. Daily 11am–9.30pm.

Taipei 101 Shopping Mall 45 Shifu Rd, ⓦ www.taipei101mall.com.tw. Taipei's smartest mall, jammed with boutiques and designer stores, restaurants (p.127) and bookstores (p.136). The basement contains Taipei's largest food court and *Jason's Market Place* (daily 10am–10pm) the best supermarket

Bamboola	大禾竹藝工坊	dàhézhúyì gōngfāng
Core Pacific Living Mall	京華城	jīnghuáchéng
EB Shoes	小格格鞋坊	xiǎogégé xiéfāng
Eslite	誠品書店	chéngpǐn shūdiàn
Franz Collection	法藍瓷	fǎláncí
Guanghua Market	光華商場	guānghuá shāngchǎng
Jade Market	建國假日玉市	jiànguó jiàrì yùshì
Jin Tai	金泰	jīntài
Lee Yao Cotton-Padded Clothing Store	李嘉棉衣店	lǐyáo miányīdiàn
Lin Tian Tong Store	林田桶電	líntiántǒng diàn
Liuligongfang	琉璃工坊	liúligōngfāng
Miramar Entertainment Park	美麗華百樂園	měilìhuá bǎilèyúan
Shiatzy Chen	夏姿服飾	xiàzī fúshì
Small Garden Embroidered Shoes	小花園	xiǎohuāyúan
Taipei 101 Shopping Mall	台北101購物中心	táiběi 101 gòuwùzhōngxīn
Taiwan Handicraft Promotion Center	台灣手工業推廣中心	táiwān shǒugōngyè tuīguǎngzhōngxīn
The Mall	遠企購物中心	yuǎnqǐ gòuwùzhōngxīn
Tian Bu	天步	tiānbù
Tittot	琉園	liúyúan
Wuching Gold Creation	吳卿金雕	wúqīng jīndiāo
Wufenpu Garment Wholesale Area	五分埔	wǔfēnpǔ
Wufenpu Garment Wholesale Area	五分埔商圈	wúfēnpǔ shāngquān
Xiao Yu	小雨	xiǎo yǔ
Zhang Yi Fang	彰藝坊	zhāng yì fāng
Zhaoheding	昭和町	zhāohédīng

for imported food. Mon–Fri 11am–10pm, Sat–Sun 10am–10pm.

Clothes

EB Shoes 96 Xining S Rd. This small shop is the home of beautifully hand-crafted Chinese-style shoes and slippers, not far from Ximen MRT (NT$400–700). Daily 10am–10pm.

Lee Yao Clothing Store 2 Lishui St. Daily 11am–9.30pm. Designer boutique popular with expats, specializing in traditional Chinese clothes with vivid floral designs. Prices range NT$1000 to NT$10,000.

Shiatzy Chen 49 Zhongshan N Rd Sec 2 ⓦwww .shiatzychen.com. Flagship store of Taiwan's top designer, famous for making chinoiserie and the *cheongsam* hip. Daily 10am–7pm.

Small Garden Embroidered Shoes 70 Ermei St (Ximen). Venerable old store with roots in 1930s Shanghai, specializing in handmade embroidered shoes in classical Ming and Qing dynasty style. Daily noon–6pm.

Wufenpu Garment Wholesale Area Near Houshanpi MRT station, Songshan. Discount clothes market, choked with everything from brand-name designers (or at least good copies of them) to absolute kitsch, as well as a variety of accessories. Daily 9am–9pm.

WUM 1, Lane 16, Zhongshan N Rd Sec 2 ⓦwww .stephanedou.com. Two shiny metallic floors full of chic, women's fashion in Stephane Dou and Chan-glee Yugin's latest boutique. Daily 10am–7pm.

Antiques, arts and crafts

Taipei has several craft centres firmly targeted at tourists, though prices and quality aren't bad and they are the most convenient way to stock up on gifts and souvenirs. If you're a serious buyer, the **antique shops** around Jianguo Road between Renai and Xinyi Roads make fascinating browsing with **Lane 291** lined with posh stores full of jewellery, paintings, carvings, and statues (many are closed Mondays). Heping East Road Section 1, east of Guting MRT station, is home to traditional Chinese **calligraphy equipment stores**: the shops at no. 77 and 123 are the best. For designer crafts try Eslite or The Mall (see p.134) on Dunhua Road.

Jade Market (under the Jianguo Elevated Freeway, between Renai and Jinan roads). Massive selection of jade jewellery, carvings and other antique stalls while the **Jianguo Flower Market** in the other direction highlights Taiwan's impressive range of semi-tropical flora (orchids for under NT$200). Both are open Sat–Sun from 8am till around 6pm.

Lin Tian Tong Store 108 Zhongshan N Rd Sec 1. Established in 1928 and specializing in Japanese-style tubs, basins and flowerpots made from *hinoki* cypress wood. The scarcity of such wood in Taiwan today accounts for the high prices, but even if you're not buying it's worth a quick look.

Liuligongfang 346 Dunhua S Rd Sec 1 ☎02/2701-3165, ⓦwww.liuli.com. Upmarket

glass sculpture studio, founded by movie star Loretta Yang in 1987. There are also showrooms in most shopping malls. Daily 9.30am–8pm.

Taiwan Handicraft Promotion Center 1 Xuzhou St ⓦwww.handicraft.org.tw. Best place for standard Chinese arts and crafts, including jewellery, porcelain, tea, fans, *cloisonné* enamelware and even traditional clothing. Daily 9am–5.30pm.

Zaoheding 60 Yongkang St. Compact warehouse packed with cheap antique stalls selling everything from old books and statues to pieces of furniture. This section of Yongkang Street is lined with antique shops – things get going at around midday and wind down after 8pm.

Cameras, computers and electrical equipment

Taipei's "**camera street**" covers Hankou Street Section 1 and the section of Boai Road south of Kaifeng Street – here you'll find all the latest in high-tech photographic equipment. **Jin Tai** (10am–6pm) at 60 Boai Road is the oldest repair shop in town: craftsman Lin Wen Ji is reputed to be able to fix anything (charges start at NT$600). Taipei is a great place to pick up computer hardware at reasonable prices, though English is rarely spoken by sales assistants (or used in manuals) and systems may not always be compatible with your home country. Try **Guanghua Market** on Civic Boulevard near Xinsheng Road (daily 10am–9pm), a warren of frenetic stalls selling computer parts, games and accessories, or the **NOVA Computer Mall** at 2 Guanqian Road, on the corner of Zhongxiao Road (daily 11am–10pm). Note that Guanghua Market is expected to move ino a new six-storey building on the corner of Bade and Xinsheng Roads, sometime in 2007.

Books

Page One, on the fourth floor of Taipei 101 Shopping Mall, is the best English-language bookshop in town, with a huge selection of novels and reference books. **Caves Books** at 103 Zhongshan North Road Section 2 is smaller but also has a good selection of China and Taiwan-related books, as well as reference/teaching materials. **Moungar** at 4, Lane 154, Guangzhou Street sells old CDs and a small selection of secondhand English books, in a converted Chinese shophouse next to *Koko's* and close to Longshan Temple. Note that **Bike Farm** (see p.138) also has a big collection of secondhand books in English. **Le Pigeonnier** at 9, Lane 97, Songjiang Rd is a comprehensive French bookstore, while **Eslite** is open 24 hours (see p.134).

Listings

Airlines Air France/KLM Asia, 9/F, 2 Dunhua S Rd Sec 1 ℡ 02/27114055; Air Macau, 6/F,134 Minsheng E Rd Sec 3 ℡ 02/27170366; Air New Zealand, 8/F, 146 Songjiang Rd ℡ 02/25678950; All Nippon Airways (ANA), 3/F, 129 Zhongshan N Rd Sec 2 ℡ 02/25215777; Asiana Airlines, 9/F, 101 Nanjing E Rd Sec 2 ℡ 02/25814000; Cathay Pacific Airways, 12/F, 129 Minsheng E Rd Sec 3 ℡ 02/27152333; China Airlines, 131 Nanjing E Rd Sec 3 ℡ 02/27151212; Continental Airlines, 10/F, 167 Fuxing N Rd ℡ 02/27195947; Dragonair, 14/F, 49 Minsheng E Rd Sec 3 ℡ 02/25182700; EVA Air, 117 Changan E Rd Sec 2 ℡ 02/25011999; Far Eastern Air Transport, Alley 123, Lane 405, Dunhua N Rd ℡ 02/33935388; Japan Asia Airways 1/F, 2 Dunhua S Rd Sec 1 ℡ 02/27765151; Malaysia Airlines 1-2/F, 102 Dunhua N Rd ℡ 02/25147888; Mandarin Airlines, 13/F, 134 Minsheng E Rd Sec 3 ℡ 02/27171230; Northwest Airlines 9/F, 2 Dunhua S Rd Sec 1 ℡ 02/27722188; Pacific Airlines, 10/F, 158 Songjiang Rd ℡ 02/25431860; Philippine Airlines, 11/F, 139 Songjiang Rd ℡ 02/25067255; Singapore Airlines, 148 Songjiang Rd ℡ 02/25516655; Thai International, 96 Jianguo N Rd Sec 1 ℡ 02/25096800; TransAsia Airways, 2/F, 150 Fuxing N Rd ℡ 02/29724599; Uni Air, 340 Dunhua N Rd ℡ 02/25185166; United Airlines, 12/F, 2 Renai Rd Sec 4 ℡ 02/23258868; Vietnam Airlines, 5/F, 59 Songjiang Rd ℡ 02/25177177.

Banks Getting cash is not a problem in Taipei: most banks will exchange foreign currency, while Chinatrust and Cathay Trust ATMs take Cirrus, Mastercard, Plus or Visa cards (not Maestro) – ATMs are also available in 7-Elevens, MRT stations and some McDonalds. HSBC has ATMs at 167 Nanjing E Rd Sec 2; at the Warner Village cinema complex in Xinyi, 16 Songshou Rd; and 1/F, 8 Xinyi Rd Sec 5. Citibank has ATMs at 117-1 Minsheng E Rd Sec 3; 101 Nanjing E Rd Sec 2; and 460 Xinyi Rd Sec 4.

Baseball Taiwan's national sport is played at Xinzhuang Stadium in the western suburbs where there are up to three games per week (take a taxi from Xinpu MRT station) and Tianmu Sports Park where around 12 games are held every year. The national CPBL league has six teams sponsored by corporations – they rotate matches between cities island-wide so there is no Taipei team as such. Check the Chinese Professional Baseball League site at ⊕ www.cpbl.com.tw.

Car rental It is possible to rent cars in Taipei, though driving in the city can be intimidating for the inexperienced. Several companies have desks the international airport, but in the city,

try Nice Rent-a-Car at 276 Chengde Rd Sec 3 (℡ 0800/999888) or Central Auto Service at 3 Chengde Rd Sec 7 (℡ 02/28280033).

Embassies/trade offices Australia, Suite 2612, International Trade Building, 333 Keelung Rd Sec 1 ℡ 02/87254100, ⊕ www.australia.org.tw; Canada, 13/F, 365 Fuxing N Rd ℡ 02/25443000, ⊕ canada.org.tw; Japan, 10/F, 245 Dunhua S Rd ℡ 02/27412116; Philippines, 4/F, Metrobank Plaza, 107 Zhongxiao E Rd Sec 4 ℡ 02/27786511, ⊕ www.meco.ph/contact.html; New Zealand, Rm 2501, 25/F, International Trade Building, 333 Keelung Rd Sec 1 ℡ 02/27576721; South Africa, Suite 1301, 13/F, 205 Dunhua N Rd ℡ 02/27153251, ⊕ www.southafrica.org.tw; South Korea, Rm 1506, 333 Keelung Rd Sec 1 ℡ 02/27588320; Thailand, 7/F, 150 Fuxing N Rd ℡ 02/27121882; UK, 8-10/F, Fu Key Building, 99 Renai Rd Sec 2 ℡ 02/21927000, ⊕ www.btco.org .tw; US, American Institute in Taiwan, 7, Lane 134, Xinyi Rd Sec 3 ℡ 02/27092000, ⊕ www.ait.org.tw.

Hospitals and clinics Most hotels will be able to help with treatment or doctors if you feel sick, and most downtown hospitals have staff that can usually speak English. The Taiwan Adventist Hospital at 424 Bade Rd Sec 2 (℡ 02/27718151) has a special clinic for foreigners with English-speaking staff towards the back of the main building known as the Priority Care Center (℡ 02/27762651) – it's NT$1000 for a walk-in registration and doctors are on duty Mon–Thurs 9–11.30am and 2-4.30pm, and 9-11.30am on Fridays and Sundays.

Internet access By 2007 most of Taipei should be covered by WLAN, the outdoor wireless Internet system using pre-paid cards for visitors (⊕ wlan .taipei-elife.net), but if you don't have a computer there are plenty of Internet cafés scattered around the city: American Pie e-café 4/F, 8 Nanyang St (24hrs; NT$40 per hour, discounts after NT$100 membership); Aztec, 5/F, K Mall, 50 Zhongxiao W Rd Sec 1 and B1, 60 Zhongxiao E Rd Sec 4 (24hrs; NT$60 per hour); Nova Computer Arcade, 2 Guanqian Rd (free Internet terminals on 3/F); Xicco, 2/F, 155 Zhongshan N Rd Sec 2 (NT$40 per hour); Skywalker Multimedia Entertainment Center B1, 119 Minsheng E Rd Sec 2 (24hrs; NT$40 per hour); Network Planet 75 Xinyi Rd Sec 3 (24hrs; NT$40 per hour).

Language courses Taipei is one of the best places in the world to study Chinese, with classes in Taiwanese also available. Serious students attend formal courses at the Center for Chinese Language & Culture Studies on Heping Rd (℡ 02/23218457, ⊕ www.ntnu.edu.tw/mtc/index.htm), but there are seven other universities that run programmes. There are also many language schools offering classes on a more casual basis, providing a useful way of obtaining extendible visas: CLI, Rm 1, 3F/, 61 Yenping S Rd (℡02/23313000); Pioneer Language Institute, 6/F, 200 Heping E Rd Sec 1 (℡02/23633535, ⓦwww.chinese.org.tw); Taipei Language Institute, 4/F, Taipei Roosevelt Center, 50 Roosevelt Rd Sec 3 (℡02/23678228, ⓦwww.tli.com.tw).

Left Luggage Taipei Main Station has coin-operated lockers tucked away in the basement, with rates starting at NT$50 per day for a small backpack-sized locker and NT$100 for larger spaces. The maximum storage time is 72 hours. Taipei Inter City Bus Terminal also has lockers (NT$30).

Libraries The National Central Library at 20 Zhongshan S Rd (Mon–Fri 9am–9pm, Sat–Sun 9am–5pm; ℡02/23619132) is Taipei's biggest. The huge periodical room on the third floor has English-language newspapers and magazines – the Rare Books Room on the fourth floor is also worth a peek. You need to show your passport at the entrance to get a one-day temporary library card to enter (over-19s only) – check bags in the free lockers. The Taipei Public Library at 125 Jianguo S Rd Sec 2 (Tues–Fri 8.30am–9pm, Sun–Mon 9am–5pm; no card needed) has a decent selection of English magazines and papers on the second floor and Internet on the first floor.

Pharmacies Taipei is littered with Traditional Chinese Medicine stores, the grandest being Beijing Tong Ren Tang at 145 Changchun Rd (ⓦwww.tongrentang.com), open daily 11–7pm.

Conventional Western non-prescription remedies (and toiletries) can be purchased in Watsons stores all over the city: try the branch next to Sogo on the junction of Zhongxiao and Fuxing Roads, or in Taipei 101 Shopping Mall.

Police The Foreign Affairs Police office (visa extensions) is at 96 Yanping S Rd near Ximending. For emergencies or reporting theft call ℡02/25554275 for English-speaking assistance.

Post office The Main Post Office is on the junction of Zhongxiao W Rd and Boai Rd (Mon–Fri 7.30am–9pm, Sat 8.30am–4.30pm, Sun 8.30am–noon). There is a post restante service at window 12.

Scooter rental Local firms seem reluctant to rent scooters to foreigners in Taipei, though Bike Farm at 7, Lane 222, Xinhai Road Section 4 (℡02/29301002, ⓦwww.bikefarm.net) is owned by an English expat and offers one month rentals from NT$2200–2600, including all servicing (daily 2–10pm). You'll need a passport and a NT$5000-7000 deposit. Daily rentals (NT$500) require a local guarantor.

Travel agents Golden Foundation at 134 Zhongxiao Rd Sec 4 has English speakers and can put together decent itineraries for touring Taiwan (℡02/27733266), while Edison Travel Service at 4/F, 190 Songjiang Rd also has English-speaking staff (℡02/25635313, ⓦwww.edison.com.tw) and operates Taipei tours. The most popular local agent for cheap air tickets and packages is Eztravel with its main office at 258 Dunhua N Rd (ⓦwww.eztravel.com.tw).

Around Taipei

The mountains and river valleys that surround the capital are loaded with attractions, making for an enticing series of day-trips or short breaks. Beitou's **hot-spring spas** are some of Taiwan's best, while hikers should find plenty to keep them busy in **Yangmingshan National Park**. The old port towns of **Danshui** and **Bali** contain a smattering of historical sights, while **Wulai** and the towns to the southeast offer a taster of the island's mountainous interior. **Yingge** is a must-see for anyone with an interest in ceramics and the temple at **Sansia** is one of Taiwan's most beautiful.

Beitou

The northern Taipei district of **BEITOU** nestles in the shadow of Yangmingshan, twenty minutes from downtown by MRT. The name derives from *beitoushe*

Beitou

Beitou	北投	*běitóu*
Beitou Hot Springs Museum	北投溫泉博物館	*běitóu wēnqúan bówùguǎn*
Hell Valley	地熱谷	*dìrègǔ*
Ketagalan Culture Centre	凱達格蘭文化館	*kǎidágélán wénhuàguǎn*
Puji Temple	普濟寺	*pǔjì sì*
Taiwan Folk Art Museum	北投文物館	*běitóu wénwùguǎn*
Xinbeitou	新北投	*xīnběitóu*

Accommodation and spas

Longnai Hot Springs Inn	龍乃湯	*lóngnǎitāng*
Open-Air Hot Springs	公共露天溫泉	*gōnggòng lùtiān wēnqúan*
Spring City Resort	春天酒店	*chūntiān jiǔdiàn*
SweetMe Hotspring Resort	水美溫泉會館	*shuǐměi wēnqúanhuìguǎn*
Whispering Pine Inn	吟松閣旅社	*yínsōnggé lǚshè*
Yitsun Hotel	逸大飯店	*yìzun dàfàndiàn*

or "witch" in the Ketagalan language, an allusion to a sorceress that once lived here, or more likely, the area's bubbling sulphur carbonate **hot springs**. Osaka merchant **Hirada Gengo** opened Beitou's first hot-spring inn in 1896, and during the Japanese occupation it became one of the island's most prominent resorts. The Japanese were particularly attracted to **Hokutolite**, a mineral-laden stone formed by the springs, and bathers still come here to enjoy its therapeutic qualities. Most visitors come for the day, taking a dip in one of the many spas in the area (as in much of Taiwan, you can't actually bathe in the hot springs at source – water is piped into spa pools and hotels), but it's also worth exploring a smattering of sights recalling Taiwan's Japanese past.

Beitou is on the Danshui MRT line, easily accessible from central Taipei. There's not much to see around the main station however, and it's best to take the branch line to **Xinbeitou** ("New Beitou"), a few minutes away and closer to the main hotels and spas.

Beitou Park and around

From **Xinbeitou** MRT station, head straight up Zhongshan Road on the north side of **Beitou Park**, a swathe of green that follows sulphuric Beitou Creek up the valley. Two hundred metres on the left is the **Ketagalan Culture Centre** (Tues–Sun 9am–5pm; free) which was established as a focus for the indigenous community in Taipei (there are around 11,000 aboriginal residents registered in the city). It has a shop on the first floor, and the exhibition on the *pingpu* tribes is especially good (see Contexts p.519), but the labelling is in Chinese only. A short walk further along Zhongshan Road on the right, **Beitou Hot Springs Museum** (Tues–Sun 9am–5pm; free) is housed in the beautifully restored public bathhouse built in 1913, complete with stained-glass windows and original bathing pool in the basement. It's the best place to learn about the history of the area. Beyond the museum take the right-hand fork in Zhongshan Road: 100m past the Open-Air Hot Springs you'll see a lane on the left leading to the Geothermal Scenic Park, otherwise known as **Hell Valley** (daily 9am–5pm; free). It's essentially a huge pool of bubbling spring water, especially impressive in winter months when it's shrouded in billowing clouds of steam. The lake is fenced off for safety reasons (the average temperature is 70°C), but locals still boil eggs and dip their feet in the scalding-hot stream by the entrance. Continue

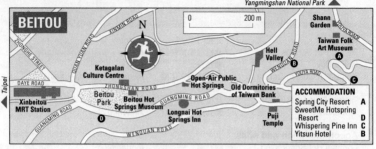

up the main street and turn left at Wenquan Road: not far on the right you'll see stone steps (take the right-hand fork) leading up to **Puji Temple** (daily 7am–8pm) a typically elegant Japanese Buddhist shrine, now rare in Taiwan. Completed in 1916 and enlarged in 1934, it's dedicated to Guanyin. On the other side of Wenquan Road you should be able to see the **Old Dormitories of Taiwan Bank**, built as a guesthouse in 1920 and now in ruins. Bear left at the next junction then turn right up Youya Road: it's a twenty-minute walk up the valley from here to the **Taiwan Folk Art Museum** which has a fascinating collection of aboriginal and early Taiwanese artefacts but has been closed since 2003 for a major renovation: it should be open by mid-2007. Next door, at 34 Youya Road, *Shann Garden* comprises a Mongolian barbecue restaurant and Japanese-style teahouse, both with grand views of Beitou below – sipping tea on tatami mats here is the perfect way to end an afternoon. Bus #230 and S25 head back to Beitou from the road outside.

Accommodation and spas

Beitou's hot-spring water is piped into **spas** all over the valley, many doubling as attractive **hotels**. Unless you're a real hot-spring fan it's usually not worth staying the night, as most places offer affordable day rates for their spa facilities. You'll normally be allowed to stay in the "public" pools (typically including sauna, steam room and a variety of hot and cold spring pools) as long as you like, and during the week you'll have them mostly to yourself. Private rooms with sunken baths are often available at the best spas, but these are pricey – at least NT$1500–3000 per hour.

Longnai Hot Springs Inn, 244 Guangming Rd. Founded in 1907 and the oldest of Beitou's traditional Japanese bathhouses (there are no rooms here despite the name), this is a no-nonsense affair where you just strip off and get into the fairly basic separate male and female indoor stone baths (NT$70 per hour, NT$40 towel). Look for the white shack-like hut below the Open-Air Hot Springs. Daily 6.30am–9pm.

Open-Air Hot Springs 6 Zhongshan Rd. Also known as the Millennium Hot Springs, this is the cheapest outdoor spa in Beitou (NT$40), featuring several mixed-sex pools that close for cleaning at regular intervals through the day (wear your swim suit). Nice location on the banks of the creek, but it can get crowded, especially at

weekends. Coin-operated lockers available. Daily 5.30–7.45am, 8.30–11.15am, 12pm–2.45pm, 3.30–6.15pm, 7–9.45pm.

Spring City Resort 18 Youya Rd ☎02/28975555, ⓦwww.springresort.com.tw. Located high on the hills above Beitou and regarded as its top resort, this modern five-star hotel offers a variety of mixed open-air pools (daily 8am–1am; NT$800) and luxury accommodation. **⑧**

SweetMe Hotspring Resort 224 Guangming Rd ☎02/28983838, ⓦwww.sweetme.com .tw. Conveniently located close to the MRT, this is one of Beitou's best contemporary spas and hotels. Luxurious indoor pools open weekdays 7.30am–12.30am and weekends 7.30am-2am – it's NT$800 for the day. **⑦**

🏃 **Whispering Pine Inn** 21 Youya Rd ⊕02/28951531. Established in 1934, this is the best of Beitou's Japanese-era inns with wooden floors and goldfish ponds creating an authentic and remarkably serene atmosphere. It's an expensive hotel, but each room has a large tatami seating area, as well as modern bedroom and bathroom with stone hot-spring bath. The

indoor men's and women's public baths are open to guests only. ❼

Yitsun Hotel 140 Wenchuan Rd ⊕02/28912121. The last of Beitou's three historic Japanese inns, set in a quiet location above the creek with charming, if a little basic accommodation. The stone bathing pools here are particularly attractive – the men-only pool is larger and open to non-guests (NT$300 per hour). ❻

Yangmingshan National Park

A comfortable day-trip from Taipei, **YANGMINGSHAN NATIONAL PARK** (Ⓦwww.ymsnp.gov.tw) sits on a geological fault line sprinkled with dormant **volcanoes**, **hot-spring spas** and well-marked **hiking trails**. The highlight is the climb up **Mount Cising**, the park's highest peak, but it also contains important historical sights – Chiang Kai-shek built his first and last homes in Taiwan here. Minibuses race between the main attractions making it unusually accessible to non-hikers, and being the only national park close to a major city, it's no surprise that Yangmingshan is Taiwan's most popular. Try to avoid visiting at weekends and during holidays, especially in the spring and summer flower-viewing seasons, when the park is at its busiest.

Exploring the park

Buses from Jiantan MRT (see Practicalities, p.145) terminate at the park **bus station** (just beyond 7-Eleven and Starbucks), close to several hotels with hot-spring spas. This is also where the **park shuttle bus** (daily 7am–5.30pm)

Yanmingshan National Park

Yangmingshan National Park	陽明山國家公園	yángmíngshān guójiāgōngyuán
Cingtiangang	擎天崗	qíngtiāngǎng
Grass Mountain Chateau	草山行館	cǎoshān xíngguǎn
Hwa Kang Museum	華岡博物館	huágāng bówùguǎn
Jhuzihhu	竹子湖	zhúzǐhú
Lengshuikeng	冷水坑	lěngshuǐkēng
Lin Yutang House	林語堂故居	línyǔtáng gùjū
Mount Cising	七星山	qīxīnngshān
Mount Datun	大屯山	dàtúnshān
Siaoyoukeng	小油坑	xiǎoyóukēng
Yangming Park	陽明公園	yángmíng gōngyuán
Yangmingshuwu	陽明書屋	yángmíngshūwū

Accommodation and spas

International Hotel	國際大旅館	guójì dàlǚguǎn
Landis Resort	陽明山中國麗緻大飯店	yángmíngshān zhōngguó lìzhì dàfàndiàn
Macao Huayi Village	馬槽花藝村	mǎcáo huāyìcūn
Yangmingshan Hostel	聯勤陽明山招待所	liánqín yángmíngshān zhāodài suǒ

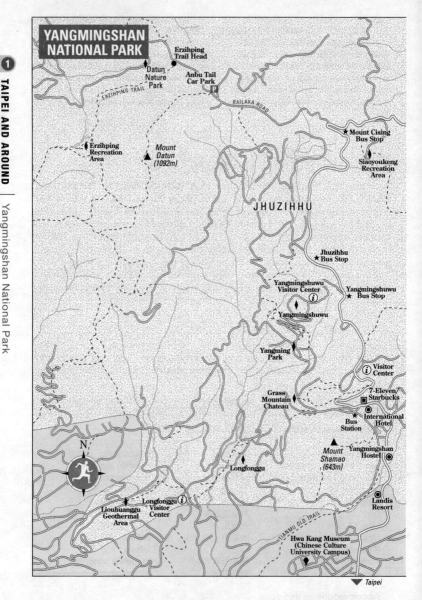

Taipei

departs every 20–30 minutes weekdays, and every 10 minutes at weekends, providing a loop service to all the main points of interest for NT$15 per trip. Weekdays you can buy a NT$60 ticket from the bus station office, which allows unlimited rides all day – at weekends it's NT$50 for six journeys. The first stop is the main park **visitor center** (Tues–Fri 9am–4.30pm, Sat–Sun 8.30am–4.30pm), which is also a surprisingly steep fifteen-minute hike, 700m from the bus station – the sidewalk path goes all the way so there's no need to

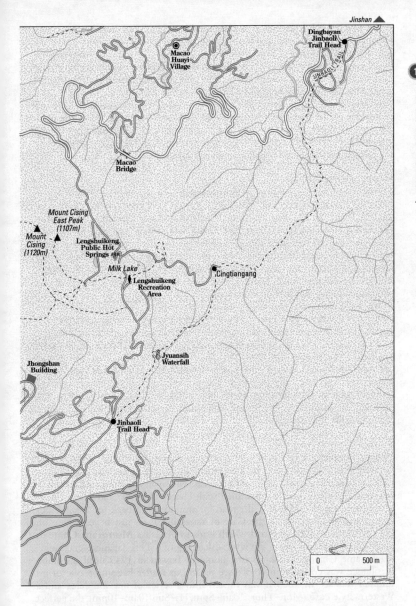

follow the road. The centre contains several exhibition rooms and provides free
information, but it's best to buy one of the more detailed maps from the shop
below if you intend to do a lot of hiking.

Mount Cising

The energetic climb to the top of **Mount Cising** (1120m) takes about two
hours from the visitor centre (2.4km) – the path is well marked and paved most

of the way, though it gets steep in places and it can get cool and cloudy on top. On a clear day, the views across the Taipei Basin and the sea to the north are spectacular. The dormant volcano was once regarded as a **holy mountain** by the Ketagalan *pingpu* tribe – a small geometric mound near the summit may have served as an altar, though it's hard to spot without a guide. On top you'll grasp why the park area used to be known as "Grass Mountain" (*Caoshan*) – the windswept peaks are covered in thick silvergrass. The park was later renamed in honour of the Ming dynasty philosopher Wang Yang-ming. From the peak you have a choice of routes down: the western path to Siaoyoukeng (1.65km) is more dramatic, lined with yellow sulphurous rocks and steaming vents, while the eastern trail leads to Lengshuikeng (1.9km).

Yangmingshuwu

The second shuttle bus stop is **Yangmingshuwu** (Tues–Sun 9am–1.30pm; NT$50), the best preserved of Chiang Kai-shek's fifteen former homes in Taiwan. From the bus stop it's a ten-minute walk down the hill to the **visitor center** (Tues–Sun 9am–4.30pm; ☏02/28611444) where you pick up a guide: tours take around one hour though you'll have to call ahead to ensure English speakers are on hand. From here it's another short walk to the house itself, once surrounded by five hundred armed guards and several tanks. The building is painted camouflage green, another security measure reflecting Chiang's obsessive fear of being attacked or kidnapped.

Originally known as the *Chung Hsing Guesthouse*, it was built in 1970 as a luxury hotel where the Generalissimo could host foreign dignitaries. Instead, it became the last home of the ailing president after Taiwan's withdrawal from the UN saw official visits dwindle. Chiang used it as a summerhouse but it wasn't opened to the public until 1998. Inside it's an odd mix of classical Chinese decor, 1970s Western design (check out Madam Chiang's pink-tiled bathroom) and extreme security: the basement was bolstered by reinforced concrete to resist air attacks, with a series of escape tunnels leading to the gardens and beyond. The contents of the house – furniture, personal items – are authentic reproductions, including a small collection of Madam Chiang's own paintings.

Yangming Park

Twenty minutes' walk downhill from Yangmingshuwu (follow signs to the "Flower Clock") brings you to **Yangming Park**, a popular subsection of the national park often packed out with tourists. The main attraction is **flowers**: in spring the gardens here are crammed with cherry blossoms and azaleas. Walk across the car park and follow the road for around 500m back towards the bus station and you'll come to the Gate of Yangming Park: just beyond here on the right is narrow Hudi Road which leads to ⚘**Grass Mountain Chateau** (daily 9am–5pm; NT$30; ⓦwww.caoshan.org.tw). This Japanese-era building became Chiang Kai-shek's first home in Taiwan in 1949 until his Shilin Residence was complete in 1950 (see p.115), thereafter becoming one of his summer retreats. In 2003 it was turned into a series of **art galleries** and a Western-style **café** (Mon–Thurs 10am–8pm, Fri–Sun 10am–10pm), the perfect spot to enjoy stunning views of Taipei. The Japanese floors, screens and inner courtyard have been artfully restored, while the former living room has become a small display area dedicated to Chiang.

Jhuzihhu to Jyuansih Waterfall

Bus stop number three is **Jhuzihhu**, a dried-up lake now ringed with vegetable and flower farms, and best visited in December, when the **calla lilies** are in bloom. Follow the signs along the road from the bus stop and you'll reach a junction in around 300m: this is the 3–4km loop road that circles the area, dotted with rustic teahouses and restaurants.

Mount Datun (1092m), the park's third highest peak (the military controls Mount Jhuzih, the second highest), is accessible from the fourth bus stop, (confusingly labelled "Mount Cising"): from here it's a 1.5km scenic hike along Bailaka Road to the Anbu Trail car park, and another 1.5km up to the top. The **Erzhiping Trail** is another 500m west along Bailaka Road, where it's a 1.7km stroll to the Erzhiping Recreation Area, good for bird-watching and butterflies (May–June).

The fifth bus stop is the **Siaoyoukeng Recreation Area**, which features a huge and highly photogenic sulphuric steam vent eating into the side of Mount Cising. Stop number six is **Lengshuikeng Recreation Area**, where you'll find free hot-spring baths (see below), and "**Milk Lake**" (Niunai Pond) with its unusual greenish white sulphur surface. The bus stops in front of the hot springs first, makes a small loop to Cingtiangang and returns to Lengshuikeng to stop outside the visitor centre. **Cingtiangang** is a wide, open plateau noted for its silvergrass and herd of cattle: there's a short but pleasant loop trail here as well as access to the more challenging **Jinbaoli Trail** (also known as Fisherman's Old Trail). The latter actually starts at the **Jyuansih Waterfall** bus stop a few kilometres south of Lengshuikeng, and meanders its way 7km north to the small village of Dingbayan on Highway 2 – it's an enjoyable hike that can take half a day, but you'll have to catch the Taipei–Jinshan bus back from here. From the waterfall stop, the shuttle bus completes the loop and ends up back at the bus station. Note that Siaoyoukeng, Lengshuikeng and Cingtiangang have small visitor centres and basic shops on site – opening times are similar to the main visitor centre.

Practicalities

The fastest way to Yangmingshan is to take the MRT to Jiantan and catch Red #5 bus (daily; 6am–11pm, NT$15), or #260 (daily; 5.10am–8pm, NT$15) on Wenlin Road just outside the station. Buses go every twenty minutes or every ten at peak times. From Beitou #230 also rattles up the hill (NT$15) and #9 goes all the way to Jhuzihhu. Taipei to Jinshan buses cut straight across the park; catch these from the Government Insurance Building stop near the junction of Gongguan and Qingdao West roads or within the park, near the bus station. Buses run 6.50am–6pm, every hour from 8am.

The park's acidic sulphur **hot springs** are some of the most famous in Taiwan. A cluster of **hotels** near the park bus station allows day-guests to use their spa facilities for a fee, though staying the night isn't good value unless you're desperate to escape the city. Most places are slightly busier in the winter, but come midweek and you'll avoid the crowds. If you're feeling adventurous try the free public pools – with separate baths for men and women you're expected to be naked.

Beyond the hotels and a couple of local diners near the bus station, **eating options** are limited in the park, so stock up at 7-Eleven or Starbucks if you want to snack. The most atmospheric places to eat are the restaurants around Jhuzihhu, and the *Grass Mountain Chateau* (see p.144).

Hotels and spas
International Hotel 7 Hushan Rd ☎02/28617100. Conveniently located close to the bus station with a distinctive stone facade, this hotel opened in

1952 making it the oldest hot-spring resort on the mountain. Just 400m from the source of untainted spring water, the separate male and female indoor public pools are fringed with attractive old stone walls (7am–9pm; NT$80; lockers NT$10). Accommodation is nothing special, but rooms come with private stone baths – you can rent these for 3hr (NT$990). ❺

Landis Resort 237 Gerzhi Rd ☎02/28616661 ⓦwww.landisresort.com.tw. Redesigned in 2003, Yangmingshan's most luxurious hotel has a stylish interior with a contemporary Japanese feel, slate walls and Zen-inspired minimalist decor in the bedrooms. Day-guests can use the spa pools, spring-water swimming pool and gym for NT$1000 (7am–10pm). Taipei buses stop outside, or it's a 20min walk from Yangmingshan bus station. ❻

Lengshuikeng Public Hot Springs (opposite the first Lengshuikeng shuttle bus stop). Separate but basic male and female pools (free) housed in attractive wooden chalets – simply walk in and strip off, leaving clothes on the shelves by the pool. There's also a shallow pool for foot-soaking outside. Lengshuikeng means "cool water pit":

at 40 degrees this is considered a relatively cold spring. Daily 9am–5pm.

Macao Huayi Village 20, Lane 251, Xuzihu Rd. Getting here is difficult but worth the effort – it's an aging resort but there are a range of outdoor spring water and volcanic mud pools to choose from and it's only NT$150 for unlimited use. It's located off the main Yangmingshan to Jinshan Highway, beyond the Macao Bridge and accessible via the Jinshan bus or by taxi – it's a very long walk from the shuttle bus route. Open 24hrs.

Yangmingshan Hostel 12 Yangming Road Sec 1 ☎02/28616601. Originally built in 1924 but renovated several times, this is actually a hotel with small, basic rooms. The public hot-spring pools (through the Chinese gate on the left) are much better, with the original stone work tastefully restored making it an atmospheric place to soak (8am–10.30pm; NT$250). Private baths with large, shiny thermometers cost NT$120 per hour (per person). Most buses stop just outside or it's a 10min walk from the bus station. ❹

Around Yangmingshan

If you have more time, it's worth exploring a couple of places on the way back from the national park, both easily accessible from the main bus route into Taipei. The **Hwa Kang Museum** (Mon–Fri 9am–4pm; free) is located within the Chinese Culture University, just over 2km south of the park bus station. The museum's collection comprises almost 50,000 historical artefacts from China and Taiwan, though only a fraction is displayed at one time. Highlights include work by painters **Zhang Da-qian** and **Pu Xin-yu**, prehistoric pottery and jade from the Peinan site (see p.422) and an original Tao canoe from Lanyu. The museum is located in the Hsiao Fong Memorial Building, a ten-minute walk along Aifu 2nd Street and Huagang Road from the university bus stop (#260) – Red #5 goes all the way into the campus. It's the first building on the left as you enter the university: the library occupies the middle block, while the museum is on the left side. You can walk back into Taipei from here via **Tianmu Old Trail,** which is clearly signposted on Aifu 3rd Street, not far from the main road. It's around 2km to the start of Zhongshan Road Section 7, where you can take bus #220 into the city.

Further south along the main bus route is **Lin Yutang House** (Tues–Sun 9am–5pm; NT$20) at 141 Yangde Road Section 2, a small but atmospheric monument to one of China's greatest writers. Lin had a peripatetic career which saw him live in the West for many years, and in 1937 he topped the *New York Times* bestseller list for a year with *The Importance of Living*. He spent the last ten years of his life in this house, dying in 1976 – he's buried in the garden. Lin's fame has faded somewhat, but the house is certainly special and commands a magnificent viewpoint over Taipei. Bus #260 and Red #5 stop outside.

Danshui and around

Set on the northern bank of the Danshui River, 20km north of Taipei, the old port town of **DANSHUI** is hugely popular with local day-trippers and tourists from the south. The chief draw is the food – at the weekends you'll

Danshui and around

Danshui	淡水	dànshuǐ
Bali	八里	bālǐ
Danshui Chang Ti	淡水長提	dànshuǐ chángtí
Fisherman's Wharf	漁人碼頭	yúrén m
Fort Santo Domingo	紅毛城	hóngmáo chéng
Fuyou Temple	福佑宮	fúyòu gōng
Guandu Temple	關渡宮	guāndù gōng
Guanyinshan	觀音山	guānyīnshān
Huwei Fort	滬尾砲臺	hùwěi pàotái
Little White House	小白宮	xiǎobáigōng
Longshan Temple	龍山寺	lóngshān sì
Malas	瑪拉斯	mǎlāsī
Martyrs' Memorial	臺北縣忠烈祠	táiběixiàn zhōngliècí
Oxford College	理學堂大書院	lǐxúe dàshūyùan
Red Castle	達觀樓	dáguānlóu
Shihsanhang Museum of Archaeology	十三行博物館	shísānháng bówùguǎn
Tamkang High School	淡江中學	dànjiāng zhōngxúe
Teng Feng Fish Ball Museum	登峰魚丸博物館	dēngfēng yúwán bówùguǎn
Yinshan Temple	鄞山寺	yínshān sì

see thousands of Taiwanese trawling up and down its wharves and old streets eagerly stuffing themselves with local specialties and enjoying carnival games. Danshui has plenty more to offer however: it's packed with historical attractions that include **Fort San Domingo** and a small but fascinating collection of sights associated with Canadian missionary **George Leslie Mackay**. Further south is the appealing temple at **Guandu**, while across the river the town of **Bali** contains one of the region's best museums, and the peak of **Guanyinshan** offers a magnificent panorama over the whole Taipei Basin.

Some history

Originally known as Huwei, Danshui literally means "fresh water", and is thought to have been the name given to the area by early Chinese seafarers. The settlement was established around **Fort Santo Domingo** (known as "Fort San Domingo" today), built by the Spanish in 1628 and later occupied by the Dutch (see Contexts p.506). By 1662 the Dutch had been driven off the island, the village growing slowly as more Chinese immigrants started to arrive in the eighteenth century. Danshui boomed after the Treaty of Beijing opened up the port to foreign trade in 1860 – **Robert Swinhoe**, the first British vice consul, arrived a year later and a customs office was in operation by 1862 (the treaty stipulated that Chinese Customs should be administered by British officers). *Hongs* such as Jardine Matheson and Buttler & Co were soon busy exporting oolong and Baozhong **tea**, but Danshui's downfall was its lack of a deepwater harbour – from 1906 it began to lose precedence to Keelung and by the 1920s had become a relative backwater. Today, in addition to a healthy tourist trade, Danshui is the home to two universities and growing numbers of Taipei commuters.

The Town

Most of the action in Danshui takes place along the **old wharf area**, packed at weekends and lined with cheap food stalls and shops (see p.150). From the MRT

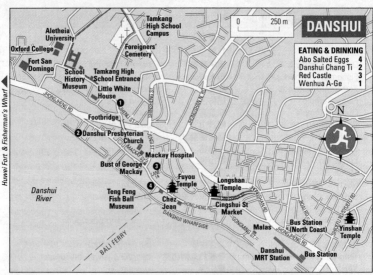

Hongshulin MRT Station & Taipei ▼

station it's possible to walk along the riverbank as far as the old Danshui Customs Wharf, just below Fort San Domingo, or take the inland route past some of the town's historical sights. Start with a quick look at **Yinshan Temple** (daily 6am–9pm), a few minutes' walk north along Syuefu Road (signposted Shiue Fu Road) just across Jhongjheng Road from the station. Established in 1822, it's the only temple in Taiwan dedicated to the Dingguang Buddha, a monk with miraculous powers who lived in China during the early Song dynasty. It's a tranquil place these days, a traditional building with a courtyard and small main shrine. Retrace your steps and turn right along Jhongjheng Road, crossing Jhongshan Road and on to the junction with Gongming Street. The narrow lane opposite leads into **Cingshui Street Market**, which has more character than the wharf area and features some tasty snack food, but closes after lunch. Turning left along Cingshui Street and then first right should take you to **Longshan Temple** (daily 5am–8.30pm), a peaceful shrine to Guanyin dating from 1858, with an elegant gold statue of the Buddhist bodhisattva in the main hall. Return to Cingshui Street and turn right: when you reach the main road ahead turn left to return to Jhongjheng Road. Turn right here and a short walk on the left is *Chez Jean* at no. 81, which has been producing Chinese-style cakes since 1935 – their hefty sesame cakes are delicious (NT$105). The grandly titled **Musee des Trois Mouquetaires** (daily 9am–9pm; free) at the back has small displays of cake-making implements labelled in French and German, and some English leaflets. A little further on the other side of the road you'll see **Fuyou Temple** (daily 5am–9pm), completed in 1796, making it Danshui's oldest and important because of the historic inscriptions on its columns and steles. The temple is dedicated to Mazu, which is not surprising given its proximity to the wharf. Opposite is the **Teng Feng Fish Ball Museum** (daily 4–9pm; free), another quirky Danshui attraction, opened by one of the town's most popular fish-ball makers and worth a quick look. More local snacks are on offer just beyond here at no. 135 – *Abo Salted Eggs* is a good place to stock up on Danshui's famous "iron eggs" (see p.150), while opposite is Lane 14 leading to the *Red Castle* (see p.151).

Memorials to George Mackay

A little further along Jhongjheng Road is the junction with Jensi Street and the bust of **George Mackay** (see box below), replete with gigantic beard. This lies opposite the narrow, unmarked lane known as **Mackay Street** leading to the white stone **Mackay Hospital** (closed to visitors), which he opened in 1897, and the current **Danshui Presbyterian Church**, built in 1933 on the site of the chapel Mackay established in 1890. It still attracts a sizeable congregation and is only open on Sundays. Keep walking and turn right at the junction ahead, then follow the road uphill, over the footbridge and straight up to Jhenli Street at Wenhua Elementary School. Turn right here and you'll see *Wenhua Ah Ge* (see p.151), while to the left is the **Little White House** (Tues–Sun 9.30am–6pm; NT$40) built between 1869 and 1876 and also known by the catchy epithet "Qing dynasty Chief Taxation Officer's Residence in Danshui". Serving as Danshui's customs house in the nineteenth century, the brilliant white colonial building was immaculately refurbished in 2005, though the rooms are a little bare – the exhibits inside provide some history and background on the site, with adequate English labelling. A little further ahead is the entrance to **Tamkang High School** (Mon–Sat 8am–4.30pm, Sun 1–5pm; free), which includes several Mackay-related sights, notably his **grave** at the far end of the campus amidst those of his immediate family. Behind this is the **Foreigners' Cemetery** (1867–1974), testimony to the town's early colonial history. Just inside the school entrance on the left is the **School History Museum** with displays on Mackay's life labelled in English. Mackay's original boys school (the precursor of Tamkang) was known as **Oxford College**, and you can still see the main building (used 1882 -1901) just inside the campus of Aletheia University, a bit further along Jhenli Road. Construction was funded by the concerned residents of Mackay's hometown in Oxford, Ontario after they found out he'd been teaching students under a banyan tree since 1872. It's not usually open to the public. From here the road swings left, and leads downhill to Fort San Domingo.

Fort San Domingo to Fisherman's Wharf

Touted as Danshui's premier historic site, **Fort San Domingo** (Tues–Sun 9.30am–10pm; NT$60) known as *Hong Mao Cheng* in Chinese ("Fort of the Red-haired Barbarians"), comprises two separate buildings. Walking up the slope from the main entrance, you'll arrive at the **fort** itself, though nothing remains of the Spanish original built 1636–38, a stone replacement for the wooden stockade they'd established in 1628. The current structure is a mixture

---

George Mackay

Canadian missionary **George Leslie Mackay**, is still fondly remembered in Taiwan for his pioneering work in the fields of education and medicine (he's famous for the somewhat gruesome achievement of having extracted over 21,000 teeth), as well as his primary task of establishing the Presbyterian church in northern Taiwan. Born in Oxford, Ontario in 1844, he came to Taiwan in 1871, and after a brief stint in Kaohsiung arrived in Danshui in 1872. In 1878, Mackay married a local woman and settled in Danshui, which was to be his home until he died in 1901. Although there was considerable resistance to his early proselytizing efforts (vividly described in his 1895 memoir *From Far Formosa*), he gathered a sufficient number of disciples to build north Taiwan's first church here in 1882, as well as a boys school (Oxford College) – his educational legacy continues at Tamkang High School.

of the Dutch fortifications completed in 1644 (and known as "Fort Anthony") and renovations (including the portico and red paint job) made after 1867 when it became the permanent **British Consulate**, leased from the Chinese government. You can explore some of the rooms inside, all well labelled in English. The red-brick **consular residence** next to the fort (built in 1891) is a typical example of the colonial-style architecture of the time, with a couple of rooms furnished in reasonably authentic Victorian decor, and more exhibits related to the site. The Brits maintained a presence here (with a brief hiatus 1941–45) until 1971.

Leaving the fort, turn right along Jhongjheng Road and in around ten minutes you should reach the turning leading to **Huwei Fort** (Tues–Sun 9am–5pm; free). The fort lies at the centre of the **Tamsui Historical Area**, highlighting some of Danshui's lesser-known sights scattered around the borders of the adjacent Taipei Golf and Country Club. Built by a German architect in 1886 for the Qing government, Huwei Fort never saw action – today it's a pristine example of a sizeable nineteenth-century gun fortification, though there's not much to do other than wander the main courtyard and clamber on the walls. Leaflets available here outline other attractions in the area, many related to the Sino-French War of 1884-5. Next door the **Martyr's Memorial** (Sat–Sun 9am–5pm; free) is a tranquil monument to Chinese Nationalist soldiers killed in conflicts since the 1911 Revolution. It was originally built by the Japanese in 1939 as a shrine to Emperor Meiji, and converted in 1974 with Ming-style architecture.

It's a boring two-kilometre walk from here to **Fisherman's Wharf**, Danshui's newest attraction at the mouth of the river, but there are also buses that ply up and down the main road from the MRT station. Restaurants and shops surround the new marina and it's a prime sunset-viewing location, but otherwise not that interesting. Catch the **ferry** back to the old wharf area (NT$40) or take the "Blue Highway" to Guandu (see box p.108).

Practicalities

Danshui is the last station on the Danshui MRT line, just 35 minutes from Taipei Main Station, making it an easy day-trip from the capital. There's little point in staying the night here, but it is a convenient starting point for trips to the north coast (see p.165). **Ferries** run from the wharf a short walk from the MRT station to Bali every 10–15 minutes (daily 6.15am–8pm, 7min; NT$18, NT$20 bicycles) and Fisherman's Wharf every 15–20 minutes (daily 9am–8pm, 12min; NT$40). Buy tickets from the booths on the wharf before boarding.

Danshui is a cheap place to **shop** for traditional Chinese clothes, handicrafts or antiques, with a few decent stores tucked in between the kitsch along Gongming and Jhongjheng Roads. **Malas** at 83 Gongming Road is owned by a member of the Bunun tribe, and the largest aboriginal handicraft store in the Taipei area: it's touristy but worth a look if you're planning to spend most of your time in the capital.

Eating

Danshui is famous throughout Taiwan for its delicious snack food. Favourites include **fish crisps** (*yu su*), sold in packets all over town, "**iron eggs**" (*tieh dan*, chicken or dove eggs boiled until they shrink, harden, and turn black), **fish ball soup** (*yuwan tang*) and seafood such as grilled squid. **Gongming Street** runs parallel to the riverside from the station and is packed with snack stalls, as is the first section of the wharf. *Danshui Chang Ti* at 9, Alley 21, Jhongjheng Road (daily 10am–midnight) is one of several pleasant cafés with outside tables towards the end of the promenade, just beyond the shady banyan trees on a quieter stretch of the river. Coffee and tea (NT$150) and light, Western-style meals and sandwiches are available from NT$240. It's signposted in Chinese but there are English menus. 🍴 *Red Castle* at 6, Lane 2, Sanmin Street, (accessible via the 106 steps at the end of Lane 14 off Jhongjheng Road), is one of the highlights of the town – built by British merchants in 1899 in colonial style reminiscent of the consular residence, today it houses a Chinese restaurant and coffeeshop (daily 11am–1am) on the third floor with one of the best views in Danshui, especially at sunset. Coffee or tea is NT$150–190. For lunch try *Wenhua A-Ge* (daily 9.30am–6.30pm) at 6-4 Jhenli Street, near the Little White House, which has been cooking up sumptuous *a-ge* (NT$25), tofu stuffed with fish and noodles, and fried like Japanese tempura, for over 100 years.

Guandu

It's worth taking a look at **Guandu Temple** (daily 5am–10pm) before heading back to Taipei, a fifteen-minute walk south from Guandu MRT station (which is just eight minutes south of Danshui by MRT) – take the Dadu Road exit (1) and follow the signs. This is one of Taipei's oldest religious sites – there's been a shrine here since 1661 with the original temple built in 1712. The **Main Hall** is dedicated to Mazu, with side altars to Guanyin and Wenchang Dijun. Behind this is a five-storey extension with halls dedicated to numerous gods, and surprisingly scenic views of Taipei. To the right side of the main hall is a **tunnel** which leads almost 100m into the hill, lined with *devas* and Buddhist carvings, emerging at a small shrine to Guanyin and a terrace with fine views of the Danshui River. A variety of stalls cash in on regular tour bus visitors and worshippers around the banyan tree outside, while just around the corner lies **Guandu Riverside Park** containing a food court and the wharf (see Blue Highway p.108). You can rent mountain-bikes here (daily 8am–7pm; NT$100 1hr).

Bali

It's a short five-minute ferry ride from Danshui to **BALI**, a fast developing suburb of Taipei on the left bank of the Danshui River. Bali was a thriving port in the eighteenth century, but after its wharves began to silt up in the 1840s business moved to the other side of the river. Today the riverbank is being developed into a series of parks and attractions dubbed the **Shore-Community-Museum** by local authorities, but the real highlight is the **Shihsanhang Museum of Archaeology** further along the coast. The town itself is an unattractive mix of light industry and residential development, but the magical views of Yangmingshan across the river more than compensate.

The town and around

Arriving by boat, you'll disembark at **Bali Wharf Street**, a smaller version of Danshui's promenade of snack stalls and carnival games. From here you can walk up the narrow lane opposite the ferry quay to Jhonghua Road and catch the R13 bus, or alternatively hire a bike and **cycle** the 4km to the archeology museum. This is not a bad idea if you have time – the route is well marked and bikes can be hired from the shop close to where the ferry docks (NT$50 per hour for mountain bikes, NT$80 for tandems). The riverside trail cuts through several parks: you'll pass the Laorong Bastion, a suitably camouflaged ex-army lookout post now used as park space, and the Zou-an Theatre, which is just a pavilion on the riverbank. More interesting are the mangrove swamps of the **Shueibizai Park** and adjacent **Wazihwei Conservation Area** further ahead. With Hongshulin across the river, these are the world's northernmost mangroves – and certainly the world's most incongruous with industrial estates just metres away; signboards along the trail provide information on local wildlife. After this you come to a junction where Bowuguan Road takes you straight to the Shihsanhang Museum, about 1km away, or you can detour up the **Guanhai Walkway** for more views of the river and return via **Wazihwei**. This is an old village by Taipei standards with a couple of buildings dating from the 1880s – most of the people here have the surname "Chang" so it's also known as "Chang Village."

Shihsanhang Museum of Archaeology

Tucked away behind the pot-shaped domes of the local water treatment plant, **Shihsanhang Museum of Archaeology** (Apr–Oct Tues–Fri 9.30am–5pm, Sat–Sun 9.30am–7pm; Nov–March Tues–Fri 9.30am–5pm, Sat–Sun 9.30am–6pm; NT$100; Ⓦ www.sshm.tpc.gov.tw) was opened in 2003 to display a fascinating collection of archeological finds dating from 200 to 1500 AD. The building itself has won several awards and comprises three distinct parts shaped from concrete and steel, while the actual dig site now lies within the treatment plant, and a small area of this is open to the public. The finds are particularly significant because it's the only prehistoric site in Taiwan to show evidence of **iron smelting** and in addition, **Tang dynasty coins** suggest the community traded with merchants from China. Perhaps the most remarkable object on display here is the mysterious **anthropomorphic jar**, one of the few artefacts ever found in Taiwan depicting a human face. The collection isn't huge but it's still impressive – it even includes **jade earrings** which experts believe were already 1,000-year-old antiques when acquired by the people at Shihsanhang. The museum also highlights the archeological process that lies behind the discoveries including excavation techniques and how, crucially, the experts made their assumptions. The Shihsanhang site was abandoned five hundred years ago and its inhabitants remain a mystery – the logical conclusion that they were the ancestors of the Ketagalan, the aboriginal tribe that occupied the area when Dutch and Chinese settlers arrived in the seventeenth century, is still debated. Most of the displays have English labels, though at present the only audio-visual presentation in English is the introductory video on the first floor.

Practicalities

To reach Bali from **Taipei** take the MRT to Guandu Station and switch to the frequent R13 **bus**, just outside exit 1 (NT$15), which swings past the wharf area and then the museum in around twenty minutes. There's plenty **to eat** around the wharf: located opposite the ferry pier, the specialty at *Sheh Family Peacock Clam* (daily 10am–9pm) is not clams, but large **mussels** cooked in basil with peacock tails painted on the shells (NT$200).

Guanyinshan

Dominating the skyline above Bali, **Guanyinshan** (612m) is the only part of the North Coast and Guanyinshan National Scenic Area (see p.164) south of the Danshui River. It's the closest thing the Taipei region has to a holy mountain, supposedly resembling bodhisattva Guanyin in repose and littered with numerous temples dedicated to the Buddhist deity. Hundreds of temples in Taiwan have been constructed with andesite rock (known as Guanyin Stone) from the mountain over the years, but quarrying is now restricted – these days it's better known for bird-watching, particularly for hawks and eagles between March and May, and the panoramic views of the Taipei Basin from the top.

Hiking trails crisscross the mountain, but the easiest way to climb the main peak is to start from **Lingyun Temple** on the south side and end up in Bali, where there are plenty of places to eat and you can catch the ferry back to Danshui. The temple was built in 1739 and dedicated to Guanyin, though the current structure is a recent construction. From here it's 2km to the top via a well-signposted stone path that passes the larger **Lingyun Zen (Chan) Temple**, built in 1882 but now looking a bit like a car park – its 11m statue of Guanyin in the main hall is one of Taiwan's largest. More rewarding is the **Guanyinshan visitor center** (daily 9am–5pm; free), which has friendly English-speaking guides, an exhibition room and video presentations on the mountain's volcanic origins, temples and history. The centre is another 1km along the road from Lingyun Temple, or an energetic 1.1km detour from the main trail down a steep path – you'll have to walk back the same way to reach the peak.

The summit of Guanyinshan is known as **Yinghan Peak**, "Peak of the Brave" or more vividly "Tough Man Peak" to encourage the scores of young army recruits that once trained here. It's actually 609m high, but the Yinghan Monument on top adds another 3m. From here it's 4.6km straight down to Bali Wharf along similarly well-marked paths and lanes – you should emerge on the main Bali highway where you turn left and walk a further 600m to the narrow lane leading to the wharf on the right.

Practicalities

To reach the southern slopes of Guanyinshan take a **bus** from Tacheng Street in Taipei, just north of Zhongxiao Road and the North Gate in Zhongzheng district. Buses depart from 6.40am daily (every 40–50min; 1hr; NT$41). The final stop is Lingyun Temple – going the other way buses depart at similar intervals until 6.10pm. Bring food with you – there's not much to eat until you get to Bali. At weekends, a **free shuttle bus** connects Bali Wharf with the Visitor centre and Lingyun Temple every 30 minutes.

Yingge and Sansia

Just 20km south of the capital, the historic towns of **Yingge** (also spelt "Yingko") and **Sansia** make a fascinating day-trip, combining the splendour of Sansia's **Zushih Temple** with some unique shopping opportunities – Yingge is Taiwan's pottery capital and overflows with over eight hundred ceramic shops

Yingge and Sansia		
Yingge	鶯歌	yīnggē
Sansia	三峽	sānxiá
Historical Museum of Sansia Town	三峽鎮歷史博物館	sānxiázhèn lìshǐ bówùguǎn
Liu Mei-shu Memorial Hall	李梅樹紀念館	lǐméishù jìniànguǎn
Sanjiaoyong Restaurant	三角湧餐飲坊	sānjiǎoyǒng cānyǐnfāng
Taipei County Hakka Museum	台北縣客家文化園區	táiběi xiàn kèjiā wénhuà yúan qū
Yingge Ceramics Museum	鶯歌陶瓷博物館	yīnggē táocí bówùguǎn
Yingge Old Street	鶯歌老街	yīnggē lǎojiē
Zushih Temple	祖師廟	zǔshī miào

and factories. If that doesn't appeal, the **Yingge Ceramics Museum** is one of the region's best and good enough to justify the twenty-minute train ride.

Yingge

YINGGE means "parrot" in Taiwanese, thought to refer to the bird-shaped rock north of the centre, but the town is best known today as Taiwan's premier ceramics manufacturing centre. The industry was founded by a Fujian immigrant called **Wu An** – legend has it that he recognized the quality of the local soil in 1805 and invited his relatives to join him in a pottery-making venture. The Wu family dominated production thereafter, until the Jianshan Ceramic Cooperative broke their monopoly in 1921 and the Japanese introduced modern kilns in the 1930s. Yingge boomed in the postwar period but like many traditional industries in Taiwan, declined in the 1980s, with tourism and the art trade keeping the dollars flowing today.

Fifteen minutes' walk from the train station, **Yingge Ceramics Museum** at 200 Wenhua Road (Tues–Fri 9.30am–5pm, Sat 9.30am–6pm; NT$100; Ⓦ www.ceramics.tpc.gov.tw) tells you everything you'd ever want to know about Yingge's history and ceramics in general, with an additional exhibition on future prospects and the use of ceramics in advanced technology – the only gripe is that the film presentations don't have English subtitles yet, though everything else has bilingual labels. For NT$50 you can take part in a regular DIY session in the ceramics studio (in the basement) – at the weekends you need to register half an hour before a class, but during the week you'll have to book ahead. The museum hosts an annual **ceramics festival** in October. To get here from the station, turn right after leaving the turnstiles, following the signs to "Wunhua Road", then turn right again when you exit the station – keep walking till you reach a crossroads. Turn left here (it's still Wenhua Road) and the museum is beyond the garage on the right-hand side.

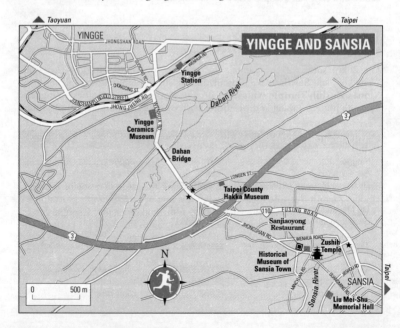

Leaving the museum, head back to the crossroads and continue under the railway bridge, taking the first left up a gentle slope: this is Jianshanpu Road, otherwise known as **Yingge Old Street** and the birthplace of Yingge ceramics, though you won't see any old buildings here. Despite the palm trees and paved road it's just a modern strip of pottery shops and snack stalls. Nevertheless, it is one of the best places in Taiwan to stock up on ceramics ranging from cheap bargains to classically designed pieces with an innovative, modern twist. Shops in Yingge tend to close around 6pm.

Practicalities

Getting to Yingge is easy: take any **train** heading south from Taipei Main Station (NT$40) – the only trains that don't stop are the express services. Moving on to **Sansia**, the #39 **bus** from Taoyuan stops at the station's Wenhua Road exit around every 15–20min (daily 6.10am–10.30pm; NT$20) and takes ten minutes, but you can also catch #702 or #19 from the stop close to the ceramics museum further along Wenhua Road. **Taxis** to Sansia from Yingge station cost around NT$150. For **food**, it's best to stick to the snack stalls and simple cafés along Old Street.

Sansia

Three kilometres south of Yingge across the Dahan River, **SANSIA** is the home of one of Taiwan's most striking temples, a stylish museum and an atmospheric old street. In the nineteenth century the town emerged as an important distribution centre for camphor and tea along the banks of the Sansia River, later developing its own cloth-dyeing industry. By the 1970s these trades were in decline, and though agriculture is still an important part of the local economy, tourism has provided a much needed boost.

Before you reach Sansia proper, it's worth stopping at the **Taipei County Hakka Museum** (Tues–Fri 9.30am–5pm, Sat–Sun 9.30am–5pm; free) located on the outskirts of town: if you're taking the bus from Yingge get off just after the Dahan Bridge and turn left down Longen Street – the museum is five minutes away. The museum is really a lavish Hakka (see p.204) cultural centre, with one very creative gallery blending multi-media installations with glass-cased exhibits, and a couple of temporary exhibition rooms. It's best to visit at the weekends, when the **performance centre** hosts various dramas, dancing and singing shows in the Hakka language. The shop on site sells attractive gifts and the **restaurant** serves decent Hakka fare, including *ban tiao* (fried noodles, NT$250), *lei cha* ("cereal tea", NT$150) and a *biandang* or special "lunchbox", served in a ceramic dish you can take away, wrapped in a multicoloured Hakka-style cloth bag (NT$299). To get into town from here, you'll have to walk back to the bus stop or flag down a taxi (NT$80).

The Town

Tucked away in the heart of Sansia, and facing the river in front of Changfu Bridge, **Zushih Temple** (daily 6am–9pm) is one of Taiwan's most beautiful. It's not far from Old Street (Mincyuan Road) at the end of narrow Changfu Street, and dedicated to popular deity Qingshui (see p.530). Though it lacks the grandeur and scale of larger temples, its lavish decor and intricate craftsmanship make this a unique showcase for temple art – for many connoisseurs it's the finest on the island. Though the temple dates from 1769 it has been rebuilt three times – the most recent renovation began in 1947 and depending on who you ask, is still ongoing. The **Main Hall** housing Qingshui's image is flanked by shrines to the Moon God on the left (West) and Sun God on the right (East). The key here is attention to detail: the temple beams are plastered in intricate carvings covered in real gold foil and it's one of the few shrines in Taiwan to use **bronze sculptures** throughout. The **dragon pillars** here are particularly ornate: there are supposed to be an incredible 156 inside, though not all have been completed – the six pillars in the central courtyard are regarded as the finest examples. If you're in Taiwan around Chinese New Year, try and visit on Lunar January 6 – the **festival** marking Qingshui's birthday is particularly colourful.

The man credited with all this artistic perfection is **Liu Mei-shu** (1902–1983), Sansia's first mayor and an exceptional painter. You can view more of his artwork and personal effects at the **Liu Mei-shu Memorial Hall** (Sat–Sun & holidays 10am–5pm; NT$50), a short walk south of the temple across Changfu Bridge. Follow the signs right onto Jhonghua Road (signposted "Junghua Road") then immediately left onto Lane 43: the hall is on the right at no.10, within a residential complex.

Mincyuan Road lies 50m behind the temple, and south of here this becomes Sansia's **Old Street** with most of the one hundred plus red-brick shop fronts dating from the late nineteenth century. It's a good place to browse for antiques and gifts and there are plenty of places to eat Sansia's most famous snack, **braised bamboo shoots**. Retrace your steps north and turn left at Jhongshan Road: the **Historical Museum of Sansia Town** (daily 9am–5pm; free) is at no.18, located in a 72-year-old shophouse. The museum provides an interesting introduction to the town's history, though it's only worth a visit if you can read Chinese.

Practicalities

Sansia is close enough to Yingge to walk but don't try it – there's no footpath on Dahan Bridge. **Buses** from Yingge should drop you on Fusing Road just north of the Sansia Bridge, from where it's a short walk along the river to the temple. It's possible to take a bus from Sansia straight back to **Taipei**: the easiest place to catch one is Fusing Road where #702 or #19 pass every few minutes and take about an hour (NT$45). Buses should stop near Ximen MRT station. In the other direction bus #702 departs from the row of bus stops on Changhua Road, north of exit 6 from Ximen MRT. For **food**, try Old Street or the *Sanjiaoyong Restaurant* at 40 Jhongshan Road, the most atmospheric **teahouse** in Sansia. It opened in 1994 but occupies an old shophouse and serves excellent tea and snacks (NT$150 for a small pot).

Wulai

Lying in a valley 25km south of Taipei, **WULAI** is the most popular day-trip from the capital, offering magnificent mountain scenery and northern Taiwan's highest **waterfall**. It's also a traditional home of the **Atayal** tribe, though the mixture of kitsch stores and dance shows on offer are aimed squarely at tourists. The new museum is definitely worth a visit though, and a short walk beyond the tourist carnival lie quiet valleys and rivers offering some beautiful **hikes** and genuine Atayal villages. Wulai is also one of three popular **hot-spring** areas near Taipei (with Beitou and Yangmingshan), though the main difference here is that the water comprises sulphur carbonate and is completely clear – the main bonus for bathers is that it doesn't have that rotten egg smell.

Wulai Hot Springs Village

The bus from Taipei terminates right in front of **Wulai Hot Springs Village** – cross the bridge over the Tonghou River ahead to run the gauntlet of tourist

Wulai

Wulai	烏來村	wūlái cūn
Doll Valley	娃娃谷	wáwágǔ
Neidong National Forest Recreation Area	內洞國家森林遊樂區	nèidòng guójiā sēnlín yóulè qū
Wulai Atayal Museum	烏來泰雅博物館	wūlái tàiyǎ bówùguǎn
Wulai Falls	烏來瀑布	wūlái pùbù
Aboriginal Restaurant	原住民美食餐廳	yuánzhùmín měishí cāntīng
Yunsian Dreamland	雲仙樂園	yúnxiān lèyuán
Xinxian	信賢村	xìnxián cūn
Xiaochuanyuan Hot Springs	小川園溫泉	xiǎochuānyuán wēnquán

Accommodation and spas

Shanggu Qingliu	溫泉會館	shànggǔ qīngliú wēnquán huìguǎn
Spring Park Urai Spa & Resort	春秋烏來	chūnqiū wūlái
Wulai Spring Resort	烏來名湯溫泉會館	wūlái míngtāng wēnquán huìguǎn

shops, snack stalls and gift stores. This is where most of Wulai's cheaper accommodation and spas are located, while the **Wulai Atayal Museum** (Tues–Fri 9am–5pm, Sat–Sun 9am–6pm; NT$50) is an absorbing introduction to the valley and the people that once dominated the area. Opened in 2005 as Taiwan's only Atayal museum, its three floors focus on history and culture, with explanations in English. Originally called Tranan, "Wulai" loosely translates as "hot spring" and comes from the Atayal word "urai" meaning poisonous. At the end of the main street you'll come to a second bridge over the wider Nanshih River, from where Wulai's public hot-spring pools (free) are clearly visible on the far right bank – the pools are carved into the rocks along the riverside and tend to get very busy. To try them, turn right when you cross the bridge and take the first path down to the river on the right.

Wulai Falls

From the Nanshih bridge you can walk to the falls in around twenty minutes or take the **miniature railway** (daily 8am–5pm; NT$50 one-way) located up the flight of steps nearby and departing every few minutes along old tram tracks. The road is rarely crowded and is closed to most vehicles – after passing a row of hotels and spas it rises along the side of a thickly wooded gorge providing fantastic views. Just after you first spot the falls you'll come to the train terminus and the second tourist village – the view of **Wulai Falls** on the far bank is certainly picturesque, and at 80m it's northern Taiwan's highest, but best during the rainy season. The *Aboriginal Restaurant* at no. 12 hosts lively **dance performances** upstairs four times a day (10.40am, 11.30am, 2.40pm and 3.30pm) – tickets cost NT$200 and can be purchased from the booth near the stone steps. The **cable car** station (daily 7.30am–8pm; NT$220 return) is a short walk up the steps, and glides across the river to **Yunsian Dreamland** (daily 8am–5pm; entry with cable car ticket) on top of the waterfall – an odd and rather faded mixture of theme park rides and gardens firmly targeted at families, tour groups, and dating couples. The *Yun Hsien Resort* (☎02/26616383, Ⓦwww.yun-hsien.com.tw; ❼) on site is expensive, but once the day-trippers leave it becomes a tranquil retreat: come midweek and all you'll hear are the

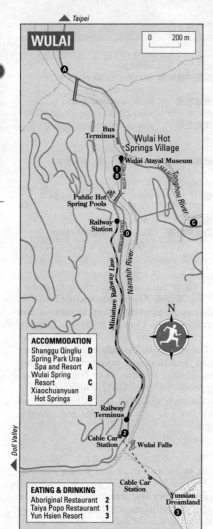

sounds of running water and the mountain forest.

Doll Valley

Walk a few minutes upstream from the falls and you'll leave most of the tourists behind. Scenic **Doll Valley** is a pleasant hour-long hike from here, along the edge of an increasingly wild and lush gorge. The name has nothing to do with dolls. One theory is that it's a corruption of the original Chinese name "Frog Valley" – the Chinese characters for Doll Valley are very similar. Follow the main road along the Nanshih River for about twenty minutes from Wulai Falls until you reach the pedestrian suspension bridge and cross to the other side – from here the path follows the left bank of the river through **Xinxian** village, to another road and eventually the car park in front of **Neidong National Forest Recreation Area** (daily 8am–5pm; NT$80). Once you've paid the entrance fee the path passes the **Xinxian Falls** on the right bank, before continuing past a dam and on to the mouth of **Doll Valley** itself, containing the middle and upper **Neidong Falls** in a gorge off the main river. It's become a popular spot for swimming in recent years, but during the week it shouldn't be too busy. From here it's possible to follow paths further up the valley to the top of the falls, though you have to return to Wulai via the same route.

Practicalities

To get to Wulai from Taipei make for **Xindian MRT Station** and take the right-hand exit to the bus stop outside. **Buses** to Wulai leave every twenty minutes (daily 5.30am–9.30pm; 40min; NT$40). Hot springs are big business in Wulai, and most spas double as hotels – the cheapest places line the main street in Wulai village, but these often have only indoor baths. *Xiaochuanyuan Hot Springs* at 32 Wulai Street (☎02/26616222) has older, tiled indoor pools for men and women, but it's not bad for a soak (daily 8am–midnight; NT$250). The free **public hot springs** by the river (see p.157) are mixed and open-air so you'll need swim suits, while the *Wulai Spring Resort* at 36 Laka Rd (☎02/26616161;

❼) has a magnificent setting above a quiet stretch of the Tonghou River, with stone and wood-finished public pools at NT$500 for unlimited use (daily 7am–11pm). The spa is fifteen minutes' walk from the bus station – turn left after the first bridge into Wulai. *Shanggu Qingliu* at 101 Wenquan Street (☎02/26616700; ❼), is just off the road to Wulai Falls in a beautiful part of the gorge. Use of the indoor and tiered outdoor public pools is NT$350. For unabashed luxury the *Spring Park Urai Spa & Resort* at 3, Yanti village (☎02/26616555, ⓦwww.springparkhotel.com.tw; ❾) is hard to beat, with Japanese-inspired rooms and private spas overlooking the river. Day guests can pay NT$1200 for one hour in a private pool or NT$850 per day (8am–midnight) for use of the lavish indoor and outdoor public pools. The bus passes the hotel just before Wulai village, about 500m further up the valley.

Outside the hotels, the most convenient **food** options are located in the two tourist villages. In Wulai Hot Springs Village, the *Taiya Popo Restaurant* at no. 14 with its bamboo decor is one of the better places to eat, though all the restaurants on Wulai Street serve up the same dishes: rice stuffed into bamboo tubes (*zhutong fan*), fried or barbecued "mountain pig" (*shan zhu*), bamboo shoots and lots of green vegetables, all nominally aboriginal fare and very tasty.

Southeast of Taipei

Taiwan's mountainous interior begins just beyond Taipei's southern suburbs, making the valleys southeast of the capital the easiest way to get a sense of its rural hinterland. **Shenkeng** is a short bus ride from city and best known for its **tofu** dishes, while the village of **Pinglin** is further south, surrounded by picturesque tea plantations and hiking trails.

Shenkeng

The old town of **SHENKENG** is an excellent place to gorge on Taiwanese delicacies. It's easy to get here by bus: #660, #236 and #251 stop along Muzha Road close to the Muzha MRT station and take 10–15 minutes (NT$15). Most of the action takes place along **Old Street**, close to the bus stop and marked by a 100-year-old banyan tree at its entrance. The street does have a few old buildings and storefronts, but it's principally noted for its gift shops and especially for its food. The chief specialty here is **tofu**, served up in a bewildering number of ways from huge vats of stewed tofu (*hong shao tofu*) to grilled tofu on sticks (*chuan shao tofu*) and even tofu ice cream. There are plenty of restaurants to choose from – no. 138–140 is one of the better options but they're all pretty good. Bamboo shoots (*lugui zhushun*) are another specialty, and a vast choice of Taiwanese desserts is also on offer, as well as traditional toys such as wooden guns and puppets. Not far from the bus stop in the opposite direction to Old Street is the **Yongan Residence** (Sat–Sun 9am–5.30pm; NT$60) a beautifully

Southeast of Taipei		
He Huan Campground	合歡露營渡假山莊	*héhuān lùyíng dùjià shānzhuāng*
Pinglin	坪林	*pínglín*
Pinglin Tea Museum	坪林茶葉博物館	*pínglín cháyè bówùguǎn*
Shenkeng	深坑	*shēnkēng*
Yongan Residence	永安居	*yǒngānjū*

maintained example of a traditional Taiwanese house built 1911–15 (the English sign is incorrect), still owned by the Huang family.

Pinglin

The small town of **PINGLIN** feels a million miles from Taipei, even with a steady trickle of tour buses rattling along its main street. In fact, it's only 20km from the edge of the city via the new Taipei-Yilan Highway. Located at the bottom of the Beishi River valley it makes a good day-trip but is also the centre of an attractive region of hiking trails and smaller sights that really require your own transport (or bike) to explore fully. Pinglin is famous principally for its tea, much of which is **Baozhong** oolong – you can see acres of tea bushes lining the hills that surround the town.

The **Pinglin Tea Museum** (Tues–Fri 9am-5pm, Sat–Sun 8.30am-6pm; NT$100) is the town's main attraction and is a good introduction to everything connected with tea in Taiwan – the only downside is that the English labelling is fairly poor ("Soar drying machine" refers to a solar drying machine for example). From the bus station keep walking along the street and you'll see the museum on the other side of the river. The museum complex also includes a shop and picturesque teahouse. For cheaper tea and food (fried **freshwater shrimps** and **fish** are the specialties here) head back to the main street where there is a huge choice of restaurants lining the roadside – main dishes are NT$50–80.

Unless new services start to use the highway, Pinglin will continue to be a long and winding hour-and-a-half ride from Taipei: buses are operated by the Xindian bus company from the stop outside the Government Insurance Building on Gongyuan Road (take exit 8 from Taipei Main Station MRT) – it's faster to catch the same bus outside Xindian MRT station (NT$96). The **He Huan Campground** (℡02/26656424) at 5-1 Shuide Village is a twenty-minute walk along the south side of the river from the tea museum if you fancy staying the night, and bikes can be hired for NT$80 per hour from here – Pinglin's 20km of **cycling trails** are worth exploring if you have time. There are also plenty of homestays in the area – ask at the museum.

Travel details

Trains

Taipei Main Station to: Changhua (18 express daily; 2hr 20min); Chiayi (12 express daily; 3hr 20min); Fulong (9 express daily; 1hr 5min); Hsinchu (16 express daily; 1hr); Hualien (14 express daily; 2hr 50min); Yilan (17 express daily; 1hr 30min); Kaohsiung (14 express daily; 4hr 30min); Keelung (frequent; daily; 40min); Sanyi (6 daily; 2hr 20min); Taichung (15 express daily; 2hr); Tainan (13 express daily; 4hr); Taitung (6 express daily; 5hr); Yingge (frequent, daily; 25min).

Buses

Buses The following gives a rough idea of duration, though heavy traffic at weekends can add more time.

Taipei to: Taiwan Taoyuan Int. Airport (daily; 45min–1hr); Jinshan (daily; 1hr); Kaohsiung (frequent; 5hr 30min); Keelung (1hr); Lugang (8 daily; 3hr 30min); Yehliu (40min); Pingsi (40min); Puli (10 daily; 3hr); Sansia (40min); Sun Moon Lake (10 daily; 4hr); Taichung (frequent; 2hr); Tainan (frequent; 4hr 30min); Wulai (daily; 40min).
Danshui to: Baishawan (20min); Shihmen (40min); Jinshan (1hr).

Flights

Songshan Airport to: Chiayi (10 daily; 45min); Hengchun (3 daily; 1hr 10min); Hualien (13 daily; 35min); Kaohsiung (40 daily; 50min); Kinmen (17 daily; 1hr); Magong (20 daily, 45min); Matzu (Nangan, 9 daily; 50min; Beigan, 3 daily; 50min); Pingdong (3 daily; 1hr); Taichung (5 daily; 35min); Tainan (15 daily; 45min); Taitung (7 daily; 50min).

North Taiwan

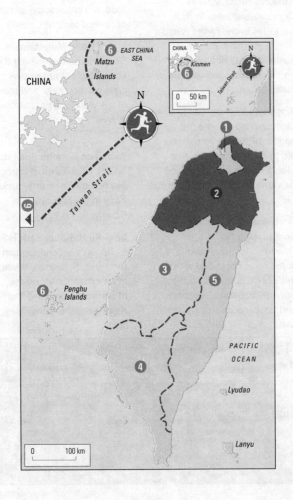

CHAPTER 2 # Highlights

* **Yeliou Geopark** View the geological oddities peppering this jagged outcrop on the north coast. See p.169

* **Keelung Night Market** Compact and easy to navigate, this is one of the island's best night markets, rich in seafood, tasty rice noodles and mouthwatering fruit ice stalls. See p.175

* **Jinguashi** Visit the Gold Museum and explore the narrow hillside streets of this old mining town, or hike up Mount Keelung for spectacular views of the north coast. See p.180

* **Northeast Coast National Scenic Area** Some of Taiwan's most dramatic coastline is contained within this scenic area, with cliff-top trails, picturesque beaches and a top-notch surfing destination. See p.183

* **Hakka culture** The north is a Hakka stronghold, with Beipu and Shengsing enchanting places to absorb Hakka culture, feast on excellent food and enjoy some *lei cha* or "cereal tea". See p.203

* **Lion's Head Mountain Scenic Area** Experience the tranquillity of this temple-covered mountain, and marvel at the world's largest statue of Milefo at Emei Lake. See p.207

* **Taian Hot Springs** Soak up one of Taiwan's most attractive hot spring resorts, tucked away in the hills of Miaoli County. See p.212

* **Shei-Pa National Park** Home to Taiwan's second-highest mountain, Syueshan, the apex of an extraordinary massif of tantalizing peaks in this rugged national park. See p.215

△ Keelung night market

North Taiwan

Northorth Taiwan is the most scenically varied part of the country. Wild terrain, fierce indigenous tribes and even wilder weather terrified early settlers, making it one of the last parts of the island to be colonized by the Chinese, primarily attracted by its timber and mineral resources. In 1949 the region was swamped by a huge influx of refugees from China, and today its jam-packed cities contain more Mandarin-speaking "mainlanders" and their descendants than anywhere else in Taiwan, providing a high proportion of Kuomintang (KMT) support.

The region encompasses Hsinchu, Miaoli, Taoyuan, Taipei and Yilan counties, part of a densely populated **urban corridor** stretching from Keelung on the northeast coast to the fast expanding cities of Taoyuan and Jhongli further west. Proximity to the capital makes the whole area highly accessible and much of it can be visited as a series of extended day-trips. Beyond this urban core lies a **dramatic coastline**, one of the north's most appealing features – a fact not lost on Taiwan's Tourism Bureau which has created two scenic areas to promote it: the **North Coast and Guanyinshan National Scenic Area** and further south, the **Northeast Coast National Scenic Area** offer spectacular scenery, some decent beaches and the **Juming Museum**, an absorbing showcase for the work of Taiwan's most celebrated sculptor. Between the two areas, the port city of **Keelung** is set in a strategic harbour surrounded by ruined fortresses and is home to Taiwan's best night market, as well as its biggest annual Ghost Festival. Inland, the **Pingsi Branch Rail Line** winds its way through a lush mountain valley, past scenic **Shihfen Falls** and **Pingsi** itself, home of Taiwan's most magical event, the release of hundreds of "heavenly lanterns" during the **Lantern Festival**. Nearby, the once booming mining towns of **Jiufen** and **Jinguashi** have been reinvented as tourist attractions, sporting atmospheric teahouses, snack stalls and museums.

Heading south, Hsinchu and Miaoli counties form the **Hakka heartland** of Taiwan, with **Beipu** and **Neiwan** providing ample opportunity to experience Hakka food and culture, and **Sanyi** renowned as the country's foremost wood-carving centre. But beyond all of this, and never far from view, lies an untamed interior of giant peaks and isolated valleys, home to the awe-inspiring **Shei-Pa National Park**, as well as the less vertiginous **Lion's Head Mountain Scenic Area**, noted for its hillside temples, and **Taian Hot Springs**, a tranquil spa retreat surrounded by great hiking country and Atayal tribal villages. With more time and preferably your own transport, you can traverse the winding **Northern Cross-Island Highway**, connecting the historic streets of Dasi with the Atayal township of Baling and Yilan on the east coast. **Yilan County** contains a handful of worthwhile stops before heading south: the attractive **Wufongci**

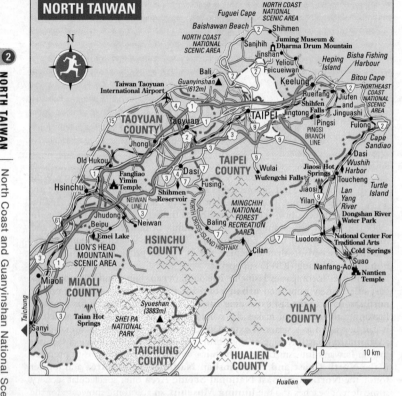

NORTH TAIWAN

North Coast National Scenic Area

Fuguei Cape

Baishawan Beach

Shihmen

NORTH COAST NATIONAL SCENIC AREA

Sanjhih

Juming Museum & Dharma Drum Mountain

Jinshan

Yeliou

Heping Island

Bisha Fishing Harbour

Bali

Feicueiwan

Keelung

Bitou Cape

Taiwan Taoyuan International Airport

Guanyinshan (612m)

Rueifang

Jiufen — and — Jinguashi

NORTHEAST COAST NATIONAL SCENIC AREA

Shihfen Falls

TAOYUAN COUNTY

Taoyuan

Jingtong

Pingsi

PINGSI BRANCH LINE

Fulong

Cape Sandiao

Jhongli

TAIPEI COUNTY

Wulai

Jiaosi Hot Springs

Wushih Harbor

Old Hukou

Fangliao Yimin Temple

Dasi

Wufengchi Falls

Toucheng

Turtle Island

Hsinchu

Fusing

Shihmen Reservoir

NEIWAN LINE

Jiaosi

Lan Yang River

Jhudong

Beipu

Neiwan

MINGCHIH NATIONAL FOREST RECREATION AREA

Yilan

Dongshan River Water Park

Emei Lake

LION'S HEAD MOUNTAIN SCENIC AREA

HSINCHU COUNTY

Baling

Cilan

Luodong

National Center For Traditional Arts

Cold Springs

Suao

Miaoli

MIAOLI COUNTY

Syueshan (3883m)

YILAN COUNTY

Nanfang-Ao

Nantien Temple

Taichung

Taian Hot Springs

SHEI PA NATIONAL PARK

Sanyi

TAICHUNG COUNTY

HUALIEN COUNTY

0   10 km

Hualien

Waterfalls, the **National Center for Traditional Arts** near Luodong and the refreshing **Suao Cold Springs**.

North Coast and Guanyinshan National Scenic Area

Taiwan's rugged coastline between Danshui and Keelung falls within the **North Coast and Guanyinshan National Scenic Area**, easily accessible from the capital and a popular destination for day-trips (Guanyinshan itself is covered on p.152). The northeast corner has the best scenery, with highlights including the **Dharma Drum Mountain** monastery, the old street and hot springs at **Jinshan**, **Yeliou Geopark's** fascinating rock formations and the entrancing modern sculptures at the **Juming Museum**.

Practicalities

All the attractions below can be visited as **day-trips** from Taipei or Keelung: the latter is worth considering as a base especially if you also want to explore

②

North Coast and Guanyinshan National Scenic Area	北海岸及觀音山國家風景區	běihǎián jí guānyīnshānguójiā fēngjǐngqū
Baishawan	白沙灣	báishāwān
Feicueiwan (Green Bay)	翡翠灣	fěicuìwān
Fuguei Cape	富貴角	fùguì jiǎo
Fuji Fishing Harbour	富基漁港	fùjī yúgǎng
Jinshan	金山	jīnshān
Cihhu Temple	慈護宮	cíhùgōng
Dharma Drum Mountain	法鼓山	fǎgǔshān
Jinbaoli Street	金包裡老街	jīnbāolǐlǎojiē
Jinbaoshan Cemetery	金寶山陵園	jīnbǎoshānlíngyuán
Jinshan Youth Activity Center	金山青年活動中心	jīnshān qīngnián huódòng zhōngxīn
Juming Museum	朱銘美術館	zhūmíng měishùguǎn
Old Grandma's Secret Garden	阿媽的秘密花園	āmā de mìmì huāyuán
San Francisco Governor Hot Spring Resort	舊金山總督溫泉	jiùjīnshān zěngtǒng wēnquán
Shitoushan Park	獅頭山公園	shītóushān gōngyuán
Sanjhih	三芝	sānzhī
Sanjhih Visitor Center	三芝遊客中心	sānzhī yóukè zhōngxīn
Shihmen	石門	shímén
Shihmen Cave	石門洞	shímén dòng
Temple of Eighteen Lords	十八王公廟	shíbā wánggōng miào
Yeliou	野柳	yěliǔ
Yeliou Geopark	野柳地質公園	yěliǔ dìzhì gōngyuán

the Northeast Coast National Scenic Area (see p.172 for Keelung bus details). From Taipei, take the MRT to **Danshui** where **buses** ply Provincial Route 2 to Keelung (daily 5.50am–8.30pm; every 20–30min; NT$150), stopping at all the main sights including Sanjhih (NT$38), Baishawan (NT$48), Shihmen (NT$60), Jinshan (NT$90) and Yeliou (NT$105), while another service, stopping at the same places, terminates at Jinshan (daily 5.40am–9.30pm; every 30min). There's also a Kuo Kuang bus from Taipei Inter City Bus Terminal to Jinshan Youth Activity Center (daily 5.40am–10.40pm; every 10–20min; NT$105) which stops at Yeliou (NT$85) and Jinshan (NT$100).

Sanjhih

The first major stop north of Danshui is the small agricultural town of **SANJHIH**, a tea and rice-growing area best explored with your own transport. If you're travelling by bus it's still worth making for the **Sanjhih visitor center** (daily 9am–5pm), a spanking new facility 2km east of the town and home to a couple of enlightening museums, both labelled in English. The first recounts the history of the area and includes a section on the north coast's earliest inhabitants, the Ketagalan (see Contexts p.519), while the **Gallery of Famous Sons** commemorates the town's most respected former residents, in particular **Lee Teng-hui**, Taiwan's first democratically elected president, and the first native Taiwanese to hold the post (see p.515). Across the park at the back of the centre is the **Yuansing Residence**, the traditional three-sided home where Lee was born. You can usually peek inside the simple central room (daily

9am–5pm), but the rest of the house remains a private residence. Most buses stop on Provincial Route 2 on the western side of town – to avoid a long walk try and find a taxi.

Baishawan

BAISHAWAN ("White Sand Bay") is a popular beach destination for Taipei residents, just twenty minutes north of Danshui by bus and 3km from Sanjhih. It's free, has the finest sand on the north coast, and from May to September it's home to regular beach parties featuring top-notch DJs – **Summer Aquarian** (ⓦwww.summer-aquarian.com; NT$800–1000) is the biggest, a slick annual event held in July here and at various beaches along the coast, including the otherwise highly commercialized resort of **FEICUEIWAN** (Green Bay), near Keelung. There's not much point visiting during the cooler months, however, although the main scenic area **visitor centre** (daily 9am–5pm; ☎02/26364503 ⓦwww.northguan-nsa.gov.tw) is at its northern end. Buses stop next to the row of shops and snack stalls on the road behind the beach.

Fuguei Cape

The next major stop after Baishawan, **Fuguei Cape** is Taiwan's most northerly point, a rugged headland topped by a stumpy fourteen-metre lighthouse. The nearest bus stop is on the main road, a few minutes' walk from **Fuji Fishing Harbour**, a compact and ramshackle dock crammed with fishing boats; a lively fish market (daily 10am–8pm) hugs the quayside, and there's a row of popular **seafood restaurants** nearby. The cape is a short walk from the back of the harbour, through a grotty car park and along the rocky coastline. The **lighthouse** was built in 1949 and is off limits, as is the military radar station nearby, but the trail offers wide ocean views and a chance to gaze at the cape itself, a battered jumble of rocks below the headland often littered with driftwood.

Shihmen and the Temple of Eighteen Lords

SHIHMEN, Taiwan's most northerly village, is another 4km beyond Fuguei Cape along the main highway, and a convenient lunch stop. The main street is lined with stalls selling the local specialty, *rouzong* (rice dumplings with chicken and mushroom, wrapped in bamboo leaves; NT$20-25); the best place to sample them is *Liu Family Rouzong* at 30 Jhongyang Road, with its special minced radish recipe. On the eastern side of Shihmen lies the topographic feature that gave the village its name ("Stone Gate"), the **Shihmen Cave**, a naturally eroded stone arch, just off the beach.

Just under 4km east of the village, the **Temple of Eighteen Lords** (daily, 24 hours) is a tiny shrine swathed in gold leaf and surrounded by a throng of small stalls and trinket sellers. It's a short walk from the bus stop on the main road, behind the highway bridge (ask to get off at the *shi ba wang gong miao*). Despite its size, this is one of the most popular temples on the north coast – not least because worshipping here is supposed to bring good luck when it comes to gambling or playing the lottery. Several legends are associated with the site, the official one being that the shrine was established in the late Qing dynasty to commemorate the faithful **dog** (the 18th "lord") of one of seventeen fishermen drowned at sea. When the bodies of the men were washed ashore near Shihmen, the dog was miraculously still alive, but overcome with grief it threw itself into its master's tomb as a sign of loyalty.

The **tomb** representing the eighteen is to the left side of the main hall lined with cigarettes placed here for the fishermen's spirits to smoke, but to get a piece of the money-making action you'll need to get your hands on one of two bronze dog statues guarding them; touch the dog's mouth for general good luck, its feet for great wealth, and the head to ensure your children grow up extra smart. Note that this tomb is a recently built reproduction – the real one is behind the shrine in the basement.

Jinshan and around

JINSHAN, 12km south of Shihmen and 24km from Keelung, is the largest town on the north coast and a good place to grab lunch or take a dip in one of its numerous hot-spring resorts. The town sits behind a small promontory which divides its two popular but unexceptional beaches. Running parallel to the east of the main thoroughfare, Jhongshan Road, is Jinshan's "old street", also known as **Jinbaoli Street** to commemorate the Ketagalan name for the area, and once the site of a busy riverside dock. Few old buildings remain, but it's a pleasant place to browse (the town is noted for its traditional cakes, wooden shoes, and baked sweet potatoes and yams). The Traditional Medicine store at no. 26, and rice shop at no. 28 are its best examples of early twentieth-century architecture. At the southern end of Jinbaoli Street is **Cihhu Temple** (daily 5am–9pm), established in 1809 and dedicated to Mazu – it's the biggest temple on the north coast, containing a plethora of statues and one central gold-faced image of the deity. The temple faces Minsheng Road, and turning left here takes you towards the beach – hail a cab or catch any bus that's heading this way if you don't fancy the 1.2-kilometre walk over the hill. The road forks a short distance ahead; the left-hand road passes the **Jinshan Visitor Center** (daily 9am–5pm) which can help with local maps, and is also close to the trailhead for hikes into **Shitoushan Park** (Lion's Head Mountain, not to be confused with the Scenic Area further south). The park encompasses most of the promontory between the two beaches, providing fine views of the Twin Candlestick Islets just offshore. At the end of the road is **New Jinshan Beach** (daily June–September 8am–6pm; NT$100), managed by the *Jinshan Youth Activity Center* (see below). The beach is no tropical paradise however, with Mandopop blaring out of strategically-placed speakers, and crowds of students enjoying various activities in midsummer, but the massive **public hot-spring pools** (daily 7am–11pm), are reasonably priced at NT$250.

The right-hand fork along Minsheng Road leads to Shueiwei Fishing Port on the south side of the promontory, and **Old Jinshan Beach**, which is free, but often littered with trash. The best thing here is the *San Francisco Governor Hot Spring Resort* at 196 Minsheng Road (daily 9am–midnight, ☎02/24082628), housed in a grey Japanese-era building built in 1938 and comprehensively renovated in 2001. The second-floor **restaurant** is a decent place to have lunch, while the attractive outdoor pools cost NT$300 (there's no accommodation).

Practicalities

Buses from Danshui and Keelung stop on Jhongshan Road in the centre of town, while the Taipei bus terminates just outside the large grey reception building of *Jinshan Youth Activity Center* near the beach (1 Cingnian Rd, ☎02/24981190; ❸). The centre offers a range of chalet accommodation, all clean and fairly spacious. Camping (tent provided) costs NT$800, or NT$500 with your own tent, while hot meals are available in the reception building. Bikes can be hired for NT$100 per hour. For **food**, the local specialty is duck noodles; you'll find them served in the bustling forecourt of the **Guangan Temple**, halfway along Jinbaoli Street (no.104). A plate of duck, with special plum sauce and fresh ginger, is NT$160, but if you're on your own they'll usually charge you less for a more manageable portion. For **tea**, try ⚘ *Old Grandma's Secret Garden* at 31 Jinbaoli Street (Sat–Sun 10.30am–2am), south of the temple, a recently restored 120-year-old Qing dynasty inn. The entrance is a narrow passageway marked by a string of red lanterns, leading to a courtyard and second-storey rooms with a balcony overlooking the back garden. Pots of tea are NT$300 or NT$120 for one, best accompanied by plates of the irresistible frozen sweet potato (NT$80).

Dharma Drum Mountain

Beautifully located in the hills above Jinshan, around 3km from the centre of town, **Dharma Drum Mountain** (daily 8am–4pm; free; ⓦ www.ddm.org.tw) is an absorbing Buddhist educational complex and monastery with extensive gardens. Established in 1989 by respected monk and scholar Master Sheng Yen, it's Taiwan's newest Chan (Zen) Buddhist foundation. Visitors are welcome but it's best to email in advance if you fancy a **guided tour** in English (free).

From the main entrance, make your way up the hill to the Reception Hall where you'll find an information desk, a gift shop and enthusiastic English-speaking volunteers. From here you can walk across to the adjacent Main Building: the third floor contains the **Founding History Memorial Hall**, which uses a suitably futuristic blend of Buddhist relics and modern technology to recount the history of Buddhism and the life of Master Sheng Yen, while the Glories of Dharma Drum Mountain on the next floor up is a vast but rather hagiographical portrait of the founder and scenes from his life. Another highlight is the **Great Buddha Hall** in the main temple of the complex, with its imposing bronze images of Sakyamuni Buddha (centre), the Medicine Buddha (right) and Amitabha Buddha (left), backed by ornate canopies carved by Japanese craftsmen.

Meditation classes are popular with expats as well as locals, and are offered in both Chinese and English; visitors can sign on for day, half-day or even two-hour sessions, most of which will incur a small charge. Lunar New Year and Buddha's birthday are the year's biggest **festivals**, and a good time to observe traditional prayers and chanting.

Bus #829 and #828 connect the main entrance (a short walk or shuttle bus ride to the Reception Hall) with Jinshan (daily 6.40am–6.25pm; every 30min) and there's a direct bus to Zhongxiao Fuxing MRT station (NT$110) and Taipei Main Station (NT$120) six times a day during the week and more frequently at weekends: the first bus leaves Taipei at 6.15am, while convenient buses leave the mountain at 1.50pm and 4.20pm. A taxi from Jinshan should cost NT$150.

Juming Museum

One of the highlights of the north coast, the **Juming Museum** (Tues–Sun 10am–5pm, May–Oct 6pm close; ☏02/24989940, ⓦ www.juming.org.tw; NT$250) lies over the ridge behind Dharma Drum Mountain. Opened in 1999 by Ju Ming, Taiwan's most celebrated sculptor, it's more a sculpture park than a museum, with most exhibits displayed around a series of landscaped gardens and ponds – it's obviously best to visit on a fine day.

From the museum **service centre,** walk down through a gallery of paintings (including Andy Warhol's "Mao Tse-Tung") to the outdoor area. The first enigmatic installation on display is **Parachute** (1987–88), part of Ju Ming's

Living World Series and a collection of life-size parachutists cast in bronze with stainless steel chutes. From here a path leads anti-clockwise around the park, lined with pieces from Ju Ming's latest Living World collection "**Armed Forces**" – this ends dramatically with a gigantic steel-frame battleship lined with sailors at the far end of the park. The real highlight however, is the sculptor's most famous work: thirty giant pieces of his extraordinary **Taichi Series**, a collection of huge, chunky figures created in the late 1970s and early 1980s. The abstract, faceless bronze forms manage to convey intense movement and the controlled energy of the Chinese martial art without resorting to minute detail. The museum's pyramid-shaped **Main Building** (closes 15min before the rest of the site) is where much of Ju Ming's early Nativist woodcarvings are displayed, along with work from Yu Yu Yang, his teacher; notable pieces include *Girl Playing with Sand*, created in 1961 using Ju Ming's wife as a model, and *In One Heart*, a vivid carving of a buffalo pulling a cart weighed down with logs. English-language documentaries about the sculptor are screened here throughout the day.

Special **buses** run to the museum from Taipei Fine Arts Museum at 8.40am and 1.10pm, returning at midday and 5pm (5.30pm in summer) – the NT$400 round-trip ticket includes admission, but call the museum first (extension 1101) to confirm times. **Taxis** from Jinshan should be around NT$200. You can walk to Dharma Drum Mountain from here, though it's around 2km by road – ask staff to point out the short cut or call a taxi.

Tomb of Teresa Teng

Hugging the slopes above the Juming Museum, **Jinbaoshan Cemetery** (daily; 24hr) has become a pilgrimage site for music fans from all over the world, the last resting place of **Teresa Teng** (Deng Lijun in Chinese), one of the most famous Chinese pop singers of all time – she died tragically in 1995, at the age of 43 after an asthma attack. Her relatively humble tomb is often littered with flowers, her ten most famous hits (including "*Will You Come Back Again*") echoing around the site on permanent loop.

Yeliou

Just to the north of the fishing village of **YELIOU** lies **Yeliou Geopark** (daily 8am–5pm; NT$50), home to a series of bizarre geological formations. The park lies on Yeliou Cape and commands stunning views across the bay to Jinshan and Yangmingshan beyond – hike to the end of the headland and you'll usually have the place to yourself. Unique rock formations litter the cape, the result of years of weathering and seismic activity - the small **visitor centre** at the entrance shows twelve-minute English videos on the geology of the area. From here, well-marked trails lead along the 1.6km headland past all of the most famous formations: rocks that resemble tofu and ginger, the unique and mystifying candle rocks and the ubiquitous mushroom rocks, the most famous of which is the **Queen's Head**, now in danger of collapse.

Yeliou's **Lantern Festival** (see p.51) is one of Taiwan's most exuberant. Local fishing boats, covered in lights and spewing firecrackers, follow each other around the harbour before eight groups of young men, each carrying one of the local temple gods on a small bamboo palanquin, dive into the freezing water and swim to the other side of the dock.

Buses stop on the main highway just outside the village – walk along the road to the right of the harbour, past the seafood restaurants till you reach the Geopark, a few minutes on the left.

Keelung and around

The port city of **KEELUNG** (pronounced "Jilong" in Chinese), sandwiched between verdant mountains and northern Taiwan's best natural harbour, is a strategic location that has been fought over by foreign powers since the seventeenth century. Though it's a typically modern Taiwanese city, home to around 400,000 people, its setting is picturesque and there's plenty to see: numerous **fortresses**, a legacy of the city's violent past, the **Fairy Cave**, one of Taiwan's most atmospheric shrines, and **Keelung Island** which provides a spectacular panorama of the coastline. The real highlights however, are Keelung's **night market**, arguably Taiwan's best and certainly its most famous, and the country's largest and most illuminating **Ghost Festival**, held every August.

Some history

The **Spanish** first established an outpost on **Heping Island** near Keelung in 1626, when the area was inhabited by the **Ketagalan**, who called it "Kelang". In 1642 the Dutch kicked out the Spaniards after a bloody siege, but abandoned their last stronghold in Taiwan in 1668. Chinese immigrants began to arrive in large numbers in 1723 and the town became an important **port** in the nineteenth century, making it a regular target for foreign powers; during the 1841 Opium War a British squadron shelled the harbour, while in the 1884-85 Sino-French War the city was occupied by the French for eight months. In 1895 Keelung was the scene of fierce resistance to the invading Japanese, while

in 1947 KMT troops from the mainland disembarked here during the 2-28 Incident. The harbour was almost completely destroyed by Allied bombing at the end of World War II, and the postwar years saw a gradual rebuilding of the facilities – it's now Taiwan's second biggest container port after Kaohsiung.

Arrival, information and city transport

Regular services from Taipei (40min; NT$43) arrive at the **train station**, conveniently located at the southwestern corner of the harbour. The main **bus stations** are all nearby. Keelung's useful **Visitor information center** (Mon–Fri 8.30am–noon, 1.30–5pm, Sat–Sun 9am–4pm; ℡02/24287664, ⓦtour-3.klcg.gov.tw) is on your right as you exit the train station and stocks plenty of English-language material – staff here can help with bus information and hotels. Chinatrust Commercial Bank has **ATMs** conveniently located in the train station and most 7-Elevens in town.

City transport

Central Keelung is best explored on foot, but to see everything you'll save time by using **local buses**. The **city bus station** is to the left of the train station as you exit, though there are plans to move it now the YM Museum has opened next door. Bus #101 trundles along Jhongjheng Road beneath Ershawan Fortress, then on to Heping Island (daily 5.50am–11.20pm; every 10–12min); #103 goes to Bisha Fishing Harbour and Badouzih Seashore Park (daily 5.50am–10.36pm; every 10–12min); and #301 goes along the northern side of the harbour to Siandong (Fairy Cave) and Baimiwang Fort (daily 5.50am–11.20pm; every 20–25min). Buses cost NT$15 per journey – make sure you have change. Taxis are available from the train station, but be prepared to negotiate the fare in advance.

Keelung and around		
Keelung	基隆	jīlóng
Big Buddha Temple	大佛禪院	dàfó chányùan
Cimetière Français de Kilung	法國公墓	fǎguó gōngmù
Cing An Temple	慶安宮	qìngān gōng
Dianji Temple	奠法宮	diànjì gōng
Ershawan Fortress	二砂灣砲台	èrshāwān pàotái
Fairy Cave	仙洞巖	xiān dòng yán
Guanghua Tower	光華塔	guānghuá tǎ
Heping Island	和平島	hépíng dǎo
Jhongjheng Park	中正公園	zhōngzhèng gōngyuán
Jhupu Altar	主普壇	zhǔpǔ tán
Keelung Island	基隆島	jīlóng dǎo
Keelung Midsummer Ghost Festival Museum	中元祭典文物館	zhōngyúan jìdiǎn wénwùguǎn
YM Oceanic Culture & Art Museum	陽明海洋文化藝術館	yángmíng hǎiyáng wénhuà yìshùgǔan
Accommodation and eating		
Evergreen Laurel Hotel	長榮桂冠酒店	chángróng guìgūan jiǔdiàn
Harbour View Hotel	華帥海景飯店	huáshuài hǎijǐng fàndiàn
Lee Hu Cakeshop	李鵠餅店	lǐhǔ bǐngdiàn
Temple Plaza Night Market	廟口夜市	miàokǒu yèshì

Moving on from Keelung

Heading south to Kaohsiung, there are only a couple of express **trains** per day and it's easier to take a local train to Taipei and transfer. Get off at Badu to pick up services down the east coast. The Keelung Bus Company station, located across Jhong 1st Road from the train station, is the hub for regular **bus** services to Yeliou (NT$44), Jinshan (NT$60), Jiufen (NT$44), Jinguashi (NT$50), Fulong (NT$100) and the Northeast Coast National Scenic Area. Long-distance services and buses to Taipei depart the Kuo Kuang Bus Station just to the right of the train station. For Danshui buses (daily 6am–8.30pm; every 20–40min), walk through the Kuo Kuang station and along Siao 4th Road to find the bus stop. The bus stops at all the main sights along the north coast: Yeliou (NT$44), Jinshan (NT$60), Shihmen (NT$90) and Danshui (NT$150). **Taxis** to Jinshan should cost NT$400. In summer, **ferries** to Matzu depart Keelung Harbour every night at 11pm, at the West Second Dock on the northern side of the harbour – buy tickets from the second floor of the passenger building in front (see p.484 for more on travelling to Matzu).

Accommodation

Mid-range accommodation in Keelung tends to be reasonably priced, though budget options in the city are unexceptional. One of the best places is the *Harbour View*, 108 Siao 2nd Road (☎02/24223131, ⓦwww.hhotel.com.tw; ❺), located on the southern side of the harbour in the centre of the city. Rooms are stylish and very comfortable, with the more expensive ones featuring excellent views of the harbour at night. The top place in town is the luxurious *Evergreen Laurel*, 62-1, Jhongjheng Road (☎02/24279988, ⓦwww.evergreen-hotels.com; ❺), on the east side of the harbour, its green tower clearly visible from most points in the city.

The City

The **harbour** remains the heart of the city, with all the main streets and buildings crammed between here and the mountains. The vibrant area south of the waterfront is where you'll find Keelung's shops, temples and restaurants, while the city's other main attractions lie either east or west of the port. Start at the **YM Oceanic Culture & Art Museum** (Tues–Sun 9am–5pm; NT$100), in the old headquarters of Yangming Marine Transport Corp, just opposite the station. The second floor contains displays about navigation and the history of ancient vessels, while the other exhibitions change every six months and focus on a range of subjects connected with ships and the ocean, particularly with a Chinese or Taiwanese slant. It's beautifully designed and well presented: everything is labelled in English and there is an army of volunteers on hand to answer queries, though the video presentations are aimed more at children.

One block south lies Keelung's busiest and most important place of worship, the **Cing An Temple** (daily 6am–10pm) – walk down Siao 2nd Road from the harbour, turn left along Jhong 2nd Road and you'll see the temple courtyard on the right, lined with food stalls. Dedicated to Mazu, the temple was established in 1780 with the most recent renovation completed in 1999. In addition to numerous ancient Mazu deities (with gold, black and brown faces), check out the shrine to five gods of wealth on the second floor of the Rear Hall, to the right. You're supposed to put a few coins into the box to get the gods' attention, the idea being you need to "invest" to enlist their help in becoming rich.

Turn right when you exit the main gate and it's a couple more blocks to Keelung's best-known shrine, **Dianji Temple** (daily 7am–10pm) on Ren 3rd Road, at the heart of the Temple Night Market (see p.175). Established in 1875 on the site of an older shrine to the Water God, the main hall dates from 1923 and is dedicated to Sage King Kaicheng – his main image sits in the central shrine. The god's birthday is on Lunar February 15, when there's a parade and plenty of festivities. The other main deity here is Tian Du Yuan Shuai (Marshal Tian Du), symbolized by a statue on the second floor of the Rear Hall, an historical figure from the Tang dynasty and a patron of *hsi-pi* music, a branch of *beiguan* (traditional "northern" music).

Jhongjheng Park and around

Perched on the hills lining the east side of the harbour, the 22m white **Guanyin Statue** in **Jhongjheng Park** (24hr) is the symbol of Keelung, and a good place to get a panoramic view of the city. The entrance to the park is on Sin 2nd Road, five minutes' walk east of the city's bulky Cultural Centre – the main trail passes several shrines and temples on the way up, skirting around the Martyrs' Shrine on the lower slopes and emerging at the **Jhupu Altar**, the grand *pudu* (spirit offering) shrine which is the focus of Keelung's Ghost Festival. The shrine was completed in 1976 and is only opened during Ghost Month, when offerings and rituals made here are supposed to appease the "hungry ghosts" that are thought to wander the earth at this time (see Festivals p.52) – the rest of the year it's worth visiting the **Keelung Midsummer Ghost Festival Museum** (Tues–Sun 9am–5pm; free) on the first floor, a small but informative exhibition about the festival, with labels in English. It's a short walk up the final stretch of hill to the Guanyin Statue from here – built on a scenic spot facing the sea, it's now part of the unremarkable **Big Buddha Temple** complex, built in 1969.

From the snack stalls at the back of the temple it's a twenty-minute walk along the road (take a left turn at the first junction), past assorted ex-military hardware, to **Ershawan Fortress** (24hr; free) dating from 1840 but rebuilt several times. This is Keelung's largest and best preserved fortress though it's little more than a series of hefty gun emplacements – the path loops around the main battlements and barrack areas behind, passing a few old tombs and a line of steep steps leading to the original gate further down the slope. This has the words "Haiman Tienxian" inscribed on the front, which roughly translates as "Dangerous Sea-Gate". From here you can walk down the hill to Jhongjheng Road along the harbour, and catch a bus back to the station, or on to Heping Island (bus #101).

One of Keelung's more unusual sites is a few metres north along Jhongjheng Road on the left, just before the junction with Zhengfeng Street. The French Cemetery, or **Cimetière Français de Kilung** (24hr) is all that remains of the graves of 600 to 700 soldiers and marines killed during the French occupation of the town in 1884–85. Estimates suggest only 270 died as a result of fighting – the majority succumbed to diseases such as malaria, cholera and dysentery. Only a few of the original tombstones remain on the far right; the main stone monument was erected in 1954 when the French government transferred the graves of two senior officers that had died in Penghu to the cemetery. French expats still hold memorial services here, with an unofficial French government representative taking part in a small ceremony held during Ghost Month. The two pillar monuments on site were erected by the Japanese.

Heping Island

Connected to Keelung via a small bridge, **Heping Island** is home to a small village (buses #101 and #102 terminate here) and **Heping Island Park** (daily

24hr; NT$60 between 9am–6pm), incorporating much of the island's wind-swept shoreline. The park's coastal trail passes some fairly wild scenery, cliffs and mushroom rocks (also known as *wan ren tou* or "thousand people heads") similar to those at Yeliou. The rocks here are not as dramatic but it's less touristy, and the heaps of flotsam piled up around the trails are vivid testimony to the power of the ocean. Look out for the **Stone Guanyin**, just off the main trail, marked by a white statue and small shrine, and opposite, the narrow **Cave of Foreign Words** where you can still see graffiti engraved by Dutch soldiers hiding from Chinese troops in 1666. The island was named Heping (which means "peace") in 1949, and it's still home to around two hundred **Ketagalan** people, mostly on the western side. The eastern part of the island has a large **Ami** community, economic migrants from the east coast.

Fairy Cave

On the other side of the harbour, ten minutes by bus from the train station, the **Fairy Cave** (daily 6am–5pm) is one of Taiwan's most distinctive temples. The site is actually a series of Buddhist shrines carved into the limestone caves facing Keelung container port – the wall carvings provide the illusion of great antiquity, unusual in Taiwan, though the temple dates from the relatively recent Qing dynasty. The cave contains four shrines; the first is dedicated to Milefo, while the second cavern features an altar to Guanyin. Behind this the main hall contains the three principal images of Buddha. To the left of the second cavern, a narrow passage through the rock takes you to another incense-filled shrine with a small stone effigy of Guanyin. The passage is very tight and may require some crawling.

Keelung Island

Keelung Island is a sharp pinnacle of volcanic rock, just off the coast and clearly visible from the hills around the city. Once a military base and off-limits

to the public, it's now a popular tourist destination, its best feature the spectacular hike up to the craggy 182m summit – the **lighthouse** on top (the only one in Taiwan to be solar-powered) has magnificent views of the coast. The island has a varied plant life (the slopes are littered with white calla lilies in the spring), but otherwise there's not much else to see and it can be a hassle getting here for individual travellers. Boats will only depart with a minimum of ten to fifteen people which can mean a lengthy wait outside of the busy weekend period. The other problem is that most trips last just two hours (including the thirty-minute boat ride there and back) which isn't really enough to climb the peak – most tourists simply follow the tour guide around the base of the island, though you are not obliged to do this.

△ View from Keelung Island

Practicalities

Most ferries to the island depart **Bisha Fishing Harbour** (NT$300 individual, NT$200 as part of a group or NT$5000 to hire the boat). The harbour is twenty minutes northeast of the city via bus #103 – get off when you see the *McDonald's* on the right and walk across the road. Tickets are sold in the Yishui Building on the edge of the marina (Tues–Sun 10am–5pm). You'll need to show your passport or ARC card. On the other side of the marina there's a popular **fresh fish market** and adjacent row of seafood restaurants – worth a try if you end up catching a ferry from here.

An alternative ferry service is operated by Yo Chi Company (☎02/24268586, ⓦwww.yochi.com.tw), which has a small terminal on the harbour opposite Keelung train station. In addition to regular boat trips to **Keelung Island** (NT$500), the company also runs a service to **Guanghua Tower** (daily departures 10am–8pm, one per hour; NT$250), a 32m lighthouse with a café on top situated on the edge of the harbour: it's a good way to see the docks up close and the café is an excellent place to view sunset. The last boat heads back at 9pm.

Eating and drinking

Keelung's **Temple Plaza Night Market** (ⓦwww.miaokow.org) on Ren 3rd Road, between Ai 3rd Road and Ai 4th Road is one of Taiwan's culinary highlights and by far the best **place to eat** in the city. The market dates from the late Japanese occupation era and fronts Dianji Temple; each stall advertizes its main dishes in English, and it's open 24 hours. The ice and fruit stalls are refreshing in summer, and while the thick soups and rice-flour noodles (*mifen*) are recommended, everything is worth a try. *Ding Bian Cuo* at no. 25-1 and 27-3 inside the temple courtyard is one of the oldest and most celebrated stalls, serving thick rice noodles in a mixed seafood broth. Not far from the market, *Lee Hu Cakeshop* (daily 9am–9.30pm) at 90 Ren 3rd Road bakes delicious crumbly pastries that look a bit like ping-pong balls, each with a variety of sweet fillings: the most popular is green bean (*ludousha bing*, NT$25 each). For something more upmarket, *Café Laurel* (buffet daily 6.30am–10pm; lounge 8–11pm) on the eighteenth and nineteenth floors of the *Evergreen Laurel Hotel*, is the perfect place to admire views of the city over dinner or drinks.

Jiufen and Jinguashi

The historic gold mining town of **Jiufen**, a short bus ride from Rueifang or Keelung, occupies a stunning hillside location with fine views of the northeast coast. It's justifiably renowned for its tasty **snack food** and atmospheric **teahouses**, though despite the hype, the town itself is architecturally fairly typical and not especially attractive. From Jiufen, the road runs 2km over the Mount Keelung ridge to **Jinguashi,** fast becoming a major tourist destination in its own right and far more interesting. Most of the town's mining-related attractions have been absorbed into the **Gold Ecological Park**, an ambitious project which combines restored Japanese buildings with old mining tunnels and ruined temples.

Both places are easy excursions from Keelung or Taipei, or can be combined in a fairly long day-trip. Jiufen is the best place to eat, and as its teahouses open stay into the early hours at weekends it's also not a bad place to spend the night, provided you can avoid the hordes that often overwhelm the place on weekend afternoons.

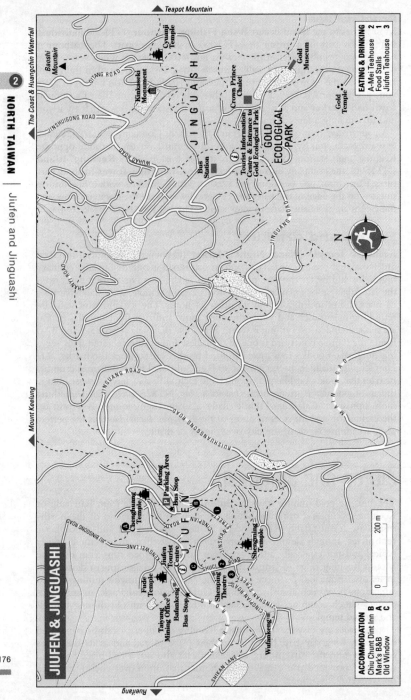

JIUFEN & JINGUASHI

▲ Teapot Mountain

Baoshi Mountain ▲

Cyuanji Temple

JINGUASHI

Kinkaseki Monument

GITANG ROAD

INSHUIGONG ROAD

WUHAO ROAD

SHANYI ROAD

◀ The Coast & Huangchin Waterfall

Crown Prince Chalet

Gold Museum

GOLD ECOLOGICAL PARK

Gold Temple

Tourist Information Centre & Entrance to Gold Ecological Park

Bus Station

◀ Mount Keelung

JINGUANG ROAD

JINGUANG ROAD

RUISHUANGGONG ROAD

MAIN ROAD

N

JIUFEN

Chenghuang Temple

Keting Parking Area
Bus Stop

JIU BINGONG ROAD

CINGBIAN LANE

B

QINGPIAN STREET

SHIHYI ROAD

JIUFEN

Taiyang Mining Office

Fude Temple

Bafankeng Bus Stop

Jiufen Tourist Centre

C

Shenping Theatre

2

JISHAN ROAD

JINSHAN STREET

Shengming Temple

SHUCI ROAD

QINGPIAN ROAD

JINSHAN STREET

Wufankeng

SHIHYI LANE

▼ Ruefang

0   200 m

ACCOMMODATION
Chiu Chunt Dint Inn   B
Mark's B&B   A
Old Window   C

EATING & DRINKING
A-Mei Teahouse   2
Food Stalls   1
Jiufen Teahouse   3

Some history

Gold was discovered in the Keelung River close to Jiufen in 1889, and in 1896 the Japanese began intensive mining in the area, dividing the land split by Mount Keelung between two government-run companies named after the officers in command: the concession operated by **Tanaka Group** became Jinguashi, while **Fujita Group** developed Jiufen. The gold ore on the Jiufen side was less pure and in 1914 the Japanese decided to sell the concession to local entrepreneur **Yen Yun-nien** who founded the Taiyang Mining Corp in 1920 and began leasing smaller chunks of land to Chinese prospectors. As a consequence, Jiufen developed haphazardly as a series of independent claims, gaining a reputation as a get-rich-quick town or **Little Shanghai** in the 1930s. Taiyang ceased all operations in Jiufen in 1971, and though artists started to settle here in the early 1980s, the good times seemed to be over – **Hou Hsiao-hsien**'s 1989 movie *City of Sadness*, in large part shot in a then atmospheric Jiufen, changed all that. The film was the first to make reference (very indirectly) to the 2-28 Incident and won the Golden Lion at the Venice Film Festival. Overnight the town became a must-see attraction, creating the tourist carnival that still exists today. In contrast, the Japanese maintained direct control over Jinguashi until 1945, the town developing in an orderly, pragmatic fashion. Its silver and especially **copper** deposits, discovered in 1905, became far more important than gold – by the 1930s the town was home to around 80,000 people with the hills honeycombed by a staggering 600km of tunnels. Mining finally ceased in 1987 when debts bankrupted the state-owned Taiwan Metal Mining Company – there's still gold in the hills but it's become too expensive to extract commercially.

Practicalities

From Taipei, the fastest option to both towns is to take a train to Rueifang (NT$80), then switch to one of the regular **buses** to Jinguashi (NT$20) which first stop at Jiufen (NT$15). The bus takes around fifteen minutes and departs from the opposite side of the road in front of Rueifang station's main (west) exit. Direct buses to both places also depart Keelung every fifteen minutes (daily 6am–9pm; 40min). The new **Jiufen Tourist Center** (daily 9am–5pm), on the main road towards the lower end of the town, has a small but informative exhibition and English-language brochures.

Jiufen and Jinguashi

Jiufen	九份	jiǔfèn
A-Mei Teahouse	阿妹茶酒館	āmèi chájiǔguǎn
Chenghuang Temple	城隍廟	chénghuáng miào
Chiu Chunt Dint Inn	九重町	jiǔzhòng tǐng
Jiufen Teahouse	九份茶坊	jiǔfèn cháfāng
Mark's B&B	馬克村莊	mǎkè cūnzhuāng
Mount Keelung	基隆山	jīlóngshān
Old Window	古窗	gǔchuāng
Shengming Temple	聖明宮	shèngmíng gōng
Wufankeng	五番坑	wǔfānkēng
Jinguashi	金瓜石	jīnguāshí
Cyuanji Temple	勸濟堂	qùanjì táng
Gold Ecological Park	黃金博物園區	huángjīn bówùyúan qū
Golden Falls	黃金瀑布	huángjīn pùbù
Teapot Mountain	茶壺山	cháhú shān

If you want to stay the night, it's best to look in Jiufen where there's plenty of cheap **accommodation**, and Cingpian Road in particular is lined with simple hotels and homestays. *Chiu Chunt Dint Inn* (T02/24967690, Wwww.9cd.com .tw; ❹) at 29 Jinshan Street is a new, centrally located place with a traditional theme, while *Old Window* (294-2 Cingpian Road T02/24062289; ❺) is a modern homestay with a fashionable rooftop teahouse. One of the cheapest places is *Mark's B&B* just off the main road at 86 Ciche Road (T02/24972889 Emarkvillage@markvillage.com.tw; ❸) – the rooms are basic, but some have superb views.

Jiufen

The narrow backstreets of **JIUFEN** are generally vehicle-free, and away from the busier areas, local life proceeds remarkably undisturbed. Most visitors get off the bus adjacent to the Keting Parking Area at the top end of town, proceeding downhill straight into **Jinshan Street** to gorge on its vast array of **snacks** (see Eating and drinking below). If you fancy some exercise before tucking in however, it's not far up the road to the trailhead for **Mount Keelung** (Jilongshan), an inactive volcano named by sailors who thought it resembled a chicken coup. On a fine day the short but steep hike to the summit (588m) offers a spectacular panorama of both Jiufen and Jinguashi.

Back in town, if you keep walking along hectic Jinshan Street you'll eventually cross Jiufen's most picturesque street, **Shuci Road**, actually a series of stone steps slicing through the middle of town and lined with teahouses and old buildings. Walk up the steps and turn left at the top to visit **Shengming Temple**, the town's most important – formally dedicated to Guan Di, it also hosts the annual Mazu festival. Return to Jinshan Street and continue downhill on Shuci Road to the junction with Cingpian Road, the most photogenic spot in Jiufen. The slightly creepy **Shenping Theatre** nearby is another site associated with the famous movie. Turn left along Cingpian Road and you'll eventually come to a small square in front of the entrance to **Wufankeng** or No.5 Mine, an evocative relic of Jiufen's mining days – it's locked up but you can still peer through the bars. Retrace your steps to Shuci Road and a short walk in the other direction along Cingpian you'll see gaudy **Chenghuang Temple**, housing Jiufen's City God. Continuing downhill, back on Shuci Road, you'll end up at a junction on the main road, with the bus stop on the opposite side.

Eating and drinking

Sampling the famous snacks on **Jinshan Street** is an essential part of any visit to Jiufen: favourites include beef noodles at no. 4, fish balls (*yuwan*) at no. 25, taro (*yuyuan*) and sweet potato balls served with ice at no. 32, herbal cakes (*caozi gao*) at *A-Lan* (no. 90) and translucent meat balls at no. 112 – if in doubt just follow the longest lines. There are also plenty of **teahouses**, and the *Jiufen Teahouse* 🎋 at 142 Jinshan Street, close to Shuci Road, is one of the highlights – make sure you get a wooden booth with a view. The building dates back one hundred years and once housed the mining bureau's headquarters. There's a NT$100 charge per person, in addition to the price of a teapot (NT$400-700) but the ambience and service makes up for the cost and the tea lasts for hours. Alternatively try the *A-Mei Teahouse* at 20 Shisia Lane (above 121 Shuci Road) on the right as you descend the steps below Jinshan Street: look out for the green exterior and red lanterns. This place featured heavily in the *City of Sadness* – a faded board showing the Chinese characters for the film marks the steps up to the entrance and is a favourite photo spot for Taiwanese tourists. Confusingly, the teahouse across the street at no. 35 is now called *City of Sadness*, though its connection with the movie is tenuous.

Jinguashi

Nesting in a small valley, just over the hill from Jiufen, **JINGUASHI** has only a handful of inhabitants and plenty of atmospheric alleys and streets to explore. Much of the old village is preserved within the absorbing **Gold Ecological Park**, an industrial heritage area that covers the western half of the valley.

Taipei buses terminate on the eastern side of the valley at **Cyuanji Temple**. Rebuilt in 1933 based on an 1896 original, the temple is noted principally for its bronze statue of Guan Di, which at 35m is one of the tallest in Asia. Steps to the right of the temple lead to the trailhead for **Teapot Mountain** (580m) which really does look like a teapot if you're standing in the right place. It's a steep 2km climb to the summit along a stone path, with a rope-assisted scramble across the scree at the top, from where the views are magnificent. Back at the temple, the lane to the left leads 200m up to an abandoned smoke tunnel and Baoshi Mountain, which is just a lookout over the valley and "**Yingyang Sea**" below – the iron ore in the river here has stained the water yellow, creating a two-tone effect in the bay below. Further down the valley the remains of the old **copper refinery** (known as "Thirteen Levels" in Chinese) make for a dramatic post-industrial landscape: the three serpent-like pipelines running up the mountainside are the world's longest smoke vents, all now abandoned, while the **Huangchin Waterfall** (or Golden Falls) nearby also gets its name from the iron and copper deposits in the river. At weekends, car park shuttle buses pass the falls (NT$15), otherwise it's a long walk down. Back at Cyuanji Temple, steps lead downhill to a narrow lane: turn right here and you'll come to a quiet park containing the **Kinkaseki Monument** and the remnants of a Japanese prisoner of war (POW) camp. A small **memorial** marks the area where 1135 Allied POWs were incarcerated between November 1942 and March 1945 – the camp was known simply as "Prisoner of War Camp No.1" or "Kinkaseki", the Japanese name for Jinguashi. From here you can wander through the town across the river and up to the Gold Park via **Old Citang Alley** or return to the temple: by the end of 2006 a trail should connect this with the Gold Museum.

Prisoner of war camps in Taiwan

Thailand's "death railway" is notorious in the English-speaking world (in part thanks to the film *Bridge on the River Kwai*), but few people are aware that the Japanese operated at least fifteen POW camps in Taiwan during World War II. More than 4300 men were incarcerated on the island, most of them British or Commonwealth troops captured in Hong Kong or Singapore, Dutch from Indonesia, and Americans from the Philippines. Life was as brutal for the POWs here as anywhere else in Asia, with each camp revolving around a system of forced labour: in Camp No.1, also known as **Kinkaseki** and the biggest, prisoners were forced to work in the Japanese copper mine in appalling conditions, while those at **Taichu Camp** (Camp No. 2) near Taichung worked on a massive flood channel – many died from starvation, disease and ill-treatment. The camps were largely forgotten after the war, but thanks to a long campaign by former prisoners and expats living in Taiwan, a memorial was erected at the Kinkaseki site in 1997, and in 1999 the Taiwan POW Camps Memorial Society was formed to research all POW camps on the island (Ⓦ www.powtaiwan.org). Several plaques have since been erected all over Taiwan, and a short memorial service takes place at Kinkaseki every year around November 11.

Gold Ecological Park

Occupying the slopes on the western side of Jinguashi, the **Gold Ecological Park** (Tues–Fri 9.30am–5pm, Sat–Sun 9.30am–6pm; NT$100; ⓦwww .gep.tpc.gov.tw) is a mixture of museums and restored mining buildings, most dating from the Japanese period. The park's **tourist office** is located at the entrance, and from here well-marked walkways lead to all the main sights. The principal trail leads past a row of food stalls to the **Environment Educational Center** containing exhibits about the geology and ecology of the area, and a short introductory film. Behind here you'll find the **Crown Prince Chalet**, a distinctively Japanese guesthouse built in 1922 for Prince Hirohito's state visit the following year, though in the end he never made it up the mountain. Just before the Gold Museum, the **Benshan Fifth Tunnel Experience Area** is a 180m section of renovated mine complete with wax exhibits – you have to join a tour to go inside (Tues–Fri 9.30am, 1.30am, 3.30am; Sat–Sun 9.30am, 10.30am, 1.30am, 3.30am, 4.30am; NT$50). From here it's a short but steep walk up to the ruined **Gold Temple** (Huanjin Miao), a Japanese Shinto shrine built in 1933 and later destroyed by fire.

Housed in the former Taiwan Metal Mining Company building at the end of the old rail track beyond the Benshan Tunnel, the **Gold Museum** focuses on the area's mining history. The highlight for many tourists is the chance to touch the **world's largest gold bar**, located on the second floor; at 220kg, it was worth over US$5m in late 2006. Suitably motivated, you can sign up for **gold panning** on the third floor (Tues–Fri 11.30am, 1.30pm, 2.30pm; Sat–Sun 10.30am, 11.30am, 1.30pm, 2.30pm, 3.30pm; NT$100). You're guaranteed to find gold dust – the museum adds some to each batch of river water used. There is also a small exhibition in the museum dedicated to the Kinkaseki POW camp (see p.179).

Pingsi Branch Rail Line

The scenic **PINGSI BRANCH RAIL LINE** splits from the main line at the village of Sandiaoling, around 8km south of Rueifang. From here, it winds its

Pingsi Branch Rail Line		
Pingsi Branch Rail Line	平溪支線	*píngxī zhīxiàn*
Rueifang	瑞芳	*ruìfāng*
Sandiaoling	三貂嶺	*sān diāolǐng*
Jingtong	菁桐	*jīngtóng*
Crown Prince Hotel	太子賓館	*tàizǐ bīngguǎn*
Palace Restaurant	皇宮咖啡簡餐	*huánggōng kāfēi jiǎncān*
Shihsunjian	石筍尖	*shísǔnjiān*
Shulang Mountain	薯榔尖	*shǔlángjiān*
Pingsi	平溪	*píngxī*
Lingjiao	嶺 腳	*lǐngjiǎo*
Lingyan Temple	靈巖寺	*língyán sì*
Siaozih Mountain	孝子山	*xiàozǐshān*
Shihfen	十分	*shífèn*
Coal Mine Museum	台灣煤礦博物館	*táiwān méikuàng bówùguǎn*
Dahua	大 華	*dàhuá*
Shihfen Waterfall	十分瀑布	*shífèn pùbù*

way almost 13km up the Keelung River valley to the atmospheric village of Jingtong, passing through the old mining communities of Pingsi and Shihfen. For much of the twentieth century this was the heart of Taiwan's **coal industry**, and, though the mines have all now closed, you'll find several reminders of its industrial past scattered around the valley. These days however, it's the mountain scenery, **hiking trails** and waterfalls that attract most of the tourists – **Shihfen Waterfall** is the biggest, and the line's most popular attraction. The valley is also the location for one of Taiwan's most captivating **lantern festivals**.

Practicalities

The line makes another good day-trip from Taipei, though you'll need two or three days to complete all the best hikes. Note that although you'll avoid the crowds during the week, far more shops and eating options are open at the weekends. The usual place to pick up a **train** is the main-line station at **Ruei-fang**, connected by regular express and ordinary trains to the capital: buy an all-day Pingsi Line pass here for NT$50, or pay per journey – the maximum is NT$30 for the Rueifang to Jingtong trip. Trains depart at irregular but fairly frequent intervals from early morning to 11pm: the last train leaves Jingtong at 10pm. An alternative from Taipei is to take the #16 **bus** which connects Muzha with Jingtong and Pingsi village (40min; NT$45), and join the railway from there. The bus departs the opposite side of Muzha Road from Muzha MRT station. Buses leave at 7.15am, 8.20am, 9.45am and 11am, thereafter at irregular intervals until 10.40pm. The last bus departs Pingsi at 9.10pm.

Shihfen and around

From Rueifang, the village of **SHIHFEN** is the third stop on the Pingsi Line, swamped at the weekends by tourists that come primarily to gawp at its celebrated **waterfall**. The falls are back towards Rueifang, on the eastern side of Shihfen, but the **Coal Mine Museum** (daily 8.30am–5.30pm; NT$200) is a worthy detour en route; follow the tracks through the centre of the village, then the road as it bears left, and you'll pass the entrance a short walk ahead. The museum is, in fact, the abandoned New Pingsi Coal Mine and processing plant, the whole thing eerily frozen in time from the day the miners stopped working. The site has two parts: the entrance stands beside the old processing plant and from here a trail follows a conveyor belt, still littered with coal, up a slope and to the end of a narrow-gauge rail line. It's a bone-shaking, painfully slow one-kilometre ride from here to the second area at the mine head, a collection of exhibition rooms (Chinese labels only) and the **mineshaft** itself, the most interesting part of the site. The shaft is gradually being restored – at the time of writing you could walk 100m into the mountain. A trail leads from the left of the tunnel entrance 3.2km up **Wufen Mountain** (757m), the highest in the valley with a weather station on top.

Continue walking along the lane in front of the museum entrance and you'll eventually hit the main road: take the lower fork across the river to the **Shih-fen Scenic Administration Office** (daily 8am–5.30pm) which has maps, information and a small café. **Shihfen Waterfall** (daily 7.30am–6pm; NT$180) is another fifteen minutes from here along a trail that starts at the back of the building and crosses the river twice before rejoining the rail tracks. En route you'll pass **Eyeglass Hole Waterfall**, named after the two hollows that have been eroded into the rock behind it. The main falls are 15m high and 30m wide, not quite Niagara, but impressive nonetheless, and wonderfully photogenic, especially in full flood. The site has become a bit of a carnival at weekends and holidays, with snack stalls and trails leading further downstream. From the entrance you can continue down the tracks through a tunnel for another 1km to catch the next train at **Dahua** station or return to Shihfen.

Pingsi and around

PINGSI is the sixth stop and one of the valley's most atmospheric villages, though there's not much to see unless you visit during the **Lantern Festival** (January or February) – the village (along with Shihfen) is home to one of Taiwan's most enchanting spectacles, the release of hundreds of "sky lanterns" or *tiandang* (see p.51). At other times you can buy and launch individual lanterns (NT$100) from shops that line the main road towards Jingtong – try no. 67 or 68. Pingsi is also surrounded by excellent **hiking trails**. Walk through the village and across the river to the main road – turn left here and in a few metres you should pass a sign-posted trail on the right leading to **Putao Mountain** and **Siaozih Mountain** (360m), both 1km away. The summit of the latter is a steep tower of rock scaled by steel ladders – the views are impressive, but don't try the climb on a wet day. A less challenging hike, but with equally fine views, begins a further 1km along the main road in the village of **Lingjiao** (take the signposted road to the left to get to the train station) and ends at **Lingyan Temple**. This route isn't well marked but it's not hard to follow: walk up through the village from Lingjiao station and stay on the road, keeping the stream on your left (ignore the tributary on the right). In around 500m you'll come to a fork in the road marked by a large temple gate – continue left until you see a path on the right marked in red Chinese characters on a yellow sign. This leads another 500m up the slope to a small lane in front of the temple. The views are worth the walk, but though the temple isn't particularly special, Taiwanese come to pray at the **Guanyin Dripping Water Cave** at the back: this is actually a small hollow in the rocks covered in stalactites, one of which supposedly resembles the Buddhist deity.

Jingtong

The old mining village of **JINGTONG** is another reminder of the valley's industrial past – mining ceased here in 1987. It's the final stop on the line or a 1.3 kilometre walk from Pingsi, along the road that follows the tracks. The small wooden **train station**, built in 1931 by the Japanese, lies on narrow **Old Street**: to the left the **Jingtong Mine Museum** (daily 10am–5pm; free) displays information about the area and the mine, though there are no English labels, while in the other direction the street is lined with small shops and a couple of cafés. Old street ends a few metres beyond at the main road overlooking the bridge – turn right here, taking the lane that leads down to the river, to the Tai Yang Club-house, also known as the **Crown Prince Hotel** (Sat–Sun 10am–5pm; NT$50) a few metres below. This beautifully preserved Japanese-style guesthouse was built in 1939 and is now the home of the Chu-Lien Meditation Centre – it is, nevertheless, very evocative of the occupation period. Once you've had a peek inside (leave your shoes at the door), keep walking around the hotel and cross the river: turn immediately right then left up an alley and you'll see the *Palace Restaurant* (daily 11am–9pm) on the right, another Japanese-era building now functioning as an attractive teahouse. The tranquil interior offers a choice of tables with tatami mats or chairs – you can order tea (NT$250–500 per pot) or light meals, though there are no English menus.

Back in the village, the area above and behind the station is dominated by the **Coal Mine Memorial Park**, the remains of the Shihdi Mine which closed in 1975. A path on the other side of the tracks leads first to the derelict coal preparation plant, topped by a small café, and further up the hill the ruins of the mine-head buildings and the main tunnel, sealed by an iron-bar gate.

The main **hikes** in the area are trails up **Shulangjian** (622m) and **Shihsunjian** (Stone Bamboo Mountain, 545m) – both offer marvellous views over the valley. The trailhead is 300m from the red-brick preparation plant: follow the road beyond the plant to a small junction and look for the lane with the fake bamboo fence. The path is marked by signs in English 200m further along the lane: Shulangjian is 1.2km while Shisunjian is 1km, though the trail continues on from the latter another 3km back to Pingsi.

Northeast Coast National Scenic Area

The **Northeast Coast National Scenic Area** incorporates some of Taiwan's most spectacular coastal scenery. Accessible by bus or train, the area can be covered as a series of lengthy day-trips from Taipei or Keelung, though **Fulong**, with its attractive **beach**, is a gateway to the region and a more convenient base for longer stays. Highlights include the network of **hiking trails** between Bitou Cape and Longdong, the surfing hotspot of **Dasi**, volcanic **Turtle Island** and the hotel at the **Lion Kingdom Museum**, a discreet getaway for Taiwanese celebrities and politicians.

The northern section of the scenic area is accessible by **bus**: the easiest option is to catch the Keelung to Fulong service (daily 4.30am–10pm, once an hour;

Northeast Coast National Scenic Area

Northeast Coast National Scenic Area	東北角海岸國家風景區	*dōngběi jiǎo hǎiàn guó jiā fēng jǐng qū*
Bitou Cape	鼻頭角	*bítóu jiǎo*
Aodi Fishing Harbour	澳底漁港	*àodǐ yúgǎng*
Longdong Bay Park	龍洞灣公園	*lóngdòngwān gōngyuán*
Longdong South Ocean Park	龍洞南口海洋公園	*lóngdòng nánkǒu hǎiyáng gōngyuán*
Caoling Historic Trail	草嶺古道	*cǎolǐng gǔdào*
Dali	大里	*dàlǐ*
Dasi	大溪	*dàxī*
Cool Surf Store	小顧衝浪俱樂部	*xiǎogù chōnglàng jùlèbù*
Dou-Dou	荳荳	*dòu dòu*
Honeymoon Bay	蜜月灣	*mìyuèwān*
Jeff's Surf Shop	"Jeff's" 衝浪俱樂部	*"Jeff's" chōnglàng jùlèbù*
Spider Surf Club	台灣蜘蛛衝浪俱樂部	*táiwān zhīzhū chōnglàng jùlèbù*
Fulong Beach	福隆海水浴場	*fúlóng hǎishuǐ yùchǎng*
Longmen Campsite	龍門露營區	*lóngmén lùyíng qū*
Yanliao Beach Park	鹽寮海濱公園	*yánliáo hǎibīn gōngyuán*
Lion Kingdom Museum	河東堂獅子博物館	*hédōngtáng shīzi bówùguǎn*
Beiguan Tidal Park	北關海潮公園	*běiguān hǎicháo gōngyuán*
Turtle Island	龜山島	*guīshān dǎo*
Wushih Harbor	烏石港	*wūshígǎng*

on the hour from 9am; NT$100), which stops at Bitou (NT$60) and all the other major sites en route. The bus departs a local hospital, passing Keelung bus station ten to fifteen minutes later: lookout for the Chinese characters for "Fulong". Alternatively Kuo Kuang runs a bus (daily 6.20am–8.20pm, every two hours) from the North Bus Station in Taipei: it terminates in Toucheng after stopping at all the major attractions between Bitou, Fulong, Dasi and the Lion Kingdom Museum.

Fulong is also accessible from Taipei by frequent **express trains** (1hr 5min; NT$132), while Dali and Dasi further south are linked to Taipei and Fulong by slower services.

Bitou Cape to Aodi

BITOU is a small fishing community that lies at the trailhead to **Bitou Cape**, a rugged outcrop of layered sandstone and one of Taiwan's most scenic pieces of coastline. From Keelung (30–40min), get off the bus before the tunnel on the edge of the village. From here there's a choice of two **hiking trails**. The **Lighthouse Trail** (1.2km) starts across the bridge over the road, but for the best views head back into the village for the **Ridge Valley Trail** (1.1km) which starts on the right side of the harbour near the temple. All the trails are well marked in English – the latter rises steeply over the top of the cape to join the main trail on the southern side. There's a small lighthouse at the end, but it's the magnificent views that make the hike worthwhile. From the lighthouse, follow the **Coastal Trail** (0.8km) along the seashore, passing a cluster of bizarre geological formations to **Longdong Bay Park** (June–October 8am–6pm; NT$100), a series of sea-fed swimming pools next to the main road. From here it's another 2km around the bay to Longdong village – the stone pools here are abalone farms. Longdong's popular **rock climbing** area is a further 1.5km around the next cape, the 30m sandstone cliffs packed with climbers at the weekends. The start of the trail to **Longdong Coastal Park** is clearly marked back in the village, climbing 100m above the cliffs and providing several stunning viewpoints. The trail ends at the main road and a bus stop, but there's a small extension that leads down to the mass of concrete below: this is **Longdong South Ocean Park** (daily 8.30am–5pm; NT$100; ⓦwww.ldsmarina.net.tw), a centre for watersports with three seawater pools open in the summer and an exhibition on local geology. The busy town of **Aodi** is a further 4km down the road, a largely unattractive fishing port famous for its wholesale fish market (daily 5–9am) and the **seafood restaurants** that line its main street.

Fulong and around

FULONG, just under 6km south of Aodi, has one of north Taiwan's best **beaches**, with heaps of fine sand surrounded by a ring of lush mountains. It's also the most convenient place to stay on the northeast coast, and famous in Taiwan for its **lunchboxes** or *biandang*, typically grilled pork or fish with a boiled egg, several types of vegetables and rice. You can buy these for around NT$50 on the train station platform or at the shops just to the left of the entrance. Since 1999 it's also been home to the Ho-Hai-Yan Rock Festival (ⓦwww.hohaiyan.com), held every July over several days, and primarily featuring bands from Taiwan and Japan – it's free and attracts up to 100,000 people. **Cape Sandiao**, 7.5km east of Fulong along the main highway, is Taiwan's most easterly point, but other than a lighthouse, there's not much to see here.

The beach

The main entrance to **Fulong Beach** is just beyond the visitor centre at the northern end of the village, a long spit of sand across the Shuangsi River: it's officially open June to October when there's a charge of NT$60, though approach the beach via the southern end of the village and you'll find a free section. The sand is fine, but tends to get covered in flotsam in the winter when it's not cleaned. While **swimming** is Fulong Beach's main draw, it sometimes gets waves suitable for **surfing** and **bodyboarding**. Although the surf here is not nearly as consistent as that of neighbouring Dasi to the south, ahead of tropical storms it's a favoured retreat of local surfers looking to escape a battering at Honeymoon Bay (see p.186). You can **rent** longboards and shortboards (NT$500 per day) and bodyboards (NT$250 per day) at the Cool Surf Store at 13-3 Singlong St (☎02/24992287), which also has a branch in Dasi.

For a change of scene, rent **boats** or hire **bicycles** (1hr NT$80, 4hrs NT$300) at the *Longmen Campsite* and follow the Longmen–Yanliao Bike Path, a 4km concrete trail across the suspension bridge over the Shuangsi River and through the dunes, north to **Yanliao Beach Park** (daily 9am–7pm; NT$60) – bikes must be left at the entrance. This beautiful beach tops Taiwan's longest continuous stretch of sand (3km) and is the spot where the **Japanese invasion** force landed in May 1895 – a stone monument commemorates those that died resisting the occupation, while information boards labelled in English and Chinese detail the main events of the initial invasion.

Practicalities

Fulong train station sits just off the main road in the centre of the village, near a cluster of basic restaurants and a convenience store. The Taipei to Toucheng bus can be picked up on the main road, while Keelung buses terminate in the car park facing the main Northeast Coast Scenic Area **visitor center** (daily 9am–5pm; Ⓦwww.necoast-nsa.gov.tw). From the train station walk to the main road and turn left – you'll see the centre across the car park on your right. There's plenty of information available and several exhibition rooms inside.

There are a few cheap but nondescript **hotels** (❷) on the main road near the station, but 500m to the north the sprawling *Longmen Campsite*, 100 Singlong Street (☎02/24991791, Ⓦlongmen.cjb.net; NT$70 entry) is better value and the biggest **campsite** in Taiwan. It's NT$800 per night for tents for four people (NT$1000 for the drive-in area) or NT$1300 for tents underneath wooden shelters. Bring your own tent and pay NT$150 less. Chalet-type rooms are also available from NT$2300 for two. There are showers, a swimming pool (NT$60) and small shop on site.

Caoling Historic Trail

The **Caoling (Tsaoling) Historic Trail** is a 9.7-kilometre path that cuts across the hills between Fulong and Dali – it's a beautiful walk with mesmerizing views of the ocean at its southern end, easily covered in half a day. The trail incorporates the only remaining section of a stone trail, built in 1807 by Taiwan's first settlers to link Danshui with Yilan; the most historic sight en route is the **Tiger Tablet**, a stone flamboyantly engraved with the Chinese character for "Tiger". The story goes that military official Liu Ming-teng made the carving in 1867 in allusion to the mythical powers tigers have to control powerful winds: you'll probably see why this is appropriate when you reach the head of the pass nearby.

The trail can be tackled in either direction, though the steepest climb is the 2.8km between Dali and the pass – the route climbs more smoothly from

Fulong, which also has more convenient rail connections. A new four-kilometre route links Fulong to the head of the main trail, though this can be tricky to follow in places. From **Fulong Station** walk to the main road and turn left – you'll see the first sign about 150m further along directing you back under the tracks. It's an easy 3km along a tarmac lane from here until the signs disappear and the road ends at two brick farmhouses – walk through the yard of the house on the left to find the concrete path on the other side. Follow this until you see a narrow trail leading down to the right, marked in Chinese – you should be OK from here, eventually coming to a bridge and the main (signposted) route on the other side. In **DALI**, the trail ends at the back of the surprisingly large **Tiangong Temple**, dedicated to the Jade Emperor and a popular pilgrimage site. Just next door the **Dali visitor center** (daily 9am–5pm; free; ☎03/9780727) houses decent exhibitions on the area and particularly its Ketagalan inhabitants, but only in Chinese. Dali train station is a short walk along the main road.

To extend the hike, take the **Taoyuan Valley Trail** from the head of the pass. This is a network of four separate routes: the first connects the Caoling Trail with the valley itself (4.5km) over Mount Wankengtou (617m). Here you have three choices: the best option is to take the five-kilometre trail to Dasi Park, a short walk from the train station and the beach at Dasi.

Dasi

South of Cape Sandiao, the northernmost foothills of the Syueshan Range rise sharply from the coast, creating a striking backdrop to the small towns that line the busy highway. **DASI**, 4km south of Dali, is a once-tranquil town that is quickly being transformed into Taiwan's premier **surf centre**. Dasi is widely considered to have the most consistent beach break in northern Taiwan, and the waves on the edge of town in **Honeymoon Bay** hold great appeal for experienced and novice surfers alike, with typically hollow faces yet enough power and speed to lend themselves to shortboards and quick take-offs. There is also usually plenty of gentle swell for novices, and due to Dasi's proximity to Taipei it can be choked with Taiwanese beginners on summer weekends – seasoned riders are better off going during the week, when they often have the beautiful stretch of black-sand beach all to themselves. Although Dasi can be surfed year-round, the biggest waves occur in **winter** – particularly in March – when faces of up to three metres can be had, though the water is cold at this time and you'll definitely need a wetsuit. Without question the most exciting swell kicks up in the days preceding one of the many **typhoons** that batter Taiwan's east coast every summer, but during these storms the water is extremely choppy and only suited to experienced surfers.

In recent years, the beach at Honeymoon Bay has also become a popular place for all-night **rave parties**, many of them organized by well-known DJs from Taiwan's major cities. In summer, there are raves here almost every other weekend, when hundreds of Taiwanese and expats converge on Dasi, more than doubling the local population. While locals have been more than accommodating, many complain about the piles of rubbish that the revellers invariably leave on the beach.

Practicalities

Cross the street after you exit the **train station**; the surf shops are about 100m to the left, while the beach is about 500m down the road to the right. Apart from the popular option of bringing your own tent and camping on the beach,

accommodation is limited to the rooms available at the town's three **surf shops**. These spartan lodgings can fill up quickly on summer weekends, so if you're planning to come at this time **reservations** are highly recommended. Two of the three offer **surfing packages** that include accommodation, meals, lessons and board rentals; if you just want to hire a board expect to pay NT$400/NT$500 per day for shortboards/longboards.

Jeff's Surf Shop at 100 Binhai Rd Sec 5 (⑦03/9781781) is run by one of Taiwan's seminal surfers and offers an excellent two-day/one-night surfing package for NT$2800. Accommodation consists of mattresses on the floor and the surf instructors here take the unorthodox approach of recommending that beginners are taught on shortboards. Next door, the *Spider Surf Club* (⑦03/9781321, ⓦwww.spidersurfing.com), 96 Binhai Rd, Sec 5, is popular with young surfers who spend weekends in the cheap but dingy basement dorm (NT$300 per bed). Their two-day/one-night surfing package is slightly more expensive, at NT$3000, but the club offers affordable memberships aimed at those planning to be regulars at Dasi; the club's website has limited English information on daily conditions. Finally, the *Cool Surf Store* at 92 Binhai Rd Sec 5 (⑦03/9781359; ❷) doesn't offer packages, but longboard rental includes a ten-minute lesson and use of the shop's showers. Accommodation consists of three small, clean doubles and a six-person dorm (NT$300 per bed).

Dasi's best **place to eat** is *Dou-Dou* (⑦03/9781147), a cosy little restaurant a few hundred metres past the surf shops, on the same side of the road. The friendly mother-daughter management serves up simple Chinese and Western dishes all day long. While sandwiches are available, house specialties are the delicious fried pork dumplings (*guotie*) and fried turnip cakes (*luobo gao*). The fresh coffee is excellent.

Lion Kingdom Museum

Around 4km south of Dasi, the 🏛 **Lion Kingdom Museum** (daily 9am–6pm; ⑦03/9780782, ⓦwww.leogroup.com.tw; NT$180), also known as the Leo Club, doubles as an exclusive **hotel** (❼), patronized by many of the country's top politicians, including the president. A mix of contemporary and southern Fujian-style architecture, the museum takes up the two basement floors and displays a portion of the six thousand Chinese stone lions collected by owner John Kao over more than thirty years – the oldest piece is from Shanxi and is over three thousand years old.

The main attraction here, however, is the **view**: watching the sunrise over Turtle Island, just across the water, is a captivating experience, assuming you can get up early enough to see it. The hotel's attractive gardens border the rocky shoreline and are a good place to relax, though during weekdays the main road next to the hotel roars with traffic. The Taipei–Toucheng bus stops a few metres away, opposite the **Beiguan Tidal Park,** a popular tour-bus destination with snack stalls and a short walkway along a rocky piece of coast, once the site of a Qing dynasty fort. You could walk back to Dasi from here, but the constant stream of trucks makes this a fairly unpleasant option.

Turtle Island

Turtle Island (Kueishan Island), around 10km off the east coast, is Taiwan's only active volcanic island, a towering mass of andesite and basalt that was until 2000 a highly secretive military base and strictly off-limits – from a distance, it does vaguely resemble a turtle emerging from the water. The island makes an interesting half-day tour, though it requires some advance planning and is extremely popular in the summer months: at the time of writing just 350 people were allowed on the island per day.

The thirty-minute boat ride to the island is part of the attraction – the views of its main peak are magnificent but you're also virtually assured sighting **flying fish** and the 300-strong pod of **dolphins** that feed in the warm, volcanic waters off the coast. Most boats spend a few minutes tailing the group though restrictions prevent them from getting too close. You may also pass through bizarre patches of light blue and milky white water, bubbling up from hot undersea springs just off the island – this is one of the much touted "eight wonders" of the island.

Once ashore most groups spend around an hour and a half being led around a cluster of sights next to **Guiwei Lake** on the island's northwest corner, and dominated by the jungle-covered peak above. The buildings here are remnants of a small fishing village founded in 1825, its inhabitants forced to move to Dasi in 1977 when the military took over. When the villagers left, they closed the local Mazu temple and took the image of the goddess with them – the army subsequently installed an image of Guanyin inside, and today the shrine has been restored and is known as **Putuoyan Temple**. A statue of Guanyin also stands on the southern side of the lake. An old army building acts as a basic visitor centre near the temple (you can buy drinks and souvenirs here), while back near the dock you can explore 800m of **army tunnels**, each leading to a gun emplacement in the cliffs. To climb the 401m summit you'll need special permission and will probably have to join a research team or university party: Mondays are reserved for these groups.

Practicalities

Weather permitting, the island is open to visitors from March to October (Tues–Sun 9am–5pm), though you need to apply to the scenic area administration for a **permit** three days in advance. The good news is that this can be done online in English (Ⓦwww.necoast-nsa.gov.tw): find the "Kueishan Island" section and follow the instructions. Alternatively, you can apply at the Dali visitor center.

Most boats leave **Wushih Harbor** near Toucheng: once you have the permit, you can just show up and take the first boat out, though they need at least twenty people to make the trip – get there before 8.30am on a weekend since the first boats leave before 9am. **Wushih Harbor visitor center** (daily 8am–5.30pm) near the marina can help with tour bookings (there were thirteen different boats at the time of writing) but if you can speak Chinese, make a reservation in advance (try ☏03/9781311 or 03/9782511 for reputable boats).

Full tours (2.5hr) cost NT$1600, while cruises around the island are NT$800 and up. **Toucheng** is accessible by express **train** from Taipei (1hr 20min; NT$189); from Toucheng station you can take a taxi (NT$100) or walk to Wushih Harbor in around thirty minutes. Turn left when exiting the station and follow the road to the main street; turn left again and follow this all the way out of town and onto Highway 2.

Jiaosi to Suao

South of Toucheng, the mountains fall back along the Lanyang River valley to open up a region of flat agricultural land and densely populated towns. Known as the Lanyang Plain, and forming the core of **Yilan County**, it contains a few worthwhile pit-stops before continuing south along the east coast.

Jiaosi to Suao

Jiaosi	礁溪	jiāoxī
Chuan Tang Hotel	泉湯旅館	qúantāng lǚgǔan
Erlong	二龍	èrlóng
Erlong Dragon Boat Races	二龍詩人節	èrlóng shīrén jié
Wufongci Waterfalls	五峰旗瀑布	wǔfēngqí pùbù
Luodong	羅東	luódōng
Chinshuei Park	親水公園	qīnshuǐ gōng yúan
Hua-Wang Business Hotel	華王商務旅館	huáwáng shāngwù lǚguan
Minsheng Market	民生市場	mínshēng shìcháng
Music Water House	音樂水屋	yīnyùe shuǐwū
National Center for Traditional Arts	國立傳統藝術中心	guólì chúantǒng yìshù zhōngxīn
Suao	蘇澳	sūào
Ba Fang Yun Ji	八方雲集	bāfāng yúnjí
Fish Market	魚市	yúshì
Jinhua Hotel	金華冷泉旅館	jīnhuá lěngqúan lǚguǎn
Nanfangao	南方澳	nánfāngào
Nantian Temple	南天宮	nántiān gōng
Suao Cold Springs	蘇澳冷泉	sūào lěngqúan
Suao Hotel	蘇澳大飯店	sūào dàfàndiàn
Yilan	宜蘭	yílán

Jiaosi and around

South of Toucheng, the resort town of **JIAOSI** is best known for its hot springs and the spectacular waterfalls just outside the city. As the main **hot-springs** area in the northeastern plains, Jiaosi is immensely popular with working-class Taiwanese, and in recent years there has been a proliferation of spa hotels, many offering rock-bottom rates. Most of these hotels have public bathing pools that non-guests can use for a nominal fee, giving you the option of having a soak after visiting the waterfalls and then moving on.

The **Wufongci (Five-peak Flag) Waterfalls**, about 4km west of the Jiaosi train station, are among the most impressive of Taiwan's accessible waterfalls and are definitely worth a side-trip if you're passing through the area. The falls consist of three separate cascades, with the upper two plummeting dramatically over sheer bluffs at least 30m high. A paved pathway leads to the falls, with a graceful **Chinese pavilion** providing a picturesque vantage point onto the middle section. From here the path climbs, with a series of concrete steps leading to the upper falls, where the stream plunges straight down over a wide cliff face, clinging closely to the moss-covered rock. The waterfalls are named after this section, as locals liken the five "peaks" in the cliff face to the five triangular banners that typically adorn the back of a war general's costume in a traditional Chinese opera. Just before the trailhead is a line of **food stalls** selling an assortment of "little eats" and beverages. To get there, a narrow road leads through the valley west of town, but it's difficult to find this road from the train station so you'd be better off taking a taxi (NT$150) there and walking back.

Jiaosi's bicarbonate hot-spring water is clear and odourless, and is piped into the dozens of **spa hotels** in town. One of those with the most elaborate public bathing complexes is the *Chuan Tang Hotel* at 218 Jhongshan Rd Sec 2 (℡03/9880606; ❺), the first hotel on the right after you exit the train station

Dragon-boating to a different beat

Every summer, usually in June, the sleepy village of **ERLONG** – about 10km southeast of Jiaosi – comes alive with Taiwan's most unusual dragon boat race, an "aboriginal-style" affair that features several twists to conventional Chinese dragon boating. The **Erlong Dragon Boat Race**, which has been held on a narrow stretch of the Erlong River for more than two hundred years, perpetuates the traditions of the **Kavalan aborigines** who pioneered the canoe-like boat race as a ritual to ease the suffering of unhappy river ghosts. In addition to being more animated and colourful than Chinese-style dragon boat races, the Erlong event takes place on a more intimate section of river, allowing you to get close to the action. Unlike the Chinese-style competition, during which participants remain seated, rowers in the Erlong races kneel on the boats' floors, facing outwards and paddling deep into the water. Most teams compete shirtless, with twenty rowers, one gong-sounder and a rudder man, all wearing matching headbands or hats. Racers paddle to the clang of a gong, with the gong-sounder perched on the boat's bow. There are no timers, judges or starters, and the winners are chosen by the **crowd** after several gruelling sprints. The long, slender canoes are veritable works of art, with yin yang symbols painted on both bow and stern, as well as on contestants' paddles. Just before the races, dragon eyes are painted on each boat's bow, incense and paper money are burnt and fireworks are set off. Only after all this are the boats carried down to the river. To get here from the Jiaosi train station, catch a **taxi** to the Erlong River: drivers will know where to take you and should charge about NT$300. Alternatively, it's easy to hitch a ride with locals heading to the races.

(the sign just says "Hotel" in English). Use of its several bathing pools with massage showers costs NT$250.

Yilan

Though it's one of the east coast's biggest towns, **YILAN** has little to offer tourists, but is an important **transport hub** for excursions to pleasant mountain villages such as **Lishan** and **Wuling Farm**, the staging point for ascents of glorious **Syueshan** (Snow Mountain, see p.221). There are two buses daily (7am & 12.40pm; NT$258) to Lishan (3hr), stopping at several villages along the way, including Wuling Farm (2hr 45min). From both Lishan and Wuling Farm, it's possible to catch a bus headed east into the **Taroko Gorge**, from where you can hop another bus on to Hualien, making for a very scenic circuit. To get to Yilan **bus station**, turn left after you exit the train station and walk for several hundred metres: you'll see it across the road to your right. If you need to stay overnight in Yilan, there is a clutch of cheap-but-shabby **hotels** about 500m to the right after you exit the train station.

Luodong and around

About halfway between Yilan and Suao is the bustling town of **LUODONG**, a major stop on the eastern railway line, known primarily for the **National Center for Traditional Arts** (9am–9pm; ☎03/9705815; NT$80) located 7km east of the train station. The privately run centre puts on daily **performances** of Chinese opera, folk dance and acrobatics, and there's a **Folk Art Boulevard** (9am–6pm) lined with shops selling expensive hand-made crafts such as wooden slippers, tea sets, glassware, candles, finger puppets, fans and jewellery. An interesting **exhibition hall** (9am–5pm; closed Mon) has in-depth explanations of many traditional arts, including those of various

△ Dragon boat race in Erlong

aboriginal tribes. The complex also includes a coffeeshop and convenience store, as well as a couple of snack bars. One of the best things to do here is to take a walk along the short concrete path that winds through the quiet marsh that the centre describes as a "wetland reserve area". It's also possible to take boat rides (9am–5.30pm; NT$50/100 one-way/return) across the Dongshan River to **Chinshuei Park** (40min return), which every summer is the site of one of Taiwan's biggest Chinese **dragon boat races**.

The centre is located at 268 Wubin Rd Sec 2, just off coastal Highway 2, making it convenient if you've got your own transport. Alternatively, **taxis** from Luodong train station cost NT$250 one-way; remember to book one for the return journey as you can't count on catching one outside the centre and there is no public transport.

Practicalities

Luodong is a convenient place to spend the night, with a huge night market and affordable accommodation. There are a few cheap **hotels** along the main Gongjheng Road that runs directly out from the **train station**, but they are old and dirty. A much better option is the *Hua-Wang Business Hotel* at 41 Jhongjheng North Rd (☎03/9544155; ③), which is spotlessly clean and excellent value, with comfortable beds and cable TV. To get there, walk down Gongjheng Road a few hundred metres until you reach Jhongjheng North Road; turn right, and it's about 200m further on your left. The **Minsheng Market**, along the second street to your left coming down Gongjheng Road from the train station, is a lively **night market** known for its cooked lamb stalls and iced desserts. About 100m north of the *Hua-Wang*, on the same side of the road, is the *Music Water House* (daily 7pm–2am; 19 Jhongjheng North Rd), a cosy **bar** with big bottles of Taiwan Beer for NT$120 and **live music** every Friday (the sign out front simply says "Pub"). There is an **Internet café** (NT$20 per hr) at 104 Gongjheng Rd, several hundred metres down Gongjheng Road from the train station, on the right-hand side, and an **ATM** in the 7-Eleven across the street from the train station.

Suao and around

With a population of around 45,000, **SUAO** is the last major town on the Lanyang Plain, and the last important stop on the east coast before Taroko Gorge and Hualien (see Chapter 5). It's not a particularly attractive place, but in the summer it's worth a pit-stop to visit **Suao Cold Springs** at 6–4 Lengcyuan Road (daily 8am–10pm; NT$70; NT$100 for private bath), some of the most attractive outdoor spring baths in Taiwan. The entrance is a short walk from Suao train station (also known as the old station): walk straight up Taiping Road, turn left at Jhongshan Road and immediately right, and the springs are a few metres to the north on Lengcyuan Road (signposted "Lingzhuan"). The spa comprises a series of grand red-brick baths, set within the stylishly converted remains of the old soda factory built by the Japanese in the 1930s to utilize the naturally carbonated water. The bubbly waters contain odourless carbonic acid, and with an average temperature of 22 degrees Celsius are very refreshing in the summer heat.

Nanfangao

Just over 1km from Suao, **NANFANGAO** is an important port and fishing harbour, with a more lively and appealing atmosphere than its neighbour, three small **fish markets** at the end of the harbour, and plenty of excellent **seafood restaurants**. **Nantian Temple** (daily 5am–9pm) is a multi-level shrine facing the harbour in the centre of town, famous throughout Taiwan for its unusually large and opulent statues of the main deity, Mazu. The images portray the goddess in imperial style, with dragon-gilded robes and rich adornments matching her formal title of "Empress of Heaven". The third floor houses the temple's most celebrated **Gold Mazu**, a large statue placed in a suitably gold-draped altar and sporting a headdress with red neon lights. The view from here, back over the dragon-smothered temple roof and harbour beyond, is worth the short climb alone. Despite its archaic appearance, the temple was completed in 1956, and the statues were created in the 1980s and 1990s.

Practicalities

Most east-coast **trains** stop at **Suaosin** station, 3km from Suao, though it is possible to catch slower trains that terminate at the old station in Suao itself. If you do end up at Suaosin, **taxis** are around NT$160 into Suao proper, but if you walk down to the bus stop on the main road you should be able to pick up a regular Kuo Kuang **bus** into town – get off near the old train station on Jhongshan Road. These buses run between Nanfangao, Suao and Luodong (daily 6am–9pm, every 30min), 13km to the north. Left luggage in the old train station is open 8am–8pm and costs around NT$20 per item per day. The 7-Eleven on the corner of Lengcyuan and Jhongshan roads has a Chinatrust **ATM**, and there's a Bank of Taiwan at 97 Jhongshan Road. To get to Nanfangao from Suao, catch a bus from Jhongshan Road, or take a taxi (NT$130). In Nanfangao buses stop in front of Nantian Temple.

There are a couple of **places to stay** if you get stuck in Suao. *Jinhua Hotel* (☎03/9962526; ❷) is opposite the cold springs at 1 Lengcyuan Road, with cheap, basic rooms, and the added bonus of spa tubs in the bathrooms. *Suao Hotel* (☎03/9969171; ❸) at 7 Sudongjhong Road is a bit more upmarket, but the rooms are showing their age; you'll find it east of the old station at the end of Jhongshan Road.

For **food**, you're better off heading to Nanfangao, but in Suao, *Ba Fang Yun Ji* (daily 8am–7pm) at 10 Jhongshan Road knocks out decent steamed or fried dumplings (NT$4 each), as well as fishball soup (NT$25), and you'll see plenty of touristy shops around the train station selling dried fish and the town specialty, jelly (jam), made with spring water – varieties include orange, tea, plum and bean. The **food stalls** next to Nantian Temple are the cheapest places to eat in Nanfangao, dishing up the town's celebrated *mahi-mahi* fishballs, as well as favourites such as *lu ruo fan* for NT$25–35. For a more substantial seafood meal, head up either side of the harbour where there are plenty of restaurants to choose from – they're all pretty good, with live fish and shellfish displayed in tanks outside. You can buy fresh sushi (NT$100) at the fish market at the end of the harbour.

Northern Cross-Island Highway

The **Northern Cross-island Highway** (National Highway 7) is one of three spectacular routes that cross the mountainous interior of Taiwan, connecting the western plains with the east coast. Accessible from the sprawling city of **Taoyuan**, the northern route starts in **Dasi** in Taoyuan County and follows the Dahan River before crossing the Syueshan Range and joining the main Yilan to Lishan road at **Cilan**, 120km away in Yilan County. Though it's not quite as dramatic as the other cross-island highways, there's plenty to see along the way, and it's the closest to Taipei – you'll need your own transport to complete the whole route however, as buses are few and only travel as far as Shangbaling. The other option is to use Fusing as a base, and explore the

Northern Cross-Island Highway

Northern Cross-Island Highway	北橫公路	běihéng gōnglù
Baling	巴陵	bālíng
Cilan	棲蘭	qīlán
Dasi	大溪	dàxī
Cihhu	慈湖	cíhú
Cihhu Presidential Burial Place	慈湖陵寢	cíhú língqǐn
Dasi Presidential Burial Place	大溪陵	dàxī língqǐn
Huang Rih Siang	日香	huáng rì xiāng
Fusing	復興	fùxìng
Fusing Youth Activity Center	復興青年活動中心	fùxìng qīngnián huódòng zhōngxīn
Shihmen Reservoir	石門水庫	shímén shuǐkù
Lalashan National Forest Zone Nature Reserve	拉拉山國有林自然保護區	lālāshān guóyǒu línzìrán bǎohùqū
Little Wulai Falls	小烏來瀑布	xiǎowūlái pùbù
Mingchih National Forest Recreation Area	明池國家森林遊樂區	míngchí guójiā sēnlín yóulèqū
Shangbaling	上巴陵	shàngbálíng
Siao Wulai Special Scenic Area	小烏來風景 區	xiǎowūlái fēngjǐngqū
Taoyuan	桃 園	táoyuán
Dunhuang Plaza	敦煌精品飯店	dūnhuáng jīngpǐn fàndiàn
Nestle Hotel	雀巢大飯店	quècháo dàfàndiàn
Taoyuan Martyrs' Shrine	桃園縣忠烈祠	táoyuánxiàn zhōngliècí

area as a series of **day-trips**: from Dasi bus station, services travel via Fusing to most points as far as Shangbaling – it's best to check timetables in Dasi. The best times to travel the highway are **early spring** when the cherry blossoms flower and **autumn** when the temperature is mild and the hills are blanketed in flaming red maple trees.

Taoyuan

TAOYUAN, just thirty minutes south of Taipei, is the most convenient starting point for journeys across the Northern Cross-Island Highway. Named after the peach trees that once covered the area, it's now the fastest growing city in Taiwan and wholly unattractive. If you have time to kill, the **Taoyuan Martyrs' Shrine** (daily 8am–5pm; free), at 200 Chengkong Road Section 3, is a bit of trek from the train station, but it's the best preserved **Japanese Shinto shrine** in Taiwan, one of over two hundred constructed by the Japanese in the 1930s. In common with the rest of Taiwan, it was rededicated to the memory of Chinese heroes in 1946, but unusually the buildings were left untouched. The shrine is located on the slopes of Mount Futou, about 3km from the station. A few buses pass the entrance but bus #5 (NT$15) goes to the nearby Taoyuan Veterans Hospital more regularly from the **city bus station** at 158 Fusing Road (just left of the junction with Jhongjheng Road). From the hospital keep walking up Chengkong Road and you'll see the stone steps leading to the shrine on the right after a few minutes. Alternatively a taxi from the station should cost no more than NT$200.

Practicalities

Regular express **trains** connect Taoyuan with Taipei (NT$66) and the rest of the west coast. The **main bus station** is two blocks behind the train station – take the underpass located just to the right of the station exit, then keep walking straight along Yanping Road to the bus station on the right. There is only one bus along the cross-island highway as far as Baling (daily 6.50am; NT$185) – note that this is also the only bus that goes to Shihmen Reservoir (NT$85). The alternative is to take a bus to Dasi where there's more choice (daily 5.50am–10.30pm, every 15–20min; NT$40).

The best **place to stay** in the centre of town is *Dunhuang Plaza* at 39 Nanhua Street (T03/3326191; ❹), a few blocks west of the station off Fusing Road, though Changshou Street, immediately left of the train station exit, is lined with cheaper accommodation: *Nestle Hotel* is slightly better than the others (5-1 Changshou St T03/3365800; ❷). There are plenty of cheap places to eat around the station, along with all the major Western chains and more upmarket **restaurants** in the shopping malls close by. Mintzu Road, a short walk from the station, is the best place for **bars**. *Itzu Restaurant* at no. 46 is an old favourite, while *Rodeo Pub* at no. 167 is another popular expat hangout. To get to Mintzu Road go straight from the station till you hit Fusing Road and turn left – Mintzu is the first major intersection. Chinatrust Commercial Bank has an **ATM** in the train station.

Dasi to Fusing

DASI (not to be confused with the east-coast surfing town) is the official starting point for the Northern Cross-Island Highway. An historic town easily accessible from Taoyuan, Dasi is worth a brief stop to explore its two old streets lined with ornate Chinese baroque architecture. Heping Road and adjacent Jhongyang Road on the northern side of the town centre are crammed with craft stores, teashops and restaurants, many selling Dasi's most celebrated snack,

dried tofu – *Huang Rih Siang* at 56 Heping Road is one of the oldest and most popular tofu sellers. The elaborate facades on display are some of the best preserved in Taiwan, most dating from the grand redevelopment of the town that began in 1912, the finely carved arches and beams etched with the names of the trading companies that once operated here. At the western end of Heping Road, you can still see the back-breaking **Old Flagstone Path**, used by porters carrying supplies down to the Dahan River, several metres below.

From Dasi the highway runs southeast to the village of **Cihhu**, famous in Taiwan as the home of the **Cihhu Presidential Burial Place** (daily 8am–5pm; free), Chiang Kai-shek's temporary mausoleum. In 1988 his son Chiang Ching-kuo was buried nearby in Touliao at the **Dasi Presidential Burial Place** (daily 8am–5pm; free), connected to the Cihhu site by a two-kilometre path. As of early 2007, the two former presidents were expected to be reburied in permanent tombs on Wujhihshan near Taipei (see box, p.101), but the two sites will be maintained as memorials containing small exhibitions on both men. The Cihhu site was built in 1959 as one of Chiang's summerhouses, and sits next to a tranquil lake (Cihhu means "Lake Kindness"). The interior, including the former bedrooms of the President and his wife has been lovingly preserved. The main **information centre** (daily 8am–5pm) is located at the car park and main entrance to the former mausoleum.

Around 18km south of Dasi, the small town of **FUSING** is the best place to stay on the highway: the *Youth Activity Center* (1 Jhongshan Rd ℡03/3822276; ⑤) operated by China Youth Corp occupies a superb location overlooking an arm of **Shihmen Reservoir**, best appreciated from the sun deck of the restaurant on site. The centre was the location of another of Chiang Kai-shek's summer retreats, though the current building is a modern construction. The rooms are simple but comfortable, all en suite with TVs and magnificent views from the more expensive rooms on the top floor. Fusing is the first stop on the highway with an obvious **Atayal** influence, with cheap eats available along the main street close to the *Youth Activity Center* – the town's specialty is green bamboo shoots. **Buses** to Fusing leave Dasi hourly through the day.

Fusing to Cilan

From Fusing, the highway follows a series of gorges created by the Dahan River deep into the Syueshan Range, with the scenery becoming increasingly wild and rugged. Around four kilometres from Fusing, **Siao Wulai Special Scenic Area** (daily 8.30am–4.30pm; free; NT$100 parking) contains the 50m **Little Wulai Falls**, Taiwan's most picturesque waterfall. You can walk down to the river in front of the falls from the main road near the tollbooth via a steep path – if you drive down to the car park, the trails lead to a variety of attractions and viewpoints above the falls. The site lies 2km off the main highway: only a couple of **buses** connect the falls to Dasi and Fusing each morning.

South of here the highway becomes narrower, ending up as a winding, single-track road. Buses (two or three per day) go as far as the village of **Baling** (500m above sea level) at the bottom of the valley and lined with several basic places to eat, and on to the Atayal settlement of **Shangbaling**, a further 200m up the mountain on a side road. The village is perched on a narrow ridge, often shrouded in mist, and has a single street lined with cheap restaurants and places to stay if you get stuck – it's especially noted for its fruits and peaches. The village is on the road to **Lalashan National Forest Zone Nature Reserve** (daily 7am–6pm; NT$150), also known as Daguanshan, an incredibly atmospheric reserve of giant cypress trees or "God Trees" (*shengmu*), 1550m up in the mountains and 12.5km from the main highway. The small visitor centre here marks the start of a 3.7-kilometre trail around 22 of the biggest trees and viewpoints. The trees survived undiscovered during the period of intense logging initiated by the Japanese – most are between five hundred and an astonishing 2800 years old, with the tallest topping out at 55m. You pay for the reserve at a tollbooth just off the main road above Baling – there's no public transport from here or Shangbaling.

Back on the main highway, the route climbs to its highest point (1250m) near the **Mingchih National Forest Recreation Area** (daily 8am–5pm; NT$120), a tranquil alpine-like mountain retreat (free of tour buses), set around a small lake. The *Mingchih Mountain Hostel* (☏03/9894104; ❻) is a relatively expensive resort hotel near the visitor centre, but also contains an attractive restaurant and café. The area was once a lumber station and is surrounded by more giant hardwoods and "God Trees". Beyond Mingchih, the road drops steeply through thickly wooded slopes, 17km to another forest reserve at **Cilan** and the end of the highway: turn left for Yilan, Luodong (see p.190) and the east coast, and right for Lishan and the Wuling Recreation Area (see p.219).

Hsinchu and around

HSINCHU, 86km south of Taipei and thirty minutes from Taoyuan, is one of the wealthiest cities in Taiwan, largely as a result of the huge revenues generated by the **Science Park** on its southeastern border. Tucked away in the heart of all this development are remnants of one of north Taiwan's oldest cities, founded in the early eighteenth century, with plenty to offer casual visitors: unusual **temples** and **traditional food stalls** reflect the city's historic roots while the absorbing **Glass Museum** is testimony to its central role in Taiwan's glass industry. It's also the gateway to the heart of Taiwan's **Hakka country**, centred on the town of Beipu.

Arrival and city transport

Hsinchu **train station**, built in 1913 and Taiwan's oldest, is at the southern end of the city, a short walk from East Gate. All the major **bus** stations are nearby along Zhonghua Road.

There are several **Internet cafés** in walking distance of the train station: *Network Planet* at 47 Dongmen Street is open 24 hours (NT$90 for 1hr) while

---

Moving on from Hsinchu

Hsinchu is on the main western rail line with regular express services to Taipei (NT$180), Taichung (NT$198) and Kaohsiung (NT$668). It's also the terminus for **Neiwan Line** trains to Neiwan (NT$44) via Jhudong (NT$25). Hsinchu's **High-Speed Rail Station** is 11km east of the city, linked to the centre by bus. Hsinchu Bus Company's **North Bus Station** is on Zhonghua Road opposite Sogo with regular services to Sinpu (for Yimin Temple, NT$30). For Jhudong (every 15 min, NT$42), bus #20 to Pu Tian Temple (10 per day) and bus #2 to Tsinghua University head to the **South Bus Station**, just to the left of the train station. Buses also depart for Taipei and Taichung from here. You'll need to change buses in Jhudong for Beipu, Lion's Head Mountain and routes south into the mountains. All the long-distance bus stations are clustered around the South Bus Station: Kuo Kuang, Free Go Bus and Howtai are among the companies offering services to Taipei and Taichung.

Hsinchu

Hsinchu	新竹	xīnzhú
Beimen Street	北門街	běimén jīe
Changhe Temple	長和宮	chánghé gōng
Chenghuang Temple	城隍廟	chénghuáng miào
Earth God Temple	東瀛福地	dōngyíng fúdì
East Gate	東門	dōngmén
Hsinchu Municipal Glass Museum	玻璃工藝館	bōligōngyìguǎn
Hsinchu Municipal Image Museum	文化局影像博物館	wénhuàjú yǐngxiàng bówùguǎn
Hsinchu Park	新竹公園	xīnzhú gōngyuán
Hsinchu Science-Based Industrial Park	新竹科學園區	xīnzhú kēxué yuánqū
Pu Tian Temple	普天宮	pǔtiān gōng
Tian Hong Temple	天宏宮	tiānhóng gōng
Tsinghua Night Market	清華夜市	qīnghuá yèshì
Zheng Family Shrine	鄭氏家祠大夫廟	zhēngshì jīa cí dàifū miào

Accommodation		
Ambassador Hotel	新竹國賓大飯店	xīnzhú guóbīn dàfàndiàn
Chinatrust Hotel	中信大飯店	zhōngxìn dàfàndiàn
East City Hotel	東城大旅館	dōngchéng dàlǚguǎn
Howard Plaza Hotel	福華大飯店	fúhuá dàfàndiàn
Shin Yuan Park Hotel	新苑庭園大飯店	xīnyùantíngyuán dàfàndiàn
Sol Hotel Downtown	迎曦大飯店	yíngxī dàfàndiàn

Eating and drinking		
An Zhi Ju	安之居	ān zhǐ jū
Black Cat Steamed Bun	新竹黑貓包	xīnzhú hēimāo bāo
Double Stars Tempura	星甜不辣	xīngtián búlà
Golden Mountain	金山	jīnshān
Guo Run Bing	郭潤餅	guō rùnbǐng
Hsinfuzhen	新復珍	xīnfùzhēn
Ya Rou Hsu	鴨肉許	yāròu xǔ
Yeh Da Li Feng Yuan	葉大粒粉圓	yèdàlì fěnyúan
Yuan Sheng Yuan Tea House	緣上園	yuánshàngyuán

South Park, 3/F, 36 Zhongzheng Road, and *Qi Yan Cheng* at 327 Zhonghua Road Section 2 are much cheaper at NT$30 per hour. **ATMs** and banks are plentiful throughout the city: Citibank has a branch at 128 Siwei Road, on the west side of downtown.

City buses depart several different stops around the train station and cost NT$15 per sector though you are unlikely to need them for sightseeing within the city. **Taxis** are plentiful in the centre of town (the meter starts at NT$90). Hsinchu has a KMT mayor, and, like Taipei, has opted for a Hanyu Pinyin Romanization system, with most roads clearly marked.

Accommodation

Hsinchu has several luxury **hotels** catering to business travellers visiting the Science Park, but it's still possible to find good discounts midweek. There are no

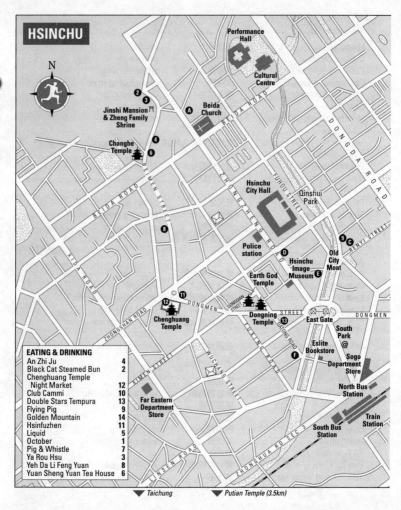

HSINCHU

N

Performance Hall

Cultural Centre

Beida Church

Jinshi Mansion & Zheng Family Shrine

Changhe Temple

Hsinchu City Hall

Qinshui Park

Police station

Hsinchu Image Museum

Earth God Temple

Old City Moat

Chenghuang Temple

Dongning Temple

East Gate

South Park @

Eslite Bookstore

Sogo Department Store

North Bus Station

Far Eastern Department Store

Train Station

South Bus Station

EATING & DRINKING

An Zhi Ju	4
Black Cat Steamed Bun	2
Chenghuang Temple Night Market	12
Club Cammi	10
Double Stars Tempura	13
Flying Pig	9
Golden Mountain	14
Hsinfuzhen	11
Liquid	5
October	1
Pig & Whistle	7
Ya Rou Hsu	3
Yeh Da Li Feng Yuan	8
Yuan Sheng Yuan Tea House	6

▼ Taichung   ▼ Putian Temple (3.5km)

hostels in the city but you'll find plenty of **cheap accommodation** located around the train station, though many of these double as "love hotels" popular with young couples – if in doubt, avoid places that advertize "short-time rates".

Ambassador Hotel 188 Zhonghua Rd Sec 2 ☎03/5151111, ⓦwww.ambassadorhotel.com.tw. Hsinchu's top five-star hotel and consequently host to a steady stream of business visitors, it occupies the 9th–24th floors of the city's tallest building, above the Shinkong Mitsukoshi department store. Rooms are modern, stylish and very comfortable, with extras including an indoor swimming pool and excellent restaurants such as *Prego* on site. ⑧
Chinatrust Hotel 106 Zhongyang Rd ☎03/5263181, ⓦwww.chinatrust-hotel.com. Fairly

generic chain hotel opposite City Hall, but with modern, comfortable rooms and decent discounts which make it a good deal midweek: the free bike rental and laundry are a bonus. ⑥
East City Hotel 1, Lane 5, Fuhou St ☎03/5222648. Decent budget option with an excellent location, near the old moat and a row of cool restaurants and bars – the entrance is just behind the *Garden 3 Restaurant*. Rooms are basic but adequate. ②
Howard Plaza Hotel 178 Zhongzheng Rd ☎03/5282323, ⓦwww.howard-hotels.com.tw.

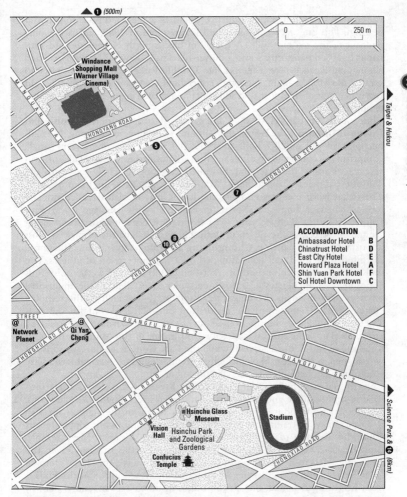

ACCOMMODATION

Ambassador Hotel	B
Chinatrust Hotel	D
East City Hotel	E
Howard Plaza Hotel	A
Shin Yuan Park Hotel	F
Sol Hotel Downtown	C

Five-star hotel with a stylish contemporary design. The rooms have modern Asian decor and are equipped with comfy armchairs, CD players and large bathtubs with mini TVs. ❽

Shin Yuan Park Hotel 11 Datong Rd ☎03/5226868. Comfortable mid-range option, not far from the East Gate and the train station. Rooms are relatively spacious, with bright but outdated blond wood decor. ❹

Sol Hotel Downtown 10 Wenhua St ☎03/5347266, ⍟www.solhotel.com.tw. Popular upmarket hotel, close to the old moat, offering sizeable weekday discounts. Spacious rooms have a few classical Chinese touches, but are otherwise modern and perfectly comfortable. Facilities include gym, free Internet and an excellent Hunan-style restaurant. ❻

The City

Hsinchu has a compact city centre, easily explored on foot. The **East Gate**, a short walk north from the train station along Zhongzheng Road, the city's main commercial street, is its most distinctive landmark and a good place to get your bearings. The gate was completed in 1829, restored in 1999, and is the only remnant of the old city walls. A couple of blocks north of here, the **old city moat** has been transformed into a flower-filled park between Linsen Road and Zhongyang Road, where it merges into Qinshui Park; it's an attractive place to wander, especially at night, lined with coffeeshops, stores and restaurants. The **old town** lies west of the moat, and still contains a smattering of historic sights and temples.

Just north of East Gate on Zhongzheng Road, **Hsinchu Municipal Image Museum** (Wed–Sun 9am–noon, 1.30–5pm, 6.30–9pm; NT$20) occupies an old cinema built in 1933: the actual museum is very small, comprising a couple of exhibition rooms behind the Movie Hall. You can take a peek inside the latter, but it's more interesting to watch one of the old Taiwanese movies screened here (Wed–Fri 7.10pm, Sat–Sun 10am & 2pm). The ticket price includes entry to the movie playing that day: occasionally foreign-language films are shown (including English-language titles) with Chinese subtitles. Retrace your steps to the East Gate and turn right along Dongmen Street; at the junction with Zhongshan Road is Hsinchu's most important place of worship, **Chenghuang Temple** (daily 4.30am–10.30pm), surrounded by food stalls and attended by a constant stream of visitors. The stalls form the city's best night market (see p.202) and add to the boisterous atmosphere – during festivals customers like to eat here while traditional opera is performed in the courtyard. Built in 1748, much of the temple's current beauty stems from the restoration of 1924: look out for the iron abacus and lurid depictions of hell on the walls, a warning to would-be criminals. The large black-faced City God image in the **Main Hall** is said to be the most senior in Taiwan, while the City God's wife and two sons are worshipped in the Rear Hall. Hsinchu's premier religious **festival** is the City God's birthday, held here on Lunar November 29.

North of Chenghuang Temple, **Beimen Street** is the city's most atmospheric thoroughfare and its earliest commercial street, lined with old shops, restaurants and teahouses. Just beyond Beida Road on the right at no. 156 is *Quan Shing*, a Traditional Chinese Medicine shop, while opposite sits **Changhe Temple** (daily 3.30am–10pm), Hsinchu's "outer" Mazu temple. Built in 1742 next to a long-silted-over wharf on the Toucian River, the nickname refers to its position just outside the city walls – the "inner" temple is on Ximen Street. The smaller Mazu statue enshrined in the **Main Hall** is from Meizhou in China, one of the oldest in north Taiwan, and is flanked by Wenchang Dijun on the left and Guan Di on the right. The Rear Hall is dedicated to Guanyin while the attached shrine to the right of the Main Hall is known as **Shuishan Temple** and dedicated to the Water God or the Great Yu, mythical founder of the Xia dynasty (2205–1766 BC), China's first. It's a short walk north of here to the end of Beimen Street, past a row of half ruined but appealing Qing dynasty buildings; **Jinshi Mansion** at no. 163 was built in 1837 for **Zheng Yong-Xi** (who became the first Taiwanese *jinshi*, or official, in 1810), while the **Zheng Family Shrine** at no. 175 is in better condition, but both are closed to the public.

Hsinchu Park

The cluster of attractions centred on **Hsinchu Park**, southeast of the station, tends to attract more tourists than the old town, though only the Glass Museum has much appeal. To walk there take the underpass to the right of the train station (opposite Sogo), then turn right and immediately left upon exiting the

Hsinchu Science Park

Hsinchu Science-Based Industrial Park (ⓦ www.sipa.gov.tw) is the engine driving Taiwan's high-tech revolution, attracting more foreign visitors than any other place on the island. These are all business people of course – government-funded tax breaks, cheap rents and infrastructure investment have attracted over 370 technology companies making this Taiwan's "Silicon Valley". The park generated around US\$30bn in total revenue in 2005, and acts as a model for schemes all over Asia, but there's not much to see for tourists. If you fancy a look anyway take bus #1 or #2 to Tsinghua University and then take a taxi to the Science Park Life Hub; the hub acts as an information centre containing cafés and a small exhibition room on the fourth floor.

tunnel. Walk across the car park to Nanda Road and turn left to Dongda Road, where you should see the garish main entrance to the park ahead on the right. The entrance leads to the **Zoological Gardens** (daily 5am–10pm; NT\$10) which occupies most of the park and is not particularly exciting. More worthwhile is the **Hsinchu Municipal Glass Museum** (Wed–Sun 9–5pm; NT\$20) to the left of the entrance, an innovative mixture of glass art exhibitions and permanent displays on the history and use of glass. There are few English labels however; the most interesting installations are the reinforced glass bridge on the second floor, and the **Jail of Glass** on the first floor with its glass walls, bars and even a glass toilet.

At the back of the park Hsinchu's **Confucius Temple** (daily 8am–5pm; free) is a quiet and abandoned-looking place dating from 1816. Enter the traditional Fujian-style compound via doors at the sides.

South of the city

If you have an extra half a day to spare, the outskirts south of the city contain a couple of unusual sights well worth exploring. Just off Guangfu Road, on the way to the Science Park, **Tian Hong Temple** (daily 6am–10pm) is one of the few shrines in Taiwan dedicated to the worship of Chiang Kai-shek and Sun Yat-sen. Built in 1976, the first floor is filled with statues and busts of both men, saved from destruction from around Taiwan. The temple is on Jiangong 1st Road, which at night becomes **Tsinghua Night Market**, popular with students from the nearby university, just across Guangfu Road. Bus #1 and #2 pass along Guangfu Road throughout the day.

Further west, **Pu Tian Temple** (daily 8am–9pm) makes for an odd excursion via bus #20, which terminates in the car park. The temple was built in 1967 to honour Guan Di, and features a 37m statue of the god garishly painted but looking decidedly faded these days. Tucked away to the left of the main temple is what has become the area's most famous attraction: the small **Matchmaker Temple** (daily 9am–5pm), adorned with pink love hearts and cutesy photos of happy couples – it's a popular place for lonely bachelors from the Science Park to pray for their dream partner.

Eating

Hsinchu has a great range of **restaurants** and **teahouses** and is renowned for its pork meatballs in soup (*gongwan*) and rice noodles (*mifen*); it's also one of the best places in Taiwan to sample "little eats" (*xiaochi*), especially at the **food stalls** in and around Chenghuang Temple and along Beimen Street.

🏃 **An Zhi Ju** 200 Beimen St. One of Hsinchu's most alluring teahouses, set inside an attractive Qing dynasty shophouse, with a series of atmospheric wooden booths: pots of tea go for NT$150–200. Daily 2pm–3am.

🏃 **Black Cat Steamed Bun** 187 Beimen St. Small take-away selling delicious steamed buns crammed with juicy stewed pork (NT$20), much tastier than the average Taiwanese *rou bao*. Daily 11am–3am.

Chenghuang Temple Night Market 75 Zhongshan Rd (inside the temple courtyard). Stalls to try include *Wang Ji O-a Jien*, which faces the main hall and specializes in oyster omelettes; just opposite, *A Cheng Hao*'s does noodles and pork meatballs from NT$30. Outside on Dongmen Street, *Guo Run Bing* sells delicious *run bing* or spring rolls stuffed with pork and mushroom (NT$35). Daily 8am–11pm.

🏃 **Double Stars Tempura** 42 Datong Rd. No frills local diner a short walk from the East Gate, serving one of the most delicious dishes in Taiwan; a selection of boiled fish balls and tofu topped in a thick, sate-like sauce (NT$40 for a small bowl). Daily 11am–11.30pm.

🏃 **Golden Mountain** 13 Jinshan 13th St ☏03/5636296. Hsinchu's most captivating restaurant, beautifully designed in the style of a Tang dynasty palace, with a variety of tasteful wooden rooms arranged around tranquil fish pools. The extensive menu ranges from Cantonese dishes (NT$100–400) to Taiwanese tea (from

NT$200), the only downside being its distant location on the other side of the Science Park. Taxis should be about NT$240 from the station. Daily 10am–midnight.

Hsinfuzhen 6 Beimen Street. Opposite Chenghuang Temple, this venerable cake-maker was established in 1898 and is famous for its deep-fried *zhuqian* meat cakes (NT$25), a mouth-watering blend of onion and pork filling with pastry, and sprinkled with sesame seeds – the sweet/sour combination is perfectly balanced. Daily 9.30am–9pm.

Ya Rou Hsu 185 Beimen St. One of Hsinchu's most famous local diners, next door to *Black Cat Steamed Bun*, serving duck noodles and plates of roast duck for over forty years; the secret is the mouthwatering special sauce (NT$40). There's also a branch at no. 54. Daily 11am–2am.

Yeh Da Li Feng Yuan 83 Beimen St. No-nonsense local place, justly popular for its sumptuous ice desserts (*da li feng yuan*) and delicious taro pudding (*yu ni*, NT$35). Daily 11am–11pm (hours can be erratic).

Yuan Sheng Yuan Tea House 186 Beimen St. Another atmospheric teahouse decorated with wooden furniture and carvings, just north of Changhe Temple and entered via a round "moon gate". The narrow interior is split in half by a fish-pond. Pots of tea start at around NT$380, but there are plenty of other cold and hot drinks on the menu (NT$150, no English). Daily 10am–3am.

Bars and clubs

Hsinchu isn't short of **bars**, fuelled by a sizeable expat population and growing numbers of party-minded locals. The most popular areas are in the centre of town around the old moat north of East Gate, and the Minzu Road spur near the canal, where you'll find a cluster of small pubs.

Club Cammi 198 Zhonghua Rd Sec 2. Best club in town, with hip-hop on Friday and Saturday (cover NT$500) and Ladies Night on Wednesday (men NT$350). Mellow lounge nights feature on Tuesday and Sunday (NT$250), while the club closes on Monday. Open 10am–4.30am.

Flying Pig 12 Wenhua St. Popular watering hole with a central location near the old moat in the heart of the city. Tends to get a bit busier than other places during the week, with pool table, and outside seating as well as dance floor inside. Cheap Tiger and Carlsberg on draught, Murphy's in cans.

Liquid 128 Sanmin Rd. Hsinchu's best lounge bar, with a classy interior featuring comfy sofas and chilled out music to accompany those cocktails and

bottled beers. Regular DJ nights at the weekends make it more like a club.

October 7, Lane 18, Guanghua St. Cosy pub in the north of the city, on a narrow lane that's rapidly becoming an alternative nightlife district. Beers from NT$150.

Pig & Whistle 102 Zhonghua Rd Sec 2 ⓦwww .pigandwhistle.com.tw. Popular British-theme pub with a big Western food menu and Guinness, Hoegaarden and Boddingtons on draught. The first floor opens from 11.30am at the weekends and 4pm weekdays, while the disco upstairs opens from 9pm till 4am or 5am at the weekends. Happy hour (two for one) applies to drinks under NT$180 till 7.30pm weekends and 8.30pm weekdays.

Around Hsinchu: Hakka country

Stretching southeast from Hsinchu, **Hsinchu County** is home to large numbers of **Hakka** people: though the ethnic group accounts for roughly fifteen percent of Taiwan's population, eighty percent of Hsinchu claims Hakka ancestry. **Beipu** is the most famous Hakka town in north Taiwan, while the **Yimin Temple** near Sinpu is the centre of Hakka religious life on the island. **Neiwan** is another Hakka village, tucked away in the mountains east of the city, and rapidly developing into a major tourist attraction.

Yimin Temple

The **Fangliao Yimin Temple** (daily 6am–9pm) or yìmín miào on Yimen Road, around 10km northeast of Hsinchu, is the original and most important Yimin temple in Taiwan, serving as the spiritual centre for the Hakka community on the island. It's a uniquely Taiwanese place and fascinating to visit, especially during a festival. The temple commemorates the Hakka militia killed during the Lin Shuangwen Rebellion of 1786–88: legend has it that the oxen pulling the cart laden with dead soldiers stopped at this site and refused to move any further. The bodies of almost 200 militiamen were buried here as a result, and you can still see the vast **burial mound** at the rear of the temple. A shrine was built on the site soon afterwards, and the Yimin cult has attracted a fair degree of controversy ever since: the militia were essentially defending their homes from Taiwanese (Hoklo) rebels, but their participation helped end the rebellion and attracted a good deal of praise from the Qing Emperor, adding to the perception among some Taiwanese, even today, that they were traitors. The **auxiliary burial mound** to the right of the original contains the bodies of over a hundred Hakka volunteers killed fighting during the Dai Chao-chun Rebellion (1862–65). All the dead warriors are venerated as gods (Yimin means "righteous people"), symbolized by the wooden tablets at the main altar.

Around Hsinchu: Hakka country

Fangliao Yimin Temple	枋寮義民廟	fāngliáo yìmín miào
Beipu	北埔	běipǔ
Beipu Old Street	北埔老街	běipǔ lǎojiē
Cihtian Temple	慈天宮	cítiān gōng
Fanpokeng Tavern	番婆坑客棧	fānpókēng kèzhàn
Jhudong	竹東	zhúdōng
Lung Yuan Pastry Store	隆源餅行	lóngyúan bǐngháng
The Well	水井	shǔi jǐng
Tangshan Lei Cha	唐山擂茶	tángshān léichá
Neiwan	內灣	nèiwān
Dashenpo	大嬸婆美食館	dàshěnpó měishíguǎn
Erjie Yejianghua Rice Dumpling	鵝姐	éjiě
Fan A-Ma Rice Dumpling	范阿嬤野薑花粽	fàn āmā yě jiānghuāzòng
Jianjhong Pharmacy	建中藥局	jiànzhōng yàojú
Liu Hsing-ching Museum	劉興欽漫畫暨發明館	liú xìngqīn mànhuà jìfā míngguǎn
Neiwan Theatre	內灣戲院	nèiwān xìyùan
Yingmu Huadao	櫻木花道內灣咖啡	yīngmù huādào ròuwān kāfēi

The Hakka

Known as *kejia ren* in Chinese ("guest families" or *haka* in the Hakka language), the **Hakka** are an ethnic sub-group of the Han Chinese family, with their own language, customs and traditions. Originally from the northern Chinese provinces of Henan and Shanxi, Hakka people began coming to Taiwan in the seventeenth century and have since developed a particularly strong identity, and several practices unique to the island. At first, Hakka migrants settled in Taipei County and along the western plains, but by the nineteenth century had moved to the areas in which they predominate today: the mountainous parts of Taoyuan, Hsinchu, and Miaoli counties, and in the Kaohsiung-Pingdong area. Scholars still argue about why this happened: in part, it was conflict with Hoklo settlers, but it was also to exploit opportunities in the camphor, tea and tobacco industries, ultimately dominated by Hakka people in Taiwan. Though few Hakka are farmers today, they're still regarded as hard workers and have a reputation for scholarship, producing some of the island's top **scholars** and **writers**: famous Hakka people include ex-president Lee Teng-hui, Soong Mei-ling (Chiang Kai-shek's wife) and film director Hou Hsiao-hsien. Chinese leaders Sun Yat-sen and Deng Xiaoping were also Hakka.

Hakka people subscribe to the same **religious beliefs** as other Chinese groups in Taiwan, but they also have their own special gods and festivals. The worship of the Yimin (mostly in north Taiwan) is unique to Taiwan (see p.203) while Taiwan has around 145 temples dedicated to the **Three Mountain Kings**, protective spirits of the Hakka and a tradition that came from Guangdong.

The **Council for Hakka Affairs** was created by the government in 2001 to help preserve Hakka culture on the island, and to ensure its language survives: there are five dialects spoken in Taiwan, with *sixian* being the most important, and the one you'll hear on train announcements. **Hakka food** is extremely popular island-wide (known for being fragrant, salty, oily and very filling), and **Hakka music**, from its traditional "mountain songs" to modern pop is thriving. **Hakka TV**, a 24-hour station, went on air in 2003.

There are three major **temple festivals** each year: the **Spring Festival** before Tomb Sweeping Day on April 5, the **Autumn Festival** at the end of October or beginning of November, and the most important, the **Yimin Festival** on Lunar July 20 – this is one of the few religious festivals to have originated wholly in Taiwan and features the infamous "God Pigs" (see box p.205).

Buses (6.40am–6.40pm; 10 per day; NT$30) to Sinpu, which stop at the temple, depart Hsinchu's north bus station. The last bus back to Hsinchu leaves Sinpu at 6pm.

Neiwan

Once a prosperous coal mining and timber transportation hub, **NEIWAN** has become one of northern Taiwan's busiest tourist centres, packed with hordes of Taiwanese at the weekends who come to enjoy the mountain scenery and local Hakka food. It's also famous for its association with cartoonist **Liu Hsing-ching**, and the **fireflies** that smother the hillsides in April and May. But despite its picturesque setting, architecturally Neiwan is nothing special, and for most foreign visitors, a day-trip from Hsinchu means lots of good food and some atmospheric places to sip coffee or tea.

Neiwan lies at the end of the **Neiwan Line**, one of Taiwan's scenic railways: trains depart from Hsinchu eleven times a day and take around 50 minutes (NT$41). There's not much to see en route, and little point in getting off before the final stop.

God Pigs

One of the most controversial of Taiwan's traditional religious practices is the rearing of **"God Pigs"**, unfortunate hogs that are fed to grotesque sizes, often so large they can no longer walk. The pigs are used as offerings to the gods – it's a particularly Hakka custom, used mostly at the Yimin Festival when literally hundreds are sacrificed. Pigs are killed the day before, by knife, and the carcass stretched over a metal cage so that by the time it reaches the temple, it looks disturbingly similar in size to a small bus. It doesn't take much imagination to work out why animal rights activists get upset about this: cases of force-feeding, alleged ill-treatment, and the relatively simplistic method of slaughter have led to increased calls for a ban over the years. Hakka groups say that it's a traditional part of their culture and that the pigs are well cared for. While it's true that the tradition of offering pigs goes back to the 1830s, intensive, modern factory methods are new; many pigs are actually bought by Hakka families at the end of the rearing process when they already sport monstrous proportions – some of the animals are worth NT$2m by time they are slaughtered.

The Town

Neiwan has a compact centre, easily navigated on foot. The train station faces Jhongjheng Road, the town's main street and lined with food stalls, restaurants and tacky tourist shops. From the station head downhill to the most attractive building in the village, the **Neiwan Theatre** (ⓦ www.nwtr.com.tw) on the left at no. 227. It's one of the few genuinely old places to have survived, a wooden cinema built in 1940: inside are a few souvenir stalls (you can buy DVDs of old Taiwanese movies here) but the main hall has been converted into a Hakka restaurant (minimum charge NT$150 per person) replete with wooden tables and a big screen which shows old movies as you eat. A bit further on, at no. 283, the **Jianjhong Pharmacy** doubles as an unofficial tourist office. Turn right at the junction with Datong Road to walk up to **Guangji Temple**, or left to the main car park area and the **Hakka Culture Hall**, which should be open by the end of 2006.

Back at the station, turning left down Jhongjheng Road takes you past several famous food stalls (see below). At the end of the road the river opens up on the right: Neiwan's famous 147m wooden **suspension bridge** is a short walk away, now open to pedestrians only. Just across the rail tracks at the back of the station, housed in a collection of old railway buildings, is the **Liu Hsing-ching Museum** (Wed–Mon 9am–5pm; NT$50) dedicated to the life and work of the renowned cartoonist (explanations in Chinese only). Liu was born in neighbouring Dashanbei in 1934 but agreed to help in the development of Neiwan by donating much of his work to the town. You'll notice his most famous characters, Brother Asan or Brother No.3 (*Ahsange*) and Aunt Dashen or Big Auntie (*Dashenpo*), as well as six models of his odd-looking Robot, splashed all over town. The mountains behind the museum are thick with **black-wing fireflies** April to May, when whole swathes of mountainside can become blanketed in tiny lights throughout the night: a narrow road leads from the village up into the hills and though you won't be alone at weekends, it's best to bring a torch.

Eating and drinking

Dashenpo at 279 Jhongjheng Road is one of Neiwan's best **Hakka restaurants**, while at the other end of the street are stalls serving special *zongzi*, a mixture of fried shrimp, mushrooms and rice wrapped in ginger lily (or *yejianghua*) leaves: at no. 45 you'll find the original store *Fan A-Ma Rice Dumpling*, while the equally as good *Erjie Yejianghua Rice Dumpling* is at no. 39, both NT$15 per dumpling. Cross the river and the opposite bank is noted for its cafés: try *Yingmu Huadao* (11am–9pm or 11pm weekends) which has tables outside among a shady grove of trees and bamboo.

Beipu

Lying around 20km southeast of Hsinchu, just north of the Lion's Head Mountain Scenic Area, the small town of **BEIPU** is the centre of Hakka culture in north Taiwan, the counterpart of Meinong in the south (see p.354). Though it's a bit touristy these days, the compact area of old buildings and teahouses around Cihtian Temple has plenty of rustic charm, and it makes an easy excursion from Hsinchu or even Taipei.

The Town

Beipu's tiny bus station is on Jhongjheng Road, a short walk from the old part of town. Walk a few metres to Nansing Street and turn right, passing some good places to try *lei cha* (see below), and on to the next junction with **Old Street**, thick with touristy shops and food stalls. The shop on the corner is **Lung Yuan Pastry Store** (9am–6pm), established in 1871 and maker of tasty sweet potato and taro cakes (around NT$150 per box). Turn left here and head towards **Cihtian Temple** (daily 5am–9pm) at the end of Old Street, established in 1830 and the town's main centre of worship. The Main Hall is dedicated to Guanyin, flanked by tablets on the right representing Sanguan Dadi, and on the left, the Sanshan Guowang (Three Mountain Kings), all Hakka favourites. Beipu's oldest and most appealing buildings are crammed into a relatively small area around the temple, a mixture of traditional red and mud-brick Chinese houses, well worth exploring. To the south, the **Jhongshu Tang**, built in 1922, is a slightly ruinous but charming Qing dynasty house with an unusual Baroque facade, eminently photogenic. Like most of the buildings here, it's still privately owned and closed to the public. Many of these houses are linked to the wealthy **Jiang family** – patriarch Jiang Siou-nuan built the grand **A-Hsin Jiang Residence**, just to the north of the temple on Miaocian Street, in a blend of Western and Japanese styles. Beyond here, on the corner of Jhongjheng Road is the traditional building known as **Jinguangfu**, the old meeting hall built in 1821, and opposite **Tianshuei Tang**, a huge Chinese mansion still occupied by the Jiang family. Jhongjheng Road becomes a narrow alley east of here, containing some of the town's most atmospheric **teahouses**.

Practicalities

The easiest way to get to Beipu is catch a **bus** to Jhudong from Hsinchu (40min), and take one of several onward services to Beipu from the Jhudong

---

Lei cha

Beipu is the best place in Taiwan to sample *lei cha*, or **"ground tea"**, a popular Hakka drink with origins in ancient China. A green tea mixed with a paste of peanuts, sesame, pumpkin and sunflower seeds, it's delicious and very filling (it's sometimes called "cereal tea"), but the modern Taiwanese spin is that you get to prepare it yourself. DIY sessions are offered at most of the teashops in town, and in general you are expected to at least have a go, the staff sometimes reluctant to pitch in. After a few minutes you'll understand why; the raw ingredients are placed into a ceramic bowl and must be pounded into an oily paste with a giant wooden pestle, a process which takes a strong arm, or preferably, several. The tea is usually served with Hakka-style *maji*, sticky rice rolled in ground peanuts.

bus station (15min; NT$22). Buses run from around 6am to 8.30pm in both directions, every twenty to thirty minutes.

Almost every **teahouse** and **restaurant** in Beipu serves classic **Hakka food** – *tong ye*, small rice dumplings served with stir-fried vegetables and soup, is particularly good here. To sample the special local tea, try the *Fanpokeng Tavern* at 35 Old Street, an attractive old teahouse with red-tiled floors, wooden tables and decorated with Chinese antiques (*lei cha* is NT$300 for two). *Tangshan Lei Cha* at 116 Nansing Street is a decent alternative (NT$500 for four). Beipu's most atmospheric teahouse is at the eastern end of Jhongjheng Road, where it becomes very narrow; *The Well* 茶 at no. 1 is a tranquil Qing dynasty building, with stone walls, wooden ceilings and rustic tables and chairs. Tea, coffee and light meals are available from NT$150.

Lion's Head Mountain Scenic Area

The Buddhist temples of the **Lion's Head Mountain Scenic Area** have been attracting pilgrims since the Qing dynasty. Shaped like a rectangle, with an area of 242 square kilometres divided between Miaoli and Hsinchu Counties, the most accessible **hiking trails** and **temples** are clustered around **Lion's Head Mountain** (Shitoushan), in the northern half of the area, and along the Jhonggang River Valley just to the south. The region is also the home of the Saisiyat people – the latter are noted for their "Ritual of the Short Black People" (see Contexts p.522). The suggested route below can be completed with a combination of buses and hiking – it's possible to see everything in a fairly long day, but there are a few places to break the journey. The other main section worth checking out is **Emei Lake**, dominated by the immense **statue of Maitreya Buddha**, one of Taiwan's highlights, in the northwestern corner of the area and also accessible by bus.

Arrival and information

The scenic area is a short drive south of Hsinchu, but taking public transport you'll need to change bus in Jhudong. **Buses** to the scenic area (35–40min; NT$45) depart Jhudong bus station five times a day: 6.40am, 10.30am, midday, 3.45pm and 4.45pm. Buses return to Jhudong at 7.25am, 11.15am, 12.45pm, 4.30pm and 5.30pm. To get to Jhudong, take a bus from Hsinchu (see p.196). Buses from Jhudong arrive a short walk from the **Lion's Head Mountain visitor center** (daily 9am–5pm; ☎03/5809296) in the northern part of the scenic area, around 6km south of the village of Emei. English-language materials and an informative video are available, but the exhibits here are labelled in Chinese only.

Lion's Head Mountain and around

There are a couple of easy hikes near the Lion's Head Mountain visitor center: the 1.7km **Tengping Historic Trail** is a lush, forested path rich in bird life which takes around an hour to complete, while a few metres further along the main road takes you to the signposted path to **Shueilian Cave**, noted for its waterfall. Moving on from the visitor centre, your best option is to hike the **Lion's Head Mountain Historic Trail** that starts nearby. It's a scenic, four-kilometre path over the hills to Cyuanhua Temple, lined with stone slabs and weaving past eleven temples, as well as smaller shrines, statues and calligraphy inscribed onto the rocks. Many of the temples are carved into the limestone

Lion's Head Mountain Scenic Area

Lion's Head Mountain Scenic Area	獅頭山國家風景區	shītóushān guójiā fēngjǐngqū
Jhunan	竹南	zhúnán
Toufen	頭份	tóufèn
Emei Lake	峨眉湖	éméi hú
Maitreya Monastery	峨眉彌勒聖地	éméi mílè shèngdì
Lion's Head Mountain	獅山	shīshān
Cyuanhua Temple	勸化堂	quànhuà táng
Lion's Head Mountain Historic Trail	獅山古道	shīshān gǔdào
Shishan Dalou	獅山大樓	shīshān dàlóu
Shueilian Cave	水濂洞	shuǐlián dòng
Tengping Historic Trail	藤坪古道	téngpíng gǔdào
Wangyue Pavilion	望月亭	wàngyuè tíng
Yuanguang Temple	元光寺	yuán guāng sì
Nanjhuang	南庄	nánzhuāng
East River Spring Garden	東江溫泉休閒花園	dōngjiāng wēnquán xiūxián huāyuán
Lao Jin Long	老金龍	lǎojīnlóng
Nanjhuang Visitor Centre	南庄旅遊服務中心	nánzhuāng lǚyóu fúwù zhōngxīn
Yu He Yuan	玉荷園	yùhéyuán

cliffs, but most of the original buildings were destroyed during the Hsinchu Earthquake of 1935, and what you see today are faithful reproductions. The path and main sites are well-marked in English. At Wangyue Pavilion, not far from **Yuanguang Temple**, about 2.5km from the visitor centre, a trail spur leads 700m to the summit of **Lion's Head Mountain** (492m) itself, with sweeping views of the valley from the top (the peak vaguely resembles a lion's head).

From the pavilion the trail drops steeply into the Jhonggang River Valley for 1km to **Cyuanhua Temple** (daily 6am–8pm), a spectacular cluster of classical-style temples and halls perched on the hillside, its tiered structure providing a wonderful close-up perspective of the elaborate, dragon-covered roofs and beams. The temple was established in 1900 as the only nominally Taoist place of worship on the mountain, primarily dedicated to the Jade Emperor and Guan Di, but in true Taiwanese style there are also shrines to Confucius and Sakyamuni Buddha. It's a beautiful location, and a good place for lunch: the canteen serves superb **vegetarian meals** for just NT$60 (breakfast 6.30–8.30am; lunch 11.50am–1.30pm; dinner 5.30–7.30pm). Opposite the canteen the temple runs a hotel, the *Shishan Dalou* (☏037/822563; ❷), which offers slightly faded but clean rooms, all en suite with TVs. The real highlight, however, are the balconies, which all have fine views of the valley below, especially beautiful in February when the cherry blossom flowers.

Moving on from the temple, follow the trail five minutes further down the slope (ignore the car park and link road on the left) to the main road (Route 124), where you should be able to pick up a **bus** to Nanjhuang, around 4.5km to the south.

Nanjhuang and around

NANJHUANG sits in the heart of the scenic area, midway up the Jhonggang River valley and 10.5km from the main visitor centre, a small, atmospheric

Hakka village that once was a major coal mining and logging centre. Today it mostly caters to tourists (and is home to one of the largest **trout farms** in Asia), with well-preserved Japanese-era wooden houses, the small but helpful **Nanjhuang visitor center** (151 Jhongjheng Road, ☎037/824570), and the best places to eat and stay in the area (see below). It also has an excellent hot-springs spa blessed with odourless sodium bicarbonate spring water. The **East River Spring Garden** (daily 9am–9pm; ☎037/825285; NT$350 for outdoor pools) is the perfect place to end the day, with a series of landscaped outdoor pools designed with a blend of Hakka, Japanese and Western styles, and rustic private baths lined with rocks overlooking the Donghe River (NT$1000 per hr; includes snacks and use of outdoor pools all day). The spa is surrounded on all sides by mountains, the only downside being the quarry nearby which generates a lot of traffic during the week. The spa is 1.5km from Nanjhuang, off Route 21 – if you don't fancy the walk, a taxi should be NT$60, but during the week the spa should be able to pick you up if you call ahead.

Practicalities

Frequent **buses** (usually every 30min) to Nanjhuang pass the bus stop below Cyuanhua Temple (see p.208). To avoid retracing your steps, take a regular bus from Nanjhuang to Jhunan (1hr; NT$65), on the main train line south of Hsinchu. The last bus departs Nanjhuang at 7.30pm.

Nanjhuang has plenty of **hotels** and **homestays**, but few decent budget options. *Yu He Yuan* at 238-1 Jhongjheng Road (❺), at the northern end of the village, is a modern homestay arranged around an attractive lotus pond with spotless, marble-floored rooms and bathrooms – the cosy pinewood rooms in the loghouse across the garden are about the same price. *Lao Jin Long* (10am–8pm; closed Tues and weekdays 2–5pm) serves excellent **Hakka food**, with set meals from NT$490 – these typically include local trout, as well as classic pork and bamboo dishes. The forty-year-old restaurant is at 1 Minzu Street, near the junction with Jhongjheng Road at the southern end of the village.

Emei Lake

Emei Lake occupies the far northwestern corner of the scenic area and contains a couple of islands in its centre. Despite the tourist hype, it's not big or especially beautiful and the main reason to come here is to wonder at the 72-metre-high **Maitreya Buddha statue** on one of the islands. In 2001, the World Maitreya Great Tao Organization (🌐www.maitreya.org.tw) began construction of the statue – set to be the tallest of its kind in the world – and a **monastery** that will accommodate both monks and nuns. The sect reveres the happy, chubby Buddha, also known as Milefo in Chinese, and the stunning bronze statue should be complete in 2007, while the first part of the monastery should be also be open to visitors.

To get to Emei Lake by public transport, you'll have to first take a **bus** to Toufen, a few kilometres east of Jhunan, and accessible by bus from Hsinchu or a direct Kuo Kuang service from Taipei. Buses depart Toufen every thirty minutes and take around thirty-five minutes (NT$40).

Sanyi and around

SANYI, in the south of Miaoli County, is Taiwan's **woodcarving** centre and a popular day-trip from Taipei, Taichung or Hsinchu. Apart from the

Miaoli Wood Sculpture Museum, the town's main attractions are its numerous woodcarving shops, selling a vast range of work from religious icons to kitsch souvenirs squarely aimed at the tourist trade. Nearby **Shengsing** offers some beautiful hiking, historic Hakka teahouses, and the photogenic ruin of Longteng Bridge. The village is halfway along a 16km loop of old mountain railway between Sanyi and Houli, now abandoned and a popular hiking trail.

Arrival and orientation

Sanyi's **train station** is inconveniently located at the far northern end of town, just off Jhongjheng Road. The built-up area south of the station is the original and fairly unattractive town centre, while most of the woodcarving shops lie a further 2km to the south, where Jhongjheng Road is known as **Shueimei Street**. The sculpture museum sits on the hillside above here in a small collection of modern buldings known as **Guangsheng Village**. **Shengsing** (Shenghsing) is quite separate from all this, tucked away in the hills to the southeast and halfway along the abandoned railway. The area is too spread out to see everything on foot, and at the weekends (when things are far livelier), a useful **minibus** shuttles between all the main sights every fifteen minutes (9am–5pm; NT$60), starting near the train station on the opposite side of Jhongjheng Road. During the week you'll have to take taxis or walk. There are no decent **hotels** in the town itself, though there are homestays – the closest major town is Miaoli though you're better off heading to Taichung for a greater choice of facilities. The best place to **eat** is Shengsing, though there are a few simple options in Sanyi itself.

The Town

Heading south along Jhongjheng Road from the train station, there's not much to see in the main part of town, though the **Sanyi Duck Treasure Shop** at 176 Chongde Road, 400m off the main road along Route 130, is one of the more unusual stores in the area. Local carvers produce a wide-range of multi-coloured wooden ducks, birds and animals here, and from NT$200 to NT$1000 (depending on size) you can paint your own model in a warehouse next door – the whole process takes about two hours. The shop is signposted in Chinese from Jhongjheng Road.

Sanyi and around		
Sanyi	三義	*sānyì*
Chen Tai Sculpture Museum	千岱博物館	*qiāndài bówùguǎn*
Guangsheng Village	廣聲新城	*guǎngshēng xīnchéng*
Miaoli Wood Sculpture Museum	苗栗木雕博物館	*miáolì mùdiāo bówùguǎn*
Sanyi Duck Treasure Shop	三義一ㄚ箱寶	*sānyì yī yā xiāng bǎo*
Sanyi Train Station	三義車站	*sānyì chēzhàn*
Shueimei Street	水美雕刻街	*shuǐměi diāokè jiē*
Shengsing	勝興	*shèngxīng*
Longteng Broken Bridge	龍騰斷橋	*lóngténg duànqiáo*
Railway Restaurant	鐵路餐廳	*tiělù cāntīng*
Shengsing Inn	勝興客棧	*shèngxīng kèzhàn*
Shanjhong Chuan Ci	山中傳奇	*shānzhōng chúanqí*

If you take the minibus, the second stop is the **Miaoli Wood Sculpture Museum** (Tues–Sun 9am–5pm; NT$60) a modern building at the end of a small strip of woodcarving shops, many doubling as teahouses and cafés. This is **Guangsheng Village**, purpose-built to accommodate Taiwan's finest wood sculptors, in order to pool their artistic (and tourist-attracting) synergies – it's also the focus of the month-long Sanyi Woodcarving Festival, usually held in October. The museum houses a small exhibition on the history of woodcarving and a collection of absorbing sculptures on the higher floors, but most of the explanations are in Chinese only. If walking, the museum is clearly signposted in English off Jhongjheng Road, 2.7km from the station.

The bus next crosses **Shueimei Street** back at the bottom of the hill, the town's main commercial woodcarving area. It's crammed with over 200 stores stretching for almost 1km, and is a good place to browse for gifts – though the most visually striking pieces are often big and expensive, there's plenty of smaller, more affordable artwork on display. **Chen Tai Sculpture Museum** (it's just a shop) at no. 336 (Ⓦ www.1000-artists.com.tw) has a huge collection of religious statues and other high-quality work.

Shengsing and around

After Shueimei Street, the bus makes the three-kilometre journey to the attractive Hakka village of **Shengsing**, but it's also a pleasant walk along narrow Route 56 or the abandoned rail tracks, particularly in the spring when the area's distinctive white **tung flowers** are in bloom – from Sanyi train station you'll see English signs to the village, though it's almost 6km from here. Shengsing was once an important transportation hub for the **camphor oil** industry, but a new tunnel meant main-line trains bypassed the village in the late 1990s.

The **old station**, completed in 1911 and once Taiwan's highest main-line station at 402m, is a picturesque wooden building at the bottom of the narrow main street. From the tracks you can still see the village's old name engraved in Chinese on the embankment, Shi Liu Fen (Sixteen Packages) – it was renamed in 1958. The road back up the hill is lined with teahouses serving Hakka food and *lei cha* (see p.206).

Suitably refreshed, you can take the bus or walk to **Longteng Broken Bridge**, just under 6km to the southeast. The hike along the old rail tracks is very pleasant, and mostly level – head south through the 726m tunnel near Shengsing station. The bridge is a red-brick viaduct that collapsed during the great Hsinchu Earthquake of 1935, and now a romantic ruin, overgrown with weeds and bushes and surrounded by lush, wooded hills. The bus makes a loop back to Sanyi station from here.

Eating

The village's oldest **restaurant** is the atmospheric 🥢 *Shengsing Inn* (daily 9am–8pm; meals from 10.30am) at 72, Lane 14, on the right just up the slope. The cosy wooden dining room was strengthened with red bricks taken from the Longteng Bridge after the earthquake. Recommended Hakka dishes include the bamboo and pork or *kejia xiaofong* (NT$230 small, NT$280 big), special tofu (NT$150/180) and the succulent duck or *zhisu ya rou* (NT$150/180). *Lei cha* is NT$100 per person, or NT$250 for a small bowl. Menus are Chinese only, but the owner's wife speaks English.

Closer to the station and facing the tracks, the *Railway Restaurant* (daily 10am–9pm) is another lovely old colonial wooden building with red-tiled floors serving tea, coffee and light meals. If the weather's good, try *Shanjhong Chuan Ci* (daily 9am–9pm), a café set on a series of wooden terraces on the slopes across the tracks where *lei cha* is NT$300 and coffee NT$150.

Taian Hot Springs

Straddling the Wenshuei River and surrounded by the mountains of Miaoli County, the **TAIAN HOT SPRINGS** area is one of Taiwan's most unspoilt resorts, offering visitors an enticing combination of challenging **hill walks** and rejuvenating **hot springs**. The springs were first developed by the Japanese, who established one of their most coveted officers' clubs here. The club is still open for public bathing, as are most of the area's hotel pools, so you don't have to stay overnight to enjoy the waters – but those who do will have more time to explore some truly remarkable mountain scenery. In addition, this area is the heartland of the **Atayal**, the country's second-largest aboriginal group, and visitors to Jinshuei Village – where most of Taian's hot-spring hotels are located – are likely to be invited to join local Atayal for a meal or a festival in neighbouring Longshan Buluo.

The hot springs are best enjoyed from October to March when the weather is cooler and drier; from the May "plum rains" and onwards through the summer typhoon season, the trails can become washed-out gullies and are extremely difficult to negotiate. Though the springs remain markedly less developed than most Taiwanese hot-springs resorts, the place is becoming increasingly popular and can get crowded on weekends.

Arrival, orientation and information

Due to the resort's relative isolation, getting here without your own transport takes some effort. Starting at Miaoli train station (connected by fast trains from Taipei), walk straight ahead about 50m to the bus station on your right; catch one of the **buses** that leave for Dahu roughly every hour, but tell the driver when you board that you want to alight at the town of **Wenshuei** (50min; NT$49). About 1km past Wenshuei, on the left-hand side of the road, is the beginning of **County Highway 62**, which winds for 14km alongside the

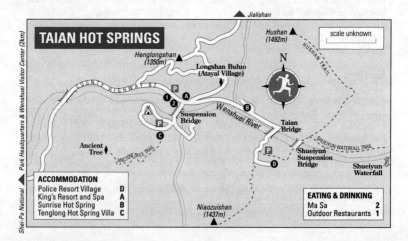

Shei-Pa National ◀ Park Headquarters & Wenshuei Visitor Center (2km)

Taian Hot Springs

Taian Hot Springs	泰安溫泉區	*tàiān wēnquánqū*
Dashihmen Waterfall	大石門瀑布	*dà shímén pùbù*
Hushan	虎山	*hǔshān*
Longshan Buluo	龍山部落	*lóngshān bùluò*
Shueiyun Suspension Bridge	水雲吊橋	*shuǐyún diàoqiáo*
Shueiyun Waterfall	水雲瀑布	*shuǐyún pùbù*
Accommodation and eating		
King's Resort & Spa	錦水溫泉飯店	*lǐnshuǐ wēnquán fàndiàn*
Ma Sa Coffee	"Ma Sa" 咖啡	*mǎ sà kāfēi*
Outdoor Restaurants	露天小吃店	*lùtiān xiǎochīdiàn*
Police Resort Village	警光山莊	*jǐngguāng shānzhuāng*
Sunrise Hot Spring Hotel	日出溫泉渡假飯店	*rìchū wēnquán dùjiàfàndiàn*
Tenglong Hot Spring Villa	騰龍溫泉山莊	*ténglóng wēnquán shānzhuāng*

Wenshuei River before it ends in a car park near the start of the area's main hiking trails. The main hot springs area, and certainly the most convenient for tourists, is at **Jinshuei Village**, about 12km down Highway 62. There are two or three local buses a day from Wenshuei to Jinshuei Village, but the schedule is erratic, so you're better off trying to get a **taxi** from Wenshuei (NT$350); if you can't find one it's possible to hitch a ride from the turnoff to County Highway 62.

Given the dearth of foreign visitors to Taian, there is no English-language information on the area, but you can pick up a very crude **Chinese map** from the *Tenglong Hot Spring Villa* just across the suspension bridge from the main road. Here, staff can advise about trail conditions and arrange **guides** for larger groups; the safety of the trails varies widely depending on the weather, so it's a good idea to ask here before setting out. There are no **ATMs** in Jinshuei Village, so be sure to take enough cash – if you're stuck, there's a Chinatrust Commercial Bank ATM in the 7-Eleven about 300m before the turnoff to County Highway 62. If you're planning to do some hiking in Taian, you could stock up on some trail snacks here, as there is only one **shop** (7am–10pm) in Jinshuei Village (at the *Tenglong Hot Spring Villa*) and it's a bit pricey.

Accommodation

Though hot-spring **hotels** and **homestays** line much of County Highway 62, **Jinshuei Village** has the best range, all within easy walking distance of the main trails. Each hotel has a **public bathing area**, most of them gender-segregated nude pools open late into the evening; most offer hefty **discounts** from Sunday to Thursday nights, when the village can be almost completely devoid of tourists. In the village centre, hugging the northern side of the road, the imposing *King's Resort & Spa* (☎037/941333; hot-spring pools NT$300; ❼) has giant rooms, many with commanding views of the river valley and some with private balconies. About 1km further up the road, the *Sunrise Hot Spring Hotel* (☎037/941988; ❼) is the swankiest option in town, featuring stylish rooms with attached stone-slab bathing tubs. The communal outdoor bathing pools are open to the public (8am–10pm; NT$350); those seeking greater privacy can rent private bathing rooms (NT$1000 for 50min). On the southern side of the suspension bridge in Jinshuei Village, the sprawling 🏥 *Tenglong Hot Spring Villa* (☎037/941002; hot-spring pools NT$350; ❸) has spacious doubles in A-frame wooden bungalows plus a small **campsite** for those with their own tents (NT$300 per tent); the staff are very knowledgeable on local hiking routes. Finally, just above the car park at the very end of County Highway 62 is the *Police Resort Village* (☎037/941175; ❷), formerly the Japanese-era officers' club which now caters mostly to Taiwanese policemen. The management is reluctant to accept overseas guests, but foreigners are most welcome to soak in the gender-segregated nude pools, the area's cheapest (8am–9pm; NT$70).

Hiking

There are several **hiking trails** around Jinshuei, the majority of which the average walker should find demanding but doable. Bear in mind that most of the paths are very steep, leaving them vulnerable to landslips during heavy rains. It's also important to note that signs are in Chinese only, and there are few, if any, distance or direction markers. Despite this, most trails are well defined and invariably flagged at regular intervals by red, white and yellow **ribbons** left by hiking clubs from all over Taiwan. As a rule, if you walk several minutes without seeing one of these markers, you should probably stop and retrace your steps. In addition to the two hikes covered below, there are a few other walks in the area, but at the time of writing the trails were in an abysmal state of disrepair; be sure to ask locals about the latest trail conditions before setting out.

Shueiyun Waterfall

The area's easiest hike – though one not to be attempted in rainy weather – is to the **Shueiyun (Water Cloud) Waterfall**, a shimmering cascade hidden behind a bend along the Wenshuei River bed. Most of the trail follows the northern side of the river bed, which remains dry for much of the year but is prone to flash floods in rainy weather. This section of the river bed is the main location for the **river tracing** outings arranged by the *Tenglong Hot Spring Villa*, so ask there about the water level before setting out – especially if you're here during the spring or summer rains.

The route begins at the car park at the end of County Highway 62. Here, the pavement ends and a dirt road continues for another kilometre or so before it reaches the **Shueiyun Suspension Bridge**, which you must cross in order to reach the trail proper. From the middle of the bridge, you can often see the **Dashihmen Waterfall** off to the right, although during dry spells it can resemble little more than a trickle. After crossing the bridge, climb the wooden steps for a couple of hundred metres until the trail enters the forest and splits into two directions (with signs in Chinese): the left-hand fork leads to the top of Hushan (see p.215), while the right-hand path drops down to the river trail to the falls. Take the right-hand trail for about 50m until you reach another sign pointing to the left; follow this path for a few minutes until you reach a rocky outcrop along the river bank. If you look closely at the rock's edge you'll find a rope you can use to lower yourself to the river bed. From here, keep to the left side of the river to reach the Shueiyun Waterfall, about 1.5km upstream: the easiest line to follow is marked by **bamboo poles** stuck deep into the ground and crested with red flags. After about thirty minutes you'll come to a big bend in the river, where the left bank runs into a giant slab of rock that rises at a fairly sharp angle – scramble up this rock about 20m and look across the river to see the falls. If the river level is really low, it's possible to cross and follow the tributary up to the base of the waterfall, where there is a clear pool, ideal for a refreshing swim. Allow yourself at least ninety minutes to make the return trip from the car park.

Hushan

The path to the top of triangular **Hushan** (Tiger Mountain) is the area's most challenging and rewarding hike, climbing steeply to the crest of this 1492-metre beauty, the tallest in the area. Though the trail is well built, the upper portion has precious few switchbacks and slices straight up the mountainside, with sturdy **ropes** anchored to trees along the way for support. The ascent is strenuous and suitable only for fairly fit hill walkers, while the descent demands strong knees. The trail begins on the far side of the Shueiyun Suspension Bridge, at the junction with the Shueiyun Waterfall path (see p.214); the left-hand fork winds through a cool, shaded forest before cutting sharply up to the top of Hushan. Between the junction and the summit the route is flagged with hundreds of red, white and yellow **ribbons**. Close to the top, the trail crosses the rocky bed of a tributary stream that can fill up rapidly in the rainy season, and you must walk up the stream bed itself for about a hundred metres before reconnecting with the trail; here it's essential to look for the trail ribbons tied to overhanging tree branches in order to keep to the path. On clear days, the **views** from the top of Hushan can be thrilling, especially looking across the river valley onto nearby Niaozuishan (Bird Beak Mountain) and beyond to the majestic peaks of **Shei-Pa National Park**. To enhance your chances of a sweeping view, it's best to start early so you can reach the top before the usual afternoon clouds and mist roll in. From the car park at the end of County Highway 62, allow yourself three to four hours for the return hike.

Eating and drinking

Apart from the hotel canteens, which tend to be pricey and uninteresting, the only places to eat in Jinshuei Village are the lively **outdoor restaurants** clustered on the north side of the suspension bridge. These establishments dish up delicious local fare, including aboriginal specialties such as **roasted mountain pig** (*kao shan zhu*; NT$100 per plate). At times it's possible to sample wild game such as deer and flying squirrel, or if you want to stick to the basics the owners can quickly whip up steaming plates of fried rice and noodles. These restaurants are popular with locals, especially **Atayal tribespeople** from nearby Longshan Buluo, who are likely to strike up a conversation with you and might even invite you to go hunting. Just up some steps on the north side of the suspension bridge is *Ma Sa Coffee* (Mon–Fri noon–9pm, Sat–Sun 9am–midnight; ☏037/941548), a breezy outdoor **café** with fabulous views of the river valley. It has a good selection of coffee (NT$100) and gourmet teas (NT$130), as well as beer and local millet wine. You also can order simple dishes such as Japanese-style curry rice (NT$130). The sign at the entrance merely says "Coffee Shop" in English.

Shei-Pa National Park and around

SHEI-PA NATIONAL PARK, an unapologetically rugged reserve of pristine mountain peaks and raging rivers, is one of Asia's most untouched expanses of wilderness and an ideal stomping ground for hill walkers of all abilities. Stretching across almost 770 sq km of the magnificent **Syueshan Range**, Taiwan's third-largest national park is studded with stunning peaks, 51 of them higher

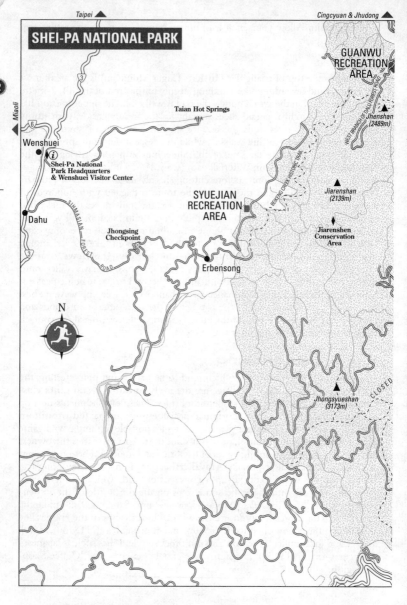

SHEI-PA NATIONAL PARK

GUANWU
RECREATION
AREA

Miaoli

Taian Hot Springs

Wenshuei
ⓘ
Shei-Pa National
Park Headquarters
& Wenshuei Visitor Center

Dahu

SHIMASIAN — FOREST ROAD

Jhongsing
Checkpoint

SYUEJIAN
RECREATION
AREA

Erbensong

N

WEST BRANCH OF DALI FOREST ROAD

Jhenshan
(2489m) ▲

BEIKONG CREEK HISTORIC TRAIL

Jiarenshan
(2139m) ▲

Jiarenshen
Conservation
Area ▲

Jhongsyueshan
(3173m) ▲

CLOSED

216

than 3000m – putting them on a par with most of the European Alps, but without the glaciation endemic to their more northerly counterparts. The park's highest peak is the range's namesake: **Syueshan** (Snow Mountain), which at 3886m is the second-tallest mountain in Northeast Asia. Despite its lofty height, it's one of the island's most accessible and rewarding climbs, with an extremely well-maintained trail that is typically open for most of the year. This path is

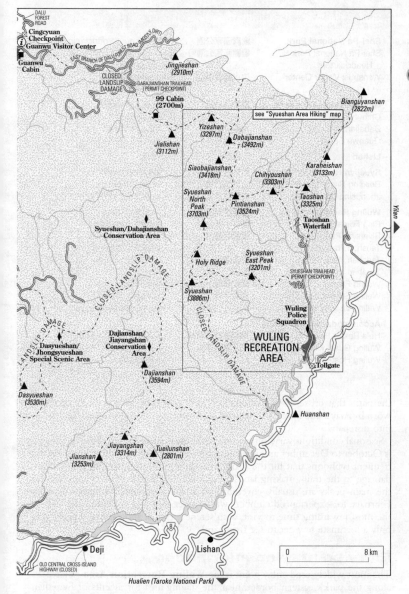

DALU
FOREST
ROAD

Cingcyuan
Checkpoint
Guanwu Visitor Center

Guanwu
Cabin

EAST BRANCH OF DALU FOREST ROAD (MOSTLY DIRT)

Jingjieshan
(2910m)

CLOSED
LANDSLIP
DAMAGE

DABAJIANSHAN TRAILHEAD
(PERMIT CHECKPOINT)

Bianguyanshan
(2822m)

99 Cabin
(2700m)

Yizeshan
(3297m)

see "Syueshan Area Hiking" map

Jialishan
(3112m)

Dabajianshan
(3492m)

Siaobajianshan
(3418m)

Chihyoushan
(3303m)

Karaheishan
(3133m)

Syueshan
North
Peak
(3703m)

Pintianshan
(3524m)

Taoshan
(3325m)

Syueshan/Dabajianshan
Conservation Area

Taoshan
Waterfall

Yilan

Holy Ridge

Syueshan
East Peak
(3201m)

SYUESHAN TRAILHEAD
(PERMIT CHECKPOINT)

Syueshan
(3886m)

Wuling
Police
Squadron

Dasyueshan/
Jhongsyueshan
Special Scenic Area

Dajianshan/
Jiayangshan
Conservation Area

WULING
RECREATION
AREA

Dasyueshan
(3530m)

Dajianshan
(3594m)

Tollgate

Huanshan

Jianshan
(3253m)

Jiayangshan
(3314m)

Tueilunshan
(2801m)

8

Deji

Lishan

0   8 km

OLD CENTRAL CROSS-ISLAND
HIGHWAY (CLOSED)

Hualien (Taroko National Park) ▼

also a grandiose gateway to the park's other mountain highlights, such as the
precipitous **Holy Ridge** that extends north from Syueshan to the 3492-metre
Dabajianshan (Big Chief Pointed Mountain), whose distinctive pyramid shape
has made it one of the country's most celebrated peaks.

Although the park has three designated **recreation areas**, much of the
remote interior remains largely undeveloped and access is limited – many of

Shei-Pa National Park and around

Shei-Pa National Park	雪霸國家公園	*xǔebà guójiā gōngyuán*
Shei-Pa National Park Headquarters	雪霸國家公園管理處	*xǔebà guójiā gōngyuán guǎnlǐchù*
Wenshuei Visitor Center	汶水遊客中心	*wénshuǐ yóukè zhōngxīn*
Guanwu Recreation Area	觀霧遊樂區	*guānwùóulèqū*
Chihyoushan	池有山	*chíyǒushān*
Dabajianshan	大霸尖山	*dàbà jiān shān*
Guanwu Cabin	觀霧山莊	*guānwù shānzhuāng*
Lishan	梨山	*líshān*
Syuejian Recreation Area	雪見遊樂區	*xǔejiàn yóulèqū*
Beikeng River Historic Trail	北坑溪古道	*běikēngxī gǔdào*
Jhongsing Checkpoint	中興檢查站	*zhōngxīng jiǎncházhàn*
Wuling Recreation Area	武陵遊樂區	*wǔlíng yóulèqū*
Ping Forest Path	蘋林小徑	*pínglín xiǎojìng*
Riverside Park	溪濱公園	*sì bīn gōngyuán*
Taoshan Trailhead	桃山登山口	*táoshān dēngshān kǒu*
Taoshan Waterfall	桃山瀑布	*táoshān pùbù*
Taoshan	桃山	*táoshān*
Wuling Farm	武陵農場	*wǔlíng nóngchǎng*
Wuling Suspension Bridge	武陵吊橋	*wǔlíng diàoqiáo*
Wuling Visitor Center	武陵遊客中心	*wǔlíng yóukè zhōngxīn*
Accommodation and eating		
Hola Resort Hotel	武陵富野渡假村	*wǔlíng fù yě dùjiàcūn*
Wuling Guest House	武陵國民賓館	*wǔlíng gúomín bīnguǎn*
Wuling Hostel	武陵山莊	*wǔlíng shānzhuāng*

the paths that crisscross the mountains were originally narrow hunting tracks worn by Atayal and Saisiyat aborigines, and some are treacherous and have fallen into disrepair.

Seasonal conditions vary, but in general the **best time** for climbing in Shei-Pa is October to December and late February to April. The May monsoons and the frequent typhoons that hit the island from June to September can cause severe damage to the trails, making landslips a concern. Though winters are cold and the main peaks are usually covered with **snow** from late December to mid-February, for experienced climbers with proper gear and crampons this can be the most rewarding time to visit, with serene views of snow-capped peaks that only a fortunate few get to see first-hand.

Entry points and information

The most widely used entry point is the **Wuling Recreation Area** (see p.219) along the park's eastern border, near the staging area for ascents of Syueshan and its neighbouring peaks. In addition to being close to these mountains, this recreation area is the only one which can be reached by public transport. The **Guanwu Recreation Area** (see p.225) in the north of the park was once its most popular entrance point – with the quickest trail access to the revered Dabajianshan – but the main road into the area was closed in the summer of 2004 after being badly damaged by typhoons and is not expected to be re-opened until mid-2008. Shei-Pa's much-anticipated **Syuejian Recreation**

Protecting park wildlife

Shielded within the mountains of Shei-Pa National Park is a staggeringly diverse array of **wildlife**, with 61 of the thousand-plus plants under park protection on the rare or endangered species lists. Of the 295 animal species in the park, 26 are found only in Taiwan and two – the **Formosan Black Bear** and the Formosan Landlocked Salmon – are endangered. Special **conservation areas** have been set up for some, especially the seriously endangered **Formosan Landlocked Salmon**, whose numbers have dwindled to only several hundred. Originally a migratory fish, this species of Pacific salmon was trapped in high mountain lakes at the end of the last ice age and has since evolved into a landlocked subspecies of freshwater fish found only in a few kilometres of streams within the park. Though the protection measures introduced since the park's 1992 establishment have largely been lauded, some – such as hunting bans on flying squirrel and wild boar – remain points of contention with Atayal tribesman in villages on the park's northwest fringes, and park officials face an ongoing battle against illegal hunting.

Area (see p.226), in the park's northwest, is in the final stages of development and is expected to finally open in late 2007. The **Shei-Pa National Park Headquarters** and its **Wenshuei visitor centre** (9am–4.30pm, closed Mon; ☎037/996100, ⓦwww.spnp.gov.tw) are rather inconveniently located along Miaoli County Highway 62, about 2km from the town of Wenshuei on the way to the Taian Hot Springs (see p.212). The visitor centre has two exhibition halls that give an excellent bilingual overview of the park's most notable attractions, and on weekdays **English-speaking staff** are on hand and can provide you with general park **maps** as well as more detailed topographical maps (Chinese only) of trails in the Syueshan area. Those wishing to climb mountains within the park can apply here for the necessary Class A mountain permits, although you must submit your application seven working days before the proposed start date of your climb (see p.56).

Wuling Recreation Area

Currently Shei-Pa's most easily accessed section, the **WULING RECREATION AREA** is the base for Syueshan climbs and is a worthwhile destination in its own right. Commonly known as **Wuling Farm**, the area was turned into an **orchard** in the 1950s and 60s by retired KMT soldiers, and still draws domestic tourists looking to buy freshly plucked peaches, pears and apples. Administration of the area is still somewhat contested, with Taiwan's **forestry bureau** also laying claim to some sections, but overall the national park service is calling the shots. Even if you don't plan to climb Syueshan, the recreation area is still worth a visit, with pleasant river valley strolls and shorter **hiking trails** open to the public.

Arrival, orientation and information

There are numerous ways to get to Wuling Farm from both the east and west coasts, and depending upon your route this trip in itself can be a major adventure. If you're planning to climb Syueshan, remember your **permit** will be valid for specific dates, and it's important to arrive in Wuling Farm the day before you're scheduled to begin your ascent to ensure you can set out on time – otherwise you might be refused entry at the trailhead.

The simplest way to reach Wuling Farm by public transport is to take one of the two daily **direct buses** (7am & 12.40pm; 2hr 45min; NT$258) that run from the east-coast city of **Yilan**. These buses return to Yilan almost immediately after arrival (around 9.10am & 2.10pm), but drivers tend to leave whenever they fancy so get to the bus stop well in advance. From this bus stop, there is one daily bus (1.40pm; NT$260) to the east-coast town of **Luodong**, and two daily commuter buses to nearby Lishan (9.20am & 3.10pm; NT$63). These buses leave Lishan for Wuling Farm at 8.30am and 1.30pm (see p.227). From the east-coast city of **Hualien** (see p.389), there are several buses daily through the **Taroko Gorge** to Tiansiang, so you also could visit the gorge on your way to Lishan and Wuling Farm.

Though the original Central Cross-Island Highway is closed, it's still possible to reach Wuling Farm and nearby areas from the west coast, using one of the other **central cross-island routes** slightly further south. The most straightforward of these is from Taichung or Shueili via **Puli**, from where buses leave hourly to **Wushe** (45min, NT$67). From here, the road winds over the stupefying pass near Hehuanshan and on to the quaint tea-growing town of **Lishan**; however, there is no public transport beyond Wushe, so you'll need your own vehicle or will have to hire a **taxi** to Lishan or Wuling Farm for roughly NT$3000. It's also fairly easy to hitch a ride between these points, and if you can only hitch your way as far as **Dayuling** – on the edge of Taroko National Park – you could wait here for one of the **minibuses** that stops on its way to Lishan from Taroko's main tourist hub of Tiansiang (see p.401).

Tolls and information

Before you enter the recreation area you'll be required to pay a NT$10 fee; the **tollgate** is shortly after the turnoff into Wuling from Highway 7. Just behind the bus stop is a **shop** (9am–5pm) with basic supplies such as instant noodles, nuts, dried fruit and bottled water. Next to the shop is the **Wuling visitor centre** (9am–4.30pm, closed Mon; ℡04/25901350), where you can get a basic map of the Wuling Farm area. The **main road** through the recreation area is sealed and heads north from the tollgate; there are short **side roads** to the two main hotels, and the winding road to the Syueshan trailhead forks left from the main road.

Wuling-area hikes

If the Syueshan climb isn't to your liking there are other hikes in the recreation area, and the park plans to build several roadside nature walks in the coming years. Just up the road from the Wuling visitor centre, a side road branches to the right and crosses the river before leading to the flat **Ping Forest Path**, an easy stroll through the **Riverside Park**. Many domestic tourists drive up the main road, stopping at various orchards along the way to pick fruit until they reach the **Wuling Suspension Bridge**, under which it's sometimes possible to spot the endangered Formosan Landlocked Salmon. It's possible to walk the entire distance, but it's about 10km each way so make sure you have enough time for the return journey. Beyond the suspension bridge the road leads to one of the area's best-known hikes, to **Taoshan Waterfall**. The four-kilometre walk climbs about 450m before reaching the 50m-high cascade; allow two to three hours for the return journey. About 1km up this path is the turnoff to the more challenging hike to **Taoshan** (Peach Mountain), which at 3325m is a serious climb that requires both time and a Class A mountain permit. If you're going to make the effort to get the permit for Taoshan, it makes sense to include it as part of a longer, multi-day trek through the Syueshan area.

Accommodation and eating

Wuling has a few comfortable if slightly pricey **hotels,** all within walking distance of the visitor centre. The best value is the *Wuling Guest House* (℡04/25901259; ⑥), which has large doubles with cable TV as well as two- and four-person cabins; a Chinese-style buffet breakfast is included in the room rate, and the **restaurant** near the hotel lobby serves lunch and dinner (NT$200 per person). A posher, more expensive option is the *Hola Resort Hotel* (℡04/25901399; ⑧), on a hill to the left of the road after you enter the recreation area. More of a package-style resort than a hotel, the *Hola* includes breakfast and dinner buffets in its room rates, but the restaurant is for guests only. There is a **campsite** (NT$400 per tent; ℡04/25901265) near the Syueshan trailhead which is used mostly by hiking clubs keen to get an early start on their climbs. While it's a convenient place to stay for climbers, you must have your own **tent** – an item that's only useful if you're planning an extended circuit along the Holy Ridge or on to Dabajianshan.

Climbing Syueshan

The 3886-metre-high **Syueshan** is one of Asia's most rewarding climbs, and though it takes a modicum of planning it's well worth the effort. The trail to the top is one of Taiwan's finest, and along the way are two trusty **cabins** with bunk-style wooden sleeping platforms (bring your own sleeping bag), nearby drinking-water sources and toilet facilities. The return journey to the summit takes most people the better part of two days, including an overnight stay in the **369 Cabin**, just less than 4km from the top. An exceptionally fit walker could make the nearly 22-kilometre journey from the trailhead to the peak and back in one long day, but most climbers choose to take their time and spend a night in the 369 Cabin. For experienced climbers with more time and their own camping equipment, this trail can be the gateway to a two- to three-day circuit over the hair-raising **Holy Ridge** and on to **Dabajianshan** or back to the Wuling Recreation Area via Taoshan – without question one of Taiwan's top treks.

Obtaining mountain permits

Though a **Class A mountain permit** is needed to climb Syueshan and the park's other mountains, Shei-Pa is one of the easiest parks in which to obtain

Climbing Syueshan		
Syueshan	雪山	*xuěshān*
Holy Ridge	聖稜線	*shèng léngxiàn*
Syueshan East Peak	雪山東峰	*xuěshān dōngfēng*
Syueshan Main Peak	雪山主峰	*xuěshān zhǔfēng*
Syueshan North Peak	雪山北峰	*xuěshān běifēng*
Syueshan Trailhead	雪山登山口	*xuěshān dēngshān kǒu*
Wuling Police Squadron	武陵警察小隊	*wǔlíng jǐngchájú xiǎoduì*
Cabins and campsites		
369 Cabin	三六九山莊	*sānliùjiǔ shānzhuāng*
Banan Cabin	霸南山屋	*bànán shānwū*
Cika Cabin	七卡山莊	*qīkǎ shānzhuāng*
Singda Shelter	新達山屋	*xīndá shānwū*
Syuebei Shelter	雪北山屋	*xuěběi shānwū*
Taoshan Cabin	桃山山屋	*táoshān shānwū*
Yundaka Shelter	雲達卡山屋	*yúndákǎ shānwū*

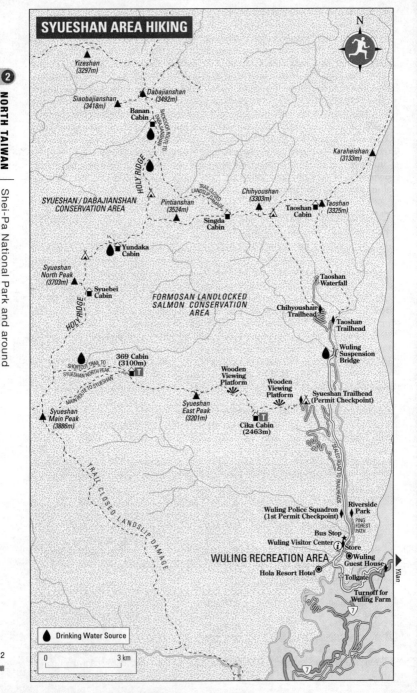

SYUESHAN AREA HIKING

N

Yizeshan (3297m)

Dabajianshan (3492m)

Siaobajianshan (3418m)

Banan Cabin

Karaheishan (3133m)

HOLY RIDGE

BACKDOOR ROUTE TO DABAJIANSHAN

TRAIL CLOSED LANDSLIP DAMAGE

SYUESHAN / DABAJIANSHAN CONSERVATION AREA

Pintianshan (3524m)

Chihyoushan (3303m)

Singda Cabin

Taoshan Cabin

Taoshan (3325m)

Yundaka Cabin

Syueshan North Peak (3703m)

Syuebei Cabin

FORMOSAN LANDLOCKED SALMON CONSERVATION AREA

Taoshan Waterfall

Chihyoushan Trailhead

Taoshan Trailhead

HOLY RIDGE

Wuling Suspension Bridge

SHORTCUT TRAIL TO SYUESHAN NORTH PEAK

369 Cabin (3100m)

MAIN ROUTE TO SYUESHAN

Wooden Viewing Platform

Wooden Viewing Platform

Syueshan Trailhead (Permit Checkpoint)

Syueshan Main Peak (3886m)

Syueshan East Peak (3201m)

Cika Cabin (2463m)

SEALED ROAD TO TRAILHEADS

TRAIL CLOSED LANDSLIP DAMAGE

Wuling Police Squadron (1st Permit Checkpoint)

Riverside Park

PING FOREST PATH

Bus Stop

Wuling Visitor Center

Store

WULING RECREATION AREA

Wuling Guest House

Hola Resort Hotel

Tollgate

Turnoff for Wuling Farm

7

Yilan

7

◆ Drinking Water Source

0   3 km

them and its conservation section – the department charged with controlling the number of visitors to protected areas – is probably Taiwan's most efficient and encourages responsible climbs of its mountains. The application procedure is the same as for other parks (see Basics p.56), and you'll need to state your proposed dates, including the night you wish to stay in the 369 Cabin. If the cabin is fully booked on the evening you desire, park officials will reserve a place for you on the next available date. Though the **application form** is most easily downloaded from the Yushan National Park website (Ⓦ www.ysnp.gov .tw), you'll still need to **post** it to the following address: Shei-Pa National Park Headquarters, Conservation Section, 100 Shueiweiping, Fusing Village, Dahu Township, Miaoli County. The park is revising its website (Ⓦ www.spnp.gov.tw) to include English-language information on climbing and trail conditions, and there are plans to implement an online English-language application procedure by 2008. Though applications are technically supposed to be received **seven working days** before the proposed start date of your climb, in practice they are often approved within a few days, and if you turn up to the park headquarters to apply in person the staff are likely to prepare your permit much more quickly.

Registration and getting to the trailhead

Before you begin your climb, you must **register** at the **Wuling Police Squadron**, a few hundred metres north along the main road from the visitor centre, on the left-hand side. Here, you'll need to produce two copies of your **permit**, together with your **passport** or ARC: a ranger will check your details and keep one copy of the permit, returning you the other copy to carry with you and show at the second permit checkpoint at the trailhead. The rangers are also likely to inspect your kit to ensure that you have the necessary **equipment** – see Basics, p.55 for a complete list of recommended climbing gear. Though all this sounds intimidating, the rangers are primarily concerned with your safety, and in practice they are exceedingly friendly to foreigners who come here to climb. It's best to arrive the day before you're scheduled to set out to allow plenty of time to check in and to arrange **transport** to the trailhead. From the visitor centre to the trailhead is a 7km walk along the main road, and, though the scenery is pleasant, the walk adds considerable time and distance to the climb and could make it a challenge for some hikers to make it to the 369 Cabin by nightfall. If the rangers are free, they might offer to drop you off at the trailhead the following morning; otherwise, you'll have to arrange a shuttle and pick-up with your hotel.

The climb

From the Syueshan trailhead it's 2km to the **Cika Cabin** (2463m), which has pit toilets and a nearby tap with a fresh water supply. From here it's a steep five-kilometre climb, mostly up stone steps, to the 369 Cabin – allow between two to five hours depending on your fitness. On a clear day this stretch offers sweeping views of more than a dozen towering peaks in Shei-Pa and Taroko National Park to the east; keep an eye out for Taroko's two tallest mountains, Cilaishan and Nanhushan (see p.406). Once you reach Syueshan's **East Peak** (3201m), the trail becomes more gradual and gives good views directly west across the valley to the Holy Ridge. About 1km further is the **369 Cabin,** which overlooks a giant valley and a vast plain to the north, making for an ideal place to relax and soak up the scenery – in late afternoon clouds often roll into the valley, creating the spectacular "**sea of clouds**" phenomenon for which Taiwan's mountains are renowned. There are no designated sleeping spaces, so you're free to grab whatever bunk you fancy. Near the cabin are pit toilets and

△ View of Nanhushan from Syueshan

a tap with fresh water – a convenient place to replenish your **drinking water**, as there are no other reliable sources between here and the summit.

Many climbers set their alarms for as early as 3am to ensure they can cover the remaining 3.9km to **Syueshan Main Peak** before dawn, and indeed watching the sun rise here, over a pinkish-blue sea of clouds below, is an ethereal experience. However, the summit can be phenomenal at any time of day, and if there is a large crowd getting up early for the sunrise it's worth sleeping in and heading to the top a bit later, when you can have it all to yourself. The last kilometre or so before the summit is quite steep, and with the high **altitude** the air is very thin, making breathing difficult for some and slowing their pace considerably. Average walkers should be able to complete the stage in two to three hours. It's important to try to reach the top by midday to allow yourself plenty of time for the descent to the trailhead, which can take anywhere from four to five hours.

The Holy Ridge: Syueshan to Dabajianshan

From Syueshan's Main Peak it's possible to set out across the **Holy Ridge**, from where you can carry on north to **Dabajianshan** or head east to **Taoshan** and back down to the Wuling Recreation Area. However, the Holy Ridge is precarious in places and there are some steep fixed-rope sections, so it's really only suited to more experienced climbers. The **Atayal aborigines** who were the first to cross this revered backbone of exposed rocks said that once a tribesman had safely negotiated his way from Dabajianshan to Syueshan he was fit to be married. Of course a Class A mountain permit is necessary for all of these, and it's essential to ask the park rangers in Wuling about the latest trail conditions and the weather forecast – the ridge is highly exposed and lightning is a real danger here.

Guanwu Recreation Area

The **Guanwu Recreation Area** has long been a busy gateway into Shei-Pa National Park but suffered a setback in August 2004, when successive typhoons caused structural damage to the forest road leading into the area, forcing officials to close it for repairs. The area is expected to be reopened in mid-2008, reinstating the main access route to the immensely popular **Dabajianshan** and resuming the heavy visitor flow that stems from Guanwu's proximity to major population centres such as Hsinchu. At around 2000m in elevation, the area is cool and densely vegetated, with one of Taiwan's most humbling old-growth forests and the island's only **Sassafras Conservation Area**. If wilderness walks are what you're after, it's well worth the effort to get here; in addition to having the safest trail to Dabajianshan, it offers several shorter **hikes** that on clear days can yield splendid vistas of the park's highest mountains – especially those along the Holy Ridge.

Arrival and information

To get to Guanwu you'll need to have your own transport, as public buses only run to Jhudong and **Cingcyuan**, the latter of which is still about 20km from the recreation area's entrance at the **Cingcyuan Checkpoint** (NT$10). Shortly after the entrance, the winding **Dalu Forest Road** splits into east and west forks; just down the east branch is the **Guanwu visitor center**, where you should enquire about trail conditions (although if you're planning to climb Dabajianshan you'll need to have already secured your Class A mountain permit). Near the visitor centre are some **short walks**, most of them to the west, along that branch of the Dalu Forest Road. The nearby **Guanwu Cabin** (☏03/5218853; ❷), originally built for loggers, has been transformed into a hostel with rustic rooms. Just below the cabin is the beginning of the 1.5-kilometre trail to the **Guanwu Waterfall**, which drops delicately down a near-vertical 30m rock face.

Climbing Dabajianshan

To get to the **Dabajianshan trailhead** from the visitor centre, you'll need to have transport for the 35-kilometre east branch of the mostly earthen Dalu Forest Road, which cuts through an amazingly diverse forest. At the trailhead is a **permit checkpoint**, where you'll need to produce two copies of your permit and your passport or ARC. For most hikers, it's a three-day return journey from here, with two overnight stays in the **99 Cabin** (reservations for the cabin will be included in your permit). The climb to the cabin, which sits at about 2700m, is fairly steep, and most walkers stop here for the night, rising well before dawn for the slog to the summit. However, as Dabajianshan has sheer faces on all sides, it's not possible to go to the very top: though the park installed **metal railings** on one side to make the ascent possible, a couple of climbers fell off and they had to be closed. Experienced climbers with adequate gear, food and the necessary permits could continue south from here, negotiating the **Holy Ridge** to get to Syueshan or heading east past Chihyoushan and Taoshan before descending into the **Wuling Recreation Area**. Most walkers, however, simply return to the 99 Cabin and spend a second night before hiking out to the road the next morning.

Syuejian Recreation Area

National park officials are planning to open the **Syuejian Recreation Area** by late 2007, giving motorists a glimpse of the park's mountain gems. The area will have a visitor centre staffed with English-speaking interpreters and park police. The natural centrepiece is the **Beikeng River Historic Trail**, which offers unobstructed views across the park, with the dramatic backdrop of the Holy Ridge in the distance. The closest settlement to the recreation area is the Atayal village of **Erbensong**, which will showcase traditional **Atayal weaving**, dancing and religious ceremonies – a plan that has courted controversy, with some arguing that the expected economic benefits for the villagers could lead to the commoditization of their culture. There is no public transport to Erbensong – you'll have to drive or hitch down the **Sihmasian Forest Road**, stopping about halfway to pay a NT$10 fee at the **Jhongsing Checkpoint**. The forest road starts at **Dahu**, just south of the park headquarters near Wenshuei.

Around Shei-Pa National Park: Lishan

Perched on the southeastern fringe of Shei-Pa National Park, the tiny village of **LISHAN** is a superb place for an overnight stop: an idyllic mountain community of apple and pear growers surrounded by picturesque **tea plantations**. Many Taiwanese make the long drive here especially for the fruit, grown at altitude and renowned for its freshness, but this is only part of the draw – the village commands sweeping **views** of Syueshan and its sisters, and visitors can also organise impromptu **excursions** to the nearby tea plantations, where bright-green tea-bush terraces cling to the plunging hillsides. Most afternoons, groups of energetic local women converge on the plantations to pick tea leaves, covered from head to toe, with conical hats fastened to their chins by brightly-coloured scarves. Paid by the weight they manage to pick, they move almost effortlessly from bush to bush, deftly filling their bamboo baskets to the brim as they chatter in a mixture of Hakka and Taiwanese.

Practicalities

The best place to stay in Lishan is the *Swallow Castle Resort & Hotel* at 46 Minzu St (℡04/25989577; ❹), where you can arrange a short trip to one of the area's most impressive plantations – but to get there you'll have to cross a yawning gorge in a partially exposed steel "**cable-cart**" used to transport tea pickers. Though not recommended for those with a fear of heights, the heart-pounding ride is actually safe provided you don't stand up or hang over the sides – and there's nothing else in Taiwan quite like it. Although the *Swallow Castle*'s rooms are a bit ostentatious, the splendid **mountain views** from the windows are more than enough to divert your attention from the tacky decor. Breakfast and dinner are available in the hotel's restaurant, and there also are some simple **Chinese food stalls** across the street where you can get basic rice and noodle dishes, as well as delicious steamed buns for breakfast. Beneath the hotel is an extensive **apple wine cellar**, where you can sample some locally made spirits. Just up the hill behind the **fruit market** in the centre of Lishan is a small **visitor centre** (9am–5pm) which has **Chinese maps** of the area and also can provide the latest information on bus times. There are two **buses** daily (8.30am & 1.30pm; NT$63) from Lishan to Wuling Farm.

Travel details

Trains

Fulong to: Dali (15 daily; 13min); Dasi (15 daily; 8min); Jiaosi (7 express daily; 25min); Suaosin (4 express daily; 1hr 5min); Taipei (10 express daily; 1hr 5min); Rueifang (7 express daily; 25min); Toucheng (7 express daily; 18min).

Hsinchu to: Jhudong (14 daily; 25min); Neiwan (14 daily; 50min); Sanyi (18 daily; 50min); Taichung (15 express daily; 1hr); Taipei (16 express daily; 1hr 5min).

Jhunan to: Hsinchu (14 express daily; 14min); Taichung (10 express daily; 50min); Taipei (14 express daily; 1hr 25min).

Keelung to: Hsinchu (2 express daily; 1hr 35min); Taichung (2 express daily; 2hr 30min); Taipei (frequent; 40min).

Luodong to: Jiaosi (16 express daily; 16min); Taipei (18 express daily; 1hr 50min); Yilan (16 express daily; 8min).

Miaoli to: Taipei (12 express daily; 1hr 30min); Sanyi (14 daily; 35min).

Rueifang to: Jingtong (14 daily; 45min); Pingsi (14 daily; 40min); Shihfen (14 daily; 30min); Taipei (16 express daily; 45min).

Sanyi to: Hsinchu (18 daily; 50min); Taichung (18 daily; 40min); Taipei (3 express daily; 2hr 15min).

Suao to: Taipei (3 express daily; 1hr 5min).

Suaosin to: Fulong (10 express daily; 1hr 5min);

Hualien (6 express daily; 1hr); Taipei (10 express daily; 2hr); Yilan (10 express daily; 18min).

Taoyuan to: Hsinchu (19 express daily; 35min); Taipei (17 express daily; 30min).

Toucheng to: Taipei (17 express daily; 1hr 20min).

Yilan to: Taipei (18 express daily; 1hr 40min); Suaosin (6 express daily; 18min).

Buses

With so many services operating in the region, most bus frequencies have not been included.

Dasi (Northern Cross-Island Highway) to: Baling (4 daily; 1hr 30min); Cihhu (20min); Fusing (40min); Little Wulai Falls (4 daily; 45min); Taoyuan (30min).

Fulong to: Bitou (30min); Dasi (35min); Keelung (1hr); Lion Kingdom Museum (40min); Toucheng (45min).

Hsinchu to: Jhudong (40min); Taichung (1hr); Taipei (1hr); Yimin Temple (10 daily; 30min).

Jhudong to: Beipu (15min); Lion's Head Mountain (5 daily; 40min).

Jhunan to: Nanjhuang (1hr).

Jinshan to: Baishawan (40min); Danshui (1hr); Dharma Drum Mountain (10min); Keelung (30min); Shihmen (20min); Taipei (1hr); Yeliou (10min).

Keelung to: Bitou (30–40min); Danshui (1hr 30min); Fulong (1hr); Jinguashi (40min); Jinshan (30min); Jiufen (30min); Yeliou (20min); Taipei (1hr).

Miaoli to: Sanyi (30min); Wenshuei (hourly; 50min).

Rueifang to: Jinguashi (20min); Jiufen (15min).

Pingsi to: Jingtong (5min); Taipei (40min).

Sanyi to: Miaoli (30min).

Suao to: Nanfangao (5min), Luodong (30min).

Taoyuan to: Baling (1 daily; 2hr 30min); Dasi (30min).

Toufen to: Emei Lake (35min); Hsinchu (20min); Taipei (1hr 20min).

Wuling Farm to: Lishan (2 daily; 15–20min); Luodong (2 daily); Yilan (2 daily; 2hr 45min).

Yilan to: Lishan (2 daily; 3hr); Wuling Farm (2 daily; 2hr 45min).

Ferries

Keelung to: Matzu (1 daily; 8hr).

Flights

Taiwan Taoyuan International Airport near Taoyuan and **Songshan Airport** (domestic flights only) in Taipei serve as the regional airports (see p.85).

Central Taiwan

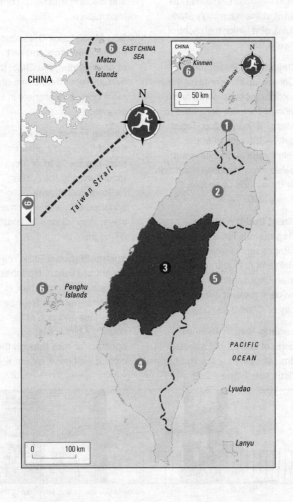

CHAPTER 3 # Highlights

✳ **921 Earthquake Museum**
Informative and poignant
memorial to the devastating
quake that hit Taiwan in 1999,
with high-tech exhibits built
around the hauntingly stark
ruins of a junior high school.
See p.248

✳**Dajia Mazu Pilgrimage**
Central Taiwan contains the
world's most colourful and
vibrant temples dedicated to
Mazu, Taiwan's chief Taoist
deity – the annual Mazu
Pilgrimage is an exuberant
celebration involving hundreds
of thousands of people.
See p.250

✳ **Great Buddha Statue,
Baguashan** Taiwan's most
famous representation of
Sakyamuni Buddha sits
atop Baguashan, with
sweeping views over the
city of Changhua. See p.256

✳ **Lugang** Historic town with
bags of charm, old streets,
craft shops, temples and tasty
"little eats". See p.257

✳ **Chung Tai Chan Monastery**
Taiwan's largest Buddhist
temple complex is an incredible
blend of modern engineering
and dazzling traditional craftsmanship. See p.273

✳**Sun Moon Lake** The ancestral
home of Taiwan's smallest
aboriginal tribe, the Thao, this
tranquil lake offers some of the
most gorgeous scenery in the
country. See p.275

✳ **Alishan Forest Railway** Take
one of the world's great train
rides into the heart of the
mountains and the Alishan
National Scenic Area, a region
sprinkled with alluring homestays, Tsou villages and pristine
hiking trails. See p.297

✳ **Yushan National Park** The
ascent of Yushan, Northeast
Asia's highest mountain, is
a lifetime ambition for many
Taiwanese and one of the
country's highlights, a
spectacular hike through the
clouds with mind-blowing
views. See p.301

△ View of Sun Moon Lake, from room at *The Lalu*

Central Taiwan

Bounded by the densely populated cities of the north, and the lush tropical plains of the south, **central Taiwan** contains the country's most magnificent scenery, making it one of the most rewarding areas to visit. This is a region principally defined by mountains: the mighty central ranges contain a vast array of tantalizing landscapes, from the mesmerizing beauty of **Sun Moon Lake** to the awe-inspiring peak of **Yushan**, Northeast Asia's tallest mountain.

Taichung is one of the most dynamic cities in the country and gateway to the region, noted for its innovative teahouses and vibrant nightlife. To the south, the flat river plains sandwiched between the hills and the sea are rich in traditional Chinese culture; worship of Taoist deity Mazu, known as Goddess of the Sea and often regarded as the country's patron saint, is more intense here than any other part of Taiwan. The towns of **Beigang** and **Dajia** are home to the most important Mazu temples on the island, and the annual Dajia Mazu Pilgrimage is Taiwan's largest religious festival. **Lugang** is one of Taiwan's oldest towns, a living museum of master craftsmen, narrow streets and temples, while the **Great Buddha Statue** in Changhua is one of Asia's biggest. The geographical centre of the island, Puli, is home to the mind-boggling **Chung Tai Chan Monastery**, a staggering monument to contemporary architecture and Zen Buddhist philosophy.

Further south, the narrow valleys and traditional Tsou villages of **Alishan National Scenic Area** lie to the east of Chiayi, an area best explored on foot or with your own transport, though it's also accessible via the **Alishan Forest Railway**, one of the world's great train rides. The scenic area's appeal is compounded by an array of attractive and highly individual homestays, while aboriginal culture is particularly strong here, with many tribal villages connected by scenic hikes through the mountains and tea fields. Alishan borders the **Yushan National Park,** offering a more challenging hiking experience, though the stunning path up its main peak is tackled by hundreds of visitors every year.

Central Taiwan comprises Changhua, Chiayi, landlocked Nantou, Taichung and rural Yunlin counties, and though **getting around** the coastal plains is straightforward given the profusion of north–south transport links, accessing remote parts of the interior can be tricky without your own transport. Buses connect the most popular destinations with the main cities, however, and distances are not huge.

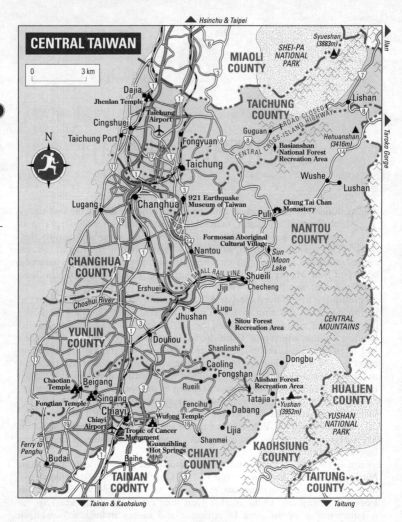

CENTRAL TAIWAN

Hsinchu & Taipei

Syueshan (3883m)

SHEI-PA NATIONAL PARK

MIAOLI COUNTY

0   3 km

Ilan

Dajia
Jhenlan Temple

TAICHUNG COUNTY

Lishan

Cingshuei

Taichung Airport

Taichung Port

Fongyuan

Guguan

CENTRAL CROSS-ISLAND HIGHWAY

ROAD CLOSED

Basianshan National Forest Recreation Area

Hehuanshan (3416m)

Taroko Gorge

Taichung Port

N

Taichung

Wushe

Lushan

Lugang

Changhua

921 Earthquake Museum of Taiwan

Puli

Chung Tai Chan Monastery

NANTOU COUNTY

CHANGHUA COUNTY

Formosan Aboriginal Cultural Village

Nantou

Sun Moon Lake

Ershuei

JIJI SMALL RAIL LINE

Shueili

Jiji   Checheng

Choshui River

Lugu

Jhushan

Sitou Forest Recreation Area

CENTRAL MOUNTAINS

YUNLIN COUNTY

Douliou

Shanlinshi

Dongbu

Caoling   Fongshan

HUALIEN COUNTY

Chaotian Temple

Beigang

Rueili

Alishan Forest Recreation Area

Tatajia

Yushan (3952m)

YUSHAN NATIONAL PARK

Fongtian Temple

Singang

Fencihu

Dabang

Chiayi Airport

Chiayi

Lijia

KAOHSIUNG COUNTY

Tropic of Cancer Monument

Wufong Temple

Shanmei

Ferry to Penghu

Budai

Guanzihling Hot Springs

CHIAYI COUNTY

Baihe

TAINAN COUNTY

TAITUNG COUNTY

Tainan & Kaohsiung

Taitung

Taichung and around

Sprawled over the flat coastal plains west of the mountains, **TAICHUNG** is Taiwan's third-largest city, the unofficial capital of central Taiwan and an important transport hub for the region. It's also regarded as the country's most attractive place to live: the climate is drier, the air less polluted, housing cheaper, and the streets greener and less crowded than Taipei or Kaohsiung. Taiwanese **tea culture** is particularly developed here; the city's appealing mix of elegant classical teahouses and stylish contemporary cafés are perfect settings for a varied range of teas. More potent liquid refreshment drives the city's dynamic **nightlife**, but there's plenty to keep you occupied during the day. Taichung's old centre still contains attractive remnants of its Japanese colonial past and a smattering of unusual **temples**, I.M. Pei's **Luce Memorial Chapel** is a striking piece of modern architecture and the **National Taiwan Museum of Fine Arts** is a world-class contemporary art gallery. Beyond the suburbs, the chief attractions are **Dajia** and its famous **Mazu Pilgrimage**, and the **921 Earthquake Museum** south of Wufong.

Taichung

Taichung	台中	*táizhōng*
Arrival and transport		
Chao Ma bus stop area	朝馬車站	*cháomǎ chēzhàn*
City Bus Station	台中汽車 站	*táizhōng qìchēzhàn*
Taichung Airport	台中航空站	*táizhōng hángkōng zhàn*
Taichung Train Station	台中火車站	*táizhōng huǒchēzhàn*
Taichung High-Speed Rail Station (Wurih)	高鐵台中站 (烏日)	*gāotiě táizhōng zhàn (wūrì)*
Accommodation		
Chin Hua Hotel	金樺大飯店	*jīnhuà dàfàndiàn*
Fuh Chun Hotel	富春大飯店	*fùchūn dàfàndiàn*
Kao Yuan Hotel	高苑旅館	*gāoyuàn lǚguǎn*
K Hotel	柯達大飯店	*kēdá dàfàndiàn*
Landis Taichung	台中永豐棧麗緻酒店	*táizhōng yǒngfēngzhàn lìzhì jiǔdiàn*
Plaza International Hotel	通豪大飯店	*tōngháo dàfàndiàn*
Splendor	金典會館	*jīndiàn huìguǎn*
Taichung Hostel C.L.C.	聯勤台中招待所	*liánqín táizhōng zhāodàisuǒ*
Taichung International Youth Hostel	台中國際青年之家	*táizhōng guójì qīngnián zhījiā*
Twinstar Hotel	雙星大飯店	*shuāng xīng dàfàndiàn*
Zaw-Jung Business Hotel	瑞君商務旅館	*ruìjūn shāngwù lǚguǎn*
Zhong Ke Hotel	中科大飯店	*zhōngkē dàfàndiàn*
The City		
Baojue Temple	寶覺寺	*bǎojúe sì*
City Hall	台中市政府	*táizhōng shì zhèngfǔ*
Confucius Temple	孔廟	*kǒngmiào*
Donghai University	東海大學	*dōnghǎi dàxúe*
Electronic Street	電子街	*diàn zǐ jiē*
Herbal Medicine Street	草藥街	*cǎoyào jiē*
International Art Street	國際藝術街坊	*guójì yìshù jiē fāng*
Jiguang Street	激光街	*jī guāng jiē*
Luce Memorial Chapel	路思義教堂	*lùsīyì jiàotáng*
Martyrs' Shrine	忠烈祠	*zhōngliècí*
Nantian Temple	南天宮	*nántiān gōng*
Nantun Old Street	南屯老街	*nántún lǎojiē*
National Botanical Gardens	國立植物園	*guólì zhíwù yúan*
National Museum of Natural Science	國立自然科學博物館	*guólì zìrán kēxúe bówùguǎn*
National Taiwan Museum of Fine Arts	國立台灣美術館	*guólì táiwǎn měishùguǎn*
Stock 20	台中二十號倉庫	*táizhōng èrshí hào cāngkù*
Taichung Park	台中公園	*táizhōng gōngyuán*
Wanhe Temple	萬和宮	*wànhé gōng*
Wenchang Temple	文昌公廟	*wénchāng gōng miào*

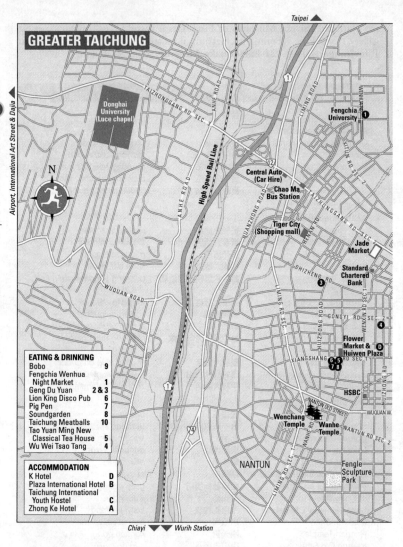

GREATER TAICHUNG

Taipei

Donghai University (Luce chapel)

N

Fengchia University ❶

Central Auto (Car Hire)

Chao Ma Bus Station

Tiger City (Shopping mall)

Jade Market

Standard Chartered Bank
❸

WUQUAN ROAD

GONGYI RD SEC 1

❹

Flower Market & Huiwen Plaza ❶

❻❺
❼❽

XIANGSHANG

HSBC

WUQUAN W.

NANTUN OLD STREET

Wenchang Temple   Wanhe Temple

NANTUN RD SEC 2

Fengle Sculpture Park

NANTUN

Chiayi ▼▼ Wurih Station

EATING & DRINKING

Bobo	9
Fengchia Wenhua Night Market	1
Geng Du Yuan	2 & 3
Lion King Disco Pub	6
Pig Pen	7
Soundgarden	8
Taichung Meatballs	10
Tao Yuan Ming New Classical Tea House	5
Wu Wei Tsao Tang	4

ACCOMMODATION

K Hotel	D
Plaza International Hotel	B
Taichung International Youth Hostel	C
Zhong Ke Hotel	A

Some history

Taichung traces its origins to a military post and village known as **Datun**, established in 1733 on the site of today's Taichung Park, but the modern city is an amalgam of several places, explaining why its oldest buildings and temples appear to be scattered all over the city – the western district of Nantun grew up around another army camp, founded in 1721 on the site of a farm that was built sixteen years earlier, and was absorbed by Taichung in 1950. Datun was briefly the **capital of Taiwan** after the island became a province of China in 1885, but local infrastructure was poor and Taipei, which was provisional capital, assumed the official role in 1894. After the Japanese occupied Taiwan in 1895 the city's name was changed to Taichung, or "Central Taiwan" and development began in

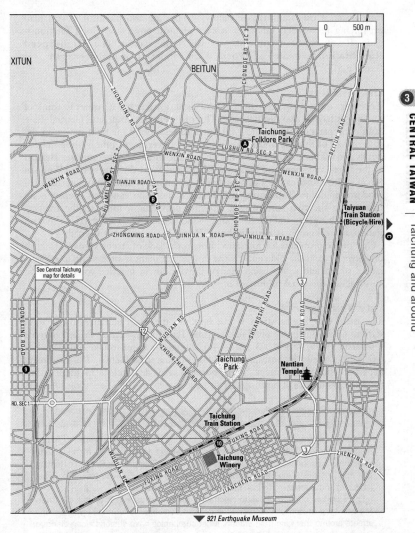

▼ *921 Earthquake Museum*

earnest, with Englishman William Barton hired to design the new road layout for the city. The economy boomed in the 1970s and 1980s, with manufacturing and particularly shoe making leading the way, and by the 1990s the commercial centre of the city had drifted west towards Taichung Port (Taiwan's third largest). The city's population topped the million mark in 2003.

Arrival, orientation and city transport

Taichung Airport is a tedious 20km northwest of the city centre: take a taxi (NT$350) or Taichung Bus #115 or #555 into the city (NT$26). Taichung is almost midway on the **Western train line** between Taipei and Kaohsiung, and the **train station** sits in the old centre of the city, close to all local and long-distance **bus** stations (see below) – taxis are also plentiful. If you plan on staying in western Taichung, note that most buses stop along Taizhong-gang Road before terminating at the train station. The **High-Speed Rail Station** is located at **Wurih**, 7km southwest of the city centre (see Basics p.31).

Orientation

Taichung covers a vast area, divided into eight districts, but it's easier to think of the city as having two distinct parts. The **old centre**, comprising Central, East, South and parts of North and West districts, lies around the train station in the eastern half of the city and is home to many government offices, shops, cheap hotels and traditional food stalls. In contrast, the modern city comprises **Beitun** to the north and sprawling **Nantun**, **Xitun** and **West** districts beyond Wuquan Road – this contains the business centre and most of Taichung's international food and nightlife. **Taizhonggang Road** is the main east–west thoroughfare connecting the two parts of the city and providing a route to the freeway, Donghai University and the harbour beyond (24km). The road starts at the train station and is known as **Zhongzheng Road** as far as Wuquan Road.

One of the problems for foreign visitors is the lack of **street signs** in English or *Pinyin* beyond the old centre – the city government is attempting to roman-ize all streets and sights using Hanyu Pinyin, but in practice you're likely to come across the usual mishmash of systems.

City Transport

The main **city bus station** is just opposite the main entrance to the train station: numerous buses ply Taizhonggang Road from here as far as Donghai University (#60, #88, #103 and #146), though it's faster to take the Dajia bus (see p.249). A few city buses, and local buses operated by Renyou Bus Company, depart Luchuan East Street. Some **buses** display destinations in English, but timetables and maps at bus stops are provided solely in Chinese – most journeys

---

Moving on from Taichung

Taichung Airport hosts charter **flights** to Hong Kong and domestic services to Taipei, Magong, Hualien, Taitung and Kinmen. For the airport, take bus #115 from Luchuan East Street, a short walk from the station (turn left off Zhongzheng Road), or Renyou bus #555 on the same street north of Chenggong Road. Express **trains** to Taipei (NT$375) and Kaohsiung (NT$470) depart throughout the day.

There are two principal areas to catch **long-distance buses** in Taichung: the **Chao Ma bus stop area** near the freeway and, more conveniently for most travellers, the streets around the main train station. Most companies have stations along Jianguo Road or Shuangshi Road: the Kuo Kuang bus station is immediately to the right of the train station, with regular hourly services to **Taipei**, **Tainan** and **Kaohsiung**; opposite on Jianguo Road is the Ubus station with a similar line-up of destinations, and Ho Hsin next door. Between here and Chenggong Road you'll find Free Go Express with services to the Taiwan Taoyuan, and on the corner, regular Quan Hang services to Puli. The Puli Express operates from Shuangshi Road. Renyou Bus runs two buses a day to **Sun Moon Lake** from Luchuan East Street – buy tickets at no. 110. Minibuses to **Lugang** depart 167 Fuxing Road Section 4, just behind the train station (take the underpass and turn left on Fuxing). Buses leave every half an hour from 6am to 10.30pm in both directions, cost NT$100 and take around one hour. For Guguan, several **buses** (NT$174; 2.5hr) depart each day from the Fongyuan Bus station, across the street from the train station and to the left.

should cost the standard single-sector fare of NT$20. **Taxis** are not a bad way to get around – the meter starts at NT$85 and you'll usually pay less than NT$220 for trips across the central part of the city. **Driving** around Taichung is particularly hair-raising, even by Taiwanese standards, but to explore the surrounding area it's useful to have your own transport (see Listings p.247 for rental firms).

Information

Taichung's principal **visitor information center** is at 2 Dacheng Street in the old centre, just off Zhongzheng Road (daily 9am–10pm; ℡04/22258988 or ℡0800/422022; ⓦwww.tccg.gov.tw), while a smaller but more convenient **information center** (daily 8am–8pm) sits near the main exit of the train station – staff at both places usually speak English. If you're aiming to stay in Taichung for a while, check out the city's growing number of expat-orientated magazines, available free at bars and restaurants. *Compass* magazine (ⓦwww .taiwanfun.com) is the most established.

Accommodation

As usual, the cheapest **hotels** in Taichung are located near the train station – things get more expensive in the western and more fashionable parts of the city. There's a reasonable selection of mid-range hotels to choose from but budget accommodation is sadly lacking, with no hostels in the centre of town. Most hotels offer free broadband access for laptop users, or use of a computer to check the Internet.

Old centre

Chin Hua Hotel 19 Liuchuan Rd Sec 3
℡04/22272257, ⓦwww.chinhua-hotel.com.tw.
Smart mid-range option just off Zhongshan Road, with friendly English-speaking staff. Japanese-style rooms come with attractive wood fittings, screen doors and big tubs, while the cheaper Chinese and European rooms are just as comfortable, though the latter's fluffy carpets and baroque decor are a little kitsch. ❹

Fuh Chun Hotel 1 Zhongshan Rd ℡04/22283181.
Good-value budget hotel, conveniently located opposite the train station in an old, slightly shabby building. Rooms are clean and come with TVs, but are otherwise what you'd expect, basic and a bit worn – the price and friendliness of the staff make it just about worthwhile for short stays. No internet. ❷

Kao Yuan Hotel 444 Zhongshan Rd
℡04/22298755, ⓦwww.kaoyuan.com.tw.
Cosy, modern business hotel in central Taichung. Rooms are compact but attractively designed in a smart, contemporary style making this one of the best deals in town. There's a slightly older and cheaper branch at 392 Zhongzheng Rd (℡04/22261566), just around the corner. ❹

Twinstar Hotel 158 Fuxing Rd Sec 4
℡04/22261811, ⓦwww.tohotel.com.tw. Convenient hotel set in a standard, anonymous building just behind the train station (take the underpass

or use the rear exit and turn left), next door to Taichung Central shopping mall. Rooms are simple but adequate, and regular promotions make this excellent value. ❸

Zaw-Jung Business Hotel 100 Fuxing Rd Sec 4 ℡04/22235838. Friendly budget hotel, set in a modern building opposite the rear exit of the train station. Standard rooms are simply decorated but comfortable, with TVs and clean wooden floors, though it's worth paying a little extra for the more spacious doubles. ❸

West district

Splendor 1049 Jianxing Rd ℡04/23298899,
ⓦwww.splendor-taichung.com.tw. Popular five-star on the edge of the Canal District, with bright, comfortable rooms, large outdoor pool and posh spa. The *Splendor Studio* (❼) has a separate entrance next door, and, though its rooms are rather characterless (designed for longer stays), the high floors offer spectacular night views of Taichung. ❽

Taichung Hostel C.L.C 400 Meicun Rd
℡04/23721954, Ⓔtaichun.hostel@msa.hinet .net. This is a budget hotel rather than a hostel, a 1950s building surrounded by pleasant gardens in the western part of town, close to the Fine Arts Museum. Rooms are plain and a little old, but clean and comfortable enough. The hostel is owned by a unit of Taiwan's military, but open to the public. ❸

Nantun

K Hotel 525 Dadun Rd ⊤04/23290055, ⓦwww
.khotel.com.tw. Stylish upper mid-range hotel
in Nantun district, around 4km from the station.
Rooms are modern and very comfortable – extras
include a small gym and giant flat-screen TVs in
the slightly more expensive deluxe rooms. ❻

Xitun

Landis Taichung 9 Taizhonggang Rd Sec
2 ⊤04/23268008, ⓦwww.landis.com.tw.
Taichung's most elegant luxury hotel, smack in the
heart of the busy western half of the city. Rooms
are stylishly decked out with natural wood and a
subtle gold colour scheme, the bathrooms swathed
in marble. Facilities include access to the Mandara
Life Club, a lavish spa and pool, as well as a couple
of swanky restaurants. ❼

North district

Plaza International 431 Daya Rd ⊤04/22956789,
ⓦaichungplaza-en.network.com.tw. Built in 1989,
this is still one of Taichung's top hotels, though
it can't compete with the newer five-stars and is
starting to show its age. All rooms feature classical
redwood furniture and there's a host of amenities
including gym, plush Chinese restaurants and a
rarity in Taichung – a decent pool. ❼

Beitun

Taichung International Youth Hostel 628 Buzi
(Puzih) Rd ⊤04/22399809, Ⓔttyh88@hotmail
.com. Taichung's only YHA-affiliated hostel has
spotless, brand new dorm beds (NT$350) and
bathrooms and is usually empty during the week.
Unfortunately this is because it's 7km out in
Beitun on the eastern fringes of town – take a taxi
(NT$200) or bus #15 from Luchuan East Street, a
short walk from the station (left off Zhongzheng
Rd). The hostel provides free bike rental, but
cycling around the city from here will make for a
hard day.

Zhong Ke Hotel 256 Chongde Rd Sec 2
⊤04/22465599, ⓦwww.zkhotel.com.tw. Modern,
relatively new hotel, with wireless Internet and
business centre for those without a computer.
Rooms are cosy, stylish and very good value – the
catch is the inconvenient location in the northern
part of the city, close to the Folklore Park, but it's a
relatively easy taxi ride from the old centre. ❻

The City

Taichung is a modern city, but there are plenty of sights tucked away between
all the development, especially in the **old centre**, **East** and **North** districts, best
explored on foot. The attractions in west Taichung are much more spread out,
and will require travelling by bus or taxi.

The old centre

The shabby **old centre** area around Taichung main train station is a bit worse
for wear, but still offers an absorbing glimpse of old Taichung's traditional
shopping streets and food stalls, as well as its finest **Japanese colonial buildings**. Start by heading to the south side of the train station, itself an attractive
building completed in 1917, to **Stock 20** (Tues–Thurs 10am–8pm & Fri–Sat
10am–10pm; free), an innovative art centre converted from old railway warehouses. Inside you'll find a café and a main gallery open to the public, while
up to eight artists in residence utilize the workshops on site. Take the underpass
under the station (right as you exit) and turn right when you emerge – the
gallery is a few metres ahead along the tracks.

Back at the station, walk north along Zhongzheng Road, past the canal on
Luchuan Street, and turn left into narrow **Electronic Street**, a pedestrianized
alley crammed with numerous electronic and computer stores – it tends to get
going after midday. Just to the north, **Jiguang Street** is the longest pedestrianized thoroughfare in the city, lined with clothes shops and snack stalls. Walk
west down either of these streets to Minquan Road and turn right, continuing
north to the junction with Shifu Road. On the north side is Taichung's **City
Hall**, completed by the Japanese in 1924. A typically meticulous imitation of
Second Empire architecture, with white stone, mansard roof and striking ionic
column facade, it initially served as the Taichung regional administration office.

The elegant white building on the other side of the road is the city's most stately colonial legacy. Built in 1920 with a handsome Neoclassical portico and domed roof, this was the original City Hall and later, the **Bureau of Transportation and Tourism** – by 2007 it should be operating as an exhibition hall or gallery.

Head back down Minquan Road to Ziyou Road and turn left – from Minzu Road onwards this becomes Taichung's **cake street** (see p.243). Walk a few blocks and turn right along Chenggong Road, continue south past Jiguang Street, and take the first left down **Herbal Medicine Street**, a series of narrow alleys lined with traditional herb stores. The subtle aromas and torpid atmosphere here make it more redolent of old Taichung than anywhere else in the city. The lanes form a small cross, with a stall (no.12) at the central axis selling refreshing **iced herbal tea** (NT$10). At Guangfu Road turn left, walk back onto Ziyou Road and turn right towards **Taichung Park**, a block to the east. Created by the Japanese in 1903 on the site of the eighteenth-century fort of Datun, it's a universe away from modern Taichung and the location of the unlikely city symbol, the twin-peaked **Wang Yue Pavilion** in the middle of the lake. Built in 1908 to commemorate the completion of the north–south rail-line, its distinctive russet-red roof tiles look a bit worn these days, but it makes a welcome retreat from the sun on sweltering afternoons. The park is a good place to be in January or February, when it plays host to Taichung's **Lantern Festival** (see p.51).

Nantian Temple

Taichung's East district has little in the way of sights, but **Nantian Temple** (daily 6.30am–10pm), just under 1km east of Taichung Park on Ziyou Road, is certainly photogenic. Dedicated to Guan Di, the main hall is fairly typical, but it's backed by a huge (48m) and slightly garish statue of the general, seated above a tiger and swathed in colourful robes. Stroking his beard – he's also known as the "Beautiful Whiskered One" – his posture is meant to convey great wisdom, as well as the loyalty and bravery symbolized by his bright red face and hands, his most distinctive features. You can climb up to the sixth floor, just below the

△ Taichung, Milefo statue

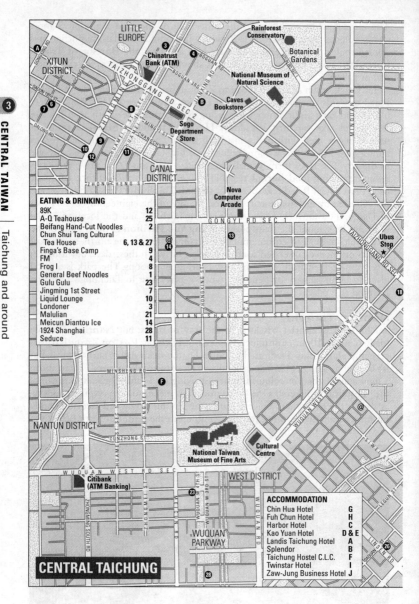

EATING & DRINKING

89K	12
A-Q Teahouse	25
Beifang Hand-Cut Noodles	2
Chun Shui Tang Cultural Tea House	6, 13 & 27
Finga's Base Camp	9
FM	4
Frog I	8
General Beef Noodles	1
Gulu Gulu	23
Jingming 1st Street	7
Liquid Lounge	10
Londoner	3
Malulian	21
Meicun Diantou Ice	14
1924 Shanghai	28
Seduce	11

ACCOMMODATION

Chin Hua Hotel	G
Fuh Chun Hotel	H
Harbor Hotel	C
Kao Yuan Hotel	D & E
Landis Taichung Hotel	A
Splendor	B
Taichung Hostel C.L.C.	F
Twinstar Hotel	I
Zaw-Jung Business Hotel	J

CENTRAL TAICHUNG

statue, to take a closer look. Bus #33 from the city bus station stops close to the temple.

North district

Old Taichung spills over into **North district**, the home of several significant temples. A few blocks north of Taichung Park along Shuangshi Road,

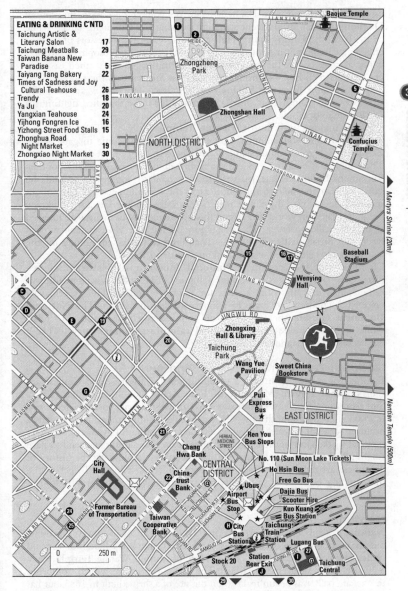

EATING & DRINKING C'NTD

Taichung Artistic & Literary Salon	17
Taichung Meatballs	29
Taiwan Banana New Paradise	5
Taiyang Tang Bakery	22
Times of Sadness and Joy Cultural Teahouse	26
Trendy	18
Ya Ju	20
Yangxian Teahouse	24
Yijhong Fongren Ice	16
Yizhong Street Food Stalls	15
Zhonghua Road Night Market	19
Zhongxiao Night Market	30

Taichung's **Confucius Temple** (Tues–Sun 9am–5pm) makes up in scale what it lacks in history. Taiwan's second-largest Confucian temple, it was completed in 1976, and, as a result, it's in relatively pristine condition – it's built in the style of the Northern Song dynasty and is a massive, palatial structure. The ceremonial entrance is the **Lingxing Gate** on Lixing Road, but this only opens for the president – everyone else enters via the small **Kuan Te Gate** on Shuangshi Road. The Dacheng Gate on your left leads to the central **Dacheng Hall**, a magnificent structure housing the Confucius tablet, while to the back, the **Chungsheng Hall** commemorates the ancestors of Confucius. The ceremony on September 28 to celebrate the philosopher's birthday is just as colourful as Taipei's and highly recommended – it's much easier to get tickets (free). Bus #41 from Luchuan East Street passes the temple. Next door, the sombre **Martyrs' Shrine** (Sat–Sun 9am–5pm; free) was a shrine for Japanese soldiers until 1945, now a memorial for those that died fighting for the Republic of China.

Twenty minutes' walk north, **Baojue Temple** (daily 8am–5pm) on Jianxing Road is one of Taichung's most popular – tourists come to gape at the 27-metre-high gold-painted statue of **Milefo**, to the far right of the compound. The temple was built in 1928 and the main hall in the centre actually honours Sakyamuni Buddha, while Japanese tourists tend to congregate around the small pavilion and stele to the left, next to the remembrance hall (you might see small, illicitly placed Japanese imperial flags here). Some Taiwanese willingly fought for Japan in World War II, and this is where many of them were interred after being killed overseas. The calligraphy on the stele is an epitaph written by former president Lee Teng-hui – Lee's brother was killed fighting for the Japanese and is enshrined at the Yasukuni Shrine in Tokyo.

Further west, the gargantuan **National Museum of Natural Science** (Tues–Sun 9am–5pm, no entry after 4.30pm; NT$100; ⓦwww.nmns.edu.tw), is Taichung's top attraction, at least for Taiwanese tourists, but it's primarily targeted at children and there isn't much labelled in English. The **National Botanical Gardens** behind the main complex is a pleasant place to relax, while the striking glass-encased **tropical rainforest conservatory** (NT$20) has become a city landmark.

National Taiwan Museum of Fine Arts

Essential for anyone with even a vague interest in Taiwanese and Chinese art, the **National Taiwan Museum of Fine Arts** (Tues–Fri 9am–5pm, Sat & Sun 9am–6pm; free; ⓦwww.tmoa.gov.tw) in West district formally reopened in 2005 after a mammoth post-921 Earthquake refurbishment. The result is a beautiful series of galleries displaying a wide range of both Taiwanese and international work. Most of the exhibits change every few months and tend to have English explanations, though the permanent gallery introducing the history of Taiwanese art on the first floor is presented solely in Chinese. To get to the museum take bus #71 from the city bus station or Renyou buses #10, #30 or #40 from Luchuan East Street.

Nantun

Nantun is a modern district, covering a vast swathe of southwest Taichung, but its roots go back to the late seventeenth century. It's here, not the old centre, that you'll find the city's oldest place of worship, **Wanhe Temple** (daily 5.30am–10pm), dedicated to Mazu. The current structure, which comprises three main halls, was begun in 1726 on the site of a shrine built in 1683, but has been renovated many times – the intricate *koji* figurines set into the walls are particularly vivid here. In front of the temple a forecourt contains a stage which hosts one of Taichung's most interesting festivals, the **Last-Name Show**, which dates from 1825. Chinese opera and dance performances start two days before Mazu's birthday on Lunar March 23 (April or May) and usually last for twelve days. Behind Wanhe Temple, **Wenchang Temple** (daily 5.30am–10pm) is the modern sister temple of an older shrine in Beitun. This version has two storeys and is dedicated not only to Wenchang Dijun (the "Emperor of Passing Exams"), but also Guan Di and Sakyamuni Buddha, and is popular with students for obvious reasons. The box in front of the main altar is stuffed with photocopies of test applications and ID cards.

A short walk north, the area around the junction of Nantun and Wanhe roads is known as **Nantun Old Street**, lined with old shophouses and a couple of cheap food stalls. Renyou buses #10, #30 or #40 from Luchuan East Street travel along Nantun Road.

Xitun

Xitun district covers a massive chunk of northwest Taichung, its main attraction the elegant **Luce Memorial Chapel** within the grounds of **Donghai University**, around 9km from the train station. Designed by lauded architect I.M. Pei, it's a breathtaking piece of engineering – completed in 1963 and named after the American missionary Henry Winters Luce, its graceful tent-like structure resembles an inverted ship's hull, or more appropriately, praying hands. It still functions as the university chapel and tends to be locked up on weekdays. The university grounds are also worth exploring if you have time, as this is probably the most attractive campus in Taiwan, with Tang dynasty themed buildings, and the main avenues lined with Phoenix trees and blossoms. Buses to the university are plentiful: #60, #88, #103, #146 and #147 run from the city bus station. Another 2.5km west from the university, **International Art Street** is an appealing place to spend an afternoon, with a range of small boutiques, craft shops, cheap clothes stores, teashops, furniture emporiums and art studios. It's beyond Donghai University and accessible via the same buses: turn right off Taizhonggang Road on Guojie Street – the entrance is next to the first 7-Eleven on the left. It's worth combining a trip out here with a visit to Dajia (see p.249) – you can hail the bus along Taizhonggang Road.

Eating

Taichung is an excellent place to gorge on both Taiwanese and international food. Traditional places tend to be focused in the old centre, with the plusher, more cosmopolitan options in the west: trawl **Wuquan Parkway** for a good selection, or **Little Europe** (a district thick with Western restaurants and bars) and the **Canal District** south of Taizhonggang Road. Local specialties include meatballs and various types of noodles, particularly beef, but for a vast spread of cheap snacks Taichung's night markets offer a good introduction – the most convenient are **Zhongxiao Night Market** on Zhongxiao Road between Taizhong and Guoguang roads south of the station, and **Zhonghua Night Market** further north. For a more eclectic range of traditional and Western snack food, popular with students, try the stalls crammed along **Yizhong Street** between Taiping Road and Yucai Street (open from late morning). Travellers with a penchant for something sweeter won't be disappointed, with Ziyou Road between Zhongzheng and Minquan roads crammed with cakeshops selling **suncakes** *(taiyang bing)*; flat, crumbling pastries filled with sweet wheat germ, honey or taro paste. The venerable *Taiyang Tang Bakery* at 23 Ziyou Road Section 2 is one of the oldest.

Old centre

A-Q Teahouse 3 Fuhou St. Atmospheric restaurant set in single-storey, wooden Japanese house, serving decent food such as beef or curry noodles (NT$90), as well as a large selection of tea (NT$90) and toast sets (NT$100).

Simple wooden tables and chairs inside, and small courtyard – ask for the English menu.

Malulian 133 Zhongzheng Rd. Best shaved ice stall in the old centre, with covered outdoor eating area and good selection of fresh, tasty toppings such as creamy taro,

A-Q Teahouse	阿Q茶舍	ā Q cháshè
Beifang Hand-Cut Noodles	北方館	běi fāng guǎn
Fengchia Wenhua Night Market	逢甲文華夜市	féngjiǎ wénhuá yèshì
Fongren Ice	一中豐仁冰	yī zhōng fēngrén bīng
General Beef Noodles	將軍牛肉大王	jiāng jūn niúròu dàwáng
Gulu Gulu	咕嚕估嚕音樂餐廳	gūlū gūlū yīnyuè cāntīng
Jingming 1st Street	精明一街	jīngmíng yī jiē
Malulian	瑪露連	mǎlùlián
Meicun Diantou Ice	美村點頭冰	měicūn diǎntóu bīng
1924 Shanghai	新月梧桐	xīnyuè wútóng
Pig Pen	犁棧	lízhàn
Taichung Artistic & Literary Salon	台中市長公館藝文之家	táizhōngshì zhǎng gōngguǎn yìwén zhī jiā
Taichung Meatballs	台中肉丸	táizhōng ròuwán
Taiwan Banana New Paradise	香蕉新樂園	xiāng jiāo xīn lèyuán
Taiyang Tang Bakery	太陽堂餅店	tàiyáng táng bǐngdiàn
Ya Ju	雅居健康素館	yǎjū jiànkāng sùguǎn
Zhonghua Night Market	中華夜市	zhōnghuá yèshì
Zhongxiao Night Market	忠孝夜市	zhōngxiào yèshì

Teahouses

Chun Shui Tang Cultural Tea House	春水堂人文茶館	chūnshuǐtáng rénwén cháguǎn
Geng Du Yuan	耕讀園	gēngdúyuán
Tao Yuan Ming New Classical Tea House	陶園茗新古典茶水空間	táoyuán míngxīngǔ diǎn cháshuǐkōng jiān
Times of Sadness and Joy Cultural Teahouse	悲歡歲月人文茶館	bēi huān suìyuè rénwén cháguǎn
Wu Wei Tsao Tang	無為草堂	wúwéicǎo táng
Yangxian Teahouse	楊賢茶館	yángxián cháguǎn

almond pudding, red bean and fruit (NT$40). Daily 10am–9.30pm.

Taichung Meatballs 529 Fuxing Rd Sec 3. This no-nonsense local diner has been serving deep-fried meatballs since the 1930s. The main event comes in small bowls (NT$30) and has a gooey, sticky texture – its translucent skin is made of a taro and rice mixture filled with pork and bamboo shoots and topped with a delicious sweet and sour sauce. Daily 10.30am–6.30pm.

Ya Ju 39 Gongyuan Rd. Modern and spotlessly clean Buddhist-inspired vegetarian restaurant with round wooden tables and calligraphy on the walls. The menu offers a decent selection of Chinese food, but there's no English menu – use the photos instead (NT$150–300 per dish). Daily 11am–2pm, 5pm–9pm.

North district

Beifang Hand-Cut Noodles 154 Meide St. Popular local lunch stop for traditional "knife-cut" noodles, thicker than the normal version, deliciously flavoured with big chunks of beef (NT$90). It's located on the north side of Zhongzheng Park – turn right off Xueshi Road before the junction with Jianxing Road. Daily 11am–2pm, 5–8pm.

General Beef Noodles 158 Xueshi Rd. The cook at this cheap and cheerful canteen has won culinary awards for his version of the Taichung classic, beef noodles (NT$70–80) – it's definitely one of the best. Not far from Baojue Temple. Daily 11am–2pm, 4pm–10pm.

Taichung Artistic & Literary Salon 125 Shuang-shi Rd Sec 1. Two-storey colonial house, once the mayor's residence, and now a pleasant café and art gallery. It's a useful pit-stop on the way to the Confucius Temple – grab a coffee or ice cream and relax in the garden or second-floor balcony. Daily 11am–10pm.

Taiwan Banana New Paradise 111 Shuangshi Rd Sec 2. An old train carriage marks the entrance to this kitsch-but-fun Taiwanese restaurant, approved as a "local museum" by the National Palace Museum in Taipei. Inside, tables are scattered along a reproduction of a 1930s street evoking old Taichung, the walls decorated in memorabilia (main dishes NT$180–200). Daily 11am–2am.

Yijhong Fongren Ice Yucai St (near Shuangshi Rd). Popular with students, this small shaved-ice stall offers mouthwatering combinations of plum ice shavings, kidney beans and ice cream (NT$25). Daily 10am–8.30pm.

West district

Finga's Base Camp 61 Zhongming S Rd. Western deli and café with outdoor seating area, on the edge of the Canal District – the sandwiches (from NT$140), salads and Mexican food (from NT$250) are the closest you'll get to the real thing this side of the Pacific. Mon–Fri 10am–10pm, Sat–Sun 8am–10pm.

Frog I 105 Huamei W St Sec 1. Mexican restaurant doubling as popular bar, with a prime location in the heart of the Canal District. Relaxed café-style interior with Guinness (NT$250) and Fosters (NT$210) on tap and decent selection of burritos and enchiladas from NT$100. At weekends check out *Grooveyard* (8pm–1am), an intimate live music venue upstairs. Daily 10am–2am.

Gulu Gulu 2, Lane 13, Wuquan W 4th St ☎04/23783128. Fun restaurant set inside a colonial-era house, owned by a Paiwan singer and serving authentic indigenous Taiwanese food. Try the grilled mountain pig (boar) with spicy boar-skin chips (barbequed outside), or set meals

(NT$260–560) and millet wine. Chinese menu only. Daily 10am–2pm, 5pm–12.30am.

Jingming 1st Street Pedestrianized shopping area lined with several pleasant outdoor cafés, making a convenient place to grab a coffee or light meal in the western part of town. Located south of Taizhonggang Road between Dadun 19th Street and Dalong Road.

Meicun Diantou Ice 176 Meicun Rd Sec 1. Best shaved ice shop in this part of town, with lavish piles of fruit and ice topped with condensed milk and coconut syrup – try the fresh mango, taro or "diantou ice" with three types of seasonal fruit (NT$50). Daily midday–11pm.

1924 Shanghai 95 Wuquan W 3rd St ☎04/23783181. One of Wuquan Parkway's many stylish, themed restaurants, with a focus on Shanghai and Jiangsu food – try the coddle pork (NT$280), eel (NT$280) and various tofu dishes (from NT$220). The atmospheric interior recalls fashionable Shanghai of the 1920s and 30s, with old posters, wooden tables and antiques. Daily 10am–1am.

Xitun

Fengchia Wenhua Night Market It's a long way from the station, but narrow Wenhua Road in front of Fengchia University is host to one of Taichung's best night markets. Stalls to look out for include barbequed shrimp, fronted by tanks of the soon-to-be cooked crustaceans (NT$20 for four), and delicious Turkish ice cream. Daily 5pm–1am.

Teahouses

Taichung is a city of **teahouses**, home to Taiwan's most successful teahouse chains and its most innovative drinks: **bubble tea** (*paomo hongcha*), a frothy black tea, was created in 1983 and **pearl milk tea** (*zhenzhu naicha*) in 1987 (milky tea with large chewy tapioca balls in the bottom), both served hot or cold and extremely sweet. Legend has it that bubble tea was created by *Yangxian Teahouse* (see p.246) by accident, and that pearl milk tea was introduced by the same shop after the owner's mother mixed gelatin balls from her market stall with leftover tea. These days the names tend to get blurred somewhat, both associated with the tapioca "pearls", and a vast range of traditional **Chinese**, **fruit** and **flower teas** accompany the original favourites.

Chun Shui Tang Cultural Tea House 17, Lane 155, Gongyi Rd; 9 Dadun 19th St (end of Jingming 1st St); 186 Fuxing Rd Sec 4 (inside Taichung Central). This modern chain has ten branches in its home town – the above are the most convenient options. Credited with bringing bubble tea and pearl milk tea to a wider world, its English menus outline the huge number of drinks available (NT$100–140), and the perfect tea accompaniment, brown sugar cake (NT$45). Daily 8am–11pm.

Geng Du Yuan 109 Shizheng Road; 251 Huamei W St Sec 2. Another Taichung chain that has

expanded island-wide, its design based on classical Suzhou gardens with tatami mats, fishponds, waterfalls, bridges and cosy tea rooms; pots of oolong start at NT$200. There are several branches in the city: Shizheng Road is the original while the Huamei store is the largest and newest. Daily 10am–2am.

Tao Yuan Ming New Classical Tea House 179 Xiangshang Rd Sec 2. One of the city's most alluring teahouses, a blend of classical Chinese wooden pavilions and fishponds with contemporary stone and concrete design. Drinks and pots of quality high mountain teas range from NT$80 to NT$250. A short walk from the Flower Market in Nantun, and close to the *Pig Pen*. No English menus (NT$100 minimum charge). Daily 10am–1am.

🏃 **Times of Sadness and Joy Cultural Teahouse** 29 Daquan St. Exquisite teahouse set in a tiny wooden Japanese house, with tatami mats, screen doors and Japanese decor. English menus feature a range of special infusions including white hair oolong, sweet osmanthus honey, green and mountain teas (NT$450 per pot), with light Chinese meals from NT$300. Daily 11am–10pm.

🏃 **Wu Wei Tsao Tang** 106 Gongyi Rd ⓦ wuwei.com.tw. Taichung's most atmospheric classical teahouse, surrounded by trees and beautifully arranged around a traditional fishpond, with wooden corridors lined with Chinese art. Teapots for one start at NT$150, NT$350 for larger groups. Daily 10am–1am.

Yangxian Teahouse 30 Siwei Rd. The place where bubble tea was invented, this pleasant teahouse became the first Chun Shui Tang chain store and retains much of its original character – the blue tablet above the entrance says "Spring Water Hall", (also *Chun Shui Tang*) written in ancient Chinese script. Daily 8am–11pm.

Bars and nightclubs

Weekends in Taichung can be raucous all-night affairs, with a host of **pubs**, sophisticated **lounge bars** and hip **nightclubs** to suit every taste. Most of the action takes place on the west side of town in the Canal District, Little Europe or further afield, so if you really want to check out the scene you're going to have to take taxis.

Bars

89K 89 Zhongming S Rd. Cosy no-nonsense bar on the edge of the Canal District, with a slightly bizarre Native American theme and an emphasis on rock. Features regular live acts and relatively cheap booze: NT$100 bottles and NT$200 for huge draught beers. Daily 8pm–4am.

FM 185 Boguan Rd. This bar and restaurant is justly popular with expats and locals alike, with first floor for drinks and a dining area upstairs, sumptuous cocktails and decent happy hour 6–8pm every night. A short walk from the *Splendor* and Sogo in the Canal District. Daily 5pm–1am, 2am weekends.

Londoner 143 Huamei W St Sec 1. Bright, modern pub in the Canal District, with small first floor bar and spacious second floor with pool table, sofas and giant TV for sports events. Old Speckled Hen (NT$160) and Stella (NT$150) on tap with weekend brunch specials NT$250. Mon–Fri 6pm–late, Sat midday–late, Sun midday–8pm.

Pig Pen 41 Daguan Rd. Taichung institution that just about pulls off its British pub theme, though serving only San Miguel on tap (NT$200) is pushing things a bit. Head upstairs to the lively disco offering a mix of live music and club nights – it's all you can drink for NT$400 on Sunday and Mondays (bottled beers are NT$150 otherwise) and NT$500 cover on weekends. Daily 6pm–2am; disco 8pm–5am.

Soundgarden 92-1 Daguan Rd (opposite *Pig Pen*). Popular late-night outdoor bar with candle-lit bench tables and stools, hip DJs, live music and basic drinks list (bottled beer NT$120) – an excellent chill-out place to start or end an evening, but all dependent on the weather. Tues, Wed, Fri & Sat 9pm–6am or later.

Lounge bars and clubs

Bobo 2 Dongxing Rd Sec 3 ⓦ www.bobonightclub .com. One of Taichung's coolest clubs, set in a glass dome with a first-floor bar and dance floor, and second-floor balcony with comfy booths (minimum charge NT$3000). Resident and international DJs spin a mix of house and hip-hop for various party nights at the weekends (NT$300), and lounge music during the week. Tues, Thurs & Sun 9pm–3am, Wed 9pm–4.30am, Fri–Sat 10pm–5am.

Lion King Disco Pub 38 Dachuan St. Cavernous club with second-floor balcony, packed most nights with DJs spinning a good mix of house and hip-hop. Drinks start at NT$150 while cover charge is NT$200, though foreigners get in free on Saturdays. Next door to the *Pig Pen*, but tends to keep going longer and more popular with a younger local crowd. Daily 8.30pm–4 or 5am.

Liquid Lounge 98 Zhongming S Rd. Fashionable lounge bar, just opposite *89K*, with stylish, softly lit interiors and plenty of comfy sofas and chairs. In-house DJs supply mellow blend of ambient and lounge music most nights, while the tempo picks up at the weekends when it becomes more like a club. Vast but pricey drinks list, though cocktails aren't bad at NT$150. Daily 6.30pm–2am.

Seduce 424 Huamei St. Lounge bar that turns into a crammed hip-hop club at the weekends, the current place to be seen for Taichung's fashion conscious. The drinks are priced accordingly, with red wine from NT$1500 per bottle (NT$200–300 minimum charge). Daily 8pm–4am.

Trendy 3/F, 1 Taizhonggang Rd Sec 1. One of the biggest and most glamorous nightclubs in Taichung, lined with sofas and illuminated with stylish fluorescent lighting – the massive sound system is superb, and VJs blend tunes with images on plasma TV screens around the club. Tues–Sun 9pm–6am, cover NT$250 weekdays, NT$350 weekends.

Listings

Airlines China Airlines, 15/F, 160 Taizhonggang Rd Sec 1 ℡04/3204718; Mandarin Airlines, 100 Minghan Rd ℡04/4254236; Uni Airways, 100 Minghan Rd ℡04/4257630; Hong Kong Express Airways, 19/F, 185 Taizhonggang Rd Sec 1 ℡04/23272358.

Cultural centres The Cultural Centre (Tues–Sun 9am–9pm; free; ℗www.tccgc.gov.tw), at 600 Yingcai Rd has a periodical reading room with English-language magazines, and several exhibition halls, the focus primarily local, contemporary painters, though there are also rooms dedicated to traditional porcelain, pottery and jade. The abandoned warehouses and factory buildings of the former Taichung Winery at 362 Fuxing Rd Sec 3, south of the station, are being developed into an atmospheric contemporary art centre and museum.

Banks There are plenty of banks and ATM machines throughout the city, and most 7-Elevens have Chinatrust ATMs: Citibank, 242 Zhongming S Rd ℡04/23726601; Chinatrust Commercial Bank, 80 Taizhonggang Rd Sec 2 ℡04/23115119 & 50 Minzu Rd; HSBC, 218 Wenxin Rd Sec 1 ℡04/24712626; Standard Chartered Bank, 598 Wenxin Rd Sec 2 ℡04/23246800.

Bookshops Caves Books is at 12 Guanqian Rd; Eslite is at 7/8F, 80 Zhongzheng Rd and 10/F, C Building, Chung Yo Dept Store. Taiwan's oldest bookstore is Ruicheng Shuju (Sweet China Bookstore) at 4-33 Shuangshih Rd Sec 1 opposite Taichung Park, though the current shop is modern, and a good place to buy gifts and stationery.

Car rental Nice Rent-a-Car, 358 Taizhonggang Rd Sec 1 ℡0800/889888, ℗www.nicecar.com.tw; Central Auto, 9 Taizhonggang Rd Sec 3 ℡04/22547000.

Cinema Warner Village has two locations: in Taichung Central at 186 Fuxing Rd Sec 4 and Tiger City at 120 Henan Rd Sec 3 (tickets NT$230).

Cycle rental You can rent bicycles at the east side of Taiyuan train station in Beitun district (Mon–Fri midday–10pm; Sat–Sun 8am–10pm; NT$30 per hour).

Hospital The biggest hospital in town is China Medical College Hospital at 2 Yude Road, off Xueshi Road in North District ℡04/22052121.

Internet access Most Internet cafés are open 24 hours. Armed Team Internet on the eighth floor of Taichung Central shopping mall is huge and not far from the station (NT$15 per hour); Corner Internet at 94 Jiguang Street is much smaller but convenient (NT$20 per hour); Goldbowl is at 166 Meicun Rd (NT$15 per hour); Nova Computer Arcade at 508 Yingcai Rd has free terminals in basement 1 (it shuts at 10pm).

Language courses Taichung is a popular place to learn Chinese. Taipei Language Institute Taichung Center on Taiping Road (℡04/22254681 ℗www.tli.com.tw) is a decent private school with a variety of classes and prices. The more established schools are attached to the major universities: the city's largest public university is National Chunghsing University (℡04/22873181; ℗www.nchu.edu.tw); apply six weeks in advance for courses at Fengchia University's Language Center (℡04/24517250; ℗www.fcu.edu.tw); the Chinese Language Center at Donghai University is also very good (℡04/23590259; ℗www.thu.edu.tw).

Pharmacies Watson's has branches at 88–90 Jiguang St, Central (℡04/22239369) and 17 Zhongzheng Rd, Central (℡04/22273218).

Police The Foreign Affairs Police (℡04/23273875) at 588 Wenxin Rd handles visa extensions (Mon–Fri 8am–5.20pm) but is also the best place to report theft if you don't speak Chinese (English speakers are usually on duty 24hr).

Post The Main Post Office is at 86 Minquan Rd (Mon–Fri 7.30am–9pm, Sat 8.30am–4.30pm, Sun 8.30am–midday).

Scooter rental Foreigners can rent scooters at Unicar (℡04/22239073), to the right of the train station as you exit, but you'll need a driving licence and ARC (NT$350–500 per day).

Shopping Try Hui Wen Plaza, off Huiwen Rd in Nantun and inside the Flower Market, for antiques (Tues–Sun 10am–9pm); Tianjin Road (North District, east of Daya Road as far as the canal), for cheap clothes and accessories; and Wenxin Jade Market on the corner of Taizhonggang and Wenxin roads (Fri–Sun 10am–6pm).

Travel agents The Visitor Center can help arrange local tours. For further afield, Elizabeth Travel Studio at 15/F, 378 Wenxin Rd Sec 1 (℡04/23298277) is popular with local expats.

Dajia	大甲	*dàjiǎ*
Jhenlan Temple	鎮瀾宮	*zhènlángōng*
Three Treasures Cultural Museum	大甲三寶文化館	*dàjiǎ sānbǎo wénhuà guǎn*
Yu Jen Shin Bakery	裕珍馨	*yù zhēn xīn*
921 Earthquake Museum of Taiwan	九二一地震教育園區	*jiǔèryī dìzhèn jiàoyù yúanqū*

Around Taichung

Before moving on from Taichung, it's worth making time for the **921 Earthquake Museum**, a poignant memorial to the victims of the great earthquake of 1999, and **Dajia**, home of one of the most venerated Mazu images in Taiwan.

The 921 Earthquake Museum of Taiwan

Located near the small town of Wufong in the village of Guangfu, roughly 14km south of Taichung train station, the **921 Earthquake Museum of Taiwan** (Tues–Sun 9am–5pm; NT$30; Ⓦwww.921emt.edu.tw) is a vivid, if sobering, introduction to the damage and destruction wrought by the massive earthquake of 1999, particularly in this part of the country. Though it has attracted a fair amount of criticism from people who say it ignores the controversial aspects of 921 (such as substandard construction) it's extremely informative and very moving.

The museum is centred on the former site of **Guangfu Junior High School** – most of the school collapsed during the quake and pictures of its mangled running track were some of the most visually shocking images in the days

---

The 921 Earthquake

All over Taiwan, but particularly in the central part of the country, you'll hear about the **921 Earthquake**: the epithet refers to the 7.3-magnitude quake that ripped across the island at 1.47am on September 21, 1999 killing 2455 people, injuring more than 8000 and destroying 50,652 buildings. It's also known as the **"Chi-Chi Earthquake"** – the epicentre was beneath the town of Jiji, 12.5km west of Sun Moon Lake. In fact, many of the casualties in Nantou County occurred during an aftershock five days later that measured 6.7 on the Richter scale, flattening buildings weakened on September 21.

Despite the heroic efforts of rescue services in the days after the disaster, the government was criticized in some places for its slow response. Though it established the **921 Earthquake Post-disaster Recovery Commission** (Ⓦportal.921erc.gov.tw) to oversee around NT$106bn in funding to help affected areas, many building contractors responsible for illegal construction – blamed for many of the deaths – have never been prosecuted. The disaster is still a sensitive issue in Taiwan – Wu Yi-feng's 921 documentary *Life* (released in 2004) received critical acclaim and left many in tears.

Earthquakes are a problem in Taiwan because the island sits on a fault line between the Eurasian and Philippine tectonic plates, causing almost constant seismic activity, though 75 percent of all quakes occur in the sparsely populated eastern half of the island. When western Taiwan is affected, the results can be catastrophic, though most buildings today can easily absorb all but the strongest tremors.

afterwards (it was mercifully empty at the time). The ruined school buildings form the outdoor area of the museum; on both sides of this are two futuristic exhibition halls packed with interactive displays labelled in English and Chinese; the **Chelungpu Fault Gallery**, which crosses the actual fault line – a clearly visible ridge created by the quake that cuts across the running track; and the **Earthquake Image Gallery** featuring a selection of audio-visual images of the quake and its aftermath, climaxing in hourly shows in a huge theatre.

You can take regular buses to Guangfu from the city bus station in Taichung: #107 stops close to the museum while #103 stops a short walk down the road in the village – both buses depart the village bus stop and run every twenty to thirty minutes (NT$35). Bus #108 goes past the entrance but this is infrequent (NT$26).

Dajia

The small town of **DAJIA**, 23km northwest of Taichung, is the unlikely home of "three treasures", a catchy label designed to attract tourists, but it's famous throughout the country for just one of them: its Mazu deity and the annual **Mazu Pilgrimage** (see box p.250), one of the largest religious festivals on the planet. Dajia's other treasures are unexceptional by comparison: humble woven hats and mats, and "crispy cakes" or butter pancakes (more like wafer-thin cookies), which are nevertheless, very tasty.

Buses arrive on Guangming Road, opposite the elegant premises of the *Yu Jen Shin Bakery* (daily 8am–10pm), Dajia's most prestigious cake shop. Inside on the second floor, the **Three Treasures Cultural Museum** (daily 9am–5pm; free) houses a small exhibition on the main attractions, though explanations are in Chinese only. You'll see "three treasures" popping up all over the Chinese-speaking world – it's an allusion to the Taoist concepts of essence, vitality and spirit. Stock up on cakes downstairs and head west along Guangming Road: at the junction with Shuntian Road you should see **Lin's Chastity & Piety Memorial Arch**, built in 1848 and honouring the virtue (read virginity) of Lin Chunniang who remained a widow for seventy years after her husband died prematurely – she was just twelve at the time.

From the Memorial Arch it's a short walk along Shuntian Road to Dajia's main attraction, **Jhenlan Temple** (daily 5am–10pm), the home of the revered Mazu deity that forms the centrepiece of the eight-day pilgrimage and month-long **Dajia Mazu Culture Festival** (ⓦmazu.taichung.gov.tw) in March and April. The original shrine was built in 1732 to house a Mazu statue brought from Meizhou in Fujian (the temple name loosely translates as "holding back the waves temple" an allusion to Mazu's power over the sea). It's been restored, rebuilt and extended many times since then, notably in 1936 and again in the 1980s when it started to rival Beigang's Chaotian Temple (see p.289) in importance. Though the original Dajia Mazu statue cannot claim to be Taiwan's oldest, its powerful supporters (including many politicians) believe that it has performed more miracles than any other, and the temple now ranks as one of Taiwan's most popular and wealthiest. The **Main Hall** houses three important Mazu deities, with the current Meizhou Mazu donated by the shrine in China in 1987 – this is made from gold and is worth around NT$120m. The temple's most attractive architectural features are the lavish algal wells above the Main Hall, plastered in gold, and the rows of *koji* pottery figures (see p.287) near the entrance.

Dajia Bus Company runs **minibuses** from Taichung train station (on the corner of Jianguo and Chenggong Roads) to Dajia (NT$80) throughout the day, but you can also pick them up on Taizhonggang Road.

Mazu Holy Pilgrimage

The annual eight-day **Mazu Holy Pilgrimage** from Dajia's **Jhenlan Temple** to **Fongtian Temple** in Singang has become one of the greatest and perhaps most bizarre of all Taiwan's religious festivals. The event has become a veritable media circus, attracting ambitious politicians (the president often turns up at the start) and even street gangs who in the past have ended up fighting over who "protects" the Goddess during the procession.

The pilgrimage traces its origins to the early nineteenth century, when Taiwanese pilgrims would cross the Taiwan Strait to the Mazu "mother temple" in Meizhou in Fujian every twelve years. The practice was suspended after the Japanese occupation in 1895 but cattle herders are believed to have restarted the pilgrimage in the 1910s, making the more permissible journey to **Chaotian Temple** in Beigang, long regarded Taiwan's most senior Mazu temple. In 1987 however, after Meizhou officials assured Dajia that its Mazu statue was equally sacred, Beigang was snubbed with a new annual pilgrimage route to what was considered a "sister" temple in Singang, 5km east.

The core **procession** comprises a series of palanquins that ferry Mazu and other senior Taoist deities 300km through rice fields and small villages, the roads lined with believers who kneel to allow Mazu's palanquin to pass over them for luck. Stops are made at smaller "branch" temples to enhance the power of local deities, and a constant stream of free drinks and food is handed out to the pilgrims trudging along behind. If you want to experience the mayhem you'll need to plan ahead – the best locations to watch the procession are in Dajia itself when it leaves town and returns eight days later, or in Singang at the end of the third day when the town becomes a massive carnival of parades and traditional performers. The statue remains in Singang for a day of celebrations (confusingly termed "Mazu's birthday" though the official birthday is Lunar March 23) before embarking on its four-day journey back to Dajia. Unfortunately it's hard to know when the parade will start until a few weeks before: the day of departure is determined by a special cast of "throwing blocks" (*zhi jiao*), on the eve of the Lantern Festival (usually in January or February). The parade itself usually takes place in **April** in the period leading up to Mazu's official birthday (see Ⓦmazu .taichung.gov.tw for the schedule).

Guguan and around

The hot-springs resort town of **GUGUAN**, around 60km northeast of Taichung, is both the first and last stop if you're coming from the west along the former **Central Cross-Island Highway** route. The once-majestic road was severely damaged by the 921 earthquake and successive typhoons, and is closed to vehicles about 2km past the town limits. The buses that used to cross the highway from Taichung and Fongyuan on their way to the mountain town of Lishan (see p.226) and beyond now make Guguan their final stop before heading back, so the town itself has become the main attraction of this revered road's western stretch.

Spread out on both sides of the scenic **Dajia River valley**, the town is best known for its alkaline carbonic acid **hot springs**, which are believed to relieve arthritis pain and make Guguan immensely popular with west-coast residents, especially in winter. Though winter weekends and public holidays are best avoided, the town is quite peaceful most other times, and even in summer the cool mountain air makes soaking in the hot springs inviting. Though the many hotel spas are the main draw cards, there are rewarding walks around town and

Guguan	谷關	gǔguān
Guguan Bus Stop	谷關公車站	gǔguān gōngchē zhàn
Guguan Visitor Center	谷關遊客中心	gǔguān yóukè zhōngxīn
Hot Springs & Culture Center	溫泉博物館	wēnquán bówùguǎn
Accommodation and eating		
Dragon Valley Hotel & Paradise	龍谷觀光大飯店	lónggǔ guānguāng dàfàndiàn
Four Season Hot Spring Resort	四季溫泉會館	sìjì wēnquán huìguǎn
Ku Kuan Hot Spring & Resort	水舞谷關渡假溫泉館	shuǐwǔ gǔguān dùjià wēnquán guǎn
Yidou Hot Spring Lodge	伊豆日式露天泡湯	yīdòu rìshì lùtiān pàotāng
Mucha Café	木柵咖啡室	mùzhà kāfēishì
Basianshan National Forest Recreation Area	八仙山國家森林遊樂區	bāxiānshān guójiā sēnlín yóulèqū
Bajing Memorial	八景紀念碑	bājǐng jìniànbēi
Basianshan Main Peak	八仙山主峰	bāxiānshān zhǔfēng
Basianshan Trail	八仙山步道	bāxiānshān bùdào
Basianshan Visitor Center	八仙山遊客中心	bāxiānshān yóukè zhōngxīn
Evergreen Trail	長青步道	chángqīng bùdào
Jinghai Temple	靜海寺	jìnghǎi sì
Shinto Shrine	神社遺址	shénshè yízhǐ
Accommodation		
Basian Lodge	八仙山莊	bāxiān shānzhuāng
Honeymoon Lodge	蜜月屋	mìyuè wū

in the nearby **Basianshan National Forest Recreation Area** (see p.253). Summer typhoons are known to send raging torrents through Guguan's river valley, in extreme cases taking riverfront hotels with them. The husks of buildings swept away during the devastating Typhoon Mindulle of July 2004 are still lodged on the banks downstream, but this doesn't deter hot-springs enthusiasts from coming.

Arrival and information

With the former Central Cross-Island Highway closed from here to Deji Reservoir to the east, Guguan is completely cut off from eastern Taiwan and the only public transport available are the several **buses** (2hr 30min; NT$174) that depart daily from Taichung's Fongyuan Bus Co stop. These buses stop en route in Fongyuan, just north of Taichung, so if you're coming by train it's much quicker to alight in Fongyuan and catch the bus from there (1hr 30min; NT$137). Guguan's main **bus stop** is on the town's eastern side, opposite the *Mucha Café* at 94 Dongguan Rd Sec 1, but drivers usually let passengers off at a couple of points before that. The same buses return to Taichung via Fongyuan until late afternoon. The **Guguan visitor center** (8.30am–5pm; ⊕04/25951496) is at 102 Dongguan Rd, Sec 1, a few minutes' walk east of the main bus stop. Its helpful staff will provide English brochures and maps and can also help you book a hotel room. The 7-Eleven on the eastern end of town has a Chinatrust Commercial Bank **ATM** which accepts international credit cards.

Accommodation and hot-spring spas

Guguan's natural hot springs are channeled into its dozen or so **hotel spas**, most of which have rooms with en-suite bathing facilities – ranging from tiny bathtubs to Japanese-style wooden Jacuzzis. **Discounts** can be had on week-nights, especially in summer, while winter rates are much higher; reservations are recommended on winter weekends. There are hotels on both sides of the Dajia River, but those on the south side – where buses arrive – are slightly more convenient as most of the town's **restaurants** are here. The hotels on the north side are accessed via a bridge on the town's eastern fringe, about a twenty-minute walk from the bus stop.

The large white complex on the left shortly after you enter town is the *Dragon Valley Hotel & Paradise* (℡04/25951369; ❼), 138 Dongguan Rd Sec 1, perched on prime real estate overlooking the river valley. Rooms are big and bright, many with fabulous river views, but rack rates are high. Still, the hotel's convenient location makes its **public bathing pools** (7am–noon & 2–11pm; NT$300) appealing if you're short of time. Its gender-segregated nude pools, designed in Japanese *onsen* style, have relaxing river views. On the river's north side, at 8 Wenquan Lane (a quiet street to the right of the main road), is the delightful *Four Season Hot Spring Resort* (℡04/25951235; ❻), in a Southeast Asian-style building with Bali-inspired outdoor bathing pools and immacu-lately clean Japanese-style doubles; a fabulous option, especially if you have your own transport. By far the town's most upscale – and expensive – hotel is the *Ku Kuan Hot Spring & Resort* (℡04/25950099; ❽) on the river's south side, at 115 Dongguan Rd Sec 1. Planned by former apprentices of the Austra-lian architect who designed *The Lalu* at Sun Moon Lake, it features beautiful rooms with smooth-slate interiors. Non-guests can soak in its spacious open-air pools (NT$300 for 90min), while those wishing greater privacy can rent their own **hot-spring rooms** (NT$1200–2500 for 90min), some with soothing waterfalls facing the pools. Near the *Ku Kuan*, at 5 Fensiao Lane (a hilly street to the right of the main Dongguan Road), is a more down-to-earth option: the ⚲ *Yidou Hot Spring Lodge* (℡04/25950315; ❼), a minimalist Japanese-style complex featuring rooms with outdoor bathing gardens, some with splendid mountain views. These rooms can also be rented for NT$800 per hour: ask for one of the **cabin rooms** with fenced-in bathing gardens as they offer more privacy. The *Yidou's* 24-hour public pools (NT$250 for unlimited time) are kept at a variety of temperatures and have invigorating massage waterfalls.

Hiking

Apart from soaking in hot springs, the other popular activity in Guguan is hiking, and while some of the town's **nature walks** were destroyed in the 921 earthquake, one is still in excellent condition. The trail starts at the suspension bridge (to the left of the post office in the town centre), turning eastward on the river's north bank and climbing over a hill which yields fine views of the gorge. After about 3km, the trail winds down to the village's northern section, ending near the *Four Season Hot Spring Resort*; from here it's a twenty-minute walk along the main road back to the town centre. On your way back, it's worth stopping by the **Hot Springs & Culture Center** (8.30am–5pm) at 102 Dongguan Rd Sec 1 – in the same building as the visitor center – to check out the bilingual exhibits on the development of Taiwan's hot springs areas. The center is surrounded by a park with a small amphitheatre where an **Atayal dance troupe** from the nearby village of Songhe gives nightly performances.

Eating and drinking

Most of Guguan's hotels have their own **restaurants**, but they tend to be expensive, and more interesting and economical options can be found along Dongguan Road on the town's southern side. Many of these small establishments specialize in fresh **mountain trout** (*zun yu*) from the Dajia River, served steamed or roasted on roadside grills – you shouldn't have trouble finding them. Some cater to Taiwanese groups, with set meals sold by the table, so you might have to negotiate with them to get smaller portions. If you want to stick to basics such as fried rice or noodles, try one of the places without fish tanks out front, as they're considerably cheaper. A couple of these are run by Atayal aborigines and dish up tribal staples such as bamboo rice, **roasted mountain pig** (*kao shan zhu*) and a variety of steamed mountain vegetables. There's little in the way of **nightlife**, but the *Mucha Café* (noon–midnight) has cold beer and cocktails starting from NT$120.

Basianshan National Forest Recreation Area

About 5km south of Guguan, the **Basianshan National Forest Recreation Area** has an extensive network of **hiking trails** and makes for a worthwhile side trip. Despite its proximity to the perennially popular Guguan, the area is blessedly tranquil, even on weekends. The former logging zone was one of the country's first forest recreation areas and is renowned for its amazing array of cypress and other coniferous trees. In addition, it's lightly and tastefully developed, with homey **holiday cabins** and hot meals available, making it a tempting place to linger if you're craving some peace and quiet. Some of the area was damaged by the 921 earthquake and the 2001 Typhoon Toraji, but the main walking trails have since been repaired and are easy to follow. Basianshan (Eight Immortals Mountain) also has central Taiwan's highest concentration and variety of **butterflies**, which can be seen extracting nectar from plants throughout the year.

Evergreen Trail

Basianshan's easiest walk is the **Evergreen Trail**, a gentle loop of just over 1km that begins and ends behind the visitor center. After skirting the wooden cabins behind the Basian Lodge and cutting through the second car park, the path passes by the tiny Buddhist **Jinghai Temple** before turning right into a cool evergreen forest that soon gives way to a towering grove of groaning **bamboo**. Just after the bamboo grove there is a side path to the left that leads to the ruins of a **Shinto shrine**, built by the Japanese to appease the spirits of loggers who died while cutting down the giant cypress trees that once filled this forest. Little remains of the shrine, which has been damaged by forest fires and the 921 earthquake, but a pavilion has been erected over the ruins. Further along the main trail and to the left is the **Bajing (Eight Scenic Spots) Memorial**, commemorating Basianshan's selection during the Japanese occupation as one of the colony's eight most scenic places. From here, the path crosses the second car park before returning to the visitor center.

Basianshan Trail

The longest, most demanding hike climbs to the top of **Basianshan Main Peak**, which at 2424m is the recreation area's highest, offering sweeping views of the mountains to the east on clear days. From the visitor center, it is 6.3km to the top, and the trail is steep in places. To start the climb, follow the Evergreen Trail until you reach the Jinghai Temple; instead of turning right, carry on straight past the shrine. The return journey can take several hours, so an early start is essential to ensure you have enough daylight. Before setting out, ask visitor center staff about the latest trail conditions.

Practicalities

There is no public transport to the forest recreation area, but if you don't have your own vehicle you can still walk or hitch from Guguan. Heading east along the former Central Cross-Island Highway from Taichung, the **turnoff** is to the right after the Duming Bridge, about 1km before Guguan. From the turnoff, it's about 1km to the **toll gate** (NT$100 on weekdays, NT$150 on public holidays; parking fee NT$100 for cars, NT$20 for motorcycles), where you'll be given a useable English map along with your ticket. From here, the partly paved road winds steeply into the hills for about 3km before reaching the **Basianshan visitor center** (7am–5pm; ℡04/25951214), where you can book **accommodation**. There is a choice of lodging options (℡04/25229696), from four-person suites in **wooden cabins** (❺) to doubles in the *Honeymoon Lodge* (❹) and cheap beds in 16- and 36-person **dorms** at the *Basian Lodge* (NT$370 per bed). **Meals** must be ordered in advance from the visitor center, with standard Chinese breakfasts (NT$50) and hot lunches and dinners (NT$100) of rice or noodles available. Some of the **hiking trails** start behind the visitor center, or you can carry on up the road for a few more minutes to the second car park, where there are signs for all the main trails. Though **camping** is technically not allowed in the forest recreation area, some visitors pitch tents on the flat grassy area just above the second car park but they refrain from building campfires.

Changhua

Just 16km southwest of Taichung, the attractive city of **CHANGHUA** is a popular destination for travellers, most of whom come to admire the famed **Great Buddha Statue** that overlooks the town centre from its lofty perch atop **Baguashan**. But while this memorable image is certainly Changhua's most remarkable attraction, the city has many other charms, from imaginative **culinary specialties** to its engrossing temples – including one of Taiwan's most archetypal Confucius temples. As a major stop on the Western rail line, Changhua is easy to reach by train from the north and south, and from here there are frequent buses to the nearby historic town of **Lugang** (see p.257). While there is plenty here to justify an overnight stay, most of the noteworthy sights are within easy walking distance from the train station, making the city a suitable stopover on your way somewhere else.

Arrival, information and accommodation

There are regular **express trains** stopping at Changhua from Taipei (2hr 20min; NT$416) and Kaohsiung (2hr 15min; NT$432) throughout the day; from **Taichung** it's only 15 minutes by train. Kuo Kuang and Ubus both have regular **express bus** services from Taipei to Changhua's **bus station**, conveniently located across the sprawling traffic circle from the train station. From here, Changhua Bus Co has frequent **shuttle buses** to neighbouring Lugang (30min).

Changhua

Changhua	彰化	*zhānghuà*
Information and accommodation		
C@ffee 101	餐飲咖啡館	*cānyǐn kāfēiguǎn*
Formosa Hotel	全台大飯店	*quántái dàfàndiàn*
Rich Royal Hotel	富皇大飯店	*fùhuáng dàfàndiàn*
Taiwan Hotel	台灣大飯店	*táiwān dàfàndiàn*
The City		
Baguashan	八卦山	*bāguàshān*
Confucius Temple	孔廟	*kǒngmiào*
Earth God Shrine	土地公	*tǔdì gōng*
Great Buddha Statue	大佛像	*dàfó xiàng*
Hongmao Well	紅毛井	*hóngmáo jǐng*
Yuancing Temple	元清觀	*yuánqīng guàn*
Eating and drinking		
An Chang Taiwanese Meatballs	安長台灣肉員	*āncháng táiwān ròuyuán*
Cat Mouse Noodles	貓鼠麵	*māoshǔ miàn*
New York Pub	紐約音樂	*niǔyuē yīnyuè*
Taiwan Cooking Specialty	台灣魯肉飯	*táiwān lǔròufàn*

The **tourist office** is at 8-1 Guashan Road (☎04/7287488), on the eastern edge of town at the base of Baguashan and the Great Buddha Statue; here the friendly, English-speaking staff can provide you with English brochures and maps. All of Changhua's main sights are along the roughly two-kilometre stretch of town between the train station and Baguashan to the east, making for a leisurely return walk of a few hours. *C@ffee 101*, a 24-hour computer game

centre and coffeeshop located behind the bus station's waiting area, offers one-hour **Internet access** when you buy a standard drink (NT$40).

There is a handful of **hotels** within walking distance of the train station; just to the right as you exit is the *Taiwan Hotel*, 48 Jhongjheng Rd Sec 2 (☎04/7224681; ❸), with clean, spacious rooms and a convenient location. A few minutes' walk southeast of the train station, at 97 Changan St, is the garish *Rich Royal Hotel* (☎04/7237117; ❷), with slightly tatty theme rooms that are nevertheless good value. About 2km south of the train station, at 668 Jhongjheng Rd Sec 2, is the more luxurious *Formosa Hotel* (☎04/7253017, Ⓦwww.formosahotel.com.tw; ❹), which has plush doubles and a range of amenities. Room rates include breakfast, use of the hotel's fitness room, Internet access and free bicycle usage (up to 3hrs).

The City

With Changhua's main sights packed in the middle of town, between the train station and Baguashan to the east, a walk down narrow Chenling Road – just southeast of the train station – will take you near most of them. Heading east on Chenling, at the intersection with Minsheng Road, is the ornate **Yuancing Temple**, originally built in 1763 and dedicated primarily to worship of the chief Taoist deity, the **Jade Emperor** (see Contexts p.531). Facing east on Chenling, turn right on Minsheng and walk about 100m until you reach the junction with Kongmen Road; to your left you'll see the stately **Confucius Temple** (*kong miao*), one of the oldest in Taiwan commemorating the ancient Chinese teacher (see Contexts p.526). First built in 1726, this well-preserved complex is a quiet haven in the heart of the city, its symmetrical layout of halls and courtyards emblematic of a classical Confucian temple, and only slightly smaller in scale than its celebrated cousin in Tainan (see p.323). Flanking the entrance to the main **Hall of the Sage** is a pair of stone columns, beautifully carved with dragon motifs. One of Taiwan's biggest ceremonies marking Confucius's birthday is held here every year at dawn on September 28. The complex's main entrances are on Minsheng Road. Head east along Kongmen and cross busy Jhongshan Road to see what remains of the 300-year-old **Hongmao (Red Hair) Well**, one of the few surviving Dutch-built wells in Taiwan. The well's crumbling stone base has been cemented over and covered by a clear glass shelter for protection, making it difficult to imagine its original incarnation. Immediately behind the well is a tiny **Earth God Shrine** (*tudi gong*) that gets much more attention from locals than the well itself.

Baguashan and the Great Buddha Statue

Rising majestically on the city's eastern fringe is the 92-metre **Baguashan** (Eight Trigram Mountain), from the top of which its crowning glory – the **Great Buddha Statue** – keeps a constant vigil over the town. Towering 22m above its brightly coloured lotus flower base, the seated likeness of the Sakyamuni Buddha has become one of Taiwan's most recognizable landmarks since its construction in 1961. The serene figure is the dominant feature of the local landscape, visible from several places in town and giving the area an enchanting ambience. Built on the former site of a commemorative tablet erected during the Japanese occupation, it is made entirely of reinforced concrete and has a hollow, six-storey interior. The inside walls, decorated with **dioramas** depicting the stages of Buddha's life, have been given a facelift, and visitors can ascend stairs leading as high as the statue's neck. Baguashan affords great views of Changhua, on very clear days yielding vistas to the sea; for this reason it was an important military lookout up until the Japanese colonial period. Behind the statue to the east is the three-storey Great Buddha Temple, the top floor of which is a superb place to watch the sun set over the Great Buddha's shoulders. Still further east is the tranquil **Baguashan Scenic Area**, interspersed with short walkways leading to pavilions and city overlooks.

Eating and drinking

Changhua is a culinary adventure in its own right, known for its **three trea-sures**: meatballs, "cat-mouse noodles" and stewed pork rice. Of these, the most sought-after by tourists are the **meatballs**, served in a translucent coating made of glutinous rice and filled with ingredients such as pork, shredded bamboo, mushrooms, egg yolk, and, in some cases, pig's liver. The best place to try them is at the intersection of Chenling Road and Changan Street – two tiny **restau-rants** occupy opposite corners of the junction and are in bitter competition. The better of the two is *An Chang Taiwanese Meatballs* at 144 Changan St. About 100m north of here, at 223 Chenling Rd, is *Cat Mouse Noodles*, so named because the restaurant's founder was said by his friends to have mouse-like mannerisms (and the Taiwanese word for "mouse" sounds like the Mandarin word for "cat"). Apart from the noodles' novel name, they are noted for the refreshingly non-oily **soup** in which they are served. **Stewed pork rice** can be found throughout the city, but one popular place to try it is the chain restaurant *Taiwan Cooking Specialty* at 307 Jhongjheng Rd Sec 2.

For **nightlife**, there are a couple of cosy pubs on Chenling Road. The hands-down favourite with expatriate English teachers is the *New York Pub*, 135 Chen-ling Rd, where rock music and videos are the nightly entertainment. Just east of here, at 65 Chenling Rd, is a considerably quieter pub named *Johnny*.

Lugang

One of Taiwan's oldest towns and ports, **LUGANG** is unusual for having preserved much of its architectural and cultural heritage, largely thanks to the efforts of its famously conservative inhabitants. Lugang's historic **temples** are wonderfully atmospheric, but much of the town's fame derives from being an excellent place to pick up traditional **handicrafts**, created by the great-est concentration of master craftsmen in the country. But while the town is eulogized in Taiwan as the epitome of classical China, its appeal tends to be exaggerated – the historic centre is relatively small, and it's surrounded by urban development that's classical modern Taiwan. Adjust your expectations accord-ingly and Lugang can still be interesting to explore – it's one of the best places to get a sense of Taiwan's early Chinese history and is an easy day-trip from Changhua or Taichung. Thanks to the gradual silting up of its harbour, one of the oddest things about Lugang today is that the Lugang River is a long walk from the old part of town, and the sea is now several kilometres away.

Some history

Lugang means "**Deer Harbour**," an allusion to the herds of deer that once roamed the Changhua plains, now long since hunted to extinction. Settlers from Fujian established the town in the early seventeenth century, and it became Taiwan's second largest after Tainan for most of the 1700s. Lugang's decline began in the late nineteenth century as the harbour began to silt up and by 1895 it was closed to major shipping: the town rapidly became a

Lugang

Lugang	鹿港	lùgǎng
Chenghuang Temple	城隍廟	chénghuáng miào
Chen's Fan Shop	陳朝宗手工扇	chén cháozōng shǒugōng shàn
First Market	第一市場	dìyī shìchǎng
Half-Sided Well	半邊井	bànbiān jǐng
Longshan Temple	龍山寺	lóngshān sì
Lugang Gate	隘門	àimén
Lukang Folk Arts Museum	鹿港民俗文物館	lùgǎng mínsú wénwùguǎn
Nine-Turns Lane	九曲巷	jiǔqǔ xiàng
Old Market Street	古市街	gǔshì jiē
Remembrance Hall	意樓	yìlóu
Sanshan Guowang Temple	三山國王廟	sānshān guówáng miào
Shih Jin-Yu Incense Store	施金玉香舖	shī jīnyù xiāngpù
Sinzu Temple	新組宮	xīnzǔ gōng
Tianhou Temple	天后宮	tiānhòu gōng
Wan Neng Tin Workshop	陳萬能錫藝工作坊	chén wànnéng xíyì gōngzuò fāng
Wenkai Academy/Civil Shrine/ Martial Temple	文開書院/文祠/武廟	wénkāi shūyuàn/wéncí/wǔ miào
Wu Dun-hou Lantern Shop	吳敦厚燈舖	wú dūnhòu dēngpù
Yu Chen Chai	玉珍齋	yù zhēn zhāi

Accommodation

Leader Landmark Hotel	立德文教休閒會館	lìdé wénjiào xiūxián huìguǎn
Matsu Temple Believer Hotel	天后宮香客大樓	tiānhòu gōng xiāngkè dàlóu
Quanzhong Hotel	全忠旅社	quánzhōng lǚshè

Eating and drinking

A Jhen Steamed Bun	阿振肉包	ā zhèn ròubāo
Ciao Wei Jhen	巧味珍	qiǎowèizhēn
Jheng Yu Jhen Cake Store	鄭玉珍餅舖	zhèng yùzhēn bǐng pù
Longshan Mian Sian Hu	龍山麵線糊	lóngshān miàn xiànhú
Old Chef's Duck Broth	老師傅鴨肉羹	lǎo shīfu yāròu gēng
Sheng Chao Wu Wei	生炒五味	shēng chǎo wǔwèi
Yi Gu Jhai	怡古齋	yígǔ zhāi

conservative backwater in the years that followed, avoiding the modernization engulfing the rest of the island until the late 1970s, when tourism gave the economy a much needed boost.

Arrival and information

Buses from Changhua terminate at the small bus station at 305 Jhongshan Road (opposite the police station), though at the time of writing there was talk of changing its location. Minibuses from Taichung travel along Jhongshan Road before terminating on Mincyuan Road, while buses from **Taipei** end up at the Ubus office a bit further along the same street.

It's possible to walk to all the main sights, but consider contacting the **Lukang Cultural Foundation** (℡04/7780096; NT$2000 for three hours) in advance to arrange a guide if you want more detailed information – English speakers are usually available at weekends. ATM and banking facilities are limited in town, so make sure you bring enough cash.

Accommodation

Accommodation in Lugang is limited, though during the week it's easy to find rooms: the best option is the *Matsu Temple Believer Hotel*, the pristine modern building just north of Tianhou Temple at 475 Jhongshan Road, with comfortable but basic singles (⊤04/7752508; ②). The cheapest place is the faded *Quanzhong Hotel* at 104 Jhongshan Road (⊤04/7772640; ②), while the only luxury hotel in town is the comfortable but rather sterile *Leader Landmark Hotel* at 588 Jhongjheng Road (⊤04/7786699; ⑥), ten minutes' walk from Tianhou Temple.

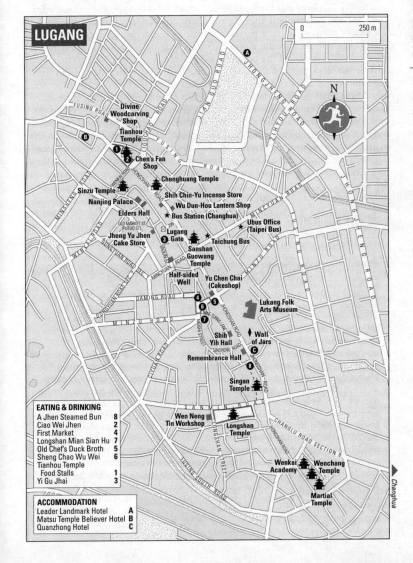

LUGANG

0   250 m

N

Divine
Woodcarving
Shop
Tianhou
Temple
Chen's Fan
Shop
Chenghuang Temple
Sinzu Temple
Nanjing Palace
Shih Chin-Yu Incense Store
Elders Hall
Wu Dun-Hou Lantern Shop
Jheng Yu Jhen
Cake Store
Bus Station (Changhua)
Lugang
Gate
Ubus Office
(Taipei Bus)
Taichung Bus
Sanshan
Guowang
Temple
Half-sided
Well
Yu Chen Chai
(Cakeshop)
Lukang Folk
Arts Museum
Shih
Yih Hall
Wall
of Jars
Remembrance Hall
Singan
Temple
Wen Neng
Tin Workshop
Longshan
Temple
Wenkai
Academy
Wenchang
Temple
Martial
Temple

FUSING ROAD
JIAN GUO ROAD
JHONGJHENG ROAD
ZHONG ROAD
FUSING ROAD
MINSHENG ROAD
JHONGSHAN ROAD
WENKAI ROAD
OLD MARKET ST (PUTUO ST)
MINCYUAN ROAD
JHONGSHAN ROAD
MINZU ROAD
JHONGSHAN ROAD
MINCYUAN ROAD
DAMING ROAD
MINZU ROAD
MEISHI STREET
NINE TURNS LANE
JHONGSHAN ROAD
SINSHENG ROAD
LONGSHAN ROAD SECT
CIVIC ROAD
FUSING SOUTH ROAD
SANMIN ROAD
LONGSHAN STREET
JHONGSHAN ROAD
CHANGLU ROAD SECTION 6

A
B

▶ Changhua

EATING & DRINKING

A Jhen Steamed Bun	8
Ciao Wei Jhen	2
First Market	4
Longshan Mian Sian Hu	7
Old Chef's Duck Broth	5
Sheng Chao Wu Wei	6
Tianhou Temple	
Food Stalls	1
Yi Gu Jhai	3

ACCOMMODATION

Leader Landmark Hotel	A
Matsu Temple Believer Hotel	B
Quanzhong Hotel	C

The Town

Lugang is a large, modern town but the historic centre is a thin wedge bordering **Jhongshan Road** from **Tianhou Temple** in the north, to **Wenkai Academy** in the south. All the main points of interest can be reached as part of a long circular walk, though if you have time it can be a rewarding place to just wander.

Tianhou Temple

Established in 1591, **Tianhou Temple** (daily 6am–10pm), at the northern end of Jhongshan Road, is one of the oldest temples in Taiwan, though the original Mazu statue (now lost) was shared among the early settlers' homes and displayed in a flimsy bamboo and brick shrine. The first solid temple was completed in 1647 and the current buildings are a result of renovations completed in 1936.

Much of the temple has a palpably archaic feel, and, though the decor is not overly elaborate, its intricate **stone carvings**, original woodwork and religious artefacts make it one of the country's most authentic. Before you go in, take a look at the depictions of foreigners on the beams on either side of the main gate: the round faces and clogs are supposed to be wicked Dutch colonizers. The **Main Hall** inside houses the chief Mazu deity (known as the "black-faced goddess" after being exposed to incense smoke for centuries), said to be one of six original statues from the Mazu mother temple in Meizhou in Fujian, brought to Taiwan by admiral **Shi Lang** in 1683. It's the smallest statue in the main shrine, honoured by several imperial tablets from various emperors hanging from the beams above. The altar through the doorway on the right honours Jing Zhu Gong, a local land god, while the Birth Goddess is worshipped on the left side – this arrangement is repeated in all Lugang's major temples. The display of weaponry on both sides of the main hall is used in religious processions to scare evil spirits, and at the back of the temple you'll find the **Temple Folk Art Exhibition** (daily 8am–5.30pm; free) housing a small collection of Mazu-related artefacts and remains of previous temple buildings.

Lugang's Living Heritage

In 1985 the Ministry of Education established the **Folk Art Heritage Awards**, also known as "Living Heritage Awards" to recognize the country's top craftsmen: the first winner was from Lugang, and the town has had six "folk arts masters", more than any other in Taiwan. Five were still living at the time of writing, but in most cases their skills have been passed on to younger family members. **Chen Wan-neng** (1942–) won the award in 1988 for his ornate **tin sculptures**. Traditional pieces can be seen at 635 Changlu Rd Section 7 while you can also view his work at the **Wan Neng Tin Workshop** (daily 9am–5pm) at 81 Longshan St, opposite Longshan Temple. **Li Sung-lin** (1906-1998) was the first winner in 1985 and regarded as the greatest master of them all, primarily in woodcarving. Many of his works can be seen in Lugang's temples, but if you call in advance (or ask your guide) you can view his exquisite sculptures in the **studio** of his son Li Bing Guei, at 28 Putuo St (Old Market Street; ☎04/7772448). **Shih Chen-yang** (1946–) is another talented woodcarver of the Quanzhou school that won the award in 1992, while **Shih Zhe-hui** (1935–) is also a woodcarver, winning the award in 1994. You can see the master at work in his **Divine Woodcarving Shop** at 655 Fusing Rd. **Wu Ching-bo** (1931–) is a fifth generation woodcarver and award winner in 1987, famous principally for religious statues. **Wu Dun-hou** (1925–) is a celebrated creator of traditional lanterns who won the award in 1988, and his **Wu Dun-hou Lantern Shop** (daily 8am–11pm) at 312 Jhongshan Road is a popular place to buy beautifully crafted Chinese lanterns.

Old Market Street

Turn left when you exit the temple and walk south along Jhongshan Road: turn right at the first junction and a little further along Wenkai Road on the left is Lugang's official Mazu shrine, established by Imperial decree in 1788 as another Tianhou Temple but known today as **Sinzu Temple** (New Mazu Temple, daily 7am–8pm). The series of narrow lanes that lead south from the temple's main entrance are collectively known as **Old Market Street**, and form what is undoubtedly Lugang's most atmospheric neighbourhood. The first stretch is known as Putuo Street; first on your left down here is **Nanjing Palace**, actually a temple dedicated to Guan Di dating from 1784, followed by **Elders Hall**, a community hall built in 1928 where local seniors gather to sing or play chess in the after-

△ Lugang, Old Market Street

noon. Beyond this the street is lined with beautifully preserved Qing dynasty buildings, many converted into touristy shops and cafés, but several still functioning as homes and workshops, giving the street an authentic edge. Lugang's **cakeshops** and bakeries are renowned for their sweet specialties, and the *Jheng Yu Jhen Cake Store* at no. 23, managed by the fourth generation of the Jheng family, is a good place to sample them – the first Jheng was head chef at *Yu Chen Chai* (see p.263). The final section south of here is Yaolin Street. The diminutive **Half-Sided Well** tucked away on the left side not far from Mincyuan Road has an interesting history – built so that the public could share the spring water bubbling up inside one of Lugang's richer homes, it's testimony to the munificence of the town's former elites.

Nine-Turns Lane

At Mincyuan Road cross over and continue south: barring a few twists and turns, you should end up at First Market and Minzu Road in around five minutes. Not far from the junction with Jhongshan Road, marked with a tiny white sign with red Chinese characters, and just to the right of a flower shop, you should see the narrow entrance to **Nine-Turns Lane** (also known as Chinsheng Lane). Named after the ninth month September, tourists are told that its thin, crooked alleyways were designed to confuse pirates and protect against the chill winds prevalent at this time of year, but most scholars believe it ran behind houses that stood, unevenly, along Lugang's harbour front. There's not a lot to see but it's one of the town's more appealing areas, especially the intriguing passageway that crosses the lane further south known as **Shih Yih Hall**, where Lugang's literati would, as the English sign explains, "recite poetry and partake in alcoholic revelry." The lane ends on Sinsheng Road but it's possible to follow tiled back alleys south from here, past the elaborate round window of the **Remembrance Hall,** and **Singan Temple** (Lugang's first Mazu shrine), before eventually reaching Sanmin Road opposite Longshan Temple.

Longshan Temple and around

With its main entrance on Longshan Street, **Longshan Temple** (daily 5am–9.30pm) is one of the most famous Buddhist temples in Taiwan, though its sobriquet of Taiwan's Forbidden City is a little misleading. It's especially noted for its exquisite **woodcarvings** – check out the eight trigram windows in the **main entrance hall** and the roof beams above. The temple is principally dedicated to Guanyin and traces its origins to a shrine founded in 1653 – it was moved to the current site in 1786 when the area was outside the town and much quieter. The original Guanyin statues were destroyed in a devastating fire in 1921, but remains of one can be found in the Folk Art Museum.

Sadly, the temple's main hall was flattened by the 921 earthquake, triggering a massive restoration project that will last for many years, making it almost impossible to fully appreciate the exceptional artwork inside – you can still visit the **Rear Hall**, finished in 2004 and currently the focus of all religious ceremonies. Guanyin is in the centre flanked by the Medicine Buddha and Jing Zhu Gong on the right, while Dizang Wang and the Birth Goddess sit on the left. You can also have a peek at the **Main Hall** restoration area which will give you some idea of the scale of the task at hand. The work is being funded by Pou Chen Corp, the world's largest shoe manufacturer and contractor for major brands such as Nike.

Before you move on, have a peek inside **Wan Neng Tin Workshop**, opposite the main temple entrance on Longshan Street (see box p.260). Turn right here back to Sanmin Road then right again to Jhongshan Road: if you've still got some energy left, there is a cluster of Qing dynasty buildings a block further south, expertly restored in 2005. **Wenkai Academy** was a school completed in 1827 and served as the focus for not only young scholars but also Lugang's famed literati for much of the subsequent 150 years. Next door the **Wenchang Temple** or "Civil Shrine" dates from 1811 is dedicated to the God of Literature, Wenchang Dijun, while finally, separated by the **Tiger Well**, is the **Martial Temple** completed the same year and dedicated to Guan Di. The main buildings are open 6am–9pm daily.

North along Jhongshan Road

It's a long walk back to Tianhou Temple from the southern end of **Jhongshan Road**, but the street has plenty of character, lined with early twentieth-century shophouses, many still home to traditional stores and master craftsmen (see box p.260). The lower end is particularly thick with furniture and coffin makers, but north of Sanmin Road the main attraction is **Lukang Folk Arts Museum** (daily 9am–5pm; NT$130): ignore the first sign on the right and instead walk to the next narrow lane, by the side of a police station at no. 108, and turn right here. This alley takes you past the "**wall of jars**", old wine jars used to build courtyard walls, and on to a bigger road – the museum is the huge baroque mansion on the left. Built in 1920, it was the home of the mighty **Koo family**, one of Taiwan's richest and most influential, until 1973 when it was turned into a museum. Though it contains a fascinating collection of everyday artefacts from the Qing and early Japanese period, most of the objects reflect the lives of the very wealthy and, one presumes, the Koos themselves. **Koo Hsien-yung** established Lugang's salt industry in the 1890s and the family still wields considerable economic clout, controlling giants such as Taiwan Cement and Chinatrust Commercial Bank.

Return to Jhongshan Road and head north to Minzu Road, where you'll see the venerable cakeshop **Yu Chen Chai** (168 Minzu Road; daily 8am–11pm) on the corner, home of phoenix eye cake, phoenix egg cake, and the comparatively prosaic green bean cake since 1877.

North of Minzu Road lies the town's modern commercial heart, but keep walking beyond Mincyuan Road and you'll find the **Wu Dun-hou Lantern Shop** at no. 312, next to the main police station (see box p.260). A short walk north on the left is the aged **Shih Jin-yu Incense Store** at no. 327-1, founded in 1756 and now owned by Shih Chi-hsun, the family's seventh generation of shop owners. Not far from here on the other side of the road at no. 366 is **Chenghuang Temple** (daily 6am–9pm), housing Lugang's City God, a small single-hall structure with a large abacus hanging above the main entrance – it's not busy these days though the mother of Acer chairman Stan Shih is said to have prayed here when the company had problems – they were subsequently solved.

The next major junction south of Tianhou Temple completes the loop: turn right here along Liouchao Road, and the second shop on the left is **Chen's Fan Shop** (400-1 Jhongshan Rd), home to exquisite, hand-painted Chinese fans. Chen Chao-zong has received many awards, though he's not yet an official "Living Treasure" – be warned that the shop seems to keep erratic opening hours.

Eating

Lugang specializes in *xiaochi* or "little eats": favourites include **oyster omelettes**, deep-fried oyster cakes and **"shrimp monkeys"** (*xia hou zi* or mud shrimp fried with basil – you'll need a vivid imagination to see the monkey), available at the snack stalls and restaurants in front of Tianhou Temple. Try the bakeries around here for **ox-tongue cake**, (*niu she bing*) a sweet flat pastry that tastes nothing like tongue, though it vaguely resembles one.

Tea, coffee and delicious **rice powder tea** (*mian cha*, NT$40) can be sampled at *Yi Gu Jhai* at 6 Putuo Street (Old Market Street), an atmospheric café in a narrow shophouse with wooden benches and Qing dynasty decor – it's a thick, sweet drink best sampled cold. **First Market** at the end of Minzu Road also has food stalls open from 6am till around 9pm. The most popular include *Old Chef's Duck Broth* at no. 159 (NT$55); *Sheng Chao Wu Wei* at no. 171, named after its main dish, a broth of shrimp, cuttlefish, pork, mushroom and bamboo shoots (NT$40); and around the corner at 84 Meishi Street, *Longshan Mian Sian Hu,* cooking up delicious vermicelli noodles with pork and dried shrimp (NT$20). *A Jhen Steamed Bun* (daily 9am–7pm) at 71 Jhongshan Road produces delicious **pork buns** with mushroom (NT$15) that are so popular it now has a branch in Japan. *Ciao Wei Jhen* just south of Tianhou Temple at 410 Jhongshan Road also serves up tasty steamed savoury buns (NT$15), founded by one of Jhen's old staff.

Jiji Branch Rail Line

The **JIJI BRANCH RAIL LINE**, beginning southeast of Changhua and stretching 29.7km to an old depot near Sun Moon Lake, is one of the country's four **narrow-gauge railways** that have been preserved for tourists. It chugs its way through some diverse countryside, stopping at a handful of **historic towns** that offer glimpses of a Taiwan that is fast disappearing. First opened in 1922 by

Jiji Branch Rail Line

Jiji Branch Rail Line	集集線鐵道	*jíjí xiàn tiědào*
Ershuei	二水	*èrshuǐ*
Asia Hotel	亞洲大飯店	*yàzhōu dàfàndiàn*
Erh Pa Shui Culture Studio	二八水文化工作室	*èrbāshuǐ wénhuà gōngzuòshì*
Fongbo Square	豐柏廣場	*fēngbó guǎngchǎng*
Fongbo Trail	豐柏山步道	*fēngbòshān bùdào*
Shoutian Palace	受天宮	*shòutiān gōng*
Songbo Ridge	松柏嶺	*sōngbòlǐng*
Taiwan Macaque Protection Area	台灣獼猴保護區	*táiwān míhóu bǎohù qū*
Jiji	集集	*jíjí*
Chi Chi Hotel	集集大飯店	*jíjí dàfàndiàn*
Jiji Holiday Village	集集渡假村	*jíjí dùjiàcūn*
Jiji Railway Station	集集火車站	*jíjí huǒchēzhàn*
Junshih Park	軍史公園	*jūnshǐ gōngyúan*
Mingsin Academy	明新書院	*míngxīn shūyùan*
Wuchang Palace	武昌宮	*wǔchāng gōng*
Shueili	水里	*shuǐlǐ*
Long Jiang Hotel	龍江大飯店	*lóngjiāng dàfàndiàn*
Yushan National Park Headquarters	玉山國家公園管埋處	*yùshān guójiā gōngyuán guánlǐchù*
Checheng	車程	*chēchéng*

the occupying Japanese to transport construction materials to Sun Moon Lake, the railway begins in the quaint town of **Ershuei** – about thirty minutes by train from Changhua – and runs west through endearing towns such as **Jiji** and **Shueili** before terminating in a rustic old depot called **Checheng**, just south of Sun Moon Lake.

The designation of the line as a scenic railway branch in 1994 has breathed new life into the towns alongside it, and over the past decade a thriving cottage tourism industry has developed, with some enterprising locals – especially in Ershuei and Jiji – offering tailor-made **excursions** to local attractions, from traditional **Fujianese farmhouses** and historic temples to nature walks through beautiful bamboo groves filled with a protected species of monkey. Much of the area is linked by easily navigable **bicycle paths**, offering another fun means of exploring the sights. And the growing numbers of family-run **homestays** – many in restored traditional homes – represent inviting accommodation alternatives.

Practicalities

The Jiji Branch Rail Line starts at the town of Ershuei on the **Western rail line**, roughly halfway between Changhua and Chiayi. Upon arrival in Ershuei, alight and follow the English signs to transfer to the narrow-gauge rail, which has eight daily trains in each direction on weekdays, with several more on weekends and public holidays. **Tickets** can be bought in the station or on the train itself: the **same-day ticket** (NT$44) allows you to alight and re-board once (a good option if you're planning to spend the night in one of the towns along the line), while the **multiple-stop ticket** (NT$80) allows you to re-board as many times as you like in a single day, making it ideal if you just want

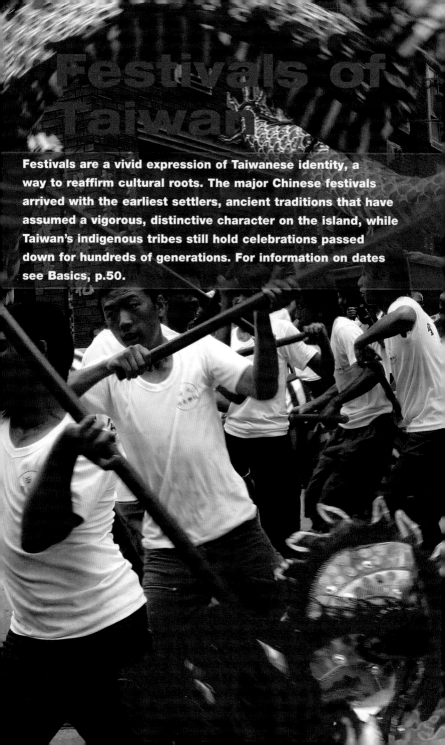

Festivals of Taiwan

Festivals are a vivid expression of Taiwanese identity, a way to reaffirm cultural roots. The major Chinese festivals arrived with the earliest settlers, ancient traditions that have assumed a vigorous, distinctive character on the island, while Taiwan's indigenous tribes still hold celebrations passed down for hundreds of generations. For information on dates see Basics, p.50.

▲ Lantern Festival

Religious Festivals

The **birthdays** of Taoist gods and goddesses are particularly exuberant affairs in Taiwan. Usually, celebrations involve several days of boisterous parades, with deities carried on palanquins to "inspect" the local area, to the accompaniment of traditional music, firecrackers, lion dances and opera singers, ending with a more formal ceremony in the temple itself. The birthdays of the Taipei **City God** (June) and **Baosheng Dadi** (March/April) tend to be the most colourful, while **Mazu's Birthday** (April) is the most fervently celebrated, particularly in central and south Taiwan where the **Dajia Mazu Pilgrimage** is one of the world's largest religious festivals. **Confucius's Birthday** on September 28 is a far more austere affair. The one-hour ceremony in Taipei begins at 6am, an elaborate combination of bright costumes, strictly observed rituals and ancient music, considered by many to be the most authentic on the planet – the attendance of the current ancestor of Confucius (77th generation) adds legitimacy.

Lantern Festival: Heavenly Lanterns and Beehive Fireworks

The **Lantern Festival** marks the end of the Chinese New Year period, with decorative paper lanterns depicting birds and beasts (usually corresponding to the upcoming year's zodiac animal) in temples and homes symbolizing hope for a bright future. Giant lanterns are displayed in all the biggest cities, but the most spectacular celebration is held southwest of Chiayi, where **Yanshuei Beehive Fireworks**, lodged in over two hundred walls or "beehives" the size of a truck, are fired into the crowds that pack the town, creating a cacophony of noise, fire and smoke throughout the night. The **Pingsi Heavenly Lantern Festival** takes place in the Keelung River valley east of Taipei, with elegant **sky lanterns** *(tiandeng)* released en masse into the night sky, creating one of Taiwan's most mesmerizing sights. The lanterns are lit by flames that make them float like balloons, each one representing a wish: white symbolizes peace, pink means happiness and orange is wealth.

▼ Yanshuei beehive rockets

Dragon Boat Festival

▲ Women's dragon boat race at Erlong

The **Dragon Boat Festival**, held in the humid months of summer (Lunar May 5, usually June), is traditionally a time for warding off evil and strengthening the body, symbolized today by **dragon boat races** held throughout Taiwan, and eating *zongzi*, balls of rice wrapped in bamboo leaves. The races commemorate a futile attempt to save a beloved ancient Chinese folk hero from drowning, over two thousand years ago. Particularly unique races take place in **Lugang**, where there's a folk festival held at the same time, and **Erlong**, near Yilan. Much smaller and intimate than other events, the Erlong rowers stand or kneel in their boats (which have no dragon heads at the prow), and rhythm is maintained by banging gongs rather than drums.

▲ Keelung, Jhupu Temple

Ghost Festival

The **Ghost Festival** is held in the middle of **Ghost Month** (Lunar July), a time Chinese believe that spirits of the dead roam the world and must be appeased with offerings of food and prayers. **Keelung** hosts Taiwan's biggest celebration, with events held throughout the month until the "gates of hell" are closed on Lunar August 1 – on Lunar July 12, Jhupu Temple is spectacularly illuminated, while on the evening of Lunar July 14, **water lanterns**, thought to guide the souls of those that have drowned to salvation, are released into the harbour after a huge parade of floats, marching bands, traditional martial arts performers and musicians.

The Big Three

The three most important holidays in Taiwan are **Chinese New Year**, the **Dragon Boat Festival** (see above) and the **Mid-Autumn Festival**. Traditional festivals tend to follow the **lunar calendar**, with families gathering on Lunar New Year's Eve for a lavish reunion dinner and exchange of "lucky money". Midnight is marked by the launch of thousands of firecrackers, and the festivities continue until the Lantern Festival fifteen days later. The Mid-Autumn Festival (Lunar August 15) originally celebrated the moon and its feminine *yin* associations, and today families and friends gather outdoors to gaze at the moon, eat mooncakes (rich pastries stuffed with red bean paste and egg yolk) and increasingly, to share a barbecue. Many Chinese would add Qingming or the **Tomb Sweeping Festival** to this list, the day when families visit ancestral graves – in Taiwan it's officially celebrated on the anniversary of Chiang Kai-shek's death, April 5.

Hakka Yimin

The **Hakka Yimin Festival**, held during Ghost Month, is unique to Taiwan, a commemoration of Hakka warriors killed in the eighteenth century. Today it's infamous for the "**God Pigs**", giant hogs reared specifically to be sacrificed at the festival. Fed to gargantuan proportions, almost a hundred pigs are slaughtered, displayed over special metal frames and arranged in front of Yimin Temple near Hsinchu on the morning of the festival. Each year the event is vehemently criticized by animal rights campaigners, who say that the ritual is extremely cruel (see p.205).

Aboriginal celebrations

Aboriginal festivals offer a rare opportunity for members of the tribe to come together and celebrate their culture. Many tribes hold **harvest festivals**, usually in the summer, while others mark important rites of passage. Rituals are enacted by clan elders, animist traditions that seek to balance the tribe's relationship with the natural and spirit worlds, usually accompanied by singing, dancing and communal feasts. The **Tsou Mayasvi Festival**, hosted annually in rotation by Tefuye and Dabang villages in February, was traditionally a celebration of warriors returning from battle, the main ceremony a series of dances culminating in the slaughter of a wild boar. **Paiwan** and **Ami** villages celebrate their harvest festivals individually with communal dancing, races, tugs of war and arrow shooting, while the **Puyuma coming-of-age festival** is marked by bouts of wrestling. The **Thao** open their harvest festival at the end of summer with "**pestle music**" created by large pestles being thumped onto wooden blocks.

▼ Jhihben, Puyuma tribe wrestlers

to have a quick look at some of the rail-side towns. You also can buy tickets at all the other stations along the line, making it possible to begin your train journey in several places, with the town of **Shueili** and the railway's western terminus at **Checheng** both accessible by the Fengrong Bus Co **coaches** that run hourly between Shueili and nearby **Sun Moon Lake** (30min; NT$42). However, note that there is not an official bus stop at **Checheng**, so if you want to start your train trip here you'll need to ask the bus driver to let you off on the main road and then walk a few hundred metres down the paved access road to the depot.

Ershuei

The railway's starting point, the town of **ERSHUEI** holds considerable allure with bucolic surroundings ideal for walking and a loosely laid-out **bicycle path** which winds through several kilometres of farmland, much of it **betel nut plantations**. The paved route – meant to be for cyclists only but also used by cautious local motorists – passes a number of folk shrines and some wonderfully well-preserved traditional **walled villas**. Most of the latter are still occupied by Hoklo families, who generally seem quite happy to let you have a look inside. To get to the beginning of the bicycle path, turn right after you exit the train station and walk about 200m until you reach the railway crossing to your right; cross the tracks and the path begins immediately to your right.

On the outskirts of town, a paved path leads through Ershuei's one sq km **Taiwan Macaque Protection Area**, home to an estimated three hundred of the energetic, bluish-grey-haired **monkeys**, who spend their days swinging from the giant bamboo trees that groan under their weight. Despite the fact that these magnificent primates are protected – and there are signs stating that feeding them is prohibited – many locals and domestic tourists insist on enticing them with all kinds of food, conditioning them to behave in a rather bold manner. The path climbs gently for about 2km up the **Songbo (Pine and Cedar) Ridge**, at the top of which sits the **Shoutian (Heaven's Acceptance) Palace**, a Taoist temple whose exterior makes for an impressive sight from a distance. However, its interior has been completely gutted by fire and is still being repaired. Still, it's definitely worth the walk to the top for the superb views of the plains and river valley below. The path, known locally as the **Fongbo Trail**, starts at **Fongbo Square**, essentially a car park about 2km from the train station, but it's tricky to find so your best bet is to catch a **taxi** here.

Practicalities

The centrally located *Asia Hotel* at 3 Guangwun Rd (T04/8793925; ❷), just in front of the train station on your left, has basic, slightly aging **rooms** that won't break the budget. A more interesting option, however, is to arrange an excursion with one of the town's small-scale **tour operators**, who typically include accommodation in a local **homestay** as part of their packages. About 300m down the main street in front of the train station, the *Erh Pa Shui Culture Studio* at 74 Guangwun Rd (T04/8792364, mobile 09/28960569; ✉mywarmday@ yahoo.com.tw) can organize walking and bicycle tours, including meals and accommodation; contact the owner, Andy Chang, who speaks some English. A small **restaurant** with basic Chinese dishes such as fried rice and noodles is at the same address.

If you just want to cycle around on your own, **bicycles** can be rented (NT$100 per day) from the shops just outside the train station. There is a Chinatrust

Commercial Bank **ATM** which accepts international credit cards in the 7-Eleven, about 200m down the main street from the train station, on the left.

Jiji

The railway's namesake, the tourist-friendly town of **JIJI** is by far the most popular stop on the line, its rustic charms drawing droves of domestic visitors searching for remnants of the Japanese colonial era. The most intact of these is the **Jiji Railway Station** itself, its simple whitewashed facade serving as one of the island's preeminent photo backdrops. Built in 1933, it was badly damaged in the 921 earthquake and had to be completely dismantled and rebuilt in strict adherence to its original design. The same red cypress beams and planks were used (although the main pillars were reinforced with steel), and the black-glazed roof tiles that were broken during the quake were replaced with those retrieved from other Japanese-era buildings in the area.

Most of Jiji's main sights are accessible via its **bicycle path**, which begins just to the right of the train station as you exit and is clearly marked with metal signs in the shape of a bicycle. Barely a kilometre along the path, across the road to the left, is the tiny **Junshih (Soldier History) Park** (6am–9pm; free), an outdoor museum filled with an array of military equipment, including tanks of different generations, anti-aircraft artillery launchers, a cargo plane and a fighter jet. Unfortunately, the only English inside are the instructions on the US-supplied F-104G fighter jet. A few hundred metres further on you'll see an ornamental Chinese archway to the right, beyond which lies the historic **Mingsin Academy**, founded in 1882 in the Neo-Confucian tradition and moved to its present location in 1902. Since 1982 it has functioned as an **architectural complex** (6am–9pm; free) with halls venerating Confucius and some of the academy's most accomplished scholars.

One of the most fascinating sights along the bicycle path is the **Wuchang Palace**, a temple which ironically rose to prominence after collapsing in the 921 earthquake. The symmetrical fashion of its collapse is intriguing – its lower walls gave way, yet its ornate, multi-tiered roof remains almost completely intact, down to the guardian statues that now watch over the ruins.

Practicalities

The closest **accommodation** option to the train station is the no-frills *Chi Chi Hotel* at 113 Minsheng Rd (☎049/2760778; ❸), just down the second street to your left after you exit the station, with basic but bright and clean doubles. Further afield but with more amenities is the *Jiji Holiday Village* at 205 Cheng-gong Rd (☎049/2762988; ❹), which is good value if you plan to spend some time here. Rooms are spotless, with big, comfortable beds, and rates include a buffet breakfast and use of the complex's **swimming pool** and spa facilities.

Jiji's signature culinary specialty is its **stinky tofu** (*chou doufu*), prized for its freshness and firm texture. The best-known place to try it is a nameless little restaurant on 7 Jhihbin St, a small alley just across Minsheng Road from the *Chi Chi Hotel*. This down-to-earth establishment, distinguished only by a Chinese sign that says "*cho doufu*", has for more than forty years served only two items: *chou doufu* topped with lightly stir-fried cabbage and steaming bowls of dried **duck's blood soup**. The standard set (NT$50) includes a plate of the tofu and a separate bowl of the soup, but you can order the tofu alone for NT$30. The place closes at 7pm sharp.

Several shops across the street from the train station rent **bicycles** (NT$50–100 per day), tandems (NT$150 per day) and motorized bikes and tiny **scooters**

(NT$150 for two hours). The gift shop just outside the train station sells crude Chinese-only **maps** for NT$10. **Internet access** (NT$20 per hr) is available at the computer game centre at 340 Minsheng Rd, about 1km down the main road from the train station on the right – it's just before the green turnoff sign for Highway 139. Note that there is no **ATM** that accepts non-Taiwanese bank or credit cards, so bring plenty of cash.

Shueili

The biggest town on the rail line, and its penultimate stop, is **SHUEILI**, a useful transport hub and home of the **Yushan National Park Headquarters** and its main visitor centre (9am–4.30pm; 300 Jhongshan Rd Sec 1; ☎049/2773121, ⓦwww.ysnp.gov.tw), where you can get excellent English-language park **maps** and brochures and apply in person for Class A mountain permits. To get to the headquarters, walk straight down Minsheng Rd from the train station for about 500m until you reach a big intersection next to the river; turn right here and walk another 500m to the next intersection – cross the bridge to the left and you'll see the large, white headquarters building on the right.

Shueili's main **bus station** is to the left after you exit the train station, directly across the street from the 7-Eleven. From here, buses leave regularly throughout the day for Sun Moon Lake (30min; NT$42), Puli (1hr; NT$98) and the mountain hot-springs town of Dongpu (1hr 10min; NT$104). Most of the **hotels** near the train station are very run-down, but one exception is the basic-but-clean *Long Jiang Hotel* at 174 Minsheng Rd (☎049/2772614; ❷), about 200m down the main road from the station on the left. There is a Chinatrust Commercial Bank **ATM** that accepts international credit cards inside the 7-Eleven just outside the train station on the left.

Checheng

The rail line terminates in a circular depot known as **CHECHENG**, whose quaint village – filled with old houses made from cypress – recalls its heyday as a bustling **logging centre**. From 1960 to 1985, the village was the headquarters of the Zhengchang Timber Co, which exploited the area's virgin cypress forests until the introduction of environmental protection measures. Today, signs of its past abound, with a defunct timber mill, a storage warehouse and water towers surrounding the train station. **Buses** running between Shueili and Sun Moon Lake ply the road on the hill above Checheng, and it's possible to alight here if you ask the driver in advance.

Sitou Forest Recreation Area

In the hills south of the Jiji Branch Rail Line, the **SITOU FOREST RECREATION AREA** is one of the island's finest, laced with easy walks through enchanting woods filled with a staggering variety of magnificent trees. Much of the area is managed by National Taiwan University's forestry department, which has cultivated several experimental groves, contributing to its remarkable variation – with species ranging from three types of bamboo to pine, cedar, red spruce, gingko, cypress and even redwood.

Covered by a leafy canopy at an elevation of over 1000m, Sitou makes for a cool summer retreat easily accessed by public transport and with ample tourist

Sitou Forest Recreation Area

Sitou Forest Recreation Area	溪頭森林遊樂區	qītóu sēnlín yóulèqū
Arched Bamboo Bridge	竹拱橋	zhú gǒngqiáo
Astronomical Observatory	天文台	tiānwéntái
Bamboo Forest	竹林	zhúlín
Conifer Arboretum	針葉標本園	zhēnyè biāoběnyuán
Fonghuangshan	鳳凰山	fènghuáng shān
Giant Cypress Tree	神木	shénmù
University Pond	大學池	dàxúe chí
Accommodation		
Castle in Red	紅樓	hōng lóu
Ming Shan Hotel	明山大飯店	míng shān dàfàndiàn
Sitou Youth Activity Center	溪頭青年活動中心	qītóu qīngnián huádòng zhōngxīn

infrastructure. Unlike so many of Taiwan's parks and recreation areas, where long hikes through often rugged terrain are required to experience different ecosystems, Sitou's core area is remarkably compact, allowing the average visitor to take in a lot in a short time. However it also offers demanding hikes that take you far away from the usual weekend crowds.

Practicalities

Sitou is easy to reach by **bus**, with Ubus offering regular direct service from **Taichung** (2hr). From **Jhushan**, just to the northwest, there are several Yuanlin buses daily to Sitou (1hr). All buses stop at the small station beside the car park, just outside the entrance to the recreation area. There are several **hotels**, most within the recreation area's boundaries, and all but one of them are run by a single luxury hotel group and are quite expensive. Although there's little in the way of budget accommodation, most of the hotels give big **discounts** on weekdays, when the trails here are virtually abandoned. The most lavish hotel is the *Castle in Red* at 10 Sanlin Lane (☎049/2612588; ⓦ www.leaderhotel.com; ⑨), an upscale resort lodge just inside the recreation area, southeast of the pedestrian entrance gate. Named because of its previous red walls and black ceramic roof tiles, its 23 rooms have beautiful hardwood floors and Jacuzzis. Considerably cheaper, the convenient *Ming Shan Hotel* (☎049/2612376; ⓦ www.mingshan .com.tw; ④), alongside the main road just outside the recreation area entrance, has a wide range of rooms as well as a restaurant, a public spa area and a 24-hour **convenience store**. Well inside the recreation area, at 15 Sanlin Lane – about 1km southwest of the pedestrian entrance – is the lovely *Sitou Youth Activity Center* (☎049/2612160; ⓦ www.cyh.org.tw; ③), the only budget alternative. Run by the China Youth Corps, the centre has a wide range of rooms, including **dorm beds** in attractive wood huts for NT$400 per person.

Meals are available in most of the hotels, but far more interesting is the assembly of **food hawkers** that sets up shop each day alongside the main road just outside the recreation area's pedestrian entrance.

The trails

The pedestrian entrance gate is just past the car park and marks the recreation area's northern boundary and the beginning of its network of easily navigable **trails** – most are paved or filled with wood chips, and those leading to the main sights are marked with distances in English. You'll also be given a basic English **map** when you buy your entry **ticket** (NT$150 on weekdays, NT$200 on weekends and public holidays).

The area's most beloved sight is the **Giant Cypress Tree**, a gargantuan beauty whose dying remains are 46m tall and 16m wide. The tree, located southeast of the entrance, is over 2800 years old, and in its twilight is serving as a gigantic backdrop for photos of the tiny tourists at its base. More commonly known as the "sacred tree", it's unique in escaping the ravages of Japanese-initiated logging that robbed the island of most of these graceful giants. To get here, walk along the main road that leads south from the entrance gate until it crosses over a stream, then take the wide pathway to your left. This well-trodden trail rises gently uphill through the exquisite **Bamboo Forest**, a mesmerizing tangle of towering green bamboo – the tree for which Sitou is famed, given its role as a leading supplier of shoots for Taiwan's massive reforestation projects. Several hundred metres past the bamboo grove the trail spills out onto a paved road directly beneath the ancient cypress. From here, you can follow the road to the east or west to get to more trails. If you turn right (heading west), you'll come to a path which leads to **University Pond**, a carp-filled body of water bisected by the **Arched Bamboo Bridge** – another favoured photo spot. This area is criss-crossed with easy trails, all of them covered by an enormous canopy of leaves that seems to mirror the blanket of colossal ferns that lines the forest floor.

For a much more challenging walk, bear left from the entrance gate along the paved road leading northeast towards the **Conifer Arboretum** and follow it for a few hundred metres until you see the stone steps rising up the hill to your left (there is no English sign). The trail climbs sharply from here into the foothills of **Fonghuangshan** (Phoenix Mountain), up the sides of which winds a steep trail of large stone steps giving lovely views of the treetops below. With each type of forest readily distinguishable from the next, the entire area resembles a soft patchwork quilt of green. After about 3km the trail comes to a paved road just below the **Astronomical Observatory**, which is closed to the public but offers good views from the wooden platforms surrounding it. If you want to hike the rest of the way to Fonghuangshan from where the trail meets the road, turn left and follow the road for about 15km until you see a narrow trail to the left – this mostly dirt path, marked only by multi-coloured ribbons, winds along a ridge for another 3km or so before reaching the mountaintop. This section of trail is poorly maintained and the overgrowth can make the going slow.

Puli and around

Located in the heart of Taiwan and surrounded by mountains, sprawling **PULI** is an obligatory stop for most buses on the way to Sun Moon Lake from Taichung and Taipei, and lies at the start of the spectacular road to Wushe and **Hehuanshan**. The best reason to break your journey here is the mind-blowing **Chung Tai Chan Monastery** on the outskirts of town, one of Taiwan's most remarkable sights. With more time and, preferably, your own transport, Puli offers an assortment of secular attractions associated with traditional manufac-turing and crafts that have flourished here for decades. Much of this is linked to the quality of the local water and surrounding natural resources – the town once produced eighty percent of Taiwan's **lacquer**, was the centre of a flourishing **paper** trade and is still the home of Taiwan's most famous **Chinese**

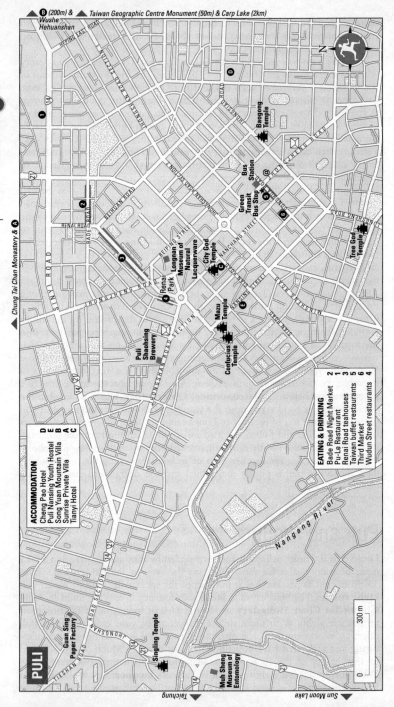

PULI

B (200m) & Taiwan Geographic Centre Monument (50m) & Carp Lake (2km)
Wushe
Hehuanshan

▲ Chung Tai Chan Monastery & **A**

HEPING EAST ROAD

ZHONGSHAN ROAD SECTION 2

HONGXIANG ROAD

D

Baogong
Temple

Bus
Station

Green
Transit
Bus Stop

BETHUAN ROAD

RENAI ROAD

BADE ROAD

SINYI ROAD

Renai
Park

Longnan
Museum of
Natural
Lacquerware

BEIPING STREET

City God
Temple **C**

NANCHANG STREET

Tree God
Temple

ZHONGSHENG ROAD

Mazu
Temple **E**

NANXING STREET

MINSHENG ROAD

Puli
Shaohsing
Brewery

Confucius
Temple

ZHONGSHAN ROAD SECTION 3

NANAN ROAD

Nangang River

Guan Sing
Paper Factory

Singling Temple

Muh Sheng
Museum of
Entomology

TIESHAN ROAD

ZHONGSHAN ROAD SECTION 3

▲ Taichung

▲ Sun Moon Lake

0   300 m

ACCOMMODATION
Cheng Pao Hotel   D
Puli Nansing Youth Hostel E
Song Yuan Mountain Villa B
Sunrise Private Villa   A
Tianyi Hotel   C

EATING & DRINKING
Bade Road Night Market   2
Pu-Le Restaurant   1
Renai Road teahouses   3
Taiwan buffet restaurants   5
Third Market   6
Wudun Street restaurants   4

Puli and around

Puli	埔里	pǔlǐ
Bade Road Night Market	八德夜市	bādé yèshì
Carp Lake	鯉魚潭	lǐyú tán
Guang Sing Paper Factory	廣興紙寮	guǎngxīng zhǐ liáo
Longnan Museum of Natural Lacquer Ware	龍南漆器博物館	lóngnán qīqì bówùguǎn
Muh Sheng Museum of Entomology	木生昆蟲博物館	mùshēng kūnchóng bówùguǎn
Pu-Le Restaurant	金都餐廳	jīndū cāntīng
Puli Shaohsing Brewery	埔里紹興酒廠	pǔlǐ shàoxīng jiǔchǎng
Taiwan Geographic Centre Monument	台灣地理中心碑	táiwān dìlǐ zhōng xīnbēi
Tree God Temple	興南宮 (樹王公)	xīngnán gōng (shùwánggōng)

Accommodation

Cheng Pao Hotel	鎮寶大飯店	zhènbǎo dàfàndiàn
Puli Nansing Youth Hostel	埔里南興旅舍	pǔlǐ nánxīng lǚshě
Song Yuan Mountain Villa	松園山莊	sōngyuán shān zhuāng
Sunrise Private Villa	眉溪曉莊別墅	méixī xiǎo zhuāng biéshù
Tianyi Hotel	天一大飯店	tiānyī dàfàndiàn

Around Puli

Aowanda National Forest Recreation Area	奧萬大國家森林遊樂區	àowàndà guójiā sēnlín yóulè qū
Chung Tai Chan Monastery	中台禪寺	zhōngtái chán sì
Cingjing Farm	清境農場	qīngjìng nóngchǎng
Hehuanshan National Forest Recreation Area	合歡山森林遊樂區	héhuān shān sēnlín yóulè qū
Lushan Hot Springs	廬山溫泉	lúshān wēnqúan
Wushe	霧社	wùshè

wines. Puli was also the birthplace of glamorous 1960s film star Chang Mei-yao – perhaps the real reason why tourist literature claims the town is famous for "water, wine, weather and women".

Arrival, information and accommodation

Puli is only accessible by **bus**, all of which stop at the bus station in the centre of town on Jhongjheng Road. Nearby, just beyond the junction with Donghua Road, there's a useful **Internet café** at 328 Jhongjheng Road, and a bit further along, the 7-Eleven on the corner contains a Chinatrust **ATM**. The main **post office** is just outside the centre at 648 Jhongshan Road Section 3, but there's a smaller branch near the Third Market at 77 Dongrong Road.

Puli is incredibly spread out, making its attractions hard to reach without your own transport – **taxis** will charge NT$150–200 for most journeys, but in practice it's best to negotiate a rate for at least half a day if you're serious about seeing everything (NT$3000 per day for four people). It's difficult to rent scooters in Puli.

Accommodation

There's plenty of choice in Puli when it comes to accommodation, but it's mostly mid- to top-range **hotels** in the centre of town, and newer

Moving on from Puli

Several companies run frequent services to **Taichung** from the bus station, including Quan Hang and the Puli Express. To **Sun Moon Lake**, you can catch regular local buses to Shuishe village, which take around thirty minutes, or the slightly faster Green Transit service from Taipei, which stops opposite Puli bus station every hour. This company is also the best option to **Taipei** (hourly services), where it terminates near Zhongxiao Fuxing MRT station. **Wushe** is serviced by hourly buses – to reach Hehuanshan and beyond you'll need your own transport.

homestays on the fringes – many of these tend to be upscale resorts rather than typical B&Bs.

Hotels

Cheng Pao Hotel 299 Jhongsiao Rd ☎049/2903333, ⓔhotelinn@ms32.hinet.net. Best hotel in town with comfortable rooms and decent pool and gym, about twenty minutes' walk from the bus station. Forty percent discounts are common during the week. ⑥

Puli Nansing Youth Hostel 311 Nansing Street ☎049/2989232, ⓔMcl.huang@msa.hinet.net. The only YHA-affiliated accommodation in Puli – look for the small YHA sign in the shop below. Comfortable doubles with a/c, cable TV, Internet, shared kitchen and bathroom are excellent value at NT$600, and the owners speak a little English. ❷

Song Yuan Mountain Villa 15-9 Neipu Rd ☎049/2993098. Located just north of the Geographic Centre Monument off Highway 14, this mini resort has spa pools and Japanese-style bedrooms in wooden chalets. It's a bit out of the way but the free bicycles are a definite bonus and the owners will pick you up from the bus station

if you call in advance (English spoken). During the week you can stay in the twelve-person room for just NT$500 (includes breakfast). ❺

Sunrise Private Villa 2-5 Shouchen Rd ☎049/2997997, ⓔpulisunrisevilla@yahoo.com.tw. Upscale homestay just outside Puli, surrounded by paddy fields and a small stream. Rooms are tastefully decorated with views across the plain, and breakfast is served in a bright sunroom – the only problem is its relative isolation, since you'll need your own transport to get here. Discounts of 25 percent during the week. ❼

Tianyi Hotel 89 Sian Rd ☎049/2998100. Centrally located budget hotel with English-speaking staff. Rooms are old and a bit faded, but come with TV and are comfortable enough, though the liberal use of white tiles all over the place is reminiscent of a public convenience. The building survived the 921 Earthquake, though minor damage is still being fixed and the lobby displays photos of the less fortunate structures in town. ❷

The Town

Most of Puli's attractions are located in the north or northwestern corners of town, a long way from the bus station and traditional centre along **Jhongjheng Road**. The areas adjacent to Jhongshan and Sinyi Roads are where you'll find most of the new development. The most appealing sight near the bus station is the Singnan Temple or **Tree God Temple**, a rare example of Taiwanese nature worship, twenty minutes' walk south on the junction of Longsheng and Nanan roads. The small but atmospheric shrine here backs onto a garden containing a large banyan tree wrapped in red ribbon, and ringed by steles.

Tucked away on the western edge of downtown Puli, the **Longnan Museum of Natural Lacquer Ware** at 211 Beiping Street (daily 9am–5pm; free) is the only remaining enterprise in Taiwan making traditional lacquers, so durable the owners claim they'll last for a thousand years. It contains a small display area with a variety of lacquered artefacts, including a 2500-year-old cup, and a shop which sells excellent gifts, but is more popular with groups for its DIY sessions – you can decorate your own chopsticks or bowl with handmade lacquer for NT$100–150.

A short walk west of the Longnan Museum, The **Puli Shaohsing Brewery** at 219 Jhongshan Road Section 3 (daily 8am–5pm; free) is the home of the **Puli Winery Corp**, producer of the famous **Shaohsing** wine originally from the town of the same name in Zhejiang, China. It's one of Puli's most popular attractions and often crawling with tourists stocking up on all manner of wine-related products, from Shaohsing ice cream and cake to Shaohsing sausage, sold on the first floor of the main building. Mildly intoxicating foods apart, there's not a lot to see here: the second floor contains exhibits on the winery and the devastation wrought by the 921 earthquake, but there are few labels in English.

Located on the western fringes of Puli, at the end of Jhongshan Road, **Guang Sing Paper Factory** at 310 Tieshan Road (daily 8.30–5.30pm; free) is also known as the Puli Taiwan Paper Museum, an attractive series of open-air workshops where you can observe the laborious process of making paper by hand. Paper goods are sold in the small gift shop on site and there's an exhibition room at the back, but otherwise it's primarily set up to accommodate school groups that have frequent DIY sessions. A bit further out of town, just off the main highway to Taichung, the **Muh Sheng Museum of Entomology** (daily 8am–5.30pm; NT$160) at 622 Nancun Road is a curious relic of Puli's once highly lucrative butterfly trade. The museum was established by **Yu Mu Sen** (1903-74) who started working for the Japanese as a butterfly catcher in 1919, and contains two floors packed with an assortment of live and dead butterflies, huge moths, insects, frogs and scorpions. Before you reach the main building you can walk through a greenhouse thick with the **Bird-winged Butterfly**, Taiwan's largest species and still endangered in the wild.

The **Taiwan Geographic Center Monument** sits northeast of the town centre on the outskirts of Puli, at the junction of Jhongshan and Sinyi roads. The park at the foot of **Hutoushan** (555m) contains a small monument topped with a thin metal pole and inscribed with the lines "clear water, clear mountain", written by ex-president Chiang Ching-kuo in 1979, but the actual centre point lies on the top of the hill a short but steep walk along the path behind this – a plaque marks the spot first identified by the Japanese in 1906. From here you can continue walking to **Carp Lake** (Liyu Tan) though you'll have to get one of the overpriced lake hotels to call a taxi to return to Puli (NT$250).

Eating

The usual range of cheap Taiwanese snacks is available at the **Bade Road Night Market**, just north of the centre, and at the **Third Market** between Donghua and Nansheng roads, a few minutes south of the bus station: Donghua Road is also lined with cheap "Taiwan buffet" diners. Renai Road is a good place to find **teahouses** and better restaurants, while **Wudun Street** just north of Renai Park is another strip of decent local eateries.

The best place to eat in town is the *Pu-Le Restaurant* at 236 Sinyi Road (☎049/2995096), north of the centre, worth a visit to experience Puli's "flower cuisine": dishes such as osmanthus flowers with shrimps, rose-petal salad and deep-fried wild ginger flowers. Justly renowned for its lavish banquets, simple sets for two start at NT$600, but it's best experienced Chinese style, in a big group (NT$4000–6000 for six).

Chung Tai Chan Monastery

Just a few kilometres north of Puli, the **Chung Tai Chan Monastery** (daily 8am–5pm; free; ☎049/2930215, ℻2930397) is one of the world's most lavish and visually stunning monuments to Chan Buddhism, fusing ancient tradition with contemporary building techniques and materials. Designed by C.Y. Lee (the architect of Taipei 101) at an estimated cost of US$110m, the monastery is worth half a day of exploring. You'll need to fax the temple (preferred over email) seven days in advance to tour the most interesting parts. A taxi here from the centre of Puli should cost around NT$200.

Chan is better known as "Zen" in the West, though you'll see few signs of the more austere Japanese version of the practice here. Chung Tai founder **Grand Master Wei Chueh** began a life of simple meditation in the 1970s in the mountains of Taipei County, and established Chung Tai Chan Monastery in 1987. Today the sometimes controversial figure (Wei Chueh offered vigorous support for the KMT in the March 2004 elections) is head of **Chung Tai World**, a Buddhist order which includes several monasteries and over eighty meditation centres located throughout Taiwan.

The monastery

The monastery complex covers 250,000 sqm dominated by the massive central building with its 37 floors, and surrounded by a series of ancillary halls and statues. The 150-metre central tower is its most distinctive feature, flanked by two sloping dormitory wings and topped by an ornate gold pearl, set on gilded lotus leaves.

From the entrance, it's a short walk to the main building and the **Hall of Heavenly Kings** on the first floor, with its impressive 12m-high guardians and colourful Milefo. They protect the **Great Majesty Hall** where Sakyamuni Buddha is enshrined, the first of three major Buddha statues in the monastery, each representing a different incarnation – this one represents the historical Buddha and the virtue of liberation, carved from Indian red granite and flanked by statues of Buddha's two main disciples. To the right is **Sangharana Hall**, where in typically eclectic Taiwan style, Taoist deity Guan Di is enshrined as temple protector, while to the left you'll find a statue of Indian monk Bodhidharma (or Damo, the 28th Buddhist patriarch and founder of the Chan school) in the **Patriarch Hall**, along with the inscribed religious lineage of the temple's founder, Wei Chueh. To go further you'll need to have arranged a guide in advance – this is highly recommended.

The fifth floor contains the **Great Magnificence Hall** housing a graceful statue of the Rocana Buddha, crafted from white jade and positioned on a real gold-covered 1000 lotus platform – the hand-painted ceiling here is particularly magnificent, in part modelled on the Mogao Caves near Dunhuang in western China. This incarnation represents the "bliss body" of Buddha, or the virtue of wisdom. From here it's customary to walk up to the ninth floor via a series of inclined corridors, eventually leading to the **Great Enlightenment Hall**, a deceptively plain shrine but the most visually striking part of the monastery. Everything here is brilliant white: the ceramic glass walls and floor, the doors, ceiling and even the statue of the Vairocana Buddha, which represents the spiritual or "dharma" body.

The sixteenth floor is usually as far as most tours go: the **Hall of 10,000 Buddhas** contains a seven-storey teak wood pagoda, facing Puli through two giant windows. The walls of the hall are decorated with 20,000 tiny copper Buddha statues, lit by optic fibres to avoid heat build-up. From here you can descend down the pilgrims' staircase, exiting the building between the drum and bell towers along a grand outdoor walkway, or if you're lucky, continue up into the sacred higher levels of the monastery – this will depend on the mood of your guide. The 31st floor is the **Sutra Treasury Pavilion**, containing the monastery's most sacred texts and decorated with soft jade carvings, while the very top, the 37th floor, is known as the **Mani Pearl** and symbolizes perfection. The shell is made of titanium, but the interior of the ball is a simple shrine finished in wood containing a small Buddha statue and is rarely open to visitors.

Elsewhere on the first floor you're free to tour the monastery's extensive collection of modern and ancient **art work** – particularly noted are the stone carvings, many "liberated" from China over the years. The monastery also runs well-respected seven-day **meditation retreats** twice a year (free) – email if you require details, though it's recommended that you have some meditation experience before applying. The only place to **eat** is vegetarian *Shang Yuan*, just outside the main gate of the monastery.

On to Hehuanshan

With the official Central Cross-Island Highway closed indefinitely after the 921 Earthquake, National Road 14 from Puli is the only link between central Taiwan and the east coast. It's a spectacular, winding road through the clouds, and one of Asia's highest, passing the 3000m mark at its uppermost point. **Buses** connect Puli and Wushe, the main village on the route, but you'll have to have a car or scooter to complete the whole journey.

From Puli, the road follows the Mei River valley to **Wushe**, an Atayal village and location of the infamous "incident" of 1930 (see Contexts p.511), though only a small monument in the centre marks the tragedy. Wushe is the best place to eat this side of the mountains (or fill up on petrol). A few kilometres before Wushe, a narrow side road leads around 25km to **Aowanda National Forest Recreation Area**, one of Taiwan's most isolated and atmospheric forest parks, but considering the hassle in getting here (you have to drive back the same way), only worthwhile December to January when the leaves of its magnificent maple trees change colour. Another spur road from Wushe leads to **Lushan Hot Springs**, a pleasant resort area nestled in the upper valley with plenty of hotels, odourless, acidic sodium carbonate waters (40–90°C) and outdoor public pools at the spring source. From Wushe, Route 14 rises steeply into the mountains, past Wanda Reservoir and at 1750m, **Cingjing Farm** (☏049/2802222; NT$100), one of the most popular of Taiwan's veterans' farms, and covered with fruit orchards, cattle fields and flower gardens. The road here is lined with homestays and restaurants taking advantage of the stunning views across the valley, but beyond the farm the road narrows dramatically. The final stretch to **Hehuanshan National Forest Recreation Area**, on the western edge of Taroko National Park, is the most scenic: the road snakes between the higher western (3416m) and eastern peaks of Hehuanshan, the former easily climbed in a couple of hours from the road. The car park opposite the eastern peak is the best place in Taiwan to see snow during the winter, and often very busy. From here the road cuts across the mountains to **Dayuling** where it forks to Taroko Gorge (see p.395) or Lishan (see p.226).

Sun Moon Lake

Hemmed in by verdant mountains in the heart of Taiwan, **SUN MOON LAKE** is the island's largest freshwater body and one of its most renowned tourist destinations. It's popular for good reason – its calm, emerald-green

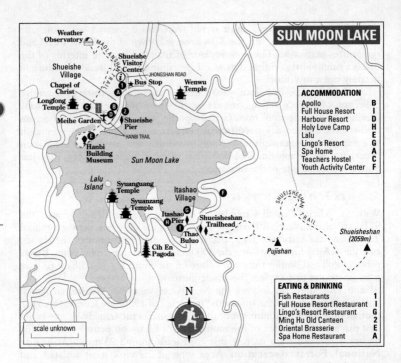

SUN MOON LAKE

Weather Observatory

MAOLANSHAN TRAIL

Shueishe Visitor Center

JHONGSHAN ROAD

Shueishe Village

Bus Stop

Wenwu Temple

Chapel of Christ

Longfong Temple

Meihe Garden

Shueishe Pier

HANBI TRAIL

Hanbi Building Museum

Sun Moon Lake

Lalu Island

Syuanguang Temple

Syuanzang Temple

Itashao Village

Itashao Pier

Shueisheshan Trailhead

Thao Buluo

Cih En Pagoda

SHUEISHESHAN TRAIL

Shueisheshan (2059m)

Pujishan

N

scale unknown

ACCOMMODATION

Apollo	B
Full House Resort	I
Harbour Resort	D
Holy Love Camp	H
Lalu	E
Lingo's Resort	G
Spa Home	A
Teachers Hostel	C
Youth Activity Center	F

EATING & DRINKING

Fish Restaurants	1
Full House Resort Restaurant	I
Lingo's Resort Restaurant	G
Ming Hu Old Canteen	2
Oriental Brasserie	E
Spa Home Restaurant	A

waters reflect the lush tiers of mountains that tower around, creating some of the country's most mesmerizing landscapes. The lake's name is inspired by its distinctive shape, with a rounded main section likened to the sun and a narrow western fringe compared to a crescent moon. Encircling it all is a 33-kilometre road, dotted with fascinating **temples** and picturesque **pavilions**, each offering a unique perspective on the waters below. The lake and its environs are also ideally suited for a variety of **outdoor activities**, from boating and canoeing to cycling and hiking. There are several well-maintained hiking trails, ranging from short, paved nature walks to longer, more rugged paths – including the tough slog up 2059-metre **Shueisheshan**.

The local **climate** is pleasant year-round, with refreshingly cool breezes in summer and moderate temperatures in winter, thanks to the shelter provided by the surrounding mountains. The lake gets its fair share of rain, but the flip side of this is the persistent morning mist and evening fog that make it so atmospheric, casting eerie shadows and creating radiant reflections. Given its abundant beauty, Sun Moon Lake draws large crowds of tourists all summer and on weekends throughout the year, seriously disrupting its serenity and sending hotel rates skyrocketing – weekdays, particularly in winter, are the best time to visit.

Swimming in the lake is allowed on only one day each year, when at least 10,000 yellow-capped Taiwanese take to the waters for the annual **Sun Moon Lake Swimming Carnival**, a three-kilometre cross-lake race that takes place around the Mid-Autumn Festival, usually in September. Held every year since 1983, the race is a spectacular sight, with most competitors using flotation devices and simply trying to reach the other side. Despite the official

Sun Moon Lake	日月潭	*rìyuè tán*
Bus Station	公車站	*gōngchē zhàn*
Shueishe Pier	水社碼頭	*shuǐshè mǎtóu*
Shueishe Village	水社村	*shuǐshè cūn*
Visitor Information Center	遊客中心	*yóukè zhōngxīn*
Accommodation		
Apollo Hotel	鴻賓大飯店	*hóngbīn dàfàndiàn*
Full House Resort Hotel	富豪群渡假民宿	*fùháoqún dùjiā mínsù*
Harbour Resort Hotel	碼頭休閒大飯店	*mǎtóu xiūxián dàfàndiàn*
Holy Love Camp	聖愛營地	*yíngdì*
Lingo's Resort	哲園名流會館	*zhéyuán míngliú huìguǎn*
Spa Home	Spa Home 飯店	*Spa Home fàndiàn*
Teachers Hostel	教師會館	*jiàoshī huìguǎn*
The Lalu	涵碧樓	*hánbì lóu*
Youth Activity Center	青年活動中心	*qīngnián huádòng zhōngxīn*
Sights		
Chapel of Christ	耶穌堂	*yēsū táng*
Hanbi Building Museum	涵碧樓博物館	*hánbì lóu bówùguǎn*
Hanbi Trail	涵碧步道	*hánbì bùdào*
Itashao Village	伊達邵村	*yīdáshào cūn*
Lalu Island	拉魯島	*lālǔ dǎo*
Longfong Temple	龍鳳廟	*lóngfèng miào*
Maolanshan Trail	貓蘭山步道	*māolánshān bùdào*
Meihe Garden	梅荷園	*méihé gōngyuán*
Pujishan	卜吉山	*bǔjíshān*
Shueisheshan	水社山	*shuǐshèshān*
Shueisheshan Trail	水社山步道	*shuǐshèshān bùdào*
Syuanguang Temple	玄光寺	*xuánguāng sì*
Syuanzang Temple	玄奘寺	*xuánzàng sì*
Thao Buluo	邵部落	*shào bùluò*
Cih En Pagoda	慈恩塔	*cí ēn tǎ*
Weather Observatory	氣象站	*qìxiàng zhàn*
Wenwu Temple	文武廟	*wénwǔ miào*
Eating and drinking		
Fish Restaurants	魚鮮餐廳	*yúxiān cāntīng*
Full House Resort Hotel Restaurant	富豪群渡假民宿餐廳	*fùháoqún dùjiā mínsù cāntīng*
Lingo's Resort Restaurant	哲園名流會館湖畔餐廳	*zhéyuán míngliú huìguǎn húpàn cāntīng*
Ming Hu Old Canteen	明湖老餐廳	*mínghú lǎo cāntīng*
Oriental Brasserie	東方餐廳	*dōngfāng cāntīng*
Spa Home Restaurant	Spa Home 餐廳	*Spa Home cāntīng*

prohibition on swimming, the rule is generally not enforced and it's easy to find suitable places for a dip.

The lake is also the ancestral home of the **Thao** (pronounced "Shao", meaning "people"), Taiwan's tenth and smallest officially recognized aboriginal tribe (see Contexts p.523). Of the estimated 540 people of Thao descent left in Taiwan, about three hundred live near the lake, and they are noted for the percussive **Pestle Music Festival** (see Basics p.53) they hold each year around the time of the Mid-Autumn Festival.

Some history

Until the early twentieth century, the lake was a shallow marsh called **Shueisha-lian**, or "where water meets sand". In 1919, the Japanese colonial administration started work on a **dam** and a system of irrigation channels to divert water into the lake for hydroelectric power generation, finally flooding the area in 1934 – and destroying the last traditional Thao community that had clung to the slopes of pyramid-shaped **Lalu Island** in the marsh's centre. Those inhabitants were forced to move to the lake's south side, into a village that was then called Bujishe and known as Dehuashe after 1945; today it's a thriving tourist village named Itashao (see p.281).

The railway and roads that had been built to transport materials for the dam's construction opened the area to further development, and after the Japanese occupation ended in 1945 the construction of a number of **cultural sights** around the lake commenced. **Chiang Kai-shek** made the lake his favoured summer retreat, spurring further cultural development that continued into the 1970s. The 921 earthquake severely damaged much of the lakeside infrastructure, levelling hotels and restaurants and rendering some hiking trails temporarily impassable. However, thanks to a concerted reconstruction campaign, the tourist villages on the lake's northern and southern shores have now surpassed their former grandeur and all the major trails have been repaired.

Arrival, orientation and information

Sun Moon Lake is easily accessed by **bus** from several cities. There are two direct buses daily from **Taichung** (2hr; NT$198), but if there is a long wait for these it's quicker to catch one of the hourly buses to **Puli** (1hr 20min; NT$135) and then get one of the regular buses from there to the lake (last one departs at 7pm; 30min; NT$51). The Fengrong Bus Co in **Shueili** has hourly direct bus service (30min; NT$42) and Green Transit has an hourly express bus from **Taipei** (3hr 30min; NT$300).

All buses to Sun Moon Lake stop in the main tourist centre of **Shueishe Village**, on the lake's northwest side, and if you don't have your own transport this is the best place to base yourself. In addition to onward transport links, it has the widest selection of hotels and restaurants and the **Shueishe visitor center** (9am–5.30pm; ☎049/2855597) at 163 Jhongshan Rd, where you can get an English map and see a short English-language film about the area. On the lake's southeast side is a slightly quieter tourist centre, **Itashao Village**, which has some very nice hotels and restaurants and is adjacent to the main **Thao community** and the trailhead for Shueisheshan. While it's less convenient if you don't have your own transport, you can still use the **tourist boats** that shuttle passengers between Shueishe and Itashao villages. Bring cash with you – while there is an **ATM** just outside the post office in Shueishe Village, it only accepts Taiwanese bank cards.

Lake tours and transport

On weekends regular round-the-lake **tourist buses** leave from Shueishe Village, stopping at the major sights; you can choose between the full circuit (NT$80) or a shorter tour around the east side of the lake, culminating at the Syuangang Temple (NT$21). Ask for the latest schedule at the Shueishe visitor center. For greater flexibility, you can hire a **taxi** in Shueishe Village (NT$400 to Itashao Village; NT$1200 for three-hour tour): the best place to catch one is near the bus stop on Jhongshan Road. For closer views of the lake, take one of the 45-minute motor **boat tours** that depart regularly from both Shueishe and Itashao piers. Solo travellers can join these for NT$300, but you must wait until the boat is full; groups of up to five people can charter a boat tour for NT$1500. In addition, **rowboats** for two people can be rented at both piers for NT$200 an hour. Foreigners can rent **scooters** at *Helio* (℡049/2850368; NT$400–500 per day), on Jhongshan Road next to the Shueishe visitor center, though you must have an international driver's licence. An increasingly popular means of getting round the lake is by **bicycle**, and a few cycling paths have been built just off the main road. The entire loop around the lake can make for a full day's ride if you stop at most of the sights, and on weekdays – when vehicular traffic is lighter – this can be a most enjoyable way to experience the lake. *Helio* also rents bicycles (NT$250 per day), as does the *Youth Activity Center* (see p.280) on the lake's southeast side, a few kilometres northeast of Itashao Village.

Accommodation

Sun Moon Lake has a broad range of **accommodation**, from the recently rebuilt lakeside hotels in Shueishe Village to some older standards near Itashao Village's waterfront. There also are several other options scattered around the lake, ranging from a rustic water-sports retreat to Taiwan's grandest luxury hotel, *The Lalu*. The most appealing places in Shueishe Village face the lake along the red brick Minsheng Road, near the Shueishe Pier. All of these have lake-view rooms with balconies, opening up splendid vistas of the lake and its soaring backdrop, Shueisheshan. **Room rates** rise dramatically during summer, as well as weekends and public holidays, making it expensive to visit at these times. The best deals can be had on winter weekdays, when you'll have the entire lake to yourself.

Shueishe Village

Apollo Hotel 3 Minsheng Rd ℡049/2855381. An attractive lakeside hotel, the *Apollo* has friendly staff, spotlessly clean rooms and small balconies affording some of the finest lake and mountain views. ⑤

Harbour Resort 11 Minsheng Rd ℡049/2855143. Next to the pier entrance, the *Harbour Resort* has bright, airy balcony rooms with great lake views and is priced similarly to the *Apollo*. ⑤

Spa Home 95 Jhongshan Rd ℡049/2855166, ⓦwww.spahome.com.tw. Near the junction of Jhongshan and Minsheng roads, this lakefront hotel caters to couples and only has doubles. Rooms facing the lake have balconies, but the hotel's highlight is its spa, and rates include a massage package. ⑧

Teachers Hostel 136 Jhongsing Rd ℡049/2855991. Up the hill behind the Chapel of Christ, the *Teachers* is more a hotel than a hostel, with spacious rooms, some featuring balconies overlooking the lake's less atmospheric western section. There are only twin rooms here, no doubles. ⑤

The Lalu 142 Jhongsing Rd ℡049/2855311, ⓦwww.thelalu.com.tw. Widely considered Taiwan's top luxury hotel, this "six-star" resort – named after the tiny island in the middle of the lake – is unabashedly devoted to pure indulgence. Easily the country's most expensive hotel, rack rates

range from NT$13,800 for a one-bedroom suite to NT$65,000 for the presidential suite. Their 35 one-bedroom suites have large living and bathing areas, with twenty-square-metre balconies commanding superb lake views. These vistas are precisely what the hotel is designed to preserve and even enhance, and all rooms feature an open construction, with giant sliding glass doors that open onto the lake and wood and stone interiors whose soft tones blend with the area's natural colours. Designed by Australian architect Kerry Hill, *The Lalu's* sleek layout – with an "infinity pool" whose waters seem to spill straight into the lake - has inspired a small boutique hotel movement in Taiwan. Another point of pride is its spa, where you can soak in flower-petal filled perfume baths or have a massage while looking out at the lake. There is also a fitness room, a teahouse and three restaurants, and discounted packages including breakfast and afternoon tea are sometimes available from Sundays to Thursdays. ⑨

Itashao Village

Full House Resort 8 Shueishe St ℡049/2850307, ⓦwww.fhsml.idv.tw. In a two-storey wooden house fronted by a peaceful garden café, the *Full House* has a slightly offbeat charm, its halls and room interiors decorated with portraits painted by the owner's wife. ⑦

Lingo's Resort 31 Shueishe St ℡049/2850055, ⓦwww.sunmoonlake.club.tw. Before *The Lalu* was built, this was the lake's top hotel, and its gorgeous lake-view rooms are thoughtfully designed, their Canadian maple-wood interiors blending nicely with the water's warm tones. Once the first port of call for domestic and foreign dignitaries – whose photos adorn the lobby walls – *Lingo's* amenities include a swimming pool, sauna, fitness room, pool tables and even a mahjong room. **❽**

Other lakeside spots

Holy Love Camp 261-10 Jhongjheng Rd ☏049/2850202, ☏04/22059715. This rustic lakeside retreat, tucked in a secluded cove a few kilometres northwest of Itashao Village, is a haven of water sports in summer, with canoeing, pedal-boating and windsurfing the main activities. The camp is accessed via a steep trail off the main

road, but the path is hard to spot and there is no parking, so call in advance to arrange a boat pick-up in Shueishe or Itashao. Single or multi-night packages including pick-up, meals and dorm-room accommodation must be made by phone with Priest An, the American who runs the camp. **❷**

Youth Activity Center 101 Jhongjheng Rd ☏049/2850070, ⓦwww.cyh.org.tw. A few kilo-metres northeast of Itashao Village, just off the main road around the lake, this hotel is popular with school groups and can be very noisy at times. However, its large, clean rooms – some Japanese-style – are great value, especially for groups, and the center rents fair-quality bicycles (NT$250 per day). The center also manages the nearby lakeside campsite, which has showers and toilets, but you must have your own tent (NT$150 per tent). **❹**

Shueishe Village and around

On the western edge of Shueishe Village are several noteworthy sights, many offering serene lake views. The set of stone steps just west of the Shueishe Pier climb to the **Meihe (Plum and Lotus) Garden**, a covered viewpoint named after the two symbols of the Taiwanese military police, who had a guard post here when the lake was Chiang Kai-shek's summer retreat. Further up the steps behind Meihe Garden is the **Chapel of Christ**, built in the 1970s for the exclusive use of Chiang and his wife, whose private residence (known as the "Hanbi Building") then occupied the hilltop just west of here, where *The Lalu* hotel now stands. Near *The Lalu's* main entrance is the **Hanbi Building Museum** (Sat–Sun 8am–5pm; free), with a fascinating collection of black-and-white photos of Chiang and a host of foreign luminaries who visited him at his lake retreat. Among the most famous are the Shah of Iran, former US President Franklin Roosevelt and Singapore's first Prime Minister, Lee Kuan Yew. There are also old photos of the lake that predate the dam's construction, giving a glimpse of what the triangular-shaped Lalu Island looked like before it was mostly submerged. All photos are labelled in English, and *The Lalu* staff will open the museum for its guests during the week upon request.

Back at the hill's base, leading west from the Meihe Garden, is the gentle **Hanbi Hiking Trail**, which makes a 1.5-kilometre loop of the shoreline surrounding the hill. A few hundred metres down the path is a **pavilion** where Chiang used to sit above a watchful armed guard – their fortified **lookout post** is still underneath the pavilion.

Around Shueishe Village

A short walk west of Shueishe Village is the **Longfong (Dragon Phoenix) Temple**, known for the **Matchmaker** statue that sits in a separate shrine just outside the entrance. The statue – Taiwan's largest Matchmaker image – was originally placed on Lalu Island in a small shrine built in the 1960s, and was a fashionable place for group weddings on National Day. After the 921 earthquake, however, it was removed from the island and taken to its less contentious location. It's still extremely popular with Taiwanese couples (see Contexts p.532). Near here is the beginning of the **Maolanshan Trail**, actually a 3km paved road that winds up the mountainside, through lovely terraces of Assam black tea bushes, to a **weather observatory** that the Japanese built on the mountaintop in 1940. Just behind the observatory you can look across a sprawling flood plain to the 1392m **Jijidashan**, whose sides were ripped apart during the 921 earthquake.

Several kilometres east of Shueishe Village, on a hill overlooking the lake's northeastern shore, is the imposing **Wenwu Temple**, dedicated primarily to learning and popular with students who come here to pray for guidance during important examinations. In the rear hall is a tablet commemorating **Confucius**, in front of which is a table covered by candle jars filled with red-paper wishes written by students. The temple's other highly venerated deity is **Guan Di** (the red-faced one in the main hall), worshipped here for his scholarly achievements (see Contexts p.529). The platform to the rear of the temple is an atmospheric place to watch the sun set over the colourful roof tiles.

Lalu Island

Tiny **Lalu Island**, just off one of the lake's southern banks, is the most sacred site of the indigenous Thao people, who believe the spirits of their ancestors dwell here. Indeed, the last traditional Thao community thrived here until 1934, when the occupying Japanese flooded the marsh from which it rose, submerging all but its uppermost point. The Japanese colonizers called it Jade Island, and after the occupation ended it was again renamed – this time by the Chinese – who dubbed it **Guanghua (Retrocession) Island**. For decades, the island served the purposes of tourism, hosting a shrine containing Taiwan's largest Matchmaker statue and at times fielding group weddings. Such development drew the ire of the Thao, who blame the felling of several of the island's trees that they considered holy for the decrease in their population. After the 921 earthquake, however, there was considerable political pressure for the island to be returned to the Thao, and in 2000 it was renamed Lalu in accordance with tribal tradition. Its shores are now protected, and only the few remaining Thao are allowed to set foot on it – visitors arriving on boat tours of the lake must disembark on a **floating pier** that encircles the island in the shape of a *bagua* (an octagon divided into eight trigrams).

Itashao Village and around

On the lake's southern fringe is **Itashao Village**, the area's second-biggest tourist centre, which thrives mostly on the dying remnants of Thao culture, with numerous shops selling traditional Thao handicrafts and items associated with the tribe's folklore. The main village is now eighty percent ethnic Chinese, and the dwindling Thao population of about three hundred remains largely segregated, tucked away behind all the tourist shops in a collection of corrugated iron huts. This **makeshift settlement** was set up to house the Thao who had lost their homes in the 921 earthquake, and though it was meant to be temporary, there still has been no agreement on where a permanent Thao village should be located. Today the only way to be sure of meeting true Thao people is to wander around this deprived area, and though the people you'll meet will be friendly you might find the experience a bit voyeuristic. Just behind the settlement is the beginning of the **Shueisheshan Trail** (see p.282).

Around Itashao Village

Several kilometres northwest of Itashao Village are two of Sun Moon Lake's most interesting sites, a pair of temples with common histories. The closest to Itashao is the **Syuanzang Temple**, named after **Xuan Zang** – China's most famous monk – whose travels in India formed the basis of the classic tale *Journey to the West*. The temple was built to house precious **religious relics** that many Buddhists believe are among Asia's most sacred, including what they claim are fragments of the remains of Xuan Zang and even of the **Sakyamuni Buddha**. These relics are enshrined in two miniature gold pagodas in the temple's main hall, with the jewel-encrusted middle pagoda holding several tiny, hardened kernels that some Buddhists believe came from Sakyamuni's ashes. The small pagoda on the right contains what some Buddhists claim is a **sliver** from Xuan Zang's skull – the sliver is said to have been looted from Nanjing by the Japanese during the Sino-Japanese War and taken to a temple in Saitama prefecture. In 1955, the fragment was returned to Chiang Kai-shek's government, and in 1958 it was moved into the newly built **Syuanguang Temple** closer to the lakeshore. This temple, 2.5km northwest of the Syuanzang Temple, occupies a tranquil position overlooking Lalu Island. However, a few years after the skull sliver was moved here, the temple was deemed too small and the relic was transferred to its present location in 1965.

Crowning the hill behind the Syuanzang Temple is the nine-tiered **Cih En (Filial Affection) Pagoda**, which Chiang had built in memory of his mother in 1971. One of the lake's major landmarks, the pagoda is accessed via a 700-metre paved pathway and commands outstanding views. The 46m-high pagoda's base is at an elevation of 954m, making the top exactly 1000m above sea level. From this point, one can look down on the Syuanzang Temple, Lalu Island and across the lake to *The Lalu* hotel, all three of which are on the same axis – most auspicious for *feng shui* believers. Ringing the **giant bell** that hangs inside the top of the pagoda is considered requisite for Taiwanese tourists.

Shueisheshan Trail

A highlight of a visit to Sun Moon Lake is the challenging hike to the top of **Shueisheshan** (2059m), by far the area's tallest mountain, the top of which provides dizzying **panoramas** of the lake and its environs that could only be beaten from a helicopter. The area's longest and most difficult hike, the **Shueisheshan Trail** winds its way up two mountains, first crossing over the densely forested **Pujishan** on its way to the prize, and is really only suited for experienced, fit hikers – the mostly dirt path is very steep in places, and the return journey should take most reasonably conditioned walkers a maximum of seven hours to complete (though it can be done in as little as five hours).

According to Thao legend, Pujishan and Shueisheshan are incarnations of two **Thao warriors**, and, as such, they are now considered guardians of the lake. For nature lovers, the trail is a real treat, offering the chance to walk through three distinct **forests** – from bamboo to hardwood to rhododendron – in an environment that has yet to be impacted heavily by tourism. There are no trail signs in English, and most of the way is flagged only with **coloured ribbons** tied to tree branches by members of domestic hiking clubs. As such, the hike should only be attempted in clear weather, and it's a good idea to ask about trail conditions in the Shueishe visitor center before you set out.

The **trail** starts at the edge of the Thao settlement behind Itashao Village, and is marked by a large stone monument inscribed with the word "Thao" in English. It begins with wide stone steps which lead several hundred metres to a fork with a Chinese sign: from here you can go left or right, as this first part of the trail is a loop. Take the left-hand path for low-lying views of the lake, and carry on up the hill until the trail turns right and flattens out. At this point, look to the left for a narrow **earthen path** hacked into the forest – the entrance is marked by dozens of hiking club ribbons. This trail is the only one that goes to the top of Shueisheshan, and if you start descending the other side of the loop you've missed the turnoff.

The first few kilometres of the dirt path are thrilling, as it snakes through a thick **bamboo forest** on the slopes of Pujishan, in some places leaving just enough room to squeeze between trees: stick to the ribbons here and you can't go wrong. After a short climb, the trail drops down the back side of Pujishan before ascending again, this time up Shueisheshan itself. Dense groves of green bamboo finally give way to a hardwood forest, at the top of which is a clearing with a **metal shack**; from here the lake views give a foretaste of what is to come. Just past the shack is a very steep section of about 1km through thick rhododendron groves. After this you must shimmy over a series of big **quartz boulders** to reach the top, from where you can see the entire lake and a wide flood plain beyond, as well as the nearby city of Puli. On the way back down, when you come off the narrow dirt path and hit the loop trail, turn left to descend the loop's other side.

Eating and drinking

There are plenty of **restaurants** in Shueishe and Itashao villages, many of them serving standard Chinese fare. Along Jhongshan Road in Shueishe, between the bus stop and the visitor center, are several fish restaurants, although these cater mostly to large groups and can be quite expensive. Individual travellers would do better to head straight to Shueishe's Minsheng Road, where there are a few small establishments with basics such as fried rice and noodles. There is a dearth of pubs in both villages, so for a **drink** your best bet is to try one of the swankier hotels or just order a beer in one of the restaurants.

Shueishe Village

Ming Hu Old Canteen 15 Minsheng Rd. This unassuming place serves up tasty Chinese staples such as fried rice and noodles, and its friendly staff can speak some English.

Oriental Brasserie 142 Jhongsing Rd ☏049/2855311. One of *The Lalu*'s three restaurants, the *Oriental* is open to non-guests and features contemporary Western cuisine throughout the week. Its Western and Asian Sunday lunch buffet (11.30am–2.30pm) is popular.

Spa Home Restaurant 95 Jhongshan Rd. More upmarket than the places on Minsheng Rd, this restaurant has a big balcony with good lake views and specializes in Western dishes, with delicious pastas and steaks.

Itashao Village

Full House Resort Hotel Restaurant 8 Shueishe St ☏049/2850307. This trendy establishment prides itself on Chinese-Western fusion dishes made completely from local ingredients. Guests can eat in the first-floor restaurant or the garden café.

Lingo's Resort Restaurant 31 Shueishe St ☏049/2850055. Popular in the evenings, *Lingo's* has a relaxing lakeside setting and an extensive menu of Chinese and Western fare. Its fresh fish dishes are the highlight, especially the steamed lake trout. The waterfront café next to the hotel's fishing pier serves alcoholic beverages and is an atmospheric spot for a drink.

Chiayi and around

Backed by the tantalizing peaks of Taiwan's mighty central mountain ranges, **CHIAYI** is the gateway to the Alishan National Scenic Area and Yushan National Park, as well as one of the country's most famous Mazu temples at Beigang. Just north of the Tropic of Cancer, it also marks the beginning of Taiwan's tropical south, and as one of the island's earliest cities, has plenty of historic temples and lively markets tucked in between the usual neon and

EATING & DRINKING

American Pie	8
Calgary Pub	1
En Dian Cookies	4
Five Cent Driftwood House	6
Golden Eagle Pub &	
Restaurant	2
Jhu Cha Lou	7
Penshuei Turkey Rice	3
Wenhua Night Market	5

ACCOMMODATION

Chinatrust Hotel	A
Guo Bao Hotel	C
Hotel Country	E
Jiaxin Hotel	D
Tongyi Hotel	B

concrete. Adding to its appeal, Chiayi's artistic legacy includes some of the country's most famous **painters** and **koji pottery** masters.

Some history

Immigrant farmers from Fujian established the first settlement in the area in 1621, though the city formally dates its creation from 1704 when the county government was moved here and the first wooden city walls were constructed. The area was originally called **Jhuluoshan**, a transliteration of *Tirosen*, a **Hoanya** word (one of the *pingpu* tribes, see p.519). Following the Lin Shuangwen Rebellion of 1787–89, Emperor Qianlong renamed the town Chiayi, an honorific title meaning "praising them for their loyalty" to reward the inhabitants for resisting the rebels. During the Japanese occupation, it gained the more creative epithet **"city of painting"** when masters such as Wu Meiling and Chen Cheng-po spearheaded the first **Nativist** art movement. With a population of around 270,000 Chiayi is now the largest city and commercial centre of Chiayi County, though the county government is located in Taibao, 15km to the west.

Arrival, orientation and information

Chiayi Airport is just over 6km south of the city near the village of Shueishang – it's best to take a taxi into the centre (NT$300) as bus times are erratic. All trains (including the Alishan Forest Railway) stop at the main **train station,** located on the western side of the city centre – all the major **bus stations** are

Chiayi	嘉義	jiāyì
Chiayi Airport	嘉義航空站	jiāyì hángkōng zhàn
Chiayi Transport Co Bus Station	嘉義公車總站	jiāyì gōng chē zǒngzhàn
Chiayi County Bus Station	嘉義客運總站	jiāyì kèyùn zǒngzhàn
Chiayi Train Station	嘉義火車站	jiāyì huǒchēzhàn
Chiayi High-Speed Rail Station	高鐵嘉義站 (太保)	gāotiě jiāyì zhàn (tàibǎo)

Accommodation		
Chinatrust Hotel	中信大飯店	zhōngxìn dàfàndiàn
Hotel Country	國園大飯店	guóyuán dàfàndiàn
Jiaxin Hotel	嘉新大飯店	jiāxīn dàfàndiàn
Tongyi Hotel	統一大飯店	tǒngyī dàfàndiàn

The City		
Beiyu Temple	北嶽宮	běi yù gōng
Chenghuang Temple	城隍廟	chénghuáng miào
Chiayi Park	嘉義公園	jiāyì gōngyuán
Cultural Center	文化中心	wénhuà zhōngxīn
Koji Pottery Exhibition Room	交趾陶館	jiāozhǐ táoguǎn
Museum of Chiayi City	嘉義市立博物館	jiāyìshì lì bówùguǎn
2-28 Memorial Park	二二八紀念公園	èrèrbā jìniàn gōngyuán

Eating and drinking		
Calgary Pub	卡加利美式餐飲	kǎjiālì měishì cānyǐn
En Dian Cookies	恩典酥本舖	ēndiǎnsū běnpù
Five Cent Driftwood House	伍角船板	wǔ jiǎo chúanbǎn
Jhu Cha Lou	竹居茶館	zhújū cháguǎn
Penshuei Turkey Rice	噴水火雞飯	pēnshuǐ huǒjīfàn

nearby. Beimen Train Station, where most of the tickets for the Alishan railway are sold (see p.295) is 1.5km further north. Chiayi's **High-Speed Rail** Station is inconveniently located near Taibao.

Most hotels and places to eat are on Jhongshan Road and the neighbouring streets that stem from the train station, and are easily accessible by foot. The most important temples are further east and require more time if walking. **Taxis** are abundant in the city centre, and the standard fare is about NT$100 for all destinations within the city. You can hire **scooters** from shops on the corner of Renai and Jhongshan Roads, just opposite the station (50cc is NT$200 for 24hr). It's a good way to explore the surrounding area and relatively hassle-free for foreigners – all you'll need is a passport and any driving licence.

There is a **visitor information center** (⊺05/2256649, ⓦ www.cyhg.gov .tw) with brochures and maps at the train station, to the left just after the exit. For information on festivals check the Chiayi City Cultural Affairs Bureau website at ⓦ www.cabcy.gov.tw. **Banks** are clustered at the main traffic circle on Jhongshan Road. For **Internet access**, try the 24-hour café close to the train station, at the corner of Sinrong and Yanping roads. Further out is the 24-hour *Chicken Internet Café* (NT$15 per hour) at 65 Tiyu Road, near the new sports stadium. Chiayi's main **police station** is at 195 Jhongshan Road (office daily 8am–midday & 1.30–5.30pm; ⊺05/2274454), with English speakers more likely at the foreign affairs division (⊺05/2220772 ext 2122). The main **post office** is at 107 Jhongshan Road in the eastern part of the city, but there's a branch near the station at 647 Jhongjheng Road.

Chiayi Airport has nine daily flights to Taipei, and at least one a day to Magong and Kinmen, all operated by Uni Air (☎052862363). Regular **express trains** connect the city to Taipei (NT$600) and Kaohsiung (NT$248), while Chiayi is also is the starting point for the **Alishan Forest Railway** (see p.297), a scenic way to reach the Alishan Forest Recreation Area.

Long-distance bus companies are congregated near the train station, along Linsen West Road: Kuo Kuang, to the left as you exit the station, has direct buses to **Taichung** and **Taipei** (every 30min, 6am–10pm). Next door, Ho-Hsin has regular buses south to **Tainan** and **Kaohsiung**. The Chiayi County Bus Station, to the right as you exit the train station, has daily buses to **Alishan** and usually three a day to Dabang (at 8am, noon and 4pm). The Chiayi Transport Co Bus Station further along Jhongshan Road has regular services to Guanzihling Hot Springs (NT$74), Beigang (NT$58), Singang (NT$42), Yanshuei (NT$88) and **Budai** (NT$75) – the latter terminates at the Penghu ferry terminal in summer. Buses to Budai depart at 8.10am, 9am and at irregular times thereafter – it takes about an hour.

Accommodation

Chiayi has a wide range of **accommodation** catering both to budget and business travellers. Most of the budget options are near the train station on Jhongjheng Road.

Chinatrust Hotel 257 Wenhua Rd ☎05/2292233, ⓦwww.chinatrust-hotel.com. Chiayi's best and most expensive hotel, set in an anonymous white modern building in the centre of town. Comfortable, five-star rooms with business centre, fitness room and free shuttle bus to the airport. **❼**

Hotel Country 678 Guangcai Road ☎05/2236336, ⓦwww.country-hotel.58168.net. Decent budget hotel, within walking distance of the station, with friendly staff and a car park in the basement. Rooms are plain but clean and comfortable. **❸**

Jiaxin Hotel 687 Jhongjheng Rd ☎05/2222280. Simple but adequate budget hotel not far from the station, with aging but reasonably clean rooms – all come with TVs and hand-held showers, though the cheapest rooms (NT$500) are very small. **❷**

Tongyi Hotel 720 Jhongjheng Rd ☎05/2252685. Cleaner and a bit smarter than some of the other budget hotels in the area, with newly renovated rooms and decent showers, but still rather basic. **❷**

The City

Chiayi's commercial heart lies along Jhongshan Road east of the train station, but the older parts of the city lie further to the southeast. The city's most important and busiest shrine is **Chenghuang Temple** (daily 5am–9.30pm), on the corner of Wufong and Guanghua roads, around 1.5km from the station and 500m from the Central Fountain in the heart of the city. Established in 1715 to worship Chiayi's City God, the current buildings date from 1940. The most valuable object inside the **Main Hall** is the plaque above the central altar which reads "Protector of Taiwan and the Ocean", awarded to the temple by Emperor Guangxu in 1887 in recognition of the great fame the City God had acquired. Take a look at the ceiling – the woodcarvings here and on the main pillars are exquisite, and the *koji* pottery figures set into the walls are equally renowned. The City God's birthday is celebrated on Lunar August 2.

Another 1.5km east, at the end of Jhongshan Road, **Chiayi Park** is the city's largest green space. The eastern part of the park was once a Japanese Shinto shrine built in 1943 – two of its elegant cypress wood temple buildings have been preserved and now function as the **Chiayi Historical Relics Museum**

(Wed–Sun 9am–noon & 1.30–5pm; free) which documents various aspects of Chiayi's history – although there is a small English leaflet available, the exhibits are labelled in Chinese only. The **Chiayi Tower** (daily 7am–8pm; NT$20), just beyond here, has good views of the city.

Back towards the train station and north of Jhongshan Road at 455 Mincyuan Road is the **Beiyu Temple** (North Hell Temple), dedicated to **Dizang Wang**, confusingly known as the King of Hell (see Contexts, p.532). Established in 1697, the current structure was restored in the 1970s. The temple's most unusual feature is its **seven-storey tower**, in which the original deity is still preserved.

North of the station

Twenty minutes' walk northeast of the train station, along Linsen West Road and across Alishan Rail Park, the **Museum of Chiayi City** (Wed–Sun 9am–noon & 1.30–5pm; free) is a lavish, modern facility containing well-presented exhibitions on geology, fossils and art, frustratingly labelled in Chinese only, but still the best place to view Chiayi's striking **stone monkeys** (second floor). Local sculptor Zhan Long started the fad in 1973, when he began to carve monkeys from fossilized rocks found in the Pachong River, and the sculptures have since become the city's most celebrated motif. The third floor is a good introduction to the city's most famous artist, **Chen Cheng-po** (1895-1947), who was killed during the 2-28 massacres in 1947. A statue of Chen sits outside the **Cultural Center** (Wed–Sun 9am–noon & 1.30–5pm; free), the older building opposite the museum and home to a library and several galleries exhibiting the work of contemporary local artists. The most interesting part of the centre, however, lies in the basement: the **Koji Pottery Exhibition Room** is a small but excellent introduction to *koji*, crammed with stunning examples of the craft. There are no English captions but even if there's no guide available it's hard not to be impressed – Kao Chi-ming's exquisite **dragon plate** is a must-see. At the weekends stalls sell *koji* outside the main entrance.

Eating and drinking

The centre of Chiayi is packed with places to eat, with street stalls lining Renai Road just across from the train station. The city's main **night market** is on

---

Koji pottery

Chiayi has been associated with **koji pottery** (also known as "Cochin") since the nineteenth century. An elaborate multicoloured style of ceramics, it was used extensively in temples to create detailed tableaux from famous Chinese stories or operas. The craft originated in southern China, evolving from the tri-colour pottery of the Tang dynasty (618–906) – scholars believe the name "koji" is the transliteration of a Taiwanese name referring to this region. Today, Taiwan is the best place to see examples of the craft since most pieces in China were destroyed during the Cultural Revolution. **Yeh Wang** (1826–1889), a master craftsman born in Chiayi, founded the Taiwanese branch of the industry, and though his work is rare these days, you can still see some of his original figures in Ciji Temple in Syuejia near Tainan (see p.333). The Japanese recognized the importance of the city when they renamed *koji*, **Chiayi-yaki**, which means "Chiayi-made ceramics" and Chiayi is still home to numerous *koji* craftsmen – in addition to its vibrant colours, *koji* is unique in that everything is handmade. **Lin Tzai-hsing** is reckoned to be the national *koji* master, and though he hails from Chiayi he now teaches in Taipei. **Kao Chi-ming** is Chiayi's most famous *koji* artist, occasionally running workshops at the Koji Pottery Exhibition Room.

Wenhua Road, with the busiest concentration of stalls south of Jhongshan Road and north of Cyueyang Road. The city isn't known for its nightlife, but there are a few pubs, all serving Western meals and snack food.

American Pie 123 Singye W Rd ☎05/2837981. Cosy pub popular with expats, serving the cheapest beer in town as well as decent nachos, burgers, chicken sandwiches and steaks. Usually open 5pm till midnight, but hours are irregular, so ring first. Closed Mon.

Calgary Pub Lane 19, 351 Guohua St ☎05/2270513. The town's main watering hole, attracting a mix of locals and expats, opened in 1998 but occupying a Japanese-era wooden building that's more than ninety years old. Cheap beers complemented by burgers, pizzas and Mexican food. The pub is along a narrow lane off Linsen West Road, just before Guohua St, and across the rail tracks. Daily 6pm–2am.

En Dian Cookies 123 Minguo Rd. "Square cookies" are a Chiayi specialty, and this fifty-year-old shop is the city's most famous place to buy them – the butter cookies are considered the most authentic. You can pick up a small packet for NT$45. Daily 9am–8pm.

Five Cent Driftwood House 844 Daya Rd Sec 1. One of three striking theme restaurants owned by a local artist, decorated with a creative mixture of battered driftwood, stone sculptures, Chinese antiques, glass, metal, and thick, wooden tables and chairs. The menu (Chinese-only) has just ten items – the pork is recommended (NT$280). Daily 10am–midnight.

Golden Eagle Pub & Restaurant 243 Ciming Rd. Homely pub and restaurant with a British theme, close to Chiayi Park. Huge selection of over 70 beers complements the extensive menu of Western and Asian comfort food – the all-day breakfasts (NT$195), burgers (NT$180) and steaks (NT$520) are excellent. Mon–Fri 11am–2pm, 5pm–2am, Sat–Sun 11am–2am.

Jhu Cha Lou 275 Daya Rd Sec 2. Atmospheric classical-style Chinese teahouse, with goldfish ponds, wooden pavilions and cosy traditional booths (pots of tea from NT$200). It's a long way from the train station on the eastern side of the city, so you'll need to take a taxi. Open 24hrs.

Penshuei Turkey Rice 325 Jhongshan Rd. Oldest restaurant serving Chiayi's signature specialty, turkey rice. The dish can be found all over the city, but this no-nonsense place is an old favourite with locals and tourists alike, centrally located near the Central Fountain (*penshui*) traffic circle. Daily 8.30am–10pm.

Around Chiayi

The main attractions around Chiayi are the hot springs at **Guanzihling** and the important temple at **Beigang**, although there are a few other low-key sights if you have more time. Those interested in the history of the region should make a quick stop at **Wu Feng Temple** (daily 8am–5.30pm), a shrine and small museum dedicated to the eponymous hero (see box p.289). It's on the

Around Chiayi

Bantianyan Zi Yun Temple	紫雲寺	*zǐyún sì*
Bi Yun Temple	碧雲寺	*bìyún sì*
Fongtian Temple	奉天宮	*fèngtiān gōng*
Guanzihling	關仔嶺	*guānzǐlíng*
Huoshan Da Sian Temple	火山大仙寺	*huǒshān dàxiān sì*
Jing Leh Hotel	靜樂館	*jìnglèguǎn*
Mutsun Spring	沐春溫泉養生會館	*mùchūn wēnquán yǎngshēng huìguǎn*
Red Leaf Park	紅葉公園	*hóngyè gōngyuán*
Toong Mao Spa Resort	統茂溫泉會館	*tǒngmào wēnquán huìguǎn*
Singang	新港	*xīngǎng*
Tropic of Cancer Monument	北回歸線標誌	*běihuí guīxiàn biāozhì*
Water Fire Cave	水火洞	*shuǐhuǒ dòng*
Wu Feng Temple	吳鳳廟	*wúfèng miào*

The legacy of Wu Feng

Though he's rarely discussed by Taiwanese today, the mention of **Wu Feng** still elicits angry dismissals from Tsou people, his story providing a rare insight into an uncomfortable chapter in Taiwan's history. The main Chinese version of the story (there are several) claims that Wu Feng was born in China in 1699 and emigrated to Taiwan with his family. He learnt the **Tsou language**, and was eventually given the position of official interpreter. By this time the Tsou had already agreed to stop the practice of head hunting, but in 1769 a serious epidemic ravaged the tribe, leading the elders to conclude that the gods were unhappy and that they should return to the old ways. In a desperate bid to stop an imminent attack on Chinese settlers, Wu Feng told the Tsou leaders that the following day a man wearing a red robe and hat would pass through their land. They could decapitate this man he said, but thereafter the Tsou must cease the gruesome practice forever. The Tsou duly ambushed the man and chopped off his head, only to discover that it was Wu Feng himself. The Tsou were so overcome with remorse, they agreed to stop head hunting forthwith.

Ironically, scholars today agree that this version was in large part fabricated by the **Japanese** in the 1920s to aid their colonization of Taiwan (the Japanese made a film *The Story of Wu Feng* in 1932 with an all-Japanese cast), and it was exaggerated further after 1949 when it was taught in primary schools across the island, remaining on the curriculum until 1988. The earliest extant Chinese record of Wu Feng's life (1855) suggests he was murdered for warning settlers about an imminent Tsou attack. In contrast, Tsou elders claim Wu was a cheat, dominating trade in the area and selling the tribe substandard goods. More extreme versions have Wu tricking the Tsou into attending a religious festival rigged with explosives, or kidnapping Tsou children in order to raise them as Chinese. Either way, it's accepted he was murdered by a small band of aggrieved tribesmen. The red outfit is dismissed as a joke: the Tsou wore primarily red clothes themselves so the idea of killing a stranger in red doesn't make sense. Most ethnic Chinese acknowledge there's something odd about his legend, but many of the older generation still believe its central tenet – that Wu Feng was a noble official that sacrificed himself to civilize the "raw" aborigines of the mountains.

main road to Alishan, fifteen minutes outside Chiayi in the village of Jhongpu. Just 3km south of the city centre, the **Tropic of Cancer Monument** marks the northern boundary of the tropics. The site has been redeveloped as an astronomical theme park and Solar Science Museum, while replicas of previous monuments (the original was built in 1908 by the Japanese) stand near the modern, fairly uninspiring incarnation. Take a taxi (NT$300) or the Putzih bus from Chiayi Transport Co Bus Station.

Beigang: Chaotian Temple

The lively **Chaotian Temple**, a short bus ride from Chiayi in the town of **BEIGANG**, is one of Taiwan's most significant religious sites. Known locally as the "**Mazu Miao**", it was first built to enshrine what many now consider the country's most powerful Mazu image. This venerated deity, blessed at the original Mazu Temple on Meizhou Island in China's modern-day Fujian Province, was brought to Beigang by settlers in the seventeenth century and has gained an ardent following of devotees.

Though many temples claim to be Taiwan's oldest, Chaotian's primary significance lies not in its age, but rather with the special place it occupies in the complex system of spirit division – in practice meaning it is one of the island's greatest **mother temples**, with a vast number of branches beneath it, reflecting the belief that its Mazu is the most sacred. As such, it's constantly filled with worshippers, making it arguably the best place in Taiwan to grasp the fundamental importance of Mazu to the Taiwanese. The most dramatic time to visit is during one of the weekends preceding **Mazu's birthday**, on the twenty-third day of the third lunar month (April 28, 2008; April 18, 2009). During this period, hundreds of groups from temples all over the island bring their Mazu images to commune with the mother deity, as this will confer greater authority on their own images. A few days before Mazu's birthday, hundreds of thousands of devotees besiege Beigang for the Goddess' annual **inspection tour**, when the image is secured in a ceremonial sedan chair and paraded around town to a chaotic backdrop of fireworks, lion dances and stilt performers masquerading as a host of other Chinese gods. These festivities reach a crescendo on the Goddess' actual birthday, when a dawn ritual is performed to thank **Mazu's parents** for bringing her into the world. This ceremony, which begins at 6am and lasts for one hour, is Mazu's biggest birthday celebration and is key to the Chaotian's importance – the images of the parents also are said to have originally come from Meizhou and are considered Taiwan's oldest such deities.

While this is certainly when the Chaotian is at its liveliest, the temple is definitely worth a visit any time, especially on Sundays, when there are always large crowds of worshippers burning incense and paper money and rattling divination sticks for other-worldly guidance. One of the most frequently performed rituals – and perhaps Taiwan's most macabre expression of religious fervour – are the **spirit-medium processions** of young men flagellating themselves, mostly on the head, with spiked, club-like objects until blood streams down their bare chests. These contemporary adherents of the ancient practice of **Wu-ism** – which holds that spirits can temporarily possess a human body, providing immunity from pain – uphold a tradition that can be traced in classical Chinese literature to the time of Confucius.

Directly behind the temple is a five-storey building with an enormous **stone statue** of Mazu on its roof, which visitors are allowed to access. Flanking Mazu are smaller statues of Guanyin and the Sakyamuni Buddha, all set within a lovely garden. From here there are excellent views of the city and the temple below.

Public **buses** (45min) leave from the Chiayi Transport Co Bus Station on Jhongshan Road every ten to thirty minutes, from 6am to 10pm. Once in Beigang, turn right after you exit the station, take your first left and carry on for about 200 metres until you reach the rear of the temple. If you need to stay overnight, the *Cinghe Hotel* at 198 Jhongshan Road (☏05/7832455; ❷) is located just behind the temple and has average rooms.

Guanzihling Hot Springs

Tucked away in the northeast corner of Tainan County but accessible from Chiayi, **GUANZIHLING HOT SPRINGS** boasts beautiful scenery, unusual hot-spring spas, picturesque monasteries and the **Water Fire Cave**, a bizarre natural wonder. The Japanese started to develop the area in 1902 – the spring water is a rare type which is found in only two other places (Japan and Sicily). It contains alkali and iodine, has a light sulphuric smell and a greyish "muddy" colour. The area was also an important centre for bamboo production until the 1940s, but these days it's better known for growing mushrooms and oranges.

Most of the spas and hotels are located within the upper and lower village on R175, south of the junction with R172 (see Practicalities p.291), but apart from a few attractive **hiking trails** here, the real highlights of the area lie in the hills outside Guanzihling.

Around Guanzihling

From the top of Guanzihling upper village it's 4.5km to the **Water Fire Cave** – take the right-hand fork (R96) off R175. The road splits again before reaching the cave – the right fork takes you above the entrance, the left below it, the cave set in a small park on the hillside between the two roads and close to a strip of food stalls. It's worth the effort to get here: the "cave" is more like a cleft in the hillside with a pool of bubbling spring water, but although it's not big, the flames smothering the rocks above the pool are a truly remarkable sight. The flames are fuelled by spontaneously igniting natural gas, shooting out of the earth. The stone carving just above it is the "Water Fire God".

Just under 2km further along R96 you should pass one of several Buddhist monasteries in the area: **Bi Yun Temple** (Blue Cloud Temple) was being renovated at the time of writing, but occupies a stunning location beneath a craggy peak with great views of the plains below. About 3km from here **Huoshan Da Sian Temple** (Great Immortals Temple) also serves as a busy monastery and is popular with tour groups: the three main halls are dedicated to various incarnations of Buddha with a couple of pagodas in the gardens outside. The complex sits on the hill just above the village of **Siancaopu** and the R172 where you can catch the bus back to Guanzihling or Chiayi: the village specializes in restaurants that roast chicken in huge clay ovens, and pumpkins and pomelos sold along the road outside town.

Practicalities

It's much easier to explore this part of Taiwan, part of the newly created **Siraya National Scenic Area**, if you have a car or scooter – the latter are easy to rent in Tainan or Chiayi. With your own transport, you can see the most absorbing temples and Water Fire Cave in a half a day. If you want to walk, note that the route above, from Guanzihling to Siancaopu, is about 12km. The hike is scenic but much of it is uphill and the road gets busy at the weekends – note also that very little is marked in English or *pinyin*.

Buses from Chiayi (1hr, NT$74) pass through the **lower village** first before terminating in a car park at the start of the **upper village**. Hourly buses are supposed to head the other way from 6.25am but it's best to check the timetable in advance.

Guanzihling's hot-spring spas all offer **accommodation** and places **to eat**, though it's usually possible to sample their spa facilities by paying day rates. The lower village is the original resort area developed by the Japanese: today it's a strip of slightly faded spas, restaurants and hotels that line the river at the bottom of the gorge. The *Jing Leh Hotel* at no. 17 (☎06/6822678; ❹) is the most historic place in town, established in 1902 with Japanese-style rooms and white-tiled spa bathrooms, located across the river at the bottom end of the lower village ($400/800 for an hour weekday/weekend). The upper village is where you'll find more **restaurants** and better, more expensive hot-spring spas. The *Toong Mao Spa Resort* at no. 28 (☎06/6823456, ⓦwww .toongmao.com.tw; ❻) is a modern behemoth a short walk up hill from the bus terminus with smart, comfortable rooms. Public pools are open 7am–9.30pm ($250). The *⚒ Mutsun Spring* at no. 27 (☎06/6823232, ⓦwww .muspring.com.tw; ❽) just next door, is the most luxurious place in the village, a beautiful Japanese-style spa and restaurant with superb views of the valley below. Private spa rooms (two people) start at NT$1200 for an hour and a half on weekdays.

Alishan National Scenic Area

Stretching from the foothills of western Taiwan to the Alishan branch of the central mountain range, the extraordinarily diverse **ALISHAN NATIONAL SCENIC AREA** covers some 420 sq km studded with picturesque **tea plantations** and inviting Tsou aboriginal villages. However, the area's main claim to fame is its mountains and the extraordinary "**sea of clouds**" views available from them. In addition, the peaks are relatively easy to access, especially compared with that of their higher, protected cousins in neighbouring Yushan National Park, for which the scenic area is the major gateway.

Confusingly, there is no single mountain called Alishan, and this name refers to all of the mountains along this branch of the central cordillera. The actual peak which attracts the most sunrise viewers is named **Jhushan**, the centrepiece of

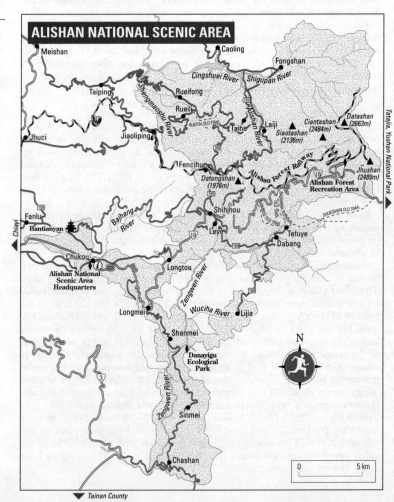

Alishan National Scenic Area

Alishan National Scenic Area	阿里山國家風景區	*ālǐshān guó jiā fēng jǐng qū*
Alishan Forest Recreation Area	阿里山森林遊樂區	*ālǐshān sēnlín yóulè qū*
Alishan Forest Railway	阿里山森林鐵道	*ā'lǐshān sēnlín tiě dào*
Jhaoping Station	沼平車站	*zhǎopíng chēzhàn*
Jhongjheng Village	中正村	*zhōngzhèng cūn*
Sianglin Village	香林村	*xiānglín cūn*

Accommodation

Alishan Gou Hotel	阿里山閣大飯店	*ālǐshān gé dàfàndiàn*
Alishan House	阿里山賓館	*ālǐshān bīnguǎn*
Catholic Hostel	天主堂	*tiānzhǔ táng*
Ciyun (Tzuyun) Temple	慈雲寺	*cíyún sì*
Gau Shan Ching Hotel	高山青賓館	*gāoshānqīng bīnguǎn*
High Mountain Museum	高山博物館	*gāoshān bówùguǎn*
Shoujhen (Shouzhen) Temple	受鎮宮	*shòuzhèn gōng*

Sights

Alishan Trail	阿里山遊覽步道	*ā'lǐshān yóulǎn bùdào*
Duei Gao Yue Forest Trail	對高岳森林浴步道	*duìgāoyuè sēnlínyù bùdào*
Jhushan	祝山	*zhùshān*
Jhushan Sunrise Trail	祝山觀日步道	*zhùshān guānrì bùdào*
Jhushan Sunrise Train	祝山觀日火車	*zhùshān guānrì huǒchē*
Magnolia Garden	木蘭園	*mùlán yuán*
Plum Tree Garden	梅園	*méi yuán*
Alishan Sacred Tree	阿里山神木	*ā'lǐshān shénmù*
Tatajia	塔塔加	*tǎtǎjiā*
Tree Spirit Monument	樹靈塔	*shùlíng tǎ*
Two Sisters Pond	姊妹潭	*zǐmèi tán*

| **Rueili** | 瑞里 | *ruìlǐ* |
| Rueitai Old Trail | 瑞太古道 | *ruìtài gǔdào* |

Accommodation

Clear Moon Guesthouse	明月的家	*míngyuè de jiā*
Ren Sheng Holiday Resort	瑞勝渡假木屋	*ruìshèng dùjiā mùwū*
Ruoh-lan Resort	若蘭山莊	*ruòlán shānzhuāng*

| **Dabang** | 達邦 | *dábāng* |
| Keupana Homestay | 給巴娜民宿 | *gěibānà mínsù* |

| **Tefuye** | 特富野 | *tèfùyě* |
| Tefuye Resort | 特富野山莊 | *tèfùyě shānzhuāng* |

Fencihu	奮起湖	*fènqǐhú*
Datongshan	大凍山	*dàtòng shān*
18 Arhats Cave	十八羅漢洞	*shíbā luóhàn dòng*

Accommodation

Arnold Janssen Activity Centre	楊生活動中心	*yángshēng húodòng zhōngxīn*
Fancylake Hotel	奮起湖大飯店	*fènqǐhú dàfàndiàn*
Liu Fu Hotel	六福賓館	*liùfú bīnguǎn*
Yahu Hotel	雅湖山莊	*yǎhú shānzhuāng*
Yeashow Hotel	雅琇山莊	*yǎiù shānzhuāng*

Laiji	來吉	*láijí*
Laiji Wall	來吉大峭壁	*láijí dàqiàobì*
Tashan	塔山	*tǎshān*
Tianshuei Waterfall	天水瀑布	*tiānshuǐ pùbù*
Bu'u Homestay	不舞工坊民宿	*bùwǔ gōngfāng mínsù*

| **Shanmei** | 山美 | *shānměi* |
| Danayigu River Ecological Park | 達娜伊谷生態公園 | *dánàyīgǔ shēngtài gōngyúan* |

the **Alishan Forest Recreation Area**, the area's main tourist hub and what most Taiwanese refer to as just "Alishan". Most visitors get to the recreation area via the spectacular **Alishan Forest Railway**, the jewel of Taiwan's narrow-gauge rail network and its only alpine rail link.

The scenic area is laced with well-marked **hiking trails**, from short nature walks to longer paths connecting quaint mountain communities such as **Rueili** with historic outposts such as the old train repair station at **Fencihu**, a favoured stop along the forest rail line. And as the ancestral homeland of the Tsou aborigines, the area is dotted with tribal villages such as **Dabang** and **Laiji**, which provide a more honest glimpse of contemporary Tsou culture than the glitzy commercial theme parks that cater to Taiwanese tourists. Finally, the scenic area is teeming with some of Taiwan's best **homestays**, with character-filled wooden rooms in idyllic mountain settings that make for a great escape from the island's often dingy urban hotels.

Alishan Forest Recreation Area

The **ALISHAN FOREST RECREATION AREA**, situated near the terminus for both the Alishan Forest Railway and buses from Chiayi, is the national scenic area's premier attraction. Its 1.75 sq km of pristine alpine forests are dotted with mostly easy walking paths and several scenic overlooks offering superb **views** of the surrounding mountains and the surreal "sea of clouds" sunrise. The area also provides easy access to **Tatajia**, in nearby Yushan National Park

(see p.301), the primary staging point for climbs of Yushan and a more serene place to take in the sunrise. However, what attracts the most domestic tourists to the recreation area are its **cherry trees**, which come into full bloom from mid-March to mid-April. On weekends during this period, the area is inundated with more than ten thousand visitors per day, completely choking walking trails and making accommodation scarce. If you visit during this season, it's advisable to come during the week, though hotel and food prices skyrocket for the entire period.

Bear in mind that given the area's 2200-metre **altitude**, it can get cold here even in the height of summer, and afternoons tend to be quite chilly once the usual midday mists roll in.

△ Alishan Forest Recreation Area, sea of clouds

Arrival, orientation and information

Alishan Forest Railway (see p.297) **trains** arrive just southwest of the main tourist centre of **Jhongjheng Village**, clustered around a sprawling car park. The **bus station** is at the car park's southern end, while directly across at the northern end is the two-storey **visitor information center** (8am–5pm; ℡05/2679917), with English-language exhibits on the area's main attractions as well as free English maps and brochures. Most of the other tourist amenities also are situated around the car park, including a **post office** (℡05/2679970) with an **ATM** although this only accepts Taiwan-issued cards (bring plenty of cash if you don't have one of these). On the car park's southwestern edge is a **health clinic** (daily 8am–5pm ℡05/2679806). Up the hill to the east of Jhongjheng Village is an area known as **Sianglin Village**, where you'll find more upscale accommodation as well as walking paths and the **Jhaoping Station** – the starting point for the Jhushan Sunrise Train.

Just outside of Jhongjheng Village, at the base of the hill along the main road towards Sianglin Village, is the forest recreation area's **toll gate** (NT$200 on weekends, NT$150 on weekdays), which is manned round the clock. The Alishan forest train (listed as the "**Alishan Express**" at the ticket booth at Jhaoping Station) leaves twice daily (1.18pm & 1.40pm; NT$399) for the descent to Chiayi.

Accommodation

Most of the forest recreation area's **hotels** are conveniently located in **Jhongjheng Village**, where you'll find a row of faceless mid-range establishments at the base of the hill behind the car park. If you don't have a reservation – usually essential during peak times – your best bet is to head here and try your luck. One with super-friendly management is the *Gau Shan Ching Hotel* at 43 Jhongjheng Village (℡05/2679716; ❹), which has clean, if slightly cramped, rooms and includes a Chinese breakfast in its rates. Though the staff have limited English, they can help you book bus tickets to Tatajia and Chiayi. The only budget accommodation is the *Catholic Hostel* (℡05/2679602; ❸) on the west side of the car park near the health clinic, which has cheap-but-basic doubles and dorm beds (NT$250). In nearby **Sianglin Village**, you'll find the area's top hotel, the *Alishan House* (℡05/2679811; ❻), set in a functional Japanese-era building with stylish rooms; if you have a reservation, the hotel staff can pick you up at the bus station. Further along the main walking path, and a stone's throw from Jhaoping Station, is the modern *Alishan Gou Hotel* (℡05/2679611; Ⓦwww.agh.com.tw; ❺), whose nearby terrace is a favoured spot for viewing the sea of clouds. Rooms are anonymous but comfortable, and its location makes for an easy early-morning stumble to catch the **sunrise train**; a shuttle bus also connects it with the bus station.

Jhushan and the "sea of clouds"

The most popular place to watch the sunrise and the famous "sea of clouds" is from the top of the 2489-metre **Jhushan** (Celebration Mountain). The quickest way up is via the **Jhushan Sunrise Train** (20min; NT$150 return, NT$100 one-way), which leaves well before dawn each morning from Jhaoping Station (check the current departure times with your hotel staff, who can also arrange a wake-up call). Despite the inevitable crowds, the carnival-like atmosphere on the train can be fun, although buying a return ticket is probably overdoing it: taking the train to the top and walking back along one of the area's forest paths is a more balanced option. For those wanting make their own way up, the peaceful **Jhushan Sunrise Trail** gently climbs through a beautiful old-growth

Alishan's red cypress trees

While the area's cherry blossoms are indeed a moving sight, most of these trees ironically inhabit a still-visible cemetery of once-mighty **red cypresses**, logged by the occupying Japanese in the early twentieth century to be turned into thousands of smoothly lacquered **tea tables**. In place of these ancient giants, many of which were well over two thousand years old when they were felled, the Japanese planted an assortment of their cherished sakura cherry trees. Sadly, apart from taking perfunctory photos before a handful of celebrated cypress stumps, most Taiwanese tourists pay scant attention to them, instead rushing to admire the cherry blossoms in an unwitting salute to the Japanese colonial legacy.

cedar forest en route to the summit. The turnoff for the trail is on the side of the road between Jhongjheng and Sianglin villages, a few hundred metres before you get to Jhaoping Station: the trailhead is crowned with an archway labelled "Jhushan Footpath". Starting from Jhongjheng Village, allow about an hour for the walk; from Sianglin Village, 45 minutes should be sufficient. There are no lights along the trail, so it's necessary to bring a torch.

Once at the **summit**, expect a barrage of Mandarin-only tourist information to be blasted through a screechy loudspeaker, while the first appearance of the sun will be signalled by the simultaneous clicking of thousands of camera shutters. Dozens of **food vendors** with pushcarts sell breakfast items ranging from boiled eggs to heated tins of coffee. If you're walking back from Jhushan and the weather is clear, the **Duei Gao Yue Forest Trail** – to the right at the first big bend in the road – offers a lovely detour through evergreen forest before it dead-ends at a **pavilion** overlooking the nearby valley. The path, which begins alongside the train tracks, is 1.65km one-way, starting from the bend in the road.

Closer to Sianglin Village are several **loop walks**, all signposted in English, offering a leisurely one- to two-hour hike through the thick forests that cover the surrounding slopes. Depending on the season, the paths are littered with flowers and **blossoms**, while a cluster of **monuments** reflects the Japanese impact on the area – particularly their belief that it was a sacred place.

Eating

You'll find plenty of **restaurants** in Jhongjheng Village, in the complex at the southern end of the car park. They invariably serve standard **Chinese fare**, from fried rice and noodles to basic stir fries, and you should be able to eat to your fill for under NT$200 even during peak season. It's possible to get breakfast, lunch and dinner at these, although breakfast is usually delayed until the groups of Taiwanese tourists have taken the Sunrise Train back down from Jhushan. At the southeastern end of the car park is a 24-hour **convenience store** where you can buy drinks and snacks for your hikes.

On to Yushan National Park

Those wanting to get further into the mountains to watch the sunrise at **Tatajia**, just inside Yushan National Park, can book a slot on one of the pre-dawn **minibus tours** (3hr return trip; NT$300) that leave from the hotel area in Jhongjheng Village about an hour before sunrise each morning. Your hotel staff can secure your seat and the minibus will usually pick you up in front of your hotel. These minibuses also make handy shuttles (NT$150 one-way) to the **Yushan trailhead** and can help you get an early start to your climb.

Alishan Forest Railway

The main transport artery through the national scenic area, the dramatic **Alishan Forest Railway** is one of Taiwan's top attractions in its own right. Easily the most spectacular of the country's narrow-gauge railways, it traverses some of the scenic area's most rugged terrain on its way from the fertile rice paddies around Chiayi to the lush **evergreen forests** of the recreation area. Starting at an elevation of only thirty metres, the train climbs to 2274m in less than three and a half hours, passing through dozens of tunnels and bridges in a journey of just over 86km. Along the way, the train chugs through three distinct climatic zones, each with markedly different ecosystems, providing an unparalleled opportunity to experience Taiwan's amazing **ecological diversity**. By the time it's all over, passengers are deposited into the depths of alpine forest – in the recreation area near **Jhushan** – where tall hemlocks tower above the gargantuan stumps of decapitated **red cypresses**. These decaying stumps are the reason for the railway, which the occupying Japanese first began to operate in 1912 to transport the precious timber from the mountains on its way to Japan. Nowadays, the train is a convenient transport option to some other parts of the national scenic area, stopping near the halfway point at **Fencihu** and also letting passengers off at **Jiaoliping**, near **Rueili**.

Practicalities

Train tickets can be bought at Chiayi's main train station – where the railway begins – or at the city's Beimen (North Gate) station, the first stop along the line. There are **two trains** daily (3hr 30min; NT$680 return, NT$399 one-way) in each direction (9am & 1.30pm from Chiayi, 1.18pm & 1.40pm from Jhaoping Station). Ticket **reservations** can be made by telephone (☏05/2768094; 8am–5pm) up to two months in advance, and this is highly recommended if you plan to visit during the cherry blossom season. If you try to get tickets at the train station and no seats are available, you can buy a **standing-only ticket**, although without a seat it's difficult to see much of the scenery along the way.

Rueili

Perched precipitously above a sheer cliff face and surrounded by tea plantations, the picturesque village of **RUEILI** is a relaxing place to soak up the highland scenery while sipping cups of fragrant tea or roaming along hiking trails. There are several outstanding nature walks near the village, ranging from short paths to pristine waterfalls to longer historic trails leading to nearby towns. One of the latter, the **Rueitai Old Trail**, connects Rueili to neighbouring **Taihe** and **Fencihu**, and represents an exciting way for more energetic travellers to get from Rueili to Fencihu before re-boarding the forest train.

Visitors will find themselves constantly being invited to drink tea with locals, many of them owners of attractive and affordable **homestays**. Though Rueili is not on the forest rail line, it's only a few kilometres from **Jiaoliping** station, and most homestay operators will pick you up there if you call in advance. You can also reach the village by **bus** from Chiayi. From March to June each year, the slopes around Rueili come alight at night, when thousands of **fireflies** put on a nightly performance considered by many to be Taiwan's most magnificent.

Rueitai Old Trail

The 6.5-kilometre **Rueitai Old Trail** snakes up some steep hills through brilliant forests of **bright-green bamboo** along the way from Rueili to Fencihu.

Once used to transport food supplies between the villages, the trail can be covered in a couple of hours and gives a good taste of the surrounding countryside while also getting you back to the forest rail line if you wish to venture deeper into the national scenic area. The **trailhead** is about 200m west of the Rueitai visitor centre, on the opposite side of the main Highway 122. The trail climbs sharply through a thick bamboo grove for much of the first 1.5km before reaching a split: the left-hand fork heads northeast about 3km to Taihe, while the right-hand path runs due south for about 5km to Fencihu.

Practicalities

The **Rueitai visitor center** at 1 Rueili Village (☏05/2501070; 8.30am–5pm), northeast of the major concentration of homestays along the main Highway 122, can provide information on area hikes and has reliable English **maps** of several nearby villages. The best places to stay are the village's superb **homestays** which add depth and character to a visit that the few run-down hotels simply can't match. In addition to offering pick-ups from nearby Jiaoliping station, most can prepare **home-cooked meals** made from local ingredients for their guests. The *Clear Moon Guesthouse* at 48 Rueili Village (☏05/2501626; ❸), with rooms surrounding a courtyard backed by an enormous family shrine, has friendly owners who make their own plum wine and are keen to share it with guests. Their main **weekday package** (NT$1200 per person) includes one night's stay, pick-up, three meals and an area tour, but you must call in advance to arrange this. More upscale, the *Ren Sheng Holiday Resort*, 79 Rueili Village (☏05/2501011, ❻www.rensheng.com.tw; ❻), is set in an attractive building and has fragrant, Japanese-style wooden rooms. Prices include pick-up, but their delicious meals cost extra. The best budget option is the *Ruohlan Resort* at 10 Rueili Village (☏05/2501210; ❻www.firefly.twtrip.net; ❷), a three-storey lodge with Western and Japanese-style rooms, some with balconies commanding sweeping views of the valley below. The owners are particularly proud of the local fireflies and arrange night viewing tours in season. Pick-up from Jiaoliping costs NT$300.

Fencihu

Roughly marking the forest railway's halfway point and about 6.5km south of Rueili by trail is **FENCIHU**, a former **train repair station** that is now one of the line's most frequented stops. The compact village spills down the hillside immediately south of the train station and has a quaint appeal, its narrow Old Street lined with curious **snack shops** and restaurants that lure visitors off the train for afternoon stopovers. Fencihu was once a haven of **hiking trails** and historic sights, but many of the trails were badly damaged during the 921 earthquake and are being repaired and upgraded with wooden boardwalks, steps and English-language signage.

The **Rueitai Old Trail** (see p.297), begins directly across the main highway from the train station, at the steep steps that wind up the hill to the remains of a Japanese-built **Shinto shrine** and beyond. The area's other main hike is the celebrated climb up **Datongshan** (1976m), which in clear weather offers extraordinary sunrise views. The trailhead is about 4km east of Fencihu along Highway 155, and some of the town's hotels offer early-morning **shuttles** here for those wishing to get a jump on the dawn. Just past the trailhead, the path splits into two, with the right-hand fork leading to the **18 Arhats Cave** – actually a sizeable sandstone rock house – just less than 2km further. The left-hand path winds to the top of Datongshan and is a moderate climb of 1.7km that takes about thirty minutes.

Practicalities

Most of Fencihu's **hotels** and restaurants are just a short walk south of the train station, scattered along the lanes stemming out from the pedestrian-only **Old Street**, itself accessible by the stairs just behind the station. It's often crowded with domestic tourists, many of whom make pit-stops simply to try local culinary delights such as traditional **jelly drinks**, **wasabi tofu** and the town specialty – the **railway lunchbox**, a Japanese-inspired arrangement of meat, vegetables, boiled egg and white rice. Hawkers on the platform sell the boxes (NT$80) to tourists arriving on the train, or you can pick them up at some of the town's hotels, most notably the *Fancylake*. At 142 Old Street is a curious **coffee/woodcarving shop** that sells cups of coffee sprinkled with a dash of aromatic wood chips. The shop owner speaks a bit of English and is always up for a chinwag.

Accommodation

Arnold Janssen Activity Centre ☎05/2561035. This Catholic hostel, down the hill from the train station, is Fencihu's only real budget option. Dorm beds go for NT$250 per person, and singles without attached bath can be had for NT$500. The Swiss sister who runs the place speaks excellent English and Mandarin and is extremely accommodating. ❶

Fancylake Hotel ☎05/2561888. The town's best-known hotel, with a wide range of wooden rooms, including a few plush Japanese-style suites. It's famous for its filling railway lunchbox, and its gregarious owner knows the history of Fencihu inside out. ❻

Liu Fu Hotel ☎05/2561776. Down the main road that runs southeast of the train station is the basic *Liu Fu*, with clean two- and four-person rooms that go for a twenty percent discount on weekdays. ❸

Yahu Hotel ☎05/2561097. Located at the far western end of the train platform, the cheap and cheerful *Yahu* has spartan but clean doubles and twins with large beds. ❷

Yeashow Hotel ☎05/2561336, ⊛www.yeashow .com.tw. Just down the steps to the left of Old St, the shiny new Yeashow has plain rooms that offer good value and very friendly management. ❸

Laiji

Several kilometres northeast of Fencihu along Highway 155 is **LAIJI**, a thriving **Tsou community** nestled near the base of **Tashan**, the barren mountain considered most holy by the Tsou. The village is well off the domestic tourist trail and, as a result, the traditional rhythms of Tsou life remain largely undisturbed. The villagers are extremely outgoing and keen to share their views on a host of political topics with outsiders, and any foreign traveller who makes the effort to get here is likely to wind up in the midst of an impromptu celebration, perhaps sampling savoury **roasted mountain pig** and drinking warm, **homemade liquor** from bamboo shot glasses.

The hills around Laiji and Tashan have great **trekking** potential, with traditional Tsou hunting trails connecting all of their main settlements. Many of these are narrow dirt tracks, however, and earthquake and typhoon damage has left them treacherous in places, but if you hire a local **guide** he can help you navigate around trouble spots. One of the area's most accessible natural attractions is the graceful **Tianshuei (Heavenly Water) Waterfall**, which plummets down the lower reaches of Tashan's southwestern side. Not far from here is the **Laiji Wall**, an exposed plate of rock with a sheer drop of about a hundred metres on one side. Called the "Sibi-sibi Cliff" in the Tsou tongue, the wall also is nicknamed "The Titanic" for its remarkable resemblance to the bow of a sinking ship. Another more challenging trail leads around Tashan all the way to the **forest recreation area** near Jhushan, but in rainy weather it can be very dangerous and even guides won't take you on this taxing two-day

Tsou language

Learn a few *Tsou* words before you visit Alishan and you'll definitely raise a few smiles, though most Tsou today speak Chinese as their first language. The most commonly used word is *aveoveoyu* (sounds like "aview-view-you"), literally "my heart is happy" and used both as a general greeting and also for "thank you". Similarly, *yokioasu* means "good health" or "good luck" and is often used when saying good-bye. Other words you might be able to use are *mafe* (delicious), *emi* (millet wine) and *zou* (good).

trek. The *Bu'u Homestay* (℡05/2661804, @abuu@mail2000.com.tw) is the best-equipped **place to stay** in Laiji and can arrange day-trips, multi-day treks and hunting excursions. It offers a good-value **package** including one night's accommodation, three authentic Tsou meals, a one-day tour and **pick-up** from Caoling, Fenchifu or Rueili for NT$1850 per person. The owner is a Tsou artist and her work is displayed throughout the homestay.

Shanmei and around

Lying at the bottom of the Zengwun River valley, a twenty-minute drive from Highway 18, the Tsou village of **SHANMEI** is rapidly becoming a popular tourist destination. The village itself has a population of just over six hundred (it means "beautiful mountain" in Chinese, and is known as "Saviki" in Tsou), though the main attraction is **Danayigu River Ecological Park** (8am–5pm; NT$80 Mon–Fri, NT$100 weekends; NT$50 parking fee; ℡05/2586994), a few kilometres up river. The valley was once a Tsou holy place, where all life was protected and hunting forbidden, but by the 1930s the Japanese had discovered the river's valuable camphor trees and it gradually became polluted. In 1989 the local community created a protected conservation area along the banks of the Danayigu River (a tributary of the Zengwun), and by 2001 revenue from tourism topped NT$10 million, with all profits ploughed back into the community.

Today the river is swarming with **"President fish"**, vivid testimony to the success of the project. The fish (*ku* in Chinese, a member of the carp family) got the nickname after Chiang Kai-shek became fond of eating them. The main **nature trail** is an easy loop along the river banks and is well marked – it takes around thirty minutes to walk without stops, and crosses the fish-packed river a couple of times. In the summer it's a good place for a swim. The park entrance area has **restaurants** that serve up traditional Tsou food and hosts regular dance performances – there's an artificial element to this, but it's not as commercialized as other places and everything is managed by local Tsou people. At the weekends there are usually shows three times a day (10.40am, 1.50pm, 3.30pm) at the **Traditional Dance Exhibition Plaza** and are included as part of the entrance fee for the park.

Practicalities

There is no bus to Shanmei, so you'll need to have your own transport or join one of the Tourism Bureau sponsored tours of the area. If you want to stay the night call the Shanmei Village Community Development Association (℡05/2513022) for details of **homestays**. You can also camp just outside Danayigu Park (NT$80). With your own car it's possible to continue south from Shanmei to the Tsou villages of **Sinmei** and **Chashan** where more hiking and traditional pavilions await.

Dabang and Tefuye

Located further along the Zengwun River valley, **DABANG** is the closest thing the Tsou have to a capital and one of the best places to get a feel for contemporary Tsou life – it's a sleepy place during the week, full of colourful wooden and corrugated iron cottages. There are a few local cafés and a couple of major streets, but the highlight is the large **Kuba Ta Tapangu** (*tapangu* means village) in the centre. With its red cypress frame raised on stilts and its thatched roof, the *kuba* or sacred hall is a visual reminder of indigenous Taiwan's cultural links with the South Pacific. You can't go inside – only male members of the tribe can enter.

A few kilometres west of Dabang, the village of **TEFUYE** is about half the size and feels a lot more isolated, containing the second Tsou **kuba**, a couple of churches and some excellent trails (see below).

Practicalities

Three **buses** a day link Chiayi with Dabang (see p.286), with departures in the other direction 10am, 2pm and 6pm. To reach Tefuye from here you'll need to hike or have your own transport. For somewhere to **stay** in Dabang, *Keupana homestay* (☎05/2511688) is a modern building surrounded by flowers and a *hufu* (wood pavilion), just below the village centre on the road to Tefuye. Rooms cost NT$400 per person – a package including tour of the area, meals and pick-up from Fencihu costs NT$1700 per person. In Tefuye, the *Tefuye Resort* (☎05/2511198, 0937651265, ℻05/2511298) can arrange guides for some of the longer hikes in the area. The hotel is 2km beyond the village in an extremely quiet spot on the hillside – during the week you'll be the only person here. One-night packages start at NT$2000 per person and include meals, transport from Dabang and tour of all the main trails – two nights costs NT$2500. Rooms are basic but comfortable with bathroom. You can walk uphill from here to Zihjhong, 9km along the **Shuishan Old Trail**, lined with beautiful *hinoki* cypress trees.

Note that at the time of writing visitors required a **Class B permit** to visit either village during festival periods: these cost NT$10 and must be obtained from Shihjhuo Police Station (it takes five minutes), but in practice you should be able to get accommodation in any of the villages to arrange this for you.

Yushan National Park

Taiwan's most untarnished breadth of backcountry, **YUSHAN NATIONAL PARK** is an archetypal mountain wilderness and the pride of both the island's national park system and the general population. A seemingly endless proliferation of 3000-metre peaks separated by yawning river valleys, the park is primarily known for the majestic **Yushan** (Jade Mountain) – at 3952m the tallest peak in Northeast Asia and a mecca for both domestic and foreign hill walkers. Yushan is often the first feature that visitors spot when they fly over the island, as its lofty peak invariably pierces through the clouds, benignly indifferent to the human tumult of the heavily populated lowlands. Indeed, with over 105,000 hectares of unbroken wilds to insulate the park from the touch of man, it retains a virginal purity that precious few places in East Asia still possess.

The vast majority of park visitors come to **climb** Yushan, the trophy peak of Taiwan, with intoxicating views that rival those of the world's highest mountains. The summit of the coveted **main peak** can be reached by two principal

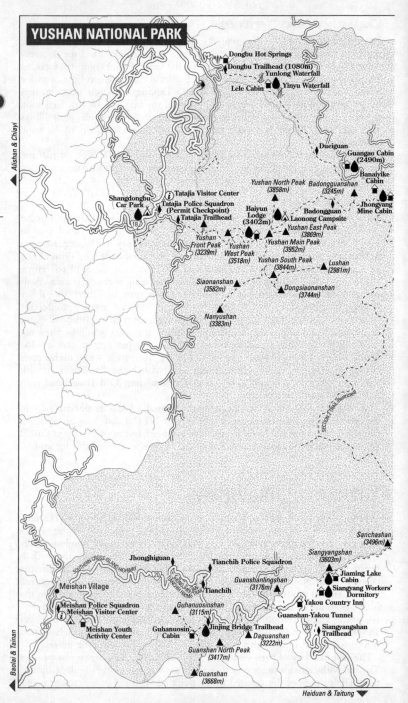

YUSHAN NATIONAL PARK

Dongbu Hot Springs
Dongbu Trailhead (1080m)
Yunlong Waterfall
Lele Cabin   Yinyu Waterfall

Dueiguan
Guangao Cabin (2490m)
Banaiyike Cabin

Yushan North Peak (3858m)   Badongguanshan (3245m)
Jhongyang Mine Cabin

Shangdongbu Car Park
Tatajia Visitor Center
Tatajia Police Squadron (Permit Checkpoint)
Tatajia Trailhead
Baiyun Lodge (3402m)   Badongguan
Laonong Campsite
Yushan East Peak (3869m)
Yushan Front Peak (3239m)
Yushan West Peak (3518m)
Yushan Main Peak (3952m)
Yushan South Peak (3844m)   Lushan (2981m)
Siaonanshan (3582m)
Dongsiaonanshan (3744m)

Nanyushan (3383m)

SECTION E TRAIL (Batongkuan)

Sanchashan (3496m)
Siangyangshan (3603m)

Jhongjhiguan   Tianchih Police Squadron
Jiaming Lake Cabin
Guanshanlingshan (3176m)
Siangyang Workers' Dormitory
Meishan Village   Tianchih
Yakou Country Inn
SOUTHERN CROSS-ISLAND HIGHWAY
Meishan Police Squadron
Meishan Visitor Center
Guhanuosinshan (3115m)
Guhanuosin Cabin   Jinjing Bridge Trailhead
Guanshan-Yakou Tunnel
Siangyangshan Trailhead
Meishan Youth Activity Center
Daguanshan (3222m)
Guanshan North Peak (3417m)

Guanshan (3668m)

Haiduan & Taitung ▼

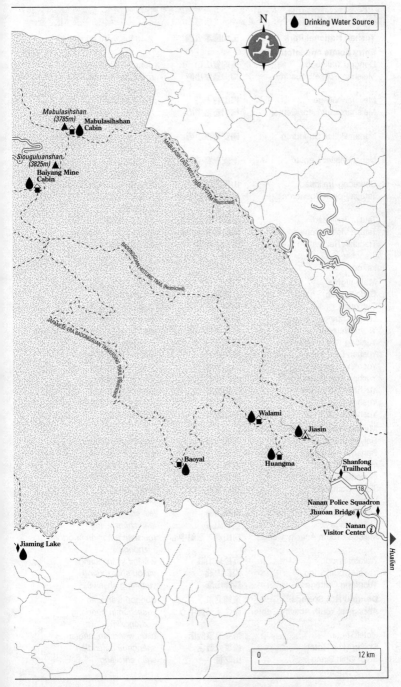

3

Yushan National Park

Yushan National Park	玉山國家公園	*yùshān guójiā gōngyuán*
Entry points and information		
Dongpu Trailhead	東埔登山口	*dōngpǔ dēngshān kǒu*
Meishan Police Squadron	梅山警察小隊	*méishān jǐngchájú xiǎoduì*
Meishan Village	梅山村	*méishān cūn*
Meishankou Visitor Center	梅山遊客中心	*méishān yóukè zhōngxīn*
Nanan Police Squadron	南安警察小隊	*nán'ān jǐngchájú xiǎoduì*
Nanan Visitor Center	南安遊客中心	*nán'ān yóukè zhōngxīn*
Shanfong Trailhead	山風登山口	*shānfēng dēngshān kǒu*
Tatajia Police Squadron	塔塔加警察小隊	*tǎtǎjiā jǐngchájú xiǎoduì*
Tatajia Trailhead	塔塔加登山口	*tǎtǎjiā dēngshān kǒu*
Tatajia Visitor Center	塔塔加遊客中心	*tǎtǎjiā yóukè zhōngxīn*
Tianchih Recreation Area	天池遊憩區	*tiānchí yóuqìqū*
Tianchih	天池	*tiānchí*
Yakou	埡口	*yàkǒu*
Main sights		
Badongguan	八通關	*bātōngguān*
Dueiguan	對關	*duìguān*
Guangaoping	觀高坪	*guāngāo píng*
Yinyu Waterfall	乙女瀑布	*yǐnǚ pùbù*
Yunlong Waterfall	雲龍瀑布	*yúnlóng pùbù*
Yushan East Peak	玉山東峰	*yùshān dōngfēng*
Yushan Front peak	玉山前峰	*yùshān qiánfēng*
Yushan Main Peak	玉山主峰	*yùshān zhǔfēng*
Yushan North Peak	玉山北峰	*yùshān běifēng*
Yushan South Peak	玉山南峰	*yùshān nánfēng*
Yushan West Peak	玉山西峰	*yùshān xīfēng*
Main cabins and campsites		
Baiyun Lodge	排雲山莊	*páiyún shānzhuāng*
Banaiyike Cottage	巴奈伊克山屋	*bānàiyīkè shānwū*
Guangao Cabin	觀高山屋	*guāngāo shānwū*
Guhanuosin Cabin	庫哈諾辛山屋	*kùhànuòxīn shānwū*
Jiasin Campsite	佳心營地	*jiāxīn yíngdì*
Laonong Campsite	荖濃營地	*lǎonóng yíngdì*
Lele Cabin	樂樂山屋	*lèlè shānwū*
Lulin Lodge	鹿林山莊	*lùlín shānzhuāng*
Meishan Youth Activity Center	梅山青年活動中心	*méishān qīngnián húodòng zhōngxīn*
Walami Lodge	瓦拉米山莊	*wǎlāmǐ shānzhuāng*
Yakou Country inn	埡口山莊	*yàkǒu shānzhuāng*
Yuanfong Cottage	圓峰山屋	*yuánfēng shānwū*
Dongpu Hot Springs	東埔溫泉	*dōngpǔ wēnquán*
Aboriginal Youth Activity Center	原住民活動中心	*yúanzhùmín húodòng zhōngxīn*
Hotel Ti Lun	帝綸溫泉飯店	*dìlún wēnquán fàndiàn*
Sheng Hwa Hotel	勝華大飯店	*shènghuá dàfàndiàn*
Shan Chih Siang	山吃香	*shān chī xiāng*

Yushan wildlife

Yushan National Park is revered by Taiwanese conservationists, who since its establishment in 1985 have worked tirelessly to protect its natural treasures. Sheltering six distinct vegetation zones, the park contains more than half of the island's endemic plant species, as well as some of Asia's rarest animal species. Chief among these is the elusive **Formosan Black Bear**, an omnivorous beast which mostly roams the foothills below 2000m. Far from being a threat, these bears are extremely rare and are seldom spotted by humans. Much more visible is the profusion of **deer species**, some of which can be seen by watchful trekkers, especially on the northern fringes of Yushan, near the beautiful high-altitude meadows of **Badongguan**. The most commonly seen of these is the diminutive **Formosan Reeve's Muntjac**, recognizable by its tan coat and stubby, single-pronged antlers.

paths, one ideal for novice hikers and the other better suited to more seasoned hill walkers. And with several other amazing mountains around Yushan and neighbouring ridges, all reachable by a well-trodden trail network, the area offers no shortage of peak-bagging prizes.

Entry points and information

Yushan National Park is by far Taiwan's largest, covering over three percent of the country and accessible by road from three sides. As such, its entry points and information centres are spread widely, making it seem like several different parks. If you're planning to climb Yushan, one of the northwestern entry points of Tatajia or Dongpu will be your gateway into the park: from Tatajia, the climb is easier and much more heavily trafficked, while the Dongpu approach is longer and more physically demanding. A **Class A mountain permit** (see p.306 and Basics p.56) is required for both, and precise planning is imperative to ensure that you can adhere to the schedule outlined in your permit. **Tatajia** is just to the east of the immensely popular **Alishan Forest Recreation Area**, to which you can get public transport (see p.286); however, there is no public bus service from Alishan to the Tatajia entrance, so you'll need to arrange a ride on one of the hotel-run minibuses that take tourists to see the sunrise at Tatajia each morning. The **Tatajia visitor center** (9am–4.30pm, closed second and fourth Tues of every month; ℡049/2702200; 118 Taiping Rd) has English maps and an exhibition hall with information on the nearby mountains and endemic flora and fauna.

Though the **Dongpu** entrance is much less trammelled and there is no visitor centre, there is a daily direct bus service from **Shueili** (see p.267) home to the **Yushan National Park Headquarters** and its main visitor centre (9am–4.30pm; 300 Jhongshan Rd Sec 1; ℡049/2773121, ⓦwww.ysnp.gov.tw). An attractive hot springs village surrounded by mountains, Dongpu is an appealing destination in its own right, and is a very convenient accommodation base for those climbing Yushan from this side.

Another quieter entry point to the park is in the southeast, at **Nanan** (see p.415), where there are worthwhile walks and a visitor centre, but you must have your own transport to get here. Over in the southwest corner, the **Southern Cross-Island Highway** skirts through a remarkably scenic section of the park, and this windy stretch of road ranks as one of Taiwan's top drives. Though it's no longer possible to get public transport all the way across the highway, there is a daily bus service from Tainan to the park entrance at **Meishankou**, where there are hotels, restaurants, a **campsite** and a visitor centre (see p.337).

Climbing Yushan from Tatajia

By far the easiest, most popular route up Yushan is from **TATAJIA**, along a well-maintained trail that is probably Taiwan's most famous hike. Though Taiwanese and even some aborigines will tell you it's an arduous two-day return climb, in reality a reasonably fit walker can make the 22-kilometre return journey from the **Tatajia Trailhead** to the main peak in one long day – provided you get an early start. Even if you think you can do the return hike in one day, it's still a good idea to make a reservation for a space in the **Baiyun (White Cloud) Lodge** (NT$220) near the summit: indeed, when you apply for your mountain permit, you'll be required to specify which night you plan to spend in the lodge, and it's nice to have the option in case the climb takes you longer than expected or you decide to scale some of the surrounding peaks.

Most of the minibuses from Alishan will drop you off near the **Tatajia Police Squadron**, where you must show two copies of your **permit** along with your **passport** or ARC. A ranger will check your details, keep one copy of the permit and give you the other copy to take with you. From here, you'll have to walk or hitch a ride up the paved access road to the actual trailhead, which will add about an hour to your journey each way. If you have your own vehicle, you can leave it in the **ShangDongpu car park** near the police squadron and either hike along the access road or try to pile in with any hiking groups that are being driven to the trailhead. For considerably more money than the minibuses, you can hire your own driver in Alishan to take you past the police checkpoint to the trailhead and could also arrange a pick-up later that evening or the next day. Some hikers **camp** overnight near the ShangDongpu car park in order to get an early start the following day, but this means you need to carry your own tent – and in practice you won't get started much earlier as you still have to wait for the police checkpoint to open for your permit details to be registered.

From the Tatajia Trailhead (2610m) to the Baiyun Lodge (3402m) is an 8.5-kilometre walk of moderate intensity, with a fairly gradual ascent. If you reach the lodge quickly, you can stash your bag inside and make a speedy ascent of Yushan's **main peak**, a steep 2.4-kilometre climb with an elevation gain of over 500m. Alternatively, you could first climb the lower 3518m **west peak** of Yushan and return to the lodge for the night. It's worth keeping in mind that the lodge, which can sleep up to ninety people and is often full, can be an incongruously hectic and noisy place to stay, and earplugs are recommended for light sleepers. Most Taiwanese hikers set their alarms for around 3am to allow ample time to reach the summit before **sunrise**; but while sunrises from the top of Yushan can indeed be momentous, during busy periods you might consider sleeping in and waiting until the mobs start to descend – you'll have more chance of solitude at the top and spend less time waiting at bottlenecks along the trail.

Climbing Yushan from Dongpu

The climb of Yushan from the hot-springs village of **DONGPU** is one of Taiwan's most challenging – and thrilling – hikes, and if you love rugged mountain experiences you should make this your first choice. The return journey is about 48km, with an elevation gain of nearly 3000m, and is suited to seasoned hill walkers with high fitness levels and heads for heights. The return journey takes the better part of three days to complete, with two overnight stays in the rustic **Guangao Cabin**. The often narrow trail winds along steep mountainsides, high above a river valley, and in several places there are dizzying drops to one side. Though the trail is fairly well maintained, some sections can be washed away during heavy rains and summer typhoons: at these times the climb can be dangerous – with landslips and falling debris real concerns – and is best avoided. At such times, park officials are unlikely to issue you a permit anyway, but if you apply during the dryer months – October through December and late February through April – the trail should be officially open and in good nick.

Arrival, information and accommodation

Dongpu is accessible from the north via **Shueili** and from the southwest through the **Alishan Forest Recreation Area** and nearby **Tatajia** – though for the latter option you'll need to have your own transport. The only direct public buses are from Shueili, where the **Yuanlin Bus Co** has eight buses daily (6am–5pm; 1hr; NT$104). All buses return to Shueili about ten minutes after arriving in Dongpu.

Though there is no **permit checkpoint** at the trailhead and in practice the path is seldom patrolled, this is all the more reason to secure the permit, as going without one means that nobody will know you're attempting the climb and will make an emergency rescue unlikely if not impossible. Applying for the permit also is the only sure way to find out about current **trail conditions**; Dongpu locals typically only know about the first few kilometres of the path, which can be walked without a permit, but generally they have no idea about the higher-elevation areas so cannot be relied on for information. If you're staying in the Guangao Cabin, you'll need to bring your own **sleeping bag** and foam or inflatable mattress.

Accommodation

Dongpu is a fun destination in its own right, and makes a great base for the Yushan climb – its hot springs something to look forward to during the arduous ascent. Though many of the town's hotels are slightly dated, with the hot- spring water piped into tiny tubs in attached bathrooms, there are a few with public indoor and outdoor bathing pools. Dongpu's top hotel – and one that is used to catering to Yushan climbers – is the ⚘ *Hotel Ti Lun* at 86 Kaigao Lane (☎049/2701616; ❺), the first hotel on the left as you enter the village from the bus stop. The *Ti Lun* has a wide range of rooms, from basic doubles to Japanese-style suites equipped with Jacuzzis. Its outdoor **public bathing pools** have excellent views of the surrounding mountains and are an ideal place to watch the sun set. If you're climbing Yushan, the hotel has a safe **left-luggage room** where you can stash all of your extra gear. One of the best deals in town is the *Aboriginal Youth Activity Center* at 64 Kaigao Lane (☎049/2701515; ❷), at the far end of the main drag through the village, about 1km from the bus stop – the last bit of road before the centre is very steep. However, it's more than worth the climb, particularly if you're on a budget, as their large doubles and twins offer great value for money, with small bathing tubs, cable TV and mountain-view **balconies**; there also are a few **dormitories**, but the price is per room so these are only a good deal if there are several people in your group. Next door, the *Sheng Hwa Hotel* at 60 Kaigao Lane (☎049/2701511; ❹) is an aging but comfortable mid-range option with outdoor hot-spring pools surrounded by lovely sakura trees.

Dongpu's main street, Kaigao Lane, is lined with small **restaurants** serving fresh **river trout** and mountain vegetables, but most cater to larger groups and are confounded by the individual traveller. One notable exception is *Shan Chih Siang* at 75 Kaigao Lane, whose friendly owners are more than happy to steam a small trout for a solo tourist.

The climb

To get to the **trailhead**, walk to the far side of Dongpu village along the main road and carry on for several hundred metres – past the national park entrance sign – until you reach the trail entrance on the left-hand side (it's marked by a large wooden sign with a trail map that is easily spotted from the road). From here, the well-marked path climbs to a narrow, partly sealed road; after about 1km you'll encounter a **Taoist temple** with a metal pavilion out front where you can buy bottled water and soft drinks. Beyond this, the trail proper begins and there is no other chance to buy supplies. Shortly after the trail narrows, there is a series of steep ledges, with thick steel guard rails along the sides, each segment bearing giant dents where boulders have come crashing down during typhoons. Once past this hair-raising section, the trail continues to hug the mountainside, and after about 3km it reaches the staggering, three-tiered **Yunlong (Cloud Dragon) Waterfall**, which plummets several hundred metres and is considered by many to be Taiwan's most beautiful cascade. To see the top two tiers at once and truly appreciate the waterfall's enormous scale, you must walk a couple of hundred metres beyond it, to where a trailside overlook gives clear views of the second tier spilling into a crystal pool hundreds of feet below. This is about as far as most Taiwanese tourists get, and it's an extremely worthwhile destination even if you're not planning to climb Yushan.

From here, the trail continues to cling to the mountainside for the next 2km, passing some steep drop-offs before reaching the grubby **Lele Cabin** (1711m), an enclosed hut with a slightly elevated wooden sleeping platform. The cabin is dirty but could be used for shelter in bad weather, and behind it is a hose through which drinking water (treatment recommended) is piped from a nearby spring. About 500m past the cabin you'll come to the **Yinyu (One Girl) Waterfall**, another multi-tiered cascade that can only be fully seen from a distance. Exactly 4km further, at the 10.3km marker, is **Dueiguan**, a patrol station during the Japanese occupation that is now recognizable by the **cherry trees** planted by the colonists. Over the next 4km you'll gain almost 500m in

△ Yushan summit

elevation before reaching **Guangaoping**, a helicopter landing pad that's only 500m from the **Guangao Cabin**, where you'll spend the night. The cabin is lightly used and very clean, and there are pit toilets and a fresh water source (treatment recommended) nearby.

To the summit

The climb from here to the summit is long and strenuous, and you'll need to start well before daybreak to allow yourself adequate time to reach the top and return to the cabin by nightfall. The first 2.3km is gradual, and you'll quickly reach the dreamlike, high-altitude **Badongguan** meadows, where if you're quiet you're likely to see some of Yushan's deer, especially the tiny Formosan Reeve's Muntjac. Here the trail to the summit forks to the right, but there is no sign indicating the turnoff: the correct trail skirts behind a tiny campsite. For the next 5.2km the trail climbs steadily, with a couple of extremely steep detours around landslip areas, until reaching the **Laonong Campsite** (3020m) alongside a creek. From here it's only 2km to the top of Yushan's main peak, but with over 930m in elevation gain left, it's one of Taiwan's most taxing bits of trail. Compounding the steepness is the altitude, with the thin air making breathing more difficult, and once onto the open rocky areas closer to the top the winds can be vicious and bitingly cold. The last kilometre or so is completely exposed, crossing a field of rocks and scree before cutting sharply left for the final 200m – girding the left-hand side of this stretch is a **chain** which can be used for support. It takes several hours to descend to the Guangao Cabin, so give yourself plenty of time to complete the return walk before dark, and be sure to carry a **headlamp** or torch. If you leave the cabin early the following morning you should reach Dongpu by mid-afternoon – just enough time to enjoy the hot springs before dinner.

Travel details

Trains

Changhua to: Chiayi (17 express daily; 50min); Kaohsiung (17 express daily; 2hr 15min); Taichung (17 express daily; 12min); Tainan (17 express daily; 1hr 35min).

Chiayi to: Alishan Forest Recreation Area (1 or 2 daily; 3hr 30min); Changhua (17 express daily; 50min); Ershuei (frequent; 50min); Fencihu (1 or 2 daily; 2hr 14min); Jiaoliping (1 or 2 daily; 1hr 39min); Kaohsiung (14 express daily; 1hr 15min); Taichung (14 express daily; 1hr 15min); Tainan (14 express daily; 40min); Taipei (16 express daily; 3hr 10min).

Ershuei to: Chiayi (frequent; 50min); Jiji (8 daily; 28min); Kaohsiung (15 daily; 2hr 30min); Taichung (frequent; 45min); Tainan (15 daily; 1hr 45min).

Taichung to: Changhua (17 express daily; 12min); Chiayi (14 express daily; 1hr 15min); Ershuei (frequent; 45min); Kaohsiung (16 express daily; 2hr 30min); Tainan (16 express daily; 2hr); Taipei (15 express daily; 2hr 5min).

Buses

With so many services operating in the region, some bus frequencies to major cities have not been included. Most inter-city buses leave every 30 min, and services to Taichung and Taipei often run 24hr.

Changhua to: Lugang (30min); Taichung (30min); Taipei (2hr 15min).

Chiayi to: Alishan Forest Recreation Area (1hr 30min); Beigang (45min); Budai (1hr); Dabang (2hr); Guanziling Hot Springs (1hr); Kaohsiung (1hr), Tainan (30min); Taipei (3hr 30min).

Dongpu to: Shueili (8 daily; 1hr).

Lugang to: Changhua (30min); Taichung (1hr); Taipei (30min).

Puli to: Shueili (1hr); Sun Moon Lake (30min); Taichung (1hr); Taipei (3hr); Wushe (45min).

Sun Moon Lake to: Puli (30min); Shueili (30min); Taichung (2 daily; 2hr); Taipei (3hr 30min).

Taichung to: Changhua (30min); Chiayi (1hr 30min); Dajia (1hr); Guguan (2hr 30min);

Kaohsiung (2hr 30min); Lugang (1hr); Tainan (2hr); Taipei (2hr); Puli (1hr); Sitou (2hr); Sun Moon Lake (2 daily; 2hr).

Ferries

Budai to: Magong (2 daily, summer only; 1hr)

Flights

Chiayi to: Kinmen (1 daily; 50min); Magong (2 daily; 30min); Taipei (9 daily; 45min).
Taichung to: Hualien (5 daily; 55min); Kinmen (10 daily; 55min); Magong (9 daily, 35min); Taipei (6 daily; 40min); Taitung (1 daily; 1hr 5min).

South Taiwan

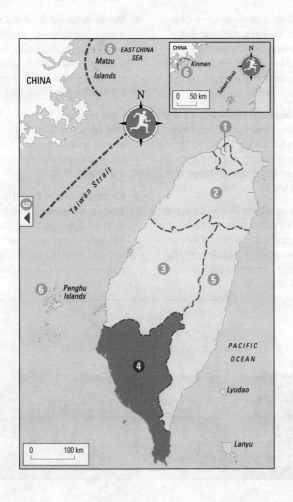

CHAPTER 4 Highlights

* **Tainan** Taiwan's former capital is a city of historic but highly active temples, and home to some of its best street food. See p.313

* **Cigu Salt Mountains** One of Taiwan's quirkiest sights, piled four-storeys high and dominating the flat, western coastline like snowy peaks. See p.333

* **Southern Cross-Island Highway** Spectacular mountain road, linking Tainan to Taitung and cutting across the southern tip of Yushan National Park. See p.334

* **Kaohsiung** Taiwan's second city is the vibrant and friendly capital of the south, with a smattering of historic sights and excellent seafood. See p.340

* **Foguangshan** Spend a day exploring the galleries, museums and stunning temples of this massive Buddhist monastery. See p.354

* **Maolin National Scenic Area** Absorb the gorgeous scenery in this mountainous area of waterfalls, hot springs, water sports and vibrant Rukai and Paiwan culture. See p.357

* **Little Liouciou Island** Kick back and enjoy the alluring rock formations on this fascinating coral island. See p.364

* **Kenting National Park** Hire a scooter and explore Taiwan's most southerly national park, with pristine surf beaches and authentic Paiwan villages scattered along County Road 199. See p.371

△ Maolin, Little Guilin

South Taiwan

anguid, tropical **south Taiwan** is a world away from Taipei, a land of betel nut plantations, pineapple groves and sandy beaches. The southern plains are home to Taiwan's oldest Chinese settlements, a bastion of Taiwanese culture and a correspondingly high proportion of independence supporters – the counties of Tainan, Kaohsiung and Pingdong are DPP strongholds and Taiwanese language is spoken everywhere in preference to Mandarin. The lush southern mountains, while not quite as dramatic as the central ranges, still offer plenty of gorgeous scenery, predominantly inhabited by the Bunun, Paiwan and Rukai tribes – the **Paiwan** maintain a particularly strong identity, their villages in the far south of the island rarely visited by travellers. Much of the region's exuberant culture is encapsulated in its **festivals**: many temples hold elaborate **boat-burning** ceremonies every three years, while the horizontal firework display at **Yanshuei** is a chaotic but exhilarating event held over Chinese New Year.

Tainan is an essential stop on any tour of Taiwan. The former capital is crammed with ornate temples, engaging historical sights and some of the best snack food in the country. From here the **Southern Cross-Island Highway** snakes east across the mountains to Taitung, a dramatic and sometimes perilous route with incredibly scenic views; it cuts through the northern end of **Maolin National Scenic Area**, no less captivating, with picturesque hot springs and the slate Rukai village of Duona, white-water rafting on the Laonong River and the stunning mountain road up to the Rukai village of Wutai. **Kaohsiung** is the biggest city in the south with a laid-back, friendly character, rapidly throwing off its grimy industrial image and close to the impressive monastery at **Foguangshan**. The narrow stub of land at the foot of Taiwan is dominated by **Kenting National Park**, with its somewhat overrated main resort but a wealth of less visited beaches and excellent surf easily accessible by scooter – the intriguing coral island of **Little Liouciou** is just off the coast.

Tainan

Historic **TAINAN**, just a few kilometres from the southwest coast, is a city of ancient monuments, delicious food, and above all **temples**: religious life has an intensity here rarely matched elsewhere, with more gods worshipped, and more festivals and rituals observed than in any other place in Taiwan. Much of this is a legacy of its former status as capital city, a title it enjoyed for over two hundred years, and particularly the seventeenth century when it was the last independent

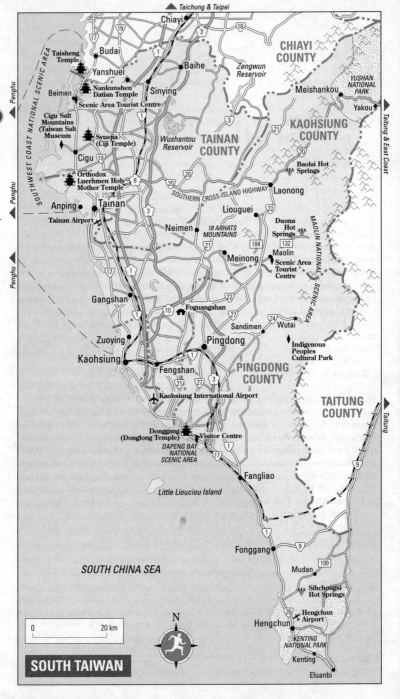

SOUTH TAIWAN

outpost of China's Ming dynasty. Although the city's most important sights are remnants of this period, the juxtaposition between modernisation and tradition here is particularly stark, with beautifully constructed classical buildings such as the Tiantan and Datianhou Temple tucked away between busy commercial streets and characterless apartment blocks.

Some history

Once the ancestral home of the Siraya *pingpu* tribe, Tainan's modern history begins with the **Dutch**, who established **Fort Zeelandia** in 1624 on a sand bar off the coast. In the seventeenth century the western half of today's city was under water, part of a huge lagoon known as Taijiang and ringed by a chain of sandy islets. Like Lugang (p.257), Tainan is a former port that is now miles from the sea, and all over town you'll be walking over old quays, filled-in canals and rivers. The Dutch called the area "Tayouan", thought to be a transliteration of the Siraya word "dayouan" (or a derivative of the Taiwanese word *tai wan*), and made it the capital of their colony (see Contexts p.506). In 1662 they surrendered to the vastly superior forces of Ming general Zheng Chenggong, also known as **Koxinga** (see box p.325) after a nine-month siege. During the period of Zheng family rule (1662–1683) Tainan prospered, many of its finest temples constructed to befit its status as an independent Chinese kingdom – in 1664, one of the last descendants of the Ming royal family, Prince Ning Jing, moved to the city. When the Zhengs surrendered to Chinese Admiral Shi Lang in 1683, the city became known as **Taiwan-Fu**, and prefectural capital of the island.

In 1823 a devastating storm led to the silting up of the lagoon, and **Anping** (the site of Fort Zeelandia) became permanently joined to the mainland. The Treaty of Beijing (1860) led to a small community of foreign merchants trading camphor, tea and opium in Anping – after the Japanese occupied Taiwan in 1895, the sale of opium and camphor became a government franchise and with the port silting up further, by 1911 most merchants had left. When Taiwan became a province in 1885, the city became known as **Tainan-Fu**, or "South Taiwan" and lost its capital status to Taipei – today it's Taiwan's fourth-largest city with a population of around 750,000. Since the end of martial law in 1987, Tainan's strong Taiwanese identity has made it a bastion of independence and DPP support (Chen Shui-bian was born in Tainan County). Ironically, the city's most notable event of recent times was the shooting of President Chen Shui-bian in March 2004 on Jinhua Road, just south of the centre.

Arrival, orientation and city transport

Tainan Airport is 5km south of the city, a short taxi (NT$200) or bus ride (NT$20) to the centre. The **train station** is located on the eastern edge of the city centre and most **buses** terminate nearby. The **High-Speed Rail station** is located near Kueijen, 10km southeast of the centre, and connected to the city by bus.

Tainan is divided into six districts with most of the sights concentrated in **Anping** and Central West: the latter encompasses most of the old walled city and forms Tainan's historic core, further divided for the convenience of tourists into **Cultural Zones**. These are easily explored on foot, with Jhongshan and Minzu roads the main commercial streets, but to access Tainan's modern shopping malls and restaurants you'll need to take taxis. The **West Gate** Area along Simen Road, and **Yonghua Road** further west are where much of the newer development is located.

Tainan	台南	táinán
Tainan Airport	台南機場	táinán jī chǎng
Tainan Train Station	台南火車站	táinán huǒchē zhàn

Accommodation

Asia Hotel	東亞樓大飯店	dōngyàlóu dàfàndiàn
Cambridge Hotel	劍橋大飯店	jiànqiáo dàfàndiàn
Guang Hwa Hotel	光華大旅社	guānghuá dàlǚshè
Hotel Tainan	台南大飯店	táinán dàfàndiàn
Hwa Mao Business Hotel	華茂商務飯店	huámào shāngwù fàndiàn
Landis Tayih	大億麗緻酒店	dàyì lízhì jiǔdiàn
La Plaza	天下大飯店	tiānxià dàfàndiàn
Puyuma Hotel	普悠瑪大飯店	pǔyōumǎ dàfàndiàn

The City

Chihkan Towers	赤崁樓	chìkǎn lóu
City God Temple	城隍廟	chénghuáng miào
Confucius Temple	孔子廟	kǒngzǐ miào
Datianhou Temple	大天后宮	dà tiānhòu gōng
Dongyue Temple	東嶽殿	dōngyuè diàn
Five Canal District	五條港區	wǔ tiáogǎng qū
Great South Gate	大南門	dànánmén
Kaiji Tianhou Temple	開基天后宮	kāijī tiānhòu gōng
Koxinga Shrine	延平郡王祠	yánpíng jùnwáng cí
Lady Linshui Temple	臨水夫人廟	línshǔi fūrén mǎ miào
Medicine Lord Temple	藥王廟	yàowáng miào
National Museum of Taiwanese Literature	國家台灣文學管	guójiā táiwān wénxúegǔan
Official God of War Temple	祀典武廟	sìdiǎn wǔ miào
Official Reception Gate	接官亭	jiē gūanting
Tiantan (Altar of Heaven)	天壇（天公廟）	tiāntán
Water Fairy Temple	水仙宮	shuǐxiān gōng
Wind God Temple	風神廟	fēngshén miào
Wufei Temple (Temple of the Five Concubines)	五妃廟	wǔfěi miào

City transport

Buses are confusing and hard to use in Tainan, with no English timetables at bus stops or on the buses themselves, though you're unlikely to need them within the old centre. The main city bus station lines the traffic circle opposite the train station. For trips outside the centre it's more convenient to take a **taxi** – the initial fare is NT$70. If you can't flag one down, there are usually plenty at the train station.

Information

The small **tourist office** (daily 8.30am–5.30pm; ☎06/2290082, ⓦtour.tncg .gov.tw) next to the train station exit has a decent selection of English-language material. *Rickshaw Magazine* is a Tainan-based publication targeting expats, and free in many hotels and bars, while *FYI South* also has decent Tainan listings. The city has opted to use the Tongyong Pinyin system, with streets well marked in English and Chinese.

Moving on from Tainan

Tainan Airport has regular **flights** to Taipei, Kinmen and Magong, while express trains run along the west-coast line to Taipei (NT$741) and Kaohsiung (NT$107) throughout the day. **High-speed rail** services depart the special station at Kueijen (see p.315). Most long-distance **buses** depart from various offices on the left side of Beimen Road, north of the train station: the first is Ho Hsin operating services to Taipei, Hsinchu, Taichung and Kaohsiung, at regular 30min intervals (24hrs): Taichung buses leave from a second office a few shops up the road. Ubus is next, offering 24hr services to Taipei and Taichung while Kuo Kuang next door also has Taichung and Taipei buses. At least one bus every hour departs the Singnan bus station on Jhongshan Road to the South West Coast National Scenic Area and Nankunshen (daily 6.10am–8.20pm; NT$104). Buses to Meishankou on the Southern Cross-Island Highway also depart daily from the Singnan bus station (7.20am, 9.10am & 3.10pm; 3hr 15min; NT$290), but for other destinations in Tainan County it's best to have your own transport. In the summer, fast **ferries** depart Anping Harbor visitor center (16, Lane 23, Singang Rd ☎06/2618333) for Magong in Penghu at 10am daily.

Accommodation

Tainan has plenty of **accommodation** conveniently located in the centre of the city, within walking distance or a short taxi ride from the station and most of the sights. The choice is limited to adequate but fairly uninspiring mid-range or budget hotels however – there are no hostels and only a couple of five-stars, both on the edge of downtown.

Asia Hotel 100 Jhongshan Rd ☎06/2226171, ⓦwww.asiahoteltaiwan.com. Tainan budget institution, with Chinese decor and slightly shabby premises not far from the station. The cheapest single rooms are tiny with newish, white-tiled bathrooms, but it's worth paying a little more for doubles which have wine-coloured carpets and redwood furniture. No Internet. ❷

Cambridge Hotel 269 Minzu Rd Sec 2 ☎06/2219911, Ⓔcamhotel2004@yahoo.com.tw. Comfortable mid-range hotel in the heart of Tainan, with clean, simply furnished standard rooms, decent buffet breakfast and free Internet access. It's worth paying a little more for the larger business or deluxe rooms. ❻

Guang Hwa Hotel 155 Beimen Rd Sec 1 ☎06/2263171. Tainan's best budget hotel, a short walk south of the station, with rooms from NT$600 and English speakers on the front desk. All rooms have TV, and bathrooms come with tub and hand-held showers. Extras include breakfast and free Internet access, while YHA cardholders get a small discount. ❷

Hotel Tainan 1 Chenggong Rd ☎06/2289101, ⓦwww.hotel-tainan.com.tw. A Tainan institution since 1964, with highly rated Chinese restaurants and comfortable rooms: it's not quite luxury standard these days, but it's convenient for trains and buses, and good value with gym and free Internet. ❻

Hwa Mao Business Hotel 23 Sinmei St ☎06/2267699, ⓦhwamaohotel.com.tw. Cheerful budget hotel in central Tainan, offering basic but bright and comfortable standard rooms: upgrade to business or Japanese rooms for more space. Extras include free coffee, Internet, laundry and bicycle hire. Located between Mincyuan and Minsheng roads. ❸

Landis Tayih 660 Simen Rd Sec 1 ☎06/2135555, ⓦwww.tayihlandis.com.tw. Tainan's top five-star hotel, its large rooms feature a contemporary minimalist style with flat-screen TVs and marble-clad bathrooms. The stylish gym (7/F) is set at the foot of a large indoor atrium, and there's a spa, pool, hip lounge bar and choice of top-notch international restaurants. ❼

La Plaza 202 Chenggong Rd ☎06/2290271, ⓦwww.laplaza.com.tw. This old hotel has been redesigned in elegant, modern Chinese style, with sleek fittings, Chinese art and bathrooms lined with grey stone; the deluxe rooms are more like mini-suites. Facilities include free Internet, breakfast, gym and coin laundry. ❻

Puyuma Hotel 7/F, 145 Jhongyi Rd Sec 2 ☎06/2275566. Cosy hotel in the heart of the old city, with modern, comfortable rooms, free laundry, Internet and small buffet breakfast. Same owners as the *Cambridge* nearby, but tends to be a little cheaper. ❹

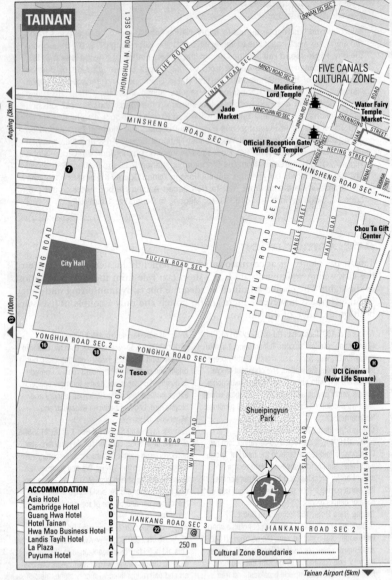

▲ Orthodox Luerhmen Holy Mother Temple (10km) & South West Coast National Scenic Area

TAINAN

Anping (3km) ◄

▲ (100m)

JHONGHUA N. ROAD SEC 1

SIHE ROAD

LINNAN ROAD SEC 1

LINNAN RD SEC 2

MINZU ROAD SEC 3

FIVE CANALS CULTURAL ZONE

Medicine Lord Temple

MINCYUAN RD SEC 2

JINHUA RD SEC 3

Water Fairy Temple Market

SHENNONG STREET

HAIAN STREET

Jade Market

MINSHENG ROAD SEC 1

Official Reception Gate/ Wind God Temple

KANGLE STREET

HEPING STREET

MINSHENG ROAD SEC 1

ROAD SEC 2

❼

JIANPING ROAD

City Hall

FUCIAN ROAD SEC 2

JINHUA ROAD SEC 2

KANGLE STREET

HAIAN ROAD

Chou Ta Gift Center

YONGHUA ROAD SEC 2

❶❻

❶❽

YONGHUA ROAD SEC 2

YONGHUA ROAD SEC 1

❶❼

UCI Cinema (New Life Square) Ⓗ

JHONGHUA N. ROAD SEC 2

Tesco

Shueipingyun Park

JIANNAN ROAD

WUNNAN ROAD

SIALIN ROAD

SIMEN ROAD SEC 2

N

ACCOMMODATION
Asia Hotel — G
Cambridge Hotel — C
Guang Hwa Hotel — D
Hotel Tainan — B
Hwa Mao Business Hotel — F
Landis Tayih Hotel — H
La Plaza — A
Puyuma Hotel — E

JIANKANG ROAD SEC 3

❷❷

@

0   250 m

JIANKANG ROAD SEC 2

Cultural Zone Boundaries ....

▼ Tainan Airport (5km)

The City

The oldest and most absorbing parts of Tainan are Anping and the cultural zones in the heart of the old city: these were created in 2005 specifically to make things easier for visitors, with city information, signs and maps tailored to each zone and well marked in English. The **Chihkan, Five Canals** and

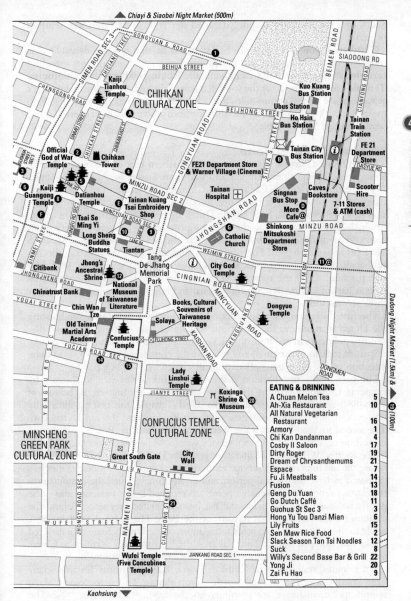

▲ Chiayi & Siaobei Night Market (500m)

CHIHKAN CULTURAL ZONE

Kaiji Tianhou Temple

Kuo Kuang Bus Station

Ubus Station

Ho Hsin Bus Station

Tainan Train Station

FE 21 Department Store

Tainan City Bus Station

Official God of War Temple

Chihkan Tower

FE21 Department Store & Warner Village (Cinema)

Scooter Hire

Kaiji Guangong Temple

Datianhou Temple

Tainan Kuang Tsai Embroidery Shop

Tainan Hospital

Singnan Bus Stop

More Cafe@

7-11 Stores & ATM (cash)

Tsai Se Ming Yi

Long Sheng Buddha Statues

Tiantan

Shinkong Mitsukoshi Department Store

Citibank

Jheng's Ancestral Shrine

Catholic Church

City God Temple

Chinatrust Bank

National Museum of Taiwanese Literature

Tang De-Jhang Memorial Park

Dongyue Temple

Chin Wan Tze

Books, Cultural Souvenirs of Taiwanese Heritage

Old Tainan Martial Arts Academy

Solaya

Confucius Temple

Lady Linshui Temple

Koxinga Shrine & Museum

CONFUCIUS TEMPLE CULTURAL ZONE

MINSHENG GREEN PARK CULTURAL ZONE

Great South Gate

City Wall

Wufei Temple (Five Concubines Temple)

Kaohsiung ▼

4 SOUTH TAIWAN | Tainan

Dadong Night Market (1.5km) & ▶

EATING & DRINKING	
A Chuan Melon Tea	5
Ah-Xia Restaurant	10
All Natural Vegetarian Restaurant	16
Armory	1
Chi Kan Dandanman	4
Cosby II Saloon	17
Dirty Roger	19
Dream of Chrysanthemums	21
Espace	7
Fu Ji Meatballs	14
Fusion	13
Geng Du Yuan	18
Go Dutch Caffé	11
Guohua St Sec 3	3
Hong Yu Tou Danzi Mian	6
Lily Fruits	15
Sen Maw Rice Food	2
Slack Season Tan Tsi Noodles	12
Suck	8
Willy's Second Base Bar & Grill	22
Yong Ji	20
Zai Fu Hao	9

Confucius Temple Cultural Zones contain the richest concentration of sights – reckon on spending at least two days to do them justice. Inevitably, Tainan's list of attractions is dominated by an overwhelming array of **temples**, most of which are architecturally beautiful but quite similar to the untrained eye – what makes them individually unique are the smaller artistic details, the historical context and various rituals that take place inside.

319

See Contexts p.532 for a more detailed description of Taiwanese temples in general.

Chihkan Tower is the best place to start, a collection of Qing dynasty pavilions built on the ruins of an old Dutch fort. From here Tainan's most appealing **temples** are just short walks away, while the **Koxinga Shrine** and **Confucius Temple** provide a locus for the southern half of the old city. Historic **Anping's** attractions are no less compact, located a brief taxi ride west of the centre. With more time, it's worth making for the northern district of **Luermen** and the world's largest Mazu temple.

Chihkan Cultural Zone

The **Chihkan Cultural Zone** covers the northern part of the old city, home to some of Tainan's finest temples and **Chihkan Tower** (daily 8.30am–10pm; NT$50), a city landmark. Chihkan is a Chinese transliteration of "Sakam", the name of the *pingpu* village that once stood here, but the name is also an allusion to **Fort Provintia**, built by the Dutch in 1653. Very little remains of the original, however, and today the site comprises two Fujianese-style pavilions constructed in the nineteenth century. The fort was captured by Koxinga in 1661 prior to his siege of Fort Zeelandia, and after the Dutch defeat, the site was gradually abandoned until a temple was built on the ruins in 1875 (the first pavilion). Over the next ten years four more buildings were constructed here as part of a Qing dynasty educational and religious complex, though only three remain today.

The first thing you'll see on entering the grounds is the **statue** symbolizing the Dutch surrender to the victorious Koxinga. It says more about twentieth-century politics than real history (the Dutchman is far too short and dressed like a Spanish captain of the time) and was actually completed in the 1980s to draw attention to the Ming general's nationalist credentials (see box p.325).

The base of the first pavilion is lined with **nine steles** sent to the city by Emperor Qianlong praising the defeat of the Lin Shuangwen Rebellion of 1786–88 (see p.508). Originally a **Sea God Temple**, the first pavilion now houses a small exhibition (Chinese only) on Koxinga and the old Dutch Fort. The second pavilion beyond is the **Wenchang Pavilion**: the first floor houses an exhibition detailing the Qing civil service system, while upstairs contains a shrine to the fourth "Wenchang" or literature god, Kui Dou Xingjun, said to aid those taking the old imperial civil service examinations. Like many Chinese deities he's supposed to have been a real person, and is said to have failed the examinations three times simply because the emperor was repulsed by his hideous looks – the poor scholar committed suicide and has been venerated ever since. Behind the pavilion on the left is all that remains of the **Peng Hu School**, built in 1886, while to the right are the red brick foundations of the **Dutch fort** – the dark red bricks were shipped from Batavia (Jakarta), the light red from Xiamen in China, and glued together by a mixture of seashells, sticky rice and sugarcane.

Ten minutes' walk north of Chihkan Tower, **Kaiji Tianhou Temple** (daily 6am–9pm) is a real gem, well worth a short detour. This is the oldest Mazu temple in Tainan (there are seventeen in the city), established in 1662. The shrine is decorated with some fascinating artwork, such as the "barbarian" figures holding up the eaves of the temple corners, and the tiled paintings at the entrance, but the real highlight is the shrine to **Guanyin** at the back. This contains one of three celebrated images of the bodhisattva in Tainan, the gold statue blackened with incense smoke over the years, her graceful pose capturing perfectly the ethos of Buddhist serenity. Walk up Chihkan Street and turn left at Chenggong Road – turn right at Zhiciang Street and the temple is at no. 12.

Official God of War Temple

The striking peach-coloured walls opposite Chihkan Tower belong to Tainan's **Official God of War Temple** (daily 6am–9pm), or literally the "Sacrificial Rites Martial Temple". The entrance is a short walk south along Yongfu Road. It's one of the city's most attractive temples, dedicated to **Guan Di**, and significant because it originally served as Prince Ning Jing's private gardens, built in 1665. He's said to have brought one of the images of the deity inside with him from China, but the temple was formally established in 1690 when it took on its current form. The **Main Hall** at the front of the complex contains the shrine to Guan Di, with an aged wooden tablet hanging from the beams above the entrance – carved in 1794, it reads *Da Zhang Fu* or "Great Man", an allusion to the fierce-looking god below. The **Rear Hall** contains tablets representing three generations of Guan Di's ancestors: on the left you'll see a small scroll inscribed with a bamboo engraving and poem said to have been penned by the general himself, though this is not the original – it's a rubbing from his tomb in China. To the left of here is a side hall containing another of Tainan's three captivating images of **Guanyin**, while around the back sits a plum tree said to have been planted by Prince Ning Jing himself.

Datianhou Temple and around

Turn immediately right when you exit the Official God of War Temple into Lane 227; known as Fortune Tellers Alley and still crammed with *feng shui* masters, it's a short walk from here to the front of **Datianhou Temple** (daily 6am–9pm). Also known as the Official Mazu Temple, it's another site with great historical significance and stands on the location of Prince Ning Jing's palace, built in 1664. Shi Lang eventually converted the palace into a shrine, honouring the goddess he believed had delivered victory in 1683. The current buildings date from 1830.

The atmospheric **Main Hall** is packed with numerous Mazu deities, while the **stele** embedded in the wall to the right was commissioned in 1685 by Shi Lang to commemorate his triumph, and is reputed to be the oldest in Taiwan. The **dragon pillars** here are rare Ming originals from the time of Ning Jing – this part of the temple is thought to have served as the private shrine where he would worship his illustrious Ming ancestors. The **Rear Hall** is dedicated to Mazu's parents, previously serving as Ning Jing's actual residence but more

The last of the Ming

All but forgotten today, **Prince Ning Jing**, one of the last descendants of China's once great Ming dynasty, rulers of China 1368–1644, died in Tainan in 1683. Chong Zhen, the last Ming emperor, hanged himself in Beijing as it was being overrun by rebel troops in 1644, and was eventually replaced by the first Manchu or Qing emperor, Shunzhi. However, several of Chong Zhen's relatives escaped to form a rival Southern Ming dynasty. Ning Jing was one of these hapless survivors. One by one, his fellow princes were defeated in battle, with the last formal pretender, Prince of Gui, murdered in 1662. Ning Jing fled to Kinmen and remained there even after Ming loyalist Koxinga sailed to Taiwan, believing that the general's retreat would mean the permanent loss of China. He was right: in 1663 he was finally persuaded to move to Tainan by Koxinga's son, Zheng Jing, becoming the nominal head of the dynasty but with little real power. In a final show of defiance he committed suicide with his household on hearing of the Zhengs' surrender to the Qing in 1683 – the dynasty died with him. Ning Jing's modest tomb is in Chuhu, south of Tainan.

famous for its grisly association with his concubines – they're supposed to have hanged themselves from the beams above, after hearing of Shi Lang's victory. The shrine to the left of the main hall contains another exceptional **Guanyin** figure, this one black-faced and robed in gold, set, rather majestically, within an attractive grotto.

Walk straight across the plaza outside the temple and turn left up Sinmei Street – the **Kaiji Guangong Temple** (daily 4am–9pm) is around 50m on the left, Tainan's oldest shrine dedicated to Guan Di and in contrast to the official temple, the place where commoners could worship. The atmospheric **Front Hall** contains the main shrine and was once the drum tower for Ning Jing's palace - the bottles of oil at the back are used to fuel lamps placed in front of the altar. Beyond here, the larger and newer **Main Hall** celebrates Guan Di in his capacity as the second Wenchang god, or god of literature.

Tiantan

Tiantan (Altar of Heaven, daily 5am–10pm), one of Tainan's most important temples, is around fifteen minutes' walk southeast from Guangong Temple. Continue south along Sinmei Street and turn left along Mincyuan Road: turn right when you come to Jhongyi Road and first left along narrow Lane 84. Despite the name, the main building is a fairly typical South Fujianese-style temple, with an elaborately carved facade and vivid dragons embellishing the double-eaved, gable and hip roof of the Main Hall. The temple is primarily dedicated to the **Jade Emperor**, but operates more like a spiritual department store, with more deities and hosting more festivals than any other in Tainan – as a consequence it's the best place to observe traditional rituals. Koxinga is thought to have built the first altar here in 1661 as a temporary measure (officially only the emperor could worship the Jade Emperor) but this was soon dismantled. Locals continued the tradition of making offerings on the site, however, and in 1854 the emperor finally agreed to the construction of a temple – it's been renovated many times since then.

The **Main Hall** is where the Jade Emperor is worshipped, and as is traditional, the god is symbolized by a tablet with his name on it – he's too powerful to be represented by a statue. Notice the tablet on the beam in front of the Main Hall, which has a single horizontal brush stroke meaning *yi* or "one" in Chinese and symbolic of the god's ultimate power – wishful DPP supporters also claim it resembles the scar on President Chen's stomach after the 2004 shooting incident.

The **Rear Hall** is crammed with smoke-stained deities – the shrine in the centre is dedicated to the San Guan Dadi, the three imperial officials of Taoism, overseeing heaven, earth and sea, but the hall's most animated occupants are the **fortune tellers** or "Red Head Masters", spirit mediums that are employed to communicate with the gods. Wearing white shirts and vivid red headgear, they usually perform rituals for a minimum donation of NT$100.

Five Canals Cultural Zone

The old merchant quarter west of Simen Road is known as Wu Tiao Gang, established beyond the old city walls in the eighteenth century as traders tried to keep up with the retreating lagoon. Dubbed the **Five Canals Cultural Zone** (though the canals are long gone), it tends to get fewer visitors than other parts of the city, but nevertheless has heaps of character. Start at **Water Fairy Temple Market**, one of the city's oldest and most traditional. Entering on the eastern side from Guohua Street, opposite Gonghua Street, you should come to its namesake, the tiny **Water Fairy Temple** (daily 6am–9pm), surrounded by a sea of meat and veg stalls and dedicated to the five water lords of ancient Chinese tradition. Squeeze inside to view the intricately carved wooden beams and Chinese characters on the back of the pillars flanking the altar; uncovered in 2004, these etchings were covered in plaster for hundreds of years and describe the origin of the temple.

Keep walking due west through the market and you'll emerge onto Haian Road; cross over, and look for narrow **Shennong Street**. This is perhaps Tainan's most traditional and photogenic street, with ramshackle, wooden houses, and at its western end, the **Medicine Lord Temple** (daily 5am–6pm). This small shrine commemorates a doctor from the Tang dynasty: his statue sits in the main hall, flanked by two pages, one holding medical books, the other a bottle of medicine. The temple was established in 1646 and is the only one in Tainan facing east, allowing it to signal the others more easily in times of trouble. Retrace your steps to Kangle Street and turn right: just across Mincyuan Road near the junction with Heping Street you'll see the **Official Reception Gate** on the right, marking the spot mainland officials would be ferried to shore to meet local dignitaries and built in 1739 – the blue stones across Heping Street mark the route of the old canal. The officials would be received in buildings later converted into the tiny **Wind God Temple** (daily 6.30am–6pm) a few metres behind: this was demolished by the Japanese but rebuilt in 1924.

Confucius Temple Cultural Zone
The southern half of the old city falls within the **Confucius Temple Cultural Zone**, littered with more temples and historic sights, and the less interesting Minsheng Green Park Cultural Zone, containing most of Tainan's Japanese-era buildings. The **Confucius Temple** (daily 8.30am–5.30pm; Ⓦconfucius .cca.gov.tw) is Taiwan's oldest Confucian shrine, established in 1666 but rebuilt many times. With its pink and russet-red walls, classical architecture and languid tree-lined forecourt, it's one of the most charming structures in the city, laid out in traditional Confucian style. As you enter, the first building on the right is the **Hall of Edification**, a school for those preparing to take provincial level exams in the Qing period. The school rules are written on a stele on the far right – among them are bans on money lending and brawling. The rare stele on the far left was inscribed with a plan of the temple and the Nanmen area shortly after the temple's foundation. The **Wenchang Pavilion** sits behind this hall, a three-storey pagoda completed in 1715 and housing gods of literature. The central **Dacheng Hall** (NT\$25), with its distinctive double-eave swallowtail roof, is at the heart of the complex. It's simply decorated inside, with just one tablet dedicated to Confucius, inscribed with "Great Teacher Spirit Tablet". As is customary, on each side are tablets to his disciples (Mencius is on the left), but what makes this temple unique are the twelve boards beautifully inscribed by various emperors and leaders of Taiwan hanging from the beams. Emperor Kangxi's "Teacher of all generations" is black and directly above the main shrine; Chiang Kai-shek wrote the blue tablet above the entrance, while to the right is the dark green eulogy from Chen Shui-bian.

Confucius's Birthday is commemorated by the **Tainan Confucius Temple Cultural Festival**, usually held over the five days leading up to the main anniversary on September 28, but the temple is unique in also celebrating the spring equinox on March 20 with another elaborate ceremony.

Fifteen minutes' walk south of the temple on Nanmen Road, the **Great South Gate** (daily 8.30am–11pm) is the best remaining example of Tainan's old defences. The double gate was completed in 1835 to replace the former wooden stockade. Continue south along Nanmen Road and turn left at

SOUTH TAIWAN | Tainan

Wufei Street to reach **Wufei Temple**, Temple of the Five Concubines (daily 8.30am–5.30pm). Set in a peaceful park, it's dedicated to the five concubines of Prince Ning Jing, who committed suicide rather than submit to the Qing in 1683. They were buried here, in what was once a cemetery outside the city walls – the burial mound is behind the temple. The tiny shrine a few metres to the left of the temple is known as **Yi Ling Chun** and commemorates the two eunuchs who also committed suicide. From here head north up Cianjhong Street, turning right at the junction with Shulin Street, passing the best remaining section of Tainan's old **city wall**. Follow Shulin Road east from here and you should emerge on Kaishan Road, just south of the Koxinga Shrine.

Koxinga Shrine and around

Dedicated to the Ming dynasty general venerated on both sides of the Taiwan Strait, the **Koxinga Shrine** (daily 8am–6.30pm; NT$50) sits in a small park off Kaishan Road. The shrine (and ticket booth) is to the right of the park entrance under the memorial arch, while the **museum** (daily 9am–5pm; entrance with shrine ticket) is straight ahead.

When Koxinga died in Tainan in 1662 his body was eventually returned to China, but local people set up a small shrine on this spot to remember him and an official shrine was built in 1874. The buildings you see today were rebuilt in Northern Chinese style in 1963.

The side corridors are lined with tablets commemorating Ming dynasty officials and generals, while the main shrine, replete with a gracious statue of Koxinga, sits in the centre. Behind this is a plum tree said to be planted by the man himself, though locals will tell you it died years ago and the current impostor is a mere forty-year-old sapling. The **Rear Hall** contains shrines to Koxinga's Japanese mother (centre) and Prince Ning Jing (right), while Koxinga's grandson Zheng Kezang, is remembered on the left. The **museum** opened in 1966 and is a little worse for wear, though all the exhibits are well labelled in English: the first floor contains a display of local folk artefacts such

△ Tainan Dutch Surrender Statue at Chihkan Tower

The life of Zheng Chenggong, traditionally known as **Koxinga** in the West (a bastardization of *Guo Xing Ye*, an official title given to him by one of the last Ming princes), is a complex mixture of historical fact, myth and politics. Born in 1624 in Japan to a pirate Chinese father and Japanese mother, he was taken to Fujian in China when he was seven and given a strict Confucian education. After the fall of the Ming dynasty in 1644, Fujian became the centre of **resistance** to the new Qing rulers and Koxinga rose rapidly through the ranks of the military, gaining honours from various Ming princes and becoming the leader of the entire resistance movement. In 1658 he was defeated in Nanjing, an event that led him to consider a tactical **retreat to Taiwan**, and in 1661 he led a sizeable fleet across the straits to remove the Dutch. Contrary to popular belief, the siege of Fort Zeelandia was characterized by a series of blunders, Koxinga's overwhelmingly superior forces taking nine months to oust the defenders. The general died a few months later in 1662, most likely from malaria, and though he was initially buried in Taiwan his body was taken back to China with his son in 1699. On the island he became known as *Kaishan Wang*, "Open Mountain King" for his supposed role in developing infrastructure and opening up the country for Chinese immigrants, and worshipped as a folk god – there are around 63 temples dedicated to him island-wide.

Today, Koxinga is eulogized not just in Taiwan but also in China (there's a huge statue of him gazing towards the island in Xiamen) for being the only Chinese general to inflict a major defeat on a colonial Western power. Those favouring **unification** claim he was the first to "take back" Taiwan, while Taiwan **independence activists** like to point out that Koxinga's family ruled an independent kingdom that had never been part of the Chinese Empire. What's often forgotten in both cases is that Koxinga's brief war with the Dutch was a relatively minor footnote to his epic struggle with the Qing regime in Beijing. Though his situation is often compared to Chiang Kai-shek's three hundred years later, Koxinga's adoption as a nationalist symbol on both sides of the straits mirrors more closely that of Sun Yat-sen. His birthday is still celebrated on August 27 with special services at the Koxinga Shrine, and you can also visit the **Jheng's Ancestral Shrine** at 36 Jhongyi Road Section 2, established in 1663 to worship Koxinga and his ancestors and still owned by the Jheng (Zheng) family.

as porcelain, puppets and Qing dynasty clothing, while upstairs you can learn about Koxinga's brief encounter with the Dutch, and his lifelong struggle against the Qing.

Facing the park on the north side of Jianye Street, **Lady Linshui Temple** (daily 6am–8.30pm), is one of Tainan's most popular shrines, particularly with women. The temple was established in 1736 to worship the Birth Goddess, but in 1852, three female deities known as the "three ladies" were added: Chen Ching Gu, or Lady Linshui, has since become the main deity, worshipped in the incredibly elaborate **Main Hall** and flanked by images of her 36 assistants, three for each month. Linshui is supposed to protect unborn children, babies and pregnant mothers – women often pray here for protection during child birth. The temple is one the main locations of the **Tainan International Chihsi Festival**, which takes place around Lunar July 7 every year (August). The festival marks the beginning of adulthood, traditionally at sixteen years old.

North of Koxinga Shrine

If you've still got some energy left, a couple of absorbing temples lie to the north of Koxinga Shrine, both associated with the Chinese underworld. From

Kaishan Road follow Chenghuang Street for around 400m to Mincyuan Road and turn right: **Dongyue Temple** (daily 5.30am–9.30pm) is at no. 110 on the opposite side. Established in 1673, the temple is principally dedicated to the Great Emperor of East Mountain (Taishan in Shandong, China). He decides which of the eighteen levels of hell to banish sinners, based on the City God's report, and holds court in the **Front Hall**. Dizang Wang occupies the **Middle Hall**, with lurid murals of hell on the walls, while the **Rear Hall**, permanently gloomy and always quiet, is the home of the "Great Emperor of Fengdu" (*Fengdu Da Dì*), the deity that rules over hell itself.

Return to Chenghuang Street and continue north to the junction with Cingnian Road, and you should see the **City God Temple** (daily 6am–5pm) on the other side at no.133. Built in 1669, it's said to be the oldest City God Temple in Taiwan and one of the most traditional, the sombre black tablet hanging from the beams in the **First Hall** reading "Here You Come", meaning everyone will be judged in time (see Contexts p.530). The City God uses an abacus to calculate individual misdeeds – you can see it behind you, hanging above the entrance, and there's another enormous example in the exhibition halls to the left of the Front Hall. Also note the shackles and torture instruments on the back on main pillars here – supposed to be a deterrent to any mischief makers.

National Museum of Taiwanese Literature

Just north of the Confucius Temple on Nanmen Road, and a short walk west of the City God Temple, the **National Museum of Taiwanese Literature** (Tues–Sun 10am–5pm; free; ⓦwww.nmtl.gov.tw) occupies the former City Hall, a striking neoclassical building built by the Japanese in 1916. It's been beautifully restored and now houses a small exhibition detailing the history of the building and a series of informative display rooms on the development of Taiwanese literature since the Japanese occupation. These are arranged thematically and augmented with examples of prose translated into English.

Anping

Anping is the oldest part of Tainan, and indeed one of the oldest non-indigenous settlements in Taiwan: this is the island of Tayouan where the Dutch built their first fortress in 1624, and where Koxinga won his famous victory 38 years later, renaming the area after his hometown in China. It's 4km from Chihkan Tower today, best reached by taxi (NT$200).

Anping	安平	*ānpíng*
Anping Fort	安平古堡	*ānpíng gǔbǎo*
Anping Oyster Shell Cement Kiln Museum	安平蚵灰窯文化館	*ānpíng éhuīyáo wénguǎn*
Anping Tree House and Old Tait & Co Merchant House	安平樹屋暨德記洋行	*ānpíngshùwū jìdéjì yángxíng*
Eternal Golden Castle	億載金城	*yìzǎi jīn chéng*
Haishan Hall	海山館	*hǎishānguǎn*
Kaitai Tianhou Temple	開台天后宮	*kāitái tiānhòu gōng*
Miaoshou Temple	妙壽宮	*miàoshòu gōng*
Old Julius Mannich Merchant House	東興洋行	*dōngxìng yángxíng*
Orthodox Luermen Holy Mother Temple	正統鹿耳門聖母廟	*zhèngtǒng lùěrmén shèngmǔmiào*
Yenping Street	延平街	*yánpíng jiē*

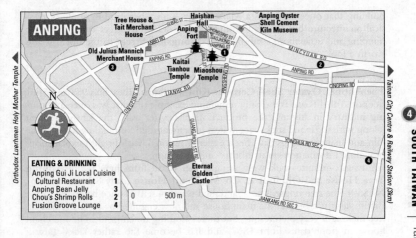

Haishan
Hall
Anping
Fort

Tree House &
Tait Merchant
House

Anping Oyster
Shell Cement
Kiln Museum

Old Julius Mannich
Merchant House ③

Kaitai
Tianhou
Temple

Miaoshou
Temple

MINCYUAN RD

ANPING RD ②

CINGPING RD

N

Orthodox Luerhmen Holy Mother Temple

YONGHUA RD SEC 2

EATING & DRINKING
Anping Gui Ji Local Cuisine
  Cultural Restaurant   **1**
Anping Bean Jelly   **3**
Chou's Shrimp Rolls   **2**
Fusion Groove Lounge   **4**

Eternal
Golden
Castle

0   500 m

JIANKANG RD SEC 3

Tainan City Centre & Railway Station (3km)

Anping Fort and around

Anping Fort (daily 8.30am–5.30pm; NT$50) is the site of Fort Zeelandia, the first Dutch settlement in Taiwan. It was established as a trading post with China in 1624, after the Dutch were kicked out of Penghu, and completed ten years later. The only substantial Dutch remains are parts of the **outer wall** along the road in front of the fort, as the imposing red-brick fortifications you see today were built by the Japanese. You can clamber up to the top where there's a small exhibition room with models of the old fort and a copy of Koxinga's treaty with the Dutch (in Chinese) on the wall. The watchtower, built in 1908, provides good views of the city.

Just south of the fort, **Kaitai Tianhou Temple** (daily 5am–10pm) has had a long and turbulent history: established in 1668, it was destroyed by the Japanese and rebuilt in 1962–1975, only to be gutted by fire and rebuilt again in 1994. Its chief claim to fame is the senior Mazu deity inside (the large statue in the middle of the back row): this is said to be one of three images Koxinga brought with him from the holy Mazu shrine at Meizhou in China – as such it has a decent claim to be the oldest Mazu statue in existence. The story goes that the three statues were created shortly after Mazu's death in 987 and seized by Koxinga during his retreat from China; two were subsequently returned but have since been lost or destroyed. Turn left along Anping Road to Gubao Street and turn right: ahead on the left is **Miaoshou Temple** (daily 6am–9pm) built in 1755 and dedicated to Baosheng Dadi. Note the two granite pillars in front of the temple, the only pair of "bat columns" in Taiwan, and the two miniature lions in front where there was once a small harbour. The second-floor hall opposite houses the temple's *wang chuan* or "spirit ship" (see Contexts p.529) – you can walk up for a closer look.

Retrace your steps up Gubao Street and turn right into narrow **Yanping Street**, the oldest commercial street in Taiwan, lined with tourist shops and snack food – it's the best place to eat in Anping (see p.330), though most of the stores are not as old as they seem. The exception is **Yong Tai Sing Preserved Fruits Store** at no. 84, dating from the Qing dynasty and still producing sticky, sweet snacks. Anping's oldest buildings are off the main street: turn left into Lane 104 (next to the old medicine shop at no. 102) and walk to Siaojhong Street to see **Haishan Hall** (daily 9am–5.30pm; free), a crumbling Qing dynasty building that once served as a Mazu shrine – it's a beautiful example of classical architecture but there's nothing much inside. This street runs parallel to Yanping and is far more atmospheric – **Jhongsing Street** to the north is also worth a look.

North Anping
The **Anping Oyster Shell Cement Kiln Museum** (Tues–Sun 9.30am–5pm; free) on Anbei Road is the only remaining example of what was once a booming industry in Anping: the production of "oyster ash", the key ingredient (along with sugar and sticky rice water) in cement used for building houses. The kiln and main buildings have been expertly restored, with English explanations providing information on its history and operation.

A twenty-minute walk west along Anbei Road from here is the **Anping Tree House** and **Old Tait & Co Merchant House** (daily 8.30am–5.30pm; NT$50). The tree house is an abandoned warehouse that once belonged to the British *hong*, just behind the main house and now engulfed by a massive banyan tree making it very picturesque, but there's nothing much inside. The merchant house in front dates from 1867, and has become the rather tacky Taiwan Pioneer History Wax Museum. Not far from here, on Lane 183 off Anbei Road, is the **Old Julius Mannich Merchant House** (daily 8.30am–5.30pm; free), the ex-premises of the German trading company: the house hasn't changed much since the 1800s, and the rooms contain an odd mix of historical exhibits and recreated colonial decor.

Eternal Golden Castle
Around 3km south of Anping Fort (NT$100 by taxi), the **Eternal Golden Castle** (daily 8.30am–5.30pm; NT$50), also known as the Er Kun Shen Artillery Fortress, was commissioned by the Qing authorities in 1876 to beef up Taiwan's defences in the wake of the Japanese attack two years before. It was designed by French engineers, built with material from Fort Zeelandia and equipped with British cannons, though only one of the artillery pieces you see today is genuine, identified by the gun sight on the barrel in the northeast corner. The fortress saw action in the Sino-French and Japanese wars, but was abandoned during the Japanese occupation. Today it's been well restored with plenty of English labelling, though other than clambering over the fortifications, there's not much to do.

Orthodox Luerhmen Holy Mother Temple
The northern district of Annan is also known as **Luermen** (or "Luerhmen"), once a narrow channel north of Anping that fed into the main lagoon between two sandy islands. Today the islands are joined together in one flat, featureless area of fish farms and industrial estates 11km from Tainan, but worth a visit for the phenomenal **Orthodox Luerhmen Holy Mother Temple** (daily 4am–9pm) or Tucheng Shengmu Miao, one of the largest temples in the world and certainly the biggest dedicated to Mazu. Built in the northern Chinese palatial style 1976-1985, it's a gargantuan complex resembling the Forbidden City in Beijing though its numerous halls are interconnected with modern steel footbridges. The **Main Hall** in the centre of the complex contains several Mazu deities: the most important is the Great Mazu in the centre, while in the gallery above sits the Marshal Mazu (left) and Official Mazu (right). The **Rear Hall** contains an image of Buddha, with Guanyin on the second floor and Jade Emperor and Matchmaker on level 3. Five Wang Ye Lords are worshipped in the **Front Hall**, statues that are said to have arrived mysteriously by boat from

China in 1913. The emphasis here is on size rather than architectural beauty, but the temple is also the centre of an ongoing dispute that reveals much about the complex and competitive relationships between temples in modern Taiwan. Koxinga's original shrine in Luermen was washed away in 1871, and the temple claims that it recovered the sacred Mazu statue inside in 1918. The rival claim is made by **Luerhmen Tianhou Temple**, south of the Luermen River, a smaller but more attractive place also claiming to stand on the original temple site: it argues that the Mazu image was kept in the local village until the new temple was completed in 1947. Academic weight points in the latter's favour, at least in terms of location, but in any case, Koxinga's grand army is likely to have had numerous official and unofficial Mazu statues with them and the Anping Mazu (see p.327) is generally accepted as the oldest and most important. You'll need your own transport to get here, or take an expensive taxi from Tainan.

Eating

Tainan has a reputation for its traditional **Taiwanese** cuisine, many of its dishes street favourites or "little eats" (*xiaochi*) that are famous island-wide. *Danzi mian* (noodles with pork, egg and shrimp) is probably the best-known dish, created in the 1890s by hawker Hong Yu Tou – the name recalls the shoulder poles he used to carry the noodles to market, while the brand he created, "Slack Season", is a reference to the slow season for fishermen, when his noodles were a way to make food last; several shops claim to be descended from his original stall. **Coffin bread** (hollowed out thick toast filled with a creamy mix of vegetables and seafood) is another Tainan specialty, a dish concocted in the 1950s when US troops were stationed nearby, but its milkfish, eel noodles, oyster omelettes and shrimp rolls are equally renowned.

Most of the traditional **food stalls** and **restaurants** are located in central Tainan, though there are plenty of contemporary and international choices on the outskirts of town, particularly along Yonghua Road Section 2, west of the

Tainan eating		
A Chuan Melon Tea	阿川冬瓜茶	āchuān dōngguā chá
Ah-Xia Restaurant	阿霞飯店	āxiá fàndiàn
All Natural Vegetarian Restaurant	全自然素食餐廳	quánzìrán sushi cāntīng
Anping Bean Jelly	安平豆花	ānpíng dòuhuā
Anping Gui Ji Local Cuisine Cultural Restaurant	安平貴記地方美食文化館	ānpíng guìjì dìfāng měishí wénhuàguǎn
Chi Kan Dandanman	赤崁擔擔麵	chìkǎn dāndānmiàn
Chou's Shrimp Rolls	周氏蝦捲	zhōushì xiājuǎn
Dadong Night Market	大東夜市	dàdōng yèshì
Dream of Chrysanthemums	夢東籬	mèngdōnglí
Fu Ji Meatballs	福記肉圓	fújì ròuyúan
Geng Du Yuan	耕讀園	gēngdúyúan
Hong Yu Tou	洪芋頭	hóngyùtóu
Lily Fruits	莉莉水果店	lìlì shuǐguǒ diàn
Sen Maw Rice Food	森茂碗粿	sēnmào wǎnguǒ
Siaobei Night Market	小北夜市	xiǎoběi yèshì
Slack Season Tan Tsi Noodles	度小月擔仔麵	dùxiǎoyuè dānzǎimiàn
Yong Ji	永記	yǒngjì
Zai Fu Hao	再發號	zàifāháo

centre. For cheap Western food like burgers or fish and chips, Tainan's pubs are probably your best bet. Similarly, none of Tainan's four traditional **night markets** are in the centre, though they are worth a visit to sample the city's traditional dishes, particularly coffin bread. Only the covered **Siaobei Night Market**, north off Simen Road Section 4, is open every night – the markets get going around 6pm and close between midnight and 1am. **Dadong Night Market** (Mon, Tues & Fri) off Linsen Road Section 2 has slightly better food than the others.

Chihkan Cultural Zone

A Chuan Melon Tea 21, Lane 227, Yongfu Rd Sec 2. Delicious melon drink stall, on Fortune Tellers Alley behind Datianhou Temple. Daily 9am–10pm.

Ah-Xia Restaurant 7, Lane 84, Jhongyi Rd Sec 2. Popular with locals, this venerable restaurant serves Chinese banquet-style food with lots of fish on the menu, but is best experienced in a group. Try the glutinous rice with crab, and assorted cold dishes – a complete set (10 dishes) will be at least NT$6000. Tues–Sun 11am–9pm.

Chi Kan Dandanman 180 Minzu Rd Sec 2. Traditional restaurant conveniently close to Chihkan Tower, with low wooden tables and rustic decor. Tasty *danzi mian* for NT$40. Daily 11am–3am.

Guohua Street Section 3 South of the junction with Minzu Road, this street is lined with famous stalls, many of which are over fifty years old: first on the left are spring rolls (*lumpia*, NT$30) and starfruit juice (NT$10); on the other side is *guobao* (pork in bun with sate sauce, NT$50–70); ask for lean meat (*shou rou*). Open from 8am until they run out, usually around 5–6pm.

Hong Yu Tou Danzi Mian 273 Simen Rd Sec 2. Tiny *danzi mian* shop with small seating area, cooking up excellent noodles with egg (NT$45) in the big pot by the door. The stall is named after the inventor of the noodles: the owner is his eldest grandson. Daily 9am–midnight.

Sen Maw Rice Food 228 Minzu Road Sec 2. Appealing old Tainan diner, with wooden school desks for tables and antiques on the walls, including porcelain bowls signed by Taiwan celebrities. The main dish here is *wah gwei*, a tasty meat pudding with pork, egg and mushroom (NT$25). Daily 9am–9pm.

Zai Fu Hao 71 Mincyuan Rd Sec 2. Best place to sample *zongzi* (sticky rice wrapped in bamboo leaves), with tasty mushroom and fresh pork fillings served in an old, no-nonsense store (NT$30–50). Daily 9am–8.30pm.

Confucius Temple Cultural Zone

Dream of Chrysanthemums 86 Cingjhong St. Classical-style restaurant offering good value *ramen*

(noodles) and variety of Chinese and aboriginal dishes like Betel Nut Chicken (NT$90–150), just north of Wufei Temple. Daily 10am–1am.

Fu Ji Meatballs 215 Fucian Rd Sec 1. Close to *Lily Fruits* and opposite Confucius Temple, this old shop sells delicious pork meatballs wrapped in glutinous rice – the slightly spicy sauce is delicious (NT$32 for two). No English menus. Daily 6.30am–6pm.

Go Dutch Caffé 18-1 Weimin St. Chilled-out backpacker café with comfy sofas, free Internet and lots of secondhand books. Decent coffee, breakfasts, pasta and pizza on offer: from the train station cross the rail line via the underpass at Beimen Rd and Weimin St – the cafe is behind you next to *Malibu* pub. Wed–Mon 9am–4pm.

🏃 **Lily Fruits** 119 Fencian Rd Sec 1. Tainan's most famous *tsua bing* (shaved ice) stall, with an incredible range of tropical fruit including guava, starfruit and mangoes served sliced, as juice, with soybean or on ice (NT$30–50). Traditional red bean toppings also served along with more indulgent banana and chocolate. Useful location opposite Confucius Temple. Daily 11am–11pm.

🏃 **Slack Season Tan Tsi Noodles** 16 Jhongjheng Rd. The *danzi mian* store owned by the family of the founder and still bearing the name of his stall, the eponymous dish (NT$50) is cooked up on a traditional stove near the entrance – with low stools and wooden tables, it's a photogenic place. Tues–Sun 11.30am–10pm.

Yong Ji 82 Kaishan Rd. This eighty-year-old shop serves excellent *lu rou fan* and fish ball soup, famous for its milkfish and sweet *hong cha* (black tea). Note it closes early. Daily 6.30am–1pm.

Anping

Anping Bean Jelly 433 Anbei Rd. Spacious canteen-style place knocking out delicious soybean pudding or *dohua* (NT$25) for over 50 years: try it with lemon juice or red beans. The downside is location – it's a short taxi ride or a twenty-minute walk from Anping Fort. Daily 9am–11pm.

Anping Gui Ji Local Cuisine Cultural Restaurant 93 Yanping St. Rustic tables and chairs with simple menu of Tainan favourites including coffin bread (NT$45) and rice cake (NT$30). Daily 11am–8pm.

Chou's Shrimp Rolls 408 Anping Rd. Tainan institution cooking up sublime shrimp rolls, lightly fried in batter tempura-style (NT$40 for two), and bowls of delicious noodles (NT$35). It has a fast-food-style system with two floors of seating and a posh restaurant on the third floor. Halfway to Anping from downtown: taxis should be NT$130 from the station. No English menu (photos). Daily 10am–10pm.

Yonghua Road

All Natural Vegetarian Restaurant 141 Yonghua Rd Sec 2. Huge modern place with excellent buffets and choice of Chinese vegetarian food (from NT$200). Located at the end of a strip of chic, contemporary restaurants on the western edge of downtown. Daily 11am–11pm.

Geng Du Yuan 23 Yonghua Rd Sec 2. A bit of a trek, but one of the most elegant classical teahouses of this Taichung chain, set in an atmospheric wooden building with cosy booths, goldfish pond and excellent tea from NT$300. Daily 11am–2am.

Drinking and nightlife

Tainan has plenty of bars, and even a couple of decent nightclubs, though things tend to be fairly quiet during the week.

Armory 82 Gongyuan S Rd ☎06/2269520 ⓦarmorypub.net. Laid-back, two-floor pub with wooden floors popular with expats and Taiwanese for its satellite TV (live sports events), live bands and dance nights. Bottled beer (from NT$100) and cocktails (NT$150) accompany a respectable menu of Chinese and Western comfort food (poutine NT$150). Daily 8pm–5am.

Cosby II Saloon 711 Simen Rd Sec 1. Small, but popular watering hole opposite *Landis* hotel, with a circular bar and an odd mix of American biker decor, dance music and satellite TV for big sports events. Western food menu and draft Warnsteiner (NT$200). Daily 10.30am–2am.

Dirty Roger 141 Dongmen Rd Sec 1. The best thing about this pub, a Tainan institution, is the huge collection of records lining the walls – if you see something you like, ask the owner and he's likely to put it on. There's table football upstairs. Daily 1pm–4am.

Espace 676 Jianping Rd. Popular lounge bar on the edge of downtown, with sleek, contemporary decor and extensive cocktail list. A taxi from the centre should cost less than NT$100. Daily 8.30pm–3am.

Fusion Groove Lounge 483 Yonghua Rd Sec 2. Tainan's top dance club, with decent DJs and packed party nights: music is predominantly funky house, breakbeat or trance. Tues–Sat 9pm–4am.

Suck 92 Sinmei St. Cosy lounge bar with comfy sofas, curtains and big screen that shows classic episodes of *Sex & the City*, with appropriate cocktails (NT$200) and beers (NT$100). Look for the rusted doors and grey slate walls, just south of Mincyuan Rd. Daily 9pm–2am.

Willy's Second Base Bar & Grill 321 Jiankang Rd Sec 2. Slightly upmarket sports bar with excellent food: try the sumptuous baby back ribs marinated in Jim Beam and Budweiser (NT$500) or any of the Tex-Mex creations (around NT$250). The Canadian owner used to play for the LA Dodgers. Tues–Sun 7pm–3am.

Shopping

Tainan has several traditional arts and crafts stores, as well as the usual plethora of modern shops and malls: **Beimen Street** south of station is the city's computer bazaar, while the best **department stores** are FE 21 at 60 Gongguan Road and 210 Cianfong Road, and the enormous New Life Square (Shinkong Mitsukoshi) at 658 Simen Road Section 1. There's even a 24hr Tesco at 16 Jhonghua West Road Section 2.

Chou Ta Gift Center 136 Jhongjheng Rd. Staple Chinese gift shop, crammed with painted vases, carvings and jewellery.

Jade Market 68–70 Linnan Rd. Similar to the markets in Taichung and Kaohsiung, this huge warehouse is full of stalls selling jade jewellery, wood carvings, statues, vases and antiques. Short taxi ride from the centre (NT$70–100). Mon, Tues & Sat 8am–4.30pm.

Solaya 41 Nanmen Rd. Cosy shop selling antique Chinese furniture and smaller, more easily carried items such as carvings and statues. Daily 1–10pm.

Tainan Kuang Tsai Embroidery Shop 183 Yongfu Rd Sec 2. Full of brightly coloured fabrics

used in temple festivals, clothing and puppets – visitors are welcome to look around and take photos, opposite the Official God of War Temple. **Tsai Se Ming Yi** 114 Minsheng Rd Sec 1 (closed Mon). Hip, ramshackle store selling curios and colourful cushions, on the corner of Yongfu Rd.
Long Sheng Buddha Statues 119 Mincyuan Rd Sec 2. Alluring store packed with intricate wood carvings of Buddhist and Taoist icons.

Listings

Airlines Far Eastern Air Transport ☎06/2904419; TransAsia Airways ☎06/2670367; Uni Air ☎06/2602811.

Banks Most 7-Elevens have Chinatrust ATMs, and Citibank has a branch at 83 Yongfu Rd Sec 2.

Books Caves Books at 159 Beimen Rd Sec 1 has a good selection of English-language books on the 4/F; Books & Cultural Souvenirs of Taiwanese Heritage at 57 Nanmen Rd has some English books (Mon–Fri 2–9pm, Sat–Sun 10am–9pm), across from Confucius Temple; Chin Wan Tze at 6 Jhongyi Rd Sec 2 (nr Youai St) is a famous secondhand bookstore (Tues–Sun 10am–10pm).

Cinema Warner Village 8/F, 60 Gongyuan Rd (inside FE21); UCI 7/F, 658 Simen Rd Sec 1 (inside New Life Square).

Hospital English-speaking staff and doctors can be found at Chi Mei Medical Center, 442 Sulin St Sec 2 or Nat ChengKung University Hospital at 138 Shengli Rd.

Internet The Yousipu chain operates several locations in Tainan charging NT$40 for 1hr: 274 Simen

Rd, 265 Jiankong Rd Sec 2, 466 Chenggong Rd, 249 & 785 Jhonghua Rd, 87 Chongdao Rd.

Left Luggage Just NT$17 per item per day: open 8am–8pm and located to the far right of the train station as you exit. Look for the English signs.

Post The main post office is at 6 Chenggong Rd, not far from the train station.

Scooter Rental Try Yuan Dong Rental Cars at 204 Cianfong Rd (☎06/2350807) – you'll have to show a driving licence and passport. Take the underpass under the train station (just left of the exit) and as you emerge it's the shop opposite: weekend prices are NT$450–600 (50–125cc) for 24hrs, but during the week you should pay around NT$200.

Tours Tainan Phoenix Culture Association (☎0930/867695, ✉elisalu@seed.net.tw) and Taoyuan Cultural Tourism Association (☎0910/819062, ✉oriform@ms4.hinet.net) have English-speaking guides that charge NT$3000 for one day or NT$1500 for half a day, plus all transport costs.

Southwest Coast National Scenic Area

Encompassing the flat, marshy stretch of coast between Tainan and the Hukou Wetlands in Yunlin County, the **Southwest Coast National Scenic Area** (Ⓦ www.swcoast-nsa.gov.tw) contains some of Taiwan's most important and oldest **religious sites**, remnants of a once thriving **salt industry**, and hundreds of fish ponds and oyster farms which make for superb **seafood**.

Southwest Coast National Scenic Area

Southwest Coast National Scenic Area	南濱海國家風景區	*nánbīnhǎi guójiā fēngjǐngqū*
Beimen	北門	*běimén*
Cigu Salt Mountains	七股鹽山	*qīgǔ yánshān*
Ciji Temple	慈濟宮	*cíjì gōng*
Mashagou	馬沙溝	*mǎshāgōu*
Nankunshen Da Tian Temple	南鯤身大天府	*nánkūnshēn dàtiānfǔ*
Syuejia	學甲	*xúejiǎ*
Taisheng Temple	太聖宮	*tàishèng gōng*
Taiwan Salt Museum	台灣鹽博物館	*táiwān yán bówùguǎn*
Wang Ye Culture Gallery	王爺信仰文物館	*wángyé xìnyǎng wénwùguǎn*

Though it can be difficult travelling here without your own transport, exploring the area by **bus** is possible: Singnan Bus near Tainan train station (see p.315) runs a service to Nankunshen via Jiali, Syuejia and Beimen, though the entire trip can take over two hours.

Cigu Salt Mountains

The coastline north of Tainan is littered with salt pans, most abandoned after the industry collapsed in the 1990s – Australia now supplies the island's salt at a fraction of the cost. A few kilometres west of **Cigu** on Highway 176 you'll see the two pyramid towers of the **Taiwan Salt Museum** (daily 9am–5.30pm; NT$100) and the famous salt mountains beyond. The museum has three floors of innovative displays covering the salt-making process, the history of the area and even a mock Polish salt mine, but there are no English labels. The **Cigu Salt Mountains** (daily 9am–5.30pm; free; NT$100 parking fee) are two ninety-thousand-tonne piles of salt four storeys high: one is now dirty brown and can be scaled via a path cut into the rock-hard sodium crystals, while the other is still pristine white and tends to get treated like snow by frolicking tourists. Though the area has become a bit of a carnival at the weekends (with stalls selling surprisingly tasty salt popsicles and even a pool where you can float, Dead-Sea-like in the brine), it's one of the most bizarre sights in Taiwan and definitely worth the trek out here – you'll need your own transport or get a taxi from the bus station in Jiali.

Ciji Temple

The small town of **SYUEJIA** is the home of **Ciji Temple** (daily 5am–10pm), noted for its exceptional artwork and great religious significance. Established in 1703, it is the oldest shrine to Baosheng Dadi (see p.530) in Taiwan. The most important deity in the **Main Hall** was brought to Taiwan by Koxinga in 1661 – it's said to be eight hundred years old, one of three originals made in China after the death of Baosheng in 1037 and now the only one in existence. It's the small statue in front of the biggest image, slightly to the right. The temple also contains over two hundred rare works of *koji*, some made by master Yeh Wang in the 1860s (see p.287) – the most important are encased in glass on the right side of the Main Hall. The temple is at 170 Jisheng Road near Jhongjheng Road, a short walk from the bus station.

Beimen and around

The tiny village of **BEIMEN**, 9km west of Syuejia, is the headquarters of the scenic area administration (daily 8.30am–5.30pm), where you can pick up maps and information. The Nankunshen bus stops in the centre of the village. Around 5km to the south, the village of Sanliaowan on Highway 174 is home to the informative **Wang Ye Culture Gallery** (daily 9am–4pm; free) which contains some interesting exhibits and camphor models of *wang chuan* ("spirit ships"), but labelled only in Chinese. It's a twenty-minute walk from the nearest bus stop. Further south, the **beach** at **Mashagou** is a real treat: decent sand and even coconut palms make this an excellent place to chill out for the day, though it can get busy in midsummer (daily May–Oct 9am–6pm; free).

Nankunshen

Three kilometres north of Beimen, in the equally small village of **NANKUN-SHEN**, lies the **Nankunshen Da Tian Temple** (daily 5am–10pm). It's the most important shrine in southern Taiwan and the centre of Wang Ye worship (see Contexts p.529) on the island, heading an organization of around 7000 branch temples. Established in 1662 and rebuilt on this site in 1817, the temple is dedicated to five senior Wang Ye gods: Li, Tsi, Wu, Chu and Fan, each with their own birthday and special annual festival attracting thousands of pilgrims (the biggest is on Lunar April 26 and 27). The original wooden statues of the gods are said to have arrived by unmanned boat, miraculously driven by the wind from China in the early seventeenth century and have since ensured the fishermen in the village abundant catches, good health and all round prosperity.

Today the temple is part of a massive religious complex, though unfortunately the main buildings are undergoing a comprehensive renovation which will not be complete until 2009: the five gods are temporarily housed in the **Entrance Hall** at the front, with Li, the "Great King", in the centre. The smaller temple to the right of the main complex belongs to the "Healthy Lord" or "Goodness Grandfather" (*gnia a gong* in Taiwanese), who looks after children. Legend has it that worshippers at the main temple must also pay their respects here or risk upsetting him. If you get stuck here, *Kang Lang Villa* (☎06/7864711; ⑤) on the far right is a pleasant place to stay the night: it's a guesthouse for pilgrims built in classical Fujianese style with basic but comfortable rooms. Unless it's a festival expect a quiet stay: there are no TVs and no breakfast, just the snack stalls in the village and around the temple.

Taisheng Temple

A further 5km north, off Highway 17 in the village of Haomeiliao, historic **Taisheng Temple** (daily 5am–9pm) contains what is generally regarded as the **first Mazu** deity to reach Taiwan: other temples claim to have older or more important images of the goddess, but this one definitely got to the island before the others. Its arrival has been dated to 1562, when a party of Chinese fishermen may have brought it to what was then a small island in a marshy lagoon: the first written record of the temple dates from 1602. Today it's a quiet, lonely spot, with five ancient Wang Ye lords worshipped in the front hall, said to be 750 years old, and the aged Mazu image in the rear hall: it's the smaller figure at the front of the shrine. Note the *hinoki* cypress wood pillars inside, which are over 140 years old.

Southern Cross-Island Highway

The spectacular **SOUTHERN CROSS-ISLAND HIGHWAY** slices across south Taiwan in a dramatic, no-nonsense traverse of the Central Cordillera that

Yanshuei beehive fireworks

An otherwise sleepy town, a short drive inland from Nankunshen, **YANSHUEI** attracts thousands to its annual **firework festival**, one of Taiwan's most famous. What makes this pyrotechnic display unique is that the fireworks – lodged in over two hundred walls or "beehives" the size of a truck – are fired horizontally into the crowds creating a cacophony of noise, fire and smoke throughout the night. Protective gear is essential if you want to participate but note that the crowds can be suffocating: around 300,000 people attend. The tradition began in 1885 when locals paraded an image of Guan Di around the town to ward off a cholera epidemic: their prayers were answered only after shooting off a ton of fireworks to 'wake' the god. Each year during the Lantern Festival, usually in February, Guan Di is once again paraded around the town before the fiery climax. **Buses** from Chiayi Transport Co Bus Station depart 6am–8pm hourly (NT$88).

leaves most travellers clutching the edge of their seats. Starting from the western coastal plains around Tainan, the highway climbs steadily to almost 2800m before dropping sharply down to the east coast, cutting through several distinct ecosystems as well as the southwestern fringe of **Yushan National Park**. Along the way are authentic Bunun aboriginal villages, abundant **hiking trails**, accessible peaks of over 3000m and relaxing hot springs – some developed, others preserved in a completely natural state. Though it's sadly no longer possible to

Southern Cross-Island Highway

Southern Cross-Island Highway	南橫公路	*nánhéng gōnglù*
Towns and villages		
Baolai	寶來	*bǎolái*
Haiduan	海端	*hǎiduān*
Lidao	利稻	*lìdào*
Meishan Village	梅山村	*méishān cūn*
Meishankou	梅山口	*méishānkǒu*
Tianchih	天池	*tiānchí*
Wulu	霧鹿	*wùlù*
Yakou	埡口	*yākǒu*
Information		
Bunun Culture Exhibition Center	布農文化展覽中心	*bùnóng wénhuà zhǎnlǎn zhōngxīn*
Meishan Police Squadron	梅山警察局	*méishān jǐngchá jú*
Meishankou Visitor Center	梅山口遊客中心	*méishānkǒu yóukè zhōngxīn*
Sights		
Changcing Shrine	長青祠	*chāngqīng cí*
Daguanshan	大關山	*dàguān shān*
Daguanshan Tunnel	大關山隧道	*dàguān shān suìdào*
Guanshan	關山	*guānshān*
Guanshanlingshan	關山嶺山	*guānshān lǐngshān*
Guhanuosinshan	庫哈諾辛山	*kùhānuòxīn shān*
Heaven's Pond	天池	*tiānchí*
Jhongjhihguan	中之關	*zhōngzhīguān*
Jhongjhihguan Trail	中之關古道	*zhōngzhīguān gǔdào*
Lisong Hot Springs	粟松溫泉	*lìsōng wēnquán*
Tianlong Suspension Bridge	天龍吊橋	*tiānlóng diàoqiáo*
Wulu Canyon	霧鹿峽谷	*wùlù xiágǔ*
Accommodation		
Guhanuosin Cabin	庫哈諾辛山屋	*kùhānuòxīn shānwū*
Meishan Youth Activity Center	梅山青年活動中心	*méishān qīngnián huódòng zhōngxīn*
Nanheng Lidao Yuenong Homestay	南橫利稻野農民宿	*nánhéng lìdào yěnóng mínsù*
Sian Fong Homestay	賢鳳民宿	*xiánfèng mínsù*
Tianchih Employee Dormitory	天池員工寄宿舍	*tiānchí yuángōng sùshè*
Tianlong Hotel	天龍飯店	*tiānlóng fàndiàn*
Yakou Country Inn	埡口山莊	*yākǒu shānzhuāng*
Eating		
Meishankou Fandian	梅山口飯店	*méishānkǒu fàndiàn*
Shenmao Store	森茂商號	*sēnmào shānghào*
Sichuan Restaurant	四川餐廳	*sìchuān cāntīng*

cross the entire highway by public transport, most places along the route can still be reached by **bus** from either Tainan or Taitung (see below).

Construction of the highway was completed in 1973, but it was not opened to the general public until 1993 and much of it remains in a perpetual state of repair, battered as it is by mudslips and **rockslides** throughout the rainy spring and summer months. During this time, particularly from late May to early September, the road's higher reaches are sometimes rendered impassable and closed for repairs. By late autumn, however, the most precarious bits usually have been patched up and stay open throughout the much drier winter.

Orientation

Though the Southern Cross-Island Highway effectively links Tainan to Taitung, the actual **Highway 20** – the road's proper name – starts on the outskirts of

Transport across the highway

It used to be possible to cross the entire highway by bus, with daily services from Tainan and Taitung connecting in Tianchih. But while the Taitung bus still terminates at Tianchih, the Tainan service now only goes as far as Meishankou, so if you're relying on these you'll have to walk or hitch the 25km between these points. Indeed, **walking** this section – as well as the fourteen-kilometre stretch of **high road** between Tianchih and Yakou – has been a time-honoured rite of passage for Taiwanese students and foreign backpackers, although mounting traffic levels are making this an increasingly unpalatable option, especially on weekends and public holidays.

From Tainan, there are three daily buses (7.20am, 9.10am & 3.10pm; 3hr 15min; NT$290) to Meishankou, leaving from the **Singnan Motor Transport** office (☎06/2223142) near the Tainan train station. Buses leave Meishankou for Tainan at 6am, 1.45pm and 2.55pm.

From Kaohsiung, there are two daily buses (6.15am & 11.10am; 3hr 30min; NT$325) to Meishankou, departing from the **Kaohsiung Bus Station** (☎07/2371230) near the train station. Buses leave Meishankou for Kaohsiung at 11.20am and 5.45pm.

From Taitung, there is one daily bus to Tianchih (6.40am; 5hr; NT$351), departing from the **Kuo Kuang Bus Station** (☎089/322027), to the east of the old train station (see p.419). The same bus leaves Tianchih for Taitung at noon, stopping at Yakou, Lidao, Wulu, the city of Guanshan and a few other villages along the way. There are also two daily buses from Taitung to Lidao (6.20am & 1.05pm; 2hr; NT$190), leaving from the **Dingdong (Mountain Route) Bus Station** (☎089/333023) and stopping at Wulu en route. Buses return from Lidao to Taitung at 9.15am & 3.20pm.

Cars, scooters and bicycles

For greater flexibility, rent a car in either Kaohsiung or Tainan and arrange to drop it off in Taitung, or vice versa. Renting a **scooter** is another option, although rental shops might turn you down if they know you're planning to take it across the island – it can be uncomfortably cold, and dangerous, in rainy weather. Highway 20 has also become a **popular bicycling** route for Taiwanese and expats alike, and it can be a rewarding – and challenging – journey, but one best left for the drier season. Anyone cycling this road should be very familiar with their bike and know how to repair it; self-sufficiency, in terms of food, water, clothing and a bicycle repair kit (see Basics p.55), is imperative.

Tainan and snakes through the mountains for 209km before terminating at Highway 9 just past the town of **Haiduan**. However, the hot-springs resort village of **Baolai** (part of the Maolin National Scenic Area, see p.362), about 85km from Tainan, is widely regarded as the Southern Cross-Island Highway's western gateway, as the road really starts to climb just beyond here. The most scenic section twists for 39km through Yushan National Park, from **Meishankou** in the west past **Tianchih** until it reaches the park boundary at the western end of the **Daguanshan Tunnel**. Just past here is **Yakou**, the road's highest point and one of the best places in Taiwan to witness the famous "sea of clouds" phenomenon. From Yakou, the road descends steeply, winding its way past the peaceful Bunun tribal village of **Lidao** and the roadside hot-springs stopover of **Wulu** on its way towards Taitung.

Meishankou

The southwestern entrance to Yushan National Park (see map, pp.302–303), **MEISHANKOU**, is the terminus for all buses from Kaohsiung and Tainan and the most tourist-orientated stop along the Southern Cross-Island Highway and well worth a stop. The national park's **Meishankou visitor center** (9am–4.30pm, closed second Tues of each month; ☏07/6866181), at no. 44-5, has English-labelled exhibits on local flora and fauna and can provide you with an excellent English brochure highlighting the main sights between Meishankou and Yakou; it also has an interesting relief map of the park on display. Next door, the tiny **Bunun Culture Exhibition Center** (same hours) contains bilingual displays on aspects of traditional Bunun life, from hunting to clothing, and includes a life-sized replica of a stone-slab house as well as a timeless collection of black-and-white **photos** of the tribespeople. Just to the east of the centre, on the same side of the highway, is the **Meishan Police Squadron**, where you can quickly obtain climbing permits for the 3000-plus-metre peaks along the Southern Cross-Island Highway. Across the highway from here is the **bus stop**, where Kaohsiung and Tainan-bound buses will pick you up (make sure you wave to ensure that the driver sees you). Behind the bus stop is a large **botanical garden**, to the side of which is a paved road leading about 2km to the actual **Meishan Village**, a bucolic Bunun settlement that is reached by crossing a towering suspension bridge.

Practicalities

Meishankou's only proper **hotel**, the *Meishan Youth Activity Center* (☏07/6866166; ❹) at no. 55 – on the left-hand side of the highway as you head east – occupies a scenic spot looking out onto nearby mountains and has spacious, comfortable rooms (the four-person **tatami rooms** are a bargain at NT$2400). A Chinese breakfast is included in the room rate, and the hotel's restaurant also serves lunch and dinner. Next door is a convenient **campsite** with slightly elevated platforms (NT$300 per tent) that can accommodate at least 24 tents (bring your own equipment). Nearby is a souvenir shop and **snack bar** where you can stock up before continuing up the highway. Just east of the visitor centre is a string of **restaurants** serving basic Chinese dishes and Bunun specialties such as roasted mountain pig (*shan zhu*) and mountain deer (*shan chang*), the latter of which costs NT$200 for a small plate. The best of these is the *Meishankou Fandian* (☏07/6866117) at no. 56, which has tasty staples such as fried rice and noodles for NT$60 and zesty stir-fries starting from NT$130. On clear days, the second-floor balcony yields splendid views of the surrounding mountains.

Mountain permits made easy

While **Class A mountain permits** (see Basics, p.56) are needed to legally climb peaks of 3000m or higher in Taiwan, requiring advance planning and usually a wait of several days, getting these precious permits is easy for four such mountains along the Southern Cross-Island Highway. In Meishankou, it's possible to have **on-the-spot permits** issued – usually in less than an hour – for ascents of **Daguanshan** (3222m), **Guanshan** (3668m), **Guanshanlingshan** (3176m) and **Guhanuosinshan** (3115m), making them the easiest peaks in Taiwan to get permission to climb. To apply, simply turn up at the **Meishan Police Squadron** (8am–10pm; ☎07/6866276) at no. 52 with your climbing gear, a **map** (available at the Meishankou visitor center) and a photocopy of your passport photo page for the police to file for identification purposes. You'll be required to complete an **application form** (available at the police station), providing your personal details, emergency contact numbers, your mobile phone number (if you're carrying one) and a brief description of your proposed route. Though most of the park police here speak little, if any, English, they'll want you to point out your **planned route** on the map. If the mountain you wish to climb necessitates an overnight stay en route, they also may want to inspect your **gear** to ensure that you have enough food, water and suitable clothing. You must pay a token NT$10 **service fee**, and if everything else is deemed acceptable you should be issued your permit in a matter of minutes. For more detailed information on individual peaks, ask for one of the English-speaking park interpreters at the front desk of the Meishankou visitor center.

Meishankou to Tianchih

For independent travellers without their own transport, the winding 25km section of road which climbs from Meishankou to **Tianchih** (2280m) – gaining almost 1300m in elevation – presents the biggest challenge of the highway crossing. However, if you aren't pressed for time and the weather cooperates, this scenic stretch of road can be one of the highlights of your journey, regardless of how you end up covering the distance. **Walking** the road is still a popular option, and it's possible to make it by foot in one day provided you get an early start, although weekend traffic can make it dispiriting and even dangerous. The bright side of all this traffic is that many drivers will inevitably stop to offer you a lift.

After about 21km you'll reach **Jhongjhihguan**, which was the site of a police station during the Japanese occupation but is now a rest area and the beginning of the short **Jhongjhihguan Trail** leading to Tianchih. The trail runs through a tranquil forest and will help you avoid the road for the last few kilometres into **TIANCHIH** (Heavenly Pond), essentially a roadside stop named after the tiny alpine lake nearby, but with one hostel that accepts foreign visitors. Beside the road is a set of steep concrete steps that lead to the **Changcing Shrine**, a stele commemorating the workers who died building the highway. To the left of the stele are some wooden steps leading up to a meadow, in the middle of which is the **Heavenly Pond**. Down the narrow road about 30m behind the stele is the only place to stay, the Forestry Bureau's *Tianchih Employee Dormitory* (☎07/6780006; ❶), which has basic rooms but absolutely nothing to eat. The English sign next to the door says "Tianchih Substation, Yujing Station, Chiayi Forest District Office".

Tianchih to Yakou

From Tianchih, the road continues to climb for another 14km to its highest point, a roadside stop named **YAKOU** (2772m) – on the east side of the

Daguanshan Tunnel – where there is an exceptional viewpoint and nearby lodging. This stretch of road is the Southern Cross-Island Highway at its most spectacular, and, accordingly, the trailheads to all four of the easily accessible **3000-metre peaks** (see box p.338) are located along this section. The most important of these is the **Jinjing Bridge Trailhead**, only 4km past Tianchih near the 139km marker. From here you can climb the area's tallest peak, the 3668-metre **Guanshan**, as well as nearby **Guhanuosinshan** (3115m). Along the trail is the **Guhanuosin Cabin**, an enclosed shelter where you can stay overnight provided you have your own sleeping bag.

About 2km past the Jinjing Bridge is **Kuaigu**, an amazing old-growth **cypress forest** that spans several kilometres of the area. At the 144km marker is the trailhead to **Daguanshan** (3222m). From here the road climbs for just over 3km before entering the six-hundred-metre-long **Daguanshan Tunnel**, the middle of which is very dark and somewhat dangerous to walk through given that there are no pavements – a torch is essential if you want to walk through it. At the other end of the tunnel is Yakou, with a viewpoint on the right-hand side of the road and a trailhead for the short-but-steep climb to **Guanshanlingshan** (3176m) on the left. On clear days, the **viewpoint** affords divine morning and evening vistas of the "sea of clouds," and nearby there are usually a few **food vendors** selling grilled sausages and stinky tofu. A few hundred metres east along the road from here is a right-hand turnoff leading down the slope for about 1km to the *Yakou Country Inn* (☎07/6866057; ④), an atmospheric wooden lodge that is the only place to stay around Yakou. Despite its rustic-looking exterior, the building's interior has been renovated and the rooms have modern furnishings. In addition to well-appointed doubles there also are eight- and twelve-person **tatami-style dorms** (NT$400 per bed). If there are enough tourists around, the lodge puts on breakfast (NT$60) as well as lunch and dinner (NT$120 each); otherwise you might have to resort to the instant noodles that are sold at the reception counter. If you're moving on to Taitung, the **bus** that leaves Tianchih at noon often arrives at Yakou as early as 12.30pm, so it's a good idea to be waiting alongside the road near the viewpoint well before then.

Lidao

About 30km southeast of Yakou is **LIDAO**, a laid-back Bunun village with a couple of welcoming homestays that can arrange excursions to the nearby Lisong Hot Springs, without question Taiwan's wildest. Lidao is also worth an overnight stay for the glimpses it offers of genuine Bunun life – and the opportunity to try freshly prepared Bunun cuisine.

Though Lidao is accessible by bus from both Taitung and Tianchih, some adventurous travellers coming from the island's western side still **walk** the thirty-kilometre stretch from Yakou, which is mostly downhill and can easily be done in a day. The village's most agreeable accommodation option is the *Sian Fong Homestay* (☎089/938038; ②) at 6-4 Lidao Village, which offers **packages** including one night's stay, dinner and transport to and from the Lisong Hot Springs trailhead for NT$1600 per person. Nearby the *Sian Fong*, at 3 Wenhua Road, is the friendly *Nanheng Lidao Yuenong Homestay* (☎089/938055; ②), which has a few basic two- and four-person rooms but doesn't usually provide dinner unless a large group has reserved meals in advance. If you're stuck for food, the adjacent **Shenmao Store** at 6-3 Wenhua Rd (☎089/938095; 6am–9pm) has **drinks** and **snacks** such as instant noodles, and the owner also can prepare staples such as fried rice and noodles for NT$60 a plate.

Lisong Hot Springs

The pristine **Lisong Hot Springs**, which form a steaming **waterfall** spilling into a small riverbed pool, are at once the most remote and unblemished of Taiwan's known thermal springs. Discovered in 2002 by Bunun hunters, there are no immediate plans to develop them. This is thanks largely to their isolation: not only are they reached via a **steep trail** which loses about 700m of elevation in only 2km, but the beginning of the trail itself can be a challenge to find. To minimize your margin for error, it's best to arrange a package with the *Sian Fong Homestay* in Lidao, or at the very least to ask its owner to drive you to the trailhead (NT$200) and point the way.

If you want to find it yourself, the trailhead is accessed by a side road which starts at the **169km marker** (there are large yellow flags that state "169km"), on the left-hand side of the road coming from Yakou. From the turnoff, it's another 2km or so to the actual trailhead, past a **farm** with some decidedly smelly pigsties. The beginning of the trail is about 200m beyond the farm, on the left-hand side of the road. The narrow path immediately starts to drop, and, given its steepness, is lined with sturdy ropes for most of the way – it's a strenuous walk in both directions, but the trail has been clearly cut so it's hard to lose your way. Once you reach the river, you'll need to wade about 100m to the left before you can see the springs pouring over a multicoloured bluff. It's safe to soak in the small pools below the falls, as they are hemmed in with rings of stacked river stones and let in some of the cool river water, but the waterfall itself is scalding hot so don't venture too close.

Wulu

The last stop of significant interest along the highway is the tiny Bunun village of **Wulu**, known chiefly for its high-end hot-springs hotel, vertigo-inducing suspension bridge and world-famous local choir. The scenery between Lidao and Wulu is impressive, as the highway passes through the striking Wulu Canyon, whose sheer walls can be seen from the road's precipitous curves. Wulu's most popular place to stay is the pricey *Tianlong Hotel* (☎089/935075; ⑥), which has private hot-springs spas in the rooms but no public bathing pools. On weekends and public holidays, the hotel often hosts performances of the **Wulu Bunun Choir**, whose traditional songs – characterized by distinctive eight-part harmonies inspired by the sounds of nature – have attracted worldwide critical acclaim. Directly behind the hotel is the **Tianlong (Heavenly Dragon) Suspension Bridge**, which crosses the Wulu Canyon at a dizzying height. The most reliable place to eat in the village is the **Sichuan Restaurant** (6am–9pm), which serves authentic Sichuan fare such as spicy noodles and stir fries (NT$60), laced with hot chillies and peppercorns, for breakfast, lunch and dinner.

Kaohsiung and around

Taiwan's second city, and one of the largest container ports in the world, **KAOHSIUNG** has been undergoing a dramatic metamorphosis in recent years, from polluted industrial centre of two million people to green city of lush parks, waterside cafés, art galleries and museums, all linked together by a spanking new transportation system. Positioned on the southwest coast with a palpably laid-back feel, its epithet as a tropical "Ocean City" is well on the way to becoming reality.

The older districts of **Zuoying**, **Yancheng** and **Cijin Island** contain plenty of historic sights and traditional snack stalls, while modern Kaohsiung is best taken in with an evening stroll along the **Love River** or a visit to soaring **85 Sky Tower** close to its bustling **shopping districts**. Forming the western boundary of the city, the ridge of hills known as **Chaishan** is the home of Kaohsiung's famously capricious troupe of monkeys, while the old **British Consulate**, overlooking the harbour, is a wonderfully atmospheric place for a cocktail.

Some history

The oldest parts of Kaohsiung are Cihou village on **Cijin Island**, established in the early seventeenth century, and the suburb of **Zuoying**, created by

Kaohsiung and around		
Kaohsiung	高雄	gāoxióng
Kaohsiung International Airport	高雄國際航空站	gāoxióng guójì hángkōng zhàn
Kaohsiung Train Station	高雄火車站	gāoxióng huǒchē zhàn
Accommodation		
Ambassador Hotel	國賓大飯店	guóbīn dàfàndiàn
Grand Hi-Lai Hotel	漢來大飯店	hànlái dàfàndiàn
Gold Chain Hotel	國群大飯店	guóqún dàfàndiàn
Hotel Kingdom	華王大飯店	huáwáng dàfàndiàn
Hotel New Image	喜悅商務大飯店	xǐyuèshāngwù dàfàndiàn
Hotel Skoal	世國大飯店	shìguó dàfàndiàn
Riverside Hotel	高雄金馬大飯店	gāoxióng jīnmǎ dàfàndiàn
Sanduo Hotel	三多大飯店	sānduō dàfàndiàn
The Splendor	金典酒店(前晶華酒店)	jīndiǎn jǐudiàn
Union Hotel	國統大飯店	guótǒng dàfàndiàn
The City		
British Consulate at Takao	高雄英國領事館	gāoxióng yīngguó lǐngshìguǎn
China Shipbuilding Corp	中國造船公司 (中船)	zhōngguó zàochúan gōngsī (zhōngchuán)
Cihou Battery	旗后砲台	qíhòu pàotái
Cijin Island	旗津島	qíjīn dǎo
85 Sky Tower	高雄85大樓	gāoxióng bāshíwǔ dàlóu
Kaohsiung Municipal Film Archive	高雄市電影圖書館	gāoxióngshì diànyǐng túshūguǎn
Kaohsiung Museum of Fine Arts	高雄美術館	gāoxióng měishùguǎn
Kaohsiung Museum of History	高雄市歷史博物館	gāoxióngshì lìshǐ bówùguǎn
San Shan Temple	三山國王廟	sānshān guówáng miào
Shoushan Nature Reserve	壽山自然生態保護區	shòushān zìrán shēngtài bǎohùqū
Temple of God of War and Education	文武聖殿	wénwǔ shèngdiàn
Tianhou Temple	天后宮	tiānhòu gōng
Xiahai City God Temple	霞海城隍廟	xiáhǎi chénghuáng miào
Around Kaohsiung		
Foguangshan Monastery	佛光山寺	fóguāngshān sì

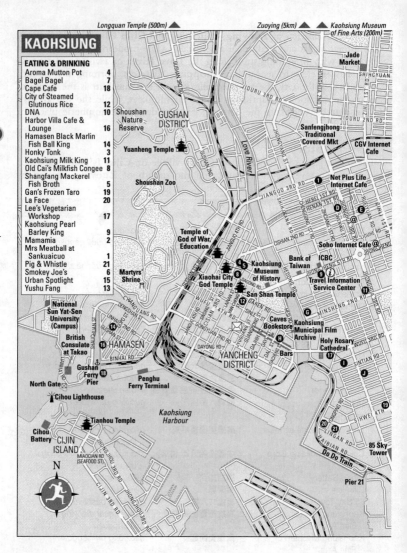

KAOHSIUNG

EATING & DRINKING

Aroma Mutton Pot	4
Bagel Bagel	7
Cape Cafe	18
City of Steamed Glutinous Rice	12
DNA	10
Harbor Villa Cafe & Lounge	16
Hamasen Black Marlin Fish Ball King	14
Honky Tonk	3
Kaohsiung Milk King	11
Old Cai's Milkfish Congee	8
Shangfang Mackerel Fish Broth	5
Gan's Frozen Taro	19
La Face	20
Lee's Vegetarian Workshop	17
Kaohsiung Pearl Barley King	9
Mamamia	2
Mrs Meatball at Sankuaicuo	1
Pig & Whistle	21
Smokey Joe's	6
Urban Spotlight	15
Yushu Fang	13

Koxinga in the 1660s as county capital, a position it maintained until the late eighteenth century. Cihou, and the harbour as a whole, was known as **Takau** (or Takow), and remained a sleepy backwater until the port was opened up to foreign companies by the Treaty of Beijing in 1860, attracting merchants eager to exploit the south's growing export trade in sugar. With them came three remarkable Brits: **Robert Swinhoe**, the famous naturalist, spent a few months in Takau in 1861 and returned in 1864, when he was appointed British Consul; **Patrick Mason**, the father of tropical medicine, arrived in 1866 as port doctor and would later teach Sun Yat-sen in Hong Kong; and missionary **James Maxwell** who lived on Cijin Island between 1865 and 1868 and established the area's first Presbyterian church.

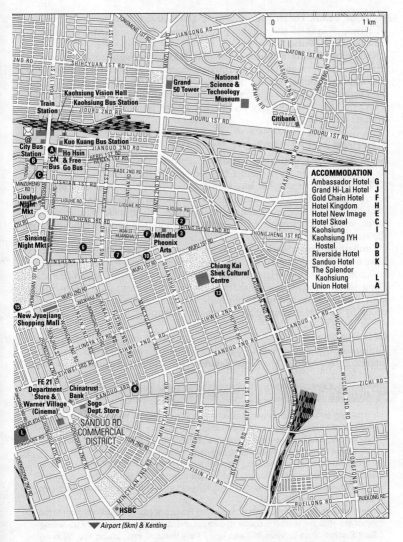

ACCOMMODATION

Ambassador Hotel	G
Grand Hi-Lai Hotel	J
Gold Chain Hotel	F
Hotel Kingdom	H
Hotel New Image	E
Hotel Skoal	C
Kaohsiung	I
Kaohsiung IYH	
Hostel	D
Riverside Hotel	B
Sanduo Hotel	K
The Splendor	
Kaohsiung	L
Union Hotel	A

▼ Airport (5km) & Kenting

Foreign trade had its dark side however: by the time the Japanese had assumed control of the city in 1895, a quarter of adult males in the south were addicted to opium. The Japanese imposed an Opium Monopoly in 1897, which effectively destroyed Western dominance of the sugar trade. They also began a major modernization programme, completing the harbour and docks in 1908 and opening the Takau Ironworks in 1919, Taiwan's first iron and steel mill. Although the city was heavily bombed by US planes in 1945, the port was rebuilt and by the late 1970s Kaohsiung was Taiwan's premier industrial centre. In 1979, the **Kaohsiung Incident** was a defining moment in Taiwan's struggle for democracy (see box p.348), and today the city is a DPP stronghold. Much of the transformation of the city in recent years was due to the vision of DPP politician **Frank Hsieh** who was mayor 1999–2005 before becoming premier of Taiwan – in 2005 the changes paid off, when Kaohsiung won the right to host the **2009 World Games**.

Kaohsiung's **name** is worth explaining: Takau is thought to derive from a Makatau (*pingpu*) word meaning "bamboo fence" – when this was transliterated into Chinese it read "beat the dog" (*da gou*), and in 1920 the Japanese changed the characters to the less offensive "Tall Hero", with the Japanese pronunciation "Takao". After 1949 the city became known by the Mandarin pronunciation of these characters.

Arrival, orientation and city transport

Kaohsiung International Airport is south of the city centre, connected to the train station by a regular bus service (every 15min; NT$12) or taxi (NT$250). The airport has international and domestic terminals containing several banks and ATM machines: the former also has a **tourist service center** (daily 9am–12.30am) in the arrival hall which can provide information on hotels, sights, and transport. Left luggage is NT$50–100 per day, depending on the size of each piece.

Kaohsiung Train Station is at the northern end of the city centre: city buses leave from the terminal outside where it's also easy to catch a taxi. The Hi-Life convenience store inside has free **Internet**. Most long-distance **buses** terminate along Jianguo Road close to the train station (see below). The **High-Speed Rail station** is located in the northern district of Zuoying, connected to the centre by bus and eventually, the new metro system.

Orientation

Kaohsiung is a big, sprawling city, divided into eleven **districts**. The most interesting for visitors are **Cijin Island** to the south, **Gushan** to the west

---

Moving on from Kaohsiung

Kaohsiung International Airport has on average forty **flights** per day to Taipei, and frequent services to Magong. You can also fly to Hualien, Kinmen and the southern Penghu slands of Chimei and Wangan. Clearly marked airport buses depart from outside the train station every fifteen minutes.

From the train station there are frequent express **trains** north to Tainan, Taichung and Taipei, and across to Taitung on the east coast via the South Line, though the new **high-speed rail** services departing Zuoying station to the north will be much faster to Taipei (see Basics p.31).

Bus stations are clustered along Jianguo 2nd Road, just east of the train station: to the left of the station exit on the corner of Jianguo and Jhongshan roads, the **Kuo Kuang East Station** offers services to Taipei every thirty minutes, and Taitung and Taichung every hour, while a little further to the left on Nanhua Street, the **Kaohsiung Bus Station** has frequent services to Donggang (NT$82), Foguangshan (daily 6.30am–9.50pm; NT$80), Meinong (NT$116) and the Kenting Express (daily 5.35am–10.40pm; NT$275), as well as buses to Meishankou (daily 6.15am and 11.10am; NT$325). Opposite, **Ubus** departs 263 Jianguo 2nd Road to Taipei and Taichung. **CN Bus**, a block closer to Jhongshan Road, runs buses to Kenting every 10min, 24hrs a day (NT$300). Note that all buses to Kenting pass the entrance to Dapeng Bay National Scenic Area.

The large **car ferry** to Magong on Penghu is a popular alternative to the faster but bumpier ride from Budai in the summer: boats take 4hrs but are far more stable (Tai Hua Ferry Co, ☎07/5515823). The terminal is in Hamasen district, off Binhai Road, connected to the train station by bus #248.

(which includes Shoushan Nature Reserve, as well as the old harbourside area of Hamasen), **Yancheng** southwest of the modern centre, and **Zuoying** to the north. The other districts cover the downtown area and suburbs to the north and south: the former is where you'll find most of the commercial activity, with Jhongshan Road the city's main thoroughfare running north–south. Navigating the streets is fairly straightforward, as most are clearly marked in Tongyong Pinyin at junctions.

City transport

Kaohsiung's sights are scattered all over the city so you'll need to use public transport to get around. The **Kaohsiung City Bus Station** is just in front of the train station: timetables are in Chinese but you can look for bus numbers and bilingual destinations on the front of the buses. Bus #248 and #100 depart from here, while #99 leaves further down Jhongshan Road on the right. Fares are NT$12 per sector. **Taxis** are plentiful and a good alternative: initial fares are NT$70. Driving isn't recommended within the city itself, but you can **rent** cars at the airport to explore further afield (see Listings, p.353).

The city **metro** or Kaohsiung Rapid Transit System (Ⓦwww.krtco.com.tw) should be up and running by the end of 2007. Two lines, Red and Orange, will crisscross the city: from Zuoying in the north to the airport in the south; and from Yancheng in the west to the eastern suburbs.

Information

Kaohsiung's **tourist office** (Mon–Fri 9am–5pm; Ⓦwww.kaohsiung.gov.tw) at 5/F, 235 Jhongjheng 4th Rd (take the lift at the back, off Chenggong Rd) has basic English leaflets and maps but it's not in a particularly convenient location – by mid-2007 there should be a new office in the train station. Free monthly magazine *FYI South* has information on upcoming events and new bars and restaurants.

Accommodation

Kaohsiung contains plenty of budget **hotels** around the train station, and for those with a bigger budget, a reasonable selection of mid-range options scattered across the newer downtown districts – all of these have broadband (ADSL) ports in the rooms, and for those without laptops, computer rooms where you can check email.

Around the station

Hotel New Image 178 Cisian 2nd Rd ⓣ07/2863033, Ⓔhotels@pchome.com.tw. Classical Chinese decor in the larger rooms adds a bit of character to this otherwise basic but comfortable mid-range option, not far from the station. Worth upgrading to the Japanese-style rooms which have beds on wooden floors. ❹.

Hotel Skoal 64 Minzuheng Rd ⓣ07/2876151, ⓕ07/2886020. Budget hotel, with basic rooms from NT$800 – small and aging, but clean enough. Includes breakfast, and within walking distance of the station. ❷

Riverside Hotel 12 Henan 2nd Rd ⓣ07/2865141, Ⓔriversd@seed.net.tw. Small but comfortable hotel, just off Jhongshan Rd south of the train station. Henan Rd runs along the south side of Canal No.2. Single rooms are adequate with newish bathrooms. ❷

Union Hotel 295 Jianguo 2nd Rd ⓣ07/2350101, ⓕ07/2351287. Popular option with travellers looking for somewhere cheap near the station, discounts can make it less than NT$1000. English spoken but breakfast is not included and rooms are showing their age. ❸

Downtown

Gold Chain Hotel 35 Minzu 2nd Rd ⓣ07/2233775, Ⓔgd233291@ms27.hinet.net. Comfortable rooms in the upscale, eastern side of the city with coin-operated washing machines on site and bicycles available at

NT$50 per hr. The ample buffet breakfast (included) is pretty decent. ❹

🏃 **Grand Hi-Lai Hotel** 266 Chenggong 1st Rd ☏07/2161766, ⓦwww.grand-hilai .com.tw. Luxurious hotel offering rooms with Neoclassical decor and floors loaded with Chinese and Western *objest d'art*; don't miss the impressive collection of calligraphy on the eighth and tenth floors and *Lobster Bar* on the 45th. Located in Kaohsiung's third-highest building, the entrance is at the back. ❽

Sanduo Hotel 107 Sanduo 3rd Rd ☏07/3323210, ⓕ07/3323208. Budget hotel with modern, clean rooms, if a little too brightly decorated, in a decent location close to the main shopping and entertainment areas downtown. Breakfast included but no Internet. ❸

🏃 **The Splendor** 1 Zihciang 3rd Rd ☏07/5668000 ⓦwww.thesplendor-tc.com. The top luxury choice in the city, thanks to its deluxe rooms and magnificent views: the hotel occupies floors 37–79 of the 85 Sky Tower. There's also a ladies-only floor and range of classy restaurants and bars – enjoy the sunset at *75 Lounge* on the 75th floor. The entrance is on Singuang Rd: check-in on the 39th floor. ❽

Yancheng and the Love River

Ambassador Hotel 202 Minsheng 2nd Rd ☏07/2115211, ⓦwww.ambassadorhotel.com.tw. Kaohsiung's first five-star, offering luxurious rooms with views of the Love River. Discounts of up to 40 percent can make this a good deal, especially given the location, though standard singles are a little small. ❼

Hotel Kingdom 42 Wufu 4th Rd ☏07/5518211, ⓦwww.hotelkingdom.com.tw. Comfortable if a little overpriced hotel with flat-screen TVs in all the rooms, popular with upmarket tour groups. Location in the heart of the old pub district is excellent though, conveniently close to the Love River. ❻

The City

Kaoshiung's best hotels, shops and restaurants are scattered around the downtown area, dominated by the colossal **85 Sky Tower**, the ideal place to get your bearings. You'll find a collection of historic sights in the older, western parts of the city; explore **Yancheng** and the **Love River**, before taking the ferry to **Cijin Island**. With more time, there's plenty to see on the slopes of **Gushan**, and around **Lotus Lake** in **Zuoying** to the north.

85 Sky Tower

One of the most iconic buildings in Taiwan, the **85 Sky Tower** looms 347.5m over downtown Kaohsiung, its striking two-legged structure based on the Chinese character *gao*, meaning tall – it was the tallest building in Taiwan from 1997 until March 2003 when Taipei 101, also designed by C.Y. Lee, was completed. The 74th-floor viewing deck (daily noon–10pm; NT$100) provides a mesmerizing panorama of the city and the harbour, especially at night. The entrance is on the southwest side of the building, next to the *Splendor* lobby. From the train station bus #100 passes the tower on its tour of Kaohsiung's major shopping malls.

Yancheng and the Love River

The **Love River** on the western edge of the city centre marks the beginning of **Yancheng**, one of Kaohsiung's oldest neighbourhoods and crammed with some of its most traditional shopping streets, food stalls and temples. The riverbank has become a spruced-up promenade in recent years, with the area between Jhongjheng and Wufu roads lined with open-air cafés and parks. Bus #248 from the station follows Jhongjheng 4th Road to the river: get off on the western side, where the former city government building has been converted into the **Kaohsiung Museum of History** (Tues–Fri 9am–5pm, Sat–Sun 9am–9pm; free). Much of the labelling here is in Chinese, but English is gradually being added and it's worth a quick look. The first floor charts the history of the city, while a special 2-28 Incident exhibition covers the bloody events of 1947 from a Kaohsiung perspective (see p.513). A short walk south along the riverbank, the **Kaohsiung Municipal Film Archive** (Tues–Sun 1.30–9.30pm; free) contains a library of almost 6000 Chinese and international films along with personal TVs for viewing them, all for free. You'll need to show your passport to gain temporary membership. The church with the white stone facade on the other side of the river, just visible through the modern buildings, is the **Holy Rosary Cathedral** (151 Wufu 3rd Rd; Tues–Sat 9am–5pm) built in 1928 on the site of Taiwan's first Catholic church and established by Spanish priest Fernando Sainz in 1859.

For a quick tour of the district's main temples head west along Sinle Street to Yancheng Street where you'll see **San Shan Temple** (daily 5.30am–10.30pm). Established in 1760 by Hakka immigrants and dedicated to the Three Mountain Kings, it's now the spiritual centre of Yancheng. During the Lantern Festival, the temple maintains the 100-year-old tradition of "**Turtle Begging**", where turtles made of ground rice are offered to the gods in remembrance of a local miracle. Worshippers pray or "beg" to take the turtles home for good fortune.

From here head north along Yancheng Street, across Dagong Street and up the narrow arcade to Fuye Road. Turn left, and just before Cisian 3rd Road on the left is the tiny but atmospheric **Xiahai City God Temple** (daily 7.30am–9.30pm), with an extra large statue of the deity in the Main Hall and *jian-nian* figures in the walls. At the end of the Fuye Road, the imposing, multi-level *Wenwu Shang Dian*, or **Temple of God of War and Education** (daily 5am–midnight), has its roots in the 1920s but is a recent 1950s construction: Guan Di, the God of War, is enshrined in the main hall, while Wenchang Dijun, the God of Literature (third floor) and Confucius (fourth floor) are worshipped above.

British Consulate at Takao

Facing the ocean on the western side of the city, the **British Consulate at Takao** (daily 9am–midnight; free) occupies a strategic point high above Lianhai Road – it's a steep climb from the bus stop (take bus #99 from the station), up to the main entrance. Contrary to what you'll read on site, evidence suggests that the red-brick colonial mansion was built between 1878 and 1879, and served as a base from which the British could administer customs until 1895, before being abandoned in 1910. Today it functions principally as a swish café and restaurant (daily 11am–midnight) with outside tables commanding superb views of the city below, beer (NT$120), decent cocktails (NT$150) and of course, English-style tea (NT$150), though the liberal display of Union Jack flags is a little over the top. The small exhibition room inside (Chinese only) contains paintings relating to the first British Consul and zoologist **Robert Swinhoe**, and several of the Taiwanese animals named after him. Swinhoe established the first consulate in 1864 on Cijin Island, but left the area in 1866 and died before the current building was constructed.

Cijin Island

Cijin Island lies between Kaohsiung Harbour and the sea, southwest of the city centre. It's the oldest part of the city with plenty to keep you busy for half a day, but the best reason for a trip out here is to enjoy the views. Take the ferry from Gushan Ferry Pier (daily 6am–midnight, every 5–10min; NT$10) – you can take bus #248 from the train station to the pier which is located in **Hamasen**, an area first developed by the Japanese and now packed with harbourside cafés. From the ferry pier you can also take **harbour cruises** at weekends (4pm & 7pm; 2hr 30min; NT$350–4000) – the city lights make the

The Kaohsiung Incident

The **Kaohsiung Incident** of December 1979 was a political watershed, often regarded as the beginning of Taiwan's democratic revolution, though there is still bitter disagreement over whether it helped or hindered the momentum for change. Opposition to Taiwan's one-party state had been growing in the 1970s and in an apparent concession, President Chiang Ching-kuo had agreed to hold legislative elections in 1979 – but at the last minute, he cancelled them. On Human Rights Day (December 10) a rally was organized in Kaohsiung in protest, activists spurred on by the arrest the night before of two workers of *Meilidao* ("Formosa" in English), a clandestine publication that was a focus for dissidents. Things quickly got out of hand as police were brought in to disperse the crowds, and violent scuffles ensued – both sides blamed each other. In the aftermath, almost every member of the unofficial opposition was arrested, culminating in the trial, in 1980, of the **"Kaohsiung Eight"** for sedition. Most were jailed for lengthy periods, but the trial was widely publicized and as a result the defendants garnered a great deal of sympathy, ultimately creating a wider base for democratic reform.

Today, the list of those involved reads like a "Who's Who" of Taiwanese politics, many becoming leaders of the *Tangwai* (Outside Party) movement and later the Democratic Progressive Party: Chen Shui-bian (elected president in 2000) and Frank Hsieh (former Kaohsiung mayor and premier) were lawyers on the defence team, while Annette Lu (vice-president from 2000), Lin Yi-hsiung (former leader of the DPP) and Shih Ming-teh (ex-DPP chairman and political activist) served five to ten years in jail. Although no one died during the incident, Lin's mother and twin seven-year-old daughters were murdered while he was in prison, a case that remains unsolved.

evening cruise more attractive. Once on the island you can hire bikes from shops near the ferry terminal for NT$30–50 per hour, but it's easy to visit all the main sights on foot. For those with more energy, 15km of **bike trails** are being developed, covering the whole island.

Tianhou Temple (daily 5.30am–10pm) is a short walk from the wharf: turn right then left along Miaocian Road. The temple is the oldest in Kaohsiung, established in 1673 and dedicated to Mazu. Note the *wang chuan* or "spirit ship", a model boat and shrine to the left of the main hall, dedicated to three Wang Ye gods thought to protect the village from disease. Miaocian Road is also known as **Seafood Street** and lined with restaurants offering a huge variety of fish and shellfish: pick out what you fancy and they'll cook it for you. The **Cihou Presbyterian Church** at no. 13 was built in 1935 on the site of James Maxwell's original church, and is where the energetic Scotsman lived in the 1860s – he so impressed the locals that it was said that if Maxwell couldn't do it, there was no way it could be done. **Cihou Battery** (daily 8am–5pm; free) is on the hill a short walk along the lanes north of here. The red-brick and concrete gun emplacement was built in the 1870s and taken by the Japanese after a short but fierce gun battle in 1895. A path leads from the battery along the ridge to the **Cihou Lighthouse** (Tues–Sun 9am–4pm; free) built in 1883 and still used today – the views from both sites are magnificent.

Shoushan Nature Reserve

The line of hills due west of the city centre forms the **Shoushan Nature Reserve**, named after the peak of Shoushan (356m), a popular hiking spot. The southern end of the ridge contains the Shoushan Zoo, Martyrs' Shrine and Yuanheng Temple, a huge Buddhist monastery, while the northern section, known by the mountain's old name **Chaishan**, is best known for its eight hundred or so **Taiwanese macaques** or rhesus monkeys, the densest such population in Taiwan. Though it's strictly forbidden to do so, people still tend to feed them, with the result that the troupes can get aggressive. During the week it's far less crowded, but don't bring food and keep a safe distance. The best way up is to take a taxi to the trail behind **Longquan Temple** on Lane 51 off Gushan 3rd Road – bus #18, #99 and #245 also pass the entrance.

Kaohsiung Museum of Fine Arts

Located in Neiweipi Cultural Park northwest of the train station, the **Kaohsiung Museum of Fine Arts** (Tues–Sun 9am–5pm; free; ⓦ www.kmfa.gov.tw) contains a series of impressive modern art galleries opened in 1994. On Sundays and holidays bus #57 makes hourly trips to the museum from the train station, and at other times bus #205 stops at the hospital nearby. Inside there are four floors of galleries, enough to keep you busy for several hours: most exhibits change every three months, but the emphasis is on modern Taiwanese painting, calligraphy and sculpture, particularly from the southern half of the country. Room 105 houses the only permanent display, the **Development of Modern Taiwanese Sculpture,** beginning with the work of Huang Tu-shui during the Japanese occupation, and featuring exquisite pieces by contemporary artists such as Ju Ming (see p.168).

Zuoying and Lotus Lake

Founded in the seventeenth century as the capital of the old county of Fengshan, **Zuoying** is today a suburban district 5km north of downtown. The main attraction is tranquil **Lotus Lake**, a relatively modest stretch of water roughly 1.5km long and 500m wide, but ringed by a handful of ancient monuments and picturesque temples and pagodas. Trains to Zuoying Station depart Kaohsiung every ten to twenty minutes (6min; NT$15). Cross the main road outside the station (ignoring the road signs to the lake), and walk straight up Shengli Road – you'll see the water after about 500m.

Little remains of old Zuoying, which once stood south of the lake, though the city wall is the best preserved in Taiwan. Known as the **Old Wall of Fengshan County**, it was completed in 1826 using bits of coral. Several sections and three gates have been restored, with the most convenient segment around the North Gate on Shengli Road, a few metres beyond the lake's southwestern corner. From here, stroll up the western shore along Liantan Road to the first pair of gaudy pagodas on the right. This is the **Dragon–Tiger Pavilion** knocked up in 1965 as an extension to Ciji Temple opposite. For good luck, enter through the dragon's mouth and exit via the tiger; inside are garish scenes of heaven and hell. A few metres ahead is the simply adorned **Spring Autumn Pavilion**, two towers built in 1953 and fronted by a statue of Guanyin on top

Zuoying		
Zuoying	左營	*zuǒyíng*
City God Temple	城隍廟	*chénghuáng miào*
Confucius Temple	孔子廟	*kǒngzǐ miào*
Beiji Xuantian Shang Di Pavilion	北極玄天上帝廟	*běijí xúantiān shàngdì miào*
Dragon-Tiger Pavilion	龍虎塔	*lónghǔ tǎ*
Old Wall of Fengshan County	鳳山舊城	*fēngshān jiùchéng*
Qiming Temple	啟明堂	*qǐmíng táng*
Lotus Lake	蓮花潭	*liánhuā tán*
Spring Autumn Pavilion	春秋閣	*chūnqiū gé*

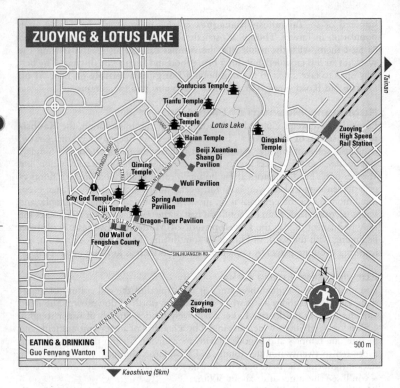

ZUOYING & LOTUS LAKE

Confucius Temple

Tianfu Temple

Yuandi Temple

Lotus Lake

Haian Temple

Beiji Xuantian Shang Di Pavilion

Qingshui Temple

Qiming Temple

Wuli Pavilion

City God Temple

Spring Autumn Pavilion

Ciji Temple

Dragon-Tiger Pavilion

Old Wall of Fengshan County

ZHONGDA ROAD

BEITZTOU STREET

YUAN RD

YUANAN ROAD

SHENGLI ROAD

SINJHUANGZIH RD.

Zuoying High Speed Rail Station

CHENGGONG ROAD

CUEIHUA ROAD

Zuoying Station

Tainan

N

EATING & DRINKING
Guo Fenyang Wanton 1

0 — 500 m

Kaoshiung (5km)

of a giant, garishly decorated dragon. Wuli Pavilion, further out in the lake, was added in 1978, with all three linked to the imposing **Qiming Temple** (daily 4.30am–9.30pm) on shore, dedicated principally to Guan Di, but hosting an array of gods including a bearded Confucius at the back of the main altar. The temple was established in 1909 and rebuilt in the 1970s.

Four hundred metres further along the lake is the impressive **Beiji Xuantian Shang Di Pavilion**, comprising a 22-metre-high statue of the Supreme Emperor of the Dark Heaven, reached via a pier lined with characters from the Chinese classic *Creation of the Gods* (*Feng Shen Yan Yi*). A short walk west along Yuandi Road from here is **Yuandi Temple** (daily 5am–9.30pm), also dedicated to the Supreme Emperor, the chief image found by fishermen in 1758 and now displayed in the central altar. The temple was established in 1666 as a shrine to Lady Linshui (see p.325), worshipped here as a goddess of lakes and rivers, and thought to give protection from drowning. Her image is kept in a shrine to the right. The temple sits in front of a small plaza – don't confuse it with Hai-an Temple which is closer to the water but far less interesting.

At the northern end of the lake is Taiwan's largest **Confucius Temple** (daily 9am–5pm) completed in 1977, though its status refers to the whole site rather than the main Dacheng Hall: it's an impressive piece of architecture but Taichung's temple is far grander. The entrance to the central courtyard is on the left (western) side, but the Dacheng Hall is only open on Confucius's birthday (September 28).

If you've still got some energy left return to Qiming Temple and turn right, then left along Beitztou Street. The bustling **City God Temple** (daily 5am–9.30pm) is a short walk on the right, dating from 1704. Check out the god's huge black abacus on the ceiling in front of the main altar. Keep walking down Beitztou Street to Shengli Road and turn right: in around 200m you'll hit Zuoyingda Road, the area's main commercial thoroughfare. Turn right here and a little further along the road, opposite *McDonald's*, is the superb *Guo Fenyang Wanton* **dumplings stall** at no. 86 (6am–midnight; NT$40–50 per bowl).

Eating and drinking

Kaohsiung is well supplied with places to **eat** and **drink**, though there are fewer international options here than in Taipei or Taichung. As usual, **night markets** provide the widest selection of cheap snacks and meals: the most famous is **Liouhe Road Night Market** (5pm–midnight) on Liaohe Road between Jhongshan Road and Zihli Road, the proliferation of Japanese food stalls here reflecting its huge popularity with Japanese tourists. **Sinsing Night Market** on Nanhua Road has more clothes stalls and some food at the southern end.

Cafés

Bagel Bagel 3 158 Minsheng 1st Rd. Located in the eastern side of downtown, deli and café with home-made bagels, sandwiches, wraps, salads, soups and smoothies from NT$120, and good-value breakfast sets under NT$100. Outdoor and indoor seating. Daily 7am–10pm.
Cape Café 109 Binhai 1st Rd. Outdoor café, just along the road from Gushan Ferry Pier with views of the harbour and Cijin Island. Minimum charge of NT$100, with coffees from NT$80 and cocktails NT$150. Also has a decent selection of Southeast Asian food. Daily 11.30am–3am.

Urban Spotlight (intersection of Jhonghua and Wufu Rds). Also known as the Outdoor Café, this is a great place to relax and people watch at the south end of Jhongshan Park, open from early afternoon till midnight or later at weekends when it tends to get busier and features live music. Serves mostly cakes, light Western snacks, teas and coffees (from NT$70). Mon–Fri 1pm–2am, Sat–Sun 10am–3am.
Yushu Fang 149-14 Heping 1st Rd. Tranquil café serving tea and coffee with lots of running water and bookshelves inside, and a slightly classical Chinese theme (NT$50–80). Daily 10am–12.30am.

Restaurants

Kaohsiung is best known for its **seafood**, with many of the oldest stalls in **downtown** and **Yancheng**, close to the pubs on Wufu Road – it's easy to point

Kaohsiung restaurants

Aroma Mutton Pot	味味香羊肉爐	*wèiwèi xiāng yángròulú*
Cape Café	好望角	*hǎowàng jiǎo*
City of Steamed Glutinous Rice	米糕城	*mǐgāo chéng*
Gan's Frozen Taro	甘家老店冷凍芋	*gānjīa lǎodiàn lěngdòng yù*
Hamasen Black Marlin Fish Ball King	哈瑪星,旗魚丸大王	*hāmǎxīng qíyúwán dàwáng*
Kaohsiung Pearl Barley King	高雄薏仁大王	*gāoxióng yìréndàwáng*
Liouhe Road Night Market	六合路觀光夜市	*liùhélù guāng yèshì*
Mamamia	瑪瑪米亞餐廳	*mǎmǎmíyà cāntīng*
Mrs Meatball at Sankuaicuo	三塊厝肉圓嫂	*sānkuàicuò ròuyúansǎo*
Old Cai's Milkfish Congee	老蔡虱目魚粥	*lǎocài shīmùyú zhōu*
Shangfang Mackerel Fish Broth	尚芳魠魚羹	*shàngfāng tuó yúgēng*
Sinsing Night Market	新興夜市	*xīnxīng yèshì*
Smokey Joe's	冒煙的喬	*màoyān deqiáo*
Urban Spotlight	城市光廊	*chéngshì guāngláng*
Yushu Fang	御書房	*yùshū fáng*

at what you want even if you don't speak Chinese. For cheap Western food try the bars listed below.

Downtown

Gan's Frozen Taro 113 Zihciang 3rd Rd. Tiny dessert store on a section of Zihciang Road crammed with enticing night market stalls. Try the frozen taro (NT$30) – sweet relief on a sizzling hot day. Daily noon–midnight.

Kaohsiung Milk King 65 Jhonghua 3rd Rd. Kaohsiung is renowned throughout Taiwan for papaya milk, popularized by this chain which was established in the 1960s. This canteen-style diner offers snacks and juices (NT$50–60) and the celebrated papaya milk for NT$50. English menu available. Daily 7am–11pm.

Kaohsiung Pearl Barley King 449 Chenggong 1st Rd. Fifty-year old store that produces sweet green bean desserts and barley drinks (NT$20) – traditional thirst quenchers especially welcome in the tropical heat. Not far from the tourist office. Daily 8am–10.30pm.

Lee's Vegetarian Workshop 145 Wufu 3rd Rd. Solid vegetarian option just across the Love River from Yancheng, with English menus and set meals (including salad bar, bread, soup, drink and dessert) from NT$260–NT$460. Mushrooms and yams seem to be central features. Daily 11.30am–2pm, 5.30–9pm.

Mamamia 186 Jhongjheng Rd 2nd Rd. Popular Italian eatery with locals and expats alike – reasonable at NT$300–400 per dish (the pasta is recommended) with fun atmosphere and friendly service. Daily 11am–1am.

Mrs Meatball at Sankuaicuo 389 Jianguo 3rd Rd. Another traditional shop that will appeal to fans of Taiwanese food: the meatballs (NT$15 per order) here are unique, cooked with soy sauce and pork to make something closer to western stew and

dumplings than the glutinous variety elsewhere on the island. Daily 6.30am–5pm.

Smokey Joe's 208 Jhongsiao 1st Rd. Decent Tex-Mex restaurant replete with adobe-looking walls, long wooden tables and decor straight out of a Tijuana *cantina*. Lunch specials from NT$220. Daily 11am–2am.

Yancheng and Hamasen

Aroma Mutton Pot 100 Fuye Road. This shop has been in business for over forty years and sells a combination of seafood and mutton hot pots, as well as a variety of other stir-fried dishes from NT$50. Daily 11am–2pm, 5pm–1am.

City of Steamed Glutinous Rice 107 Daren Rd. Cheap local shop that's over fifty years old, producing mouth-watering bowls of glutinous rice topped in pork or fish with cucumber (NT$25). Daily 9.30am–10.30pm.

Hamasen Black Marlin Fish Ball King 27 Gupo St (between Linhai Rd and Gushan St). This celebrated food stall is located in the forecourt of Da Tian Temple in Hamasen – locals reckon they serve the best fish ball soup in the country and though that might be pushing it, the food here is superb and a bargain at NT$25 per bowl. Daily 10am–6pm.

Old Cai's Milkfish Congee 201 Lainan St. This small restaurant sells not only congee but whole milkfish cooked in ginger, a Kaohsiung specialty – delicious and easy to order. Near Dagong Rd. Daily 6.30am–2pm, 5pm–8pm.

Shangfang Mackerel Fish Broth 72 Fuye Rd. Tasty fried fish balls served with soup noodles in the heart of Yancheng's "temple street." Set lunches from NT$100 or bowls from NT$40. Daily 9.30am–7.30pm.

Drinking and nightlife

DNA 4/F, 77 Minsheng 1st Rd (right side of Jinmen Rd). Popular bar and nightclub, with decent sound system and DJs making this one of the better dance venues in town. Daily 10pm–3am; all you can drink on Fridays (NT$500 men, NT$300 women).

Honky Tonk 2/F, 101 Jhongjheng 2nd Rd. Unpretentious bar with pool table, at the top of a narrow staircase off the main street and the haunt of both locals and expats. All you can drink for NT$600 at the weekends – don't lose your glass because you'll have to pay again. Daily 6pm–6am.

La Face 233 Siwei 4th Rd. Lounge bar cum-restaurant with a mixture of Thai and Italian food, and a

big selection of pizza (NT$220), burgers, over fifty cocktails, wine and cigars. Sun–Thurs 6.30pm–2.30am, Fri–Sat 6.30pm–4am, closed Tues.

Pig & Whistle 199 Siwei 4th Rd ⓦwww .pigandwhistle.com.tw. This Kaohsiung institution features an English-style pub with Corona (NT$150), Guinness (NT$240) and Carlsberg (NT$190) on tap and classics such as fish and chips (NT$280) on the first floor, busy nightclub upstairs and a more relaxed "Luxury Lounge" on the third floor. Daily 7pm–3am.

Wufu 4th Road Traditional nightlife area in Yancheng, and still home to numerous pubs and restaurants, though these days it's looking a little tired and tends to be frequented by an older expat crowd. Plenty of cheap beer deals and happy hours from 5pm to 8pm however: *Night Owl* at no.88 is a cosy place next to *Focus Pub*, with a popular happy hour, while friendly *Oxford Music Pub* (just off Wufu at 111 Dayi St), is an expat stalwart.

Shopping

Kaohsiung is second only to Taipei as a place to **shop**, with plenty of department stores as well as cheaper markets and gift shops. In addition to those listed below, there are several other specialty streets: Dalian Street north of the station is good for **shoes**, Singjhong Street north of Sanduo 3rd Road is lined with **flower stalls** and Jianguo 2nd Road south of the station is packed with **computer stores**.

Jade Market On the corner of Zihli Rd and Shihcyuan Rd. Similar to Taichung's jade market, this vast hall is crammed with not just jade, but antique stalls selling statues and jewellery.
Mei Li Tan Artefacts 190 Wufu 2nd Rd. Taiwanese arts and crafts shop, in the centre of downtown. Mon–Sat 10.30am–7pm.
New Jyuejiang Shopping Mall Lanes between Wenhang 2nd Rd and Renjhih St, just south of Wufu 2nd Rd. The narrow streets in this area are crammed with fashionable stalls, upmarket boutiques and coffeeshops, the best place to check out local street fashions. It's a bit like Taipei's Ximending.

Sanduo Road Commercial District Chief shopping zone in the modern, southeast side of downtown between Jhongshan and Wenheng Rds, containing Sogo, FE21 and Shinkong Mitsukoshi department stores; the alleys nearby are packed with clothes stores.
Sanfengjhong Traditional Covered Market Stretches from Zihli Rd to Jhonghua Rd, just north of Jianguo 3rd Rd and west of the train station, crammed with stalls selling all sorts of traditional Chinese snacks and dried foods.
Sinle Street Narrow pedestrianized street in Yancheng packed with traditional gold and jewellery stores between Lainan St and Yancheng St, and fabric sellers further east.

Listings

Airlines China Airlines ☎07/2826141; Mandarin Airlines ☎07/3320608; TransAsia Airways ☎07/3359355; Eva Airways ☎07/5369301; Uni Airways ☎07/7911000; Dragon Airlines ☎07/2016647; Far Eastern Air Transport ☎07/3371388; Thai Airways ☎07/2155871; Cathay Pacific ☎07/2827538; Malaysia Airline System ☎07/2369348; Singapore Airlines ☎07/2270653.
Banks/ATMs There are plenty of banks and ATMs in Kaohsiung, many located inside 7-Elevens. HSBC has a branch in the Baochen Enterprise Building, 6 Mincyuan 2nd Rd (☎07/3377333) while Citibank is at 502 Jiouru 1st Rd (☎07/3916000).
Books Caves Books is at 76 Wufu 4th Rd.
Car rental Hertz Car Rental is at 23 Jhongshan 4th Rd (☎0800/015168) south of the airport while Central Auto is at 81 Changcian Rd (☎07/8020800).
Cinema Warner Village is at 13/F, 21 Sanduo 4th Rd (inside FE21).
Hospital The Kaohsiung Medical University Chung-Ho Memorial Hospital at 100 Zhiyou 1st Rd

has out-patient clinics (☎07/3208181; Mon–Fri 8.30am–noon, 2–5pm & 6–8.30pm).
Internet access CGV on Jianguo 3rd Rd just west of the station (24hrs; NT$20/hr); eSoho on the junction of Jhongjheng and Rueiyuan Rds (NT$10/hr); Net Plus Life at 193-10 Cisian 2nd Rd (24hrs; NT$15/hr).
Left luggage Coin lockers are available at the train station and come in three sizes: NT$30, NT$120 or NT$150 for 24hr.
Police For emergencies, visa renewal and lost and found contact the Foreign Affairs Police at 260 Jhongjheng 4th Rd (☎07/2154342; Mon–Fri 8am–noon & 1.30–5.30pm, Sat 9am–noon).
Post The post office at 2-2 Jianguo 3rd Rd is conveniently located to the right of train station exit (daily 8am–5pm).
Theatre and performing arts Try expat-run Mindful Phoenix Arts at 165 Jhongjeng 2nd Rd (☎07/2230581, ⓦwww.mindfulphoenix.com) for classes including kung fu, salsa and tai chi, and weekend theatre in English. The Chiang Kai-shek Cultural Center at 67 Wufu 1st Rd hosts concerts and contains several art galleries.

Around Kaohsiung: Foguangshan Monastery

One of several wealthy Buddhist foundations established in Taiwan since the 1960s, **Foguangshan Monastery** (daily 8.30am–10pm; museums and galleries Tues–Sun 8.30am–5pm; free; ℗07/6561921, ⓦwww.fgs.org.tw) is a vast complex of grand temple architecture, giant statues and extensive collections of Buddhist art. Around 25km northeast of Kaohsiung, it's an absorbing day-trip from the city, with regular buses making it easy to reach.

The monastery is the home of the Foguangshan International Buddhist Order, founded in 1967 by **Master Hsing Yun**, an enigmatic monk from China who has spent his life travelling and teaching his unique brand of "Humanistic Buddhism". He's still based at the monastery, though Venerable Hsin Pei became abbot in January 2005. Today Foguangshan is part monastery, with around three hundred monks and nuns, and part educational complex with over a thousand students at its on-site university and high school campus. Many people come here to study or participate in the monthly seven-day **meditation retreats** (see website), but there's plenty to see for casual visitors. Starting at the **Non Duality Gate** at the front of the monastery, take a look inside the **Foguangshan Treasury Museum** on the right, packed with Buddhist art, carvings and cultural relics. From here climb straight up the hill towards the stunning **main shrine** or "Great Hero Hall": it contains three 7.8-metre Buddha statutes (Amitabha, Sakyamuni and Bhaisajya-guru or Medicine Buddha), beautifully cast in bronze and surrounded on all sides by a staggering 14,800 smaller Buddha images lit by tiny lights and displayed within an intricate latticework of carved wood. If you stay the night (see below), be sure to catch morning prayers and chanting which take place here at 5.50am every day.

The main building behind the shrine is the **Tathagatha Hall** which contains an **art gallery** in the basement, a **museum** (not much English) on the second floor and the **Buddha's tooth relic**, donated by a Tibetan monk in 1998 and housed temporarily on the fourth floor (open only on weekends – a special hall for the relic is being built behind the main site). The other highlight is the 36-metre **statue of Amitabha Buddha** on the east side of the complex (an area known as "Great Buddha Land"), the iconic symbol of the monastery and approached by a road lined with 480 smaller statues.

Practicalities

Buses from Kaohsiung Bus Station terminate just outside the main monastery gate. There are several teahouses (the tea is free) and cafés serving delicious **vegetarian food** on site and outside the main gate, and you can also stay at the very comfortable *Pilgrim's Lodge* just below the main shrine (NT$2000) – **rooms** are all en-suite with cable TV. Note, however, that you are expected to dress modestly (no shorts or miniskirts). Plenty of staff speak English and a host of foreign languages, but guided tours (recommended) need to be arranged in advance. You'll hear the word *Amitofu* everywhere you go: this is another name for Buddha ("boundless light") and has become a catch-all for thank you, bless you, or hello. The most interesting **festivals** are Chinese New Year (January or February) and Buddha's Birthday (usually in April).

Meinong and around

The rural town of **MEINONG**, around 40km northeast of Kaohsiung, lies in the centre of the Shuang River plain and at the heart of **Hakka culture**

Meinong	美濃	měinóng
Chung Li-ho Memorial Museum	鍾理和紀念館	zhōnglǐhé jìniànguǎn
Guang Hsing Guo Wang Gong	廣興國王宮	guǎngxīng guówánggōng
Meinong Folk Village	美濃民俗村	měinóng mínsú cūn
Meinong Hakka Museum	美濃客家文物館	měinóng kèjiā wénwùguǎn
Yuan Hsiang Yuan Cultural Village	原鄉緣紙傘文化村	yúanxiāngyúan zhǐsǎnwén huà cūn
Accommodation and eating		
Renzih Homestay	人字山莊	rénzì shānzhuāng
Shuangfengdu Homestay	雙峰渡假民宿	shuāngfēngdùjià mínsù
Meinong Traditional Hakka Restaurant	美濃古老文物客家菜	meínóng gǔlǎo wénwù kèjīa cài

in the south – ninety percent of its inhabitants claim Hakka ancestry and the majority still speak their traditional language. As with Beipu in the north, Meinong is celebrated for its fabulous **Hakka food**, but has the additional appeal of producing exquisite traditional-style, oil-paper **parasols**. The countryside around the town is different too: it's exceptionally tranquil, still dotted with nineteenth-century red-brick houses, paddy fields and banana plantations. Having your own transport is definitely an advantage as things are spread out, and hiring a bike is a sensible option given the signposted network of **cycling trails** in the area – pick up a map from the Hakka Museum or any homestay. March is the best time to come, when the weather cools and fields of flowers are in bloom.

Meinong was founded by brothers Lin Feng-shan and Lin Guey-shan in 1736, gradually forcing out the local Rukai tribe and Hoklo settlers to create the Hakka enclave that exists today. The local **tobacco industry** was established in 1939 and boomed in the 1970s and 1980s, creating much of the area's wealth, but after Taiwan joined the World Trade Organization in 2002 local producers were unable to compete and most of the farms have closed – today you'll see only a few ruined tobacco towers outside the main town. Meinong's multi-coloured parasols make beautiful gifts, though the traditional Chinese craft only took off here in the 1920s.

The Town

A short walk south of the bus station, Meinong's **Old Street** (Yongan Road) begins at **Dongmen** (East Gate) at its eastern end, a defensive work originally constructed in 1755 but rebuilt several times since. A few metres away, in a small garden overlooking the river, is one of over two hundred **Earth God** shrines in the Meinong area: known as "Bogong" locally and the town's most important deity, the god is symbolized by a tablet rather than a figure. The 150-year old tree shading the site was killed by the concrete around the shrine – a new one has been planted behind it.

From here Old Street follows the course of the Shuang River, once an important trade route, though it's little more than a stream today – you can still see the remains of the **old wharf** behind the **Tianhou Temple** a short walk from the East Gate, along a lane parallel to the main road. Further along at no. 178 is **Lin Cheun-yu's House**, home of Meinong's richest family and much bigger than it looks from the street. Lin family members still live here but don't mind visitors having a peek inside the older parts of the complex at the front – much

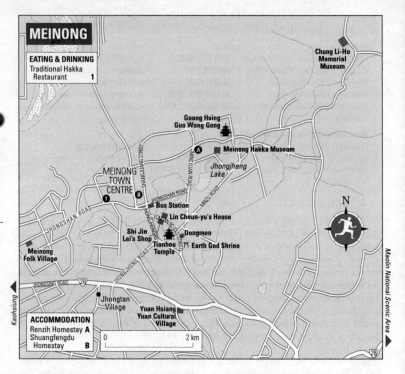

MEINONG

EATING & DRINKING
Traditional Hakka
Restaurant   1

Chung Li-Ho
Memorial
Museum

Guang Hsing
Guo Wang Gong

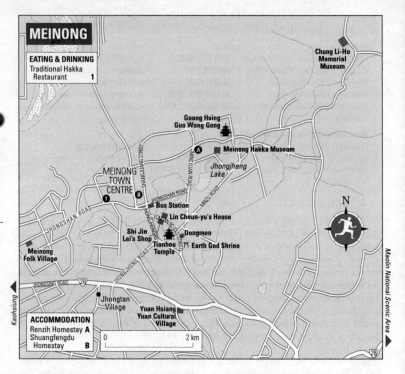 Meinong Hakka Museum

Jhongjheng
Lake

MEINONG
TOWN
CENTRE

Bus Station

Lin Cheun-yu's House

Shi Jin
Lai's Shop   Dongmen

Tianhou   Earth God Shrine
Temple

Meinong
Folk Village

JHONGSING ROAD

Jhongtan
Village

Yuan Hsiang
Yuan Cultural
Village

ACCOMMODATION
Renzih Homestay **A**
Shuangfengdu
Homestay **B**

0   2 km

N

of this is in dire need of renovation. Opposite at no. 177 is the workshop of master tailor **Shi Jin Lai** who was born in 1909 and still makes traditional **blue Hakka clothes**. Everything is made by hand: simple shirts or blouses cost NT$1000–1200. Northeast of the centre, just beyond Jhongjheng Lake on Minzu Road, lies the **Meinong Hakka Museum** (Tues–Fri 9.30am–4.30pm; Sat–Sun 9am–5pm; NT$60), housing an interesting collection of exhibits, including a mock tobacco tower. Everything is labelled in Chinese only, but there are English leaflets.

Practicalities

Meinong's small **bus station** is in the centre of town at the junction of Jhong-shan and Jhongjheng roads, with buses to Kaohsiung (daily 5.35am–8.45pm every 30min; NT$131) and seven daily services to Liouguei in the Maolin National Scenic Area. Staying overnight in Meinong is a good idea, especially as many of the **homestays** in the area offer **bike rentals**. The best is *Renzih Homestay* at 66-5 Mincyuan Road (⏂07/6614684; **❸**) with comfortable rooms in a two-storey house in a tranquil area northeast of the centre. The owners speak some English, are very knowledgeable guides and will pick you up from the bus station (⏂0912/199926). Bikes are NT$100 per day. Another good place, with free bicycle hire, is the *Shuangfengdu Homestay* at 8 Shangjuang Street (⏂07/6820839; **❷**), a ten-minute walk from the bus station with dormi-tory beds for NT$250–300. For **food**, try local Hakka specialties such as *ban tiao* (fried noodles) and *lien* (wild lotus), available at the atmospheric *Meinong*

Traditional Hakka Restaurant (*Meinong Gu Lau Ke Jia Cai*) at 362-5 Jhongshan Road, on the west side of town. This part of Jhongshan Road is the best place to look for **shops** selling oil-paper parasols.

Around Meinong

In addition to traditional Hakka houses and farms scattered between the paddy fields and banana groves, there are plenty of tourist-orientated shops lining the main roads in the countryside around Meinong. The most popular can be found in the **Meinong Folk Village** (daily 8am–6pm summer, 8am–5.30pm winter; free), a few kilometres outside Meinong at 80, Lane 421, Jhongshan Road Section 2. It's a bit tacky but not bad if you want to buy Hakka souvenirs, especially the famous **oil-paper parasols**; large ones go for around NT$700–900, while you can make your own small version for NT$330 at the weekends (ask at the shop at the end of the street). South of Meinong, on Route 28 on the edge of Jhongtan, **Yuan Hsiang Yuan Cultural Village** at 147 Jhongsing Rd Sec 1 (Mon–Fri 8.30am–5.30pm, Sat–Sun 8.30am–6.30pm; free) is a similar complex of shops and restaurants with an excellent collection of Hakka artefacts on the second floor and slightly more authentic crafts for sale.

A short ride east of the Hakka Museum you'll find the **Guang Hsing Guo Wang Gong**, Meinong's Three Mountain Kings temple, often packed on special days or weekend mornings with locals praying for good luck: these gods are supposed to be particularly munificent when it comes to protecting cars from theft or accident. If you can read Chinese the **Chung Li-ho Memorial Museum** (Tues–Sun 9am–5pm; free) northeast of here in Guanlin village is worth a look. Chung, author of the acclaimed *Lishan Farm* (1960), was a pioneer in the field of Taiwanese literature in the 1950s, a Hakka writer who helped inspire the postwar Nativist movement.

Maolin National Scenic Area

The **MAOLIN NATIONAL SCENIC AREA**, stretching across a sizeable expanse of hilly southern Taiwan, has broad appeal for travellers with a diverse range of mountain scenery, aboriginal cultures, hot springs and ample opportunity for outdoor activities. Concentrated in the foothills to the east of Tainan and Kaohsiung, its major centres are accessible by public transport, making them ideal for day-trips. The scenic area's heart is the **Maolin Recreation Area**, which includes the attractions alongside curvy **County Highway 132** from Maolin Village to Duona, an aboriginal village known for its unspoiled outdoor hot springs. This region is the traditional homeland of the **Rukai aboriginal tribe**, known chiefly for their hunting prowess and their signature **slate-slab houses**. The scenery here is superb, with dense virgin forests, butterfly-filled valleys, sprawling suspension bridges and waterfalls at nearly every turn. South of the recreation area is the aboriginal stronghold of **Sandimen**, where the **Paiwan** and Rukai tribes live in harmony. From Sandimen, restricted **Highway 24** twists and turns east into the mountains to the seldom visited Rukai village of **Wutai**, representing a rare opportunity to familiarize yourself with their distinctive culture, architecture, food and drink.

Adventure sport ranks high on the agenda of many visitors to the area, and the **Saijia Aviation Park** near Sandimen is widely regarded as one of Asia's top **paragliding** sites (see Basics p.357). **White-water rafting** is another popular activity, and the towns of **Laonong** and **Baolai** – in the north of the national scenic area – host a steady stream of rafting groups during the rainy summer months. With several **hot-springs hotels**, Baolai, at the Southern Cross-Island Highway's western edge, is a relaxing overnight stopping point for those making their way over this exhilarating road (see p.334).

Maolin National Scenic Area

Maolin National Scenic Area	茂林國家風景區	màolín guójiā fēngjǐngqū
Maolin National Scenic Area Visitor Center	茂林國家風景區遊客中心	màolín guójiā fēngjǐngqū yóukè zhōngxīn
Maolin Recreation Area	茂林遊憩區	màolín yóuqìqū
Towns and villages		
Baolai	寶來	bǎolái
Duona	多納	duōnà
Liouguei	六龜	liùguī
Maolin Village	茂林村	màolín cūn
Sandimen	三地門	sāndìmén
Shenshan	神山	shénshān
Shueimen	水門	shuǐmén
Wutai Village	霧台村	wùtái cūn
Sights		
18 Arhats Mountains	十八羅漢山	shíbāluóhàn shān
Dragon Head Mountain	龍頭山	lóngtóu shān
Duona High Suspension Bridge	多納高吊橋	duōnà gāo diàoqiáo
Duona Hot Springs	多納溫泉	duōnà wēnquán
Laonong River	荖濃溪	lǎonóng xī
Maolin Park	茂林公園	màolín gōngyuán
Purple Butterfly Valley	紫蝶幽谷	zǐdié yōugǔ
Saijia Aviation Park	賽嘉航空運動飛行場	sàijiā hángkōng yùndòng fēixíngchǎng
Snake Head Mountain	蛇頭山	shétóu shān
Accommodation and eating		
Dian Mi Restaurant	甸咪餐廳	diànmī cāntīng
Dreamer Hostel & Restaurant	夢想之家民宿餐廳	mèngxiǎng zhī jiā mínsù cāntīng
Fongshan Agricultural Activity Center	鳳山市農會茂林會員活動中心	fèngshānshì nónghuì màolín huìyuán huódòng zhōngxīn
Fun Chen Resort Hotel	芳晨溫泉渡假村	fāngchén wēnquán dùjiàcūn
Gumula Homestay	咕木啦民宿	gūmùlā mínsù
Salabo Leisure Village	撒拉伯休閒山莊	sālābó xiūxián shānzhuāng
Rafting Outfitters		
Baomei Rafting Company	寶美泛舟有限公司	bǎoměi fànzhōu yǒuxiàn gōngsī
Laonong Whitewater Rafting Company	荖濃泛舟有限公司	lǎonóng fànzhōu yǒuxiàn gōngsī
Pingdong	屏東	píngdōng
Pingdong Bus Station	屏東公車站	píngdōng gōngchē zhàn
Pingdong Train Station	屏東火車站	píngdōng huǒchē zhàn

Maolin Recreation Area

The **MAOLIN RECREATION AREA**, covering the region around County Highway 132, is a quiet haven of butterflies, waterfalls, suspension bridges and natural hot springs that makes a great retreat from the rigours of urban Taiwan. The quickest way to get to here by public transport is via the transport hub of **Pingdong** which is connected to Kaohsiung by frequent trains (20min; NT$31). From Pingdong there are regular **buses** (1hr; NT$102) to Maolin Village (the Pingdong bus station is about 100m to the left of the train station after you exit). All buses first stop at the recreation area's **tollgate** (6am–10pm; NT$70), where you'll need to pay the entrance fee before being driven about 2km further to Maolin Village proper. Just to the right of the tollgate is the **Maolin National Scenic Area visitor center** (9am–5pm; ☎07/6801488, ⓦ www.maulin-nsa.gov.tw), where you can get English **maps** and brochures on the scenic area, but the Chinese-only exhibits here are scant and the staff speak very little English. However, workers at the information desk can arrange accommodation in **homestays** in Maolin Village and Duona, so it's worth a stop here if you haven't already lined something up. Most visitors prefer to stay overnight in **Duona**, which has the allure of its nearby outdoor hot springs. In Maolin Village itself, the only hotel-style accommodation is the *Fongshan Agricultural Activity Center* at no. 16 (☎07/6801115; ❸), across the road from Maolin Park; rooms here are basic but clean. There is no public transport along County Highway 132, so to explore the area you'll need to rent your own vehicle, walk or hitch.

Purple Butterfly Valley

Across the road from Maolin Village is **Maolin Park**, in an area known as the **Purple Butterfly Valley** – so named because it's one of the major winter sanctuaries of four species of butterfly, one of which sports strikingly purple wings. Every winter, from December to February, dense flocks of butterflies converge in these protected valleys from different breeding sites, the surrounding hills sheltering them from the wind. Following closely behind them are thousands of Taiwanese butterfly lovers, meaning that accommodation in Maolin Village can be scarce during this period, especially on weekends. Throughout the winter, Maolin Park is a popular place to witness thousands of butterflies clinging to vegetation, at times carpeting the entire valley. The most arresting time to see them is at daybreak, when the rising sun wakes them and their wings begin to flutter en masse.

County Highway 132: Maolin Village to Duona

Winding **County Highway 132** climbs the 15km from Maolin Village to Duona in grand style, roughly following the contour of the meandering **Jhoukou River** and slicing through soothing mountain scenery. This area gets abundant rainfall for much of the year, especially during summer and the spring "plum rain" season, sparking a proliferation of **waterfalls**, from sleek roadside cascades to multi-tiered torrents spanning entire hillsides. Alongside the road are several stopping points, many with small car parks and short trails to scenic viewpoints and suspension bridges. And, just a few kilometres before the road dead-ends in the mountains is the Rukai village of **Duona**, one of the last bastions of their traditional slate-slab houses.

Alongside the road and in the river valley are several distinctive geographic features, but the most celebrated of these is **Dragon Head Mountain**, actually a rounded hillock situated near a river bend about 9km from Maolin Village.

Though it's visible from the main road, there is a short side road leading to the riverbank, where there is an elevated wooden viewing platform said to be the best vantage point for deciphering the "dragon head" shape. Nearby is the **Duona High Suspension Bridge**, the area's largest, which yields sweeping views of the river valley and is well worth walking across. About 1km further up the main road is the **Snake Head Mountain**, another hillock lodged on a dramatic turn in the river.

Duona and around

About 5km past the viewpoint on to Snake Head Mountain is the rustic village of **Duona**, which is becoming increasingly kitted out for tourism and is an excellent base for excursions to the nearby Duona Hot Springs (see below). A friendly place to stay is the ⚑ *Gumula Homestay* at no. 90 (☎07/6801509; ❷), down a narrow road to the left of the main street in the middle of the village. The Rukai owner speaks some Japanese but little English, yet he has no problems looking after his foreign guests and can lead you to the beginning of the trail to the hot springs. He'll also let you sample some of his home-made **millet wine** (NT$200 per bottle), which is slightly sweet and about five percent alcohol by volume. Duona is a great place to try Rukai cuisine, with outdoor **barbecue stalls** serving up an assortment of meat grilled on smooth, fire-heated slate slabs. For a slightly more formal experience, try the *Dian Mi Restaurant*, on the right-hand side of the main street just after the village entrance – you'll know it by the slate-slab grills out front.

Accessible via a short trail at the village's northern end are the **Duona Hot Springs**, one of the few outdoor springs in Taiwan to have escaped commercial overdevelopment. The springs (free) have been harnessed in pools cut into the rocks alongside the river and make for a relaxing soak, while the adjacent river pool is an ideal place to cool down. If you don't want to walk the trail from the

△ Maolin, Slate-slab barbecue near Duona Hot Springs

village, you can drive the remaining few kilometres until the road dead-ends in a gravel **car park** (cars NT$50, scooters NT$20) just above the springs. Next to the car park are several food stands, most dishing up the Rukai's specialty **grilled sausages**. There are also a couple of dingy guesthouses here, but the ones in Duona are much cleaner.

Saijia Aviation Park

About a thirty-minute drive south of Maolin Village on County Highway 185 is the **Saijia Aviation Park** (℡08/7992221), Taiwan's first paragliding site and one of Asia's most popular launching points. Saijia is widely considered to consistently have the best flying conditions of all the island's major paragliding spots, and with Taiwan's largest landing zone it's ideal for novice pilots. The main flying season here is from September to April, and it gets crowded on weekends during this period. The land here is private property, and the land-owner is amenable to pilots using the site, but its administration has changed a few times in recent years; it has most recently come under the informal control of a local microlight and tandem paraglider who asks all users to make a NT$50 **donation**. Keen to tap in on the site's popularity, Maolin National Scenic Area officials are trying to gain administration rights through legal channels and are planning to open a **second launch site** on a small hilltop just north of the main launching area.

It's possible to **camp** for free on the grounds near the site if you have your own tent, and many domestic pilots do so in order to get an early start. Most foreign pilots, however, opt to stay overnight in Kaohsiung or Pingdong and drive here, often renting **minivans** in Kaohsiung (see p.353).

Highway 24: Sandimen to Wutai

About 5km south of the Saijia Aviation Park on County Highway 135 is **Sandimen**, an aboriginal community nestled where the western plains meet the mountains, and the heartland of the Paiwan tribe. While busloads of Taiwanese tourists come here to visit the slightly commercialized Aboriginal Culture Village nearby, Sandimen is also the gateway to the spectacular nineteen-kilometre stretch of **Highway 24** leading to the remote Rukai village of **Wutai** – one of the national scenic area's highlights. Though a **permit** is required for both foreigners and non-local Taiwanese to gain access to the area, it's free and easy to obtain with a little advance planning. It's well worth the effort – the road winds through some truly amazing scenery, with steep roadside drop-offs framed by **rushing waterfalls** at almost every turn. And Wutai itself is a real treat, with Taiwan's most undiluted Rukai culture and several friendly **homestays** which will arrange permits for foreigners who make overnight reservations.

The homestay with the most experience arranging permits is the *Dreamer Hostel & Restaurant* at 36 Jhongshan Lane (℡08/7902312; ❹). The owner, named Dugu, can speak passable English and can arrange to pick up guests from Sandimen. Another safe bet is the *Salabo Leisure Village* at 14–6 Shenshan Lane (℡08/7902277 or ℡08/7361962; ❹), which is actually located in the tiny Rukai settlement of **Shenshan**, on the left-hand side of the road about 2km before you reach Wutai (just past the 38km marker of Highway 24). In addition to arranging permits and transport, both of these homestays can whip up tradi-tional **Rukai meals** if you reserve them several hours in advance. Wutai and the seven other Rukai villages along this section of Highway 24 are renowned for their stately stone-slab houses, whose walls are made from stacks of thin slate slabs, each pressed tightly against the next. From Sandimen, the first 5km along

Highway 24 are open, but just after the 26.5km marker the road is blocked by a checkpoint, and anyone without a permit will be turned back here.

County Highway 184 to Baolai

In the north of the Maolin National Scenic Area, picturesque **County Highway 184** cuts through some interesting scenery and makes a pleasant access route to the first stops along the Southern Cross-Island Highway: Laonong and Baolai. The best-known geographic features along the road are the **18 Arhats Mountains**, an extremely photogenic series of craggy, round-topped mountains nicknamed "**Little Guilin**" due to their resemblance to the world-famous karst mountains of Guilin and Yangshuo in southern China. While falling short of their mainland Chinese counterparts in size and scale, these hills – on the left several kilometres before the town of **Liouguei** – certainly add considerable atmosphere to the drive. Several kilometres further, the section of the **Laonong River** between the Sinfa Bridge and the hot-springs resort town of Baolai is one of Taiwan's most popular **white-water rafting** routes.

Baolai

The hot-springs town of **BAOLAI**, considered the western gateway to the Southern Cross-Island Highway, is also the **starting point** for all white-water rafting trips along the Laoning River. The eighteen-kilometre non-technical stretch between Baolai and the Sinfa Bridge has an elevation loss of 230m and typically takes about two hours to raft, making for a relatively gentle introduction to Taiwan's white water. Several Baolai-based rafting **operators** can arrange cheap and cheerful excursions for groups of six to eight people, and if you arrive in smaller numbers they can often slot you in with other groups, especially during the summer high season. One of the most reputable is the **Baomei Rafting Company** (℡07/6882580), in the centre of Baolai. Also worth a try, just a few doors down from the *Baomei*, is the **Laonong Whitewater Rafting Company** (℡07/6882996). For groups of six people, both companies offer excursions at a price per head of NT$600 (Mon–Fri), NT$700 on weekends and public holidays. An attractive **place to stay** in Baolai is the *Fun Chen Resort Hotel* (℡07/6881229; ❺) at 132 Jhongjheng Rd, directly across the street from the *Baomei Rafting Company*. The *Fun Chen* has spotless rooms and comfortable hot-springs pools in riverside cabins.

South from Kaohsiung

Along the busy coastal highway heading south from Kaohsiung to Kenting National Park are several worthwhile attractions, suitable as stopovers on an extended excursion to the island's tropical southern tip or as day-trips from Kaohsiung. Much of this area has been placed under the administration of the **Dapeng Bay National Scenic Area**, slated to become one of Taiwan's top tourist destinations, with a golf course, water theme park and an international marina offering ferry services to the Philippines in various stages of development. For the time being, however, the area remains relatively low-key, with the fishing town of **Donggang** featuring some of Taiwan's finest seafood and **Little Liouciou Island** making for a relaxing retreat from city life. As for **Dapeng Bay** itself, work is underway to transform the sheltered lagoon into a watersports paradise, but at the moment boat tours of the surrounding mangroves and oyster farms are the main draw. Just before the highway reaches Kenting

National Park, **Sihjhongsi Hot Springs** and **County Road 199** make a worthy detour, offering characterful spas and beautiful countryside dotted with Paiwan villages.

Donggang

About an hour's bus ride south of Kaohsiung, **DONGGANG** is a frenetic fishing port best known for its formidable annual haul of the highly prized **Pacific bluefin tuna** – whose soft underbelly yields what the Japanese reverently refer to as *toro*, the fatty, lighter-coloured flesh that makes the finest cuts of **sashimi**. While in the past much of the catch was put on ice and immediately flown to Japan, in recent years Taiwanese demand for the fish has risen and the town's Bluefin Tuna Cultural Festival – held every May and June since 2001 – attracts thousands of domestic tourists eager to sample it and other marine specialties. Though its superb **seafood restaurants** are the main attractions, the lively **Donggang Fish Market** is Taiwan's most visited, and its ornate **Donglong Temple** is one of South Taiwan's most venerated.

The Town

Most buses from Kaohsiung conveniently stop at the corner of Jhongshan and Guangfu roads, the latter of which is known as "**seafood street**" and is brimming with excellent restaurants. One of the finest is also the oldest – *Dongsheng Restaurant* at 66 Guangfu Rd Sec 2 (☎08/8323112), with exquisite fare at reasonable prices. The tuna sashimi here is *toro* at its best, while the **Sakura shrimp fried rice** – one of Donggang's signature dishes – is a tasty and filling treat. The tiny Sakura shrimp is one of the town's "three marine treasures", along with bluefin tuna and the **oilfish**, whose roe is baked into delicate cakes that can be dipped in a distinctive garlic and radish sauce. The oilfish itself also makes for a nice sashimi.

To more fully appreciate the scale of the town's fish trade, visit the frenzied **Donggang Fish Market** (9.30am–noon, closed second Mon of each month) along waterfront Fongyu Street. Here you'll find weathered old women hurling all manner of marine life into giant heaps ahead of the animated wholesale auctions conducted in thick Taiwanese dialect. To get there by foot, head northwest along Jhongshan Road until you reach Yanping Road; turn left here, cross the Fongyu Bridge and keep straight for a few hundred metres until the road dead-ends in front of the market.

Donglong Temple

About midway between the main bus stations and the fish market, and framed with a majestic gold-plated archway, the **Donglong Temple** at 21-1 Donglong St is the centre of Donggang religious life and attracts a continuous procession of worshippers – particularly fishermen – who pray for safety from the storms that frequently ravage the Taiwan Strait. The temple's most exalted deity, and

Donggang		
Donggang	東港	*dōnggǎng*
Donggang Fish Market	東港魚市場	*dōnggǎng yú shìcháng*
Donggang King Boat Festival	東港王船節	*dōnggǎng wángchúanjié*
Donglong Temple	東隆宮	*dōnglóng gōng*
Dongsheng Restaurant	東升餐廳	*dōngshēng cāntīng*

the one to which such prayers are considered requisite, is **Wen Hong**, a folk god who is generally perceived as part of Taiwan's vast pantheon of **protection deities** (See Contexts p.525).

Originally from northeast China's Shandong Province, noted scholar Wen Hong rose to prominence after he and 35 fellow academics rescued a Tang dynasty emperor during an attack on an imperial tour. He was later assigned as governor of Shanxi Province, and during his tenure he consolidated his reputation as a protector by breaking up a ring of bandits. In recognition of this feat, the emperor awarded Wen Hong the highest official rank and sent him and his 35 scholarly comrades on a **maritime tour** to extol the virtues of Tang culture. However, all of them perished in a shipwreck in the Taiwan Strait and the aggrieved emperor ordered the entire country to build temples in their honour and commissioned the construction of an enormous ship named "Lord Wen", which was set afloat with 36 tablets commemorating the victims. According to legend, this vessel often mysteriously appeared along the coast of Fujian and Zhejiang provinces during storms to help guide fishing boats in distress. Over the centuries, Wen Hong gained a loyal following among Fujianese fishermen, and during their mass migrations to Taiwan in the seventeenth century he was regarded as their principal guardian.

To give thanks for the safe passage of their ancestors, local devotees stage the dramatic **Donggang King Boat Festival** outside the Donglong Temple once every three years. In the year preceding the festival, local craftsmen build a large wooden vessel and fill it with replicas of everyday items such as cars, clothing, houses and offerings of meat. During the course of the seven-day festival, the Wen Hong deity is taken on an extended "**inspection patrol**" – when it is finally returned to the temple the model craft is set ablaze along with all its contents in honour of Wen Hong's return to heaven. The next **boat-burning ceremony** will take place in October 2009.

To get here from the main bus stations, walk northwest along Jhongshan Road a couple of hundred metres until you reach Donglong Street; turn left here and you'll soon see the gilded archway in front of the temple.

Practicalities

Donggang's centre is fairly compact, with its restaurants, fish market and Donglong Temple all within walking distance of the two main **bus stations** on busy Jhongshan Road, the town's primary thoroughfare. The frequent **buses** (1hr) from Kaohsiung will let you off anywhere on Jhongshan Road, or you can get out at one of the stations, each a short walk from the **Donggang Port** – from where there are regular **ferries** to nearby Little Liouciou Island. To get to the port, walk northwest along Jhongshan Road for about 1km until you reach Chaolong Road; turn left here and walk another few hundred metres until you see the two ferry terminals on your right.

Little Liouciou Island

The gem of the Dapeng Bay National Scenic Area, delightful **Little Liouciou Island** makes for a convenient, relaxing retreat from the din of the west-coast cities. The only one of Taiwan's offshore islands whose surface is completely composed of **coral**, it's covered with curious rock formations and caves and offers seemingly endless sea views. Some people make it a long day-trip from Kaohsiung, but it's better to stay overnight and explore at your leisure. There is abundant tourist infrastructure, including hotels, restaurants and a seaside **camping area** that could easily take honours as Taiwan's finest.

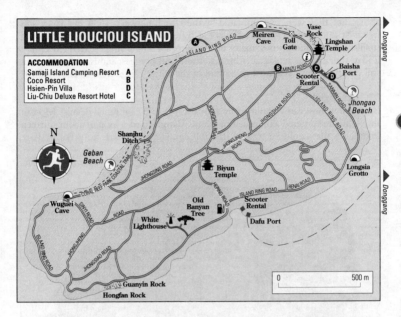

Liouciou literally means "drifting ball", as early settlers from mainland China likened the island to a ball awash in the sea. Though it was originally settled by

Little Liouciou Island

Little Liouciou Island	小琉球	*xiǎo liúqiú*
Baisha Port	白沙碼頭	*báishā mǎtóu*
Dafu Port	大福漁港	*dàfú yúgǎng*
Accommodation		
Samaji Island Camping Resort	沙馬基島露營渡假區	*shāmǎjīdǎo lùyíng dùjiàqū*
Coco Resort	椰林渡假村	*yēlín dùjiàcūn*
Hsien-Pin Villa	賢濱山莊	*xiánbīn shānzhuāng*
Liu-chiu Deluxe Resort Hotel	白龍宮休閒渡假旅館	*báilóng gōng xiūxián dùjià lǚguǎn*
Sights		
Biyun Temple	碧雲寺	*bìyún sì*
Geban Beach	蛤板灣	*gébǎn wān*
Guanyin Rock	觀音石	*guānyīn shí*
Hongfan Rock	紅番石頭	*hóngfānshítóu*
Jhongao Beach	中澳海灘	*zhōngào hǎitān*
Lingshan Temple	靈山寺	*língshān sì*
Longsia Grotto	龍蝦洞	*lóngxiā dòng*
Meiren Cave	美人洞	*měirén dòng*
Old Banyan Tree	老榕樹	*laoróng shù*
Shanjhu Ditch	珊瑚群礁	*shānhú qúnjiāo*
Vase Rock	花瓶石	*huāpíng shí*
White Lighthouse	白燈塔	*bái dēngtǎ*
Wuguei Cave	烏鬼洞	*wūguǐ dòng*

aborigines, they were exterminated by the Dutch between 1636 and 1645, and it wasn't until the 1770s that Fujianese fishermen began arriving, establishing small fishing communities, many of them comprising a single extended family. Today, tourism has replaced fishing as the island's biggest industry, but there is still plenty of fresh **seafood** to be had in the main village next to Baisha Port.

The island

Liouciou is most easily explored by **scooter** (see p.367 for rental details). Most of the sights are scattered alongside the **Island Ring Road**, a loop of about thirteen kilometres that could be walked in a full day. Heading north from Baisha Port,

△ Little Liouciou, Vase Rock

the first feature you'll encounter is **Vase Rock**, a mushroom-shaped mound of eroded coral that has become the symbol of the island – an obligatory stop for Taiwanese tourists in search of the definitive Liouciou photo. Just inland behind Vase Rock is the **Lingshan Temple**, dedicated to a collection of Wang Ye gods. From the temple steps there are outstanding views of the Taiwan Strait. Further along the ring road, **Meiren (Beauty) Cave** is actually a series of coral grottoes eroded by the sea – a paved shoreline pathway cuts through them. The next notable attraction along the road is one of the island's best, **Shanjhu (Mountain Pig) Ditch**, a narrow labyrinth of coral cliffs choked by overhanging tree roots so named because mountain pigs are said to have once roamed here. For a closer look at the cliffs, stroll along the raised wooden walkway that loops inland from the ring road. Well into the "ditch" are some small rock houses where locals sought shelter during a US bombing raid towards the end of World War II.

Some of Liouciou's best views can be had further down the coast, at the **Wuguei (Black Ghost) Caves**, a spectacular string of eroded seaside grottoes connected by a well-built pathway that offers sublime sea views. The caves' macabre name stems from a massacre the Dutch committed against a group of local cave-dwelling aborigines (at times referred to simply as "dark people") in retaliation for the slaying of a few Dutch sailors (though the sign at the entrance incorrectly attributes the massacre to the English). Further around the ring road, on the island's southwest coast, is a stretch of coral formations that imaginative islanders liken to people and deities. Chief among these are **Hongfan (Indian) Rock** and **Guanyin (Goddess of Mercy) Rock**. About 2km further east, up a hilly road to the left, is Liouciou's **White Lighthouse**, built by the Japanese during the occupation period. On the way to the lighthouse is a short side road that leads to the impressive **Old Banyan Tree**, which seems to strangle the diminutive shrine upon which it dwells.

If you're dying for a dip in the sea, about the only stretch of sand that isn't fringed with razor-sharp coral is **Jhongao Beach**, a few minutes' walk south of Baisha Port. From here there are fine night-time views of the lights of Kaohsiung.

Practicalities

From Donggang Port, two **ferry operators** run daily services to the island from 7am to early evening, although their ferries call at different places on Liouciou. The private United Ferry Service (☎08/8325806) – the first one you'll encounter as you head down Chaolong Road from Jhongshan Road – has nine daily departures (40min; NT$210 one-way, NT$410 return) to Liouciou's main **Baisha Port**, near most of the tourist facilities. However, its last ferry is at 5.30pm, so if you miss it you'll need to catch the slightly slower 6.45pm Liouciou Township Ferry (☎08/8613048; 50min; NT$180 one-way, NT$350 return), which has five daily departures to the secondary **Dafu Port**, just over 3km from the main village at Baisha. On the ferry, you're likely to be approached by affable local touts renting **scooters** (NT$300 per day), which are vastly preferable to walking around the island in the summer heat. Although you also can rent scooters from vendors at both ports, you probably won't be able to wrangle much of a discount from them, and on weekends and during the summer you'd be wise to strike a deal with one of the ferry touts to ensure that you get a scooter. No licences are required.

Accommodation

There are several **hotels** near Baisha Port, but many of them are faceless, white-tiled monstrosities catering to Taiwanese tour groups. One of the exceptions is the homey *Hsien-Pin Villa* at 206-1 Sanmin Rd (℡08/8611230; ❸), just up the flight of steps to the left as you exit the ferry pier. A short walk from Jhongao Beach, this tiny hotel has clean doubles and a very friendly owner, though no English is spoken. To the right as you leave the ferry pier is the *Liu-chiu Deluxe Resort Hotel* at 272 Sanmin Rd (℡08/8612536; ❹), which has several rooms with nice hardwood floors. Considerably further afield is Liouciou's finest indoor accommodation, the cosy *Coco Resort* at 20-38 Minzu Rd (℡08/8614368; ❺). A twenty-minute walk up the main road from Baisha Port, the *Coco* has several whitewashed bungalows shaded by palm trees. But by far the most atmospheric option is the *Samaji Island Camping Resort* 🏕 (℡08/8614880; ❸ including breakfast), on a breezy oceanside knoll along the Island Ring Road about 3km from Baisha Port. Here there are several fashionable **bungalows** that sleep two, as well as numerous elevated wooden platforms for pitching tents (some with wooden rain shelters). **Camping** costs NT$200 per person if you have your own tent or NT$350 a head for tent/sleeping pad/bag rentals. With breakfast and a toiletry kit included in the price, it's a great deal.

Dapeng Bay

A few kilometres south of Donggang lies **DAPENG BAY**, actually a shallow lagoon sheltered from the sea by a two-kilometre sand bar. Linked to the ocean only by a narrow channel, the lagoon's waters are consistently calm, and it's unusually well protected from the northeast winter monsoon. With placid waters and reliably sunny weather, tourism officials are touting this former oyster farm area as a potential water-sports haven and have launched a massive dredging and clean-up project to make it suitable for activities such as water-skiing, kite-surfing and windsurfing. In the meantime, a section of the lagoon is open for canoeing and sailing, and there are daily passenger boat excursions as well as tours of historic sites around the lagoon.

Practicalities

From Kaohsiung, the easiest way to get to Dapeng Bay is to take a Kaohsiung to Kenting **bus** and alight at the national scenic area entrance along Highway 17, a few kilometres south of Donggang. Coming from Donggang, it's best to take a **taxi** (NT$100) to the entrance, where admission tickets (NT$100) are sold. Beyond the entrance to the right is the **Dapeng Bay National Scenic Area Visitor Center** at 169 Datan Rd (9am–5pm ℡08/8338100, ⓦwww.tbnsa.gov .tw), which has English **maps** and brochures and an English film on the scenic area's highlights. Though a hotel complex is being planned, for the time being the only accommodation option near the lagoon is a small **campsite**, but you'll need to have your own tent to stay here. An international marina is being built, and by 2010 officials plan to have regular **ferry services** to Little Liouciou Island and Kenting National Park, as well as to locations in the Philippines.

Boat tours (1hr; NT$150) of the lagoon, including a short side-trip into some adjoining mangroves and a stop at the last remaining oyster farm, start

Dapeng Bay		
Dapeng Bay	大鵬灣	*dàpéngwān*
Dapeng Bay National Scenic Area Visitor Center	大鵬灣國家風景區遊客中心	*dàpéngwān guójiā fēngjdng qū yóukè zhōngxīn*

from the pier, about 500m straight past the visitor centre; there is no fixed schedule, with boats waiting until they are full before leaving. In the middle of the oyster farm is an islet formed by discarded oyster shells, on top of which is a stilt-house **restaurant** where you can sample a variety of home-grown oyster delicacies. It's also possible to join tours of the many decommissioned **military sites** surrounding the lagoon, including several heavily fortified structures built by the Japanese; ask inside the visitor centre for these.

Sihjhongsi Hot Springs

Just north of Kenting National Park, the hilly **SIHJHONGSI HOT SPRINGS** area offers a cool respite from the scorching heat of Taiwan's deep south and is drenched in divine scenery and off-the-beaten-path attractions. Though there is a profound lack of public transport here, most visitors tack this area onto their Kenting itineraries, taking advantage of the ease of renting **scooters** in Kenting town (see p.372) and making it part of a mammoth two-wheeled circuit. The area's elevation and abundant vegetation mean it's usually several degrees cooler here than in the simmering coastal lowlands, and on winter nights it can get downright chilly – making it a perfect time to "*pao wenquan*" (soak in hot springs).

During the Japanese occupation, Sihjhongsi was one of the colonists' most prized hot-spring areas, renowned for the therapeutic effects of its clear **sodium carbonate waters**. Today, the hill resort is restful, with much less development than most of the island's better-known hot-springs areas. The emphasis here has remained on the springs themselves, which are believed to help relieve the symptoms of arthritis, athlete's foot and even gastrointestinal disorders. Indeed, the spring water here is safe to drink, and the sodium carbonate bubbles lend themselves to a litany of **refreshing beverages** – which explains the fizzy nature of the special coffee and tea served up at some local resorts.

Sihjhongsi's location in the foothills along the national park's northern fringe – the heartland of the **Paiwan aboriginal tribe** – also makes it an ideal base for exploring the many tribal villages along narrow **County Road 199**. With no public transport traversing this road, it remains delightfully underused and makes for a most pleasant scooter ride.

Practicalities

To get to Sihjhongsi from Kenting town or **Hengchun** – where it's also easy to rent scooters – drive north along **Highway 26 West** to just before Checheng

Sihjhongsi Hot Springs		
Sihjhongsi Hot Springs	四重溪溫泉	sìchóngqī wēnquán
County Road 199	199 縣道	yījiǔjiǔ xiàn dào
Damei Village	大梅村	dàméi cūn
Dashan Hot Spring Spa & Farm	大山溫泉農場	dàshān wēnquán nóngchǎng
Hueisiang Lianlian Hot Spring Hotel	茴茴戀戀溫泉會館	huíhuí liànliàn wēnquán huiguǎn
Mudan Village	牡丹村	mǔdān cūn
Shihmen Historic Battlefield	石門古戰場	shímén gǔzhànchǎng
Shihmen Reservoir	石門水庫	shímén shuǐkù
Yuansiang Hot Spring Restaurant	緣鄉溫泉餐廳	yuánxiāng wēnquán cāntīng

and then head east along County Road 199 for several kilometres until you reach the springs. There are several **hot-spring hotels** along the main road, but most of these are of the concrete-box variety, with spring water piped into large bathtubs in the rooms. More attractive options can be found near **Damei Village**, the left-hand turnoff for which is marked by a small sign at the far end of town. About 1km down this road on the left is the gleaming new *Hueisiang Lianlian Hot Spring Hotel* at 1-16 Damei Rd (℡08/8824900; ❾), with spotless doubles and outdoor **public bathing pools** (NT$200 per person). An offbeat alternative is the *Dashan Hot Spring Spa & Farm* at 60-1 Damei Rd (℡08/8825725; ❹), with a modest **bird farm** of chickens, ducks and ostriches to complement its hot-springs pools. Its well-appointed doubles are clean and comfortable, and its public outdoor bathing pools (NT$150 per person) are in a relaxed setting. To get here, drive to the far side of Damei Village and turn left on the dirt road leading up the hillside (marked with a sign in Chinese). After about 100m, the road forks – take the path to the left and you'll quickly be in the hotel car park.

If you don't plan to stay overnight, a good option for a soak and a meal is the *Yuansiang Hot Spring Restaurant* at 85 Wuncyuan Rd (℡08/8824071), the public complex on the left as you enter Sihjhongsi town. Here there are public pools (NT$200 per person) and private two-person rooms (NT$600 for 1hr 30min).

County Road 199

Winding northeast through the mountains beyond Sihjhongsi, **County Road 199** is a fascinating attraction in its own right, a narrow sealed track that crosses pristine **highland scenery** before sweeping down to the island's splendid southeastern seaboard. Along the way, it passes by Paiwan tribal villages that remain largely untouched by Taiwanese tourism, and it's possible to cross over to the east coast by scooter from Sihjhongsi in about an hour and a half.

Heading east from Sihjhongsi, as you begin to climb, is the **Shihmen Historic Battlefield**, where, in 1874, a defiant group of Paiwan tribesmen defended themselves against a 3600-strong, Samurai-led expeditionary force of Japanese seeking reprisal for the 1871 killing of 54 shipwrecked Japanese sailors. There is a stele here with an inscription commemorating what has come to be known as the **Mudan Incident** (see Contexts, p.508). Just to the east is **Mudan Village** itself, an excellent place to try authentic Paiwan fare, characterized by an astounding array of mountain vegetables. Even though Mudan – called "*Shihmen*" in Mandarin – has not been spoiled by tourism, there are a few shops where you can buy **handmade Paiwan crafts** for bargain prices.

Past the enormous **Shihmen Reservoir**, the road climbs sharply into the mountains, offering fantastic views down to the plains below. Here the road narrows to single-track, so if you want to cross over to the east be sure to allow yourself plenty of daylight. Along this stretch are some of Taiwan's most untarnished **aboriginal villages**, where the Paiwan language and traditions still thrive for their own sake, rather than the consumption of Taiwanese tourists. If you stop in one of these villages, listen out for the local language, its monotonal rhythms bearing no resemblance to any Chinese dialect – a taste of what island life was like before centuries of Chinese migration. Gradually the road starts to descend to the east coast, where you can take the east-bound branch of County Road 199 through the **Syuhai grasslands** to Highway 26 East. From here you can travel south into Kenting National Park or north to Highway 9, which leads to the eastern city of Taitung.

Kenting National Park

Straddling Taiwan's southern tip and bounded by sea on three sides, **KENTING NATIONAL PARK** attracts several million visitors each year, most of them lured by its warm tropical climate and magnificent white-sand beaches. Taiwan's first national park, Kenting covers most of the **Hengchun Peninsula**, which sits at the confluence of fault lines and tectonic plates. As a result, the peninsula has been pushed, pulled and twisted into a complex network of low-lying mountains, grassy meadows, steep cliffs, sand dunes and elaborate coral formations. Despite its remarkably varied natural scenery, much of it is overlooked by visitors, the majority of whom relish the amusement-park atmosphere of the main tourist area around **Kenting town** and nearby **Nanwan** (South Bay). With so many tourists clinging to these more developed spots, much of the park remains relatively quiet – even during peak periods such as summer and Chinese New Year – making it simple to escape the crowds with the help of a **scooter**, easily rented in Kenting town.

The park's beautiful beaches are definitely its biggest drawcard, and though the ones closest to Kenting town and Nanwan are often coated with sunbathers, it's not hard to find your own stretch of fine white sand in a more secluded setting. Kenting is known as Taiwan's premier **surfing** destination (see box p.376).

Kenting differs from Taiwan's other national parks, being considerably more developed, with a population of over 20,000 and much of the land remaining

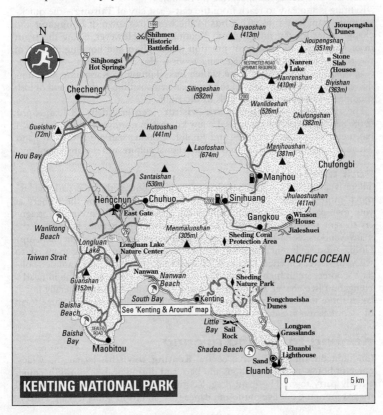

KENTING NATIONAL PARK

0   5 km

in private hands. But while a stretch of its splendid southern coastline has been inundated with white-tiled hotels and go-kart tracks, some other coastal spots and inland areas are heavily protected and remain off-limits to tourists who haven't obtained permits from park officials. These ecological and landscape **protection areas** harbour features such as inland coral reef, seashell-sand beaches and even a seven-hundred-year-old aboriginal village. The park is also a **bird-watching** paradise – more than 26 species of predatory birds have been recorded here and it's recognized as one of Asia's most active sites for raptor migration. September and October is the time to see hawks and egrets, while the waterfowl-viewing season lasts from November to March.

Arrival and information

The nearest **airport** to the park is at **Hengchun**, just north of Kenting town, to which it is connected by regular shuttle buses. TransAsia Airways (☏02/29724599) flies from Taipei's Songshan Airport to Hengchun every Tuesday and Saturday (1hr 10min; NT$2203). Many visitors also arrive via **Kaohsiung Airport**, from where **buses** to Kenting town (2hr 30min; NT$250) leave every twenty minutes. If you arrive in Kaohsiung by train, a handful of bus companies near the train station offer regular direct services to Kenting town. Kaohsiung Bus Station has frequent buses (daily 5.35am–10.40pm; NT$275), while CN Bus has 24-hour service (NT$300).

Kenting is also easy to reach from the east-coast city of **Taitung** – the quickest route from here is to take a **bus** to the west-coast town of **Fonggang** and change buses for the final leg into Kenting town. However, taking the **train** from Taitung to the west-coast junction of **Fangliao** and hopping on one of the regular onward buses to Kenting town is also a convenient – and scenic – option. The **South-link Line**, which links Taitung to Kaohsiung via Pingdong, affords sweeping views of the southeastern coastline to the left and of lush mountains and plunging waterfalls to the right.

The **Kenting National Park visitor center** (daily 8.30am–5pm; ☏08/8861321) at 596 Kenting Rd, a few kilometres northwest of Kenting town, has useful maps and brochures, and English-speaking staff are always on hand. There also are interesting exhibits on aboriginal culture and the area's geology.

Park transport

There is an infrequent **bus service** to various spots within the park, but it's much more convenient to hire your own transport and enjoy the scenery at your own pace. Kenting town is one of the easiest places in Taiwan for foreigners to rent **scooters** (NT$500 per day, not including petrol), both from the many vendors along the main drag or from your hotel (at a slight mark-up). Unlike most such rental shops in Taiwan, few of those in Kenting town ask to see your driver's licence. However, at weekends and during the summer holidays scooters are in high demand, so you might consider renting one in nearby Hengchun (see above). Although the rental companies here are generally not as lax as those in Kenting town, it's usually possible if you leave them some form of identification as a deposit.

Kenting town and around

Undoubtedly the park's nerve centre, **Kenting town** has by far the widest range of hotels, restaurants, shops and bars, and during peak seasons it becomes a lively party town. The main drag, Kenting Road, is packed with **clubs** and **discos** pumping out live music and dance mix, and **food stalls** serving a dizzy-

Kenting town and around

Kenting

Kenting town and around	墾丁	*kěndīng*
Kenting National Park Headquarters	墾丁國家公園管埋處	*kěndīng guójiā gōngyuán guánlǐchù*
National Park Police	國家公園警察	*guójiā gōngyuán jǐngchá*
Dawan Beach	大灣	*dàwān*
Siaowan Beach	小灣	*xiǎowān*
Frog Rock Marine Park	青蛙石海洋公園	*qīngwāshí hǎiyáng gōngyuán*

Accommodation

Caesar Park Hotel	墾丁凱撒大飯店	*kěndīng kǎisā dàfàndiàn*
Catholic Kenting Student Activity Center	天主教墾丁學生活動中心	*tiānzhǔjiào kěndīng xúeshēng húodòng zhōngxīn*
Chateau Beach Resort	夏都沙灘酒店	*xiàdū shātān jiǔdiàn*
Kenting Youth Activity Center	救國團墾丁青年活動中心	*jiùguótuán kěndīng qīngnián húodòng zhōngxīn*

Eating and drinking

Amy's Cucina Inn	Amy's 住宿酒吧餐廳	*Amy's zhùsù jiǔbācāntīng*
Amy's Pasta House	Amy's 意大利麵館	*Amy's yìdàlìmiàn guǎn*
Ocean Blue	海餐廳	*hǎi cāntīng*
Warung Didi	迪迪小吃	*dídí xiǎochī*
Eluanbi	鵝鑾鼻	*éluánbí*
Eluanbi Lighthouse	鵝鑾鼻燈塔	*éluánbí dēngtǎ*
Sand	沙點民宿	*shādiàn mínsù*
Nanwan	南灣	*nánwān*
Beach House	南灣海館	*nánwān hǎiguǎn*
Bossa Nova Café	巴沙諾瓦餐廳	*bā shā nuò wà cāntīng*
Fu Dog Surf & Dive	"Fu Dog" 潛水衝浪	*"Fu Dog" qiánshuǐ chōnglàng*
Sail Rock	船帆石	*chuánfān shí*
Mingjun Holiday Centre	明君渡假中心	*míngjūn dùjiā zhōngxīn*
Whale Coast Hotel	鯨鯊海岸高級民宿	*jīngshā hǎi'àn gāojí mínsù*
Ya Ge Tourist Home	亞哥旅遊之家	*yàgē lǚyóuzhījiā*

ing array of "little eats" line the road in the evenings. There are also myriad **souvenir stands** and shops, selling everything from earthy bead necklaces to Kenting T-shirts and trendy swimwear. Unfortunately, the beach scene lags behind all this: the longest stretch of sand, **Dawan (Big Bay) Beach**, has been leased by the national park to the luxury *Chateau Beach Resort* and is firmly off-limits to all but its overnight guests. Access to this beach is blocked by the sprawling hotel complex's walls, and surfing and other water sports are strictly prohibited. For the time being, the only beach in Kenting town that is open to the public is the much smaller **Siaowan (Little Bay) Beach**, directly across Kenting Road from the *Caesar Park Hotel*. Given Kenting town's extraordinary tourist numbers, this beach suffers from chronic overcrowding and the shallow part of the bay is a complete free-for-all of swimmers, surfers and snorkellers. The biggest danger here is the **jet-skis** that rip through the water, often coming

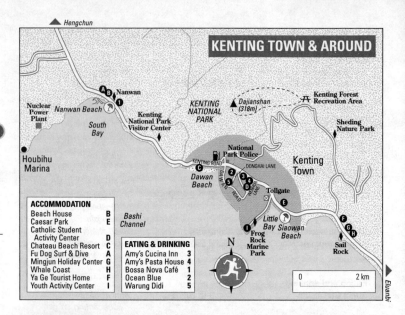

Kenting Town & Around map

ACCOMMODATION

Beach House	B
Caesar Park	E
Catholic Student Activity Center	D
Chateau Beach Resort	C
Fu Dog Surf & Dive	A
Mingjun Holiday Center	G
Whale Coast	H
Ya Ge Tourist Home	F
Youth Activity Center	I

EATING & DRINKING

Amy's Cucina Inn	3
Amy's Pasta House	4
Bossa Nova Café	1
Ocean Blue	2
Warung Didi	5

end map labels: Hengchun, Nanwan, Nuclear Power Plant, Nanwan Beach, South Bay, Houbihu Marina, Kenting National Park Visitor Center, Kenting National Park, Dajianshan (318m), Kenting Forest Recreation Area, Sheding Nature Park, National Park Police, Kenting Road, Dawan Beach, Donghai Lane, Dawa Road, Wenhua Lane, Kenting Town, Tollgate, Little Bay, Siaowan Beach, Frog Rock Marine Park, Sail Rock, Bashi Channel, Eluanbi, 0 2 km

dangerously close to bathers. Though their use is technically illegal within park boundaries, insufficient penalties mean their operators can pay the fines and still make a profit, so these disruptive craft continue to be a menace.

For the country's growing legions of rock music fans, Kenting town has become the site of one of Taiwan's biggest annual rock festivals – **Spring Scream** (Ⓦwww.springscream.com) – held every April for more than a decade. Popular with Taiwanese and expatriates alike, this five-day event showcases both international and home-grown talent and is consistently the country's biggest gathering of foreigners, with English teachers from all corners of the island converging on Kenting town for days of unbridled indulgence.

Practicalities

Most **public buses** terminate at the southeast end of town before turning around for their return journeys to major cities. Most of them let passengers alight wherever they request; to catch one, simply stand alongside Kenting Road and flag it down. For money, all of the 7-Elevens in Kenting town have Chinatrust Commercial Bank **ATMs**.

Accommodation

Even on the busiest days it's possible to find **accommodation** in Kenting town, although prices can almost double on weekends and holidays. At these times, the human and vehicular traffic can be almost unbearable, so if you're looking for a quieter getaway you'll be much better off heading a bit further southeast to nearby Sail Rock or Eluanbi (see p.377).

Caesar Park Hotel 6 Kenting Rd ☎08/8861888, Ⓦwww.caesarpark.com.tw. One of Kenting town's top hotels, the *Caesar* is popular with families because of its child-orientated amenities, including free baby cribs and a kids' play area. Its restaurants are popular with non-guests. ❻

Catholic Kenting Student Activity Center 2 Wenhua Lane ☎08/8861540. Clean, well-run hostel offering good value, with dorm beds (NT$350) and affordable doubles. Given that it's located in the middle of Kenting town, it's more relaxed than most of Taiwan's Catholic-run hostels

– the gate remains open all night and drinking is allowed, provided that guests behave respectfully. ❸

Chateau Beach Resort 451 Kenting Rd ☎08/8862345, ⓦwww.ktchateau.com.tw. On the northwestern edge of Kenting town, this five-star luxury resort is the area's most exclusive hotel, controlling all of beautiful Dawan (Big Bay) Beach and restricting access to all but its overnight guests (see p.373). Rooms are spacious and plush, many with fantastic views of Big Bay. The giant beach-side pool has an attached bar. ❾

Kenting Youth Activity Center 17 Kenting Rd ☎08/8861221, ⓦwww.cyh.org.tw. Although this China Youth Corps-run hotel caters mostly to student groups and Taiwanese families, its unique design and location make it an interesting option. Built in the layout of a traditional Fujian village, it features elaborate building facades and ornate roofs as well as clean, modern rooms. Tucked down a lane off Kenting town's main strip, the complex is fairly quiet. Non-guests can gain access to the adjacent Frog Rock Marine Park (NT$30 per vehicle) via the tollgate at the lane's entrance. ❺

Eating and drinking

In addition to the many food stalls along Kenting Road, there are numerous **restaurants** specializing in a broad range of cuisine, but for many foreigners the highlight is the Western-style establishments serving favourites such as **pizza** and **pasta**.

Amy's Cucina Inn 131-1 Kenting Rd ☎08/8861977. This quaint, red-brick, Italian-style eatery serves up some of Kenting town's tastiest pizza and pasta.

Amy's Pasta House 21-3 Kenting Rd ☎08/8861679. Cosy restaurant on the southeast end of town, close to Siaowan (Little Bay) Beach. Offers an extensive English menu of Western-style dishes (different ownership from *Amy's Cucina Inn*).

Ocean Blue 111 Kenting Rd ☎08/8862600. In the heart of Kenting Road's dancing district,

this restaurant-cum-bar starts late and stays open until the wee hours on weekends and most summer nights.

Warung Didi 176 Dawan Rd ☎08/8861835. This Southeast Asian restaurant is one of Kenting town's best, both for food and atmosphere. Owned by a Malaysian Chinese, the house specialties are authentic Malay and Thai curries, and there is a respectable wine selection. 5.30pm–1am, closed Tues.

Nanwan (South Bay)

About 6km northwest of Kenting town, **Nanwan (South Bay)** is a busy strip of small hotels and surf shops just across the road from the bay and its famous Nanwan Beach. The place is slightly less frantic than Kenting town itself, with similarly priced small hotels, and the **surf shops** have cheap **dorm bunks** that are available to all tourists, regardless of whether they're taking surf lessons or renting boards. The welcoming *Beach House* at 230 Nanwan Rd (☎08/8880440; ❶) is a small surf shop with a **café** and eleven dorm beds available on a first-come, first-served basis. Longboards (NT$500 per day) can be rented here, and **Internet** usage is free for guests. The help-ful owner can also arrange more upscale accommodation in Eluanbi, near Taiwan's southern tip. Just next door, *Fu Dog Surf & Dive* at 232 Nanwan Rd (☎08/8897141; ❶) is the area's longest-running surf shop, owned by an American expat. Cheap dorm beds (NT$350) are available here, as are longboard (NT$500 per day) and shortboard (NT$400 per day) rentals. **Surf lessons**, including board rental, cost NT$1000. The shop also offers **scuba-diving lessons** (NT$1500) and PADI/NAUI certification (NT$10,000). An atmospheric place to eat or drink is the *Bossa Nova Café* at 100 Nanwan Rd (☎08/8897137), with a range of coffees, juice drinks, bottled beers and cocktails, not to mention the standout views of South Bay. The house specialty – hot and spicy chicken with Thai sauce (NT$220) – is delicious, as is the spicy shrimp coconut curry (NT$300).

In search of southern surf

Kenting has become synonymous with **surfing** in the Taiwanese psyche, as the typically gentle beach breaks along the southern coast are ideal for beginners. Though experienced riders might find the average conditions in the park's crowded southern fringe to be lacking in challenge, there are enough lesser-known beach, reef and river-mouth breaks elsewhere in the park to keep a surf trip here interesting – especially a few days before a summer typhoon makes landfall. And if Kenting doesn't deliver the swell you desire, you can always head a bit further north to the seldom-surfed breaks in the **Taitung/Chenggong** area (see p.412) or even to the northeast coast hotspots around **Dasi** (see p.185) and **Fulong** (see p.375).

Kenting's most popular surfing spot is **Nanwan (South Bay) Beach** (see p.375). The waves here are chronically soft and subject to close-outs, but they are good for beginners to practise their paddling and take-offs – and the handful of surf shops have no shortage of **longboards** for rent and also offer lessons and accommodation (see p.375). But while Nanwan can make for a good base, seasoned surfers might find the scene a bit posey. For slightly more consistent surf, drive around the coast road to the park's Pacific side, where the shallow bay and river mouth near **Jialeshuei** can dish up some sweet barrels. The black-sand beach here is a nice place to camp, but if you're tentless there's a friendly surfer's hostel about 200m up the road. The homey *Winson House* at 244 Chashan Rd (℡08/8801053; ⓪), run by one of Taiwan's best-known surfers, has communal **dorm beds** (NT$300 per person) and eleven expensive rooms that sleep four to six people. The hostel also rents **surfboards** (NT$800 full day/NT$500 half day) and **bodyboards** (NT$500 full day/NT$300 half day). Basic **meals** are available if you order ahead.

For more advanced surfers, it often pays to head just northeast of the park on County Road 200, where the beaches around **Gangzih** can yield some exciting swell – often with scarcely any other surfers in sight. All of the beaches here are well suited for **camping** but there is no private accommodation. To the north, coastal **Highway 26 East** cuts through some stunning seaside scenery, passing several surfable beaches along the way. If you find waves here, you're guaranteed to have them all to yourself.

Sail Rock

A few kilometres south of Kenting town, **Sail Rock** is a comparatively laid-back cluster of hotels and Chinese restaurants looking out over an arresting stretch of coral-lined coast. A few hundred metres west of the hotel strip is a beach, while directly across from the main hotels is the village's namesake, a massive slab of eroded coral jutting from the water in a formation said to resemble a **Chinese junk sail**. Locals have also likened the rock's side-view to the profile of late US President Richard Nixon, so it's alternatively known as "Nixon's Head". The reef that encircles this towering chunk of coral is home to an astonishing array of **tropical fish** and has become a popular **snorkelling** spot, although the jet-skis that encroach on this area from their base at the nearby beach can make it a slightly unnerving pastime. The ledges at Sail Rock's lower reaches are favoured launch pads for jumping into the teal-green waters below during high tide.

Practicalities

The row of **hotels** across from Sail Rock represents an attractive – and cheaper – alternative to those in Kenting town, and the atmosphere is much more relaxed. Many hotel rooms here have **seaview balconies** that offer great views of southern Taiwan's sublime sunsets. In addition, several of the hotels rent **snorkelling equipment**. You may be asked to hire a wet suit and life jacket, even in the heat of summer, but the water is invariably warm and there are rarely any jellyfish; however, it's worth renting neoprene booties to protect your feet when walking out onto the coral. The *Mingjun Holiday Centre* at 678 Chuanfan Rd (℡08/8851301; ⑤) has ten immaculate rooms, half of them with seaside balconies; its first-floor **seafood restaurant** is reasonably priced and serves basic dishes such as fried rice. The *Whale Coast Hotel* at 606 Chuanfan Rd (℡08/8851606; ⑥) has three expensive seaview rooms and several more reasonably priced non-seaview doubles. The village's best deal is the unassuming *Ya Ge Tourist Home* at 686 Chuanfan Rd (℡08/8851241; ❸). The basic-but-clean doubles with seaview balconies are a bargain and include **breakfast**. There is no English sign for the hotel and the owners speak little English, but they're friendly and are happy to rent basic snorkelling equipment at a discount.

Eluanbi

Several kilometres southeast of Sail Rock, past a procession of go-kart tracks, is **Eluanbi**, Taiwan's southernmost village. Less than 1km from the island's **southern tip**, the village comprises a couple of hotel resorts catering to domestic tour groups and a handful of hip private hotels. The area's defining landmark is the **Eluanbi Lighthouse** (daily 7am–5.30pm; NT$40), built in 1882 under the direction of English engineer John Ropinald. One of several English-designed lighthouses in Taiwan, this whitewashed structure is heavily fortified, with a trench around its perimeter and several gun emplacements in the tower itself. To get here, take the road leading up the hill to the right just past the village until you reach the car park at the top. A footpath from here leads to the lighthouse; beyond this is another trail leading to a **boardwalk** which winds around the coast, giving close-up views of the coral reef that has long protected Taiwan's southern tip from amphibious invasion.

On the left-hand side of the road as you enter Eluanbi from Sail Rock is *Sand* at 230 Shadao Rd (℡08/8851107, ⓦwww.sand.com.tw; ⑥). An elegantly designed **boutique hotel** it combines stone-slab minimalism with all the amenities of a five-star resort. With only eleven rooms – seven of them doubles – reservations are recommended.

Exploring the park

Amazing **natural attractions** are scattered throughout Kenting National Park. A nice route would be to make a roughly **anti-clockwise circuit** of the park, first exploring the inland areas north of the main entrance near **Dajianshan** before heading southeast along the coast and around Taiwan's southern tip. A drive north from here along the park's eastern shore provides unparalleled panoramas of the **Longpan Grasslands** and **Fongchueisha Dunes** on your way to the intriguing coastal coral formations at **Jialeshuei**. From there, a clockwise mini-circuit around the park's remote northeast section gives a glimpse of its more hilly country, and from there you can travel due west past the natural gas fires at **Chuhuo** on your way to idyllic white-sand beaches such as **Baisha**, on the park's far southwest fringe – one of the finest places to watch the sunset.

Inland loop: Dajianshan to Sail Rock

The entrance (free) to the park's main **inland area** is through the **archway** on the north side of the main intersection at Kenting town's western edge. From the archway, a solitary road climbs northeast, with **Dajianshan** (Big

Kenting National Park sights

Kenting National Park	墾丁國家公園	kěndīng guójiā gōngyuán
Baisha	白沙灣	báishā wān
Chuhuo	出火	chūhuŏ
Dajianshan	大尖山	dàjiānshān
East Gate	東門	dōngmén
Fongchueisha Dunes	風吹砂	fēngchuīshā
Gangkou	港 口	gǎngkŏu
Jialeshuei	佳樂水	jiālè shuǐ
Jioupengsha Dunes	九硼砂	jiŭpéngshā
Hengchun	恒春鎮	héngchūn zhèn
Kenting Forest Recreation Area	墾丁森林公園	kěndīng sēnlín gōngyuán
Longpan Grasslands	龍磐公園	lóngpán gōngyuán
Maobitou	貓鼻頭	máobí tóu
Nanren Lake	南仁湖	nánrén hú
Nanrenshan	南仁山	nánrénshān
Shadao	砂島	shādǎo
Sheding Nature Park	社頂公園	shèdīng gōngyuán
Winson House	周文生衝浪教學會館	zhōuwénshēng chōnglàng jiàoxúe huìguǎn

Point Mountain; 318m) in constant view on the left. Rising sharply from sea level, the pyramid-shaped mountain is the park's leading landmark. About 4km up the winding road a car park signals the entrance to the **Kenting Forest Recreation Area** (8am–5.30pm; NT$150), a 435-hectare maze of trails, ranging from short nature walks to two more challenging **hikes** to the top of Dajianshan. While the latter two hikes afford unfettered views of the entire park, the trails are often closed due to landslip damage, so inquire at the national park visitor centre before setting out. The gentler approach is from the mountain's northern side, while a much steeper trail switches back up its southern flank. The forest recreation area is renowned for its cave-like formations and lush **botanical gardens** featuring more than 1200 species of plants. A network of easy walking paths runs through the gardens, which were established during the Japanese occupation and include a mix of indigenous and exotic species. A highlight is the **Valley of the Hanging Banyans**, which slices through a succession of limestone cliffs covered in hanging banyan tree roots.

Just southeast along the same road, the **Sheding Nature Park** (8am–5pm; free) also features a system of walking paths, this time through valleys of inland coral reef, limestone caves and even grasslands. The nature park, once home to the **Paiwan tribe** of aborigines, now hosts legions of colourful butterflies as well as chirping cicadas for much of the year. Even the road through this area gives glimpses of the giant **uplifted coral formations**, and as it circles down the mountain towards the southeast shore it yields clear views of the coastline around Sail Rock (see p.376).

The southeast coast: Shadao beach to Jialeshuei

Back on the coast road heading southeast from Kenting town, you'll pass the pristine **Shadao beach**, composed almost entirely of sand from seashells, coral and marine microorganisms known as foraminifers. This beach, with an unusually high calcium carbonate concentration of almost 98 percent, is protected, but there is an adjacent exhibition hall with a **viewing platform**. The coast road continues around Taiwan's southern tip, past the village of Eluanbi (see p.377), before curving sharply north and clinging to the **cliffs** and **dunes** along the park's Pacific shoreline.

A scooter ride here is pure pleasure, in places affording simultaneous views of the Bashi Channel to the west and the Pacific to the east. Along the way are numerous spots to pull off the road and admire the open scenery of areas such as the **Longpan (Dragon Rock) Grasslands**, and, a bit further north, the **Fongchueisha (Wind-blown Sand) Dunes**, which spill hundreds of feet from the roadside to the coral reef below. Carry on north along this road until it forks at Gangkou and turn right to reach **Jialeshuei**, a string of fantastic **coral formations** that locals liken to an array of animal shapes. There is a tollgate (7am–6pm; NT$50) just before the beginning of the coral outcroppings. About 500m before the tollgate is the confluence of a sandy bay and a river mouth that has some of Kenting's best surfing (see p.376)

The hilly northeast: to Jioupengsha Dunes and back

For a taste of the park's remote, **hilly northeast**, return to Gangkou and head northwest to the tiny town of **Sinjhuang**. From here, County Highway 200 runs west towards Chuhuo and northeast into the hills; follow this lightly travelled road through the village of **Manjhou** and past sleepy Paiwan hamlets, far removed from the tourist hordes in Kenting town. Most of the forest to the east of this road is an ecologically protected area containing **Nanren (Southern Man) Lake** and **Nanrenshan** (Southern Man Mountain), both of which can be reached via a narrow access road which eventually peters into a trail. To enter this area you need to obtain a permit at the national park visitor centre.

Several kilometres further northeast, and just outside of the national park boundary, are the shimmering **Jioupengsha Dunes**; from here, you'll need to go back the way you came or drive due south along the bumpy old **coastal track** that runs directly back to Jialeshuei. This road is technically off-limits to tourists, but the rule is not enforced and it makes for an exciting detour (be sure you have plenty of petrol). To the west of the track as you head south is a highly protected heritage area centred on an archeological excavation of thirty-one **stone-slab houses** estimated to be about seven hundred years old. Archeologists believe these houses belonged to what they call the **South Paiwan civilization**, which they stress is markedly different from the modern Paiwan tribe. Access to the site requires a permit, which small groups can arrange at the park visitor centre.

The west: Chuhuo to the southwest beaches

From Sinjhuang, take County Road 200 west for several kilometres until you reach the **natural gas fires** at **Chuhuo**, just before the sizeable town of Hengchun. Caused by methane escaping through fissures in the shale, the fires are ringed off by shallow fences and can be visited for free. Although they're more impressive at night, you can usually see them during the day. Just west of Chuhuo, on the outskirts of **Hengchun**, is the **East Gate**, the best-preserved section of an imperial Chinese city wall left in Taiwan. Hengchun was built in the 1870s – near the twilight of the Qing dynasty – as a **walled city**, and all four of its city gates remain intact in their original locations. However, the East Gate is by far the most impressive as it still has a lengthy stretch of wall adjoining it.

South of Hengchun, accessible via the main Highway 26 from Fengkang, is the park's largely untrammelled southwest corner, ringed with alluring and often empty **beaches**. To get here, turn south when you see the sign for **Maobitou**, a friendly village next to another patch of eroded coastal coral formations named after a host of animals. The highlight of this area – and indeed of the park as a whole – is the glorious white-sand beach at **Baisha (White Sand) Bay**. Unlike the beaches closer to Kenting town, which are perennially packed with people and unsightly umbrella forests, Baisha looks and feels like the quintessential tropical beach, with glistening sands seeming to melt into the turquoise sea – **sunsets** here are truly outstanding.

Travel details

Trains

Fangliao to: Kaohsiung (5 express daily; 1hr 10min); Taitung (3 express daily; 1hr 20min).
Kaohsiung to: Fangliao (5 express daily; 1hr 10min); Pingdong (9 express daily; 20min); Taichung (14 express daily; 2hr 30min); Tainan (17 express daily; 30min); Taipei (15 express daily; 4hr 30min); Taitung (5 express daily; 2hr).
Tainan to: Chiayi (14 express daily; 40min); Kaohsiung (17 express daily; 30min); Taichung (14 express daily; 2hr); Taipei (15 express daily; 4hr).

Buses

With so many services operating in the region, inter-city bus frequencies have not been included. Most buses leave every 30min, and services to Kenting, Taichung and Taipei often run 24hr.
Kaohsiung to: Donggang (1hr); Foguangshan (40min); Kenting (2hr); Meinong (1hr); Meishankou

(2 daily; 3hr 30min); Taichung (2hr 40min); Taipei (5hr); Taitung (3–4hr).
Kenting to: Kaohsiung (frequent; 2hr).
Pingdong to: Maolin (frequent; 1hr); Sandimen (Sat & Sun every 20min; 1hr); Shueimen (frequent; 1hr).
Tainan to: Kaohsiung (40min); Meishankou (3 daily; 3hr 15min); Nankunshen (hourly; 2hr); Syuejia (hourly; 1hr); Taichung (2hr); Taipei (4hr 30min).

Flights

Kaohsiung Airport has international flights to several cities including Hong Kong, Bangkok, Manila and Tokyo (see Basics p.27).
Hengchun to: Taipei (3 daily/twice weekly; 1hr 10min).
Kaohsiung to: Cimei (2 daily; 20min); Hualien (3 or 4 daily; 45min); Kinmen (5 daily; 55min); Magong (19 daily; 35min); Taipei (40 daily; 50min); Wangan (2 weekly; 25min).
Tainan to: Kinmen (2 daily; 50min); Magong (4 daily, 25min); Taipei (15 daily; 45min).

5

The east coast

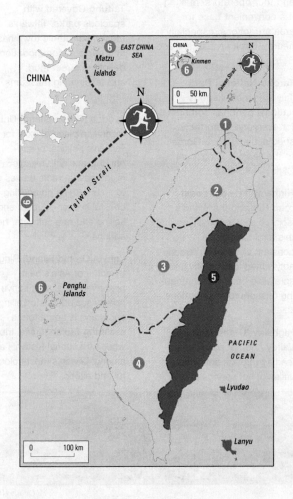

CHAPTER 5

Highlights

* **Hualien** The east coast's largest city retains a relaxed holiday feel, with a wide range of restaurants, hotels and tour operators, making it a convenient base for area attractions, especially nearby Taroko National Park. See p.385

* **Taroko National Park** Taiwan's most famous national park has something for everyone, from the spectacular Taroko Gorge to the seaside Cingshuei Cliffs. See p.395

* **Highway 11 – the coast road** Hugging the island's isolated eastern coastline, this rural road yields constant views of its remarkably varied topography, from sprawling beaches to intriguing offshore rock formations. See p.407

* **Highway 9 – the East Rift Valley** Another scenic road leading through an inviting valley of hot springs and outdoor recreation areas, including popular white-water rafting and paragliding spots. See p.412

* **Taitung** Covered with spacious parks, Taiwan's most multi-ethnic town has affordable accommodation, delightful street food and fascinating museums. See p.416

* **Lyudao (Green Island)** Until recently a place of exile for Taiwan's political prisoners, this ancient volcanic island now attracts droves of tourists with its compelling coastal scenery, superb snorkelling and rare saltwater hot springs. See p.425

* **Lanyu (Orchid Island)** Ringed by some of Asia's best-preserved coral reef, Lanyu boasts secluded snorkelling spots and is home to the seafaring Tao aboriginal tribe, whose traditional festivals are among Taiwan's most colourful and exotic. See p.432

△ Cingshuei Cliffs

The east coast

Nowhere in Taiwan shatters the myth of the island as an industrial waste-land more resolutely than its pristine **east coast**, a haven of Arcadian charms cut off from the country's crowded west and north by the cloud-piercing Central Cordillera. While the region is best known for the awe-inspiring **Taroko Gorge** – the centrepiece of **Taroko National Park** – it encompasses a broad array of geological wonders. The plunging **Cingshuei Cliffs** in the north of Taroko are among Asia's most magnificent, while the East Coast and East Rift Valley **national scenic areas** are defined by picturesque landscapes. The main cities of **Hualien** and **Taitung** are fairly slow-paced and well equipped for tourism, with numerous companies offering tours of nearby attractions. And just off the coast of Taitung are two exotic Pacific islands, both easily accessed by air and sea and fringed with coral suitable for snorkelling and diving. The closer, **Lyudao** (Green Island), was a centre of exile for political prisoners during the White Terror of the 1950s while, the less touristy **Lanyu** (Orchid Island) is home to the Tao people – by far the most isolated of Taiwan's aboriginal tribes.

With mountains, rivers, ocean and islands all in close proximity, the east coast is naturally a paradise of **outdoor pursuits**. Taroko National Park offers some of Asia's best hiking and mountain climbing, while the coral-fringed sea offers limitless opportunities for surfing, snorkelling and diving. Kayaking and **white-water rafting** on rivers such as the Siouguluan has become increasingly popular during the rainy season, while in dry weather river tracing has a devoted following. Further inland, in the East Rift Valley, are some of the region's top take-off spots for **paragliding**, and a growing number of cyclists are pedalling their way down the coast.

The region is also visibly marked by ethnic diversity, with Taiwan's densest concentration of **indigenous people**: seven officially recognized tribes are represented here, and their relative isolation has enabled them to preserve many of their traditional beliefs, languages and practices. The stretch between the cities of Hualien and Taitung is the heartland of the **Ami** – the country's largest tribe with around 140,000 members – and scattered throughout are villages of the Atayal, Bunun, Paiwan, Puyuma, Rukai and Tao people. The tribespeople are invariably foreigner-friendly, most of them hungry for recognition and eager to share their cultures with outsiders. Visiting the area during a **festival** period – the busiest of which is in July and August – gives a fascinating glimpse into a seldom seen side of Taiwan.

Though the area is most easily explored with your own transport, a combina-tion of train and bus journeys can get you up and down its entire length.

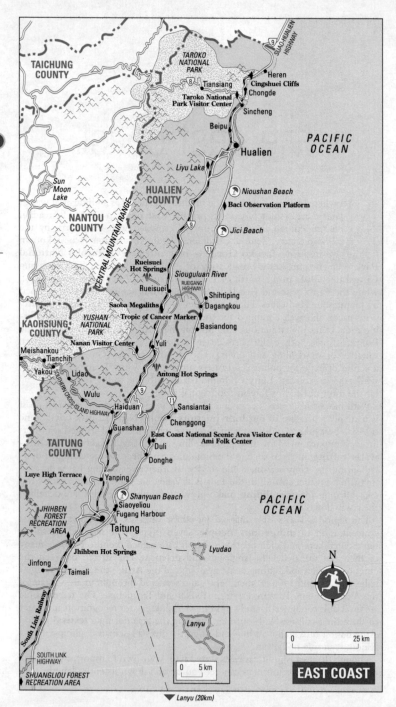

TAICHUNG
COUNTY

TAROKO
NATIONAL
PARK

Tiansiang

Taroko National
Park Visitor Center

Cingshuei Cliffs
Chongde

Heren

SIAO-HUALIEN
HIGHWAY

9

Sincheng

Beipu

PACIFIC
OCEAN

Hualien

Liyu Lake

HUALIEN
COUNTY

Nioushan Beach

Baci Observation Platform

Sun
Moon
Lake

NANTOU
COUNTY

Jici Beach

CENTRAL MOUNTAIN RANGE

Rueisuei
Hot Springs

Siouguluan River

9

11

Rueisuei

RUEIGANG
HIGHWAY

Shihtiping

Dagangkou

YUSHAN
NATIONAL
PARK

Saoba Megaliths

Tropic of Cancer Marker

Basiandong

KAOHSIUNG
COUNTY

Nanan Visitor Center

Yuli

Meishankou

Tianchih

Yakou

SOUTHERN CROSS-ISLAND HIGHWAY

Lidao

Wulu

Antong Hot Springs

9

11

Sansiantai

Haiduan

Chenggong

Guanshan

East Coast National Scenic Area Visitor Center &
Ami Folk Center

TAITUNG
COUNTY

Duli

Donghe

Luye High Terrace

Yanping

PACIFIC
OCEAN

JHIHBEN
FOREST
RECREATION
AREA

Shanyuan Beach

Siaoyeliou

Fugang Harbour

Taitung

Lyudao

N

Jhihben Hot Springs

Jinfong

Taimali

South Link Railway

Lanyu

0   5 km

0   25 km

SOUTH LINK
HIGHWAY

SHUANGLIOU FOREST
RECREATION AREA

EAST COAST

▼ Lanyu (20km)

Some history

Known to early Chinese settlers as the "mountain back", the east coast has always been a backwater and its history has been defined by its isolation from the island's more accessible – and arable – regions. The formidable geographic barriers helped to stem the encroachment of the Han Chinese, and while many of the west-coast *pingpu*, or plains aborigines, began assimilating into Hakka and Hoklo cultures as early as the seventeenth century, the east-coast tribes were largely left to themselves until the twentieth century.

Although the influence of outsiders was briefly felt when the **Spanish** attempted to mine gold near present-day Hualien in the early 1600s, the first significant non-native settlements weren't established until the 1850s, when small groups of **Chinese farmers** began migrating to the Hualien area. However, these agrarian communities were but far-flung pockets of Chinese culture, and it wasn't until after the **Japanese occupation** that a concerted effort was made to develop the region. The narrow, dusty path that connected Hualien to the north was widened into a proper road in the 1920s, with tunnels cut through the cliffs – forming the foundation for today's heart-stopping Suao-Hualien highway. Meanwhile, the Japanese built a handful of narrow-gauge rail links between important settlements, and by 1926 had united them into what was then called the **Eastern Railway Line**, linking Keelung in the north to Taitung in the south. By that time, Taitung had already been transformed into a pivotal base for Japan's military expansion into the tropics, and in 1930 the **Huatung Highway** connecting Hualien and Taitung was opened.

Under the Japanese, sugar processing plants and wood mills were established in the Taitung area, for the first time drawing large numbers of Chinese labourers to the east coast – a migration that was made easier by the opening of a highway looping around Taiwan's southern tip in 1932. The opening of the **Central Cross-Island Highway** in 1960 further contributed to the area's development, particularly around Hualien and in 1972 the winding **Southern Cross-Island Highway** was completed, connecting Tainan to Taitung via a hair-raising climb over the mountains and making the area more accessible to tourists (see p.334). Finally, the 1991 opening of the **South-link Line** connecting Kaohsiung with Taitung by rail, together with the 1982 widening of the tracks between Hualien and Taitung, made travel to the east coast easier from all sides of the island.

Hualien

The biggest city on the east coast, **HUALIEN** sits on a mountain-fringed plain 110km south of Suao, making an ideal base for expeditions to Taroko National Park. It's also one of the world's major producers of **marble** (as well as jade and cement), and elegant stonework is used liberally all over the city to adorn temples, pavements, the airport and even the train station. The relatively large numbers of tourists passing through means Hualien has a laid-back, holiday town atmosphere, with a growing number of teahouses, attractive restaurants and tasty local specialties to try, as well as a handful of absorbing temples and an inexpensive stone market.

Some history

Hualien has a relatively short history, making it something of a frontier town: **Chinese settlers** from Danshui established the first village in 1851, but conflicts with various aboriginal tribes, including a fierce battle with the **Sakizaya**, resulted in the colony being abandoned twice and only in the 1890s

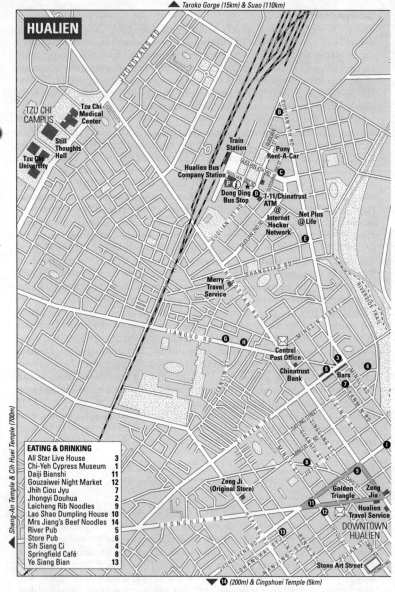

▲ Taroko Gorge (15km) & Suao (110km)

HUALIEN

Tzu Chi Campus

Tzu Chi Medical Center

Still Thoughts Hall

Tzu Chi University

Train Station

Pony Rent-A-Car

Hualien Bus Company Station

Dong Ding Bus Stop

7-11/Chinatrust ATM

Internet Hacker Network

Net Plus @ Life

Merry Travel Service

JIANGUO RD

Central Post Office

Chinatrust Bank

Bars

Zeng Ji (Original Store)

Golden Triangle

Zeng Jia

Hualien Travel Service

DOWNTOWN HUALIEN

Stone Art Street

EATING & DRINKING

All Star Live House	3
Chi-Yeh Cypress Museum	1
Daiji Bianshi	11
Gouzaiwei Night Market	12
Jhih Ciou Jyu	7
Jhongyi Douhua	2
Laicheng Rib Noodles	9
Lao Shao Dumpling House	10
Mrs Jiang's Beef Noodles	14
River Pub	5
Store Pub	6
Sih Siang Ci	4
Springfield Café	8
Ye Siang Bian	13

Sheng-An Temple & Cih Huei Temple (700m)

▼ ⑭ (200m) & Cingshuei Temple (5km)

did a permanent settlement take hold. The **Japanese** had a strong impact here, the region becoming an immigration zone for poor Japanese families during the occupation era, but Hualien remained a remote place for much of the twentieth century: it wasn't until the 1920s that the Japanese hacked out a road to replace the old track to Suao; the Central Cross-Island Highway was completed in 1960; and the rail line from Taipei opened in 1980. Today Hualien is a city of

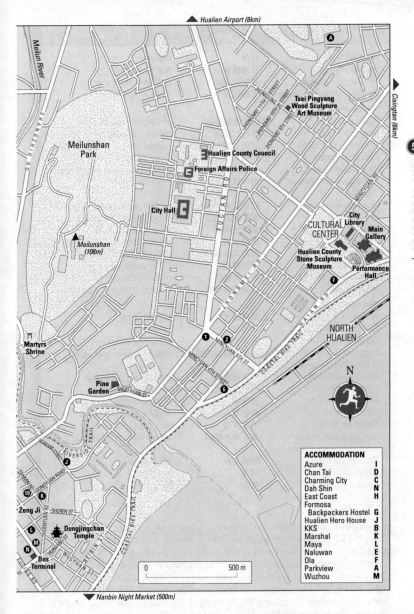

Hualien Airport (6km)

Cisingtan (6km)

Meilun River

SHANGZHIH RD

Meilunshan Park

Meilunshan (108m)

JHONGMEI 11TH STREET

JHONGMEI 10TH STREET

JHONGMEI 9TH STREET

Tsai Pingyang Wood Sculpture Art Museum

Hualien County Council

Foreign Affairs Police

City Hall

FUCIAN RD

JHONGMEI RD

MINCYUAN RD

City Library

CULTURAL CENTER

Main Gallery

Hualien County Stone Sculpture Museum

Performance Hall

F

NORTH HUALIEN

Martyrs Shrine

Pine Garden

SHUEI YUAN ST

MINCYUAN 5TH ST

MINCYUAN 4TH STREET

COASTAL BIKE TRAIL

N

SIN SHING RD

LOGNGYUAN ROAD

HUAKANG TRAIL

RIVERSIDE TRAIL

J

ZHONGHUA RD

Zeng Ji

SHUREN ST

L

M

N

Dongjingchan Temple

JHONGSHAN RD

JHONGJENG RD

Bus Terminal

WUCYUAN RD

COASTAL BIKE TRAIL

0   500 m

ACCOMMODATION

Azure	I
Chan Tai	D
Charming City	C
Dah Shin	N
East Coast	H
Formosa Backpackers Hostel	G
Hualien Hero House	J
KKS	B
Marshal	K
Maya	L
Naluwan	E
Ola	F
Parkview	A
Wuzhou	M

Nanbin Night Market (500m)

THE EAST COAST | Hualien

110,000, unique in having almost equal numbers of Hakka, Hoklo, mainlander and aboriginal citizens: the latter are primarily Atayal and Ami.

Arrival, transport and information

Hualien Airport is 6km north of the city, equipped with a tourist office (daily 8am–9.30pm; ☎03/8210625), ATM and car rental desk in the arrival hall. The

387

Hualien	花蓮	*huālián*
Hualien Airport	花蓮機場	*huālián jīchǎng*
Hualien Train Station	花蓮火車站	*huālián huǒchēzhàn*
Visitor information centre	旅遊服務中心	*lǚyóu fúwù zhōngxīn*
Accommodation		
Azure Hotel	藍天麗池飯店	*lántiān lìchí fàndiàn*
Chan Tai Hotel	仟台大飯店	*qiāntái dàfàndiàn*
Charming City Hotel	花蓮香城大飯店	*huālián xiāngchéng dàfàndiàn*
Dah Shin Hotel	大新大旅社	*dàxīn lǚshè*
East Coast Hotel	東岸精緻商務旅館	*dōngàn jīngzhì shāngwù lǚguǎn*
Formosa Backpackers Hostel	青年民宿	*qīngnián mínsù*
Hualien Hero House	花蓮國軍英雄館	*huālián guójūn yīngxióngguǎn*
KKS Hotel	國廣興大飯店	*guóguǎngxīng dàfàndiàn*
Marshal Hotel	統帥大飯店	*tǒngshuài dàfàndiàn*
Maya Hotel	瑪亞旅店	*mǎyà lǚdiàn*
Naluwan Hotel	那魯灣旅店	*nàlǔwān lǚdiàn*
Ola Hotel	洄瀾客棧	*huílán kèzhàn*
Parkview Hotel	美崙大飯店	*měilún dàfàndiàn*
Wuzhou Hotel	五洲商務旅館	*wǔzhōu shāngwù lǚguǎn*
The City		
Abode of Still Thoughts	靜思精舍	*jìngsī jīngshè*
Cihhuei Temple	慈惠堂	*cíhuì táng*
Dongjingchan Temple	東淨禪寺	*dōngjìngchán sì*
Hualien County Stone Sculpture Museum	花蓮石雕博物館	*huālián shídiāo bówùguǎn*
Meilunshan Park	美崙山公園	*měilúnshān gōngyuán*
Pine Garden	松園別館	*sōngyuán biéguǎn*
Sheng An Temple	勝安宮	*shèngān gōng*
Still Thoughts Hall	靜思堂	*jìngsī táng*
Stone Art Street	石藝大街	*shíyì dàjiē*
Tsai Pingyang Wood Sculpture Art Museum	蔡平陽木雕館	*càipíngyáng mùdiāoguǎn*
Tzu Chi Campus	慈濟園區	*cíjì yuánqū*
Zeng Jia	曾家	*zēng jiā*
Zeng Ji	曾記	*zēng jì*

airport bus into downtown operates every half hour from the terminal (8.30am–7pm; NT$20), while tour buses to Taroko also stop here twice a day – ask the tourist office for details. A **taxi** into the city should cost around NT$250–300.

Hualien's **train station** lies over 2km northwest of downtown; left luggage (8am–8pm) is to the right of the exit, while ATM machines can be found in the ticket hall. Hualien Bus Company services from Taroko and Taitung stop just outside, while Dingdong Bus Company has a small stop a few shops down in front of a restaurant. Note that most Hualien Bus Company services terminate in the smaller downtown bus station (called the "terminal") at the end of Jhongshan Road, closer to the shops, bars and restaurants.

The city does have a bus system but services are infrequent and difficult to use for non-locals: it's easy to walk around central Hualien but for longer excursions plan to use taxis or hire transport. **Taxis** are supposed to use the meter: pay around NT$150 for trips downtown from the station. **Scooters** can be hired from a variety of shops around the train station: a good option is Pony Rent-A-Car Group (81 Guolian 1st Road) to the left of *Ching Yeh Hotel*: in theory you need a driver's licence but a passport usually does the trick. It's NT$500 per day for 125cc.

Information

The **tourist office** (daily 8am–10pm; ☎03/8360634, ⓦwww.hlhg.gov.tw) in front of the train station is well stocked with English-language material and helpful English speakers. Most hotels offer free **Internet access**: if not try *Internet Hacker Network* (NT$30 per hr) at 39 Guolian 2nd Road or *Net Plus Life* at 41 Guolian 5th Road (NT$25 per hr). There are plenty of **banks** in Hualien and most 7-Elevens have **ATMs** inside. The main **post office** is at 92 Jhongshan Road (daily 9am–5pm). Tongyong Pinyin street signs are gradually being introduced in Hualien, though you'll still see the old MPS2 system used in places.

Tours and activities

Organised **tours** of the region save the hassle of arranging transport but are best suited for those short of time: you'll be whisked through scenic spots at breakneck speed. The Tourism Bureau sponsors tours of the east coast, Taroko and East Rift Valley operated by local tour company Merry Travel Service (549-2 Jhongshan Rd; ☎03/8355447), departing the airport and tourist office every day: you can also ask about **whale watching** tours (April–October; NT$800) at the tourist office and most hotels.

Hualien is a growing base for a range of **adventure sports** and **activities** along the east coast. The Hualien Surf Club (☎03/8711245, ⓔraveleoman@ yahoo.com.tw) can arrange classes and rent boards, while the Calvin Cycle Outdoor Explore School (☎03/8357992, ⓔoutdoor@outdoor-taiwan.com) runs kayaking, biking, climbing and river tracing trips for groups of ten or more. The *Formosa Backpackers Hostel* has good links with both organizations. Hualien's popular **Coastal Bike Trail** runs from Nanbin Park in the south to Cisingtan (Chihsingtan) Beach 15.8km to the north, and is a pleasant way to travel between the two places. Rent bikes at your hotel or shops along the coast – you'll find a couple on the stretch south of the Meilun River.

Moving on from Hualien

Far Eastern Air Transport (☎03/8265702) and TransAsia Airways (☎03/8261365) operate regular flights to Taipei from Hualien Airport throughout the day, while Mandarin Airlines (☎03/8268785) flies to Kaohsiung and Taichung. Hualien is a major stop on the **Eastern Line** with regular express services to Taipei, Yilan and Taitung. Hualien Bus Company runs **buses** to Taroko National Park visitor center every half hour from the downtown terminal and train station (daily 5.30am–9.30pm, 1hr; NT$71) and seven times daily to Tiansiang (1hr 30min; NT$145) midway up the gorge, starting at 6.30am. There's just one bus to Lishan daily at 9.30am (5hr; NT$357). Five buses a day run to Taitung (NT$450) via the East Rift Valley (5.10am, 7.10am, 9.10am, 12.10pm, 4.10pm). The 10.20am bus is the only service along the coast (4hr). A few stores down from the Hualien Bus stop, Dingdong Bus Company offers three daily services to Taitung (NT$447) via the coast road (4.35am, 1pm, 2.20pm): the restaurant next to the bus stand sells tickets from 10am.

Taxis and touts around the train station will offer to drive you on a short tour of Taroko Gorge: expect to pay at least NT$2000 for 3 hours. At the time of writing all bus services to Taipei and Suao had ceased, which means the only way to experience the coast road north and the Cingshuei Cliffs is to drive yourself or take a tour.

Accommodation

Accommodation is plentiful in Hualien, though as elsewhere in Taiwan, **budget hotels** are harder to find. Apart from a couple of decent options closer to downtown, the cheapest hotels tend to be close to the train station in the northwestern part of the city, which is convenient if you're passing through or hiring a scooter, but otherwise a bit dead. The harbour area north of the Meilun River contains several top-class hotels, but once again, transport is a pain and you'll spend a lot on taxis staying here. **Mid-range hotels** have really taken off in Hualien and offer the best value, with a host of new and comfortable places scattered all over town.

Train station area

Chan Tai Hotel 83-1 Guolian 1st Rd
☎03/8330121. Convenient budget option, across from the slightly more expensive *Chin Yeh* opposite the train station. Rooms are plain but adequate. ❷

Charming City Hotel 19 Guoshing 2nd St
☎03/8353355, ⓔhotel_n@hotmail.com. Hualien's only boutique hotel, with stylish rooms and a blend of contemporary Asian and Art Deco themes. Discount schemes can bring the cost under NT$2000, and it's within sight of the train station. ❼

KKS Hotel 223 Guolian 5th Rd ☎03/8338882. New hotel just north of train station offering some good deals (weekdays NT$1600–2000), popular with tour groups. Comfortable rooms come with polished stone floors. ❼

Naluwan Hotel 7-3 Guolian 5th Rd
☎03/8360103. Modern hotel, a short walk from the station, with an aboriginal theme and Ami staff. Spacious rooms are decorated in a slightly quirky style, with wooden floors, bold colours and large beds topped with a mini canopy. Free Internet. ❻

Downtown

Azure Hotel 590 Jhongjheng Rd ☎03/8336686, ⓦwww.azurehotel.com.tw. Elegant hotel popular with well-heeled tourists, though the 45 percent discounts available online make it good value mid-week. The compact rooms are stylishly furnished, with marble-clad bathrooms and great views of the city from the large French windows. ADSL ports available if you have your own computer. ❼

Dah Shin Hotel 101 Jhongshan Rd ☎03/8322125 Backpacker-friendly budget hotel, with plenty of maps, information and helpful staff. Rooms are basic but clean and very cheap, and the location at the southern end of town is handy for bike trails and the bus terminal. ❷

East Coast Hotel 128 Jianguo Rd ☎03/8332889, ⓔservice@ec-hotel.com.tw. Attractive new hotel set in a grand building on the edge of downtown. Stylish rooms feature traditional Chinese touches such as redwood furniture, but the slightly more

expensive Japanese rooms with futons and pine-wood floors are also good value after discounts. ❼

🏃 **Formosa Backpackers Hostel** 206 Jian-guo Rd ☎03/8352515, ⓔformosahostels @yahoo.com. Excellent modern hostel with friendly English-speaking owners who can set you up with tours, surf groups, kayaking, whale-watching and car/scooter rentals. The marble-floored dorms are modern and spotlessly clean. Extras include free tea and coffee, a shared kitchen and free pick-up from airport, train or bus stations if you call ahead. Dorm beds are NT$350, and there's a Japanese futon double room. The location isn't bad, a short walk from downtown and the bars on Linsen Road. ❷

Hualien Hero House 56 Huagang ☎03/8324171. Comfortable budget accommodation a short walk from downtown, with dorm beds (four per room) NT$400 and several doubles. All rooms have TVs and bathrooms. Serves as a hostel for members of the military, but open to the public. ❸

Marshal Hotel 36 Gongyuan Rd ☎03/8326123. This huge hotel with porthole windows and a slight aboriginal theme is the poshest place in downtown, though big discounts reflect its age. Rooms are a little faded but still good quality, and facilities include free Internet and a decent spa and pool. ❼

Maya Hotel 516 Fujian St ☎03/8326171. Budget hotel with a Bali-meets-China theme and the pleasant *Mango Tree Café* on site. It's an old building, but rooms are relatively cheap and have been attractively refurbished. ❸

Wuzhou Hotel 84 Jhongshan Rd ☎03/8332292. This cosy hotel at the end of Jhongshan Road opened in 2005, with a smart stone facade and great value discounts mid-week (NT$1600, or tatami rooms from NT$600 per person). ❻

North of the Meilun River

Ola Hotel 11 Haian Rd ☎03/8227188, ⓔolahotel @ms58.hinet.net. Bright hotel overlooking a palm-fringed section of the seafront, though views of the ocean are obstructed somewhat by the cement loading port in front. Rooms are disappointingly plain

considering the Surrealist theme in the lobby and café, but the free bike hire is handy for the Coastal Bike Trail opposite. **⑥**
Parkview Hotel 1-1 Linyuan Rd ☏03/8222111, ⓦwww.parkview-hotel.com. Hualien's top luxury hotel, with all the extras including pool, spa, landscaped gardens and tennis courts. Rooms are extremely comfortable, but standard five-star fare. There's a free shuttle bus from the airport, but otherwise it's a trek from downtown – the lavish buffets (NT$450–550) and *dim sum* restaurant on site are the most convenient dining options. **❽**

The City

Jhongshan Road connects the relatively sleepy train station area to **downtown Hualien**, home to most of the city's bars, restaurants and shops; the best place to pick up locally produced marble is **Stone Art Street** (Mon–Sat 2–10.30pm, Sun 10am–10.30pm), towards its southern end. The "street" is in fact a large compound of market stalls selling cheap marble carvings and statues, fossilized coral and wood, and precious stone and jade jewellery, at the junction of Boai Street and Chongcing Road. Touristy **dance shows** are held here every evening (8.10–9.10pm; free) by local Ami people.

From Stone Art Street return to Jhongshan Road and keep walking east along Huagang Street to reach **Dongjingchan Temple** (daily 5am–5pm), a tranquil Buddhist shrine. The entrance is on Wucyuan (Wuchiuan) Street, just to the left of the junction with Huagang Street. The main hall contains three golden Buddha statues, several massive geodes and is plastered with local marble, making it unusually opulent (take your shoes off if you want to go inside).

Hualien's **Golden Triangle** commercial district is formed by Jhongshan, Jhongjheng and Jhonghua roads just north of here. This is where most of the city's famous *muaji* stores are located, selling sticky rice cakes with delicious fillings also known as *mashu*. From Jhongshan Road, heading west along Jhonghua your first stop should be **Zeng Jia** at no. 27, the sixty-year-old store that started it all; many cakeshops in Hualien use the name Zeng (or "Tseng") in their title but this is the original, established by Tseng Shui-gang in the 1940s. Back at the junction of Jhongshan and Jhonghua roads is one of many bright yellow **Zeng Ji** *muaji* stores, probably the most popular brand in town (the original is at 4 Minguo Road). The founder is Dong Cheng Chou, the son-in-law of the original Tseng – the cakes here are always fresh and best eaten within two days.

Sheng An Temple and Cihhuei Temple

Around 2km west of the Golden Triangle, along Jhonghua Road, are the most important Taoist temples in Hualien, regarded as the "Lourdes of Asia" for their power to heal the sick. They can be a little tricky to find: turn right off Jhonghua by the canal along Cih Huei (Tsz Huei) 1st Street then first right at Sheng An 2nd Street (marked by a large stele): turn left along Cih Huei (Tsz Huei) 3rd Street after around 200m, and you'll reach **Sheng An Temple** (daily 4am–9.30pm). A modern, garish building completed in 1950, it's dedicated to the chief Taoist goddess **Queen Mother of the West** (Wang Mu Niang Niang) and significant because in 1949 the goddess is supposed to have spoken on this spot through the body of a young man in a trance. **Cihhuei Temple** (daily 5.30am–9.30pm) next door is dedicated to the same goddess, but this shrine belongs to another sect and here she's known as Jinmu Niang Niang ("Golden Mother"). Cihhuei has over a thousand branch temples in Taiwan and overseas, and though it looks older and is far more beautiful (the main hall is inlaid with marble), it was consecrated at the same time as Sheng An and completed in 1963. The busiest time here is on the eighteenth day of the second lunar month,

when thousands of pilgrims believe the goddess accords special healing qualities. The large four-storey hall at the back of the temple is where many of the
pilgrims stay during this period, while the top level contains a shrine dedicated
to the Jade Emperor and intricate wood carvings.

North of the Meilun River

The area north of downtown across the Meilun River is a sleepy, modern district
containing the city government buildings, most of the best hotels and a handful of sights. It's dominated by **Meilunshan Park**, a 108-metre mound of lush
vegetation, clearly visible from most parts of the city and crisscrossed by pleasant
trails, mostly at its northern end (marked only in Chinese), to avoid the military
base on top. Hualien's **Martyrs' Shrine** (open 24hrs) sits at its base at the end of
Linsen Road, the elegant main hall inlaid with marble. You'll most likely have to
peek through the glass though, as this part opens to the public just twice a year
(March 29 and September 3). Further south, on a bluff overlooking the river,
the **Pine Garden** (daily 9am–5pm; free) is a former Japanese Navy command
centre completed in 1944, just in time to host send-off parties for Japanese
kamikaze pilots at the end of World War II. These days the main building serves
as a series of art galleries while the **café** (daily 9am–8pm) in the gardens outside
is a tranquil place to contemplate the city and port below. The building lies at
the end of Shuei Yuan Street off Jhongmei Road. Another 1km north of here,
Hualien's **Cultural Centre** is a complex of four buildings surrounded by a
sculpture park near the coast: facing Mincyuan Road is the city library and to the
right the **Hualien County Stone Sculpture Museum** (Tues–Sun 9am–noon
& 1.30–5pm; NT$20) containing a small but visually appealing collection of
contemporary carvings, and a historical section labelled in Chinese only. Behind
here on the left is the **main gallery** (same hours) which houses local art and a
small collection of aboriginal artefacts on the second floor. Anyone interested in
aboriginal art should arrange to visit the grandly titled **Tsai Pingyang Wood
Sculpture Art Museum** (☎03/8226423) at 180 Jhongsing Road further north:
Tsai Pingyang is Chinese but taught himself Ami and Taroko (Truku) carving
techniques, and though his work is not wholly traditional, his creations are
certainly exquisite. His old workshop has been absorbed by a condo development and all that remains is his small shop across the road – call in advance to
be sure of catching him.

Tzu Chi Campus

Northwest of the city and the train station, near the junction of Jhongshan and
Jhongyang roads, sits the **Tzu Chi Campus,** home of the **Tzu Chi Foundation** (ⓦ www.tzuchi.org), the world's largest charitable Buddhist organization.
Located in between the Tzu Chi Medical Centre and the Tzu Chi University is
the striking **Still Thoughts Hall** (daily 8.30am–5pm; free), a modern temple-
like structure completed in 2001. A combination of contemporary and classical
architecture, its most distinctive feature is the roof, with its triple eaves decorated with 362 bas-relief *feitian*, or celestial beings based on the Buddhist sutras
and the famous Mogao Caves in China. Several absorbing exhibition halls on
the first floor highlight the foundation's activities in charity, medicine, education and culture, and there are usually English-speaking guides on hand (free).
You also can visit the main hall upstairs which acts as a meeting hall rather than
a temple, and have a free lunch at the **vegetarian cafeteria** (11.30am–1pm)
in the building behind it.

Tzu Chi was founded in 1966 by **Venerable Master Cheng Yen**, a nun
who still lives and works in Hualien, to put into practice her interpretation of

Taiwan's National Parks

To protect its natural and historic treasures, Taiwan has established six national parks, which together account for 8.5 percent of its total land area. They include some of the country's most spectacular sights from soaring cliffs to alpine mountains and aboriginal villages to well-preserved Chinese architecture.

Mountains

▲ Syueshan signpost under snow

With 258 peaks rising above 3000m, Taiwan is one of the most mountainous places on earth – making it a climber's paradise. Most of the highest mountains are within national parks, with **Yushan National Park** boasting the tallest of them all: **Yushan** (Jade Mountain), which at 3952m is the loftiest peak in northeast Asia. Despite its daunting height, Yushan can be accessed via a well-maintained trail, making it an extremely popular and worthwhile climb. While Yushan receives most of the fanfare, mountain-choked **Shei-Pa National Park** comes a close second, with 51 peaks over 3000m. Though many of these are off-limits, the 3886m **Syueshan** (Snow Mountain) and adjacent **Holy Ridge** can be scaled with some advance planning. And while **Taroko National Park** is best known for its magnificent gorge, its towering western hinterlands are teeming with challenging climbs such as Cilaishan and **Nanhushan**.

Beaches

Though Taiwan is surrounded on all sides by beaches, few are as protected as the sandy shores of **Kenting National Park**, where shimmering **sand dunes** often stretch hundreds of metres from the sea. Set against turquoise waters – highlighted by well-preserved offshore coral reef – these dunes are atmospheric places to watch sunrises and sunsets, and some are suitable for strolling. While several of Kenting's beaches have uniquely high percentages of calcium carbonate and have been made off-limits to visitors in order to protect them, there are still plenty of beaches open to the public for sunbathing and swimming. Among the most popular are **Siaowan**, in Kenting town, and the beautiful white-sand beach at **Baisha**, on the park's western fringe.

▼ Kenting National Park, Baisha Beach

Historic Preservation

As well as scenery, Taiwan is keen to protect its rich historic and cultural heritage. For example, **Kinmen National Park** has been established to preserve its imperial Chinese monuments and hybrid Chinese-European architecture. Having been shelled by mainland China for decades, Kinmen also bears the scars of war, and several battlefield memorials and museums have been erected to honour the fallen. Historic roads also are being preserved throughout Taiwan, one example of which is the **Badongguan Historic Passage**, a Qing-dynasty military route that traverses Yushan National Park. Important archeological sites are scattered across Taiwan, some of them under national park protection. Among the most significant is a 700-year-old settlement of stone slab houses, believed to have belonged to the **South Paiwan aboriginal civilization**, which is being excavated in Kenting National Park.

▲ Kinmen Guei Pavilion in Jincheng

The Most Visited

While the primary function of Taiwan's national parks is the protection and conservation of precious natural resources and historic sites, they also are intended to serve as educational and recreational areas, and some attract droves of visitors each year. The most visited – and the best known outside of Taiwan – is **Taroko National Park**, with its awe-inspiring **Taroko Gorge** drawing increasing numbers of domestic and foreign tourists each year. With its steep cliffs and smooth marble walls, the 20km gorge offers truly world-class scenery, putting it on the itinerary of most foreign visitors. Enveloping the island's southern tip – and ringed by beautiful golden-sand beaches – **Kenting National Park** also packs in the crowds, especially during summer, but its warm tropical climate means it's a pleasant place to visit year-round. With low-elevation mountains laced with hiking trails – most within walking distance of Taipei's city centre – **Yangmingshan National Park** continues to be the favoured stomping ground of the capital's residents.

▼ Taroko National Park, Taroko Gorge

Ecological Protection Zones

All of Taiwan's national parks have **ecological protection zones** designed to preserve threatened species of flora and fauna. Among the best-known such zones are those to protect the endangered **Formosan Landlocked Salmon** in Shei-Pa National Park, which also has a zone to preserve the **Taiwan Sassafras** tree. Kenting National Park has several such zones, some sheltering ancient coral beds, others shielding pristine beaches from human degradation so they can be studied by scientists. Kinmen hosts more migratory birds than any other place in Taiwan, and its **Shuangli Wetlands Area** has been set aside to protect them. **Yangmingshan** is a hotbed of post-volcanic activity, and some of its areas with fumaroles and volcanic fissures are protected zones.

Aboriginal Areas

With many of Taiwan's indigenous inhabitants long relegated to the island's mountainous interior, pockets of the highlands remain strongholds of **traditional aboriginal culture** and fall within the boundaries of various national parks. Though the parks' strict conservationist laws are at stark odds with time-honoured aboriginal **hunting practices** – still a source of tension in some areas – poaching of protected species is on the wane. The most celebrated aboriginal hunters are the **Atayal tribe**, some of whom still live in parts of Shei-Pa and Taroko national parks, and the **Bunun tribe**, who inhabit the fringes of Yushan National Park. In the north of Kenting National Park, broad swaths of land are occupied – and even farmed – by members of the **Paiwan tribe**, and a drive along scenic **County Road 199** will reveal a side of the island that few Taiwanese even get to experience. Travellers who make the effort to visit isolated aboriginal villages within the parks are certain to gain rare insight into their timeless ways of life.

▼ Relief of Atayal village at Longshan Buluo, Taian

Humanistic Buddhism (see p.527); now there are over four million members worldwide. You can visit her original temple, known as **Abode of Still Thoughts** at 21 Kanglo Village, north of the city off Route 9, but you'll need your own transport to get there. It's signposted "Tzu Chi Academy" from the main road, 1.2km north of the Beipu Road intersection. The spiritual home of the foundation, the temple is surrounded by its administrative headquarters and a tranquil nunnery.

Eating

In addition to *muaji*, Hualien is known throughout Taiwan for *bianshi*, a type of wanton or dumplings in soup, filled with pork and shrimp, while its night markets are also a good place for cheap eats. The most convenient is **Gouzaiwei Night Market** on Zihyou Street south of Jhonghua Road, while **Nanbin Night Market** on the coast south of downtown is bigger but harder to get to without your own transport. At the top end, the city has started to develop a more sophisticated restaurant scene in recent years, with many renovated wooden Japanese-era buildings now serving as fashionable cafés.

Chi-Yeh Cypress Museum 106 Jhongmei Rd. Not a museum, but an attractive Chinese restaurant, teahouse and woodcarving showroom in an old Japanese-style wooden house. No English, but menus have photographs of the main dishes and sets (NT$250–300). Daily 10am–10pm.

Jhih Ciou Jyu 69 Datong Rd. Pleasant teahouse with simple, classical Chinese-style decor and wooden tables, on the junction with Sanmin Road. Tea and coffee from NT$50. Daily 10.30am–12.30am.

Jhongyi Douhua 2 Mincyuan 5th St. Popular local eatery not far from the *Astar Hotel*, specializing in *douhua*, a tasty soybean dessert mixed with syrup and peanuts (NT$25). It's especially delicious with lemon juice in the summer. Daily 11am–11.30pm.

Daiji Bianshi 120 Jhonghua Rd. One of Hualien's most celebrated *bianshi* dumpling shops, a no-nonsense local canteen with a special recipe

handed down within the Dai family from the Japanese era (NT$50). Daily 7.30am–12.30am.

Laicheng Rib Noodles 544 Jhongjheng Rd. No-fuss diner serving delicious bowls of noodles with a fried pork chop in soup, topped with green onions and pieces of leek (NT$50). Daily 10.30am–10pm.

Lao Shao Dumpling House 3-2 Sanmin Rd. Small local restaurant opposite the *Marshal Hotel*. The specialties are steamed pork dumplings (*shui-jiao*); it's NT$90 for ten. It also knocks out decent staples such as fried rice and noodles – there's an English menu and free ice tea. Daily 10am–2pm & 4.30pm–8.30pm.

Mrs Jiang's Beef Noodles 128 Jhongjheng Rd. Made famous by visits of late president Chiang Ching-kuo, this traditional place with wooden tables cooks up big bowls of sumptuous beef noodles (NT$80); the soup is spicy and delicious, though the meat might be a little fatty for

Hualien eating and drinking		
All Star Live House	歐斯達	ōusīdá
Chi-Yeh Cypress Museum	奇業檜木館	qíyè guìmù guǎn
Daiji Bianshi	戴記扁實店	dàijì biǎnshí
Gouzaiwei Night Market	溝仔尾夜市	gōuzǎiwěi yèshì
Jhih Ciou Jyu	知秋居	zhīqiūjū
Jhongyi Douhua	中一豆花	zhōngyī dòuhuā
Laicheng Rib Noodles	來成排骨麵	láichéng páigǔ miàn
Lao Shao Dumpling House	老邵餃館	lǎoshào jiǎoguǎn
Nanbin Night Market	南濱夜市	nánbīn yèshì
Mrs. Jiang's Beef Noodles	江太太牛肉麵店	jiāng tàitài niúròumiàn diàn
Si Shang Ci	思想起	sīxiǎngqǐ
Stone Pub	石頭族樂園	shítóuzú lèyuán
Ye Siang Bianshi	液香扁食店	yè xiāng biǎnshí diàn

some. Mrs Jang's son now runs the place but the matriarch still totters around at lunchtime. Daily 10am–2.30pm, 5–8.30pm.

🏃 **Sih Siang Ci** 87 Datong St. Upmarket restaurant set in a beautifully converted old wooden house at the end of Datong Street near the river, serving Chinese and Japanese food (from NT$180), as well as tea and coffee. Note that meals are only served 11.30am–1.30pm and 5.30–8.30pm. No English menu. Daily 11.30am–midnight.

🏃 **Ye Siang Bianshi** 42 Sinyi St. The most famous *bianshi* shop in Hualien, another one patronized by Chiang Ching-kuo and established more than seventy years ago. Bowls of the tasty dumplings get dished out automatically when you sit down (NT$50). Daily 8am–10pm.

Drinking

Hualien has a growing number of atmospheric places to sip coffee or tea, but its **nightlife** is fairly subdued. **Linsen Road** between Jhongshan and Mingli roads is lined with several decent pubs and lounge bars, but it's likely to be very quiet during the week – bars rarely open before 7 or 8pm. The *All Star Live House* at 81 Mingli Road (daily 8pm–4am) is a friendly bar just off Linsen Road, with happy hour till 9pm, live bands and a menu of reasonable snack food. The *Springfield Café* at 209 Boai Street is a another converted Japanese-era wooden house serving tea or coffee, close to the main shopping streets in downtown, while the *Stone Pub* on Haian Road and Mincyuan 4th Street (daily 11am–1am; ☏03/8331103) is a laid-back bar on the seafront framed by two banyan trees and offering various beers (Taiwan Beer NT$220), tea and snacks. It's best to go later in the evening when the traffic on Haian Road has thinned out, and the cement port lights below seem far more exotic.

Around Hualien

Before heading to Taroko Gorge, it's worth taking a day to explore **Cisingtan Beach** to the north and **Cingsiou Temple** further south, though it's best to have your own transport. **Liyu (Carp) Lake** is around 16km southwest of the city and a popular day-trip for city residents who come to fish, hire pedal boats, hike around the lake or up Liyu Mountain (601m). The scenery isn't bad, but despite being Taiwan's largest natural lake it's still relatively small and considering the hassle involved in getting here only worthwhile if you have lots of time. The exception is during the Dragon Boat Festival (June), when the lake hosts exuberant dragon boat races.

Cisingtan Beach

Around 6km north of Hualien, **Cisingtan Beach** is rapidly being developed as a tourist attraction, though it's covered with shingle and sits next to a major airforce base. There are a couple of attractive parks at its northern end however, and though it's not a popular place to swim, it is possible to **surf** here if the waves pick up (see p.389). It's also the end of the coastal bike trail and the site of an annual **manbo** or sunfish festival (April/May).

Around Hualien		
Cisingtan	七星潭	qīxīngtán
Chihsingtan Katsuo Museum	七星柴魚博物館	qīxīng cháiyú bówùguǎn
Cingsiou Temple	慶修院	qìngxiūyùan
Jian	吉安	jíān
Liyu Lake	鯉魚潭	lǐyútán

The southern section of the beach borders Cisingtan village with several cafés on the seafront and **Chihsingtan Katsuo Museum** (daily 9am–8pm; free; ⓦwww.katsuo.com.tw) on the main road. *Katsuo* is dried bonito (small tuna), sliced into thin flakes and a staple of Japanese cooking. Today Cisingtan's old *katsuo* processing factory has been reborn as a working tourist attraction, and though the "museum" is just a small exhibition on the history of the fish and the local area, it's housed in an atmospheric wooden storehouse with the busy processing area clearly visible on one side. Labels are in Chinese only, but it's worth sampling the product via steaming bowls of noodles or fishballs served at the **café** on site.

Cingsiou Temple

Around 5km southwest of Hualien, close to the town of Jian, **Cingsiou Temple** (Tues–Sun 9am–noon, 2–5pm) is Taiwan's best preserved and most beautiful Japanese Buddhist temple, tangible evidence of the strong Japanese presence here before World War II. It was built in 1917 to serve as the spiritual centre for immigrants from Kyushu, mostly poor farmers that were relocated as part of a controversial government scheme begun in 1909. Derelict for many years, the complex was skilfully restored in 2003: the wooden main hall is surrounded by a garden containing 88 statues, representing the equivalent number of "distresses" in human life and recalling Kyushu's 88 Shingon temples. These line one of Japan's most famous pilgrimage routes – for information about this and the temple watch the English DVD in the shop at the back. The temple is at 345 Jhongsing Road, 1km off Jhongyang Road.

Taroko National Park

Framed by sheer seaside cliffs and majestic inland mountain peaks, **TAROKO NATIONAL PARK** is Taiwan's most diverse national park and one of the island's top tourist destinations. Covering 92,000 hectares, Taroko is second only to Yushan National Park in size, with terrain that rises steadily from sea level in the east to lofty heights of over 3700m in the west, with one of the world's most wondrous river gorges cutting right through the middle. The amazingly narrow **Taroko Gorge** is the park's namesake and main attraction, and for good reason: stretching some 20km, with marble walls that soar several hundred metres above the Liwu River – often blocking out the sky – the canyon offers some of Taiwan's most awe-inspiring scenery, from crystal-clear waterfalls plunging down the rock faces to ethereal canvasses of ferns swaying gracefully in the wind as they hang from hairline cracks in the stone. Walking through some sections of the gorge is akin to stepping into an ancient Chinese scroll painting, with water cutting fantastic formations across the marble-cake cliffs and lushly vegetated outcrops draped in heavy bouquets of mist. Alongside the winding road through the canyon are several easy **walking paths**, providing superb vantage points for some of the most spectacular features and giving a greater sense of scale.

Though the gorge is Taroko's claim to fame – and the main tourist magnet – it comprises only a small part of the park, which also has an easily navigable network of hiking trails, outdoor hot springs and some of Taiwan's most challenging mountain climbs. And with the vast majority of visitors limiting their tours solely to the gorge, the rest of the park remains delightfully underused. Near the main tourist centre of **Tiansiang** are the outdoor **Wenshan Hot**

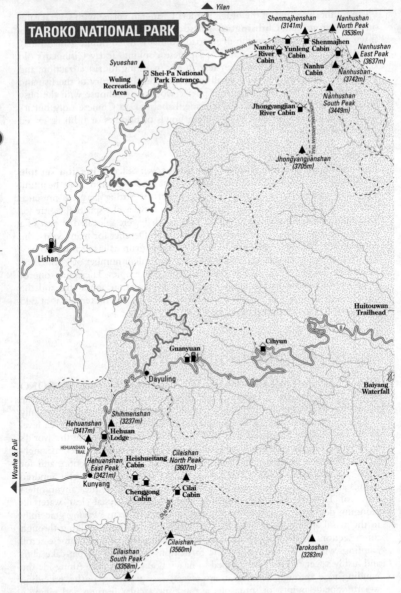

Springs, with bathing pools carved into the marble river bed. Other hiking trails lead through peripheral canyons, across lengthy suspension bridges, to roaring waterfalls, picturesque Chinese pavilions and shrines, and remote villages of the **Truku (Taroko) aboriginal tribe**, the indigenous inhabitants after whom the park is named. Formerly considered part of the Sedeq sub-group of the Atayal tribe, the Truku became officially recognized as Taiwan's twelfth indigenous

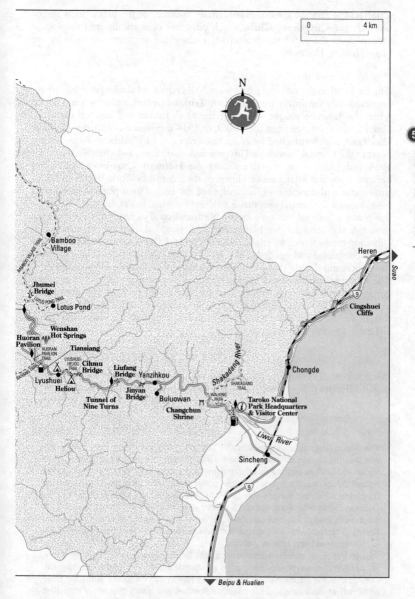

0   4 km

N

Bamboo Village

Jhumei Bridge

Lotus Pond

Wenshan Hot Springs

Huoran Pavilion

Tiansiang

Cihmu Bridge

Lyushuei

Heliou

Liufang Bridge

Yanzihkou

Jinyan Bridge

Tunnel of Nine Turns

Buluowan

Changchun Shrine

Shakadang River

Taroko National Park Headquarters & Visitor Center

Liwu River

Sincheng

Chongde

Cingshuei Cliffs

Heren

Suao

Beipu & Hualien

ethnic group in 2004 (see Contexts p.523). Though the Truku, traditionally known for their hunting prowess and weaving skills, once populated many river valleys within the park's current boundaries, few remain today. Most of those still living inside the park are located in Buluowan and the Bamboo Village.

For avid hill walkers and mountaineers, the park's wild western countryside boasts two of Taiwan's most coveted mountain climbs: those of the rugged

Cilai Ridge and the revered **Nanhushan.** Another of the park's finest attractions are the **Cingshuei Cliffs**, which plummet dramatically into the Pacific Ocean along the park's northeastern boundary and are accessible only by the Suao–Hualien Highway.

Some history

The land within the national park's boundaries remained almost pure wilderness, impacted only minimally by indigenous **Truku hunters**, until the early 1900s, when the Japanese sought to exploit the area's timber and mineral resources. Despite stiff resistance from the Truku, in 1914 the Japanese built the **Hehuan Old Trail**, which stretched from the east-coast city of Hualien to Wushe in the heart of the Central Cordillera. This path was maintained and improved between 1914 and 1935, when it was renamed the **Hehuan Crossover Road** and became a popular hiking route. However, their defeat in World War II and their subsequent withdrawal from Taiwan spelled the end of their plans to complete a road through the central mountains to the west coast. It was not until 1956 that this plan was revived, this time by the **Nationalists.** For nearly four years, more than five thousand former Nationalist soldiers toiled away at the road, often chiselling through rock by hand, until the **Central Cross-Island Highway** was finally completed and opened to the public in 1960. Conditions were extremely dangerous, and during the course of construction more than 450 workers died. The **Changchun (Eternal Spring) Shrine** not far from the entrance to the gorge was built in their memory. Due to a concerted push by conservationists in the early 1980s, and against the will of developers who had sought to build a dam in the gorge as part of a massive hydroelectric project, the land was set aside as Taiwan's fourth national park in 1985.

Entry points, information and transport

Bounded on all corners by paved highways and bisected by the extraordinarily scenic **Highway 8** – along the easternmost section of the original Central

---

Ancient history brought to the surface

The Taroko Gorge is a living museum of Taiwan's geological history, with the **marble** that lines the canyon considered to be the island's most ancient layer of rock. Formed about 250 million years ago after the metamorphosis of magma from undersea volcanic eruptions, the layers of marble, schist and gneiss are believed to have been pushed to the earth's surface after the Philippine Oceanic Plate subducted under the Eurasian Continental Plate some 6.5 million years ago. The significant crustal uplift around this area of Taiwan's east coast, together with the rapid downcut of the **Liwu River**, combined to form the gorge, and the erosion resistance of the marble has led to its narrowness and unique U-shape.

Given the broad elevation differences within Taroko National Park, there are a variety of distinct **ecosystems**, harbouring an abundance of plant and animal species. One third of the vascular plants endemic to Taiwan can be found within the park, while half of the island's native mammal species and ninety percent of its native bird species also are present here. In the mid- to high-elevation regions there are plenty of **Formosan Wild Boar**, though they tend to be difficult to spot, and sightings of the **Formosan Reeve's Muntjac** – a diminutive species of deer – are much more common. Those sticking to lower-elevation areas are more likely to encounter excitable gangs of the **Formosan Macaque**, commonly known as the Formosan rock monkey.

Taroko National Park	太魯閣國家公園	*tàilǔgé guójiā gōngyuán*
Cingshuei Cliffs	清水斷崖	*qīngshuǐ duànyá*
Liwu River	立霧溪	*lìwù qī*
Taroko Gorge	太魯閣峽谷	*tàilǔgé xiágǔ*
Arrival, orientation and information		
Buluowan	布洛灣	*bùluò wān*
Dayuling	大禹嶺	*dàyǔ lǐng*
Taroko National Park Visitor Center	太魯閣國家公園遊客中心	*tàilǔgé guójiā gōngyuán yóukè zhōngxīn*
Taroko Handicrafts Exhibition Room	太魯閣手工藝展覽室	*tàilǔgé shǒugōngyì zhǎnlǎnshì*
Tiansiang	天祥	*tiānxiáng*
Siangde Temple	祥德寺	*xiángdé sì*
Accommodation		
Catholic Inn	天祥天主堂來賓宿舍	*tiānxiáng tiānzhǔtáng láibīn sùshě*
Grand Formosa Taroko	天祥晶華假酒店	*tiānxiáng jīnghuá dùjià jiǔdiàn*
Heliou Campsite	合流營地	*héliú yíngdì*
Lyushuei Campsite	綠水營地	*lùshuǐ yíngdì*
Tiansiang Youth Activity Center	天祥青年活動中心	*tiānxiáng qīngnián húodòng zhōngxīn*
Hiking trails		
Baiyang Waterfall Trail	白楊瀑布步道	*báiyáng pùbù bùdào*
Bamboo Village Trail	竹村步道	*zhúcūn bùdào*
Changchun Shrine Trail	長春祠步道	*chāngchūn cí bùdào*
Huitouwan Trailhead	迴頭灣登山口	*húitóuwān dēng shānkǒu*
Huoran Pavilion Trail	豁然亭步道	*huōrán tíng bùdào*
Lotus Pond Trail	蓮花池步道	*liánhuā chí bùdào*
Lyushuei-Heliou Trail	綠水合流步道	*lshuǐ héliú bùdào*
Shakadang Trail	砂卡礑步道	*shākǎdāng bùdào*
Tunnel of Nine Turns Trail	九曲洞步道	*jiǔqū dòng bùdào*
Wenshan Hot Springs Trail	文山溫泉步道	*wénshān wēnquán bùdào*

Cross-Island Highway – Taroko National Park can be reached from several directions, making it one of Taiwan's most accessible wilderness areas. While it can easily be entered – and even traversed – by **public buses**, to cross the entire park you'll need to plan your onward route carefully to ensure you make your connections. For maximum flexibility, **renting a car** – or a scooter for the hardy – would be ideal, allowing you to see much more of the park while stopping at the myriad picturesque spots along the way. Though those with their own transport often make a day-trip of driving through the gorge itself, most foreign travellers – especially those relying on public buses – spend at least one or two nights in Tiansiang, taking time to enjoy some of the park's many trails. Those wishing to truly explore the area – including its remote west – could easily spend several days here.

From the east

Most visitors start from **Hualien** (see p.385), where there is ample accommodation, car and scooter rentals, taxis and regular **public bus** service through the park's **main entrance** along coastal Highway 9. While Hualien is certainly the most convenient transport hub, if you're coming by train along the **Eastern Line** and don't want to transit here, it's possible to alight at the town of **Sincheng**, about 5km from the park's main entrance. But though Sincheng is closer to the park than Hualien, it's lacking in tourist infrastructure and if you arrive late you might have trouble sourcing transport into the park until the next day. If you can get to Sincheng before early afternoon, however, you should be able to catch one of the buses headed into the park from Hualien – most stop here en route to the park headquarters and the main tourist centre of Tiansiang (see p.401).

From the west

It's also possible to enter the park from its **western boundary** via roads heading from both the north and west, and these invariably make for a dramatic arrival. Buses run daily along **Highway 7** from the northeast coast city of **Yilan** to Wuling Farm (see p.219) and **Lishan** (see p.226), where the cross-park minibus starts its return journey all the way to Hualien train station. Departure times heading east are: Lishan (3pm), Dayuling (4pm), Tiansiang (6.25pm) and Sincheng (7.30pm).

Without question the most exhilarating way to get to Taroko is to travel from the west coast along one of the **central cross-island routes**, although one section is not serviced by public buses so you'll need to have your own car or hitch. Starting from **Taichung**, there are regular buses to **Puli** (see p.269), from where buses leave hourly to **Wushe** (45min; NT$67). However, there are no buses on the stretch from Wushe to **Dayuling** (the first point inside the park where the bus coming from Lishan regularly stops), but you can hire a taxi in Wushe for about NT$3000, and it's fairly easy to hitch here as well. It is well worth the effort: this section, which bypasses beautiful **Hehuanshan**, is Taiwan's most mind-blowing road, and on clear days it offers the most impressive mountain scenery that can be seen in the country from a vehicle.

Information

The **Taroko National Park Headquarters and visitor center** (8.30am–4.45pm, closed second Mon of each month and Lunar New Year's Eve; ⊤03/8621100, ⓦwww.taroko.gov.tw) is located just inside the main entrance, and most public buses will let you off on the road just below it (a walk of about 100m). If you're planning to spend some time in the park, it's well worth stopping here to gather free **maps** and brochures, as well as to find out about the latest **trail conditions**: though the park's trails are well maintained, heavy seasonal rains and the resulting landslips result in occasional closures, so it's important to ensure they are safe before setting out. There is always at least one **English-speaking interpreter** on duty who can brief you on trail conditions, bus schedules and even help you plan your route. In the centre is a café and **souvenir shop** where you can buy English books on the park.

Hiking from park entrance to Tiansiang

There are some nice **hikes** that start near the visitor centre, and some people who get here early enough walk the entire 18km of Highway 8 between the park entrance and the main tourist village of Tiansiang. However, the road through the gorge is winding and narrow, with several pitch-black **tunnels**, and walking can be dangerous in places, especially on weekends and public holidays, when giant tour buses churn the route at blistering speeds. Rather than walking solely on the road, it's preferable to hike along the **pedestrian**

paths that skirt Highway 8 until they finish and then wait for a taxi or hitch a ride to the next roadside trail. As you'll inevitably have to walk through at least some of the tunnels, it's important to carry a torch.

Park transport

From Tiansiang, there are several daily buses back to Hualien, as well as one daily **westbound minibus** that plies along Highway 8 through the park's highlands before heading north to **Lishan** (2hr 45min; NT$236) via the roadside village of **Dayuling**. The minibus leaves daily from the Hualien train station at 9.30am, the park headquarters at 10.30am and Tiansiang at 11.15am, and the driver will let you off at the trailheads for the Wenshan Hot Springs (NT$20), the Bamboo Village (NT$23) and the Huoran Pavilion (NT$27), making it a great shuttle option for hikers.

△ Taroko National Park

Tiansiang

The tiny tourist village of **TIANSIANG** somehow manages to accommodate most of the overnight visitors to Taroko National Park while remaining remarkably free of tacky overdevelopment. With only three hotels and an array of open-air buffet-style restaurants, the village retains a strong rural flavour, and on weekdays it can feel decidedly relaxed. There is little to do in Tiansiang itself, but it makes a convenient base for exploring the park's main trails, and many visitors find themselves spending several nights here. Everything is within easy walking distance from the **bus stop**, with the clutch of overpriced Chinese **buffet restaurants** located next door – at these you simply fill your plate with what you want and the staff will weigh it, charge you and then stick your food in the microwave before serving it.

Directly across the main road from the bus stop is the **Tiansiang visitor center** (9am–4pm, closed second and fourth Mon of each month), where you can pick up free maps and brochures on park trails, but it's seldom staffed with English speakers. Next door to the visitor centre is the town **post office** (Mon–Fri 8.30am–noon & 1–3.30pm), which sells postcards and can handle international parcels. Near Tiansiang's eastern entrance, on a hillside reached by a suspension bridge, is the **Siangde Temple**, a Buddhist place of worship run by a handful of resident monks. Near the temple is a giant whitewashed statue of Guanyin (see Contexts p.528) and a graceful **pagoda** which visitors can climb for fine views of the surrounding valley.

Practicalities

Tiansiang's three **hotels** tend to fill up quickly on weekends, public holidays or during the summer high season, so if you visit during one of these times, be sure to book a room in advance. The *Catholic Inn* at no. 33 (☎03/8691122;

❷) is Taroko's only budget option, with doubles – some with balconies overlooking the valley – and no-frills dorm beds for NT$250 per head. At the opposite end of the price scale is the *Grand Formosa Taroko* at no. 18 (Ⓦwww .grandformosa-taroko.com.tw; ℡03/8691155; ❼), the park's only five-star hotel, which has large rooms with marble bathrooms, a bar, a café and two pricey restaurants – one with average Western fare, the other serving tasty Chinese standards. But the best all-around accommodation is the 🏕 *Tiansiang Youth Activity Center* at no. 30 (℡03/8691111; ❸), on the hill at the village's western edge, just past the *Catholic Inn*. The centre has a wide range of rooms and prices, starting from spotless dorms at competitive rates to tasteful Japanese-style doubles and honeymoon suites with balconies looking out on the river. Room rates include a Chinese-style **breakfast**, and the restaurant also serves lunch and dinner. Inside the hotel complex is a souvenir shop, a snack bar serving decent coffee and a very handy coin-operated **washing machine** and dryer.

Camping around Tiansiang

There are no **campsites** in Tiansiang itself, but just a few kilometres to the east are two places where you can camp for free, provided you have your own tent. Located in Heliou and Lyushuei, at either end of the 2km Lyushuei-Heliou Trail (see p.403), both have calming views of the Liwu River. The one at **Heliou** is older and slightly better equipped, with clean **showers**, toilets and elevated wooden platforms for tents. The site at **Lyushuei** is a bit more primitive, but its shielded location is serene and tranquil. From here it's only about 3km to Tiansiang. Buses from Hualien can drop you off at either campsite, but you must let the driver know in advance.

Hiking trails

There are at least a half-dozen good **hikes** in the Taroko Gorge and the vicinity of Tiansiang, making many of the park's natural attractions very accessible to the average visitor. Several of these hikes are short and relatively flat, providing great opportunities for stretching the legs and taking in some of the gorge's most scenic spots. A few of them are more challenging, with steep hill sections and trailside drop-offs, and these are sometimes closed due to landslip damage, so ask for updated conditions at the visitor centre near the main entrance before you get started.

Shakadang Trail

One of Taroko's easiest walks, the mostly flat **Shakadang Trail** hugs the bank of the delightful Shakadang River, filled with translucent pools and time-worn boulders. To get to the **trailhead**, walk west from the park headquarters, through the tunnel with a pedestrian walkway. After about 1km, just after you exit the tunnel, there is a set of stairs on the right; descend these to the river's edge and you're at the start of the trail. The path sticks to the river for 4.4km, passing a small Truku village that has been all but abandoned. At the 4.4km point, the trail climbs to another former Truku village; from here, it's about 1.5km to the trailhead for the **Dali-Datong Trail**, which leads to a pair of far-flung Truku villages. However, the trail climbs steeply, with many switchbacks, and a mountain permit is required to venture beyond the 4.4km marker. Allow about three hours for the return hike.

Changchun (Eternal Spring) Shrine Trail

Another easy walk, the scenic **Changchun Shrine Trail** is only 1.4km from one end to the other, and can be started from the car park that overlooks the shrine itself or from the main road about 2km from the park headquarters. Coming from the headquarters, the trail starts under an arch to the left of the main road, and if you go in this direction there is slightly less climbing involved. After crossing a suspension bridge there is a short climb before you reach an aging **Chan (Zen) Buddhist monastery** and a nearby pagoda with commanding views of the river. From here, the trail skirts the edge of a cliff before descending a steep flight of stone steps to the rear of the dignified **Changchun Shrine**, which straddles an elegant cascade, a picture of perfect harmony between man and nature – perhaps fitting for a memorial dedicated to the 450-odd workers who perished while battling against nature to build the Central Cross-Island Highway. The shrine is one of the park's most recognizable landmarks, and, as such, is a requisite stop for all tour buses, whose passengers pile out throughout the day to make the short walk from the car park for a perfunctory photo shoot. If you start your hike from the car park, you'll have to huff up the steep steps behind the shrine to carry on.

Tunnel of Nine Turns Trail

This paved pathway is the park's **premier hike**, following a stretch of the original road through the narrowest part of the gorge, providing unparalleled vantage points on the river, the smoothly **sculpted marble** with its ornate patterns and the precipitous canyon walls. The wide 1.9-kilometre path has been cut into the cliff and much of it is sheltered by a cave-like overhang, making it walkable even on rainy days. Heading west, the path starts on the left-hand side of the main road, about 14km from the park headquarters, and can easily be walked in a half-hour. **Buses** from Hualien will let you off here if you tell the driver in advance, but once you reach the other end of the trail you'll still have to find onward transport; **taxis** congregate here at times, but in their absence you'll either have to walk, hitch or wait for the next public bus that comes through the gorge. If you're coming from the Changchun Shrine it's about 5km westbound along the main road to the trailhead.

Lyushuei–Heliou Trail

This mostly flat **earthen trail** runs for 2km above a cliff overlooking the highway, offering clear views of the Liwu River. Closer to Lyushuei, the path has been cut straight into the cliff but is shielded by a guard rail so the way is relatively safe. Just before arriving in Lyushuei the trail winds through the remnants of an old **camphor forest**, with some aging specimens of this valuable tree visible from the path. The walk takes just over half an hour and can be started from either Heliou or Lyushuei, both of which have free public **campsites** (see p.402). In Lyushuei, which is only 3km from Tiansiang, there is a **snack bar** where you can buy drinks. The trailhead at Heliou is only a couple of kilometres from the western end of the Tunnel of Nine Turns Trail, so if it's early enough in the day you could walk along the main road to get here; alternatively, a taxi can get you here in a few minutes.

Huoran Pavilion Trail

The 1.9-kilometre walk from Tiansiang to the **Huoran Pavilion** is very steep, with an elevation gain of 450m. The trail begins almost directly across from the entrance to the *Tiansiang Youth Activity Center* and almost immediately begins to climb, with the loose dirt path making it a fairly strenuous undertaking for the average visitor. Towards the top, the trail follows the spine of a hill, with steep drops on both sides protected by rope netting. If the weather is clear, the **views** of the valley from here are superb. Allow yourself at least an hour for the climb. If you'd prefer to descend this trail instead, you can catch the 11.15am **minibus** (NT$27) from Tiansiang and ask the driver to let you off at the Huoran Pavilion, which marks the finish at the high end of the trail. However, the descent can be hard on the knees so it's not necessarily an easy way out. If you choose to climb to the pavilion and want to return via the main road, note that it's an 11km walk that goes through several long, dark tunnels.

Baiyang Waterfall Trail

This beautiful walk leads to the **Baiyang Waterfall**, which turns into a raging torrent during periods of heavy rain and can be quite a sight to behold. To get to the trailhead, walk westbound along the main road from Tiansiang for 860m until you see a long **tunnel** on the left; walk through this 380-metre tunnel and carry on for another 2km, through a few shorter tunnels, to reach the waterfall. Cross the bridge leading to the **wooden platform** for direct views of the falls. Beyond here the trail used to lead to a pair of "water curtain tunnels" – so-named because water drips from their roofs – but they were damaged during the 921 earthquake and park officials do not plan to reopen them. The hike from Tiansiang to the falls and back takes about two hours.

Wenshan Hot Springs Trail

These unique **hot springs**, situated in the middle of the Dasha River and fenced in by rings of marble, are accessible via a short trail that descends from the main highway about 3km west of Tiansiang. The path begins just before the entrance to the first major tunnel coming from Tiansiang, on the right-hand side. Steps lead down to the river, where you must cross a **suspension bridge** and walk along the cliff until you reach the springs. There is a changing room nearby. If you don't wish to walk the road to the trailhead, you can take the 11.15am **minibus** (NT$20) from Tiansiang and ask the driver to let you off at the entrance.

Bamboo Village and Lotus Pond Trails

These secluded walks are a little harder to reach than the others in the area, but they are certainly worth the effort. The **Huitouwan trailhead**, which marks the beginning of both paths, is about 5km west of Tiansiang by the main road and is situated along a hairpin bend behind the bus stop. To walk here along the main highway, you'll have to pass through a handful of dark tunnels, so a torch is essential. To cut down some of the distance, you can catch the 11.15am **minibus** (NT$23) from Tiansiang and ask the driver to let you off at Huitouwan. The trail is exciting from the onset, as the beginning has been cut into the rocky face of a towering cliff overlooking the Dasha River, and there are sheer drop-offs all along this stretch. Carry on for about 2km, crossing one suspension bridge, until you reach a **second suspension bridge** called Jhumei: this is the point where the trail forks into two paths, the riverside one leading to the Plum Garden and Bamboo Village and the one across the bridge climbing steeply to the Lotus Pond. Provided you get an early start and are in good physical shape, it's possible to make the return journey to the Bamboo Village and climb up to Lotus Pond on your return in one day.

From the Jhumei Bridge, it's about 8km along the riverside trail to the **Bamboo Village**, a Truku settlement consisting mostly of bamboo houses. There is little to see in the village, but the section of river underneath the lofty suspension bridge you must cross just before you get there is one of the park's finest **swimming spots**; to get to the riverbank, take one of the narrow paths on the right-hand side of the trail shortly after you cross the bridge. About halfway between the Jhumei Bridge and the Bamboo Village is **Plum Garden**, another tiny Truku village. From the Huitouwan trailhead to the Bamboo Village is almost 10km and takes at least two hours in each direction.

If you've time and energy for the climb up to **Lotus Pond**, cross the Jhumei Bridge and start the terribly steep ascent up the dirt path, where the earth has been secured by wooden planks embedded into the ground. Beyond this stage, the trail follows a winding, grassy road up the hill for several hundred metres before flattening out for the final stretch to the Lotus Pond, which is covered in green algae – the walk is mainly notable for the **lush forests** along the way. From the Jhumei Bridge turnoff it's about 4km to the pond, so allow ample time to complete the return journey and still walk the 5km stretch of road back into Tiansiang before it gets dark.

Buluowan

Once a cradle of Truku civilization, **BULUOWAN** is now a tiny tourist village devoted primarily to the preservation – and sale – of the tribe's **traditional arts**. The small community of Truku here makes a living producing handmade crafts, which are on display in the **Taroko Handicrafts Exhibition Room** (9am–4.30pm, closed first and third Mon of each month). This is a good place to see women giving demonstrations of traditional loom weaving, while the men are engaged mostly in bamboo and rattan basket weaving. Buluowan, which means "echo" in the Truku tongue, has in recent years become a symbol of the revitalization of their culture. The village is about 2km off the main highway and is accessed via a steep, curvy road, the turnoff for which is some 9km from the park entrance. Most **buses** that run between Hualien and Tiansiang make side-trips here on their ways in and out of the gorge.

Cingshuei Cliffs

The staggering **Cingshuei Cliffs**, located along a precarious stretch of the **Suao-Hualien Highway** just inside the park's northeastern boundary, are among the east coast's most visually compelling attractions. Spanning a 21-kilometre section of the Suhua coastline between the hamlets of Chongde and Heren, these sheer cliffs plunge straight into the turquoise waters of the Pacific Ocean – in places from heights of almost 1000m – forming one of Asia's most dramatic coastal scenes. Once known as one of Taiwan's "eight wonders", the cliffs have been admired since the Qing dynasty, when the first road was hacked into them – a 174-kilometre track between Suao and Hualien that became known as the **Old Suhua Road**. Today, this road is heavily trafficked, with endless convoys of trucks spewing exhaust into the air and making it a perilous journey for cyclists, motorcyclists and motorists alike. The series of long **tunnels** carved straight through the cliffs is an engineering marvel, with each tunnel opening up to another invigorating view of more bluffs and sea.

Unfortunately for visitors, there are no public buses between Suao and Hualien, so the only way to see the cliffs is to hire your own transport. Cars and scooters can easily be rented in Hualien (see p.389), from where it's about an hour's drive to the cliffs. If you drive yourself, especially if you go by **scooter**, it's wise to leave early in the morning so you can make the return trip before the traffic starts to pick up around 9am. Just past the 176km marker is a car park with some of the best views of the cliffs surrounding the Chongde Delta.

Cilai Ridge

The jagged saw-tooth protrusion known as the **Cilai Ridge**, not far from the park's southwestern entrance near **Hehuanshan**, is one of Taroko's most striking features and represents one of Taiwan's most challenging climbs. The narrow,

Cilai Ridge

Cilaishan	奇萊山	*qílái shān*
Cilai Cabin	奇萊山屋	*qílái shānwū*
Chenggong Cabin	成功山屋	*chénggōng shānwū*
Hehuanshan	合歡山	*héhuān shān*
Hehuan Lodge	合歡山莊	*héhuān shānzhuāng*
Heishueitang Cabin	黑水塘山屋	*hēishuǐtáng shānwū*

craggy ridge connects several outstanding peaks, with steep drops on both sides, making it an exhilarating and sometimes dangerous climb. While the **trail** that runs over the ridgeline is well marked and in good condition, with no serious technical sections requiring the use of ropes, the main danger is in the fact that it is so exposed to the elements and subject to abrupt weather changes. Over the years, several climbers have fallen to their deaths after losing their footing in thick mists, while typhoon-force **winds** from the nearby Pacific have actually blown a few people off the ridge. In light of these risks, park officials are conservative in issuing the **Class A mountain permits** required to legally climb in this area (see p.407).

The main **trailhead** is just inside the park's southwest entrance, near the **Hehuan Lodge**, a full-service mountaineering station with rooms and food. However, the lodge is very expensive and the food is mediocre, and most climbers prefer just to pitch their tents nearby the night before they start their hikes. There are several cabins along the trail, but most groups try to make it to the **Cilai Cabin** for the first night so they can get an early start on the ridge and **Cilai North Peak**, the highest at 3607m. After negotiating the ridge, the majority of climbers return to Cilai Cabin for a second night before descending to the road on the third day. The safest time to climb here is in late **autumn**, when the summer typhoons have ceased and the weather is drier and less windy.

Nanhushan

Tucked away in Taroko's remote northwest corner is **Nanhushan**, commonly called "**Nanhu Dashan**", Taiwan's fifth-tallest peak at 3742m and the favourite of most Taiwanese climbers. Despite its reputation, it's very seldom scaled due to its isolation and inherent technical difficulties, although seasoned climbers are unlikely to find it overly challenging. Like the Cilai Ridge, the biggest obstacle here is the **harsh weather**, as Nanhushan is pelted with strong winds, rain or snow for an average of about two hundred days a year, making some key sections of the trail arduous. For hardy climbers, this is all part of the mountain's appeal and summiting Nanhushan is a rite of passage for Taiwan's

Nanhushan

Nanhushan	南湖山	*nánhú shān*
Jhongyangjian River Cabin	中央尖溪山屋	*zhōngyāng jiān qī shānwū*
Nanhu Cabin	南湖山屋	*nánhú shānwū*
Nanhu River Cabin	南湖溪山屋	*nánhú qī shānwū*
Shenmajhen Cabin	審馬陣山屋	*shěnmǎzhèn shānwū*
Yunleng Cabin	雲稜山屋	*yúnléng shānwū*

committed mountaineers. Another reason why the mountain is so loved is for its classic beauty, with its triangular summit covered in deep snow for most of each winter. Indeed, winter is a popular time to climb Nanhushan, although this is only for experienced climbers, and, at the bare minimum, **crampons** are essential for the higher regions.

Park officials are extremely cautious about issuing the mandatory Class A **mountain permit** for Nanhushan, as given its remoteness it is very difficult and expensive for them to perform rescue operations (see above). Occasionally, domestic climbing clubs make trips up Nanhushan, and the best way to find out about these is to ask at some of the **outdoor shops** on Zhongshan North Road in Taipei. The mountain can be reached from the north and south, but the **southern route** – which begins at the Bamboo Village Trail (see p.404) – is often closed due to landslips caused by heavy rains. The more common route – and the one that starts closer to the peaks – is from the **north**, via a trailhead just off Highway 7 between Yilan and Lishan.

Hualien to Taitung: two routes

Just to the south of Hualien is a crossroads, giving a choice of **two routes** south to **Taitung** running either side of the Coastal Mountain Range. **Highway 11** hugs the coast, passing through prime aboriginal territory, pockmarked with idyllic fishing villages, rice paddies and herds of water buffalo cooling off in roadside pools; while **Highway 9** turns inland through the **East Rift Valley**, a volcanic zone of hot springs, forest reserves and the Siouguluan River, Taiwan's most popular **white-water rafting spot**.

Highway 11: the coast road

Though the countryside along coastal **HIGHWAY 11** remains one of Taiwan's most laid-back places, it is becoming increasingly popular as word of

East Coast	東部海岸	*dōngbù hǎi àn*
East Coast National Scenic Area	東部海岸國家風景區	*dōngbù hǎi àn guójiā fēngjǐngqū*
Ami Folk Center	阿美文化村	*āměi wénhuà cūn*
Baci Observation Platform	芭崎瞭望台	*bāqí liàowàng tái*
Basiandong	八仙洞	*bāxiān dòng*
Chenggong	成功	*chénggōng*
Dagangkou	大港口	*dà gǎngkǒu*
Donghe	東河	*dōnghé*
Dulan	都蘭	*dūlán*
Jici Beach	磯崎灣	*jīqí wān*
Jinzun Beach	金樽灣	*jīnzūn wān*
Nioushan Beach	牛山灣	*niúshān wān*
Rueigang Highway	瑞港公路	*ruìgǎng gōnglù*
Sansiantai	三仙台	*sānxiān tái*
Shanyuan Beach	杉原灣	*shānyuán wān*
Shihtiping	石梯坪	*shítīpíng*
Siaoyeliou	小野柳	*xiǎo yěliǔ*
Sincheng	新城	*xīnchéng*
Tropic of Cancer Marker	北迴歸線標誌	*běihuí guīxiàn biāozhì*

its beauty spreads. Almost the entire road is part of the **East Coast National Scenic Area**, which continues to tastefully develop the coastline with viewing platforms, visitor centres and well-designed campsites. There are a few buses that ply this route daily, starting from both Hualien and Taitung, and if you have plenty of time they can be a relaxing way to check out the coast and meet many of the indigenous inhabitants who rely in part on this form of transport. However, if your time is limited, it's preferable to rent private transport in Hualien. If you're visiting in late summer and hope to witness some of the many aboriginal **festivals** held each July and August, private transport is essential – indeed, one of the joys of coming at this time is whipping from one festival to another on a **scooter**, soaking up the boundless seascapes along the way.

Nioushan and Jici beaches

Within 40km south of Hualien along Highway 11 are two of the area's finest beaches. The first, about 30km from Hualien, is **Nioushan (Cow Mountain) Beach**, a secluded stretch of sand that dead-ends into the rounded Cow Mountain. Unlike some of the other east coast beaches, this one remains undeveloped and is an ideal spot to relax and enjoy some solitude. At times the swell is suitable for **surfing**, although experienced surfers are only likely to be challenged here during a tropical storm. To get here, you'll need your own transport – given its proximity to Hualien, it makes for an excellent day-trip by scooter or car.

About 10km further south, enveloping a bay surrounded by leafy hills, is the three-kilometre-long **Jici Beach**, which is considerably more developed than Nioushan and can get crowded in summer, when there are lifeguards on duty. The beach, near the 37km marker of Highway 11, is equipped with toilets, shower facilities and elevated wooden platforms for **camping**, although you're advised to bring your own tent. The water in the sheltered bay is considerably calmer than that of many other east coast beaches, making it a favoured **swimming** spot. Another interesting feature of this beach is the changing colour of the sand: during the lower tides of summer, it's mostly a dusty golden colour, while the higher tides of winter churn up dark stones and sand from the seabed, giving the beach a dark grey hue. About halfway between the Nioushan and Jici beaches, near the 32km marker, is the **Baci Observation Platform**, which commands a panoramic view of the coast to the south.

Shihtiping and Dagangkou

Another 30km or so to the south, near the 66km marker, is **Shihtiping** (Stone Stair Terrace), a one-kilometre-long stretch of volcanic rock that has been eroded into terraces and other curious formations. The surrounding area is popular for **fishing**, and the **Shihtiping visitor center** (9am–5pm) has exhibits on local marine life and other natural resources. A circular walkway allows visitors to inspect the rock formations more closely, and there are raised wooden platforms for camping – again, bringing your own tent is advisable.

Just south of Shihtiping is **Dagangkou**, which lies at the enormous estuary of the Siouguluan River and is the termination point for the white-water rafting trips that are conducted almost daily during the summer. Here, County Highway 64, more commonly known as the **Rueigang Highway**, cuts across the coastal mountains, following the Siouguluan River for 22.5km until Rueisuei, the starting point for white-water rafting trips (see p.414). This scenic road is a worthwhile endeavour in itself, offering frequent glimpses into the gorge below, but there is no bus service so it's only possible by private transport – it makes for an excellent scooter or bicycle ride. Carrying on down the coast, just south of Dagangkou, a towering **white monolith** shaped like a sundial marks the point where the road crosses the **Tropic of Cancer** – once past this you are squarely in the tropics.

Basiandong

A few kilometres further south, near the 78km signpost, are the **Basiandong** (Caves of the Eight Immortals), a collection of more than a dozen **grottoes** carved into the seaside cliffs and one of Taiwan's most important archeological sites. Formed when waves eroded indentations in the volcanic rock during a period of tectonic uplift, the caves now stand as high as 150 metres above sea level. In 1968, a number of **stone-age artefacts** such as tools made of animal bones and stone were found in some of the grottoes, giving evidence of a prehistoric culture that was named "**Changpin Culture**" due to its location in present-day Changbin Township. Carbon-14 tests on the artefacts dated some as far back as thirty thousand years ago, placing the culture in the Paleolithic

△ Caves of the Eight Immortals

period and making the hunter-gatherers the earliest people known to have inhabited Taiwan.

Today, most of the caves have been turned into Buddhist and Taoist shrines and filled with scores of religious deities. Wooden walkways with steps leading up the cliff face link the caves, and from the highest ones there are outstanding sea views. At the entrance (free) is the **Basiandong visitor center** (9am–5pm), which has some basic information in English about the caves and the artefacts they have yielded. About 50m south of the entrance is a clutch of souvenir vendors and **snack stalls**, where you can buy drinks and basic meals such as fried rice and noodles. All of the **buses** that travel between Hualien and Taitung stop just outside the car park (NT$30), and from here it's possible to catch any of these in either direction. If you're headed on to Taitung, you also can catch one of the local commuter buses that start just north of here and terminate in Taitung (2hr 30min; NT$253). Exact change is required for these buses, which stop here hourly in the summer.

Sansiantai

South of Basiandong, the road crosses a flat plain, passing by several unusual rock formations along the coastline. By far the most famous of these is the **Sansiantai** (Three Immortals Platform), a series of small islets crowned with three rocky outcroppings named after a trio of legendary Taoist sages who, according to local lore, once visited the area. The turnoff, near the 112km marker, leads to a car park (NT$30) and a lengthy footbridge with several arches spanning the shallow water that separates the islets from the mainland. Though the bridge tends to be packed with Taiwanese tour groups on weekends and during the summer, it's worth crossing it to reach the **boardwalks** that skirt the islets, thereby leaving the crowds behind. These walkways circle around both sides of the first outcropping before ending partway around the second. If you walk around the right side of this one along the stony shore, past some wooden stairs leading up to tiny caves, you'll come to another set of stairs that climb to a small **lighthouse** – from here there are superb views of the third "immortal", framed by the blue sea beyond. Much of this area is surrounded by coral reef, sheltering an amazing array of tropical fish and making for some of the east coast's best **snorkelling**. However, there is nowhere nearby to rent equipment, so you'll need to bring your own, and it's a good idea to stay close to the coastline. Beside the car park is the **Sansiantai visitor center** (9am–5pm), which has English-language exhibits on local geology and marine life. Several food, drink and souvenir stalls are nearby.

Chenggong and around

Just south of Sansiantai, near the 117km signpost, is the sizeable fishing town of **CHENGGONG**, which boasts one of Taiwan's liveliest **fish markets** and some of the freshest seafood anywhere on the island. Inhabited by a mix of Chinese, Ami and members of the officially unrecognized *pingpu* Siraya tribe (see Contexts p.519), Chenggong has a population of about twenty thousand, making it the largest coastal settlement between Hualien and Taitung. Every afternoon at about 3pm, the local fishermen return to the town's Singang Fishing Port to unload and sell the day's catch. These entertaining **auctions**, usually in full swing before 4pm, are a highlight of a visit here, with swarthy, Betel-nut-chewing auctioneers rattling off prices in a maelstrom of Mandarin and Taiwanese, while weather-beaten fishmongers hack up the catch. One of the best times to visit is during the **swordfish** season in October, when scores of the pointy-proboscis fish are put on auction each day. Next to the fishing dock is a small market with a variety of local fish specialties, the most famous of which are the delicious dried fish slices. Just up the hill behind the market is the **National Taitung Oceanarium** (Sun–Fri 8.30am–6pm & Sat 8.30am–8.30pm; NT$200), which has aquariums filled with several rare species of mullet, shark and skate. Highway 11 runs through the middle of Chenggong, and alongside the road are several small **restaurants** that serve up some of Taiwan's tastiest seafood for lunch and dinner.

About 12km south of Chenggong, near the Ami village of **Duli**, is the East Coast National Scenic Area headquarters, which has a **visitor centre** (9am–5pm) with a broad overview of the east coast's main attractions. The headquarters, near the 129km marker, include the sprawling **Ami Folk Center** (9am–5pm, closed Tues), an open-air museum with reconstructions of historic Ami buildings. The centre, managed by Taitung County's Aborigine Social Welfare Commission, also has a variety of traditional Ami handicrafts for sale.

Shanyuan Beach and Siaoyeliou

Just north of Taitung, near the 158km signpost, is the delightful **Shanyuan Beach**, one of the east coast's most picturesque and also one of the safest for swimming. You must pay NT$60 to enter the main section of golden-sand beach, but this includes use of toilets and shower facilities. **Camping** is possible here, and in summer tents can be rented for NT$400. **Water-sports** are popular here, and you can hire windsurfing equipment, inflatable rafts, sailboats and jet skis – on weekends and hot summer days the water can get crowded, and jet-skis pose a significant hazard to swimmers and windsurfers. The swell here is subject to closeouts, and surfers would do better to explore some of the secluded spots further north (see box p.412). There also is some intact coral reef at the north and south ends of the beach that is well suited for **snorkelling**. On a grassy hill overlooking the beach's southern end is the superb *Zorba Garden Italian Restaurant* at 129 Fusan Rd (11.30am–11.30pm; closed Wed; ☎089/281276), which specializes in zesty Italian fare, including piping-hot bread with olive spread. Mains, such as delicious lasagna and lamb chops, start from about NT$300, and there is also the east coast's best selection of European wines. The restaurant has a shady patio and a garden with one of Taiwan's most seductive sea views.

About 6km south of Shanyuan, and marking the southernmost point of the East Coast National Scenic Area, is **Siaoyeliou** ("Little Yeliou"), a smaller version of the fanciful geological marvel Yeliou (see p.169) in northern Taiwan. Known for its surreal coastal **rock formations**, composed of a rare mix of sandstone and shale that is easily eroded by wind and waves, this is one's of the area's most scenic spots and also offers a very attractive accommodation alternative to the hotels of Taitung – one of Taiwan's most charming **campsites**, perched on a grassy plateau overlooking the sea. With elevated wooden platforms (Sun–Thurs NT$280; Fri–Sat NT$350), attached barbecue pits and toilet and shower facilities, this breezy campsite is vastly underused, and you might have it all to yourself even in the height of summer. At the time of writing, it was being operated by the scenic area administration, and campers were required to register and pay at the **Siaoyeliou visitor center** (9am–5pm), next to the car park. However, until the scenic area finds a private vendor to run the campsite, you'll need to have your own tent. Behind the visitor centre are walkways leading to the rock formations, which have been given names such as "tofu rock," "mushroom rock" and "honeycomb rock". By the car park is a shelter that houses souvenir stalls and snack shops selling instant noodles and drinks.

Taitung's secret surf spots

Though the better-known beach breaks along the northeast coast and around Taiwan's southern tip get most of the hype – and most of the crowds – the island's strongest, most consistent **surf** can be found along the fifty-kilometre stretch of coastline north of Taitung. Most of the best spots are shielded from the road by small villages, keeping them the closely guarded secrets of a hardcore handful of expat surfers living in Taitung. As there are absolutely no surf shops in the area, you'll need to bring your own board and plenty of wax, and it's best to arrange your own transport so you can explore the coast at your leisure.

The biggest waves are generally near reef or rocky areas which require considerable experience to surf safely, but there are also some smaller beach breaks that are ideal for beginners. The closest to Taitung, and the easiest for novice surfers, is near the Ami village of **Dulan**, near the coastal highway's 146km marker. To get to this sandy beach, which has small but consistent waves, cross the bridge just north of Dulan and turn east on the third lane to your right. A couple of kilometres further up the road, just north of the village of **Singcheng**, are the area's top summer breaks. Just past the village, when the coastal road starts to veer eastwards, you'll see a statue of a giant custard apple alongside the road – the first right after this leads to the shore. At the northern end is reef, while the southern end is mostly sandy. Another kilometre or so to the north, near the **141.5km marker**, there is a narrow lane leading down to the shore, where you'll find two howling breaks: one left and one right (be prepared to kick out early because there are loads of rocks close to shore); if you reach Longchang village then you've gone too far north. For some pure beach action, head north another 5km until you reach the popular **Jinzun Beach**, 3km of fine dark sand with some usually rideable waves close to shore. Be careful of paddling too far out, as the seabed drops off sharply here and there is a formidable riptide. Finally, if you're an experienced surfer and are here in winter or just before a typhoon, you won't want to miss the **Donghe River mouth** – the turnoff is just north of Donghe village before you reach the Donghe Bridge. Though there are rocks on either side of the estuary, if you have some groundswell from a tropical storm you should get some lovely river-mouth barrels.

Highway 9: the East Rift Valley

Heading southwest from Hualien, rural **HIGHWAY 9** cuts through the **East Rift Valley**, a haven of hot springs sandwiched between the Coastal Mountain Range and the eastern fringe of the Central Cordillera. Most of the valley falls within the **East Rift Valley National Scenic Area**, and English-language signs have been set up for many attractions. The valley's biggest claim to fame is **white-water rafting**, and its Siouguluan River attracts more rafters than any other river in Taiwan (see box p.414). Note that the valley also provides access to **Yushan National Park** and the **Southern Cross-Island Highway**.

The **train** from Hualien to Taitung passes through the valley, but many of the main sights aren't near train stations. Likewise, while both the Dingdong and Hualien **bus** companies have daily service through the valley, stopping at most towns, many of the sights are along side roads that are hard to get to by local buses. Given this, if you want to visit several places it's much more convenient to arrange private transport – or even a specialized tour – in Hualien (see p.389).

Rueisuei Hot Springs

About 4km northwest of the Rueisuei train station are the **Rueisuei Hot Springs**, thought to be the only ones in Taiwan that are carbonated. The

East Rift Valley	花東縱谷	*huādōng zònggǔ*
East Rift Valley National Scenic Area	花東縱谷國家風景區	*huādōng zònggǔ guójiā fēngjǐngqū*
Antong Hot Springs	安通溫泉區	*āntōng wēnquánqū*
Guanshan	關山	*guānshān*
Haiduan	海端	*hǎiduān*
Luye High Terrace	鹿野觀望台	*lùyě guānwàng tái*
Nanan Visitor Center	南安遊客中心	*nán'ān yóukè zhōngxīn*
Rueisuei	瑞穗	*ruìsuì*
Rueisuei Hot Springs	瑞穗溫泉區	*ruìsuì wēnquánqū*
Rueisuei Rafting Service Center	瑞穗泛舟服務中心	*ruìsuì fànzhōu fúwù zhōngxīn*
Saoba Megaliths	掃叭石柱	*sǎobā shízhù*
Siouguluan River	秀姑巒溪	*xiùgūluán qī*
Southern Cross-Island Highway	南橫公路	*nánhéng gōnglù*
Yanping	延平	*yánpíng*
Yuli	玉里	*yùlǐ*
Yushan National Park	玉山國家公園	*yùshān guójiā gōngyuán*
East Rift Valley: Accommodation		
Antong Hot Springs Hotel	安通溫泉大飯店	*āntōng wēnquán dàfàndiàn*
Hongye Hot Springs Hotel	紅葉溫泉大飯店	*hóngyè wēnquán dàfàndiàn*
Rueisuei Hot Springs Villa	瑞穗溫泉山莊	*ruìsuì wēnquán shānzhuāng*

iron-rich spring water has a yellow tint and an average temperature of 48°C; it's said to be effective in treating rheumatism and some skin rashes. Some Taiwanese also believe that if women bathe regularly in this type of water it will increase their chances of bearing a male child, hence the large number of newlyweds who come here to soak. In 1919 the Japanese developed the springs into a resort, with a hotel including public bathing areas; this hotel, now known as the *Rueisuei Hot Springs Villa* at 23 Hongye Village (☎03/8872170; ④), has added an open-air bathing pool and this, as well as the other public pools are open to non-guests, with the price based on the amount of time you want to bathe. To get here from the train station, take a taxi and tell the driver you're going to the "outer hot springs" (*wai wenquan*). About 2km further northwest is another Japanese-developed hot-springs resort, the *Hongye Hot Springs Hotel* (☎03/8872176; ③), which has clear, odourless alkaline water with an average temperature of 47°C. Here, the spring water is pumped into private bathhouses. The cost for non-guests to use the pools is NT$70 for thirty minutes. If you take a taxi, tell the driver you're going to the "inner hot springs" (*nei wenquan*).

Back on Highway 9, about 2km south of the Rueisuei train station, the **Saoba Megaliths** stand alongside the road. The pair of two-metre-high stone columns is thought by archeologists to be remnants of the Peinan civilization that thrived in the valley some five thousand years ago. According to local legend, however, they are actually the incarnations of incestuous twins who tried to escape the wrath of their tribe and were turned to stone. Nearby, a white monolith shaped like a sundial denotes the point where the valley road crosses the **Tropic of Cancer**: there is an identical marker alongside the coast road.

Rafting the Siouguluan

The **Siouguluan River** is Taiwan's premier white-water rafting spot, and for many a wet and wild trip down it is the highlight of their visit to the East Rift Valley. Running 104km from its source near Siouguluan Mountain to the Pacific estuary at Dagangkou, it's eastern Taiwan's longest river, and the main 24-kilometre rafting route can be an exciting run for amateurs after prolonged rains or a typhoon. But the best bit is definitely the scenery – the river cuts through a **deep gorge** in the coastal mountains and is surrounded by steep vertical cliffs in many places, with your raft providing an unparalleled perspective on the immensity of it all.

Depending on the water level, the trip usually takes three to four hours, including a lunch break at the Ami village of **Cimei**, and by the end you'll be soaking wet. Though the rafting season depends mostly on the level of rainfall, it generally runs from early April to late October. Most trips start at the town of **Rueisuei**, about halfway between Hualien and Taitung on Highway 9. All trains running through the East Rift Valley stop here. Though most travel agents in Hualien can arrange rafting trips, including return transport, equipment rental and lunch, for about NT$950 per person, they usually only charge about NT$750 if you have your own transport to and from Rueisuei. It's also possible to arrange trips in Rueisuei itself, and near the main start point at the Rueisuei Bridge is the **Rueisuei Rafting Service Center**, 215 Jhongshan Rd Sec 3 (April–Oct 8am–4.30pm; closed Nov–March), where there are several private rafting operators. However, most of them have branches or representation in Hualien (see p.389), and unless you're with a group of six or more people it can be time-consuming to arrange a trip here, as individual travellers might have to wait to join a Taiwanese group. If you take the train from Hualien to Rueisuei, it's complicated to get from the train station to the rafting service centre by bus, so you're better off taking a taxi for the four-kilometre ride. Both the Dingdong and Hualien bus companies that ply this route from Hualien make stops at Rueisuei, but you'll have to take a local bus to get from town to the rafting centre, and again it might be easier to take a taxi. It's possible to pitch a tent on the lawn outside the rafting centre.

Each June the river is the site of the annual International Siouguluan River Rafting Race, organized by the Tourism Bureau. But while this race was originally a truly international event, with competitive rafters flown in from around the world, the costs became too high and since 1994 only foreigners based in Taiwan have been invited to give the race its "international" flavour.

Antong Hot Springs

The **Antong Hot Springs**, about 8km southeast of **Yuli**, a major stop on the Hualien–Taitung train line, were discovered by loggers in 1904 in the Antong Creek. The springs still well up in the stream at temperatures ranging from 60 to 66°C and can be enjoyed by bathers for free. Though the water is clear, it smells strongly of hydrogen sulphide. The part of the stream that's best for bathing is below the *Antong Hot Springs Hotel* at 36 Wencyuan Rd (T03/8886108; ❹), which has doubles with private baths. All trains through the valley stop at Yuli station, from where you can get a taxi to the springs; however, some trains stop at Antong station, much closer to the springs, so ask before you get off at Yuli. The Dingdong and Hualien buses will also get you closer to the resort, as they stop a short walk from the springs.

Yushan National Park: the eastern corridor

Immediately south of Yuli, just past the 294km marker of Highway 9, is the turnoff to scenic Highway 18, which winds its way to the eastern entrance of

Yushan National Park (see p.301). This peaceful, little-visited fringe of the park is a worthwhile detour for those with private transport. About 8km from the turnoff is the **Nanan visitor center** (9am–4.30pm; closed second Tues each month), where you can get English information and detailed trail maps for this section of the park. About 6km further, the road ends at a trailhead for the **Walami Trail**, which can be hiked without a mountain permit. Less than 2km up the trail is the magnificent **Shanfong Waterfall**, which plunges below a suspension bridge. Some 3km further on is **Jiasin**, an overlook with fine views of the valley to the east – the return trip to Jiasin takes about half a day, but if you want to linger you can camp here, provided you have your own tent. If you wish to walk the entire 14km to **Walami**, it's possible to stay overnight in a solar-heated shelter there and make a two-day trip of it, but you should first ask at the visitor centre to ensure there is enough space, as the shelter only holds thirty people and is popular with hiking clubs; you'll also need your own sleeping bag. Beyond Walami is the often treacherous Japanese-era **Badongguan Traversing Trail** (see map, pp.302–303), which crosses the entire park and eventually hooks up with the main routes to Yushan from the northwest. This trail has sustained serious structural damage and can be dangerous, so access is heavily restricted, with a **Class A mountain permit** and a local guide (usually a Bunun tribesman) required. It can take several days to cross the park on this trail, so extensive planning is necessary; ask about trail conditions and permits at the visitor centre.

South to Taitung

Back on Highway 9, about 30km south of the turnoff to the Nanan visitor center, is **Haiduan**, near the eastern entrance to the stunning **Southern Cross-Island Highway**, one of Taiwan's most thrilling drives. Officially designated as Highway 20, this 169.5km-long road climbs over the southerly reaches of the Central Cordillera – including the southern tip of Yushan National Park – before ultimately descending to the west-coast city of Tainan (see p.313). A few kilometres south of here is the old logging town of **Guanshan**, now best known for the scenic twelve-kilometre **bicycle path** that loops around the city. A good place to start is the riverside park (NT$50), where you can rent three-speed bicycles starting from NT$150 a day.

Near the southern end of the East Rift Valley, about 18km north of Taitung, is a small road that heads west to **Yanping**, near which is an idyllic **Bunun** village, offering a genuine glimpse of the tribe's culture and heritage. If you have your own transport, this is a fascinating side-trip, whether you just stop by to sample some authentic Bunun cuisine or camp or stay overnight in the village's hostel, which has several well-kept **cabins** (❸). Cradled near the confluence of the coastal and central mountains, the village is a relaxing retreat overlooking a tributary of the Beinan River, and on weekends the tribe puts on one of the most authentic aboriginal song and dance shows (Sat & Sun 10.30am & 2pm; free) in Taiwan. If you're here at lunchtime, the **set lunch** (NT$200) is great value, with a generous spread of Bunun specialties such as thin-sliced roast mountain pig (*kao shan zhu*), oven-baked sweet potatoes, sticky rice dumplings wrapped in shell ginger leaves, sweet ground millet soup and a glutinous millet cake dessert – all washed down with a thimble of locally made sweet millet wine. In the centre of the village is a spacious **craft workshop** where you can watch traditional handicrafts being made – many of them, including some exquisite woodcarvings, are sold in the adjacent shop.

Tea-plantation paragliding

The **Luye High Terrace**, crowning the highest point of the Luye oolong tea plantation to the north of Taitung, is widely considered Taiwan's top summertime paragliding site. The plateau here drops off sharply into an expansive agricultural plain, providing pilots with several kilometres of unfettered cross-country flying potential. Southerly winds are required for flying, and local and overseas pilots converge here en masse on most sunny summer weekends to wait out the wind. While the majority of pilots here are members of the hundred-strong Chinese Taitung Aerosports Association (℡089/353201), Taiwanese and expat pilots come from all over the island, and the sport is also extremely popular with flyers from Hong Kong, Japan and South Korea. There is no **fee** for independent pilots to use the site, but before you'll be allowed to take off you must produce a C-grade **pilot's certificate**; otherwise, you can go with one of the many **tandem pilots** who turn up on Saturday mornings throughout the summer. Each July or August, the site hosts an **international paragliding competition** that attracts some of the world's most accomplished pilots – for more information on this event visit ⊛www.wingstaiwan.com.

Behind the launching pads is a **teahouse** where you can sample the local oolong tea and also can rent equipment for **camping** in the lot just outside. The cost to camp is NT$500 if you bring your own tent, while spacious four-person tents are rented for NT$800 per night, with sleeping bags and foam pads costing an additional NT$50 per person. The turnoff to the terrace is along Highway 9, about 19km north of Taitung, and, as there is no public transport to the site, it's essential to hire your own vehicle. Another option is to contact the local paragliding association and arrange to carpool with pilots based in Taitung.

Taitung and around

Stretched across an open plain between lush mountains and a whitecap-coated sea, **TAITUNG** is Taiwan's most arresting city and is an essential base for exploring the southeast coast and the dreamy Pacific islands of **Lyudao** and **Lanyu** that lie offshore. With a population of 110,000 and a rapidly improving public transport system, it has the laid-back feel of a town half its size. Filled with leafy parks and promenades, it retains an aura of calm that is only disrupted by the morning and evening fighter-jet drills that originate from the nearby air base. Even in the tropical summer heat, the robust ocean breezes have a cooling effect that is absent in most Taiwanese cities. Taitung also trumps Hualien as the island's most multicultural town, with at least a half-dozen **indigenous tribes** tilting the balance between native and Hakka and Han Chinese cultures. With significant numbers from the Ami, Bunun, Rukai, Paiwan, Puyuma and Tao tribes, it has a remarkably ethnic flavour – something you'll taste the moment you set foot on one of its streets. Just to the south are the immensely popular **Jhihben Hot Springs**, with a range of resorts to suit most budgets, and the adjacent Jhihben Forest Recreation Area for some leisurely hiking options.

Some history

Taitung is one of Taiwan's youngest cities: it wasn't until the early twentieth century that the occupying **Japanese** began to develop it as a base for their Pacific expansion. During this period, sugar refineries and wood mills were set up in the area, spurring the first large-scale migrations of **Chinese labourers** to the east coast. In 1930, the Huatung Highway between Hualien and Taitung was opened, and the 1932 completion of the road looping around the island's

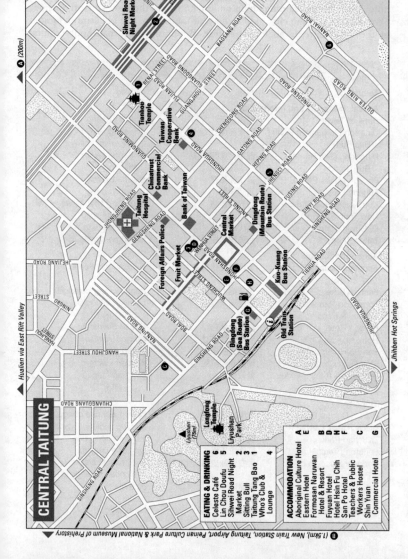

CENTRAL TAITUNG

EATING & DRINKING

Celeste Café 6
Lin Chou Doufu 5
Sihwei Road Night Market 2
Sitting Bull 3
Taitung Tang Bao 1
Who's Club & Lounge 4

ACCOMMODATION

Aboriginal Culture Hotel A
Eastern Hotel E
Formosan Naruwan Hotel & Resort B
Fuyuan Hotel D
Hotel Hsin Fu Chih H
San Po Hotel F
Teachers & Public Workers Hostel C
Shin Yuan Commercial Hotel G

Beinan River
Pipa Lake
Black Forest Park
Seaside Park

Hualien via East Coast Highway
Hualien via East Rift Valley

N
0   200 m

Sihwei Road Night Market
Tianhou Temple
Taitung Hospital
Chinatrust Commercial Bank
Taiwan Cooperative Bank
Bank of Taiwan
Foreign Affairs Police
Fruit Market
Central Market
Dingdong (Mountain Route) Bus Station
Kuo-Kuang Bus Station
Dingdong (Sea Route) Bus Station
Old Train Station
Longfong Temple
Liyushan Park

Jhihben Hot Springs

(1.5km), New Train Station, Taitung Airport, Peinan Culture Park & National Museum of Prehistory

A (200m)
B

south ushered in successive waves of settlement from west coast towns such as Changhua, Chiayi and Tainan. Many of these migrants were **Hakka**, and by the 1960s they had become one of the city's main ethnic groups. In recent decades, increasing numbers of **aborigines** have moved to Taitung from nearby villages in search of greater economic prospects, making the town a true melting pot.

Arrival, transport and information

Taitung Airport is about 7km northeast of the city centre and has a **visitor information Center** (℡089/361111), an ICBC ATM and a **car rental** counter in the arrivals hall. The **airport bus** to the old train station downtown operates almost hourly from the terminal (7.55am–7.35pm; NT$20), but it's notoriously erratic. Taitung's train station, known as the **new station**, is about 6km northeast of the city and is where all trains stop. The old station, located in the city centre, is no longer in use. Buses run every half-hour (20min;

Taitung		
Taitung	台東	*táidōng*
Arrival, transport and information		
Bank of Taiwan	台灣銀行	*táiwān yínháng*
Dingdong (Mountain Route) Bus Station	鼎東客運(山線)站	*dīngdōng kèyùn (shānxiàn) zhàn*
Dingdong (Sea Route) Bus Station	鼎東客運(海線)站	*dīngdōng kèyùn (hǎixiàn) zhàn*
Foreign Affairs Police	警察外事課	*jǐngchá wàishìkè*
Fugang Harbour	富岡漁港	*fùgāng yúgǎng*
Kuo Kuang Bus Station	國光客運站	*guóguāng kèyùnzhàn*
New Train Station	新火車站	*xīn huǒchē zhàn*
Old Train Station	舊火車站	*jiù huǒchē zhàn*
Taitung Airport	台東豐年機場	*táidōng fēngnián jīchǎng*
Accommodation		
Aboriginal Culture Hotel	原住民文化會館	*yuánzhùmín wénhuà huìguǎn*
Eastern Hotel	東之鄉大飯店	*dōngzhīxiāng dàfàndiàn*
Formosan Naruwan Hotel & Resort	娜路灣大酒店	*nàlùwān dàjiǔdiàn*
Fuyuan Hotel	富源大飯店	*fùyuán dàfàndiàn*
Hotel Hsin Fu Chih	新福治大旅社	*xīnfúzhì dà lǚshè*
San Po Hotel	三博大飯店	*sānbó dàfàndiàn*
Shin Yuan Commercial Hotel	馨園商務旅館	*xīnyúan shāngwù lǚ guǎn*
Teachers & Public Workers Hostel	公教會館	*gōngjiào huìguǎn*
The city		
Peinan Culture Park	卑南文化公園	*bēinán wénhuà gōngyuán*
Black Forest Park	台東森林公園	*táidōng sēnlín gōngyuán*
Liyushan Park	鯉魚山公園	*lǐyúshān gōngyuán*
Longfong Temple	龍鳳寶玉塔	*lóngfēng bǎoyùtǎ*
National Museum of Prehistory	國立台灣史前文化博物館	*guólì táiwān shǐqián wénhuà bówùguǎn*
Pipa Lake	琵琶湖	*pípá hú*
Seaside Park	海濱公園	*hǎibīn gōngyuán*
Tianhou Temple	天后宮	*tiānhòu gōng*

NT$20) from the new train station to the main city **bus terminal**, the Ding-dong (Sea Route) Bus Station, next to the old train station. There are two other bus stations in Taitung, each servicing a different geographic area. **Taxis** from the new station to the old station, or to anywhere in the downtown area, usually cost about NT$200, but if you arrive late at night expect to pay around NT$300.

City transport

Taitung has a **bus system**, but it's difficult to use if you don't read Chinese, and the downtown area is fairly compact and easy to walk around. However, the **Dingdong (Sea Route) Bus Station** (℡089/333443), next to the old train station, has frequent buses to the new train station and points on the outskirts of town. There is usually a clutch of **taxis** around the old train station, and drivers generally prefer to negotiate a flat rate rather than use the meter. To get

Moving on from Taitung

Taitung's transport links with the rest of the island have expanded significantly in recent years, with regular air, rail and bus connections to major destinations in the south and west, north along the east coast and East Rift Valley, as well as regular ferries and flights to Lyudao and Lanyu.

Far Eastern Air Transport (℡089/390388) and Uni Air (℡089/362625) operate regular **flights** from Taitung Airport to Taipei throughout the day, while Mandarin Airlines (℡089/362669) has daily flights to Taichung. Daily Air Corp is the only carrier with service to Lyudao (15min; NT$1091 one-way) and Lanyu (25min; NT$1408 one-way); phone reservations aren't possible, so you'll have to turn up at the Taitung Airport (or the Lyudao or Lanyu airports) to try your luck.

Taitung is a major stop on the **Eastern Line** and is the starting point for the **South-link Line** that connects the city with Pingdong and Kaohsiung in the west. There is regular express service to **Hualien** (NT$355), and several slower trains each day make frequent stops at towns in the East Rift Valley. There are several express trains daily to **Kaohsiung** (2hr 45min; NT$280) via Pingdong. To get to **Kenting town**, take the train to Fangliao and then catch one of the regular buses that run south from Kaohsiung.

The **Dingdong (Sea Route) Bus Station** (℡089/333443) has regular service to destinations along the coastal Highway 11. There are three buses daily to Hualien (6.10am, 8.30am & 1.40pm), while seven buses a day make a return trip to **Cheng-gong** (1hr; 7.50am, 10am, 5pm, 6pm, 7pm, 8pm & 9.30pm); it's possible to take one of these and catch one of the several Chenggong–Hualien buses for the remainder of the journey to Hualien. To the east of the old train station, the **Kuo Kuang Bus Station** (℡089/322027) has useful service in all directions, including two overnight buses to **Taichung** via Kaohsiung (6hr 30min; 10.30pm & 11.15pm), five buses daily to Chenggong (1hr; 4.30am, 5.30am, 12.40pm, 5.40pm & 7pm; NT$125) and one bus daily to **Tianchih** (5hr; 6.40am; NT$351), roughly the halfway point along the **South-ern Cross-Island Highway** to Tainan. There are also nine buses daily to **Kaohsiung** (4hr); the quickest way to get to **Kenting town** by bus is to take one of these to Fong-gang and transfer to one of the many buses headed south from there.

The **Dingdong (Mountain Route) Bus Station** has frequent buses to points on Highway 9 in the **East Rift Valley**, including Chihshang, Fuli and Guanshan, as well as two daily to Lidao (6.20am & 1.05pm) on the Southern Cross-Island Highway. It also has several buses each day to villages south of Taitung and runs eleven buses daily to Jhihben Hot Springs. There are sixteen daily buses to the new train station.

There are regular **ferry services** from Fugang Harbour, a few kilometres north of Taitung, to the offshore islands of **Lyudao** and **Lanyu** (see p.427).

from the old station to anywhere inside the city should cost between NT$70 and NT$100. If you want to visit the town's environs it's best to take a taxi or hire your own transport. **Scooters** are the easiest way to get around the greater Taitung area and can save you a lot of time and hassle, in addition to being a pleasurable means of exploring the coast and East Rift Valley. At only about NT$300 per day to rent, they work out far cheaper than using taxis and buses, especially if you're travelling outside of the city. However, Taitung is the hardest city on the island for foreigners to hire scooters, as most of the rental companies require an Alien Resident Certificate with a Taiwan address in addition to a Taiwanese or international driver's licence (see Basics p.33). The best places to try your luck are the **scooter rental shops** on either side of Sinsheng Road as you head southeast from the old train station.

Information

The **Taitung County Travel Service Center** (9am–5pm; ☎089/359085) is in the old train station and has an assortment of English-language brochures and maps of the area, including the offshore islands and sights along the east coast. If you're here in July or August, when villages of the Ami tribe and other indigenous groups are holding **harvest festival** celebrations, the centre's staff might be able to point you in the right direction. The best place to exchange foreign currency is the **Bank of Taiwan** at 313 Jhongshan Rd, which also has an **ATM** that recognizes most international debit cards. A few of the downtown 7-Elevens have Chinatrust Commercial Bank ATMs. The **Foreign Affairs Police** are at 268 Jhongshan Rd (☎089/334756).

Accommodation

Given the growing popularity of the southeast and the offshore islands, the number of tourists visiting Taitung has risen in recent years, and it's a favourite of Taiwanese students during summer holidays – so there is ample **budget accommodation** alongside Jhongshan Road as you head northeast from the old train station. The rooms at these tend to be small and dingy, but staff at some will help you book **ferry tickets** to Lyudao and Lanyu and can arrange transport to the ferry pier at nearby Fugang Harbour. Outside the city centre, but closer to the new train station and the airport, are a couple of **mid-range options**, as well as a gleaming five-star hotel.

Aboriginal Culture Hotel 10 Jhongshan Rd ☎089/340605. Run by friendly local aborigines of various tribes, this hotel makes up for its slightly inconvenient location about 1km north of the city centre with ambience. The large Japanese-style rooms are kept immaculately clean and offer the best value for money in town. ❸

Eastern Hotel 374 Jhongshan Rd ☎089/310171. Conveniently located budget option, with small but clean rooms and cable TV representing good value. ❷

Formosan Naruwan Hotel & Resort 66 Lianhang Rd ☎089/239666, ⓦwww.naruwan-hotel.com .tw. Located in the city's northwest, a short taxi ride from the airport and new train station, this five-star hotel has lavish, airy rooms with all the usual amenities. Included in the complex are restaurants,

a nightclub, a shopping area, a spa and massage centre and a saltwater swimming pool. ❼

Fuyuan Hotel 72 Wenhua St ☎089/331136. Tucked away in a tiny lane just off Jhongshan Road, the family-run *Fuyuan* is the best of the budget options, with bright, spotless rooms with cable TV that are marginally cheaper than the more tatty hotels nearby. The friendly managers speak very basic English but can nonetheless help you book ferry tickets to Lyudao and Lanyu for no additional fee. ❷

Hotel Hsin Fu Chih 417 Jhongshan Rd ☎089/331101. The *Hsin Fu Chih*'s furnishings are getting worn and the beds are rock-hard, but doubles are fairly clean and cheap and are an option if everything else is full. ❷

San Po Hotel 393 Jhongshan Rd ☎089/324696. Doubles are slightly more upmarket than the other hotels nearby, but this hardly justifies the fact that they cost almost twice as much. ❸

Shin Yuan Commercial Hotel 402 Jhongshan Rd ☎089/325101. Features spartan, compact rooms with cheap fittings, but is reasonably clean and conveniently located right next to the Dingdong (Sea Route) Bus Station. ❷

Teachers & Public Workers Hostel 19 Nanjing Rd ☎089/310142. A hotel rather than a hostel, with bright, spacious rooms offering reasonable value for travellers. It's often packed out during summer holidays as it offers steep discounts to students and teachers. ❸

The City

Taitung's most compelling attraction is its scenery, and its expansive **parks** are the best places to appreciate the city's privileged position between mountains and sea. The largest, and the one closest to the downtown area, is **Liyushan (Carp Hill) Park**, less than 1km northwest of the old train station. Covered in trees, it's a shady retreat crisscrossed with concrete walking paths, some with steps leading up to the spine of 75-metre-high Liyushan, named because imaginative Chinese settlers fancied a resemblance to the auspicious fish. A path along the backbone of Liyushan leads to several lookout points offering 360-degree panoramas of the city, and is an ideal place to catch Taitung's cooling afternoon breezes. At the base of the hill, and accessible via several paths, is the imposing **Longfong (Dragon Phoenix) Temple**, a Buddhist sanctuary popular with both worshippers and the retirees who practice *taichi* in its courtyard every morning. In the complex is a multi-storey pagoda which visitors are allowed to climb.

Covering Taitung's southeastern flank is the sprawling **Seaside Park**, with commanding views of the coastline and numerous walking paths and bicycle tracks. The park, about 2km east of the old train station, is filled with aboriginal sculptures and woodcarvings, and has a cycle path that loops around the peaceful **Pipa Lake** and links up with the adjacent **Black Forest Park**. Over in the northeastern part of town, alongside bustling Jhonghua Road, is the ornately carved **Tianhou Temple**, erected in honour of Mazu. Richly decorated, it attracts large numbers of local devotees on weekends – and especially on Mazu's birthday, when an animated celebration is held here.

National Museum of Prehistory

One of Taiwan's best museums, the **National Museum of Prehistory** (Tues–Sun 9am–5pm, last entry 4.40pm; NT$80; Ⓦ www.nmp.gov.tw) was created primarily to house the fascinating horde of Neolithic artefacts dug up from the Peinan Culture Park (see p.422), around 7km away. The museum also provides a thorough introduction to Taiwan's rich prehistoric history as a whole, and information on all its major archeological sites via two permanent exhibitions: **Natural History of Taiwan** and **Taiwan's Prehistory**. The large, futuristic halls combine contemporary design and technology with a fascinating collection of exhibits, models and dioramas to present each section in English and Chinese. The first exhibition explains the geological and ecological development of the island over millions of years, while the second takes a chronological journey from the first known humans in Taiwan (Tsochen Man) through to the early Iron Age, two thousand years ago. The exquisite **jade** ornaments and **pottery** taken from the Peinan site have their own exhibition areas, but the most startling finds are the distinctive **stone coffins** and moon-shaped **stone pillars**, the latter reminiscent of the stone circles of Northwest Europe. The museum also has an exhibition on the **Indigenous Peoples of Taiwan**, charting the development of Taiwan's modern aboriginal tribes and how they might relate to the island's prehistoric peoples.

The museum is inconveniently located around 8km west of the city centre: you can either take a train to Kanglo Station (8 daily; 5min) and walk (7min) or take a taxi (NT$200) from there. Alternatively there are three buses daily (7.40am, 11.10am & 4.20pm; 20min; NT$27) to the museum from the Dingdong (Sea Route) Bus Station next to the old train station.

Peinan Culture Park

Once the location of a flourishing Neolithic community, **Peinan Culture Park** (free) is now a major archeological site and a series of landscaped open spaces, also containing another absorbing exhibition hall managed by the Museum of Prehistory. The Japanese began working here in the 1940s, but most excavation was carried out in the 1990s, and today it's the largest and most productive archeological site in Taiwan, yielding over twenty thousand artefacts (mostly pottery) and 1600 slate coffins. The park's informative **visitor centre** (Tues–Sun 9am–5pm; NT$10), contains a sunken area displaying **stone coffins** and an exhibition dedicated to the people that once lived here, between 1500 and 300 BC. Archeologists have been able to surmise an astonishing amount about this community of hunters and farmers, although there is still disagreement over whether they were the ancestors of any of today's aboriginal tribes: the local Puyuma people call themselves "Beinan", but some anthropologists think the Paiwan or the Ami are more likely to be related to the prehistoric Peinan culture.

Elsewhere in the park, the two-level **observation deck** offers fine views over the area, while the **stone pillar** or standing stone is the only artefact left in its original location – archeologists think this may have marked the centre of the village. The houses that once stood here were made of schist and wood, with roofs of bamboo and straw and an average size of 69 square metres. Each had an attached storehouse, but common granaries were also scattered around the village. You'll need a vivid imagination to picture any of this today however, as nothing remains above ground, though it's possible to observe archeologists working on a section of the village in the southern corner of the park. The park is at the back of the new station in the northern suburbs of Taitung – just follow the road round (right as you exit) and under the bridge (10min).

Eating

Given its diverse ethnic mix, Taitung has an eclectic assortment of eating options, many of them visible at the myriad roadside food stalls throughout the city. Every Sunday night, the whole of Sihwei Road between Jhonghua Road and Guangfu Road is blocked off for the lively **Sihwei Road Night Market**, where you can find all of Taitung's specialty dishes. One of the most popular treats, but not one for the finicky, is the **pig's blood soup** (*zhu xie tang*), a thick broth filled with diced cubes of congealed pig's blood. Another local favourite

Taitung eating and drinking		
Celeste Café	海濱咖啡館	*hǎibīn kāfēi guǎn*
Fruit Market	水果市場	*shuǐguǒ shìcháng*
Lin Chou Doufu	林臭豆腐	*lín chòu dòufǔ*
Puyuma Yuanshi Buluo	普悠瑪原始部落	*pǔyōumǎ yuánshǐ bùluò*
Sihwei Road Night Market	四維路夜市	*sìwéi lù yèshì*
Sitting Bull	紅番區	*hóngfān qū*
Taitung Tang Bao	台東湯包	*táidōng tāngbāo*
Who's Club & Lounge	胡氏餐廳	*húshì cāntīng*

is **bamboo tube rice pudding** (*tongzi migao*), glutinous rice filled with pork or mushrooms and steamed in a bamboo tube. Taitung is also known for its amazing variety of **fruit**, the most famous of which is the **custard apple**, also known as the "Buddha Fruit" for its likeness to the hair coils common to many East Asian representations of the Sakyamuni Buddha. The best place to find it is along "**Fruit Market**", the long stretch of Jhengci Road between Jhongshan and Boai roads that is lined with dozens of fruit vendors each day.

For the best **dumplings** in town, stop by the unassuming little shop named *Taitung Tang Bao* (the sign says "Taitung Soup Stuffed Buns" in English), at the corner of Jhonghua Road and Renai Road, directly across the street from the Tianhou Temple. Here, you can eat your fill of fresh dumplings (NT$50 for eight) while watching worshippers file into the temple – which is particularly atmospheric at night, when it's awash with colourful lights. In the evenings, several **food stalls** set up shop on either side of the temple's Jhonghua Road entrance. *Lin Chou Doufu* at 130 Jhengci Rd (3.30pm–midnight), tucked down narrow Jhengci Road between Fujian and Guangdong roads, is legendary with locals, as much for its eccentric owner as for its unique **stinky tofu**. As if to underscore the pungency of his deep-fried tofu (NT$30 for small portion; NT$100 for large), which is made from green beans rather than the usual soya, the owner wears camouflage fatigues and a gas mask when preparing food for customers. For Western-style food, the *Celeste Café* (Mon–Fri 4pm–1am, Sat–Sun 2pm–1am), opposite the Seaside Park near the corner of Datong and Nanhai roads, is a relaxing place for dinner or an afternoon **pasta** fix (NT$150 for lasagna or spaghetti). The café specializes in **fruit tea** (NT$150 per pot), with more than twenty types, and has excellent coffee (NT$100) as well as beer (NT$100 per bottle) and wine (NT$160 per glass).

The best place to try freshly prepared **Puyuma tribe** specialities is *Puyuma Yuanshi Buluo* (Original Tribe), an atmospheric open-air restaurant built in the style of a traditional Puyuma village. It's located several kilometres northwest of Taitung in the hillside village of **Lijia**, offering splendid night-time views of the city lights below. Open only for dinner (nightly 6pm–10.30pm; reservations recommended ☎089/382700), it's a fitting place to cap off a late-afternoon visit to the nearby National Museum of Prehistory. To get to the restaurant, catch a taxi in front of the museum; expect a fare of about NT$100.

Drinking

Though Taitung tends to be fairly sedate at night, there are interesting options for both a quiet drink and a late-night dance. The town's hippest **bar** is *Sitting Bull* at 74 Wenhua St (nightly 6pm–3am; ☎089/347200), next to the *Fuyuan Hotel* just off Jhongshan Road (its sign says "Music Bar & Restaurant" in English). Run by some clued-up young aboriginal entrepreneurs and decorated with posters and off-the-wall photos of indigenous folk heroes from the American West, it's a good place to get a feel for the cultural revival that's taking place among the urbanized aborigines of Taiwan's southeast. It also has upbeat music, bottled beer starting from NT$150 and South American **wine** at NT$900 per bottle. If you fancy a boogie, the city's most happening **disco** is *Who's Club & Lounge* at 323 Jhonghua Rd (8pm–5am; ☎089/320618), which is popular with locals and usually doesn't come to life until after 10pm. It's owned by an American expat who previously ran the now-defunct *Gringo Hostel* and *Amigo Pub*.

Around Taitung: Jhihben Hot Springs

The **JHIHBEN HOT SPRINGS**, in a long river valley about 20km south of Taitung, are among the finest in Taiwan, and the crowds they attract certainly bear

Jhihben Hot Springs	知本溫泉區	*zhīběn wēnquánqū*
Banyan Shaded Trail	榕蔭步道	*róngyìn bùdào*
Cingjue Temple	清覺寺	*qīngjúe sì*
Dong Tair Spa Hotel	東台溫泉飯店	*dōngtái wēnquán fàndiàn*
Forest-view Suspension Bridge	觀林吊橋	*guānlín diàoqiáo*
Four-faced Buddha Hot Springs Spa	四面佛露天浴池	*sìmiànfó lùtiān yùchí*
Hotel Royal Chihpen	知本老爺大酒店	*zhīběn lǎoyé dàjiǔdiàn*
Hoya Hot Springs Resort & Spa	知本富野渡假村	*zhīběn fùyě dùjiācūn*
Jhihben National Forest Recreation Area	知本森林遊樂區	*zhīběn sēnlín yóulèqū*
Ming Chuan Hotel	明泉旅遊山莊	*míngquán lǚyóu shānzhuāng*
Rainbow Resort	泓泉溫泉渡假村	*hóngquán wēnquán dùjiācūn*
Songquan Holiday Hotel	松泉渡假山莊	*sōngquán dùjiā shānzhuāng*
Yunshanyuan Campsite	雲山園露營區	*yúnshānyuán lùyíngqū*

out this reputation. Developed into a resort by the **Japanese** in the early twentieth century, it's one of the country's oldest hot-springs resort areas and its **sulphur carbonate waters** are believed to be some of the island's most therapeutic, effective in treating everything from arthritis to intestinal disorders (the colourless, odourless spring water is drinkable). Though in its early days bathers soaked in the riverbeds, where the springs emerged at temperatures of more than 100°C, today all of the natural springs have been tapped and are pumped into the proliferation of luxury resorts that are popping up along the valley entrance. Despite this, the area retains considerable charm, and further inland the development starts to diminish, as do the crowds. At the end of the main Longcyuan Road – which cuts straight through the valley – is the tranquil **Jhihben National Forest Recreation Area**, which has attractive scenery and several easy walking paths.

Practicalities

While renting a car or scooter will give you much more flexibility, it's also fairly easy to reach Jhihben by **bus** from Taitung: eleven buses leave daily (6.05am–6.35pm) from the Dingdong (Mountain Line) Bus Station, although some of these turn around just past the valley entrance, so if you plan to go further inland be sure to confirm where the terminus is before you buy your ticket.

Whether you arrive via Highway 9 or Highway 11, as you enter the valley you're likely to be greeted by a welcoming party of indigenous people on scooters, entreating you to stay at their hot-springs hotels. Most of these places are near the highway turnoff, an overdeveloped area of faceless high-rises. If all you're after is a quiet soak, you'll do better going to the far end of the valley, near the entrance to the serene Jhihben National Forest Recreation Area where there are several more down-to-earth options. Camping is not allowed inside the forest recreation area, so if you want to rough it the best option is the **Yunshanyuan Campsite** (☎089/510769), which has an outdoor swimming pool and a hot springs bathing area and mostly caters to groups with six-person tents available for NT$880 per night (around half that if you bring your own). The narrow turnoff to the campsite is on the right-hand side of the road as you head towards the recreation area, about 1km before the entrance.

If you don't plan to stay overnight, it's possible to soak in some of the hotels' **public pools** for a nominal fee. One of the cheapest, most convenient options is also Jhihben's oldest hot-springs development: the *Four-faced Buddha Hot Springs Spa* at 32 Longcyuan Rd (☎089/514316), named after the Thai-style, four-headed Buddha statue in the courtyard outside the entrance. The Japanese-style complex has several pools (NT$200 per person, unlimited time), including a variety of **massage showers**, and is open 24 hours from Friday to Sunday; it's also open from Monday to Thursday, but hours vary in accordance with their pool-cleaning schedule.

Hot-spring hotels

Dong Tair Spa Hotel 147 Longcyuan Rd ☎089/512290. A favourite of Taiwanese families and tour groups, with large rooms and one of the valley's biggest open-air bathing areas; tends to be crowded. **⑥**

Hotel Royal Chihpen 113 Lane 23, Longcyuan Rd ☎089/510666. Jhihben's poshest hotel, with 183 rooms equipped with private Jacuzzis. Occupying the side of a hill just off the main Longcyuan Road, the complex includes a swimming pool, recreation area, putting greens, an archery range and an outdoor stage where touristy Puyuma dance performances are held nightly. Non-guests can soak in the public bathing pools for as long as they want for NT$350. **⑧**

Hoya Hot Springs Resort & Spa 30-2 Longcyuan Rd ☎089/515005. A five-star option close to the river valley entrance and within walking distance of the main stretch of overpriced Chinese restaurants. **⑦**

Ming Chuan Hotel 267 Lane 2, Longcyuan Road ☎089/513996. A cheap and cheerful option, on the hill directly across from the forest recreation area entrance. Facilities are basic but clean, with a small outdoor bathing pool, but some of the motel-style rooms and private cabins look out onto the valley's best scenery, including the Forest-view Suspension Bridge and the spectacular waterfall that comes crashing down behind it. Price includes breakfast at the riverside café below the hotel. **③**

Rainbow Resort 139 Lane 11, Longcyuan Rd ☎089/510150. Reasonable mid-range option located up a hilly lane above Longcyuan Road, with sweeping views of the river valley; price includes breakfast. **⑤**

Songcyuan Holiday Hotel 135 Lane 6, Longcyuan Rd ☎089/510073. Small, family-run hotel with attractive rooms offering excellent value. Located up a very steep lane, about 100m off the main road. Breakfast costs an extra NT$50. **③**

Temple and forest trails

In addition to hot springs, the valley has other worthwhile attractions, both man-made and natural. Sharing a hillside with the *Hotel Royal Chihpen*, up Lane 23 just off Longcyuan Road, is the peaceful **Cingjue Temple**, which houses a pair of exquisite **Buddha statues**: one carved of white jade from Myanmar and the other a bronze image from Thailand. There is a small monastery nearby, and the resident monks frequently meditate inside the temple.

The highlight of the valley is where the road ends and the **Jhihben National Forest Recreation Area** (July–Sept 8am–6pm, Oct–June 7am–5pm; NT$100) begins. The area is accessed by the **Forest-view Suspension Bridge**, which looks out onto a magnificent multi-tiered **waterfall**. At the tollgate you can get an English-language brochure with information and a basic map of the trails, all of which are well marked and easy to follow. The **Banyan Shaded Trail**, a leisurely walk of just over 2km, remains cool even in summer, sheltered as it is by old-growth forest – including seventeen hundred-year-old banyans. In some sections, **Taiwanese macaques** can be seen leaping from tree to tree.

Lyudao (Green Island)

A verdant Pacific gem about 33km east of Taitung, **LYUDAO** (Green Island) flourishes with tropical vegetation inland and a jaw-dropping abundance of

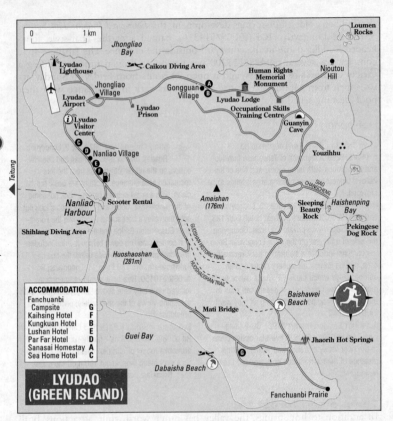

colourful **marine life** amid the nourishing coral that skirts most of its shore-line. Formed by ancient volcanic activity, the island is also surrounded by sedimentary rock, which wind and water have sculpted into some of Taiwan's most mesmerizing **coastal scenery**. Its beauty and relative accessibility – a twelve-minute flight or fifty-minute ferry ride from Taitung – have made it an immensely popular tourist destination, with a holiday feel at stark odds with its recent history as Taiwan's principal place of exile for political prisoners. Site of the notorious **Lyudao Lodge**, where tens of thousands were held without proper trials and routinely tortured during the **White Terror** period of KMT single-party rule (see Contexts p.513), the island is now equally well known for some of Taiwan's finest **snorkelling** and **diving**. It also boasts the atmospheric Jhaorih Hot Springs, one of only two known natural **saltwater hot springs** in the world (the other is near Mount Vesuvius in northern Italy).

Given its small size – an eighteen-kilometre sealed road loops round it – Lyudao can easily be explored by scooter or taxi, and many Taiwanese opt to fly in for a day-trip before returning to Taitung for the night. Despite this, it gets very crowded during the **summer holidays**, and especially on weekends, when tourist numbers easily dwarf the island's summer population of just over two thousand. In contrast, during the **winter** months, there is a sharp decline in the number of visitors, and ferries and flights are prone to last-minute cancellations

Ferries to Lyudao and Lanyu

It's easy to get to **Lyudao** and **Lanyu** by ferry, with a half-dozen **ferry operators** offering regular services from Fugang Harbour, a few kilometres north of Taitung. In summer, boats to **Lyudao** (40min; NT$400 one-way, NT$800 return) leave every two hours or so throughout the day, so it's possible to buy tickets at the pier. However, given Lyudao's popularity, on summer weekends they are usually all full in advance, so if you're going at this time book your ticket through your hotel in Taitung. Some hotels offer this service free to guests and will arrange your transport to Fugang Harbour.

All ferries to **Lanyu** first stop at Lyudao, and if you want to visit both it's possible to buy a ticket allowing you to stop off at Lyudao on either leg of the journey (NT$1500). From Lyudao, it's another 1hr 40min to Lanyu, and the seas here can get very choppy, especially in winter. During tropical storms and throughout the winter months, boats run sporadically and are frequently cancelled.

due to inclement weather. If you come during this time, you're likely to have the island mostly to yourself, but many tourist facilities are closed and it's hard to arrange snorkelling trips unless you've brought your own kit.

Some history

Archeological evidence suggests that humans inhabited Lyudao as early as 1000 BC, and it's thought to have been an important **transmigration point** for various Austronesian peoples. According to aboriginal myth, it was known as *Sanasai*, and the Ami, Kavalan and Ketagalan tribes believe their ancestors used it as a land bridge for migration. The first **Han Chinese** immigrants arrived in the early 1800s and named it *Huoshaodao*, or "Fire-burned Island", in reference to the fires that locals would light to help guide fishing boats to shore (the island's highest point, at 281m, is named *Huoshaoshan*). In the early 1930s, the occupying Japanese built processing plants for dried fish, which was shipped to Japan. By the 1970s, the raising of **Sika deer**, prized commercially for their antlers, had become a boom industry, and at one point there were more of these diminutive creatures than people. Though this industry has been in decline on Lyudao since 1986, there are still plenty to be seen, and today they are something of a tourist attraction. In the main village of Nanliao, some hotel and restaurant owners keep them as pets, sadly leashing them up for photo opportunities.

Arrival, transport and information

Lyudao Airport (☎089/671261) is less than 1km north of Nanliao Village, the island's main tourist centre. In summer, touts will greet you, offering deals including accommodation, food, scooter rental and snorkelling trips. The same is true if you arrive by ferry at **Nanliao Harbour**, about 1km south of the village. These all-in-one arrangements can be good value, but the downside is that they're luck of the draw, and you might wind up with a dingy room, only to find yourself being shunted around on an overcrowded snorkelling outing the next day.

For greater freedom, it's best to rent a **scooter** from one of the many rental shops near the ferry pier, or from one of the airport touts, and set about looking for a room on your own. Scooters usually cost about NT$300 per day, not including petrol, but the price jumps to NT$400 on summer weekends, when they can often be completely rented out. If you arrive late in the week and plan to stay through the weekend, make sure you'll be able to keep your scooter for

Lyudao (Green Island)

Lyudao	綠島	*lǜdǎo*
Lyudao Airport	綠島機場	*lǜdǎo jīchǎng*
Lyudao Visitor Center	綠島遊客中心	*lǜdǎo yóukè zhōngxīn*
Nanliao Harbour	南寮漁港	*nánliáo yúgǎng*

Accommodation

Fanchuanbi Campsite	帆船鼻露營區	*fánchúanbí lùyíngqū*
Kaihsing Hotel	凱薪飯店	*kǎixīn fàndiàn*
Kungkuan Hotel	公館大飯店	*gōngguǎn dàfàndiàn*
Lushan Hotel	綠山飯店	*lǜshān fàndiàn*
Par Far Hotel	雙發渡假飯店	*shuāngfā dùjiā fàndiàn*
Sanasai Homestay	珊納賽	*shānnàsài*
Sea Home Hotel	海洋之家渡假村	*hǎiyáng zhījiā dùjiā cūn*

The island

Caikou Diving Area	柴口潛水區	*cháikǒu qiánshuǐqū*
Dabaisha Beach & Diving Area	大白沙潛水區	*dàbáishā qiánshuǐqū*
Gongguan Village	公館村	*gōngguǎn cūn*
Guanyin Cave	觀音洞	*guānyīn dòng*
Guoshan Historic Trail	過山古道	*guòshān gǔdào*
Human Rights Memorial Monument	將軍岩人權紀念園區	*jiāngjūn yán rénchuán jìniànyuánqū*
Huoshaoshan Trail	過山步道	*guòshān bùdào*
Jhaorih Hot Springs	朝日溫泉	*cháorì wēnquán*
Jhongliao Village	中寮村	*zhōngliáo cūn*
Lyudao Lighthouse	綠島燈塔	*lǜdǎo dēngtǎ*
Lyudao Lodge	綠島山莊	*lǜdǎo shānzhuāng*
Lyudao Prison	綠島監獄	*lǜdǎo jiānyù*
Nanliao Village	南寮村	*nánliáo cūn*
Nioutou Hill	牛頭山	*niútóu shān*
Occupational Skills Training Center	職能訓練所	*jìnnéng xùnliànsuǒ*
Shihlang Diving Area	石朗潛水區	*shílǎng qiánshuǐqū*
Siao Changcheng	小長城步道	*xiǎo chángchéng bùdào*
Youzihhu	柚子湖	*yòuzǐ hú*

Eating and drinking

| Chi Tang You Yu | 池塘有魚 | *chítáng yǒuyú* |
| Mei Er Mei | 美而美 | *měi ér mě* |

the duration: large student groups often book scooters in advance, and if this has already been done you'll be asked to return yours when they arrive. Most vendors will give you a scooter that is practically on empty so be sure to fuel up at the **petrol station** near the ferry pier. A whirlwind **taxi tour** around the island, with perfunctory stops at the main sights, will cost a minimum of NT$500, more during crowded weekends. You also could **walk** around the loop road, or bits of it, but in summer the searing heat and relentless scooter traffic could make this an unpleasant endeavour.

The **Lyudao visitor center** (8.30am–5.30pm; ☎089/672026), across the road from the airport and just north of Nanliao Village, has crude maps and some English-language information. The staff can arrange snorkelling and diving trips and also make reservations for the excellent **campsite** near the island's southern tip (see p.429). In addition, you can also buy a multi-use **bus ticket** (NT$100) here that allows you unlimited rides for a three-day period on the public bus that makes a circuit around the loop every thirty minutes or so (7am–6pm). There are thirteen bus stops around the island – roughly one for every kilometre.

Accommodation

The bulk of **accommodation** on Lyudao is concentrated in congested Nanliao Village, which teems with Taiwanese tourists all summer, especially on weekends, when the overwhelming influx of visitors severely disrupts the island's serenity and most hotels here are fully booked. If you'll be here on a summer weekend, call a few days ahead of time – or have your hotel in Taitung call for you – to ensure you'll have a room. A more relaxed alternative to Nanliao is **Gongguan Village** in the north of the island, where there is a handful of small hotels near one of the top snorkelling and diving spots. Even quieter is the shady **Fanchuanbi Campsite** in the south, between the Jhaorih Hot Springs and Dabaisha Beach, where you can pitch a tent on grass (NT$150) or elevated wooden platforms (NT$350). Reservations should be made at the visitor centre, and staff there can direct you to a private vendor if you need to rent tents, sleeping bags and foam mattresses: six-person tents usually go for about NT$200, but the price varies according to the vendor. Mosquitoes abound at the campsite, so bring plenty of repellent.

Nanliao Village

Kaihsing Hotel 102–12 Nanliao Village ☏089/672033. Lyudao's biggest – and busiest – hotel, catering mostly to domestic tour groups; discounts are routinely given in winter. ❺

Lushan Hotel 102–6 Nanliao Village ☏089/672243. Next door to the *Kaihsing*, the *Lushan* offers a range of clean doubles, twins, triples and some Japanese-style dorm rooms with tatami mats, ideal for groups of young people. ❹

🏃 **Par Far Hotel** 146 Nanliao Village ☏089/672552. By far the best deal on Lyudao with bright, spotlessly clean rooms – some with superb sea views. Given the great value it offers, the *Par Far* is often fully booked, so if you want to stay here you should have your hotel in Taitung call to make a reservation (the affable woman who runs it doesn't speak English). ❸

Sea Home Hotel 39 Nanliao Village ☏089/672515. Immaculate, breezy rooms with sea views, but much more expensive than the *Par Far* and management are reluctant to discount in summer; breakfast is included. In winter, sizeable discounts can be had. ❻

Gongguan Village

Kungkuan Hotel 2–10 Gongguan Village ☏089/672799. Upmarket hotel with spacious, well-appointed rooms and very comfortable beds; some of the most expensive rooms have views of coastal rock formations. ❻

Sanasai Homestay 1 Gongguan Village ☏089/672788. Just across the street from the *Kungkuan* is this slightly cheaper option with seven clean rooms, three of which have sea views; breakfast is included, and reservations (Chinese only) are recommended. ❹

The island

A good place to start a tour is the **Lyudao Lighthouse**, on the island's northwest corner and one of its most prominent landmarks. Accessible via a side road from Jhongliao Village, it's a dramatic place to watch the sunset. It was built in 1938, a year after the US cruise liner *SS President Hoover* ran aground on an offshore reef, prompting villagers to stage a valiant rescue effort. In gratitude, the US Government financed the construction of the lighthouse, which sustained serious damage during World War II a few years later. The existing structure was partially reconstructed by the KMT. Along the main ring road to the east are three former **prisons** that have come to symbolize the White Terror period of martial law (see box p.430).

In the island's northeast corner is **Nioutou (Ox-head) Hill**, a rock at the edge of a grassy plateau that offers great views of the coastline. Just south of here is **Guanyin Cave**, a water-eroded limestone opening containing several stalactites and stalagmites: one of the latter is said to resemble Guanyin, the Goddess of Mercy, and is wrapped accordingly in a flaming red robe. Legend has it that during the Qing dynasty a fisherman in peril was led to shore near here by a mysterious light emanating from the cliffs. The area was then searched by locals, who found the stalagmite and likened it to Guanyin sitting on a lotus: deducing that this must have been the source of the life-saving light, they pronounced the spot sacred and today it is in important pilgrimage point. South of the cave, a steep, winding road leads down to an extraordinary stretch of wave-beaten coral coastline, surrounded by towering crags just offshore. The sheltered, sandy area just inland is an abandoned aboriginal settlement known as **Youzihhu**, where several derelict **old dwellings** are slowly succumbing to the encroaching vegetation. The area is one of the island's most atmospheric, and given that it's largely hidden from view of the main road, it remains refreshingly free of the

Remembering the White Terror

In the minds of many Taiwanese, especially the elderly, Lyudao's natural beauty is far overshadowed by its brutal recent past as the primary place of imprisonment, torture and execution during the country's **White Terror** (see Contexts p.513). This, the most paranoid period of martial law under KMT single-party rule, was a crippling campaign to purge the island of those viewed by Chiang Kai-shek's regime as politically questionable. Although in the late 1940s and early 1950s it was mostly targeted at those suspected of being **communist spies** for the mainland, eventually students, intellectuals and professionals accused of criticizing the government were rounded up, tortured and interrogated before being imprisoned or executed. During this time, more than ninety thousand people were arrested and at least half were put to death, usually by a gunshot to the heart. Some of Taiwan's best and brightest were killed, and Chiang's regime treated both native Taiwanese and immigrants from mainland China with equal ruthlessness. From 1951 until the end of martial law in 1987, more than twenty thousand political prisoners were shipped to Lyudao, where they were held in the notorious **Lyudao Lodge**, the now-crumbling facility just east of Gongguan Village. Here, inmates were routinely tortured and often confined to damp underground bunkers where they were eaten alive by mosquitoes. Some were held for more than thirty years before being freed, and an estimated one thousand were executed here. The prison, sometimes called **"Oasis Villa"** in English, is off-limits to visitors, but curious tourists come to try to get a glimpse inside the complex. There is talk of turning it into a museum to remind Taiwan's younger generation of the sacrifices that were made prior to the country's rise to democracy. For the time being, however, the **Human Rights Memorial Monument** across the road is designed to serve this purpose. The words on the graceful stele, by writer Bo Yang, who spent twelve years in prison here, read: "During that era, how many mothers have cried through the night for their children imprisoned here?"

To the west of Lyudao Lodge, between Gongguan and Jhongliao villages, is the Lyudao **Prison**, a maximum-security complex built in 1971 to hold Taiwan's most dangerous convicts, including some of the island's infamous organized crime bosses. Under pressure from President Chen Shui-bian and Vice President Annette Lu – both former political prisoners held on Lyudao – the prison has been ordered shut and inmates have been moved to facilities on the Taiwanese mainland. The same is true of the Occupational Skills Training Centre, a rehabilitation centre for convicts, located just east of the Lyudao Lodge.

student-driven scooter armadas that race round the island. Further south along the main road is **Siao Changcheng** (Little Great Wall), a short path tracing the spine of a hill to a lookout point, and indeed bearing some resemblance to a stretch of Great Wall winding towards a guard tower. It's a quick walk to the lookout point, from where there are truly majestic views of the shoreline to both the north and south. Jutting out of the Haishenping Bay to the south are two giant **rock formations** named Sleeping Beauty Rock and Pekingese Dog Rock.

Carry on south and you'll come to the trailheads of two footpaths that eventually link up and lead over the hills in the island's centre before dropping down behind Nanliao Village on the west side. The first is the **Guoshan Historic Trail**, a short but quiet walk of less than 2km that runs into the maintenance road leading north to Nanliao Village. The second, the **Huoshaoshan Trail**, begins across the road from beautiful **Baishawei Beach** and skirts the eastern flank of 281-metre Huoshaoshan, the now-extinct volcano whose eruption created the island. However, the mountaintop has a military radar installation and is strictly off-limits: this trail also meets up with the maintenance road heading north to Nanliao.

Jhaorih Hot Springs

Near Lyudao's southern tip are the **Jhaorih Hot Springs** (March–Oct open 24hr, Nov–Feb 6am–10pm; NT$200; ☎089/671133), which rank as one of the world's most unusual hot-springs areas. The saltwater hot springs are created by a rare phenomenon: the tide carries seawater into coral crevices, where it's funneled deep underground, heated geothermically and pressurized back to the earth's surface. Here, it has been harnessed into three circular **seaside-bathing pools**, each with different temperatures that allow you to adjust gradually to the hottest one: the range is typically 53–93°C, and once you get too hot you can clamber into the sea to cool down. The combination of salt and sulphur – the main mineral in the water – is thought to be most salubrious. During the scorching-hot summer, when a daytime soak would be anathema to most, the pools are open 24 hours, allowing you to come for a late-night dip and stay through to the **sunrise**, as the waves crash against the surrounding tidal flats. Just inside the entrance are changing facilities and an open-air spa pool with several gushing **massage showers**.

Snorkelling and diving

Snorkelling is another highlight of the island, ringed as it is by remarkably intact coral that teems with tropical fish. The sheer diversity of marine life here easily rivals or surpasses many better-known snorkelling areas in Southeast Asia, making it a real treat if you can manage to avoid the summer weekend crowds. If you plan to snorkel, it's recommended that you bring your own kit: mask, snorkel and neoprene booties (to protect your feet from sharp coral) should be sufficient. However, at times **jellyfish** can be a problem, in which case you can easily rent a wetsuit from one of the many snorkelling and diving operators in Nanliao and Gongguan villages. The best spots are close to shore and an easy wade out and unless you're a weak swimmer or are uncomfortable in the ocean, it's best to avoid the organized snorkelling trips arranged by local operators. Due to the pervasive Taiwanese fear of deep water, such outings will entail a group of several dozen people, clad in life vests and linked together by a rope forming a line across the shallow water with each participant waiting for a turn to look through the hole of a ring buoy at whatever fish might be swimming by at that moment. Even if you only rent equipment from these operators, they may try to insist that you adhere to their safety protocol – it's best to tell them up front that you merely want to rent some gear and make your own way. Ironically, the cautious nature of these local outings has left much of the coral incredibly well preserved, with only the wading tracks where groups line up being trampled.

The best-known snorkelling spots are Caikou and Shihlang, both of which have gentle currents and are very safe. The stretch of reef near **Dabaisha Beach** in the southwest also has excellent snorkelling, but as currents here are less predictable it's better suited to strong swimmers and scuba divers. The most easygoing operators are near Gongguan Village, not far from the **Caikou Diving Area**. Serious **scuba divers**, or those wishing to learn, will have problems with the local operators unless you speak fluent Mandarin; though the diving here is definitely worth the effort in coming, you'd be better off trying to arrange your trip in advance. One operator specializing in diving trips off the coast of Lyudao is *Green Island Diving* (Ⓦwww.greenislanddiving.com), which runs **hammerhead-shark**-spotting excursions off the island's southern tip from January to March of each year. For scuba instruction, a reputable company is the Taichung-based *Taiwan Scuba* (Ⓣ09/23818469, Ⓦwww.taiwanscuba .com), which offers **PADI certification** courses.

Eating

Both Nanliao and Gongguan villages are filled with **seafood restaurants**, although some tend to cater to large tour groups, making it difficult for independent travellers and small groups to order specific items. At the northwestern end of Gongguan Village are a couple of open-air **barbecue restaurants** with festive atmospheres and plenty of grilled seafood: in summer, these places draw the party crowd, especially university students putting away their share of Taiwan Beer. In Nanliao Village, the restaurant most amenable to foreigners is *Chi Tang You Yu* at no. 150 (noon–2pm & 6pm–midnight), which serves up tasty seafood and has a relaxing seafront patio on the first floor. The most popular dish here is the garlic octopus (*suan xiang zhangyu*). A great spot for a light **breakfast** of egg pancakes (*dan bing*) is *Mei Er Mei* at no. 103–1 (5am–noon), which also has a breezy upstairs balcony with splendid sea views.

Lanyu (Orchid Island)

Jutting sharply out of the sea some 91km southeast of Taitung, **LANYU** (Orchid Island), is one of Taiwan's most precious places, overflowing with unbridled beauty and holding endless cultural fascination. This volcanic island is mostly a green-velvet mountain, surrounded by a flat, narrow strip of alluvial plain that stretches into some of the most unspoilt **coral reef** in all of Asia. In addition to its astounding natural allure, Lanyu is the sole domain of Taiwan's purest aboriginal tribe: the seafaring **Tao** or "Dawu" (see Contexts p.522), whose isolation has allowed them to preserve much of their traditional heritage. Despite all this – and the fact that it's fairly easy to reach for most of the year – remarkably few travellers make it to Lanyu, but those who do find themselves enchanted by its many charms, and some consider it the most memorable part of their travels in Taiwan. Much of the appeal is its sheer simplicity: apart from a budding seasonal tourism business, there is no industry on the island and it remains blessedly free of development. There are few tourist sites per se, with the main attractions being the rich tropical scenery, the Tao villages with their

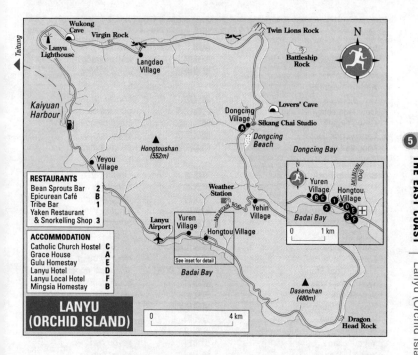

signature **semi-subterranean houses**, and some of the world's most under-rated **snorkelling**. Even in the height of summer, when nearby Lyudao is choked with tourists, Lanyu is quiet and peaceful, a place to relax and absorb its timeless rhythms.

Some history

Lanyu's history has long been defined by its remoteness, with its native Tao inhabitants left mostly to themselves for the better part of eight hundred years. Traditionally a peaceful seagoing people with strong cultural and linguistic links to the Philippines' **Bantan Islands**, the Tao's relations with outsiders were mainly limited to small-scale trade with Bantan islanders and eastern Taiwan's coastal **Ami tribe** until their initial contact with Dutch colonists in the early seventeenth century. The tribe has for centuries made its livelihood from **fishing** and taro farming, gradually adding millet and sweet potatoes to the crops they have cultivated along the thin belts of fertile land between the mountains and the sea. Though there were infrequent conflicts between villages, the tribe as a whole maintained its cohesion through social conventions, particularly its strict code of **taboos**: many of these related to respect for life and protection of nature, which helped ensure a sustainable supply of the resources necessary for their survival.

During the **Japanese** colonial period, the occupiers were intrigued with Tao culture and did little to influence it, although an error by a Japanese anthropologist led to the misnaming of the tribe as the "**Yami**" (which merely means "people") – a name that stuck until recent years. Things began to change for the Tao after the KMT seized power, when boatloads of Han Chinese were sent to the island in an attempt to Sinicize the tribe. Although the Tao fiercely resisted

Lanyu (Orchid Island)

Lanyu	蘭嶼	*lányŭ*
Kaiyuan Harbour	開元港	*kāiyuángăng*
Lanyu Airport	蘭嶼機場	*lányŭ jīchăng*

Accommodation

Grace House	恩典居	*ēndiăn jū*
Gulu Homestay	古魯民宿	*gŭlŭ mínsù*
Lanyu Hotel	蘭嶼別館	*lányŭ bièguăn*
Lanyu Local Hotel	蘭嶼民宿	*lányŭ mínsù*
Mingsia Homestay	明霞民宿	*míngxiá mínsù*

The island

Battleship Rock	軍艦岩	*jūnjiàn yán*
Dongcing Beach	東清灣	*dōngqīng wān*
Dongcing Village	東清村	*dōngqīng cūn*
Dragon Head Rock	龍頭岩	*lóngtóu yán*
Hongtou Village	紅頭村	*hóngtóu cūn*
Langdao Village	朗島村	*lăngdăo cūn*
Lanyu Lighthouse	蘭嶼燈塔	*lányŭ dēngtă*
Lovers' Cave	情人洞	*qíngrén dòng*
Sikang Chai Studio	希岡菜工作室	*xīgāngcài gōngzuōshì*
Twin Lions Rock	雙獅岩	*shuāngshī yán*
Virgin Rock	玉女岩	*yùnǚ yán*
Weather Station	氣象觀測所	*qìxiàng guāncèsuŏ*
Wukong Cave	五孔洞	*wŭkŏng dòng*
Yehin Village	野銀村	*yěyín cūn*
Yeyou Village	椰油村	*yéyóu cūn*
Yuren Village	漁人村	*yúrén cūn*

Eating and drinking

Bean Sprouts Bar	荳芽菜酒吧	*dòuyácài jiŭbā*
Epicurean Café	無餓不坐	*wú'é bùzuò*
Tribe Bar	部落酒吧	*bùluò jiŭbā*
Yaken Restaurant & Snorkelling Shop	茶坊	*yaken cháfāng*

the campaign, intermarriages did take place, slightly diluting their genetic purity and blurring once-clear lines of ancestry. In 1966, the KMT banned the Tao's traditional **underground homes** and had them torn down and replaced with concrete buildings. However, the shoddy construction and above-ground design of these structures made them vulnerable to the formidable typhoons that hit the island each year, and many were destroyed, forcing the government to lift the ban in 1980.

Despite the government's assimilation efforts, the Tao have been more successful than any other Taiwanese aboriginal group in preserving their old ways of life, and time-honoured customs are still routinely observed. A few villages consist almost exclusively of the stone semi-underground dwellings, and some elderly men still wear traditional **loincloths**, though the number is rapidly diminishing. The rite of passing along massive **silver helmets** from father to son is still observed, though the younger generation is losing interest in this custom and the art of silversmithing is in danger of dying out. One conventional practice that looks set to stay is the building of handmade **wooden canoes**, the intricately carved and colourfully painted vessels that, more than anything else, have come to symbolize the sea-hardy character of the Tao people (see p.438). Still, modernization is taking its toll, with Lanyu's estimated three-thousand-strong Tao population dwindling fast as young men forsake silver helmets and loincloths in favour of baseball caps and blue jeans and leave the island in search of greater economic prospects. Another threat, and one which has catapulted Lanyu into the international news headlines over the years, is the presence of 98,000 barrels of low-level **nuclear waste** that the Taiwan Power Company has stored on the island's southern tip since 1982. Locals believe that some of the storage containers have begun to leak, killing many fish, and for years there have been vehement protests calling for removal of the waste (see Contexts p.523).

Arrival, transport and information

Lanyu Airport (℡089/732220) is about 2km north of **Hongtou (Redhead) Village**, the island's main commercial hub, with the biggest choice of hotels and restaurants. In summer, you're likely to be greeted by touts offering you accommodation and scooter rental: most are friendly and will give you a lift into Hongtou Village, although chances are they'll drop you off at their home-stay. Expect a similar reception if you arrive by ferry at **Kaiyuan Harbour**, several kilometres north of Hongtou Village. Though the touts here might at first seem a bit off-putting, keep in mind that scooters are seldom available for rent at either the airport or harbour, and if you decline their services you could wind up on a long, hot walk into Hongtou Village.

The **vehicle rental** shop is alongside the main road, just below the *Lanyu Hotel*. **Scooters** cost NT$400–500 per day, depending on how new they are; however, if you agree to rent a scooter for three days or more, you should be able to bargain them down to about NT$350 a day, payable in advance. Make sure there's enough fuel in the tank to at least get you to the island's only petrol station, next to the harbour. While a scooter is ideal for a sunny summer day, if you're visiting in winter or during a rainy spell you might consider the more comfortable option of renting a **car** for about NT$1500 a day. A few **bicycles** are also available for rent here (NT$150 per day), and these make for a pleasant way to tour around the mostly flat 37-kilometre sealed road that loops round the island. There are no taxis, but a **bus** makes four daily loops round the island, starting from **Yeyou Village**, about 2km south of the harbour. The bus stops at all villages – and basically anywhere so long as you ask the driver in advance. If you want to flag it down you'll need to make your intentions fairly obvious. Many villagers depend on this bus, and though it's not a particularly quick or convenient way to get around, it's a great way to rub elbows with the locals. The round-island road is not heavily trafficked and can make for a nice, if long, **walk**, but it can be uncomfortably hot in summer and intolerably wet during the winter.

Given Lanyu's undeveloped nature, there is no tourist office, but some hotels can provide you with basic maps. The friendly owners of the *Tribe Bar* in Hongtou Village (see p.439) speak some English and are excellent sources of information on Tao culture and festivals.

Accommodation

Lanyu's major villages all have ample **accommodation**, but the places best suited for independent travellers are in Hongtou Village and the adjacent Yuren Village, while quaint Dongcing Village on the island's sparsely populated east side has a cosy **homestay** offering delicious home-cooked meals. Most of the accommodation is basic but clean, and on average it's the cheapest in Taiwan.

Hongtou Village

Gulu Homestay 135 Hongtou Village ℡089/732584. Though it's a bit tricky to find, this tiny homestay has two bright, well-kept rooms with double beds and a shared bathroom that offer some of the best value on the island. To get there, go straight to the top of the hill along the road in front of the *Yaken Restaurant*; at the top, turn right and it's about 20m further on the left. Alternatively, ask for directions at the *Tribe Bar*. ➊

Lanyu Hotel 45 Hongtou Village ℡089/731611. Overpriced concrete box catering mostly to Taiwanese tour groups, but an acceptable option if everything else is full. Guests can order breakfast (NT$100), lunch (NT$200) and dinner (NT$200) in advance. It also conducts bus tours round the island (minimum of eight people) for NT$300 a head, and snorkelling outings from NT$400 per person. ➍

Lanyu Local Hotel Directly across the main road from the hospital ℡089/731601. Offers half a dozen rooms, including a large, bright dormitory (NT$400 per bed). Guests can make themselves at home on the rooftop patio, which has sweeping ocean views. ➌

Yuren Village

Mingsia Homestay 77 Yuren Village ℡089/731623. Adjoining the *Epicurean Café* and run by the same family, this homestay has six rooms and can hold up to twenty people; reservations are recommended in summer. ➊

Catholic Church Hostel In the centre of the village. Lanyu's cheapest accommodation, but also its most spartan with only thin mattresses on the floor of its three basement rooms (shared bathroom and kitchen facilities). To stay here, ask anyone in the village for the church's caretaker. NT$200 per person.

Dongcing Village

Grace House 69 Dongcing Village ℡089/732885. Immaculate homestay run by the family of the village's Presbyterian minister, a hospitable Tao man who speaks excellent Mandarin and English. A true homestay, rooms are in the family house, with air conditioning on the first floor and breezy six-person rooms upstairs. Guests here can share traditional, home-cooked Tao meals with the family, though you must let them know in advance. If you make a reservation, the owner's son can give you a lift from the airport or ferry pier; alternatively, rent a scooter in Hongtou Village and drive here yourself. Note that alcohol and cigarettes are prohibited, and there is a 10pm curfew. ➋

The island

Lanyu is mostly devoid of designated tourist sight, and one of the best things to do is to simply take a scooter or bicycle round the island, stopping at your leisure to swim, snorkel or just soak up the captivating coastal scenery. The surrounding igneous rock has been sculpted by wind and water into curious formations, the best known of which is **Dragon Head Rock**, at Lanyu's southeastern tip. Other distinctive stone configurations, all on the north side, are **Battleship Rock**, **Twin Lions Rock** and **Virgin Rock**. Just past Virgin Rock is the **Wukong (Five-hole) Cave**, a series of five grottoes eroded into petrified coral. The Tao once called these grottoes the "Home of Evil Spirits" and forbade women and children from coming here.

One of the most exciting things to do is to take a ride over the winding **mountain road** that connects Hongtou and Yehin villages, with each bend offering a new perspective on the coastline far below. Near the top of the pass is a turnoff to an extremely steep bit of road that leads to Lanyu's **weather station**, which commands astounding views of Dongcing Bay to the east: sunrises here are truly spectacular. The intriguing **Yehin Village** is the only community on the island that still has more **semi-underground homes** than modern structures. These dwellings, dug into the earth, fortified with low walls of wood or stone and covered with thatched roofs, still withstand the test of the typhoons that rip through the Pacific each year. Close to many homes are **sitting platforms** with thatched roofs, where villagers while away balmy afternoons chatting, playing cards, chewing Betel nut – and, for the men, often drinking copious amounts of alcohol. The village is

△ Lanyu Traditional Canoe

Lanyu's colourful festivals

Every year, Lanyu's villages are swept up in traditional **festivals**, considered by many to be the most colourful and exotic in Taiwan, and certainly the most profound and vivid expressions of the enduring Tao identity. The three major events are listed below.

The **Flying-Fish Festival**, which takes place every spring – usually in March – just before the flying-fish season begins, is essentially a coming-of-age ceremony for young Tao males that also is viewed as the harbinger of a plentiful summer flying-fish catch. During the festival, young men dressed in loincloths, steel helmets and breastplates chant for the return of the flying fish before they paddle out to sea in their canoes. The flying fish is an important figure in Tao mythology, and it was historically felt that the more flying fish a young man could catch, the greater his merit to a would-be bride.

The **Millet Harvest Festival**, usually held in mid-June, is a vibrant extravaganza highlighted by an ancient dance performed by the men and the surreal **hair dance** of long-haired Tao women. The latter, which entails the synchronized, dervish-like whirling of long locks of hair by women in a circle, is an unforgettable sight.

Boat-launching festivals are much harder to track, as they are only held when a village has finished building a handade canoe, and the completion dates for these are always very rough estimates (but usually in the warmer months). However, if your visit coincides with the christening of a new canoe, you're in for a real treat. The ornate vessels are built through a painstaking process of binding 27 separate pieces of wood together without a single nail that typically takes two to three years to complete. Once a canoe has been built, intricately carved and painted in red, white and black, villagers hold a monumental **feast** in preparation for the ceremonial launch. Once everyone has finished eating, the canoes are carried down to the sea, where the men perform an elaborate dance in the water before paddling out into the open ocean.

strikingly photogenic, but be careful if people wander into your viewfinder, as many Tao don't want their likenesses captured on film and you could find yourself becoming decidedly unwelcome.

A few kilometres north of Yehin is the dazzling **Dongcing Beach**, with fine white sand and some of Lanyu's safest swimming. Nearby is Dongcing Village, with its inviting homestay and one of Taiwan's oddest art studios; the **Sikang Chai Studio** at 38 Dongcing Village (℡089/732793), inside a weather-beaten waterfront shack adorned with a motley array of ornaments, has a curious selection of Tao-influenced **woodcarvings** and sculpture, many with maritime themes. The owner, a young Tao fisherman–cum–artist who renders his Chinese name as "Sikang Chai", should be happy to show you around his shop, which is closed most mornings while the artist is out fishing for a living. If you'd like to buy some original art, it's best to come in the afternoon; if the studio is locked up, ask in the village for the owner by name. In front of the village along the waterfront is Lanyu's largest collection of traditional **wooden canoes**, each exquisitely carved and painted in red and white.

In the island's north is **Langdao Village**, another idyllic Tao community with numerous semi-underground houses and handmade wooden canoes.

Snorkelling and diving

The combination of untainted coral reef and the Japan Current, which brings in all manner of tropical marine life, makes Lanyu an ideal place for snorkelling and diving, and even in summer you can usually have an entire section of reef all to yourself. One distinctive aspect of Lanyu's coral is that it is home to an abundance of amazingly beautiful **sea snakes**, which are easy to spot even when snorkelling but tend to keep their distance and are not considered very dangerous. The most common snake sports zebra-like black-and-white stripes, and sighting one of these is an exhilarating experience. Though superb snorkelling can be had all over the island, the two spots that are easiest to access and which consistently have the greatest variety of fish are on the northern shore, between Twin Lions Rock and Langdao Village (see map p.433). Most hotels in Hongtou Village can arrange **snorkelling trips**, but it's not necessary to participate in these if you have rented your own transport. The most flexible operator is based at the *Yaken Restaurant* (see below), which can arrange both snorkelling and diving trips or just rent you a mask, snorkel and neoprene booties (NT$150 per day). For a **guided trip** of about two hours, the cost per person is NT$400 without a boat and NT$600 with a boat that takes you to some fantastic outlying reef where you're virtually guaranteed to spot sea snakes.

Eating and drinking

Lanyu has a delightful bundle of **restaurants** and **bars** in Hongtou and Yuren villages, where you can sample traditional Tao fare and fresh seafood or simply usher in a summer evening with a cold beer. However, some of these establishments close during the winter. The island's most outstanding restaurant is the 🍴 *Epicurean Café* at 77 Yuren Village (11.30am–2pm & 6–11.30pm; ☎089/731623). The Tao food here is excellent, and from April to August the kitchen serves up a set meal (NT$250) of **sun-dried flying fish**, local veggies, taro and a drink. The patio upstairs is a relaxing spot for an after-dinner beverage. Another place that often serves Tao cuisine is the *Tribe Bar* at 48 Hongtou Village (☎089/732540; 11am–2.30pm & 6.30–11.30pm), in the heart of Hongtou Village. On summer evenings, it's usually packed with tourists eager to try its nightly set dinners (NT$300) of fresh fish, vegetables, taro and tea. Sometimes the chef likes to experiment with Southeast Asian ingredients, giving the sets a Thai flavour. Reservations are recommended in summer. The best place for **breakfast**, including morning tea or coffee, is the friendly *Yaken Restaurant* at 38 Hongtou Village (6am–7pm; ☎089/731635), just across from the post office. In addition to delicious dumplings, steamed buns and egg pancakes (*dan bing*), they also do Western breakfasts such as omelettes with toast and bacon or ham. For lunch, they can prepare passable hamburgers and spaghetti. Locals flock here throughout the day for their **iced milk tea**. The owners are very helpful and can arrange scooter rental as well as snorkelling outings. A great place for afternoon or **evening drinks** is the open-air seaside *Bean Sprouts Bar* (April–Oct noon–midnight; closed in winter), perched above the beach in front of Badai Bay about midway between Yuren and Hongtou villages. This bar, with comfortable **hammocks** strung up alongside it, has a wide selection of **cocktails** and bottled beers, as well as coffee and tea.

Travel details

Flights

Hualien to: Kaohsiung (3–4 daily; 55min); Taichung (3–5 daily; 55min); Taipei (12 daily; 40min).
Taitung to: Taipei (7–9 daily; 50min); Taichung (4 daily; 1hr 10min); Lyudao (3 daily; 15min); Lanyu (6 daily; 25min).

Trains

Hualien to: Fulong (5 express daily; 2hr); Luodong (14 express daily; 1hr 20min); Suaosin (8 express daily; 1hr); Taipei (14 express daily; 2hr 50min); Taitung (9 express daily; 2hr 40min).
Taitung to: Hualien (9 express daily; 2hr 40min); Kaohsiung (5 daily; 2hr 45min); Pingdong (4 daily; 2hr 20min); Fangliao (4 daily; 1hr 40min); Taipei (6 daily; 5hr 45min).

Buses

Hualien to: Lishan (1 daily; 4hr 30min); Taroko National Park Visitor Center (frequent; 25min); Taitung (9 daily; 3hr); Tiansiang (7 daily; 1hr).
Taitung to: Chenggong (12 daily; 1hr); Fonggang (9 daily; 3hr); Guanshan (3 daily; 1hr); Hualien (9 daily; 3hr); Jhihben (11 daily; 40min); Kaohsiung (11 daily; 4hr); Lidao (2 daily; 2hr); Taichung (2 nightly; 6hr 30min); Tianchih (1 daily; 5hr).
Tiansiang to: Dayuling (1 daily; 2hr); Hualien (7 daily; 1hr); Lishan (1 daily; 2hr 45min).

Ferries

Taitung (Fugang Harbour) to: Lyudao (every two hours in summer; 40min); Lanyu (every two hours in summer; 2hr 20min).

6

The Taiwan Strait Islands

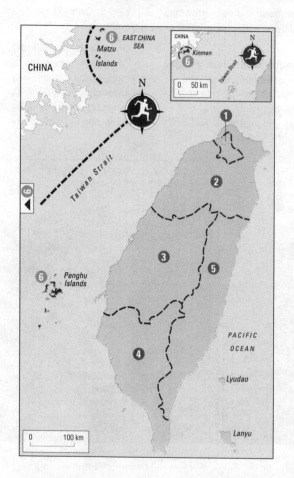

CHAPTER 6 # Highlights

* **Penghu's main islands**
  Explore the historic and
  cultural sights of Penghu,
  Baisha and Si islands on a
  scooter. **See p.454**

* **North Sea Islands (Penghu Archipelago)** Snorkel in
  turquoise waters surrounding
  Sianjiau and Mudou islets.
  See p.458

* **South Sea Islands (Penghu Archipelago)** Spend the
  night at Wangan Island,
  the annual nesting site of
  the endangered Green Sea
  Turtle. **See p.459**

* **Kinmen** Extensive tunnels,
  war museums, ancestral halls
  and unique hybrid architecture. **See p.463**

* **Beigan (Matzu Islands)** Stroll
  secluded beaches, sample
  superb seafood and stay the
  night in Cinbi Village. **See
  p.490**

* **Dongyin (Matzu Islands)**
  The most dramatic scenery
  in the Matzu Islands, with
  sheer cliffs plunging to the
  sea, capped by the lonely
  Dongyong Lighthouse. **See
  p.497**

△ Matzu, View from Yuntai Mountain on Nangan

6

The Taiwan Strait Islands

he **TAIWAN STRAIT ISLANDS**, sprinkled across the windswept channel that separates Taiwan from the People's Republic of China, comprise some of Taiwan's most treasured territory and hold endless fascination for both casual holidaymakers and Chinese history buffs. With enormous geopolitical significance that far transcends their tiny sizes, the islands to this day form a natural buffer between the two "Chinas", two rival ideologies and two diametrically opposed systems of government. Though most of the world knows of them only vaguely for their roles in the struggle between communism and capitalism – and now between totalitarianism and democracy – in opening to the outside world they are starting to be recognized for their rich historic and cultural heritages as well.

Kinmen and the Matzu Islands, all huddled just off the mainland Chinese coast, were once among the world's most austere **Cold War flashpoints** but are now becoming the main bridges for closer economic, political and cultural ties between Taiwan and the People's Republic. Despite the damage caused to these islands by heavy PRC bombardment in the 1950s and 60s, many historic monuments and relics remain largely intact, testifying to their prolific histories and strategic importance as maritime trading entrepots. **Kinmen**, an island of extensive tunnels and imposing military installations, is also an archeological haven, with well-preserved **Ming dynasty constructions** and entire villages of hybrid **Chinese-European houses**. Closer to the main island of Taiwan, the **Penghu Archipelago** is littered with ruins from the Dutch colonial period as well as successive Chinese regimes, and boasts some of Asia's most magnificent **golden-sand beaches** and unspoilt coral reefs. In the warmer months, regular commuter ferries allow for easy island-hopping here, opening up possibilities for a variety of water sports, from the region's most underrated **snorkelling** and diving to some of the world's most celebrated **windsurfing**. In addition, the curious **basalt columns** that buttress the sheer cliffs of many of Penghu's islands give them a mysterious, primordial dimension and make them eminently photogenic.

All of the Taiwan Strait islands are becoming increasingly easy to get to, with frequent flights for most of the year and fairly convenient ferry connections during calm seas. With such a broad range of attractions and activities, most tourists who take the time to visit these extraordinary islands find them among the main highlights of their visits to Taiwan.

The Penghu Islands

The windswept **PENGHU ISLANDS** are considered national treasures by the Taiwanese, who invariably gush over their storied histories, striking topography, searing heat and, perhaps most of all, brilliant fine-sand **beaches** that attract legions of holidaymakers every summer. Situated in the south of the strait, the sprawling archipelago stretches some 60km north to south and

40km east to west, encompassing 64 islands – only twenty of which are still inhabited. The major population centres are on the **main islands** of Penghu, Baisha and Si – the large landmasses that comprise the island chain's heart. Sprinkled to the north and south of here are distinct groups of islets called the **North Sea Islands** and the **South Sea Islands**, accessible by ferries operating from two separate hubs. The largest island – and the archipelago's namesake – is **Penghu**, whose main town of **Magong** is the primary entry and exit point for most tourists.

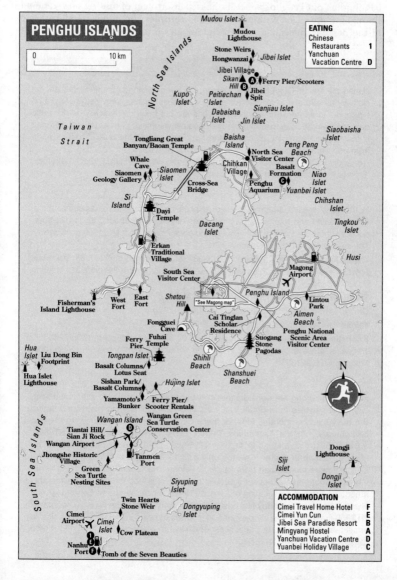

The Penghu Islands are continually buffeted by strong **northeasterly winds** that have weathered away their rock foundations, creating some of their biggest attractions – the magnificent **basalt mesas** that rise sharply from the sea in astonishing arrays of temple-like columns. The winds also make Penghu a major mecca for **windsurfing**, particularly in winter, when Magong hosts one of the sport's premier international competitions. The islands are also havens for other **water sports** such as sailing, sea kayaking, fishing and surfing. In addition, the **coral reefs** are home to an amazing variety of tropical marine life, making **snorkelling** one of the most popular tourist activities.

Rounding out Penghu's appeal is the rich assortment of historic sites scattered throughout the chain. With more than 165 **temples**, the archipelago boasts one of the densest concentrations of religious sites in the country. Allow yourself

Getting to the Penghu Islands

During the March–October tourist season, the Penghu Islands are eminently accessible by air and sea from Taiwan's major west-coast cities – provided there are no typhoons. In **winter**, transport connections are cut back dramatically as domestic demand dwindles due to strong winds and colder weather. For most visitors, Magong is the main arrival point, its airport and ferry pier fielding the bulk of traffic to and from mainland Taiwan.

In addition, the biggest of the South Sea Islands – **Wangan** and **Cimei** – both have airports that host frequent flights from mainland Taiwanese cities.

By air

In the busy season, Magong can be reached **by air** daily from Taipei, Taichung, Chiayi, Tainan and Kaohsiung, with services running from about 7am to mid-afternoon. Flights take thirty to fifty minutes and prices range from NT$1350 to NT$1850. The airlines operating from each city are:

Taipei: Far Eastern Air Transport ☏02/33935388, Magong ☏06/9249388; TransAsia Airways ☏02/29724599, Magong ☏06/9218500; Uni Air ☏02/23583131, Magong ☏06/9216350

Taichung: Mandarin Airlines ☏04/4254236, Magong ☏06/9216966

Chiayi: Uni Air ☏05/2862363, Magong ☏06/9216350

Tainan: Uni Air ☏06/2602811; Magong ☏06/9216350

Kaohsiung: Far Eastern Air Transport ☏07/3371388, Magong ☏06/9249388; TransAsia Airways ☏07/3359355, Magong ☏06/9218500; Uni Air ☏07/7911000, Magong ☏06/9216350

By sea

Ferries to Magong are considerably cheaper than flying and are still convenient, with daily services from Budai (just west of Chiayi), Tainan and Kaohsiung during the busy summer months. Most of these don't run from late October to the end of February, but the **Taiwanline Taihua Ferry** from Kaohsiung (5hr, NT$660, ☏07/5615313) and Magong (4.5hr; NT$629; ☏06/9264087) has a year-round service, though in winter it makes only four to five trips per week. Though the sailing time is longer than from Budai or Tainan, the *Taihua Ferry* is much larger – holding more than a thousand people, plus vehicles – so the ride is considerably smoother. From the beginning of Chinese New Year to the end of September, the **Huaci Shipping Company** has one ferry daily from Tainan (2hr; NT$750 economy/ NT$950 first class). The shortest option in terms of sea-travel time is the *All Star*, a small ferry that runs from Budai (west of Chiayi) to Magong daily from mid-March to early October (1hr; NT$650).

at least a week if you want to see the most significant sights and visit several outlying islands.

Some history

Their location in the middle of an important navigation route has for centuries put the Penghu Islands in the path of **colonial invaders**. Though they were used as transit points as early as the late tenth century, archeological evidence suggests that the first hamlets were not formed until the early twelfth century, In 1281, shortly after the **Mongols** conquered China and founded the Yuan dynasty, they set up an official garrison to govern Penghu – making it the first part of what is now Taiwan to be subjected to mainland authority.

During the late Ming period, Penghu's population began to rise dramatically as droves of **southern Fujianese** fled the political and military upheaval on the mainland. It was during this time that the **Dutch** became the first Europeans to lay claim to Penghu, setting up a temporary base in 1604. Even though the Ming court had officially turned its back on the islands, upon hearing of the arrival of the Dutch fleet the government expelled them under threat of force. After failing to seize other outposts in the South China Sea, the Dutch returned in 1622, reoccupied the main island of Penghu and built a fort near Magong. In response, Ming forces in 1624 attacked the Dutch fort, and, after eight months of fighting, the Dutch signed a treaty that actually allowed them to build outposts on the main island of Taiwan in exchange for leaving Penghu.

In 1661, when Ming loyalist **Koxinga**'s fleet was en route to Taiwan to kick out the Dutch and regroup for its larger goal of restoring Ming sovereignty, they used Penghu as a base and a garrison was later established here. But their rule over the islands was short-lived: Qing dynasty admiral **Shi Lang** convinced Emperor Kangxi that Taiwan should be incorporated into the empire – in large part to tighten control over anti-Qing rebels – and in 1683 the admiral seized Penghu in a naval battle. Just over two hundred years later, in 1884, the **French** briefly occupied Penghu, but their rule was cut short when the Qing ceded the islands to **Japan** in the 1895 Sino-Japanese Treaty of Shimonoseki. Just over fifty years later, the archipelago again fell into Chinese hands, when the **National-ists** seized it during their retreat from mainland China.

Following the lifting of martial law in 1987, Taiwanese began to visit and the islands have continued to grow in popularity, now ranking as one of the country's top tourist destinations. In recognition of the island chain's natural and historic significance, it was officially designated a **national scenic area** in 1995.

Orientation and transport

For purposes of transport, the archipelago is divided into three parts: the **main islands** of Penghu, Baisha and Si, all connected by bridges; the **North Sea Islands**, reached by ferry from the North Sea visitor center on Baisha; and the **South Sea Islands**, served by ferry from the South Sea visitor center in Magong. While most of the main north and south sea islands are accessible by ferry and easily covered by scooter (which can be rented upon arrival), the main islands have limited public transport, with infrequent bus services tailored to locals rather than tourists. As such, you'll need to rent a **scooter** if you want to see the main sights outside of Magong. Alternatively, **taxis** can be hired in Magong, but a full-day tour is likely to cost a minimum of NT$3000, more

The Penghu Islands	澎湖群島	*pénghú qúndǎo*
Arrival and information		
Baisha Sea Tourist Centre	白沙海遊客中心	*báishāhǎi yóukè zhōngxīn*
Cimei Airport	七美機場	*qīměi jīchǎng*
Magong Airport	馬公機場	*mǎgōng jīchǎng*
Ming Yang Company	名揚育樂開發有限公司	*míngyáng yùlè kāifā yǒuxiàn gōngsī*
Nanhu Port	南滬港	*nánhù gǎng*
North Sea Visitor Center	北海遊客中心	*běihǎi yóukè zhōngxīn*
Penghu National Scenic Area Visitor Center	澎湖國家風景區遊客中心	*pénghú guójiā fēngjǐngqū yóukè zhōngxīn*
South Sea Visitor Center	南海遊客中心	*nánhǎi yóukè zhōngxīn*
Tanmen Port	潭門港	*tánmén gǎng*
Wangan Airport	望安機場	*wàng'ān jīchǎng*
Wangan Green Sea Turtle Conservation Center	望安綠蠵龜觀光保育中心	*wàng'ān lǜxīguī guānguāng bǎoyù zhōngxīn*
The islands		
Baisha Island	白沙島	*báishā dǎo*
Cimei Islet	七美嶼	*qīměiyǔ*
Hua Islet	花嶼	*huāyǔ*
Hujing Islet	虎井嶼	*hǔjǐngyǔ*
Jibei Islet	吉貝嶼	*jíbèiyǔ*
Mudou Islet	目斗嶼	*mùdǒuyǔ*
Penghu Island	澎湖本島	*pénghú běndǎo*
Si Island	西嶼	*xīyǔ*
Sianjiau Islet	險礁嶼	*xiǎnjiāoyǔ*
Siaomen Islet	小門嶼	*xiǎoményǔ*
Tongpan Islet	桶盤嶼	*tǒngpányǔ*
Wangan Island	望安島	*wàng'ān dǎo*
Yuanbei Islet	員貝嶼	*yuánbèiyǔ*

during peak periods. However, taxis can be useful for shorter trips to and from the airport (NT$200–300), or from Magong to the North Sea visitor center (NT$500–600).

Scooter rental

Scooters are the most convenient and cost-effective way to get around the main islands, but many rental shops in Magong refuse to rent them to foreigners who don't have a valid Taiwanese driver's licence and an ARC. While this rules out most tourists, some hotels are happy to help overseas guests rent scooters, though they often prefer you to take a tiny 50cc contraption that is considerably slower than the 125cc standard bearer. For example, the staff at the *Jhongsin Hotel* in central Magong could help arrange a rental from an affiliated shop just down the street if you make it clear that you plan to stay in their hotel for a few days. In such a case, the rental shop owner will still want to see some sort of driver's licence and will require you to leave some form of identification as a deposit. If you do rent a scooter, it's best to keep it for a few days, as you can use it to get to the North and South Sea visitor centres and leave it in the nearby car parks if you plan to stay overnight at one of the outlying islands. As scooter rental is generally NT$250/$350 per day for 50cc/125cc machines, this works out dramatically cheaper than taking taxis, for which the minimum charge will be a flat NT$200.

Magong

By far the archipelago's biggest town, **MAGONG** is the major transport hub and has an abundance of hotels, restaurants and **historic monuments.** The downtown area itself is easy to navigate on foot, so you can duck into the narrow lanes that permeate the old centre.

Arrival and information

Magong Airport is about 8km east of the town itself. There is an **airport bus** (30min; NT$15) that makes a few trips downtown each day, but the service isn't timed with arrivals from major cities and even locals don't seem to rely on it. If you have booked accommodation, some hotels include a **pick-up service** in the price; otherwise, take a **taxi**, which should cost about NT$300 to the city centre (the return journey is generally cheaper, ranging from NT$200 to NT$250). If you arrive by **ferry**, most of the hotels are a short walk from the pier; alternatively, some will offer to pick you up if you've reserved ahead.

Just west of the main ferry pier is the **Magong Harbour Terminal Building**, where you can buy return ferry tickets to mainland Taiwan. The desk (daily 8.30–11.30am & 1.30–4.30pm) for the Taiwanline *Taihua Ferry* is on the ground floor, directly across from the main entrance. For the Huaci Shipping Company, the desk (daily 8am–6pm; ☎06/9279999) is on the first floor, just to the left inside the main entrance. Finally, the *All Star's* office (daily 8am–6pm; ☎06/9269721) occupies the terminal building's twelfth floor.

Halfway between the airport and Magong, the **Penghu National Scenic Area visitor center**, 171 Guanghua St (daily 8am–5.30pm; ☎06/9216521), is an excellent place to visit before you head out to the islands. In addition to maps and information, there are interesting exhibits on Penghu culture, geology and marine life. Ask one of the guides at the reception desk for a free interpretive tour of the visitor centre. There are also **visitor centres** for the North Sea Islands (see p.458) and South Sea Islands (see p.459), the latter located at Magong's Third Ferry Pier.

Magong is the only place in the Penghu Islands with **banking** services. As few venues outside of Magong accept credit cards as payment, it's essential to make sure you have enough cash before you leave the city. Many of the 7-Eleven shops have **ATMs**, as does the Bank of Taiwan at 24 Renai Rd, which has the only **foreign-currency exchange** desk. The local **Foreign Affairs Police** at 36 Jhihping Rd can help with visa extensions.

If you're interested in **surfing** or **windsurfing**, stop by Liquid Sport, 36 Huimin 1 Rd (11am–9pm), which rents surfboards ($800 per day) and windsurfing equipment ($1500 per day). Two-hour **windsurfing lessons**, including all equipment, cost NT$1500.

Accommodation

Magong is awash with **hotels** but rooms can become scarce during the June-August school break and on weekends in late spring and early autumn. If you come during one of these busy periods, **reservations** are recommended.

Magong	馬公	*mǎgōng*

Arrival, transport and information

Bank of Taiwan	台灣銀行	*táiwān yínháng*
Bus Station	客運站	*kèyùn zhàn*
Foreign Affairs Police	警察外事課	*jǐngchá wàishìkè*
Guolong Car Rental	國隆旅遊租車	*guólóng dàyóu zūchē*
Magong Harbour Terminal Building	馬公港務大樓	*mǎgōng gǎngwù dàlóu*
Main Ferry Pier	主碼頭	*zhǔ mǎtóu*
Penghu Public Hospital	衛生署澎湖醫院	*wèishēngshǔ pénghú yīyuàn*
South Sea Visitor Center	南海遊客中心	*nánhǎi yóukè zhōngxīn*
South Sea Ferry Pier	南海碼頭	*nánhǎi mǎtóu*

Accommodation

Baohwa Hotel	寶華大飯店	*bǎohuá dàfàndiàn*
Dongsin Homestay	東信民宿	*dōngxìn mínsù*
Fu Lu Shou Hotel	福祿壽飯店	*fúlùshòu fàndiàn*
Hotel Ever Spring	長春大飯店	*chāngchūn dàfàndiàn*
Hwa Shin Palace Hotel	華馨大飯店	*huáxīn dàfàndiàn*
Jhongcing Hotel	中慶大旅社	*zhōngqìng dàlǚshè*
Jhongsin Hotel	中信大旅社	*zhōngxìn dàlǚshè*
Jhongsing Hotel	中興大飯店	*zhōngxīng dàfàndiàn*
Jih Lih Hotel	日立大飯店	*rìlì dàfàndiàn*
Penghu Youth Activity Center	澎湖青年活動中心	*pénghú qīngnián huádòng zhōngxīn*
Sheng Kuo Hotel	勝國大飯店	*shèngguó dàfàndiàn*

The city

Beichen Temple	北辰宮	*běichén gōng*
Chiang Kai-shek Retreat	蔣中正別墅	*jiàng zhōngzhèng biéshù*
Cianyi Tang Chinese Traditional Medicine Business	乾益堂中藥行	*gānyìtáng zhōngyàoháng*
Confucius Temple	孔廟	*kǒng miào*
Four Eyes Well	四眼井	*sìyǎn jǐng*
Guanyin Pavilion	觀音亭	*guānyīn tíng*
Guanyinting Cingshuei Recreation Park	觀音亭親水遊憩區	*guānyīn tíng qìngshuǐ yóuqìqū*
Jhongyang Street	中央街	*zhōngyāng jiē*
Magong City Wall	馬公城牆	*mǎgōng chéng qiáng*
Martyrs' Shrine	忠烈祠	*zhōngliè cí*
Penghu Reclamation Hall	澎湖開拓館	*pénghú kāituò guǎn*
Shihgong Ancestral Hall	施公祠	*shīgōng cí*
Shuncheng Gate	順承門	*shùnchéng mén*
Tianhou Temple	天后宮	*tiānhòu gōng*
Well of a Thousand Soldiers	萬軍井	*wànjūn jǐng*

Eating and drinking

Dao Siao Mian	刀削麵	*dāoxiāomiàn*
Freud Pub	弗洛伊得酒吧	*fúluò yīdé jiǔbā*
Hei Sha Tang	黑砂糖	*hēi shātáng*
Night Food Stalls	夜市小吃攤	*yèshì xiǎochī tan1*
Renai Siao Chih	仁愛小吃	*rén'ài xiǎochī*
Sha Ai Jhuang	傻愛莊	*shǎ'ài zhuāng*
Sunny Colony Pub	陽光殖民地酒吧	*yángguāng zhímíndì jiǔbā*
Yongda Vegetarian Restaurant	永達素食館	*yǒngdá sù shíguǎn*

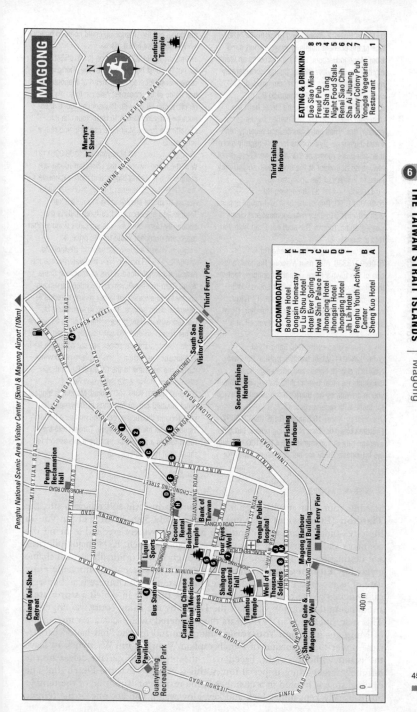

MAGONG

N

Penghu National Scenic Area Visitor Center (5km) & Magong Airport (10km) ▲

Confucius Temple

Martyrs' Shrine

SINSHENG ROAD

SINMING ROAD

SINTIAN 1ST RD

Third Fishing Harbour

BEICHEN STREET

SHUEIYUAN ROAD

HAIFU ROAD

Third Ferry Pier

South Sea Visitor Center

SINGGANG NORTH STREET

YULONG ROAD

Second Fishing Harbour

WENPU ROAD

JHONGHUA ROAD

JHONGJHENG ROAD

SHUDE ROAD

MINGYUAN ROAD

JHIHPING ROAD

Penghu Reclamation Hall

JHONGSIAO ROAD

JHONGHSING ROAD

SHUDE ROAD

JHONGSHAN ROAD

MINSHENG ROAD

SANMIN ROAD

MINTYUAN ROAD

CHONGCING STREET

GUANGMING ROAD

JIANGUO ROAD

Bank of Taiwan

Beichen Temple

Scooter Rental

Liquid Sports

HUIMIN 1ST ROAD

Penghu Public Hospital

LINMIN ROAD

First Fishing Harbour

LINHAI ROAD

Magong Harbour Terminal Building

Main Ferry Pier

Chiang Kai-Shek Retreat

MINZU ROAD

Bus Station

Cianyi Tang Chinese Traditional Medicine Business

Shihgong Ancestral Hall

Four Eyes Well

Tianhou Temple

Well of a Thousand Soldiers

HUIAN ROAD

HUIMIN 1ST ROAD

MINTSU ROAD

FUGUO ROAD

Shuncheng Gate & Magong City Wall

JINGUO ROAD

JINGFU ROAD

SINFU

IESHOU ROAD

Guanyin Pavilion

Guanyinting Recreation Park

0   400 m

ACCOMMODATION
Baohwa Hotel   K
Dongsin Homestay   F
Fu Lu Shou Hotel   H
Hotel Ever Spring   J
Hwa Shin Palace Hotel   C
Jhongcing Hotel   E
Jhongsing Hotel   D
Jhongsing Hotel   G
Jih Lih Hotel   I
Penghu Youth Activity   B
  Center
Sheng Kuo Hotel   A

EATING & DRINKING
Dao Siao Mian   8
Freud Pub   4
Hei Sha Tang   3
Night Food Stalls   5
Renai Siao Chih   6
Sha Ai Jhuang   2
Sunny Colony Pub   7
Yongda Vegetarian   1
  Restaurant

Baohwa Hotel 2 Jhongjheng Rd ☎06/9274881. One of the poshest hotels in town, a short stroll from Magong Harbour, offering discounts on weeknights. The sea-view rooms, though considerably more expensive, are highly recommended. ❺

Dongsin Homestay 12 Jhongsing Rd ☎06/9279123. Just down the street from the *Jhongsin Hotel* (below), and owned by the same person, this small hotel has several recently renovated Japanese-style rooms for only slightly more than the basic rooms at the *Jhongsin*. There is not always an attendant at the front desk, so you may need to enquire at the *Jhongsin*. ❷

Fu Lu Shou Hotel 31 Jhongsing Rd ☎06/9271290. One of the best mid-range options, with extremely friendly management and clean, if slightly aging, rooms. The staff here can help you rent a scooter. ❸

Hotel Ever Spring 6 Jhongjheng Rd ☎06/9273336. Also near Magong Harbour, and one of the town's more upmarket options, featuring gleaming rooms with Internet access. With breakfast included in the room rate, it's fairly priced, even during the height of summer. There are several rooms with harbour views, all at a price. ❹

Hwa Shin Palace Hotel 40 Sanmin Rd ☎06/9264911. While hardly a palace, the *Hwa Shin* is a decent option and offers significant discounts on most weeknights, even in summer. If you're arriving by air, there's a free shuttle service for those with reservations. ❹

Jhongcing Hotel 16 Sanmin Rd ☎06/9273832. Features basic doubles at varying prices, but the average rate in summer is about NT$1000, including breakfast. There are better places to stay for

the price, but the *Jhongcing* could come in handy if everywhere else is full. ❷

Jhongsin Hotel 22 Jhongsing Rd ☎06/9272151. One of the best budget options, the *Jhongsin* is conveniently located in the heart of Magong and has some of the cheapest rates in town. As a result, it can fill up with Taiwanese students, so enquire early in the day to raise your chances of getting a room. Staff here can help you rent a scooter. ❷

Jhongsing Hotel 82 Mincyuan Rd ☎06/9261121. With the same owner as the *Jhongsin*, rooms are comparable if slightly bigger and more expensive. ❷

Jih Lih Hotel 25 Huimin 1st Rd ☎06/9265898. Across from the alley leading to the Beichen Temple and adjacent outdoor food stalls is the spotlessly clean *Jih Lih*, with spacious doubles that represent excellent value for the price. ❹

Penghu Youth Activity Center 11 Jieshou Rd ☎06/9271124. Located near the waterfront along peaceful Jieshou Road is this comfortable China Youth Corp-run hotel, which has fifteen spacious doubles and a variety of larger rooms catering to different-sized groups. Though in summer it is packed with student groups, they tend to fill up the larger rooms so doubles can usually be had. From November to January, prices are cut almost in half. The location is perfect if you're planning to windsurf in the bay next to the Guanyin Pavilion. ❹

Sheng Kuo Hotel 2-12 Syueyuan Rd ☎06/9273891. With 130 rooms, Magong's biggest hotel is kitted out for busloads of Taiwanese tourists. Though the rooms are large and airy, better value can be found elsewhere. Thrown into the room rate is a shuttle service from the airport for those with reservations. ❹

The town

Starting your tour at Magong's most important historic and religious site, the **Tianhou (Empress of Heaven) Temple** (daily 5am–8pm), will put you in the city's oldest quarter. Dedicated to **Mazu**, it's widely credited as being the country's oldest surviving Mazu temple – and, as such, it's a major pilgrimage destination for Taiwanese tourists. Though it was originally a small shrine erected by **Fujianese fishermen** at the end of the sixteenth century, the exact date of its inception is disputed. The earliest date for which there is archeological evidence of the temple's existence is 1604, the year in which a **stone stele** announcing the eviction order of the Dutch by the Ming court was engraved. This stele, unearthed in 1919, bears the weathered twelve-character inscription of Ming general **Shen You-rong**'s smug demand for the "red-haired barbarians" under the command of Dutch captain Wijbrand van Waerwijck to leave the island without a fight. Faced with the prospect of certain defeat by the infinitely larger Ming imperial forces, this is exactly what the Dutch did. The original stele is housed in a chamber at the rear, right-hand side of the temple, but is usually kept under lock and key. However, if you ask one of the temple attendants they might let you have a look. While the stele proves that the temple existed at this site before the Dutch arrived, the structure itself has undergone numerous renovations. In 1922, during the Japanese occupation, a distinguished mainland **Chinese artisan** was hired to oversee the engraving of the present-day structure's elaborate wooden beams – the Chinese artistry, coupled with the Japanese influence, led to the elegant fusion of styles that makes this one of Taiwan's most visually captivating temples.

Down the narrow lane to the right of the Tianhou Temple, then almost immediately to the right, is the so-called **Well of a Thousand Soldiers**, with a modern concrete exterior that seems to belie the story behind it. When Qing general **Shi Lang** arrived on Penghu, his troops were not immediately welcomed by the locals, who refused to share their limited water. Studying the landscape, the crafty general discovered a water source at this spot and, making a display of praying to Mazu for water, he stuck his sword in the ground here, ordering troops to dig for water, which they found almost immediately. The well has long since gone dry. A few feet further down the lane and to the left is the **Shihgong Ancestral Hall**, built in honour of General Shi in 1688.

Follow the lane as it veers left and you will shortly run into the pedestrian-only **Jhongyang Street**, Magong's oldest and now a busy hive of craft shops. At the head of the street is a tiny square, the centrepiece of which is the **Four Eyes Well**, said to have been dug as early as the fifteenth century. Locals believe there is a "Well Mother God" inside, and many come here to pray every month. Believers also use the well water to wash the bodies of loved ones after they die.

On the square next to the well is the **Cianyi Tang Chinese Traditional Medicine Business**, 42 Jhongyang St (7am–9pm), an attractive old multistorey building filled with aromatic medicinal herbs. A bit further north, tucked into an alley between Huimin First Street and Jhongjheng Road, is the **Beichen Temple**, dedicated primarily to the worship of Chu Wang Ye, one of the so-called "pestilence gods" (see Contexts p.529). In front of the temple is a busy outdoor **night market** with several food stalls.

The outskirts

Several hundred metres north, on Jhihping Road, is the **Penghu Reclamation Hall** at 30 Jhihping Rd (10am–10pm, closed Mon & last day of each month; NT$30), once the residence of the county magistrate and now a museum with exhibits on Penghu history and culture.

A few hundred metres south on Jieshou Road is the **Guanyin Pavilion** (daily 5am–8pm). First built in 1696, this small temple is dedicated to **Guanyin**, the Goddess of Mercy, and is an important place of Buddhist worship. Although the temple structure itself has been levelled twice during respective wars with the French and Japanese, the **old bell** inside is original, dating back to 1696. In front of the temple is the expansive **Guanyinting Recreation Park**, located along a bay that is one of the world's best windsurfing spots and the site of international **windsurfing competitions**.

Head south until you reach the **Shuncheng Gate** and a short segment of the old **Magong City Wall**, both completed by Qing forces in 1889 after the war with the French prompted them to step up security. Once part of a network that encircled the entire city, these were the only sections to be spared when the Japanese pulled down the wall in order to build the Magong Port. Climb up the Shuncheng Gate for good views of the sea, and take a stroll through the **abandoned village** adjoining the gate and old wall.

Eastern fringe

To the east of Magong, along Sinsheng Road, is the austere **Confucius Temple** (daily, courtyard open 24hrs). This site originally housed the **Wenshi School**, built by the Qing in 1766 as Penghu's only centre of higher learning. The school was converted into a Confucius temple during the Japanese occupation. Access to the main courtyard is via a pathway to the right of the temple. Closer towards town on Sinsheng Road is the **Martyrs' Shrine**, now a mere shadow of its former grandeur as the towering structure withers from benign neglect.

Eating and drinking

Magong is renowned for its **culinary specialties**, ranging from fresh seafood and dried snacks to signature noodle dishes and ice desserts. There are a number of small outdoor **night markets** where you can sample cheap local food such as seafood noodles, pumpkin rice noodles and deep-fried tofu. Alternatively, the upmarket seafood **restaurants** specialize in several-course meals for large parties. Among the seafood delights that Penghu is most famous for are steamed grouper, raw lobster, abalone and "five-flavour" balloonfish.

Dao Siao Mian 30 Jhongshan Rd. Penghu's most famous noodle joint, this tiny, unassuming place specializes in so-called "knife-cut noodles", shaved out in thick, wide slabs and fried with meat or vegetables (NT$50 per plate). (9.30am–6.30pm, closed Thurs)

Hei Sha Tang 27 Fuguo Rd. Magong's best-known ice dessert shop continues to serve up its specialty eight-flavour delight, with all the little treasures hand made on site. The shop's name means "black sugar", as brown sugar is one of the key ingredients. In winter, hot red bean and brown-sugar soups are served.

Renai Siao Chih 73-1 Renai Rd. This tiny place is famous for its Taiwanese meatballs, wrapped in a glutinous coating (NT$30 for two), and is usually packed with student tourists.

Sha Ai Jhuang 14 Sinsheng Rd. This slightly more upscale restaurant/teahouse, in a renovated house that originally belonged to Penghu's first county chief, has great atmosphere. The interior is lavishly decorated with local crafts, the staff are outgoing, and the menu is unique, with items such as "cactus noodles" (NT$180, only in summer) and "coral pancakes" (made with carrot, egg and sugar, NT$50). There is an extensive list of freshly squeezed juices from NT$120, and cocktails start at NT$170. The restaurant's name roughly translates as "stupid love pub" – a reference to the fact that the owner is the youngest in a family of seven siblings.

Yongda Vegetarian Restaurant 27 Sinsheng Rd. This basic serve-yourself Buddhist restaurant has mediocre vegetarian fare for cheap prices (8am–2pm & 4–7.30pm).

Freud Pub 2-1 Sinsheng Rd. One of Magong's longest-running bars, the *Freud* has by far the city's most extensive drinks list, with a huge selection of whiskies/white liquors and a range of imported bottled beers costing NT$120–170. Basic cocktails are NT$140, and the house special "Absolutely Drunk" ($300) – mixed with five different spirits – is reminiscent of a university punch party. Bartenders are happy to play requested numbers from the formidable collection of CDs and MP3 files (11am–2am).

Sunny Colony Pub 4 Lane 3, Jhongjheng Rd. Tucked away down narrow Lane 3, with an English sign visible from Jhongjheng Road, is this popular bar, with dim lighting, comfortable seating and loud, upbeat music. One of the house specials is cactus juice spiked with rum, but they're pricey at NT$180 per drink (6pm–2am).

The main islands

Elsewhere on **Penghu Island**, as well as on **Baisha** and **Si** islands to the north and northwest, is a good mix of attractions, from cultural sites to often empty beaches, and one could easily spend a fair few days exploring them by scooter.

Aimen Beach	隘門沙灘	*ài'mén shātān*
Baoan Temple	保安宮	*bǎo'ān gōng*
Cai Tinglan Scholar Residence	蔡進士第	*cài jìnshìdì*
Chihkan Village	赤崁村	*chìkàn cūn*
Cow Plateau	牛母坪	*níumǔ píng*
Dayi Temple	大義宮	*dàyì gōng*
East Fort	東嶼古堡	*dōngyǔ gǔbǎo*
Erkan Traditional Village	二崁聚落	*èrkàn jùluò*
Fisherman's Island Lighthouse	西嶼燈塔	*xīyǔ dēngtǎ*
Fongguei Cave	風櫃洞	*fēngguì dòng*
Fuhai Temple	福海宮	*fúhǎi gōng*
Hua Islet Lighthouse	花嶼燈塔	*huāyǔ dēngtǎ*
Jhongshe Historic Village	中社古厝	*zhōngshè gǔcuò*
Jibei Spit	吉貝沙嘴	*jíbèi shāzuǐ*
Jibei Village	吉貝村	*jíbèi cūn*
Lintou Park	林投公園	*líntóu gōngyuán*
Lotus Seat	玄武岩柱狀節理	*xuánwǔ yánzhùzhuàng jiélǐ*
Mudou Lighthouse	目斗嶼燈塔	*mùdǒuyǔ dēngtǎ*
Peng Peng Beach	澎澎灘	*péngpéng tān*
Penghu Aquarium	澎湖水族館	*pénghú shuǐzúhuǎn*
Shanshuei Beach	山水沙灘	*shānshuǐ shātān*
Shetou Hill	蛇頭山	*shétóu shān*
Siaomen Geology Gallery	小門地質博物館	*xiǎomén dìzhì bówùguǎn*
Sikan Hill	西崁山	*xīkàn shān*
Sishan Park	西山公園遊憩區	*xīshān gōngyuán yóuqìqū*
Suogang Stone Pagodas	鎖港子午寶塔	*suǒgǎng zǐwǔ bǎotǎ*
Tiantai Hill	天台山	*tiāntái shān*
Tomb of the Seven Beauties	七美人塚	*qī měirén zhǒng*
Tongliang Great Banyan	通梁古榕	*tōngliáng gǔróng*
Twin Hearts Stone Weir	雙心石滬	*shuāngxīn shíhù*
West Fort	西嶼西台	*xīyǔ xītái*
Whale Cave	鯨魚洞	*jīngyú dòng*

Accommodation

Cimei Travel Home Hotel	七美旅行家旅館	*qīměi lǚxíngjiā lǚguǎn*
Cimei Yun Cun	七美漁村餐旅民宿	*qīměi yúcūn cānlǚ mínsù*
Jibei Sea Paradise Resort	澎湖之美海上樂園	*pénghúzhīměi hǎishang lèyuán*
Mingyang Hostel	名揚山莊	*míngyáng shānzhuāng*
Yanchuan Vacation Centre	岩川育樂	*yánchuān yùlè*
Yuanbei Holiday Village	員貝渡假村	*yuánbèi dùjiācūn*

Penghu Island

Winding south and then west along a narrow peninsula, the area of Penghu Island known as **Pengnan** is filled with historic sites and also has some of the archipelago's finest scenery. Head east out of town along Guanghua Street and turn south at the junction of Highway 201 to find the **Cai Tinglan Scholar Residence**, the tastefully restored house of Penghu's only *jinshi*, or scholar, who passed the third-degree imperial civil service exam during the Qing dynasty. A revered academic and public official, Cai Tinglan was best known for his adventures in Southeast Asia – in 1835, his ship was blown off course by a typhoon while returning to Penghu from the Fujian port of Xiamen. His ship eventually came aground in central Vietnam, from where Cai travelled overland back to China. His written account of the journey, *Miscellaneous Notes from the Southern Seas*, is still referenced by scholars of Southeast Asian studies. The official, a statue of whom is in the courtyard, had the residence built in 1846. Along the lanes behind the residence are many crumbling **Fujian-style houses** surrounded by walls built of coral.

A few kilometres further south on Highway 201 is the small fishing village of **Suogang**, whose centrepieces are the two eleven-metre **Suogang Stone Pagodas**, pyramid-shaped towers believed to drive away evil spirits and provide protection during natural disasters. The pagodas, one called the "north tower" and the other the "south tower", are in separate locations around the village so you may need to ask someone to point you in the right direction.

About 2km southwest of Suogang is the popular **Shanshuei Beach**, with fine sand, clear water and a gentle break that is suitable for surfing in winter. A bit further west is the picturesque **Shihli Beach**, which stretches around an exceptionally calm bay and is a popular swimming spot. Continue westbound on Highway 201, along the narrow peninsula whose coastline is formed of cooled basalt magma, until you reach the **Fongguei Cave**, actually a wave-carved hole in the rock that comprises a natural chute through which water rushes at high tide, often creating a spectacular plume.

Head back east until you see the sign for **Shetou (Snake Head) Hill** and turn left to climb to this once heavily fortified point. Here, a Dutch admiral had Penghu's first **Western-style fort** built in 1622, shortly after his fleet reoccupied the island. A short path leads to a few remnants of the structure, but these are far overshadowed by the splendid views across the bay to Magong.

Husi

The central and eastern sections of Penghu Island comprise an area known as **Husi**, a broad swath of flat land filled with farmland, parks and the beautiful **Aimen Beach**, accessed via a short road that branches to the south from Highway 204. This long expanse of golden sand can get packed out on weekends, but on weekdays it's usually deserted. The bay here is ideal for swimming and a variety of water sports, and there are nearby toilet and shower facilities. Just east of here is **Lintou Park**, the only place in the archipelago where trees grow in abundance, providing nearby farms with much-needed shelter from the wind. A path leads through the park to a long stretch of beach that links up with Aimen to the west. At the edge of this beach is a **granite stele** with an inscription commemorating the landing here in 1895 of the Japanese navy.

Baisha Island

Directly north of Penghu Island, and connected by a sprawling bridge, is the island of **BAISHA (WHITE SAND)**, best known for its aquarium and the North Sea visitor center – the transit point for excursions to the North Sea Islands. The recently expanded **Penghu Aquarium**, 58 Chihtou Village (daily 9am–5pm; NT$200), gives a good overview of the archipelago's abundant marine life. The main highlight is the transparent underwater tunnel that allows visitors to watch fish swim overhead.

To the west along Highway 203 is the **Tongliang Great Banyan**, whose enormous roots form a magnificent canopy that stretches some 660 metres above and beyond the entrance to the **Baoan Temple** (daily 5.30am–6pm). More than three hundred years old, the sprawling tree is one of Asia's biggest temple-bound banyans and far overshadows the temple itself. The shops nearby are famed for their **"purple ice" treats** made from cactus.

Si Island

Southwest of Baisha, and linked to it by the Cross-Sea Bridge, is **SI (WEST) ISLAND**, which is littered with historic sites and has some of the archipelago's finest scenery – making it a perfect place for an afternoon scooter ride. Just after the bridge, a turnoff to the right leads to the tiny islet of **Siaomen**, where you'll find the **Whale Cave**, a basalt cliff whose underbelly has been worn by waves into a noteworthy archway – prompting imaginative locals to liken the formation to a beached whale. Nearby is the **Siaomen Geology Gallery**, at 11–12 Siaomen Village (daily 8am–5pm), with exhibits on the islands' predominant geological features.

Head back out to Highway 203 and cross over it to take the road leading to Jhuwan Village, home of the visually impressive **Dayi Temple** at number 75 (daily 5.30am–6pm). The temple is dedicated to Guan Di (see Contexts p.529). Further south down Highway 203 is the **Erkan Traditional Village**, a mostly crumbling compound of old houses with basalt foundations and coral walls, the oldest dating back to 1690. Though many of the buildings are in a state of profound disrepair, some of them have been renovated and are still inhabited.

Closer to the island's southern tip are two **Qing dynasty forts**, the East Fort and West Fort, completed in 1887 after the war with the French convinced the Qing that additional defences were needed. The smaller of the two, the **East Fort**, is accessed via a narrow track just beyond Neian Village – the path turns to dirt before you reach the whitewashed battlement, which lies in the middle of a partially restricted military zone. It's possible to wander inside here, as there is no entry gate to the compound. The much larger **West Fort**, 278 Waian Village (summer 7.30am–6.30pm, winter 8am–5.30pm; NT$25), a bit further southwest along Highway 203, is easier to find and captures most of the tourist traffic. The walls were made of a mixture of mud, black-sugar water and glutinous rice.

At the island's southern tip, next to a military base and adjacent firing range, is the **Fisherman's Island Lighthouse** (9am–4pm, closed Mon). Originally built in 1779, the seven-storey structure was the first stone lighthouse in what is now Taiwan. It was rebuilt in its current Western style in 1875. The lookout point from the edge of the grassy plateau next to the lighthouse is a serene place to watch the sunset.

△ Fisherman's Island Lighthouse

The North Sea Islands

The smattering of tiny islets in the north of the archipelago, known collectively as the **NORTH SEA ISLANDS**, have broad appeal, with white-sand beaches, basalt formations and some of Taiwan's top snorkelling spots. The biggest and most popular of these is **Jibei**, a water-sports haven and a major windsurfing destination. Smaller islets such as **Sianjiau** and **Mudou** are not much more than specks of coral and sand surrounded by blue sea, and are superb places for snorkelling and diving. On islets such as Jibei and **Yuanbei**, which is famous for its basalt columns, it's possible to spend the night, and many visitors opt for this so they can enjoy the beaches at their leisure.

The departure point for all of these islands is the **North Sea visitor center** (daily 6.30am–5.30pm; ☎06/9933082), on the waterfront near Chihkan Village on Baisha. At the centre you can get maps and information, and in summer there are numerous **ferries** from here to Yuanbei, Peng Peng Beach, Sianjiau, Jibei and Mudou. Most of these are run by private operators who offer **multi-stop tours** of the islets, usually including the option of snorkelling or other water sports such as sea kayaking and jet-skiing. Prices for these tours range from NT\$250 for single-island trips to over NT\$1000 for multi-island excursions including water-sports activities. The range of options and schedules can be confusing, and few of the operators speak English, so it's best to first approach the main **information desk** (at the far end of the hall to the left of the entrance) and tell the staff there where you'd like to go. They'll then lead you to the operator specializing in tours to the island(s) of your choice.

Yuanbei Islet

Just southeast of the visitor centre is **Yuanbei Islet**, a geological work of art jutting from the sea. The name means "round shell", and when you sail around the eastern side you can immediately see why – a collection of long, narrow **basalt columns** comes together at the shoreline in the shape of a seashell.

Some operators simply sail around Yuanbei to give passengers a view of the basalt formations. If you want to stay longer or spend the night, be sure to ask before you buy your ticket. The best place to stay is the *Yuanbei Holiday Village* (☎06/9933065; ❸), which has clean doubles and offers lunch and dinner if you give advance notice.

Peng Peng Beach

Idyllic **Peng Peng Beach** is actually a stretch of glistening offshore **sand bars** between Yuanbei and nearby Niao Islet. The water here is remarkably clear, making it prime **snorkelling** territory. Most of the multi-islet boat tours include a stop here, mooring offshore while you wade or swim to the beach. The area also is becoming a favoured destination for sea kayakers who paddle over from Baisha or Husi. In summer, about three-quarters of the beach is made off-limits to visitors in order to protect nesting terns, leaving only the northeast tip for tourist activity.

Sianjiau Islet

Sianjiau (Danger Reef) Islet is surrounded by spectacular **coral reef** and is rich in marine life, making it another favoured snorkelling and diving location. In addition, the blinding **white-sand beaches** here are probably the archipelago's most stunning.

Some boats starting from the visitor centre will stop here en route to Jibei to allow passengers to swim, snorkel or participate in a range of other water sports. The operator with the sign "Ming Yang Co" (☎06/9932362) specializes in water-sports tours to Sianjiau and Jibei. A return ticket to both islets is NT$400, including use of snorkelling equipment.

Jibei Islet

The largest and most popular islet, **Jibei** is covered in golden-sand beaches, and home to the spectacular **Jibei Spit**, a mini-peninsula of sand that stretches out into the teal-blue waters for almost 1.5km. Fortunately, most tourists tend to congregate on the beach to the right – where most of the watersports activity is concentrated – leaving the spit itself refreshingly devoid of people. It's located a few kilometres west of the ferry pier, and just beyond it is **Sikan Hill**, which gives good views of the series of beaches to the north.

Practicalities

All kinds of **water-sports** equipment can be rented on the main beach. **Accommodation** on the islet is not cheap in summer, but the hotels that stay open in winter offer discounts of up to half-price. About halfway between the ferry pier and the Jibei Spit is the *Mingyang Hostel*, 182 Jibei Village (☎06/9911113; ❹), with about a dozen cabins with double beds. It fills up quickly in summer so it's best to call in advance. Next to the Jibei Spit is the immensely popular *Jibei Sea Paradise Resort*, 187 Jibei Village (☎06/9911313; ❺), which also has cabins with double beds. The location is ideal if you're planning to engage in water sports – or if you just want to wake up next to the beach. The section of Jibei Village to the right as you leave the ferry pier has several small **restaurants** with reasonably priced Chinese dishes as well as local seafood specialties. Return ferry tickets to Jibei cost NT$250, and the trip takes about fifteen minutes.

Mudou Islet

The archipelago's northernmost islet, tiny **Mudou** is dominated by a towering **lighthouse** built in 1899 to safeguard ships negotiating the shallow reefs nearby. These **reefs** are now the biggest draw for tourists – the visibility here is nothing short of amazing. In the waters on the islet's north side are some deeper sections with channels and caves well suited to **scuba diving**.

It's only possible to get to Mudou by ferry during high tide, and most of the operators don't include the islet on their circuits. One company that specializes in snorkelling and scuba-diving trips to Mudou is the Baisha Sea Tourist Centre (☎06/9215115), which offers trips daily during summer. A full-day outing costs about NT$900, including snorkelling gear, and includes stops at Sianjiau and Jibei if time permits.

The South Sea Islands

Dozens of landmasses comprise what are known as the **SOUTH SEA ISLANDS**, but only five are regularly accessible by public or private ferries. While there are certainly some notable historic sites on these islands, the overwhelming focus of most is on the natural environment, particularly the curious **basalt formations** that decorate their fringes.

The two islets closest to Penghu Island – **Tongpan** and **Hujing** – are best known for the signature basalt mesas that line their perimeters, while the larger islands of **Cimei** and **Wangan** have a wider range of attractions and make for rewarding overnight destinations (the latter two are both accessible by air from mainland Taiwan). **Ferries** to these islands leave from the **South Sea visitor center** (daily 6.30am–5.30pm; ☎06/9264738), just across the street from Magong Harbour's Third Ferry Pier. Here also is an assortment of operators offering a variety of tours, and again the best way to cut through the confusion is to approach the main **information desk** across the hallway directly in front of the entrance. Even in the height of summer, the only South Sea Islands with frequent ferry services are Tongpan, Hujing, Wangan and Cimei, while there are a few ferries a week to tiny **Hua Islet**, known for its lighthouse. Most private operators offer multi-island tours including short stops at Tongpan and Hujing and longer visits at either Wangan or Cimei, giving you the option of staying overnight at these.

Tongpan Islet

About fifteen minutes by boat from Magong Harbour, the tiny inhabited islet of **TONGPAN** is best known for the vertical cliffs of symmetrical **basalt columns** that surround it, giving it the nickname "the Yellowstone Park of Penghu". Most boats only stop here for forty to fifty minutes, which makes trying to get round the whole islet a bit of a slog – if you follow the tour guides assigned to most boats, they'll take you to some of the islet's finest columns. The **Fuhai Temple**, located near the pier, is dedicated primarily to the pestilence god Wen Wang Ye (see Contexts p.529) and is the archipelago's most popular shrine.

Most ferries heading south to Wangan or Cimei make Tongpan their first stop. On summer mornings there are sometimes boats going just to Tongpan, or to it and Hujing, for about NT$80.

Hujing Islet

Just southeast of Tongpan is **Hujing** (Tiger Well), also known for its towering mesas of **basalt columns** but with the added attraction of **Japanese military tunnels** from World War II. The most visually striking – and accessible – of these columns line the road that leads up the hill to the west. Indeed, this side of the islet is the only one that's open to tourists, as the east side is dotted with off-limits military installations. Follow the road to the right of the pier to reach **Sishan (West Mountain) Park**, home to a line-up of imposing basalt columns to the left of the road. If you look closely here you can see the openings of tunnels dug by Japanese soldiers. At the top of the hill is a viewpoint looking out onto the sea and a few small concrete buildings covering the entrances to some of the tunnels – one of which is the former **bunker** of Japanese **Admiral Isoroku Yamamoto**, who had a formidable underground fort built here to serve as the headquarters for his nation's invasion of South Pacific countries.

Most multi-island boat tours stop here for less than an hour, so if you want to have a good look around you'll need to get motorized transport. Most Taiwanese tourists get shuffled onto a **minivan** for an additional cost of NT$100, but you can also rent one of the many **scooters** lined up near the pier for NT$120.

Wangan Island

The archipelago's fourth-largest island, **WANGAN** is one of the highlights of a visit to the Penghu Islands, with secluded beaches, one of Taiwan's best-preserved traditional fishing villages and the chain's only nesting sites for the endangered **Green Sea Turtle**. As with several of the other islands, the best way to get around here is by scooter, especially if you want to see all the main sights.

One of the island's biggest treats is the captivating **Jhongshe Historic Village** on the west side – quite possibly Taiwan's most complete collection of historic houses. Written records of the village date back about two hundred years, to the Kangxi period of the Qing, but locals claim it was first established about three hundred years ago. Though there is a small aging population, most of the houses have long since been abandoned, leaving the tiled roofs and coral walls to collapse. The upside of this neglect is that the village has retained its original dynastic layout, giving it a timeless aura. Some of the houses are slowly being restored; chief among these is the **Jheng Family Residence**, in the north of the village, with a facade richly decorated in traditional Chinese symbols. Just north of the village is **Tiantai Hill** (53m), an excellent spot for a panoramic view of the island. On top of the hill is Sian Ji Rock, where, according to legend, the footprint of Lu Dong Bin – one of the most renowned of China's "Eight Immortals" – is said to be embedded. According to the tale, the footprint was left after Lu stopped to relieve himself while walking through the Taiwan Strait. His other footprint is allegedly on top of a cliff on the east side of nearby Hua Islet.

About 1km north of the ferry pier is the **Wangan Green Sea Turtle Conservation Center** (daily 8.30am–5.30pm), a free museum with exhibits on all marine turtles endemic to the region. Wangan's beaches are the only nesting sites in Penghu where endangered Green Sea Turtles return regularly to lay eggs, and the museum is mostly geared towards educating visitors about the importance of not disturbing them. The turtles usually mate in March and April, so they typically crawl onto Wangan's **southwestern beaches** in May and June to lay eggs. If you're visiting during this time, or even later in the summer, there's a chance you could see them. However, access to these beaches is often restricted at this time.

Practicalities

It's possible to **fly** between Wangan and Kaohsiung. **Daily Air Cor** (Kaohsiung ☎07/8014711, Magong ☎06/9221838) offers one-way flights (35 min; NT$1921) in a small propeller-driven plane on Tuesday and Friday mornings. Multi-island boat tours (NT$500) starting from the South Sea visitor center call here for up to two hours as part of their circuits, but to really gain an appreciation of the island it's best to stay overnight. In good weather this is easy, as there is a 7am **public passenger ferry** to Magong (40 min; NT$200) each morning, allowing you to spend an entire afternoon on Wangan and still get back to Magong in time to catch a boat to another island. Regardless of whether you stay overnight, you'd do well to rent a **scooter**, as the sights are spread out over the island. The cost is NT$150 for two hours or NT$300 for the day, including a full tank of fuel – no driver's licence is required. Apart from scooters, the other transport option is to join a group of Taiwanese tourists on a whirlwind **minivan tour** for NT$100.

The best place to stay on Wangan is the ⚑ *Yanchuan Vacation Centre*, 60–2 Jhongshe Village (☎06/9991440; ❸), which has waterfront bungalows and discounts heavily during the off-season. The management is extremely friendly, and the **restaurant** serves up delicious multi-course seafood sets to guests who reserve in advance – a bargain at only NT$150 per head.

Cimei Islet

One of the best-known islets, **CIMEI** has some of the area's most stunning scenery, with **steep cliffs** plunging down to craggy coastlines. Despite being the archipelago's southernmost islet, it gets swamped with domestic tourists in summer and the giant tour buses and legions of scooter-revving students greatly disrupt the tranquillity. Cimei means "Seven Beauties" and relates to a legend about seven Ming dynasty maidens who were attacked by Japanese pirates while doing laundry at a well. Rather than surrender their chastity they jumped to their deaths inside the well, which was later filled and covered with a tomb in their honour. Shortly afterwards, seven trees began to grow around the site. The **Tomb of the Seven Beauties** (NT$30) is a mandatory stop for Taiwanese tourists, and it's worth a visit just to observe some of the rituals that take place here. Carry on around the islet's hilly east coast until you get to the **Cow Plateau**, a beautiful stretch of grassland looking out onto some of the Penghu Islands' best coastal scenery.

Located at the base of a cliff on the islet's northeast corner is the **Twin Hearts Stone Weir**, a traditional **fish trap** made of stones piled into the shape of two large hearts. Although the archipelago is covered in stone weirs, this one is the most famous and now sees far more tourists trampling over it than fish.

Practicalities

Given Cimei's popularity, **Daily Air Corp** (Kaohsiung ☎07/8014711, Magong ☎06/9221838) has two flights daily (30 min; NT$1817 one-way) on propeller-driven aircraft from Kaohsiung to Cimei in summer. Multi-island **ferry tours** (NT$550) starting from the South Sea visitor center make Cimei their last port of call before returning to Magong, usually allowing passengers an insufficient hour and a half to look around. If you really want to soak up the scenery you'll need to spend the night at one of the hotels near the ferry pier, but if time doesn't allow for that it's best to rent a **scooter** for a quick spin round the island. Scooters are for rent at the ferry pier, costing NT$150 for a short time and NT$300 for the day, including petrol. Alternatively, you can board a **bus** (NT$100) for a dizzying tour in Mandarin and Taiwanese.

The best **accommodation** on Cimei is the *Cimei Travel Home Hotel*, 38 Nangang Village (☎06/9971265; ❸), along the road to the right of the ferry pier. A less expensive option closer to the pier is the *Cimei Yun Cun*, 18 Nangang Village (☎06/9971888; ❷), with affordable doubles and beds in seven-person dorms for NT$300. The first-floor **restaurant** here serves up cheap Chinese fare, and there's free Internet access for guests. There are also a handful of basic Chinese restaurants directly in front of the pier.

Hua Islet

The Penghu Islands' westernmost point, tiny **HUA (FLOWER) ISLET** is the archipelago's oldest, and the only one whose base rock is composed of **granite** rather than basalt. The inhabited islet is known primarily for its picturesque **lighthouse** and is also a popular **fishing spot**. Atop a cliff on its eastern fringe is a rock that legend holds bears the footprint of Lu Dong Bin, one of China's "Eight Immortals". Lu's other footprint is on nearby Wangan Island (see p.461).

Despite its small size, Hua is accessible by **public ferries** (NT$250) starting from the South Sea visitor center, but there are only four per week so you would need to spend at least one night on the islet.

Kinmen

The islands of **KINMEN**, huddled just over 2km off the mainland Chinese coast, are among Taiwan's most fascinating travel destinations, with a wealth of historic, cultural and culinary delights rolled into one of the most heavily fortified places on earth. Best known as the front line in the struggle between Mao Zedong's Communists and Chiang Kai-shek's Nationalists over control of China, the main islands of Kinmen and **Lieyu** are seemingly impregnable fortresses, surrounded by offshore minefields and a sobering ring of anti-landing spikes. Yet within this harsh exterior, and in between myriad military sites, some of Taiwan's most emblematic culture thrives, largely undiluted by outside forces and the encroachment of modernism. For visitors, almost every glance is likely to yield enigmatic juxtapositions, from golden fields of sorghum laced with menacing anti-parachute pillars to quaint seaside fishing villages hiding vast networks of underground tunnels – all testaments to the remarkable preservation of a culture despite decades of routine physical destruction.

The closest chunk of Taiwanese territory to mainland China, Kinmen has for centuries harboured Chinese civilization and holds an impressive concentration of precious antiquities, from **Ming dynasty memorial arches** to Qing-inspired burial mounds fronted by rows of masterfully carved stone sculptures. Amidst all the imperially commissioned monuments are Kinmen's signature folk icons, the most common of which are the intriguing stone **wind-lion lord statues** (*fengshiye*) that for centuries have watched over the island's villages and are believed to protect them from the ravages of heavy winds and storms. Another of the island's unique features are the villages of peculiar "**Western-style houses**" (*yang lou*), actually European-Fujianese hybrid structures built by prosperous Kinmen natives who made their fortunes in Southeast Asia and were enamoured with the European architecture they saw in colonies such as Singapore and Malacca. Despite the prolonged bombing campaign that the PRC waged against this tiny island, many of these villages remain well-preserved, while others have been tastefully restored and serve as living museums; some of the houses have been converted into rustic **homestays**, offering travellers an offbeat opportunity to stay in period-specific accommodation. In recognition of Kinmen's outstanding cultural heritage, in 1995 much of the island became Taiwan's sixth **national park** – the only one dedicated to the preservation of historic monuments and battlefield memorials. With the lifting of martial law in 1987 and greatly improved political and economic relations between Taiwan and mainland China, many once-important **military sites** have been decommissioned and are now open to the public, giving tangible insights into the grim reality that for Kinmen's hardy residents has only recently begun to brighten.

Some history

Though archeological evidence suggests that Kinmen was inhabited as early as 6500 years ago, it was not until 317 AD that the first traceable ancestors of contemporary **Kinmen clans** moved to the island to escape turmoil in central China. This settlement was on a small scale however, and the island remained a cultural backwater until the Tang dynasty, when the ancestors of twelve clans, led by **Chen Yuan**, arrived to breed and raise horses in 803. The horse-breeding efforts met with limited success, and much of Kinmen's development over the next few centuries consisted in the establishment of **oyster farms**. In 1297, a

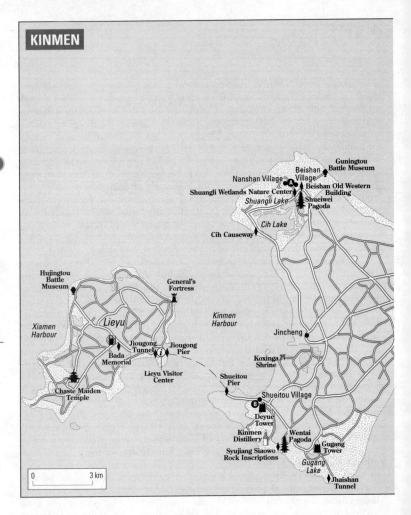

KINMEN

Guningtou
Battle Museum
Beishan
Village
Nanshan Village
Beishan Old Western
Building
Shuangli Wetlands Nature Center
Shueiwei
Shuangli Lake
Pagoda
Cih Lake
Cih Causeway

Hujingtou
Battle
Museum
General's
Fortress
Kinmen
Harbour
Xiamen
Harbour
Lieyu
Jincheng
Jiougong
Tunnel
Jiougong
Pier
Bada
Koxinga
Memorial
Shrine
Lieyu Visitor
Shueitou
Center
Pier
Shueitou Village
Chaste Maiden
Temple
Deyue
Tower
Kinmen
Wentai
Distillery
Pagoda
Gugang
Syujiang Siaowo
Tower
Rock Inscriptions
Gugang
Lake
0   3 km
Jhaishan
Tunnel

salt mine was set up to supply the mainland, and after this the island became
a popular hiding place for Chinese and Japanese **pirates**. The marauding of
these pirates became such a problem that in 1387 a massive project was started
to build battlements and moat to defend against them. In the 1640s, the Ming
loyalist general **Koxinga** occupied the island and used it while preparing his
navy to fight against the Qing forces that had overrun China. During his reign,
many of the island's indigenous trees were felled for use in shipbuilding, leaving much of Kinmen barren and subject to the severe winds that dominate the
Taiwan Strait.

After the **Opium War** in 1842, when the nearby city of Xiamen became
one of China's five **treaty ports**, many Kinmen residents began travelling to
Southeast Asia via Xiamen to do business, in the process amassing considerable wealth that they used to build lavish, European-inspired houses back at

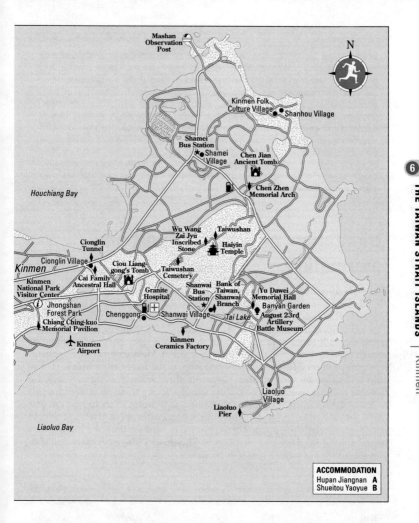

home. But when the Sino-Japanese War broke out in 1937, **Japanese forces** immediately seized the island and occupied it for eight years, bringing to an end its most prosperous period. In 1949, Kinmen bore the brunt of another invasion force, this time from Chiang Kai-shek's retreating **Nationalist army**, which used the island as the front line in its preparations to recover mainland China from Mao Zedong's Communists. On August 23, 1958, the Communists launched a brutal **artillery attack** on Kinmen, firing almost 475,000 shells in 44 consecutive days of bombing. The shelling continued intermittently for the next twenty years, and Kinmen became the subject of headlines around the world. Since the lifting of **martial law** in 1987, Kinmen has undergone a small-scale renaissance, with promising economic ties to mainland China being forged, setting the stage for a new period of growth and development.

Reminders of Kinmen's recent military past

When driving around Kinmen, it's hard to miss the ubiquitous **anti-parachute stakes** that stud almost all of the island's open spaces. Ominous reminders of the daily threat of invasion that the islanders lived under for decades, these four-metre-high cement poles are usually spaced about 10m apart, and each is crowned with a sharp steel spike, waiting to impale any airborne invaders. Similarly, all of Kinmen's open beaches are lined with seemingly endless rows of daunting **anti-landing barriers** embedded deep into the sand, designed to thwart amphibious attacks. These long metal spikes are tilted at angles that allow them to be submersed during high tide, but at low tide they jut out across broad swathes of sandy shoreline, adding a menacing dimension to these otherwise attractive beaches. Much of Kinmen's coast has been heavily mined, and **landmine warning signs** should be taken seriously.

Orientation, arrival, transport and information

There are fifteen islands in the Kinmen Archipelago, with twelve under Taiwanese administration and three under mainland Chinese control. Only the two biggest – Kinmen and Lieyu – are inhabited by civilians and open to visitors. The main island, Kinmen, is shaped like a dumbbell, spanning only 3km from north to south in its centre and as much as 15km from north to south in its eastern portion. From east to west it's about 20km. Most visitors make the main commercial hub of **Jincheng** their first stop, as the majority of hotels, restaurants and shops are located here. Given the sheer amount of sights – and the fact that they are spread out across the island – seeing them all might prove to be a stretch, especially if your time is limited. By renting a **scooter** or car, you could probably take in most of the main attractions in about five days; double that if you're relying on public buses. If you're pressed for time, the historic sites in and around Jincheng and characterful **Shueitou Village** certainly will give you a solid idea of what Kinmen is all about.

Kinmen arrival, transport and information		
Kinmen	金門	*jīnmén*
Lieyu	烈嶼	*lièyǔ*
Arrival, transport and information		
Bank of Taiwan, Shanwai Branch	台灣銀行	*táiwān yínháng*
Kinmen Airport	金門機場	*jīnmén jīchǎng*
Kinmen National Park Visitor Center	金門國家公園遊客中心	*jīnmén guójiā gōngyuán yóukè zhōngxīn*
Liaoluo Pier	料羅碼頭	*liàoluó mǎtóu*
Lieyu Visitor Center	烈嶼遊客中心	*lièyǔ yóukè zhōngxīn*
Shamei Bus Station	沙美公車站	*shāměi gōngchē zhàn*
Shanwai Bus Station	山外公車站	*shānwài gōngchē zhàn*
Shuangli Wetlands Nature Center	雙鯉溼地自然中心	*shuānglǐ shīdì zìrán zhōngxīn*
Shueitou Pier	水頭碼頭	*shuǐtóu mǎtóu*

6

Kinmen is the only one of the Taiwan Strait islands that is not accessible by a regularly scheduled passenger ferry service, so for most tourists the only way to get here is to fly. The good news is that there are **daily flights** throughout the year from five west-coast cities, with four domestic carriers to choose from. Return tickets typically cost between NT$3200 and NT$3500, with one-way fares starting from NT$2000. **Uni Air** (☎082/324481) flies fo Kinmen from Chiayi, Kaohsiung, Taichung, Tainan and Taipei, **TransAsia Airways** (☎082/321502) from Kaohsiung and Taipei, **Mandarin Airlines** (☎082/328000) from Taichung and Taipei and **Far Eastern Air Transport** (☎082/327339) from Taipei.

While there is an irregular **ferry service** between **Kaohsiung** and Kinmen's **Liaoluo Pier**, it's devoted to cargo for much of the year and usually only takes passengers during holidays and busy summer months. Though it will cost you around half the price of an air ticket, the journey takes about ten hours and the seas are routinely choppy. In addition, finding out if ferry tickets are available can be quite a hassle, as you'll need to call the **Kaohsiung Port Authority** (☎07/5216206) and it's unlikely you'll find an English-speaker there.

Arrival

Kinmen Airport is located just over 4km from the centre of Jincheng. Near the main exit is a **visitor information centre** (8am–6pm), with a formidable array of English **maps** and brochures on Kinmen's main attractions. Just to the left is an **ICBC ATM**, which accepts most international cards apart from American Express or Visa (bring plenty of cash if you use these cards). There is also a **post office** (Mon–Fri 8am–noon & 1–4.30pm, closed Sat & Sun) which can send parcels internationally. There are plenty of **taxis** which can take you to the centre of Jincheng for about NT$200. Alternatively, take **bus #3** (19 times daily, 6am–7.50pm; 25min; NT$12 one-way), but note that it also runs in the opposite direction to the village of Shanwai, so make sure Jincheng is displayed on the flashing billboard behind the front window. The bus takes a rather circuitous route but ends up conveniently at Jincheng's main bus station. The airport bus stop is about 25m to the right after you exit the terminal.

Transport

The most convenient way to get around the island is by **scooter**. The best place to rent them is **Sin Jin Yue Scooter Rentals**, immediately south of the traffic circle between Minsheng Road and Wangdu West Road in Jincheng. The family-run business is very foreigner-friendly and can rent scooters (NT$400 per day, discounts for multiple-day rentals) to foreigners provided they can produce a valid international driver's licence.

With the exception of the airport service, public **buses** are painfully slow and require careful planning to get to the main sights. Jincheng has regular **bus services** to Shanwai and Shamei, the next-biggest villages which are located near several worthwhile attractions. The most useful route is between Jincheng and Shanwai, which is serviced by buses #1 (7.50am–4.30pm) and #2 (7.40am–8.30pm).

Information

The **Kinmen National Park visitor center** (8.30am–5pm), in the centre of the island not far from the airport, has interesting bilingual exhibits on local history and culture. The **Kinmen Post Office** (4 Minsheng Rd; Mon–Fri 7.30am–5pm, Sat 8–11.30am, closed Sun) is across the street from the main bus station in Jincheng. Although there are **ATMs** scattered across the island, many will not accept international cards, though MasterCard would be your best bet. The most reliable one on Kinmen is an unassuming 24-hour dispenser for **Land Bank**, located across Minsheng Road from the main bus station in Jincheng, between the Catholic Church and 7-Eleven. The other safe bet is the 24-hour ATM at Jincheng's main **Bank of Taiwan branch** (162 Mincyuan Rd; Mon–Fri 9am–3.30pm, closed Sat & Sun), which is the only place on the island where you can change foreign currency and traveller's cheques.

Accommodation

The vast majority of Kinmen's accommodation is concentrated in the bustling commercial district of Jincheng, the most convenient place to stay on the island, with plenty of clean yet faceless **hotels** a short walk from the main bus station. For something with a bit of charm and atmosphere, it's well worth opting instead for one of the growing number of family-run **home-stays**. Featuring private rooms in restored traditional village houses across the island, homestays are excellent value, offering hotel-standard amenities such as comfortable beds and spotlessly clean linen – all in an historic home that oozes with character. **Breakfasts** of Kinmen specialties such as sticky thin noodles and the local version of Cantonese rice porridge are usually included in the room rate, and the owners will pick you up at the airport or ferry pier if you reserve a room in advance. Though it might take a little effort to book these in advance, it could reap big dividends for non-Chinese speakers, as the hosts can help you rent scooters, direct you to the main sights and inform you of any festivals or cultural activities that may be taking place during your visit.

Hotels

Hai-Fu Grand Hotel 85 Mincyuan Rd ☎082/322538. One of Jincheng's higher-end options, with bright, clean rooms and cable TV. Prices include breakfast, and hotel staff will pick you up at the airport or ferry pier if you make arrangements in advance. ❸

Hong Fu Hotel 169–175 Minzu Rd ☎082/326768. Conveniently located close to Jyuguang Road, Jincheng's historic artery, but the rooms are very basic, and those overlooking busy Minzu Road tend to stay noisy day and night; if you stay here, ask for a room away from the road. ❷

King Ring Hotel 166 Mincyuan Rd ☎082/323777. Jincheng's biggest – and most expensive – hotel, with a hundred rooms, some of which face the sea and command views of mainland China on clear days. Breakfast costs an extra NT$200 (four times what you'd pay at a stall in the town centre). Given its size, it caters to tour groups and is often packed out. ❹

Kinmen Hotel 172 Minzu Rd ☎082/321567. Jincheng's best option in terms of convenience, cleanliness and value for money. About the same price or cheaper than the town's other hotels, but with better-kept rooms, comfortable beds and cable TV. Free ADSL is available to guests, as is a modest breakfast of coffee and a steamed bun. Like the *Hong Fu*, it's located close to the town's historic sites and rooms overlooking Minzu Road can be noisy. ❷

Shang Bin Hotel 35 Mincyuan Rd ☎082/321528. Rooms here are basic and showing their age, and those not facing the road are a bit dark, but it's one of Jincheng's cheapest options. ❷

Ta Chen Hotel 16 Minsheng Rd ☎082/324851. A short stumble from Jincheng's bus station and a stone's throw from the town's main sights, rooms here are very clean and offer good value – if you can get past the hideous pastel wallpaper and ersatz paintings of Victorian Europe that eerily line the hallways. ❷

Kinmen accommodation

Hotels

Hai-Fu Grand Hotel	海福大飯店	*hǎifú dàfàndiàn*
Hong Fu Hotel	宏福大飯店	*hóngfú dàfàndiàn*
King Ring Hotel	金瑞大飯店	*jīnruì dàfàndiàn*
Kinmen Hotel	金門旅館	*jīnmén lǚguǎn*
Shang Bin Hotel	上賓飯店	*shàngbīn fàndiàn*
Ta Chen Hotel	大成飯店	*dàchéng fàndiàn*

Homestays

Shueitou Yaoyue	水頭邀月	*shuǐtóu yāoyuè*
Hupan Jiangnan	湖畔江南	*húpàn jiāngnán*

Homestays

Kinmen's most picturesque village also boasts its most memorable accommodation option: the 🏠 *Shueitou Yaoyue* (85 Shueitou Village; ☎082/375242 or ☎0929/121008, ⓦhome.kimo.com.tw/joeyroland1117; ❶), with three guest rooms surrounding the courtyard of a beautifully restored family home. One of the island's first such homestays, its rooms have been gracefully restored, and one features an authentic wood-canopied bed frame that is almost eighty years old. The price is per person, rather than per room, making it slightly better value for solo travellers than couples or groups, but it's still one of Kinmen's cheapest abodes. Room rates include breakfast, and the owner will pick you up and drop you off at the airport. She also can help arrange **scooter rental** and will let you use one of the four house **bicycles** for free. However, it's often full, so reservations are highly recommended. The helpful owner, Ms Zhang Yu, speaks enough English to make you feel comfortable. Another appealing option is the *Hupan Jiangnan* (5-1 Nanshan Village; ☎082/373978 or ☎0939/725883, ⓦvicoo.myweb.hinet.net; ❶), in a restored traditional house not far from the Shuangli Wetlands Nature Center in the heart of Nanshan Village. There are five guest rooms, two with **lofts** that are ideal for families or large groups. Though prices are per person, guests in the rooms with lofts can get discounted rates for those staying upstairs. Prices include **breakfast**, and the owner can arrange free transfers to and from the airport.

Jincheng and around

JINCHENG's core is a labyrinth of narrow lanes and alleys, twisting their way through a hodgepodge of curious old houses and an amazing assortment of tiny temples and shrines. The best way to absorb the delights of this compact area is to take a walk and let yourself get lost – before long you'll come out on one of the town's few major streets and can get reorientated. Most of the best-known attractions are situated around Jyuguang Road and quaint Mofan Street, both of which have some superb little restaurants.

The old centre

The present design of **Mofan Street** dates back to 1925, when two rows of brick buildings were erected in the Western-influenced style popular at that

Jincheng	金城	jīnchéng

Arrival, transport and information

Bank of Taiwan	台灣銀行	táiwān yínháng
Chunghwa Telecom	中華電信局	zhōnghuá diànxìn jú
Jincheng Bus Station	金城車站	jīnchéng chēzhàn
Post Office	郵局	yóu jú
Sin Jin Yue Scooter Rentals	新敬業機車出租	xīn jìng yè jīchē chūzū

The City

Guei Pavilion	奎閣	kuí gé
Jhusi Shrine	朱子祠	zhūxi cí
Jyuguang Tower	莒光樓	jǔguāng lóu
Mofan Street	模範街	mófàn jiē
Ciou Liang-gong's Maternal Chastity Arch	邱良功母節孝坊	qiū liánggōng mǔ jiéjiào fāng
Wu River Academy	浯江書院	wújiāng shūyuàn

Eating and drinking

Bar Sa	吧薩	bāsà
Chao Wei Siang	巧味香	qiǎo wèi xiāng
Hong Lou	戀紅樓	liàn hóng lóu
Jide Seafood Restaurant	記德海鮮餐廳	jì dé hǎixiān cāntīng
Ke Die Zijia	蚵嗲之家	kē dié zhī jiā
Laoliou Siaoguan	老六小館	lǎo liù xiǎoguǎn
Mei Chih Vegetarian Restaurant	美治素食館	měichì sù shíguǎn
Shouji Guangdong Jhou	壽記廣東粥	shòujì guǎngdōng zhōu

Shopping

Kinmen Distillery	金門酒廠	jīnmén jiǔchǎng
Maestro Wu's Steel Knives	金合利鋼刀	jīn hé lì gāng dāo

time, with arches lining the entranceways. All the entrances to the establishments on this street have uniform "five-foot way" verandas, modelled after the codes adopted by British urban planning officials in Singapore during its colonization period in the 1880s. This enchanting little street now houses the hippest of Kinmen's teahouses-cum-bars (see p.473). Framing the main intersection of nearby Jyuguang Road is **Ciou Liang-gong's Maternal Chastity Arch**, the largest surviving monumental archway in Taiwan (and mainland China's Fujian province). **Ciou Liang-gong**, a Kinmen native who rose through the Qing military ranks to become commander-in-chief of the navy stationed in China's Zhejiang province (see p.478 for more on the commander), ordered the imposing, intricately carved arch built in 1812 as a tribute to his mother's devotion to his father – she refused to remarry during the 28 years between her husband's death and hers. The archway, which overlooks the city's historic heart and is surrounded by some of Jincheng's best restaurants, is an excellent landmark among the maze of streets. A few minutes' walk from here is the two-storey **Guei Pavilion**, built with eight sides to mirror the shape of a *bagua*, the octagonal *feng shui* tool used to determine the most auspicious settings in traditional Chinese interior design. During the Qing dynasty, aspiring civil servants would come here to pray for guidance

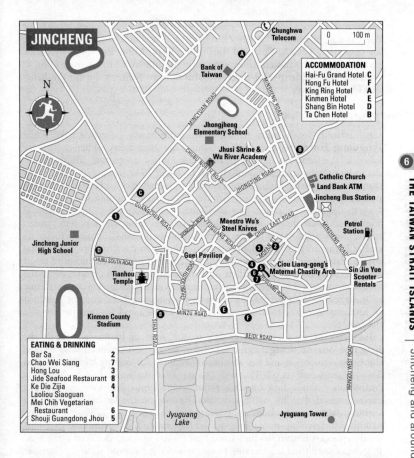

during imperial examinations. The pavilion is tricky to find: to get here from the memorial arch, walk northwest along Jyuguang Road about 100m, until you reach 27 Jyuguang Rd on the left-hand side. Here, a narrow alley less than one metre wide runs for about 20m before intersecting another small lane – keep to the right for another 30m or so and you'll come to an open courtyard with the pavilion in the centre. Just before you reach the pavilion, on the right, is a derelict two-storey *yang lou* built in 1933 by a local family upon their return to Kinmen from Southeast Asia.

Further north along Chubu North Road is the **Jhusi Shrine**, situated at the rear of the renovated **Wu River Academy** – a school built in 1780 as one of the four imperial centres of learning established on Kinmen during the Qing dynasty. The shrine was erected in honour of the Neo-Confucian scholar **Zhu Xi** (1130–1200), who during the Southern Song dynasty successfully helped to revitalize key tenets of Confucian thought after more than a thousand years of stagnation. A firm proponent of the idea that human nature is essentially good and can be refined through self-cultivation, based primarily on the study of **Confucian classics**, Zhu Xi and his circle of scholars at the **White Deer Grotto Academy** – near Lushan in China's modern-day Jiangxi province – codified what is now widely considered to be the Confucian canon Though Zhu Xi's teachings were unorthodox during his time, they became favoured during the Yuan, Ming and Qing dynasties, and many young Kinmen males were strongly influenced by them, leading to a proliferation of **imperial degree holders** from Kinmen during the Ming and Qing dynasties.

The outskirts

On Jincheng's southeastern fringe, overlooking nearby Jyuguang Lake, is the **Jyuguang Tower**, built in 1953 to honour the Nationalist soldiers who were killed in the ferocious fighting against Communist troops that culminated in the latter's surrender near Guningtou in October 1949 (see p.476). The three-storey, sixteen-metre-high tower was built in the style of a **classical Chinese palace tower** and is strikingly similar to those surrounding the Forbidden City in Beijing. As the first classical Chinese-style building to be constructed after Chiang Kai-shek's retreat to Taiwan, the tower became a potent symbol of the Nationalist desire to regain control of mainland China, and today it's one of Kinmen's most popular tourist attractions. On the first floor is a **tourist office** (8am–10pm) with some English brochures. On the first and third floors are interesting **bilingual exhibits** on Kinmen's history and culture, while the second floor is devoted exclusively to the wide variety of cormorants endemic to the region. There are excellent views of Jyuguang Lake and the outskirts of Jincheng from the third-storey balcony. Buses #3 and #6 stop just outside the tower.

Tucked away in a peaceful garden to the west of Jyuguang Lake is the **Koxinga Shrine**, a large memorial to the Ming loyalist general who resisted the Qing occupation and has also been credited with ousting the Dutch from Taiwan (see Contexts p.507). Inside is a statue of the general with a fearsome countenance, while four intricate **reliefs** carved into the stone walls depict events attributed to his military career. The one on the left as you enter the shrine speaks volumes about the popularized view of Koxinga as an anti-colonial liberator: two big-nosed, long-haired Dutchmen bow before him in frightened, repentant postures as they hand him a scroll of surrender. Across the road in front of the shrine is a viewing platform looking out onto Kinmen Harbour. Bus #7 stops along the road leading past the shrine, but you'll still have to walk due west for several hundred metres.

Eating and drinking

Jincheng is packed with delightful places to eat – the area between central Jyuguang Road and Mofan Street is teeming with **food stalls** and tiny **restaurants**, with the highest concentration clustered around Ciou Lianggong's Maternal Chastity Arch. Among Kinmen's most famous **specialties** are the handmade thin noodles (*mian xian*) that can be seen drying on racks all over town and so-called *Guangdong jhou*, a local approximation of Cantonese congee. Street-side shops sell locally made hard "tribute candies" (*gong tang*) by the bucketful, including the popular peanut candy made from a mix of malt and home-grown peanuts – which, due to poor soil quality, are small but prized for their rich flavour and texture. And while Jincheng has a distinct lack of **nightlife** – retaining a curfew-like atmosphere after dark – a couple of the trendier joints on Mofan Street can get lively, usually after the consumption of their curious **cocktails** made with Kinmen *gaoliang* (sorghum liquor).

Bar Sa 13 Mofan St. This tiny teahouse-cum-restaurant doubles as a low-key drinking establishment, serving up its own cocktails (NT$100) made from *gaoliang* and a variety of fruit juices. Each concoction is named after local military features such as the *kengdao* (tunnel).

Chao Wei Siang 39 Jyuguang Rd Sec 1. The best place in Jincheng to try handmade thin noodles, served in big, steaming bowls of soup with fresh oysters (*ké cài miàn xiàn*). It's conveniently located, clean, and offers bowls of the noodle (NT$50) without the chopped pig intestine that crops up in most of the town's other *miàn xiàn* diners. 7am–7pm

Hong Lou 22-24 Mofan St. Almost directly across the street from *Bar Sa*, it's another trendy teahouse-bar-restaurant decorated with an eclectic array of local artefacts, from miniature *fengshiye* to old movie posters and period mainland Communist kitsch. The house cocktail is *Mao Zedong nai cha* (milk tea spiked with a healthy dose of *gaoliang*), served in a pint glass (NT$70) or one-litre schooner (NT$100). Occasionally local folk artists perform animated acoustic sets in the evening. 10am–11pm

Jide Seafood Restaurant 253 Minzu Rd. Favoured by locals for its fresh seafood but with a wide selection of dishes, from fried rice and noodles to aboriginal standards and well-known mainland Chinese recipes with a Kinmen twist.

Most dishes start from about NT$150. 11am–2pm & 5pm–midnight

Ke Die Zijia 59 Jyuguang Rd Sec 1. Just behind Ciou Liang-gong's Maternal Chastity Arch is this immensely popular snack stall, which sells everything from deep-fried oyster fritters (NT$20) to scrumptious sweet balls (NT$10) filled with pastes made of green bean, red bean and peanuts. 2–7pm

Laoliou Siaoguan 65 Mincyuan Rd. This friendly family-run eatery specializes in seafood and caters more to groups than individual travellers – try the fish hotpot (NT$400) that can feed up to six. 11am–2pm & 5–9pm

Mei Chih Vegetarian Restaurant 55 Jyuguang Rd Sec 1. Excellent Buddhist vegetarian restaurant, with a buffet selection as well as stir-fries and noodles made to order. The vegetable fried rice (NT$60) is delicious. 8.30am–7pm

Shouji Guangdong Jhou 50 Jyuguang Rd Sec 1. Kinmen's most famous breakfast spot, specializing in the local version of Cantonese congee, served in huge bowls (NT$60) and usually eaten with fried bread twists (*youtiao*). The family-run establishment has been in business for almost ninety years, and the owners are proud of their congee-making heritage, which began when some of their clan emigrated to southern Guangdong province. 7am–12.30pm

Shopping

Kinmen's most famous product is its fiery **Kinmen gaoliang liquor**, made from local sorghum and most commonly available in 38- or 58-proof

Getting an edge on the enemy

By far the most unique of Kinmen souvenirs – and the most telling of its recent history – is the amazing range of **cutlery** forged and fashioned from melted-down **artillery encasements** left over from mainland attacks. With more than 970,000 shells having pounded Kinmen over a twenty-year period, there is a seemingly endless supply of raw materials, and industrious locals have learnt how to make a living from designing **knives**, meat cleavers, axes and even swords from the spent casings. As this cottage industry has grown, it has attracted considerable worldwide media attention, even being featured on the BBC and CNN. Though you'll find the cutlery for sale in shops all over Jincheng, usually starting at about NT$800 for a basic knife or meat cleaver, the creations of **Maestro Wu's Steel Knives** are widely considered the finest. Founder Wu Chao Hsi, son of an iron caster who learned tool-making techniques in Xiamen during the Qing dynasty, carried on the family tradition during the years of mainland bombardment, transforming the exploded casings into magnificent instruments. His business continues to thrive, with outlets all over Kinmen and a glitzy **showroom** on a small square just off Jyuguang Road, a few minutes' walk from Ciou Liang-gong's Maternal Chastity Arch. The showroom is a good place to buy the cutlery, and staff there also can arrange tours of their **workshops**.

incarnations. Shops all over Jincheng sell the liquor in ornate ceramic bottles, while the **Kinmen Distillery** (8am–noon & 1.30–5.30pm) near Shueitou (see below) has the largest selection and regularly holds liberal **sampling sessions**. Prices here are similar to those in Jincheng shops, although the wider selection means the distillery also has some expensive designer versions (NT$1800) in beautiful ceramic vases. Prices for ordinary half-litre bottles start at about NT$350, while those in ceramic containers start from NT$550. **Gift boxes** with small bottles in various proofs also are available.

Shueitou Village and around

Southwest of Jincheng, along the road that leads to the Shueitou Pier, lies the sublime **SHUEITOU VILLAGE**, home of Kinmen's best-preserved **yang lou**, the European-Fujianese hybrid houses that have become one of the island's hallmarks. Ever since moneyed Shueitou emigres began returning to the village in the 1920s and 30s and started building elaborate houses inspired by the colonial architecture of Malaysia and Singapore, Kinmen residents have had a saying: "Just because you're as rich as a Shueitou person doesn't mean you'll be able to build a house as beautiful as a Shueitou house." The village's architecture – both the *yang lou* and the purely traditional **southern Fujianese houses** – is indeed impressive, and remains remarkably intact. The *yang lou*, though viewed by locals as Western, are in fact curious combinations of colonial European and Fujianese styles, with interiors arranged in accordance with Chinese concepts of **geomancy** and outside walls lavishly decorated with reliefs, inscriptions and tiles – approximating the facades of the colonial buildings of Southeast Asia that so impressed these enterprising emigres. As testaments to their affluence, the wealthiest of these residents added features such as statues, columns and balconies with graceful balustrades, and a leisurely stroll through the village will give you a close-up view of some of this painstakingly detailed ornamentation. Gregarious elderly residents are quite likely to invite you inside some of these dwellings for fragrant cups of Chinese tea, allowing you to experience some of Taiwan's unrivalled tea hospitality while also getting a glimpse of Fujianese interior design.

Shueitou's largest estate is the **Youtang Villa**, built in 1766 by Huang Jyun, the head of the village's founding Huang clan and also Kinmen's richest resident of the day. But the village's best-known landmark – and the building considered by many locals to be Kinmen's most beautiful *yang lou* – is the eleven-metre-high **Deyue (Moon Grasping) Tower**, built in 1931 by businessman Huang Huei-huang to protect his estate from burglary. Essentially a glorified gun emplacement, the four-storey tower has no staircase, with each floor connected to the next by a removable wooden ladder. During the decades of fighting with mainland China, the tower was used for military purposes, and underneath it are said to be tunnels leading to nearby buildings. Near the tower is the **Stories of the Overseas Chinese Hall** (8am–5pm), a small museum with fascinating exhibits (Chinese and English) highlighting the histories of some of the village's overseas Chinese families, the majority of which sought their fortunes in Singapore.

Shueitou has a handful of **homestays** in tastefully restored traditional houses, the most reputable of which is the *Shueitou Yaoyue* (see p.459). Bus #7 from Jincheng stops just outside the village.

Around Shueitou Village

Southeast of Shueitou Village is the serene stone **Wentai Pagoda**, built in 1387 and one of Taiwan's oldest surviving relics. The only one of Kinmen's three ancient stone towers still in existence, the solid granite structure sits atop an enormous boulder, cutting a solitary figure above the surrounding trees. Some local tourist guides, as well as official tourist literature, dubiously claim that this five-storey hexagonal tower was built during the early Ming as a spot for that dynasty's founding emperor – known as Hongwu – to observe **constellations**. Hongwu never visited Kinmen, but the stone tower may well have been a marker for heavenly worship, as characters carved on the northeast side of its third level state: "the star of literature shines high in the sky." Underneath these characters is a time-worn relief of **Wenchang Dijun** (known as the God of Literature; see Contexts p.536) kicking a vessel said to resemble the Big Dipper.

Kinmen sights

August 23rd Artillery Battle Museum	八二三戰史館	bā èr sān zhànshǐ guǎn
Bada Memorial	八達樓子	bādá lóuzi
Banyan Garden	榕園	róng yuán
Beishan Old Western Building	北山古洋樓	běishān gǔ yáng lóu
Beishan Village	北山村	běishān cūn
Cai Family Ancestral Hall	蔡氏祠堂	cài shì cí táng
Chen Jian Ancient Tomb	陳健古墓	chén jiàn gǔmù
Chen Zhen Memorial Arch	陳禎恩榮坊	chén zhēn ēnróng fáng
Chiang Ching-kuo Memorial Pavilion	蔣經國紀念館	jiǎng jīngguó jìniàn guǎn
Cih Lake	慈湖	cí hú
Cionglin Tunnel	瓊林坑道	qióng lín kēngdào
Cionglin Village	瓊林村	qióng lín cūn
Ciou Liang-gong's Tomb	邱良功墓園	qiū liánggōng mùyuán
Deyue Tower	得月樓	déyuè lóu
General's Fortress	將軍堡	jiāngjūn bǎo
Gugang Lake	古崗湖	gǔgāng hú
Gugang Tower	古崗樓	gǔgāng lóu
Guningtou Battle Museum	古寧頭戰史館	gǔ níng tóu zhànshǐ guǎn
Haiyin Temple	海印寺	hǎiyìn sì
Hujingtou Battle Museum	湖井頭戰史館	hú jǐng tóu zhànshǐ guǎn
Jhaishan Tunnel	翟山坑道	zháishān kēngdào
Jhongshan Forest Park	中山紀念林	zhōngshān jìniàn lín
Jiougong Tunnel	九宮坑道	jiǔgōng kēngdào
Kinmen Ceramics Factory	金門陶瓷廠	jīnmén táocí chǎng
Kinmen Folk Culture Village	金門民俗文化村	jīnmén mínsú wénhuà cūn
Koxinga Shrine	延平郡王祠	yánpíng jùnwáng cí
Mashan Observation Post	馬山觀測站	mǎshān guàn cè zhàn
Nanshan Village	南山村	nánshān cūn
Shueitou Village	水頭村	shuǐtóu cūn
Shueiwei Pagoda	水尾塔	shuǐwěi tǎ
Tai Lake	太湖	tài hú
Taiwushan Cemetery	太武山公墓	tàiwǔ shān gōng mù
Taiwushan	太武山	tàiwǔ shān
Wentai Pagoda	文台寶塔	wéntái bàotǎ
Wu Wang Zai Jyu Inscribed Stone	毋忘在莒勒石	wú wàng zài jǔ lè shí
Syjiang Siaowo Rock Inscriptions	虛江嘯臥碣群	xūjiāng xiào wò jié qún
Yu Dawei Memorial Hall	俞大維紀念館	yú dàwéi jìniàn guǎn

However, Kinmen historians say the pagoda's main function was to serve as a navigational marker for ships plying the nearby shallow waters. About 50m west of the pagoda are the **Syujiang Siaowo Rock Inscriptions**, credited with being the most exquisite calligraphic engravings on Kinmen. According to legend, they were carved into the rock face in honour of **Ming general Xujiang**, who was said to enjoy the sea views from this spot. The characters read: "Xujiang shouts while lying here."

Just southeast of the Wentai Pagoda is **Gugang Lake**, an atmospheric setting for a walk, surrounded as it is by weeping willows and the elegant **Gugang Tower**. Southeast of here are the **Jhaishan Tunnels** (8.30am–5pm), blasting on which began in 1961, at the height of cross-Strait tensions. As the area is composed of solid granite gneiss, the A-shaped tunnels took five years to complete, but by the time they came into usage they could safely shelter up to 42 **supply boats** during intensive artillery attacks, becoming a crucial lifeline for the island. Due to falling water levels, the tunnels have not been used for over thirty years and are now open to visitors, who can walk through the dimly-lit corridors for free. An assortment of **anti-aircraft cannons**, machine guns and supply boats are on display in front of the entrance. **Bus** #6 from Jincheng stops just outside Gugang Lake and the tunnels.

The northwest peninsula

Nowhere are the scars of **warfare** more evident than Kinmen's **northwestern tip**, where the coastline bristles with anti-amphibious landing barriers and once quiet fishing villages lie in ruins. But while the area is the best place to gain insight into the bleakness of daily life during the decades of bombardment, it's not all doom and gloom: important historic and cultural relics have survived, and the Cih and Shuangli lakes are among Taiwan's most famous **bird-watching spots**. The area's best-known attraction is the **Guningtou Battle**

△ Kinmen Relief at Guningtou Battle Museum

Museum (8.30am–5pm), located near the beachfront that was the site of one of Kinmen's earliest and bloodiest ground battles. At around 2am on October 25, 1949, a ragtag force of more than ten thousand Communist soldiers sailed towards Kinmen in fishing boats, finally landing on the northwest coast amid an intensive barrage of artillery fire. They were greeted with a wall of Nationalist troops, and after more than a day of fighting the Nationalists succeeded in pushing the Communists into a corner around Guningtou. The mainland sent reinforcements but wave upon wave of men were mowed down upon landing on the beach. After another day-and-a-half of brutal clashes, most of the Communists had been killed and about nine hundred remaining soldiers surrendered. In total, more than fifteen thousand soldiers from both sides were massacred. The museum's collection consists primarily of a dozen enormous **oil paintings** depicting the struggle's defining events, along with a smattering of documents, photographs, weapons and other war memorabilia. Equally interesting are the large **bronze relief sculptures** of soldiers in action that line the walls on both sides of the entrance – exhibiting a predilection for Soviet-style socialist realism that both the Nationalists and Communists shared. **Buses** #10, #11 and #26 stop in a car park near the museum entrance.

Beishan and Nanshan Villages

In the northern corner of nearby **Beishan Village** is the **Beishan Old Western Building**, a bullet-hole-riddled *yang lou* that has become a symbol of the Nationalist victory at Guningtou. Seized early in the conflict by the Communists, who turned it into a **command post**, it was eventually recaptured by the Nationalists after a series of vicious battles. Though there's little to see here but a few crumbling old walls, it's an important point of pilgrimage for patriotic Taiwanese. There is no English sign marking the building. Beishan Village itself is still inhabited, but it looks as though it hasn't fully recovered from all the shelling, with many old homes still lying in ruins. Buses #10 and #11 stop just outside the village. Just to the southwest, alongside the road between Beishan and Nanshan villages, is the **Shueiwei Pagoda**, a quadrilateral granite tower erected in 1695 upon the recommendation of a geomancer who predicted it would help stem the **flooding** that once routinely destroyed crops planted on this corner of the island. At the pagoda's top level, each of the four panels is engraved with a Chinese character: the three facing in the direction of the sea – "Buddha," "The Way" and "Follower" – were believed to ward off evil spirits, while the fourth character, "Treasure", faces inland to symbolize prosperity. Nowadays, the pagoda seems rather forlorn in its marshy location on the edge of Shuangli Lake, on the left-hand side of the road as you head towards Nanshan Village. Near the pagoda, about 100m up a small lane that heads north to the western side of Beishan Village, is one of Kinmen's most celebrated **wind-lion lord statues** (*fengshiye*), which are believed to protect crops and villages from wind damage.

At the southern entrance to Nanshan Village is the **Shuangli Wetlands Nature Center** (8.30am–5pm), a two-storey facility with exhibits (Chinese and English) on local flora and fauna, with particular emphasis on some of the more than 250 species of **migratory birds** that stop at nearby Shuangli and Cih lakes throughout the year. The best period for bird-watching is November through March. Buses #10 and #11 stop near here. **Homestays** in renovated old houses are opening up in Nanshan to accommodate the growing numbers of tourists: *Hupan Jiangnan* (see p.469) is one of the nicest. The saltwater **Cih Lake** is widely considered Kinmen's best all-round bird-watching spot, and the

Cih Causeway that now cuts the lake off from the sea is the best place to see the rows of anti-amphibious landing spikes that line the beaches of the island's exposed northwest corner.

Jhongshan Forest Park and around

The **Jhongshan Forest Park**, the wooded area just south of the Kinmen National Park visitor center (see p.467), is a peaceful evergreen forest lined with paved pathways for short nature walks. The main attraction is the **Chiang Ching-kuo Memorial Pavilion** (8.30am–5pm), at the park's southern end. Dominating the pathway leading to the pavilion is a giant **bronze statue** of Chiang Ching-kuo (see Contexts p.513), the son of Chiang Kai-shek, who commanded troops on Kinmen and eventually succeeded his father as president. Inside the pavilion is a bust of the younger Chiang, as well as displays of numerous gifts presented to him by foreign dignitaries and **photographs** outlining events from his political career. For the pleasure of his biggest admirers are displays of items from his wardrobe, as well as key utensils from his personal **grooming kit**, including such essentials as razors, a comb, hair cream and a bottle of his favourite cologne. **Bus #1** from Jincheng stops outside the national park visitor centre.

Northeast of Jhongshan Forest Park is the fascinating **CIONGLIN VILLAGE**, renowned equally for its ancestral halls and the extensive network of tunnels. During a period of the Ming dynasty, Cionglin was Kinmen's most prosperous village, inhabited by the scholarly **Cai clan**, and its seven **ancestral halls** (*ci tang*) represent the largest concentration on Kinmen. The grandest of these – and indeed the most visually striking on the island – is the **Cai Family Ancestral Hall**, situated in the heart of the village. Also known as the Eleven Generation Ancestral Hall, its interior is lavish, with intricate woodcarvings and large lanterns looming from the ceiling. Directly behind the altar in the main hall are several rows of **ancestral tablets** – a testament to the longevity of the

Imperial praise for a pirate-fighter

Just southeast of Cionglin Village is **Ciou Liang-gong's Tomb**, the elaborate burial complex of the celebrated naval commander who ordered the construction of the memorial arch to his mother in Jincheng (see p.470). The well-preserved memorial to the commander and his wife is a classic example of a **Qing-era tomb** compound, complete with a ceremonial arch and a **spirit way** - two rows of stone-hewn animal and human figurines in pairs, standing opposite each other along the path to a giant **earthen burial mound**. As one of only a couple of such complexes in existence in Taiwan, it's well worth a visit, especially if you've never been to an imperial tomb in mainland China. Ciou Liang-gong was born to a poor family on Kinmen. His father died when he was young, so he joined the military and quickly became renowned for his **pirate-fighting prowess**. His reputation for fearlessness spread to the mainland, and he was continuously promoted, eventually being given the title of "baron" and appointed commander-in-chief of the naval fleet stationed in the mainland province of Zhejiang. Such was his fame that he was granted an audience with Emperor Qing Ren Zong (commonly known as **Jia Qing**) in 1817; however, during the return journey to Zhejiang from the Forbidden City he fell ill and died. Upon hearing of the tragedy, Jia Qing ordered a memorial funeral to be held and had the burial complex built in 1819.

Cai clan. Cionglin's other main claim to fame is its **tunnels**, most of which were dug by village residents, earning it the nickname "battle settlement". The main **Cionglin Tunnel** is an extensive underground refuge that winds directly under the village for several hundred metres. One entrance, on the village's northern edge, is open to the public, but there's nothing in English to mark the tunnel so look out for the sign stating "Kinmen National Park, East District Administrative Station". Inside the **station** (8am–noon & 1–5.30pm; NT$10), the attendant will turn on the tunnel lights and lead you downstairs to the entrance – from there you're on your own. The narrow tunnel can be claustrophobic, and during rainy periods puddles of water collect on the floor, all of which usually contribute to a brisk walk to the end, a turnstile on the village's outskirts. On the fringe of the village look out for the impressive *fengshiye* standing guard.

Eastern Kinmen

The hilly terrain northeast of Ciou Liang-gong's Tomb gives rise to **Taiwushan**, which at 253m is Kinmen's highest mountain and a popular walking area, with several worthwhile attractions here and around nearby Shanwai and Shamei villages. In the broad valley at the mountain's western base is the sprawling **Taiwushan Cemetery**, built in 1953 to consolidate the scattered graves of fallen Nationalist soldiers into a unified memorial park. Graceful stone bridges spanning lily ponds lead to a **martyrs' shrine**, behind which is the enormous cemetery, filled with thousands of headstones laid into the gently rising hillside. On the cemetery's north side is the beginning of the **Taiwushan Footpath**, a paved pedestrian-only road leading to the mountaintop. Just over 1km up the path is the famous **Wu Wang Zai Jyu Inscribed Stone**, a massive smooth-faced outcrop inscribed with the four characters of Chiang Kai-shek's oft-recited rallying cry to reclaim the Chinese mainland. The slogan, which literally means "Forget Not the Time in Chu", refers to the ancient military achievement of **General Tian Dan**, who retreated to the territory of Chu to regroup and train his troops before recovering their former territory of Qi during the Zhou dynasty. Chiang ordered the characters inscribed in the stone in 1952, exhorting civilians and soldiers alike to be inspired by Tian Dan's historic example.

Further up the footpath is the **Haiyin Temple**, which first was built near the top of Taiwushan during the Song dynasty, between 1265 and 1274. Originally a Taoist shrine, during Ming dynasty renovations the Taoist statuary was replaced with Buddha images. However, the temple was destroyed during the August 23 Artillery Battle in 1958 and a new one was built in the current location. At the temple's front left side is the **Shihmen Guan** (Stone Gate Pass). From here you can continue to follow the footpath as it descends to Taiwushan's northeastern base or retrace your steps to the entrance near the cemetery.

Shanwai and around

Kinmen's second-largest settlement, **SHANWAI** is mostly populated with young soldiers and is mainly useful to tourists as a transport hub, with a bus station offering services to nearby attractions. With numerous restaurants, it's also a convenient place to stop for lunch or dinner. The **Kinmen Ceramics Factory** (8am–noon & 1–5pm), just west of Shanwai, is known for making some of the most precious ceramics in Taiwan, and its showroom has an impressive variety of wares for sale. Among the most distinctive are the *gaoliang* **vessels**, which start from about NT\$800, and the small **wind-lion lord statuettes** which cost around NT\$150 each.

About 2km south of Shanwai is **Tai Lake**, a favoured recreation area of locals and an important breeding ground for cormorants and osprey. On the lake's northeastern side is the **August 23rd Artillery Battle Museum** (8.30am–5pm), which chronicles the crippling battle that began on the eve of August 23, 1958, when Communist forces launched an artillery attack against Kinmen and Lieyu that lasted 44 days, firing almost 475,000 shells and destroying 2649 buildings. The attack, which ushered in years of bombing between the two sides, placed Kinmen squarely into the global tussle between communist and capitalist countries – as evidenced by the United States' unequivocal support of Chiang Kai-shek and sustained supply of weaponry to Nationalist forces. The museum provides an excellent overview of the bombardment and its aftermath, including fascinating exhibits about the prolonged **propaganda war** between the two sides. Most of the displays have English captions, and there is a variety of black-and-white photos and video footage from the period. Nearby is the **Yu Dawei Memorial Hall** (8.30am–5pm), built in honour of the Republic of China's first minister of defence. A distinguished intellectual, Yu earned a PhD in philosophy from Harvard before continuing his studies at Berlin University, where he was eventually discovered by a Nationalist talent scout and offered a government position. Next to the two museums is the **Banyan Garden**, a popular picnic spot filled with some enormous banyan trees.

Shamei and around

The village of **SHAMEI** has a bus station and is a useful transit point for some of the sights in the island's northeast corner, although to see everything you'll need to hire taxis or have your own transport. About 3km north of Shamei, right on the island's northeasterly tip, is the **Mashan Observation Post** (8am–6pm), a heavily fortified station from which Taiwanese troops keep tabs on the mainland. Just past the entrance gate – where there is an armed guard who may ask you to leave your passport with him – you'll enter a long tunnel leading to a pillbox offering clear views of some inhabited **PRC islands** less than 2km away. Inside the pillbox are **high-powered binoculars** that can give you close-up views of the islands and the mainland and Taiwanese fishing boats that freely ply these waters. No buses go this far, so if you don't have your own transport you'll need to catch a taxi in Shamei. Some 4km southeast of the Mashan Observation Post is the **Kinmen Folk Culture Village** (8am–5pm; NT\$50) at **Shanhou**, a spectacularly photogenic collection of well-preserved **southern Fujian-style houses**. The village contains sixteen traditional houses, all interconnected and aligned in perfect symmetry, accessible via a neatly organized network of narrow lanes. Many of the family homes are still occupied by friendly old people who may invite you to sit for tea in one of their spacious courtyards. The wooden beams above the entrances to the homes are masterfully carved, as are the ornate ceramic gables underneath the houses' classic **swallowtail eaves**. The village, which also has an **ancestral hall** and a school, was built by the wealthy **Wang clan**, some of whose members were overseas merchants who made their fortunes in Japan. The entire complex took more than twenty years to build and was completed in 1900. Buses #25 and #31 from Shamei stop at the entrance gate.

About 3km southwest of Shanhou, along the road to Yangchai Village, are a couple of **Ming-era monuments** that are considered the oldest in Taiwan. The first one you'll encounter as you head south is the **Chen Jian Ancient Tomb**, a small burial complex built in honour of Kinmen native Chen Jian, whose stellar performance in imperial examinations sparked a distinguished career as a public official on the mainland. Although Chen and his wife are buried in China, his hat and gown are interred here. The tomb is hard to find: as you head south along the main road towards Yangchai you'll come to a small road on the left that leads about 1km to the tiny village of **Dongheng**. At the far end of the village, down a short **stone path** to the right, is the tomb, which also serves as a grazing area for the village goats. About 1km further south along the main road to **Yangchai**, on the left side of the road just before you reach the village, is the **Chen Zhen Memorial Arch**, dedicated to Chen Jian's father, who was highly respected by the Ming court. About 100m to the right of the arch is a colourfully painted *fengshiye*. A small temple also has been built nearby.

Lieyu

Commonly known as "Little Kinmen", **LIEYU** – the small island just west of Kinmen – was relentlessly shelled by the PRC for decades, and much of it still lies in ruins. Many of its old villages have been completely decimated and the island remains heavily fortified, with most of its perimeter bristling with land-mines and strictly off-limits. Despite this, villages are slowly being rebuilt and decommissioned **military installations** are opening up to tourism, making it a fascinating place for a day-trip. Lieyu is easy to reach, with **ferries** (15min; NT$48) leaving from the Shueitou Pier every half hour (7am–6pm). All ferries will allow you to bring a bicycle or **scooter** on board, highly recommended as the sights are fairly spread out and there is no public transport on the island. Bus #7 runs from Jincheng to the Shueitou Pier.

Upon arrival at **Jiougong Pier**, the first building you'll see is the **Lieyu visitor center** (8.30am–5.30pm) on the hill to the left. The centre is small and the exhibits are all in Chinese, but there's a coffeeshop and souvenir stand inside. Just to the right of the visitor centre is the entrance to one of Lieyu's most compelling attractions, the **Jiougong Tunnel** (8.30am–5.30pm), commonly referred to as the "Sihwei Tunnel". Blasted into solid granite in the 1960s to transport and shelter personnel and rations, it was dug out in a double-T configuration, with four exits to the sea and five connecting tunnels leading to piers. The 790-metre-long main tunnel was decommissioned and handed over to Kinmen National Park in 1998. Near the tunnel entrance is a **bicycle stand** (8am–noon & 1–3pm) allowing free use of bikes provided you leave some form of identification. It's a good idea to take a bike if you didn't come with a scooter, as the rest of the sights are scattered around the island and accessible via an 18-kilometre **bicycle loop**. As you head north on this loop, the first attraction you'll encounter is the **General's Fortress**, an abandoned command outpost situated on a lonely stretch of golden-sand beach. This sizeable fort, a pivotal command centre during the August 23rd Artillery Battle, offers clear views across the Kinlie Channel to Kinmen. Underneath the fort is a string of **gun emplacements**, a munitions warehouse and former living quarters. Further around the loop on the island's northwestern corner is the **Hujingtou Battle Museum** (8.30am–5.30pm), mostly of interest because of the unparalleled views it provides of the gleaming mainland Chinese city of **Xiamen**. The museum itself consists primarily of hundreds of **photos** of Chiang Kai-shek and his son Chiang Ching-kuo inspecting troops and walking alongside bare-breasted Nationalist frogmen. There also are weapons on display, as well as **battle diagrams** and oil paintings depicting battle scenes, but all exhibits are labelled in Chinese. In the back of the museum is a fortified **observation post** with two pairs of high-powered binoculars through which you can see the stunning scale of development across the water in Xiamen. On the main road heading back towards the Jiougong Pier is the **Bada Memorial**, a replica of a **Great Wall tower** that stands in the middle of a four-way intersection near Sizai Village. The replica was built in 1963 by a local regiment nicknamed the "Great Wall troops" to honour seven Chinese soldiers who died in a 1933 battle against the Japanese at a strategic section of the Great Wall near **Gubeikou**, about 125km from Beijing. On top of the tower replica are statues of the seven soldiers brandishing weapons.

The Matzu Islands

Poised tantalizingly close to the coast of mainland China's Fujian province, the **MATZU ISLANDS** are second only to Kinmen in their proximity to the PRC – a fact which explains the formidable displays of **military force** on most of them. Tucked away in the northwest corner of the Taiwan Strait, the archipelago – which faces the mouths of China's mighty Min and Lien rivers – is geographically, historically and culturally distinct from mainland Taiwan. Its inhabitants' ancestors originally migrated from **northern Fujian**, and here more than anywhere else their traditional ways of life are preserved. In addition to upholding their fishing heritage, most of the islanders speak the **Minbei dialect**, commonly referred to in English as the "Fuzhou" dialect – it's markedly different from the "Minnan" (Southern Fujian) dialect that's predominantly spoken throughout Taiwan.

Although the archipelago comprises nineteen islands and islets, most of them are not inhabited by civilians and remain off-limits to visitors. However, six of them are open to tourists, each with a distinct flavour and appeal. While the main island and tourist centre **Nangan** has the greatest variety of attractions, the less crowded **Beigan** has the best beaches and examples of northern Fujian architecture. For their part, the hilly **Dongyin** and **Siyin** – which are connected by a causeway – feature the most striking topography, and the sister islands of **Dongjyu** and **Sijyu** are brimming with historic landmarks. In fair weather, they can easily be reached via **ferries** originating at Nangan, but you should allow at least a week if you want to visit all of them at a leisurely pace. Given the distance required to travel here from mainland Taiwan, it makes sense to take your time and soak up the atmosphere at each one.

Although the entire archipelago is named "Matzu", locals and Taiwanese tourists routinely refer to the biggest, most visited island of Nangan as "Matzu" as well: according to legend, the Chinese goddess **Mazu**'s dead body washed ashore on one of its beaches.

The best period to visit is from late May to September, as warm weather and clear visibility allow for regular flight and ferry services. The islands are shrouded in thick fog from March to early May and battered by heavy winds throughout the winter, making air and sea connections highly erratic at these times. In addition, colder winter temperatures make wheeling around on a scooter a less comfortable option, though those looking for seclusion might find the winter months an appealing time to visit.

Some history

The Matzu Islands were first settled, on a small scale, in the mid-1300s, when **fishermen** from China's Fujian province used them for shelter during stormy weather and eventually set up permanent bases. The first significant wave of migration came in the early 1400s, when **northern Fujianese** began fleeing the mainland to escape the turmoil brought about by the expansionist policies of Ming dynasty emperor Yongle, setting the tone for future patterns of migration. During this period, members of the crew that accompanied Muslim eunuch **Admiral Zheng He** on his celebrated western voyages established homes on some of the islands, significantly raising their profile and strengthening their ties with the mainland. However, the heaviest migration took place in the 1600s, when boatloads of mostly northern Fujianese refugees began arriving in the wake of the **Manchu invasions** from northeastern China. These migrations consolidated the northern Fujian character of the islands, which still feature the same traditional religious practices, language, food and architecture.

Throughout much of the Qing dynasty the islands were plagued by **piracy**, with periodic raids forcing many settlers to at least temporarily abandon their homes. Unlike the rest of Taiwan, the Matzu Islands were never colonized by the Japanese, and they remained sleepy fishing outposts until 1949, when the retreating **Nationalists** seized them along with **Kinmen** and built numerous **military installations** to fend off advances by mainland **Communists**. In August 1954, the Nationalist government sent 15,000 troops to Matzu, instigating an artillery bombardment by the Communists. The shelling continued steadily until 1956, when the United States supplied the Nationalists with sophisticated weaponry that effectively countered the Communist offensive, and the bombing continued only sporadically until August 1958, when the Communists resumed a massive artillery attack on the island and threatened to **invade**. The US responded by deploying its **Seventh Fleet** to the Taiwan Strait, providing naval aircraft that enabled the Nationalists to establish control of the region's airspace. These actions placed the Matzu Islands and Kinmen at the centre of the Cold War standoff between the US and the China–USSR axis, capturing the world's attention. In October 1958, Communist Party Chairman **Mao Zedong** proposed a deal: if US warships stayed away from the mainland coastline, the Communists would only bomb the Strait islands on odd-numbered days. The offer was rejected at first, but two years later the Americans and Taiwanese agreed and the alternate-day shelling continued until 1978.

Martial law wasn't lifted on Matzu until 1987, but since then the military presence has been gradually scaled back and local businesses have increasingly turned towards **tourism**. Several former military installations have been opened to tourists, and old northern **Fujian-style villages** are slowly being restored. In recognition of the islands' unique history and culture, the archipelago was designated the **Matzu National Scenic Area** in 1999, and since then there has been a continuous effort to make the major sights more accessible. These days most places of interest are marked with English signs, many with detailed historical information. In 2001 Matzu and Kinmen received an economic boost with the implementation of the **Three Small Links** agreement, which allows local residents to engage in limited direct travel and trade with mainland China.

The Matzu Islands are among Taiwan's most remote destinations, but with time and planning they might well be a highlight of your trip. Although during the winter and the March–May foggy season transport is often spotty, in summer there are regular **air** and **sea** connections that are only cancelled in the event of a typhoon. Whether you're flying or taking the ferry, the most reliable months are July and August, although this is also when the crowds of Taiwanese tourists reach their peak.

By sea

The **ferry** is a fairly convenient and fun way to get to the islands, and is the only means of transport to **Dongyin**. The waters of the Taiwan Strait are generally calm and the ferry is large, so your risk of seasickness is minimal. There is **one nightly ferry** to Matzu, departing from the northern port of **Keelung** every night at 11pm, calling at **Dongyin** at 6am and arriving at **Nangan** at around 8.30am. The same ferry leaves for the return journey to Keelung about an hour later, but note that it only stops at Dongyin on **alternate days**, so if you want to visit this island it's best to make it your first port of call. It's worth noting, however, that in winter and during the March-to-May foggy season this ferry is often cancelled, so it's only a reliable means of transport from June to September. Services are operated by the **Tai Ma Boat Company**, whose offices are on the second floor of the passenger building at the West Second Dock in Keelung. To get there, turn left as you exit the Keelung train station and walk straight for a few hundred metres – the building is directly in front of the road where it begins to veer left. It's best to reserve your **ticket** at least one day in advance, but same-day purchases are possible. In all cases, however, you must make your **reservation** during the daytime (8.30am–noon & 1–5pm) and then return at 8.30pm on the evening you're scheduled to leave to actually pay for the ticket (steerage NT$400, dorm NT$650–800, quad NT$1000, twin NT$1200) ahead of the security check and boarding. You'll need to show your **passport** when reserving and paying for your ticket, as well as before you board the boat. During summer, reservations also can be made by **phone** (Keelung ☏02/24246868 ext 2, Nangan ☏0836/26655, Dongyin ☏0836/77555), but only in Chinese, and you also must fax the office a photocopy of your passport.

By air

If you're visiting outside the summer months **flying** is a more reliable option, although during the March–to-May foggy season flights are also frequently cancelled. **Uni Air** (Taipei ☏02/25185166, Nangan ☏0836/26511, ⊛www.uniair.com.tw) has eight flights daily from **Taipei** to **Nangan** (Taipei–Nangan NT$1951, Nangan–Taipei NT$1861) from June to August; from September to May the number of daily flights is cut to seven. If you wish to buy a round-trip ticket, however, you'll have to pay double the Taipei-Nangan fare, so it's cheaper to buy another one-way ticket in Nangan. Major credit cards are accepted at the Uni Air counter in Nangan airport.

Uni Air (Taichung ☏04/26155199) also has one flight daily from **Taichung** to **Nangan** (NT$2320) and four flights daily (NT$1951) from **Taipei** to **Beigan** (☏0836/56578).

Inter-island ferries

Unfortunately, it isn't possible to hop directly from one island to another, as **local ferries** originate from Nangan's **Fuao Port**. This means you'll have to return to Nangan after visiting each island to catch a ferry to another one. The only exception is that most of the ferries from Nangan to **Dongjyu** call at nearby **Sijyu** along the way, so it's possible to alight at Sijyu and then catch an onward ferry later to Dongjyu.

While there are usually daily ferries from Nangan to the other islands from June to August, weather permitting, at other times of year schedules can be cut back considerably. For local ferry schedules, check the "Arrival and accommodation" section under each island.

Nangan

The largest of the Matzu Islands, **NANGAN** is the administrative and cultural centre and captures the vast majority of the area's tourist traffic. With the archipelago's primary **port**, it's also the centre of the military and commercial supply chain, and since the opening of the **Nangan Airport** in 2003 it has displaced nearby Beigan as the main hub for tourist flights.

Nangan has a wide range of sights, from former **military installations** that have been opened to the public to restored **traditional stone houses** and one of Taiwan's most famous distilleries. It's also a place of legend, where the earthly body of the goddess **Mazu** is reputed to have washed ashore – and the Tianhou Temple in Matzu Village contains the sarcophagus in which locals claim her clothes are still buried.

Arrival, information and accommodation

Whether you arrive by ferry at **Fuao Port** or by air at **Nangan Airport** – both on Nangan's eastern end – you'll need to find some form of motorized transport if you plan to stay somewhere with character. Though there typically are queues of **taxis** (minimum of NT$150 for trips to a single destination) in front of both the port and airport following the arrival of a ferry or aeroplane, their usefulness can be limited depending upon the place at which you intend to stay. In most cases – especially if you want to stay at one of the interesting homestays in one of the island's villages – your best option is to rent a **scooter** and drive yourself there. Scooter **rentals** are widely available for about NT$500 a day, and given that none of the vendors require a driver's licence – or indeed any identification – these are an accessible, affordable and enjoyable way for foreign tourists to get round the island independently. One of the best places to rent a scooter is at the *Holiday Hotel* (T0836/25515; ❸) at 96 Fuao Village, a short walk from the ferry pier or a few minutes' taxi ride from the airport. At this hotel, the only passable lodging option in Fuao Village, rentals of well-maintained scooters with a full tank of fuel and a helmet are NT$500 per day or NT$300 for four hours.

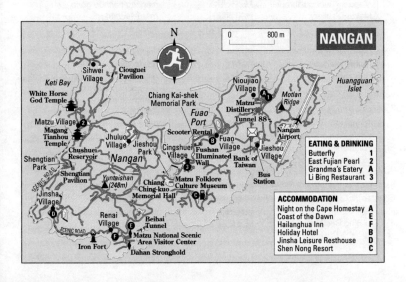

Nangan	南竿	*nángān*

Arrival, transport and information

Bank of Taiwan	台灣銀行	*táiwān yínháng*
Bus Station	客運站	*kèyùn zhàn*
Fuao Port	福澳港	*fúào gǎng*
Matzu National Scenic Area Visitor Center	馬祖國家風景區管理處	*mǎzǔ guójiā fēngjǐngqū guǎnlǐchù*
Nangan Airport	南竿機場	*nángān jīchǎng*

Accommodation

Coast of the Dawn	日光海岸	*rìguāng hǎi'àn*
Hailanghua Inn	海浪花客棧	*hǎilànghuā kèzhàn*
Holiday Hotel	假期大飯店	*qiàqī dàfàndiàn*
Jinsha Leisure Resthouse	津沙休閒空間	*jīnshā xiūxián kōngjiān*
Night on the Cape Homestay	夜宿海角	*yèsù hǎijiǎo*
Shen Nong Resort	神農山莊	*shénnóng shānzhuāng*

The island

Beihai Tunnel	北海坑道	*běihǎi kēngdào*
Chiang Ching-kuo Memorial Hall	經國先生紀念館	*jīnggúo xiānsheng jìniàn guǎn*
Chiang Kai-shek Memorial Park	蔣中正紀念公園	*jiǎng zhōngzhèng jìniàn gōngyuán*
Chushuei Reservoir	儲水澳水庫	*chùshuǐ ào shuǐkù*
Cingshuei Village	清水村	*qīngshuǐ cūn*
Ciouguei Pavilion	秋桂亭	*qiūguì tíng*
Dahan Stronghold	大漢據點	*dàhàn jùdiǎn*
Fuao Village	福澳村	*fú'ào cūn*
Fushan Illuminated Wall	福山照壁	*fúshān zhàobì*
Iron Fort	鐵堡	*tiěbǎo*
Jhuluo Village	珠螺村	*zhūluó cūn*
Jieshou Village	介壽村	*jièshòu cūn*
Jinsha Village	津沙村	*jīnshā cūn*
Magang Tianhou Temple	馬港天后宮	*mǎgǎng tiānhòu gōng*
Matzu Distillery	馬祖酒廠	*mǎzǔ jiǔchǎng*
Matzu Folklore Culture Museum	馬祖文物文化館	*mǎzǔ wénwù wénhuà guǎn*
Matzu Village	馬祖村	*mǎzǔ cūn*
Nioujiao Village	牛角村	*niújiǎo cūn*
Renai Village	仁愛村	*rén'ài cūn*
Shengtian Park	勝天公園	*shèngtiān gōngyuán*
Shengtian Pavilion	勝天亭	*shèngtiān tíng*
Sihwei Village	四維村	*sìwéi cūn*
Tunnel 88	八八坑	*bābā kēng*
White Horse God Temple	白馬文武大王廟	*báimǎ wénwǔ dàwáng miào*
Yuntaishan	雲台山	*yúntái shān*

Eating and drinking

Butterfly	蝴蝶屋	*húdié wū*
East Fujian Pearl	閩東之珠藝術文化休閒餐廳	*mǐndōngzhīzhū yìshù wénhuà xiūxián cāntīng*
Grandma's Eatery	依嬤的店	*yīmó de diàn*
Li Bing Restaurant	儷儐餐廳	*lìbīn cāntīng*

In addition to being the most cost-effective way to get you to your hotel or homestay, scooters also are essential if you want to explore Nangan, for which you should allow yourself at least **two days**, as the numerous sights are scattered across the island. Taxis are another transport option for sightseeing, but with most rides to a single destination costing a minimum of NT$150 you would spend a lot of cash using them for this purpose. However, some drivers offer whirlwind tours starting at about NT$500 an hour.

It's a good idea to bring enough **money** for your entire stay in the Matzu Islands, as there is only one bank with an **ATM** that accepts major credit cards: the **Bank of Taiwan**, 257 Jieshou Village, on the steep hill that heads northwest out of the settlement. It's also possible to change money here. Next door, at number 258, is the **Military Post Office**.

The **Matzu National Scenic Area visitor center** (8am–5.30pm; ℡0836/25630, ⓦwww.matzu-nsa.gov.tw) is off to the left before the entrance to the Beihai Tunnel complex in the south of the island, about a fifteen-minute scooter ride from either the airport or ferry pier. But with few exhibits and no English maps, your time would be better spent visiting the **Matzu Folklore Culture Museum** at 135 Cingshuei Village (see p.488).

Accommodation

Though there are about a dozen villages on Nangan, most of the attractive **accommodation** options are concentrated in only a few of them. If you arrive by ferry, there are a handful of fairly run-down old **hotels** in Fuao Village, a few minutes' walk from the pier. These establishments charge a premium due to their proximity to the port, but with the exception of the *Holiday Hotel* (see p.485) none are worth the price, and you'll do much better heading to one of the atmospheric **homestays** at either Jinsha or Nioujiao village.

Indeed, restoring traditional Fujianese **stone houses** and turning them into tourist homestays has become something of a fad on Nangan, with such renovations being undertaken in an increasing number of villages. Though rustic, these homestays have tremendous character and are excellent value compared with most of Nangan's expensive yet faceless higher-end accommodation.

Coast of the Dawn 1-1 Renai Village ℡0836/26666. Along the main road to the east of Renai Village, Nangan's swankiest abode features modern, chic rooms overlooking the Beihai Tunnel entrance and the coastline beyond. Price includes breakfast, and dinner is available in the hotel restaurant. ❺

Hailanghua Inn 64 Renai Village ℡0836/22568. New eighteen-room hotel, immediately to the south of the village's Tianhou Shrine, with six good-value sea-view rooms and scooter rental. ❸

🏃 **Jinsha Leisure Resthouse** 71 Jinsha Village ℡0836/26189. By far the best deal on Nangan, featuring several rooms in beautifully restored traditional houses scattered throughout idyllic Jinsha (Sandy Ford) Village, nestled on a tiny bay on Nangan's southwest side. The office and excellent restaurant are tucked into an alley – turn left at the far end of the village and you'll see it to the left. If you don't mind climbing steps, ask for the rooms on the hilltop to the right as you enter Jinsha – all have aromatic wooden interiors, some

command sweeping bay views, and one has an attached balcony. ❷

Night on the Cape Homestay 143 Nioujiao Village ℡0836/26125. Not far from the airport, in Nioujiao (Cowhorn) Village, is Nangan's first restored-house homestay, renovated with an eye for aesthetics. As a result, it's become popular with trendy young Taiwanese tourists in search of a slice of history, and its handful of rooms can fill up quickly so it's a good idea to call in advance. Follow the English sign to *Grandma's Eatery*, a restaurant with the same owner, to ask about rooms. ❸

Shen Nong Resort 84-2 Cingshuei Village (℡0836/26333). Alongside the main road, roughly halfway between Fuao and Renai villages – and close to the island's petrol station – the multistorey *Shen Nong* is good value, with actual prices that are exactly half of the listed rates. Though a bit sterile, its rooms are big, clean and comfortable, and some offer broad views of the island. However, the nearby military firing range can be very distracting. ❸

The island

As with all of the Matzu Islands, much of the enjoyment on Nangan is in riding a scooter or just walking around select bits. The sights are spread out, so it's best to visit all the attractions in each area while working your way round the island in order to avoid backtracking. Starting from Fuao Village, for example, a convenient **circuit** would be to head southwest on the main road before making a clockwise loop around Nangan's sight-filled western half.

Outside Fuao Village: Nationalist monuments

To get a feel for the unfulfilled aspirations of the KMT, an ideal place to start your tour is the **Fushan Illuminated Wall**, on the hilltop just outside Fuao Village along the road headed southwest. The imposing whitewashed wall is emblazoned with four giant red characters that comprise an old idiom meaning "sleep with one's sword ready" – an ominous warning of the Nationalists' unrealized plans to invade the mainland and overthrow the Communist government that had forced them to flee their homeland. The characters were ordered inscribed by Chiang Kai-shek during a 1958 inspection of Nangan. From the viewing platform in front of the wall, one can see a poignant reminder of Chiang, as well as of his failure to achieve the defining objective he had inscribed on the wall – a towering yet forlorn **statue** of the Generalissimo himself looking out towards the Chinese mainland that he never reclaimed. The statue forms the core of the **Chiang Kai-shek Memorial Park**, just across the main road from the Illuminated Wall. To get to the car park to the rear of the wall, follow the sign that says "Always on the Alert" in English, apparently the national scenic area administration's preferred translation of the symbolic slogan.

Jieshou Park to Renai Village

Continue southwest along the main road until you reach Cingshuei Village, then take the left-hand road through the village to get to **Jieshou Park.** On the left-hand side of the road as you head southwest is the multistorey **Matzu Folklore Culture Museum** (9am–5pm, closed Mon; free), which gives a better introduction to the Matzu Islands than all of the national scenic area visitor centres combined. The exhibits on the first floor have explanations in Chinese, English and even Spanish, but unfortunately those on the upper floors are only labelled in Chinese. Just past the museum, also on the left-hand side of the road as you drive southwest, is the **Chiang Ching-kuo Memorial Hall**, a two-storey pavilion dedicated to the former president and son of Chiang Kai-shek.

Further southwest, around Nangan's most southerly point near **Renai Village**, are the island's major decommissioned **military sites**, all of which are being promoted as tourist attractions. To get here from Jieshou Park, head southwest until the junction with the main road, then turn left and drive due south – there are signs for Renai Village. East of the village is the 700-metre **Beihai (North Sea) Tunnel** (9am–5pm; free), built as a shelter for military vessels and ammunition. Getting to the tunnel entrance is a bit daunting, as you must turn left through a **checkpoint** manned by heavily armed soldiers – this is one of only three checkpoints in the Matzu Islands that tourists are allowed to pass. A few hundred metres south of the tunnel is the **Dahan Stronghold**, a recently decommissioned labyrinth of underground fortifications that lead through a granite hill to some abandoned gun emplacements overlooking the ocean. It's worth the short walk through these for the sea views alone.

Just west of Renai Village, on the scenic road that winds along the coast, is the so-called **Iron Fort**, a former **bunker** carved into a rocky outcrop that once served Matzu's amphibious forces. Inside are living quarters and plenty of strategically placed sniper points. Near the fort is a lookout point where, in summer, tanned Taiwanese naval frogmen clad only in red shorts keep watch over the bay below.

Coastal road: from Renai Village to Matzu Village

The scenic **coastal road** that runs between Renai and Matzu villages is a worthwhile attraction in its own right, yielding sweeping sea views and making for a superb walk or scooter ride. About halfway between the two villages is the lovely **Jinsha Village**, a living museum of traditional northern **Fujianese stone houses**, many of which have been restored to their original grandeur. In addition to its aesthetically pleasing architecture, the village surrounds a beautiful rocky bay, is filled with gregarious locals and boasts Nangan's finest **homestay** (see p.487). Despite all of its charm, Jinsha's isolation at the base of a steep hill has kept it well off the main tourist circuit.

A few kilometres beyond Jinsha Village is the 10-hectare **Shengtian Park**, which features Nangan's most remarkable seaside scenery. In the middle of the park, next to the **Chushuei Reservoir**, is the tastefully designed **Shengtian Pavilion**, a Tang dynasty-style structure built by soldiers in 1990. With its graceful flying eaves and natural hues, the pavilion blends in perfectly with its natural surroundings and is a relaxing place to enjoy some solitude.

A couple of kilometres further along the coastal road is the intersection with the main road, which drops sharply to the left to enter **Matzu Village**, home of the nationally famous **Magang Tianhou (Empress of Heaven) Temple**. According to one local legend, the earthly body of the Chinese goddess **Mazu** washed ashore on the adjacent beach, now dominated by a garish display of naval landing craft. The villagers are said to have recovered Mazu's body and buried it in the **stone coffin** embedded in the temple floor directly in front of the altar. Locals like to debate whether her remains are still in the coffin: some say it now holds only the clothes recovered from Mazu's body, while others maintain it actually contains the remains of Mazu's drowned father. Regardless of the coffin's contents, one thing everyone agrees on is that it's the only part of the temple with historic significance: while the building itself was first constructed at the end of the Qing dynasty on the site of a much smaller shrine, it has been renovated and expanded several times since then. Despite this, locals claim the coffin is still laid in its original location. Given the site's historic import, it's a requisite stop for Taiwanese tourists and draws a steady stream of worshippers.

Just north of Matzu Village, on the road that leads to **Sihwei Village**, is the tiny **White Horse God Temple**, devoted to two Qing dynasty generals whose bodies floated ashore at nearby Keti Bay in the late 1800s. Villagers buried the bodies, and shortly after they were interred one of the generals reputedly instructed the villagers through a spirit medium to build a temple in his honour. Locals believe that the temple deity now provides protection for boats in the bay, as a mysterious warning light is said to flash across the water every time a storm is approaching. If you double back to Matzu Village and then drive southeast on the main road you'll pass **Yuntaishan**, the island's highest point at 248m and a favoured place to watch the sun set. From the top, there are unparalleled views of Nangan and nearby islands, and accordingly there is an active **military observation post** bristling with soldiers. Tourists are welcome to photograph the scenery to the north, but if you turn your camera towards the guard station you're likely to have your camera confiscated and you might even get arrested.

Matzu Distillery and Tunnel 88

On Nangan's northeast corner is the well-known **Matzu Distillery** (Mon–Fri 8.30–11.30am & 1–5pm, Sat–Sun 3–5pm), a fitting place to cap off a long day of sightseeing. Here you can sample some of Matzu's fiery **gaoliang sorghum liquor** as well as the milder *laojiu*, a traditional rice spirit. Although there is no actual distillery tour, if you follow a Taiwanese tour group inside you can taste some of the samples provided. If you stay with the group a bit longer, you can follow it into nearby **Tunnel 88**, a former air-raid shelter that is now used for the fermentation and storage of the strong-smelling spirits. The tunnel, the entrance to which is lined with giant decorative jars, is usually locked up and is only opened for the Chinese-language tours. Both the distillery and tunnel are near the traffic circle at the entrance to Nioujiao Village.

Eating and drinking

Nangan is an outstanding place for **eating**, with inexpensive restaurants in many villages offering authentic **northern Fujian cuisine**. One of the best places to sample such fare is the *East Fujian Pearl* at 22 Matzu Village (10am–2pm & 5–9pm; ☎0836/22900), which specializes in seafood. The house specialty is the **"Buddha's hand" clams**, so named because the prongs on their shells are thought to resemble the fingers of the Buddha. Cooked with a healthy dose of *laojiu*, this dish exemplifies the red-marinated cooking style for which Matzu is famous. Be sure to ask for a demonstration of how to open the shells before you begin your meal. A more expensive option is the homey *Grandma's Eatery* at 143 Nioujiao Village (10am–2pm & 5–10pm; ☎0836/26125), an atmospheric and often lively joint set in a wonderfully restored Fujian-style stone house. The emphasis here is fittingly on traditional northern Fujian dishes, with **red-marinated seafood** taking centre stage. The fishball soup is a favourite of the crowds of Taiwanese tourists that converge on the place for dinner. It's also a popular drinking hangout, particularly for those with a taste for *laojiu*. The small, unpretentious *Li Bing Restaurant* at 107 Cingshuei Village (☎0836/25198) is a favourite of locals and soldiers, who flock here in the evenings for fresh seafood and the house specialty – big, juicy **dumplings**. Meals here are cheap and portions are generous.

Though there is a shortage of dedicated **drinking** establishments on Nangan, one good place for a drink is *Butterfly* (5–11pm; ☎0836/26609) at 72-1 Nioujiao Village, down the hill and directly across the street from *Grandma's Eatery*. This bar and restaurant serves a respectable selection of **cocktails** and bottled beers in a relaxed environment.

Beigan

The archipelago's second-largest island, **BEIGAN** is filled with charming villages and superb scenery, including several **secluded beaches** with dramatic mountain backdrops. Beigan once boasted the Matzu Islands' only airport and was the nerve centre for tourism, but since the 2003 opening of the Nangan Airport it has played second fiddle to its bigger neighbour to the south, and its atmosphere is sleepy by comparison. Though some tourists still fly to Beigan from Taipei, many arrive by ferry from Nangan and spend at least one night in a rustic village homestay.

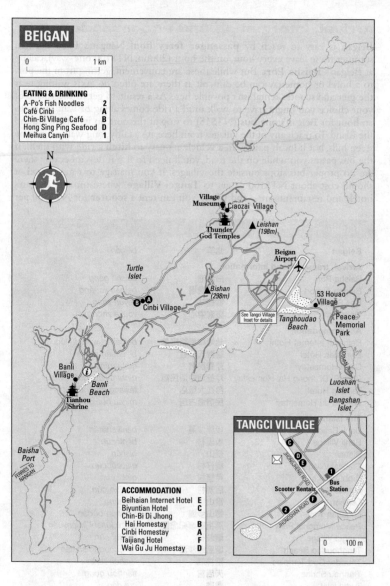

BEIGAN

0   1 km

EATING & DRINKING
A-Po's Fish Noodles	**2**
Café Cinbi	**A**
Chin-Bi Village Café	**B**
Hong Sing Ping Seafood	**D**
Meihua Canyin	**1**

N

Village Museum
Ciaozai Village
Thunder God Temples
Leishan (198m)

Turtle Islet

Beigan Airport

Bishan (298m)

See Tangci Village Inset for details

53 Houao Village

Tanghoudao Beach

Peace Memorial Park

Cinbi Village

Luoshan Islet
Bangshan Islet

Banli Village

Banli Beach

Tianhou Shrine

Baisha Port
FERRIES TO NANGAN

ACCOMMODATION
Beihaian Internet Hotel	**E**
Biyuntian Hotel	**C**
Chin-Bi Di Jhong Hai Homestay	**B**
Cinbi Homestay	**A**
Taijiang Hotel	**F**
Wai Gu Ju Homestay	**D**

TANGCI VILLAGE

JHONGSHAN ROAD

Scooter Rentals

Bus Station

JHONGSHAN ROAD

0   100 m

In many respects, Beigan is a microcosm of the Matzu Islands themselves: mountainous, dependent on **fishing** and tied to its traditional ways of life. The sharp relief of the hilly terrain makes farming challenging at best, and most of the island's inhabitants squeeze their livings from the sea, with tourism providing a secondary boost. Beigan's villages are another highlight, with the archipelago's most picturesque northern **Fujian-style stone houses**. Some of these buildings have been renovated as hotels, and staying overnight in one greatly enhances the experience of being here.

Arrival, information and accommodation

Beigan is easy to reach by **passenger ferry** from Nangan's Fuao Port. In summer these leave every hour, on the hour (20min; NT$100 one-way), calling at Beigan's **Baisha Port**. But while these are convenient, getting from the port to a hotel or homestay can be difficult as there are often no taxis waiting near the pier and scooter rental isn't possible here. As a result, to get to the village of your choice you might have to walk until a ride comes along or wait for up to an hour for Beigan's one **bus** (NT$15) to stop at the port on its circuit around the island. To reach any of the villages from here, it's a fairly long walk over some steep hills, but if locals pass by in a vehicle it's easy to **hitch** a ride with them. If the bus passes you while on the road, you'll need to flag it down because there are no proper bus stops outside the villages. If you manage to catch a **taxi**, it should cost about NT$100 to get to **Tangci Village**, where most of Beigan's hotels and restaurants are – and where you can rent a **scooter** for NT$500 per

Beigan

Beigan	北竿	*běigān*
Arrival, transport and information		
Baisha Port	白沙港	*báishā gǎng*
Beigan Airport	北竿機場	*běigān jīchǎng*
Bus Station	客運站	*kèyùn zhàn*
Visitor Information Center	遊客中心	*yóukè zhōngxīn*
Accommodation		
Beihaian Internet Hotel	北海岸網路旅館	*běihǎi'àn wǎnglù lǚguǎn*
Biyuntian Hotel	碧雲天旅社	*bìyúntiān lǚshè*
Cinbi Homestay	芹壁民宿	*qínbì mínsù*
Chin-Bi Di Jhong Hai Homestay	芹壁地中海民宿	*qínbì dìzhōnghǎi mínsù*
Taijiang Hotel	台江大飯店	*táijiāng dàfàndiàn*
Wai Gu Ju Homestay	民宿懷古居	*mínsù huáigǔ jū*
The island		
Banli Beach	坂里沙灘	*bǎnlǐ shātān*
Banli Village	坂里村	*bǎnlǐ cūn*
Bishan	壁山	*bìshān*
Ciaozai Village	橋仔村	*qiáozǎi cūn*
Cinbi Village	芹壁村	*qínbì cūn*
Houao Village	后澳村	*hòu'ào cūn*
Leishan	雷山	*léishān*
Luoshan Trail	螺山步道	*luóshān bùdào*
Peace Memorial Park	馬祖軍事紀念園	*mǎzǔ jūnshì jìniànyuán*
Tangci Village	塘岐村	*tángqí cūn*
Tanghoudao Beach	塘后道沙灘	*tánghòudào shātān*
Thunder God Temples	雷神廟	*léishén miào*
Tianhou Shrine	天后宮	*tiānhòu gōng*
Turtle Islet	龜島	*guī dǎo*
Eating and drinking		
A-Po's Fish Noodles	阿婆魚麵	*ā pó yǔmiàn*
Café Cinbi	芹壁咖啡廳	*qínbì kāfēitīng*
Chin-Bi Village Café	芹壁地中海咖啡廳	*qínbì dìzhōnghǎi kāfēitīng*
Hong Sing Ping Seafood Restaurant	鴻星平海鮮樓	*hóng xīng hǎixiān lóu*
Meihua Canyin	梅花餐飲	*méihuā cānyǐn*

day (no licence required, helmets mandatory). A scooter is critical if you wish to stay in one of the restored stone-house hotels, as they are on the island's north side, separated from Tangci by a taxing hill. A scooter also is the most convenient means for sightseeing, but if you can find a taxi the driver might be willing to give you a two-hour tour for about NT$1000.

An advantage of arriving by air is that the **Beigan Airport** is located next to Tangci, a very short walk from the town's main hotels. However, the schedule for flights into Beigan is much more erratic than for Nangan: the Beigan Airport runway is only 890m long, too short for an instrument-based landing system, so pilots must fly by sight and the only planes from Taiwan that can land here are the 37-seaters owned by Uni Air.

Along the road from Baisha Port to Tangci, just behind Banli Beach, is a small **visitor information center** (8am–5pm), but it seems mostly designed to promote certain local businesses by offering their brochures.

Accommodation

Your choice of **accommodation** is limited to the uninspiring but convenient hotels in Tangci or one of the two traditional stone-house homestays in captivating Cinbi Village, on Beigan's north side.

Tangci Village

Beihaian Internet Hotel 240 Jhongjheng Rd ☎0836/55034. Features dark but clean rooms, each with its own computer and free broadband Internet access. ❸

Biyuntian Hotel 255 Jhongjheng Rd ☎0836/55461. Just down the street from the *Beihaian*, the *Biyuntian* also has all of its rooms equipped with computers and broadband Internet access – and not only are its rooms cheaper than those of the *Beihaian*, they're also cleaner and brighter. ❷

Taijiang Hotel 200 Jhongjheng Rd ☎0836/55256. While the *Taijiang* has seen better days, its price includes breakfast and a pick-up from the ferry pier for those with reservations – making it one way to overcome the shortage of transport from Baisha Port. ❷

Wai Gu Ju Homestay 129 Tangci Village ☎0836/55426. A cheap and cheerful homestay in the heart of Tangci, not far from Jhongjheng Road. If you want to stay here, ask at the *Hong Sing Ping Seafood Restaurant* (see Eating p.495), which has the same owner. ❷

Cinbi Village

Cinbi Homestay 49 Cinbi Village ☎0836/55456. One of Taiwan's most distinctive accommodation options, and Matsu's most interesting place to stay, the Cinbi is perched on a terrace in the midst of the village, with rooms in restored old stone houses that simply ooze with character. Rustic but clean, with comfy beds and traditional windows that frame splendid views of nearby Turtle Islet and the sea beyond, these rooms have a timeless appeal. Rates are good value on weekdays and during the off-season, and discounts are offered for multiple-day stays. Ask at the attached *Café Cinbi* (see Eating p.495), which serves excellent meals on a relaxing veranda. ❸

Chin-Bi Di Jhong Hai Homestay 54 Cinbi Village ☎0836/56611. A few buildings west of the *Cinbi Homestay* is this newcomer to the rustic-restoration game. Unlike the original *Cinbi*, however, the *Di Jhong Hai's* structures aren't made from old stones and only look rustic from the outside. The interiors of the rooms are modern, which could explain why they're more expensive. Ask at the adjoining *Chin-Bi Village Café* if you want to stay here. The homestay also offers pick-ups from the airport or ferry pier if you have a reservation. ❹

The island

Starting from Baisha Port and heading northeast, the first stretch of sand you'll encounter is beautiful **Banli Beach**, at the edge of Banli Village. Some enterprising locals offer **jet-ski** and **quad bike** rentals, but there are usually only takers on summer weekends. There are shower and toilet facilities here. At the southwest end of the beach is a tiny **Tianhou Temple** dedicated to Mazu.

To the east of Tangci Village, which has hotels, restaurants and food shops but little in the way of tourist attractions, continue east along the main road, past the airport, until you reach **Tanghoudao Beach**, a long spit of sand that forms a natural causeway between Tangci and Houao Village to the east. The bay here is considerably calmer than the one at Banli Beach, and, as such, it's Beigan's favoured swimming spot.

Houao Village and the Peace Memorial Park

Houao Village is a small fishing community with some beautifully restored stone-slab houses and is a nice place for a stroll, especially around dusk, when elderly villagers typically come out to socialize. **Number 53** is a northern Fujian-style house with a painstakingly restored interior, and if the welcoming owner is there she is usually happy to show visitors around.

Behind the village, up the steep road heading southeast, the **Peace Memorial Park** is being built around a handful of decommissioned army outposts. The park, designed to commemorate Beigan's recent military history, is centred on a group of hilltop pillboxes and now-derelict gun emplacements.

Ciaozai and Cinbi villages

Nestled in the island's northwest corner is **Ciaozai (Little Bridge) Village**, so named because of the many small bridges that span the gullies carrying runoff from nearby **Leishan** (Thunder Mountain). While most villages in Matzu were settled by northern Fujianese, Ciaozai is unique in that it was founded by fishermen from the southern part of the province. Once Beigan's biggest, most affluent village, these days it's not much more than a laid-back fishing settlement. In the village's centre is a small **museum** (9am–5pm) with displays of old fishing equipment and models of Fujianese fishing boats. Ciaozai also is noted for having more **temples** than any other village in the Matzu Islands.

To the west of Ciaozai Village along the main road is the unmistakable **CINBI VILLAGE**, with terrace upon terrace of two-storey **stone houses** tumbling

down a hillside to the sea – arguably the archipelago's most picturesque community. Spending a night in one of Cinbi's rustic **homestays** (see Accommodation p.493) is highly recommended, but even if you don't stay here it's definitely worth a stroll through its narrow lanes and up its steep steps. If time permits, a short swim across the shallow water to **Turtle Islet** – actually a granite outcrop in the middle of the bay – yields unrivalled views of the village as well as of the sea to the north.

Bishan

For a bird's-eye view of Beigan's eastern half, nearby **Bishan** – at 298m the Matzu Islands' highest hill – is the place to go. Near the top is an **observation point** looking out over Tangci and Houao villages, as well as the airport, making a perfect place to watch the small planes make their precarious

△ Matzu, Cinbi Village on Beigan

landings. You can drive a scooter up the road or walk to the top along the challenging stone-stair path that starts behind Tangci.

Eating

Given its reliance on fishing, Beigan is an excellent place to try fresh **seafood** at reasonable prices. The island is most famous for its **fish noodles**, made from corn starch and pressed fish such as eel and drum. To see the noodles being hand made and dried in the sun, stop by *A-Po's Fish Noodles* (9am–5pm), at 168 Jhongshan Rd in Tangci Village. This unassuming little shop is run by a friendly old woman who is happy to give demonstrations. You can buy a bag of the noodles here for only NT$80. If you want to try a hot bowl of these noodles, the best place in Tangci is the *Hong Sing Ping Seafood Restaurant* (11.30am–2pm & 5–8pm) at 242 Jhongjheng Rd. At lunchtime it can be crowded with Taiwanese tourists making day-trips from Nangan.

Just across the street from the airport exit is the spartan *Meihua Canyin* (10am–1.30am), at 272 Jhongshan Rd, which caters to local soldiers with cheap noodle and rice dishes starting from NT$40.

On the island's north side is one of Beigan's best places to eat, *Café Cinbi* (10am–9pm), at 49 Cinbi Village. The fish noodles here are fresh and tasty, and you can enjoy them on a veranda looking out onto Turtle Islet and the sea.

Dongyin and Siyin

Matzu's most visually compelling islands are **DONGYIN** and **SIYIN**, two hilly tracts of land connected by a causeway at the archipelago's northernmost point.

Dongyin and Siyin		
Dongyin	東引	*dōngyǐn*
Siyin	西引	*xīyǐn*
Arrival, transport and information		
Dongyin Visitor Center	東引遊客中心	*dōngyǐn yóukè zhōngxīn*
Jhongjhu Port	中柱港	*zhōngzhù gǎng*
Accommodation		
Lao Yue Hotel	老爺大飯店	*lǎoyé dàfàndiàn*
Mingjian Star Hotel	明建星大飯店	*míng jiàn xīng dàfàndiàn*
Sinhua Hotel	昕華飯店	*xīnhuá fàndiàn*
Yingbin Hotel	盈賓休閒旅館	*yíngbīn xiūxián lǚguǎn*
The island		
Andong Tunnel	安東坑道	*āndōng kēngdào*
Beihai Tunnel	北海坑道	*běihǎi kēngdào*
Dongyong Lighthouse	東湧燈塔	*dōngyǒng dēngtǎ*
Kai-shek Bridge	介石橋	*jièshí qiáo*
Martyred Maiden Cliff	烈女義坑	*liènǚ yīkēng*
Thanksgiving Pavilion	感恩亭	*gǎn'ēn tíng*
Thread of Sky	一線天	*yīxiàn tiān*
Eating and drinking		
Jhen Shan Mei	珍膳美餐廳	*zhēnshànměi cāntīng*
Shandong Siao Guan	山東小館	*shāndōng xiǎoguǎn*

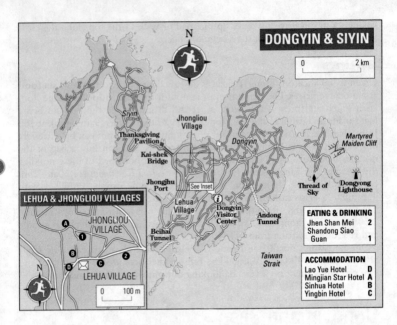

Characterized by sheer **granite cliffs** that plunge dramatically down to the sea, the scenery here is sublime – especially on the larger island of Dongyin, where most of the sights and all of the tourist amenities are located. Dongyin also has some standout historical sites, such as the solitary **Dongyong Lighthouse** that dominates the island's far eastern tip.

The islands have an illustrious history, with their first settlements dating back to the Yuan dynasty, when Fujianese fishermen often used them as a base during stormy weather. During the Ming dynasty, many of the crew that accompanied Muslim eunuch admiral **Zheng He** on his groundbreaking voyages established homes here, and some locals claim this ancestry with pride. Due to their isolation, the islands get comparatively few tourists and locals tend to go well out of their way to make them comfortable. And, though both islands are still heavily militarized, even the soldiers are exceedingly friendly to the few visitors who make it here.

Arrival, information and accommodation

The easiest way to get here from mainland Taiwan is on the **Keelung–Nangan ferry**, which stops at Dongyin's **Jhongjhu Port** every morning en route to Nangan (see Getting to the Matzu Islands p.484). If you want to get here from Nangan, your only option is the 9.30am **Nangan–Keelung ferry** which stops at Dongyin on alternate days. Tickets cost NT$285, and the boat usually arrives around noon. There is no public transport on the islands, so you'll probably need to rent a **scooter** or hire a **taxi** for sightseeing – walking is a possibility, but Dongyin is several kilometres in width and it would take the better part of a day to see the main sights on foot.

There are no scooter rentals at Jhongjhu Port, but it's possible to rent them in the nearby villages of **Lehua**, **Nanao** or **Jhongliou**, all of which are clustered together on the hill that rises from the harbour and are a short walk or taxi ride from the pier. All of Dongyin's **hotels** and **restaurants** are concentrated in these three adjoining villages, and some hotels will rent scooters for NT$500 a day without needing to see any identification.

For security purposes, all visitors are required to **register** at the **Dongyin visitor center** (8am–noon & 1.30–5.30pm), 160–1 Lehua Village, before visiting some of the sights, particularly the Thread of Sky viewpoint. Staff at the front desk will take down your name and passport number and provide you with a **permit** that you must show guards at the entrance to the Thread of Sky. The visitor centre has interesting English-captioned exhibits on the islands' history.

Accommodation

All of Dongyin's **accommodation** is centred in the villages of Lehua, Nanao and Jhongliou, and consists of standard but affordable hotels whose management will often book onward ferry tickets for you without charging commission.

The *Lao Yue Hotel*, 29 Lehua Village (☏0836/77168; ❸), has small but clean rooms, some with views onto the harbour. Further up the hill, the *Mingjian Star Hotel*, 66 Jhongliou Village (☏0836/77180; ❷), has basic rooms, some with computers and free Internet access; the management will help you book your onward ferry ticket without charging commission. Near the post office, the *Sinhua Hotel*, 46 Lehua Village (☏0836/77600; ❷), is good value and has a restaurant and free Internet café – it's a short walk from here to the ferry pier. Slightly more expensive, the *Yingbin Hotel*, 78 Lehua Village (☏0836/76336 ; ❸), is another inviting option, with very clean rooms and management who can arrange scooter rental and book your onward ferry ticket without taking a commission.

Dongyin

Most of **DONGYIN**'s sights are situated along the main road that winds east of the three villages, but one – the **Beihai (North Sea) Tunnel** – is located to the south of Jhongjhu Port and accessed by a paved road leading south from the visitor centre. Built in the 1970s to provide refuge for small naval vessels during rough seas and artillery attacks from mainland China, the tunnel is considerably smaller than its namesake on Nangan, at only 150m in length, but it's still worth a visit. Like its Nangan counterpart, it was hollowed out with only hand tools and blasting powder. It was opened to tourists in 2000, when eight **bronze statues** of army tunnel builders were erected at the deep end in memory of those who died building it. The statues, lined up along a ledge and bathed in fluorescent light, give the tunnel an eerie feel.

Further east, about 1km past the visitor centre, the much larger **Andong Tunnel** cuts deep through the heart of a hill before ending up at some vertical **cliffs** on Dongyin's southern coast. Here, from rounded openings looking out over the sea, there are views of the island's rugged shores to the northeast. This tunnel, once used to house soldiers and all manner of military equipment, descends for about 700m at an angle of 30 degrees. Along the way you'll see old barracks, officers' quarters, ammunition depots and even a former animal pen where pigs were raised to feed the hungry troops. The return walk to the cliffs takes about an hour.

A few kilometres northeast of the Andong Tunnel along the main road is one of Dongyin's most celebrated examples of eroded coastline – the so-called **Thread of Sky**, a vertical, narrow crevice between two sharply angled cliff faces that yields only a fragmentary glimpse of the sea beyond. Listening to the waves crashing against the rocks here is obligatory for Taiwanese tourists: the four-character **inscription** on the cliff means "hearing waves at the crevice of heaven". Young soldiers at the entrance will ask to see your permit before escorting you down to the viewpoint.

A bit further along the main road, on the left-hand side as you head east, is another evocative section of coastline known alternately as **Suicide Cliff** or **Martyred Maiden Cliff**, as according to legend a young woman leapt to her death here during the Qing dynasty to escape from pirates. You can walk out to the edge of this sea-eroded cliff, which plunges more than 100m to the rocks below. A guardrail is in place to keep visitors from falling.

Crowning the island's far eastern tip is the highlight of a visit to Dongyin – the **Dongyong Lighthouse**, a whitewashed beacon of functionality perched above several lonely tiers of grassy, windswept terraces. Built by **British engineers** in 1902, the lighthouse and accompanying complex of buildings were designed in an eighteenth-century English style, complete with a weather vane and lightning rod. A concrete path leads up to the lighthouse, and you can wander around the former residential and office buildings to the rear. From this vantage point, the lighthouse seems to jut straight out into the blue sea beyond. Below the lighthouse, a paved path leads to a gun emplacement with two old **cannons** once used for signalling to ships during foggy weather. They fell into disuse with the advent of the foghorn.

Eating

Dongyin's best **eating** places are down-to-earth little joints that serve up mostly northern Chinese specialties. For dinner, try *Jhen Shan Mei*, 93 Lehua Village (2–9pm), whose friendly owner learned how to make dumplings and other northern Chinese dishes in Beijing – it's best to ask him what his nightly special is. The most popular place for breakfast is the *Shandong Siao Guan*, 38 Jhongliou Village (6am–3pm), which has morning goodies ranging from steamed buns and fried bread sticks to rice porridge and hot soy milk.

Dongjyu and Sijyu

At the southernmost point of the Matsu Islands are **DONGJYU** and **SIJYU**, two tiny specks of land originally called "East Dog" and "West Dog" because they were said to resemble canines when viewed from the sea. The islands, whose names mean "East Chu" and "West Chu", were symbolic of Chiang's ambitions to reclaim the mainland (see also Kinmen p.463)

Both islands are relaxing places to hang out, with ample accommodation and restaurants, and they're easily accessible by ferry from Nangan. In good weather, and especially during the busy summer tourist season, there are several **ferries** each day to Dongjyu and Sijyu from Nangan's Fuao Port (50 min, NT$140). If you want to see both, the way to do it without having to double back to Nangan is to start with Sijyu, spend the night there, then catch one of the six daily ferries that leave on the hour, every other hour (7am–5pm; 10 min, NT$20), stopping off at Dongjyu on the way back to Nangan.

Dongjyu

The larger of the two islands, **DONGJYU** can nevertheless still be covered on foot in several hours. However, with few trees it gets scorching hot in summer,

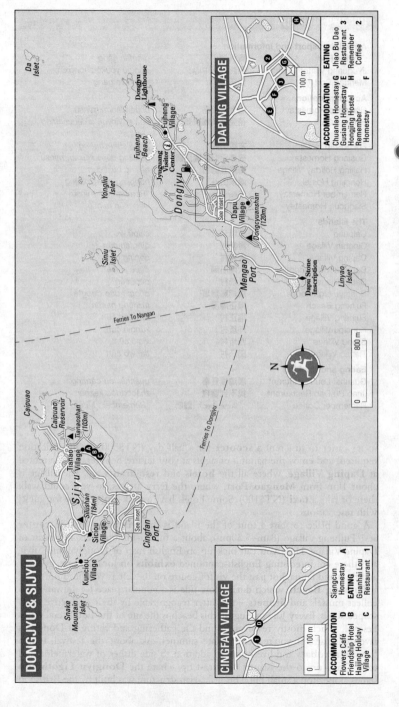

DONGJYU & SIJYU

Caipuao

Caipuao Reservoir

Tianaoshan (103m)

Tianao Village

Silushan (184m)

Sijyu

Siciou Village

Kunciou Village

Snake Mountain Islet

Cingfan Port

Ferries To Dongjyu

CINGFAN VILLAGE

ACCOMMODATION
Flowers Café
Friendship Hotel   **B**
Haijing Holiday   **D**
Village
Siangcun Homestay

EATING
Guanhai Lou   **C**
Restaurant   **1**

0   100 m

DAPING VILLAGE

ACCOMMODATION
Chuanlao Homestay **G**
Gusiang Homestay   **E**
Hongjing Hostel   **H**
Remember
Homestay   **F**

EATING
Jhao Bu Dao
Restaurant   **3**
Remember
Coffee   **2**

0   100 m

Da Islet

Dongjyu Lighthouse

Fujheng Village

Fujheng Beach

Jyuguang Visitor Center

Dongjyu

Dapu Village

Dongcyuanshan (120m)

Mengao Port

Dapu Stone Inscription

Yongliu Islet

Siniu Islet

Linyao Islet

Ferries To Nangan

N

0   800 m

Arrival, transport and information

Cingfan Port	青帆港	qīngfān gǎng
Jyuguang Visitor Center	東莒遊客中心	dōngjǔ yóukè zhōngxīn
Mengao Port	猛沃港	měngwò gǎng

Accommodation

Chuanlao Homestay	船老大民宿	chuán lǎodà mínsù
Flowers Café	花兒音樂咖啡餐坊民宿	huā'er yīnyuè kāfēi cānfāng mínsù
Friendship Hotel	友誼山莊	yǒuyì shānzhuāng
Gusiang Homestay	故鄉渡假休閒民宿	gùxiāng dùjiǎ xiūxián mínsù
Haijing Holiday Village	海景渡假村	hǎijǐng dùjiàcūn
Hongjing Hostel	鴻景山莊	hóngjǐng shānzhuāng
Remember Homestay	"Remember" 民宿	"Remember" mínsù
Siangcun Homestay	鄉村民宿	xiāngcūn mínsù

The islands

Caipuao	菜埔沃	càipǔ wò
Cingfan Village	青帆村	qīngfān cūn
Daping Village	大坪村	dàpíng cūn
Dapu Stone Inscription	大埔石刻	dàpǔ shíkè
Dapu Village	大埔村	dàpǔcūn
Dongjyu Lighthouse	東莒島燈塔	dōngjǔ dǎo dēngtǎ
Fujheng Beach	福正海灘	fúzhèng hǎitān
Fujheng Village	福正村	fúzhèng cūn
Kunciou Village	坤坵村	kūnqiū cūn
Siciou Village	西坵村	xīqiū cūn
Tianao Village	田沃村	tiānwò cūn

Eating and drinking

Guanhai Lou Restaurant	觀海樓餐廳	guānhǎi lóu cāntīng
Jhao Bu Dao Restaurant	找不到客棧	zhǎobùdào kèzhàn
Remember Coffee	"Remember" 咖啡	"Remember" kāfēi

so it's easier to just rent a **scooter** for a half-day (NT$300, no identification required) and enjoy the handful of sights at your leisure. Scooters can be rented at **Daping Village**, where all the **hotels** and **restaurants** are. The village is about 1km from **Mengao Port**, where the ferry arrives, so you could walk there or take a **taxi** (NT$100). Some hotels have a **pick-up service** for guests with reservations.

A good place to start a tour of the island is the **Jyuguang visitor center** at 1 Fujheng Village (8am–5.30pm), about a fifteen-minute walk northeast of Daping Village. Here you can pick up an English map of Dongjyu and Sijyu, and there are interesting English-captioned **exhibits** on local culture, geology and flora and fauna. Just past the visitor centre on the left as you head northeast is **Fujheng Beach**, which during low tide is a popular place for Taiwanese to collect mussels and **limpets** – the latter recognizable by their distinctive oval-shaped shells. Every July or August, this beach is the site of the Equilateral Venus Festival, which mostly revolves around the gathering and eating of Dongjyu's favoured clam. If you're here in late summer, ask about the festival, which features **acrobats** and live music in addition to side dishes of watermelon and tofu. Carry on to the island's northeast tip, where the **Dongjyu Lighthouse** stands alone atop a small hill. This utilitarian structure was built by the British in

1872 to help with the navigation of ships engaged in the **Opium Wars**. It now overlooks a grassy plain dotted with abandoned pillboxes. Below the lighthouse there used to be **four cannons** used for signalling to ships in the fog, but they have been removed and are now on display in the Matzu Folklore Culture Museum on Nangan (see p.488).

Near the island's southwest corner is **Dapu Village**, an abandoned fishing settlement that has been completely restored. The **stone buildings**, which have been rebuilt in eastern Fujianese style, essentially comprise an open-air museum and lack the character of some of the archipelago's inhabited communities. However, the village is located on an isolated, rocky promontory and makes for quite a sight when viewed from a distance. Further south, at Dongjyu's southern tip, is the **Dapu Stone Inscription**, a tablet with a 42-character engraving commemorating the capture of pirates by a Ming dynasty general. Below the pavilion built around the tablet is a set of wooden steps leading to a flat stretch of rocks that leads gently to the sea. This spot, another favoured shellfish-gathering area, is a nice place to watch the sunset.

Practicalities

All of Dongjyu's **accommodation** and **restaurants** are in tiny Daping Village, most of them a stone's throw from each other. The *Chuanlao Homestay* at number 55-1 (℡0836/88022; ❷) has recently been renovated and has big, comfortable doubles. **Scooters** can be rented here for NT$300 for a half-day, and, if you are a guest, the owner will let you take one for an hour's loop round the island at no cost. The *Gusiang Homestay* at number 79 (℡0836/88080; ❷) was the first to open on Dongjyu, but it has been well maintained and its eight rooms are good value, especially the bright sea-view ones on the third floor. In the north of the village, at number 5, is the *Hongjing Hostel* (℡0836/88033; ❷), with clean, airy rooms and the island's most comfy beds. Alternatively, the *Remember Homestay* at number 68 (℡0836/88397; ❷) has four immaculate, breezy rooms with beautiful wooden ceilings – reservations are recommended, and a pick-up at the pier is included in the price. To stay here, ask at the adjacent *Jhao Bu Dao Restaurant* (℡0836/88030), which opens for lunch and dinner whenever tourists are around. Its **seafood** and **tofu dishes**, made from local ingredients, are excellent.

The village's other eatery is *Remember Coffee* at number 21 (℡0836/88030), which has decent coffee and Western-style food such as toast and spaghetti.

Sijyu

The smallest of the Matzu Islands, **SIJYU** today is but a shadow of its former self, its once bustling **Cingfan Port** now serving the slow trickle of tourists who visit here. Sijyu has long been a pivotal **command post** and has absorbed more than its share of artillery fire from mainland China. It continues to be of immense strategic importance, and a strong military presence remains. The island's heyday was during the **Korean War**, when the Western Enterprise Co of the US – a front for the CIA – stationed spies here to collect intelligence on mainland China, ushering in loads of Western goods and decadence. The main Cingfan Village was flooded with bars, ballrooms and brothels, earning it the nickname "**Little Hong Kong**". After the Korean War ended, the village reverted to its prior sleepy self.

There aren't many tourist sights on Sijyu, and the best thing to do is take a **walk** around the island, which can easily be covered in a few hours. On its northeast corner is **Caipuao**, once the favoured place for villagers to gather laver. Heading west along the road from here you'll encounter sweeping ocean views.

Practicalities

Ferries from Nangan arrive at Cingfan Port, a few minutes' walk from Cingfan Village. Most of the **hotels** are located in **Tianao Village**, over the hill to the northeast of Cingfan, which has the island's only places to eat. Given this, if you stay at one of the Tianao hotels, you'll need to walk to Cingfan for meals. Though it's hardly worth getting a **scooter**, they can be rented in Cingfan (NT$300 half-day/NT$500 full-day).

The nicest place to stay in Tianao is the *Friendship Hotel* at number 67 (℡0836/89107; ❸), where there are bright, clean rooms. The owner speaks a tiny bit of English and will be so happy to see a foreign face that he may offer to give you a free **taxi tour** of the island. Nearby, at number 68-3, is the *Haijing Holiday Village* (℡0836/88125; ❷), a decent budget choice with basic rooms. On the first floor are a few computers with **Internet** access. The village's cheapest option is the tatty *Siangcun Homestay*, at number 55 (℡0836/88116; ❸), but rooms here are dank and dark.

Across from the post office in Cingfan Village is the *Flowers Café*, at number 23 (℡0836/89265; ❸), a **homestay** with four spotless rooms. There is an attached **restaurant** and **café** which serves good coffee. For **seafood** and simple rice and noodle dishes, try the *Guanhai Lou Restaurant* at number 40 (10am–8pm), tucked away in a tiny square in the heart of the village.

Travel details

The number of air and sea connections to the major islands of the Taiwan Strait can vary significantly throughout the year, and the frequencies below are what can be expected in the busy March-to-October season.

Flights	Ferries
Chiayi to: Kinmen (1 daily; 50min); Magong (2 daily; 30min)	**Budai to:** Magong (1 daily, mid-March to early October; 1hr)
Kaohsiung to: Cimei (1–2 daily; 35min); Kinmen (6 daily; 55min); Magong (13–15 daily; 35min); Wangan (twice weekly; 35min)	**Kaohsiung to:** Kinmen (1 daily in summer; 10hr); Magong (1 daily in summer, 4–5 weekly in winter; 5hr)
Magong to: Cimei (1 daily; 15min)	**Keelung to:** Dongyin (1 nightly, June–September; 7hr); Nangan (1 nightly, June–September; 9hr 30min)
Taichung to: Kinmen (9 daily; 55min); Magong (5–7 daily; 35min); Nangan (1 daily; 1hr 5min)	**Nangan to:** Beigan (hourly in summer; 20min); Dongjyu (several daily in summer; 1hr); Dongyin (3–4 weekly, June–September; 2hr 30min); Keelung (1 daily, June–September; 9hr); Sijyu (several daily in summer; 50min)
Tainan to: Kinmen (2 daily; 50min); Magong (3–4 daily; 30min)	
Taipei to: Beigan (3 daily; 50min); Kinmen (11–16 daily; 55min); Magong (9–13 daily; 55min); Nangan (7 daily; 50min)	**Sijyu to:** Dongjyu (six daily in summer; 10min)
	Tainan to: Magong (1 daily, Chinese New Year to September; 2hr)

Contexts

Contexts

A brief history of Taiwan

T
aiwan has an exceptionally short recorded history by Asian standards, starting with the arrival of the Dutch in 1624. Though the Taiwanese have a long tradition of rebellion and resistance, they've rarely been masters of their own fate, what ex-president Lee Teng-hui calls the "Taiwanese Sadness"; in addition to the Dutch, the island has been occupied by the Spanish, mainland Chinese, Japanese and briefly the French. Today it all boils down to one question: is Taiwan part of China? Inevitably, historians tend to interpret Taiwan's past quite differently according to their answer.

Prehistory

Archeologists have identified fourteen prehistoric cultures in Taiwan, and though it would seem logical to regard these as antecedents of the aborigines (see p.518), it's been hard (and controversial) to prove such links. What is agreed is that humans have inhabited the island for thousands of years, arriving in a series of migrations from mainland Asia; the simple bone, horn and stone implements found on the east coast and dating from 30,000 to 50,000 years ago represent the **Changpin Culture**, Taiwan's first, while **Tsochen Man**, who lived between 20,000 and 30,000 years ago, is the earliest remains of a human found in Taiwan. The **Shihsanhang** people were the last of these cultures and the only one to possess iron-smelting capabilities, flourishing 200–1500 AD. By this time the indigenous tribes recognized today were well established, having been in Taiwan for at least four thousand years, and the first temporary **Chinese settlements** were starting to emerge with small groups of fishermen and pirates thought to have been the first to arrive, sometime in the sixteenth century. Though vague references are made to the island in Chinese sources from the Sui dynasty (581–618 AD), and an official party on their way to the Ryukyu Islands made a brief landing in 1292, it was regarded as a wild, uninhabitable place and largely ignored by mainland China.

The beautiful island

Portuguese sailors, passing Taiwan on their way to Japan in the sixteenth century, named it **Ihla Formosa**, "the beautiful island". In the West, Taiwan was referred to as Formosa until the 1950s, and the name is still used by companies, hotels and museums today. The origin of the Chinese word **Taiwan** is less clear, though Ming dynasty negotiators used the name in their treaty with the Dutch in 1624. It seems likely that it stems from the aboriginal word "Taiyan", which meant alien, or early Chinese references to the island as "Dayuan", pronounced "Dai Wan" in Fujianese. The Dutch named the Tainan area "Tayouan" as a result – this became known as "Taiwan-fu" in the seventeenth century, the term gradually applied to the whole island. Since 1949 its official name has been the "**Republic of China**", but locals rarely use this in practice.

The Dutch

The **Dutch** were the first foreign power to develop Taiwan in an organized way, providing the earliest written accounts of the island and its population. The **Dutch East India Company** had established a base in Indonesia in 1619, and eager to raid the coast of China and extract favourable terms of trade, occupied **Penghu** in 1622. In 1624 the Chinese attacked, and in the subsequent truce, agreed that the Dutch could have Taiwan if they abandoned Penghu (though whether this means the Ming dynasty regarded Taiwan as part of its territory is still debated).

The Dutch made a base at **Anping** (near Tainan), where they found a small group of Chinese settlers, and well-established indigenous tribes. As Dutch rule spread across the island, many of the latter were converted to Christianity, but relations were often hostile: in 1629 the aborigines at Madou massacred some Dutch soldiers, resulting in a brutal punitive campaign between 1635 and 1636 which brought much of the southern plains under Dutch control. Farming was developed on a large scale for the first time, with tomatoes, mangoes, cabbages, rice, sugar cane and water buffaloes introduced, but the greatest Dutch legacy was **Chinese immigration**: the Dutch needed Chinese labour and settlers to build a successful colony, offering land (to rent, not to buy) to farmers who made the voyage across the Taiwan Strait. When the Dutch arrived in 1624, they estimated only one thousand to 1500 Chinese were living on the island, but 38 years later the figure had increased to over fifty thousand. These farmers had to pay a five to ten percent levy on profits, a head tax, and sales tax on commodities like butter and alcohol. These high taxes and resentment of Dutch authority led to a series of **rebellions**, notably in 1652, when a plot by local leader **Guo Huai-yi** was exposed before he had time to properly organize his force of 16,000, and at least 4000 were killed by an army of Dutch and aboriginal warriors – the colonial tactic of divide and conquer has been used with great effect in Taiwan ever since.

Who are the Taiwanese?

Around 98 percent of Taiwanese citizens today claim descent from Han Chinese immigrants from mainland China. In the sixteenth century they came primarily for commercial reasons: in the south they were mostly **fishermen**, while in the north they **traded** with aboriginal tribes for sulphur, deer hides, and gold. Over eighty percent of immigrants came from Quanzhou and Zhangzhou prefectures in Fujian province: the descendants of these people form the Taiwanese or **Hoklo** majority today, around seventy percent of the country. Taiwan's smaller **Hakka** population hails from Guangdong province, migrating in the early eighteenth century, and now forming fifteen percent of the population. Taiwan's "mainlanders" (*waishengren*) came with Chiang Kai-shek in 1949, political migrants from the eastern provinces of Zhejiang and Jiangsu, but including people from almost every major region in China – they now represent around thirteen percent. Though Taiwan's **indigenous population** is officially just two percent of the total, it's worth remembering that very few Chinese women crossed the Taiwan Strait in the early years of colonization, and that in reality, most Hoklo Chinese have some aboriginal blood – as this will almost certainly be on the mother's side it's rarely recognized. Some studies suggest that up to sixty percent of Taiwanese have aboriginal genes.

The Spanish

Spain had carved out a profitable colony in the Philippines in the 1560s, and were eager to expand their trade with Japan – Taiwan seemed perfectly located midway along the sea routes, and in 1626 they occupied **Heping Island** near modern-day Keelung and built Fort San Salvador. In 1628 a second base at **Danshui** was established, Fort Santo Domingo. The Spanish had a fairly miserable time in Taiwan. The local aborigines proved impossible to subdue, the tropical, wet weather was debilitating, and profits from deer hides and the sulphur trade meagre. In the 1630s the Dutch launched a series of violent assaults on the Spanish forts, and with Japan now closed to foreign trade the whole venture seemed pointless. In 1638 Danshui was abandoned and in 1642 the Dutch occupied Heping Island, forcing the Spanish back to Manila.

The Zheng dynasty

In 1661, Chinese general **Zheng Chenggong**, also known as Koxinga, attacked the Dutch capital at Tainan with 25,000 men as part of a strategic retreat from mainland China. He'd been fighting a civil war on behalf of the Ming dynasty, who were toppled by the Manchurian Qing dynasty in 1644 (see box, p.325). After a nine-month siege, he secured the Dutch surrender in February 1662, kicking them off the island and establishing an independent Chinese state that included Penghu.

Koxinga died later that year, but his son, **Zheng Jing**, ruled as "King of Taiwan" until 1681. Tainan was developed as an imperial capital, Dutch land privatized, and Chinese-style taxation, administration, education and finance introduced. The Chinese population continued to expand, reaching around 100,000 in the 1680s, but after Zheng Jing's death, fighting between his sons, **Zheng Kezang** and **Zheng Keshuang**, weakened the kingdom. In 1683, the Qing regime in China decided to bring the Zhengs to heel. **Admiral Shi Lang** led the Qing navy to a devastating victory in Penghu, and by the time he reached Tainan, Keshuang, who had won the leadership struggle with his brother, had no stomach for a fight. The Zheng kingdom was handed over without further bloodshed, the "King" pensioned off to a small palace in Beijing.

The Qing era

At first, Qing Emperor Kangxi wanted to force Taiwan's Chinese inhabitants back to the mainland and abandon the island. Shi Lang managed to persuade him that it was worth keeping, primarily as a defensive measure, but also to develop its potentially rich resources, and in 1684 Taiwan was officially admitted into the **Chinese Empire** as a prefecture of Fujian province. Taiwan, or at least the part of it inhabited by Chinese farmers, was ruled by the Qing for another 212 years.

Early Qing rule

From the start, the Qing administration segregated the aboriginal and Chinese sectors of the island, banning interracial marriages and limiting contact, abrogating all responsibility over indigenous areas – this would have dire consequences in 1871 (see p.508). The Qing's **passive approach** to governing Taiwan meant that despite travel restrictions, illegal immigration flourished. The growing Taiwanese population became resentful of corrupt officials, who typically served three to five years in a place they considered the end of the earth and ripe for plunder. Morale within the relative tiny militia kept on the island was low and it's no surprise there were 159 major incidents of civil disturbance during the Qing era, several of them serious rebellions against imperial authority.

Rebellion

Rebellion in the early years of Qing rule was motivated primarily by political factors, while economic grievances became more important in the nineteenth century. In the most serious cases, troops from the mainland were required for the Qing to regain control, an expensive undertaking that exasperated the emperors. In the **Zhu Yi-gui Rebellion** of 1721, where Zhu (a duck farmer) managed to occupy Tainan and declare himself king, a mainland army only restored order six months later. Taiwan's most serious insurgency was the **Lin Shuangwen Rebellion** of 1786–88, when Lin's "Heaven and Earth Society" mobilized tens of thousands in an attempt to overthrow the government and reinstate the Ming dynasty – Lin ruled Taiwan for over a year, and was finally defeated by a combination of mainland, Hakka and aboriginal troops.

Between 1780 and 1860 Taiwan underwent an **agricultural revolution** as more land was cultivated for rice and sugar cane, but tensions grew between the now increasingly large immigrant communities – the Qing era saw hundreds of bitter fights and brawls between Chinese settlers, some of them, like those in Taipei and Keelung in the 1850s, resulting in scores dead.

The Nineteenth Century: Taiwan opens up

In the nineteenth century, the Qing dynasty was weakened by a series of external crises, all of which affected Taiwan. In 1841 the British shelled Keelung during the **Opium War**, and in 1854 US Commodore Matthew Perry, the man that forced the Japanese to open its markets, anchored off Keelung and urged the US government to occupy the island – he never received a formal response, and no action was taken. Finally, the **Treaty of Beijing** (1860) forced China to open its ports to foreign trade: in Taiwan, only Anping and Danshui were included, but in the 1860s the list was expanded to include the deeper harbours at Keelung and Takao (Kaohsiung). These ports subsequently attracted a mix of missionaries such as **George Mackay** (see box, p.149), and merchants and officials, many of them British – the latter administered customs and represented the other Western nations, including the US from 1875. In 1868 the Qing monopoly on **camphor** was abolished, and this, along with a huge upsurge in **sugar** and **tea production** (the latter encouraged by entrepreneurial Englishman **John Dodd**), created a boom in exports in the 1870s, dominated by the foreign *hongs* or trading companies.

The Mudan Incident

It wasn't just the Europeans and Americans that wanted a piece of China. The **Japanese**, modernizing incredibly fast after the Meiji Restoration in 1868, were eager to match the West in every way, including imperialist ambition. Taiwan, as one of the closest territories to Japan, was a natural target. In 1871 a ship from the Japanese-held Ryukyu Islands ran aground near the southern tip of Taiwan. The 66 survivors stumbled on the **Paiwan** village of **Mudan**; traditional accounts suggest the sailors were mistaken as enemies and attacked by the villagers, though the Paiwan version claims that at first they helped the men, and only attacked after they had fled the village at night, confusing the tribe. Either way, 54 sailors were beheaded in the melee. After the survivors finally returned to Japan, the government spent the next three years demanding the Qing regime take action – the Qing claimed that the Paiwan were beyond their jurisdiction. In 1874 the Japanese took matters into their own hands, sending a punitive force to Taiwan, resulting in a series of bloody encounters and **massacres** in several Paiwan villages. The Qing government deployed an army to Taiwan from the mainland, but war was narrowly avoided: instead the Chinese paid the Japanese compensation for the dead men and expenses for the operation. The attack shocked the Qing into a review of their Taiwan policy, Imperial Commissioner **Shen Baozhen** initiating a building programme of forts around the island (1874–1875), reversing the immigration policy to boost the Chinese population, and proposing the establishment of Taipei. The dead Paiwan were largely forgotten.

The Sino-French War and provincial status

In 1884 Taiwan became involved in another war, this time a conflict between China and France over Vietnam. French troops raided the Danshui area, and managed to capture Keelung for over six months. The general credited with holding them back was **Liu Mingzhuan**, regarded as hero in Taiwan and more recently in China, where he's buried in Hefei and is one of only a handful of Qing officials rehabilitated by the Communist Party. After the war in 1885, Taiwan was finally given **provincial status**, and Liu was appointed its first governor. Generally regarded as a progressive and dynamic leader, Liu began the modernization of the island in earnest, building railways, developing coal mines and improving infrastructure. He was less successful in pacifying the mountain tribes however, and after forty military missions and heavy Chinese casualties, Taiwan's wild hinterland remained virtually independent. After his replacement in 1891 by Shao You-lian, attempts to modernize were stymied and momentum was lost.

The Sino-Japanese War and the Taiwan Republic

In 1894 China became embroiled in a war with Japan over the sovereignty of Korea. Though none of the fighting took place near the island, China's defeat in 1895 led to the **Treaty of Shimonoseki**, a humbling agreement in which the Qing regime agreed to hand over Taiwan and Penghu to the Japanese. Shocked at this apparently casual abandonment of the island, a group of wealthy and educated Chinese in Taiwan pressed the recently appointed governor, **Tang Jing-song**, into declaring an independent **Taiwan Republic** on May 15, 1895. Tang was made president, and a cabinet appointed; the new nation even had a flag and stamps printed. Japan had no intention of letting its first colony slip away that easily however, and landed a force of twelve thousand men on the north of the island on May 29. Lacking the stomach for a fight, the regime collapsed almost immediately, Tang fleeing back to the mainland ten days after his inauguration. After overcoming the Republic's army with relative ease, the

Japanese marched into Taipei without a fight on June 7, beginning the period of **Japanese occupation**.

The Japanese occupation

The **Japanese** ruled Taiwan for fifty years, a period of colonial exploitation but also of unparalleled economic development: by the time the KMT took control in 1945, Taiwan was a model economy, far more modernized than China. In recent years the period has been undergoing a thorough reassessment: under Chiang Kai-shek (as in China today), children were taught that Japan was a wicked, imperialist power, but many older Taiwanese compare the Japanese favourably with what they see as the equally alien and cruel KMT regime. Though it's certainly true that Japanese rule could be beneficial and even enlightened, especially in the 1920s and early 1930s, Taiwan was developed primarily to benefit Japan – it's also the case that the initial occupation was fiercely resisted, and violently imposed.

The Japanese invasion and Taiwanese resistance

The Japanese army took five months to suppress formal resistance to their occupation (Tainan surrendered on October 21), a violent campaign in which 14,000 Taiwanese died, but it took another seven years before they mopped up smaller bands of guerrillas or "bandits". Resistance was fiercest in Yunlin and Chiayi, and for the first time Chinese fought with aborigines in numbers.

In 1898 the appointment of **Governor Kodama Gentaro** and his chief administrator **Goto Shinpei** signalled a change in tactic and the imposition of "bandit laws" – 32,000 Taiwanese were punished under this authoritarian piece of legislation and, with the combined expansion of the police force, guerrilla resistance was wiped out by 1902. Though armed rebellion was rare thereafter, Taiwanese continued to protest Japanese rule through a series of riots and strikes, most notably during the **Beipu Affair** in 1907, when local farmers protested the monopolization of the camphor industry by Japanese companies. During the 1920s there was a series of attempts to petition the colonial gov-

King of the bandits

Lin Shao-mao was one of the most successful "bandits" who resisted the Japanese, becoming a Taiwanese legend in the process. Born in 1866 in **Pingdong** County in the south of the island, Lin became an outlaw after a brief stint as a Qing dynasty official, but after the Japanese invasion in 1895 he used his bandit experience to organize guerrilla resistance. This culminated in successful attacks on Donggang in 1897, and Chaojhou in 1898 with an army of two thousand that included Paiwan and Hakka troops as well as Taiwanese. In 1899 the Japanese launched a vicious counter-offensive, massacring around two thousand villagers in the area, and by the end of the year Lin had agreed to surrender, albeit on very favourable terms: he was allowed to rule his own fiefdom near Fengshan, free of Japanese taxation, a situation that allowed him to become extremely rich. For the Japanese however, such deals were temporary expedients: in May 1902 they launched a final crackdown on all remaining "bandits", laying siege to Lin's base and killing him and all his troops – around one thousand more were executed in the aftermath.

ernment for a Taiwanese assembly, without success, and the **Taiwan Cultural Association**, formed in 1921, organized large-scale events to encourage a sense of identity in the face of continued Japanization. Left-wing movements were tolerated by the colonial authorities in the late 1920s, and included the Taiwan Peasant Association (1926) and Labourers Association (1928); the **Taiwan Communist Party** was established in 1928, and included the independence of Taiwan as one of its aims, though it remained a secretive and underground group. The Japanese increasingly cracked down on left-wing movements after 1931, and after full-scale war broke out in China in 1937, all popular organizations were banned.

Economic development

The arrival of Kodama and Goto in 1898 had signalled a shift in Japanese policy, blending the harsh suppression of resistance with a moderate approach to those that cooperated. Goto instituted an ambitious programme of **economic development**, building factories, harbours, railways, highways and bridges, as well as introducing medical schools and hospitals. He also established a central **Bank of Taiwan** in 1899, stabilizing the currency, and encouraged the development of rice and sugar exports to Japan – the European *hongs* were gradually forced out. Kodama was governor until 1906, but development continued: the appointment of **Den Kenjiro** in 1919, Taiwan's first civilian governor-general, ushered in a period of relatively enlightened colonial government that lasted until 1936, when militarism started to dominate Japanese politics.

The Wushe Incident and aboriginal resistance

The Japanese were the first rulers of Taiwan to undertake a comprehensive study of the mountain-dwelling aborigines, but also to demand their complete subjugation – in order to exploit Taiwan's rich **lumber** and **camphor** resources, they had to control the mountains. After a series of military campaigns (1911–14), when Bunun and Atayal areas were especially hard hit, policemen were stationed in every village and a school system established, making Japanese compulsory for all aboriginal children. Such policies angered tribal leaders, and in October 1930, a misunderstanding at a wedding provided the spark for an **Atayal** uprising led by **Chief Mona Rudao** at **Wushe** in central Taiwan. The local school - which was holding a sports day - was attacked, the Atayal warriors slaughtering 132 Japanese men, women and children (and two Chinese by mistake). Japanese reaction was swift: an army of 2700 was sent, along with trackers from rival Atayal clans, to hunt down the rebels, a campaign which took fifty days, involved aerial bombing and poison gas and left around 644 Atayal dead – Chief Mona Rudao, along with almost three hundred other warriors, opted to hang himself rather than surrender. In the aftermath most of the local villages were wiped out, the Japanese offering bounties to other Atayal warriors to mop up resistance, leading to further massacres of those that surrendered. Rudao's body was taken to Taipei and only given a formal burial in 1981 – a special 20-dollar coin was minted in his honour in 2001.

World War II

War in China from July 1937 meant that Japanization was intensified, traditional Chinese customs banned and Chinese writing suppressed. To feed the Japanese war machine Taiwan was transformed into a giant military-industrial base, a policy that created an economic boom. At first the war left the island

Takasago Volunteers

In 1974, the discovery of a man in the Indonesian jungle, described as "the last Japanese soldier from World War II" made headlines around the world. In fact, the soldier was an **Ami tribesman** from Taiwan called Suniyon, who had joined the **Takasago Volunteers** in 1943. Recruitment of indigenous tribesmen into the Imperial Army was largely covered up after the war, but between four thousand and eight thousand men are thought to have fought and almost half were killed. After the Wushe Incident, the Japanese regarded aboriginal warriors as excellent fighters, and ironically many volunteers came from the devastated Atayal region. After the war many of them were enshrined via Shinto ritual at the Yasukuni Shrine in Tokyo (along with over 27,000 other Taiwanese) without family consent, and many Taiwanese aborigines still visit Japan to protest.

physically untouched, but between 1942 and 1944, an estimated six thousand Taiwanese volunteered to fight for the Japanese, including 1800 members of the aboriginal **Takasago Volunteers** (see box above). In 1944, a further 22,000 Taiwanese were conscripted and by the war's end an estimated 200,000 personnel were involved in war-related activities including over seven hundred "**comfort women**" forced to serve as sex slaves – around 30,000 Taiwanese died. The island was also home to fifteen **Allied POW camps**, including the notorious **Kinkaseki** (see box, p.179). Heavy US bombing destroyed Keelung and Kaohsiung harbours and many other parts of the island between 1944 and 1945, but when the Japanese surrendered in August 1945, Taiwan was still occupied – the last governor, Ando Rikichi, committed suicide soon after.

Return of mainland rule and the 2-28 Incident

According to the terms of the **1943 Cairo Declaration** agreed (but not signed) by Franklin Roosevelt, Winston Churchill and Chiang Kai-shek, Taiwan was returned to China after Japan's surrender in 1945 though the mainland had changed dramatically since it handed the island to Japan in 1895. The Qing dynasty had been overthrown by revolutionaries led by **Sun Yat-sen**, creating the **Republic of China** in 1911 and the Chinese Nationalist Party in 1912, commonly known as the **Kuomintang** (KMT). The KMT held power in China, on and off, for the next twenty years, and from the 1920s was led by Generalissimo **Chiang Kai-shek.** The party had been involved in a fierce civil war with the rival Communist forces of Mao Zedong since 1927, only briefly put on hold during the struggle with the Japanese, and when **Chen Yi** was appointed the Chinese governor of Taiwan in 1945, he promptly began stripping Taiwan of all its industrial wealth in order to bolster the KMT's renewed campaign against the Communists. Methods were often brutal, and the Taiwanese quickly came to resent the brusque and corrupt officials sent to replace the Japanese. Meanwhile, the 480,000 Japanese inhabitants of Taiwan, many of whom had been born on the island, were told to leave by April 1946 – the KMT confiscated all Japanese real estate and property left behind.

The 2-28 Incident

The **2-28 Incident** began in Taipei on February 27, 1947, when a local vendor selling smuggled cigarettes was roughed up by Monopoly Bureau officers – in the ensuing fracas a bystander was shot and killed. The next day, a large crowd gathered outside the local police station, and fearing attack, the police opened fire, killing more civilians. Protests, strikes, riots and school closures spread across the island until March 8, when reinforcements from the mainland arrived to restore order in a bloody crackdown that took at least 28,000 lives (estimates vary wildly), and initiating forty years of martial law known as "White Terror". During this period, all discussion of the massacre was banned, and today it's still the source of heated debate among Taiwanese, especially the elderly, many of whom regard the KMT as murderers. No one has ever been charged over the incident, though Chen Yi was recalled to China in disgrace, and Chiang later had him executed.

The Republic of China: the Kuomintang and martial law

In 1949 the Communists finally defeated Chiang's Nationalist forces, and the remnants of his army retreated across the Taiwan Strait – almost two million "mainlanders" arrived in Taiwan to establish the last outpost of the **Republic of China**. Chiang Kai-shek became president in 1950, a post he held until his death in 1975. During martial law, opposition parties and Taiwanese language was banned, mainlanders dominated positions of authority and Chiang had statues of himself built in every town. Although the economy began to flourish in the late 1970s (see box p.514), resources in the early part of KMT rule

---

The Chiang dynasty

Chiang Kai-shek and his family have had a greater impact on modern Taiwan than any other. Chiang ruled the island for 26 years, though it's his activities in China pre-1949 that appear most colourful to outsiders and the focus of most biographies. Born in Zhejiang province in 1887 and trained as a soldier, he worked his way up to the position of general and then leader of the KMT in the 1920s, in part due to his wife's connections (**Soong Mei-ling** or Madam Chiang) and links to the Shanghai mob. By the time of his flight to Taiwan in 1949, his position as Generalissimo was unchallenged. After his death in 1975 and a brief but fruitless attempt at influencing politics, Madam Chiang moved to the US, dying in New York in 2004 at the age of 106. Chiang's only son **Chiang Ching-kuo** (by his first wife – he had no children with Mei-ling) was president between 1978 and his own death in 1988. Ching-kuo married Russian-born **Faina Epatcheva Vahaleva** (1916–2004, known as Chiang Fang-liang) in 1935, but their three sons died shortly after Ching-kuo and only their daughter is still alive, living in the US. In the early 1990s, Chiang Kai-shek's adopted son **Chiang Wei-kuo** briefly mounted a political challenge to Lee Teng-hui, but the Chiang family were falling out of favour and he died in 1997. That wasn't the end of the Chiangs however. Ching-kuo also had two illegitimate sons: one of them, **John Chiang**, who used his mother's family name Chang until March 2005, is now the family's unofficial political heir in Taiwan, serving as a member of the Legislative Yuan since 2002.

were primarily earmarked for defence and stockpiled for an eventual invasion of China. In reality, Taiwan's independence, as today, was made possible solely by **US support**. The conflict against Communism in Korea and later Vietnam ensured that US administrations backed Chiang's anti-communist KMT as an important ally – President Truman sent the Seventh Fleet to patrol the Taiwan Strait in the 1950s and stationed troops in Taiwan, but despite a vicious assault (see p.465) on **Kinmen** and **Matzu** in 1954 (which was repulsed by Taiwanese troops), and the heavy bombardments of 1958 (during which China announced it would only shell Kinmen on odd-numbered days) major conflict was avoided. In 1951 Japan signed the **Treaty of San Francisco** with the Allies, formally ending World War II and officially giving up sovereignty over Taiwan, but without specifying who to – a fudge which provides plenty of bitter debate today. Independence activists want the date of the treaty – September 8 – to become **Taiwan's Independence Day**.

Withdrawal from the United Nations

Taiwan became increasingly isolated in the 1970s. Mao Zedong's People's Republic of China (PRC) was finally admitted to the United Nations in 1971, but rather than share a seat, Chiang's Republic of China **withdrew**, a move which was to have serious implications in the years to follow. In 1972 President Nixon made an historic visit to China, and in December 1978 the unthinkable happened – President Carter switched US recognition to the PRC, severing formal relations with Taiwan. Much of the world has since followed suit. Though the **Taiwan Relations Act** ensured the US would still supply the island with weapons, US troops left and with the re-conquest of China now impossible, the KMT began to commit more resources to infrastructure and economic development, creating one of the world's most dynamic economies.

The Taiwan Miracle

Perhaps the greatest achievement of KMT rule was economic reform, laying the foundations of what became known as the **Taiwan Miracle** – the rise from developing nation status to seventeenth-largest-economy in the world in the early twenty-first century. **Land reform** in the 1950s was a crucial first step, resulting in the opening up of new land to farmers, and increased agricultural yields and incomes. From 1951 to 1964 the US supplied Taiwan with around US$1.5bn in non-military aid, much of this channelled to infrastructure projects and investment in the **textile industry**, Taiwan's first big export success story. **Education** was another factor, the KMT building new schools and universities in the 1950s. In the 1960s the government initiated an aggressive export-orientated at strategy: liberalizing the financial system and setting up a stock market, increasing manufacturing and creating export processing zones (Kaohsiung was the first in Asia). Between 1960 and 1970 Taiwan became the world's fastest-growing economy, averaging 9.7 percent GNP growth a year. In the 1980s, Taiwan began to produce high-quality electronics, especially **semiconductors** and **computers**, and though it has few recognisable domestic brands (Acer and BenQ the obvious exceptions), chances are that your PC or laptop contains components made by Taiwanese companies – however, all their production factories are now in mainland China where Taiwan is the largest investor (US$60bn as of 2003). Today the service sector accounts for around two thirds of GDP, while agriculture accounts for just 1.86 percent and industry around thirty percent.

Democracy

After Chiang Kai-shek's death, the now largely forgotten **Yen Chia-ken** became president in 1975, but in 1978 Chiang's son, **Chiang Ching-Kuo** took over and ruled till his own demise in 1988. Chiang Ching-kuo is a complex figure, presiding over a period of unprecedented economic growth and eventual political liberalization in Taiwan, while remaining dedicated to KMT hegemony and the goal of reunifying China.

Opposition to one-party rule and KMT corruption (dubbed "**Black Gold**" because of notorious links with local mafia) grew in the 1970s. The *Tangwai*, or "outside the party" movement, involved students and academics at first, almost all of them Taiwanese; members started by contesting local elections, but government oppression led to the 1979 **Kaohsiung Incident**, now regarded as a landmark in Taiwan's democracy movement (see box, p.348) and the trial of the "Kaohsiung Eight" which garnered much public sympathy. Between 1980 and 1985 however, progress was limited: the Chiang regime continued to crackdown on dissent, though informal opposition grew. In September 1986 the leaders of the *Tangwai* movement illegally established the **Democratic Progressive Party** (DPP). In response President Chiang lifted martial law in July 1987 and press restrictions were removed in January 1988. Much of this was due to US pressure, but with growing opposition inside Taiwan, Chiang seems to have genuinely accepted the need for change.

KMT chairman **Lee Teng-hui** became Taiwan's first native-born president in 1988, ushering in a period of reform and the end of formal hostilities with China in 1991. **Student demonstrations** in Taipei in 1990 led to more democratic concessions, and though the DPP made gains in the Legislative Yuan, Taiwan's **first free presidential election** in 1996 was won by incumbent Lee. This despite intimidation from China, which tested missiles close to the island to mark their disapproval of Lee's growing independence sympathies. Though retired from government, Lee remains an enigmatic and active figure, despised by many in China and even Taiwan – once a KMT loyalist, he's now the spiritual father of the independence movement and an outspoken critic of China.

In 2000, in a landmark election, the KMT lost power for the first time in almost fifty years: **Chen Shui-bian** of the DPP, a lawyer by training who earned his political stripes defending dissidents in the Kaohsiung Incident, became president with 39.3 percent of the vote, beating independent and ex-KMT member James Soong (36.84 percent) and KMT candidate Lien Chan (23.1 percent). The peaceful change of regime was vindication of how far Taiwan had come – the world's first Chinese democracy, while a little green and rough around the edges, was largely created by the Taiwanese themselves in a dramatic rebuttal to pundits who claimed democracy was alien to "Asian Values".

Taiwan today: the struggle for political identity

Since the election of 2000 Taiwan's **struggle for political identity** has become the primary issue of the day. Whilst ordinary Taiwanese and especially its youth have continued to develop a very recognizable identity in terms of

As of December 2006, Taiwan in its official guise as Republic of China, and bolstered by considerable sums of financial aid, was recognized by only twenty-four states: Belize, Burkina Faso, Costa Rica, Dominican Republic, El Salvador, Gambia, Guatemala, Haiti, Honduras, Kiribati, Malawi, Marshall Islands, Nauru, Nicaragua, Palau, Panama, Paraguay, Saint Kitts and Nevis, Saint Vincent and the Grenadines, Sao Tome and Principe, Swaziland, Solomon Islands, Tuvalu and the Vatican City. The problem lies in the oft repeated mantra of **"One China"** which can be interpreted in myriad ways; Taiwanese officials (mostly KMT) claim that there is "one China controlled by two governments". The simplest interpretation is largely semantic: that only one country can call itself China, which means that while Taiwan continues to use its official "ROC" moniker most nations will recognize the far larger People's Republic of China. This ignores the far thornier territorial interpretation of "One China" favoured by the mainland, which states that the territory of Taiwan (along with Tibet and Xinjiang) is part of the PRC no matter what you call it.

music, pop culture, food, fashion and art, Taiwan's status in the world remains unclear, its **relationship with China** its most challenging problem.

The status quo

The China debate reflects a very real and passionate **divide** across Taiwanese society although you're unlikely to see much expression of this on the streets. Around 75 percent of Taiwanese remain in favour of what's called the "**status quo**": that is, the current situation where Taiwan is de facto independent, but unrecognised as such in much of the world (ten percent favour reunification and fifteen percent formal independence). Though in part driven by fear of what China might do to a formally independent Taiwan, the status quo is acceptable because in practice Taiwan operates much the same as any other sovereign nation. The obvious exceptions are at the Olympics, when Taiwanese athletes compete under the embarrassing designation "Chinese Taipei", and its lack of representation at the UN.

The status quo is dependent on two things: the idea that Taiwan is the "Republic of China" – that is, an alternative China rather than an entirely different nation – and most of all, on China itself, which regards Taiwan as a "**renegade province**". A symbol of formal independence would be to change the island's official moniker to the Republic of Taiwan – a move China has threatened to meet with war. On the other hand, China has indicated it is content to maintain the status quo, and therefore the de facto independence of Taiwan (though of course this would never be admitted publicly), as long as Taiwan keeps the door open for eventual reunification.

Given this, most politicians support the status quo position, masking a fundamental division between many KMT and DPP supporters: the real issue remains **unification** versus **formal independence**.

Stalemate

Taiwan's highly adversarial political parties are drawn into two alliances, broadly reflecting their positions on China: the **pan-greens** (which has no relation to the Green parties of the West) including the DPP and pro-independence Taiwan Solidarity Union; and the opposition **pan-blue coalition** comprising the KMT led by **Ma Ying-jeou** (the ex-Taipei mayor that many pundits tip for the presidency in 2008), the People's First Party led by James Soong, and the marginal New Party. Many pan-blues believe that Taiwan ought to be, at some stage, united with the mainland, while independence-minded pan-green members want a truly sovereign nation and membership of the UN.

In 2004 Chen Shui-bian won re-election by just thirty thousand votes (50.3 percent), after an **assassination attempt** that many opposition members believe was staged. As a result, the pan-blue coalition has never really accepted the result. Despite stating his determination to see out his four-year term, Chen's presidency hit new lows in 2006, after corruption allegations involving his close aides as well as family members led to widespread calls for his resignation. In May he relinquished control of cabinet matters to premier **Su Tseng-chang** (likely to be the DPP candidate in the 2008 presidential election), while an opposition attempt to have him recalled failed in June, after DPP legislators refused to vote. Though the pan-greens control the presidency, the pan-blue coalition controls the legislature – government remains effectively **deadlocked**.

Until Taiwan's status is resolved, political progress is likely to remain sluggish, though it's surely an irony that despite achieving democracy, the fate of Taiwan's 23 million people is largely in the hands of China, the world's most populous but non-democratic state, and UN members like Tuvalu, the world's smallest. Despite all the progress of the last twenty years, "Taiwan's Sadness" looks set to linger.

Taiwan's indigenous peoples

More commonly known as **aborigines** or *yuanzhumin* ("original inhabitants") in Chinese, Taiwan's **indigenous peoples** represent just two percent of the island's 23 million people. The apparently small size of many tribes is deceiving – although the number of "pure" aboriginal people is small, many Taiwanese have aboriginal blood, often on the mother's side, but such ancestry is rarely acknowledged and often covered up for fear of social stigma. Things have improved over the last ten years, but Taiwan's indigenous population still suffers discrimination and remains very much at the bottom of the country's economic and social ladders. One of the key differences between the aboriginal population and the Chinese is religion: thanks to an aggressive missionary effort, the indigenous population is now almost completely **Christian** (mostly Presbyterian); a proliferation of churches and a Christian graveyard is an easy way to tell if you are in an aboriginal village.

Origins

Taiwan's indigenous tribes form part of the **Austronesian** cultural and linguistic family, an umbrella term for ethnic groups inhabiting a vast area of the Asia-Pacific region – the aborigines speak ancient languages known as the Formosan branch of the family, while peoples from Madagascar to Easter Island speak Malayo-Polynesian. The **origins** of Taiwan's aborigines are still fiercely debated, though most agree that they are descendants of Neolithic peoples that have inhabited the island for thousands of years. Early Western and Japanese anthropologists believed that the aborigines had migrated from Southeast Asia, while others, primarily mainland academics, have proposed that migrations came from China, thereby emphasizing the historic links between the two places. However, the most radical theory, and the one currently in favour in Taiwan, claims that the island is in fact **the homeland of all Austronesian people** – that migrations from Taiwan would eventually, over thousands of years, colonize the entire Pacific. Linguist Isidore Dyen (though he's since changed his mind) suggested this might be the case in 1963, when he identified Taiwan as having the greatest concentration of Austronesian languages. The theory was popularized in the 1990s by the work of Peter Bellwood, and jumped on by Taiwanese independence activists who relished the opportunity to promote a separate identity from China; though the theory suggests the ancestors of the aborigines did migrate from the mainland in the distant past, this was long before the creation of China and the tribes developed independently on the island before launching migrations south.

Current situation

Taiwan's aborigines have been treated poorly since the arrival of the Chinese and the Europeans in the seventeenth century. The formation of the **Alliance**

of Taiwan Aborigines in 1984 marked the formal beginning of the indigenous political movement, which focused on the return of traditional land, the right to be called *yuanzhumin*, rather than *shanbao* or *gaoshanzhu* ("mountain people") and a demand for self-government. In 1988, with the support of the Presbyterian Church, the **Return Our Land Movement** was born, and by mid-1991 this had evolved into the Aboriginal Constitutional Movement. With the end of martial law in 1987 and a greater interest in Taiwanese history in the 1990s came a reappraisal of policy: in 1994 *yuanzhumin* was adopted by the ROC Constitution and a cabinet-level **Council of Indigenous Peoples** was established in 1996 to oversee aboriginal affairs (currently headed by Walis Pelin, an Atayal), though self-government was ruled out and the council is still criticized for doing too little; most of its efforts have been focused on increasing **education**, though many aborigines still end up with low-paid work, particularly on construction sites in the cities. The DPP has made some progress in championing aboriginal rights since it came to power in 2000, though most aborigines (who tend to only speak Mandarin Chinese) still vote for the KMT, suspicious that the DPP favours Taiwanese-speakers. In 2001, the Ministry of Education added **aboriginal classes** to the schools language curriculum (in aboriginal areas), but in practice lesson time is limited and the incentives to learn poor.

In 2005, **Frank Hsieh** (who was premier at the time), admitted his great-grandmother was a Ketagalan aborigine. Hsieh made the revelation on August 1, designated **Indigenous Peoples Day**. The same year the **Indigenous Television Network**, a 24-hour TV station dedicated to aboriginal news, documentaries and entertainment was launched, one of the requirements of the Aboriginal Education Law (2000).

The Tribes

As of January 2007, there were thirteen **official indigenous tribes** in Taiwan: the Ami, Atayal, Bunun, Kevalan, Paiwan, Puyuma, Rukai, Saisiyat, Sakizaya, Tao, Thao, Truku (Taroko) and Tsou. Being recognized as an official tribe brings public recognition and government subsidies for community projects, but the process has been highly controversial and is based largely on simplistic classifications established by Japanese anthropologists in the 1920s.

During the Qing era, aborigines were classified as either *sheng fan*, "raw" or uncivilized barbarians who inhabited the mountains, or *shu fan*, "cooked" or civilized tribes that lived on the plains and generally paid taxes. Although most aborigines primarily associated themselves with their village and locale, in the 1920s the Japanese grouped the *sheng fan* into nine core "mountain" tribes. The plains aborigines were referred to collectively as *pingpu*: until very recently these people were considered totally assimilated by the Han Chinese and even today many Taiwanese will tell you that there are no *pingpu* left on the island – quite untrue. The reason for this is that most *pingpu* tribes have yet to gain official recognition as distinct ethnic groups, partly because they have ceased to speak tribal languages and maintain limited cultural traditions. This has been changing: in addition to the acknowledgment of *pingpu* tribes (like the Kevalan), those regarded as subgroups of larger "mountain" tribes are becoming recognized as distinct communities (the Thao were once considered part of the Tsou, the Truku part of the Atayal). The **Ketagalan**, **Makatau** and **Pazeh**, supposedly extinct *pingpu* tribes, are currently pushing for official recognition. Depending on how you classify them, there are at least nine officially unrecognized *pingpu* tribes: Babuza, Hoanya, Ketagalan (which includes the Basay, Luilang and Trobiawan clans), Kulon, Papora, Pazeh, Qauquat, Siraya (including the Makatau), and Taokas.

The thirteen official tribes are usually distinguished by traditional dress, rituals and exotic customs such as headhunting which have long died out, and though you will see bright costumes, singing and dancing at festivals, little of this has much bearing on contemporary aboriginal life.

Ami

The **Ami** are Taiwan's **largest tribe** with around 140,000 members, concentrated along the east coast between Hualien and Taitung, and roughly divided into Southern, Northern and Central (Siouguluan River) groups. The **Harvest Festival**, known as *Ilisin*, is the most important Ami event, usually taking place in July or August and marking New Year: each village holds its own celebration, lasting from one to seven days. Although Taitung city contains the largest concentration of Ami people, there are numerous Ami villages along the east coast and East Rift Valley, notably **Cimei** near Rueisuei, and **Dulan**, which is around 15km north of Taitung. Dulan is the largest Ami settlement on the southern coast and regarded as a centre of Ami culture – its annual **Art Festival** (October) acts as a magnet for traditional performers. The Ami are particularly well known for their **musical** traditions, producing Mandopop star Van Fan and alternative rocker Chang Chen-yue – more familiar to Western audiences, New Age dance project Enigma sampled an Ami performance group singing the traditional "Song of Joy" (without their permission) on their 1993 single "**Return to Innocence**", which was later used to promote the 1996 Atlanta Olympics. The Ami singers sued the group and reached an out-of-court settlement in 1998. The Ami word for "welcome", *naruwan*, was adopted by the Tourism Bureau in 2004. The Sakizaya was once considered part of the Ami, but became the thirteenth officialy recognized tribe in January 2007.

Atayal

The **Atayal**, meaning "genuine person" or "brave man", is the second largest tribe and the most widely spread, inhabiting the mountainous northern half of Taiwan. Its population of around 61,000 is divided into two main clans: the Seediq or **Sedeq** in the east and **Atayal** proper in the west. Despite their geographical dispersion, the Atayal have offered the most resistance to colonization over the years, gaining a reputation as fierce fighters after the 1930 Wushe Incident. In 1999, the Atayal opposed the creation of the Qilanshan National Park (later called **Makao National Park**) as it threatened local land rights, and a compromise deal was later quashed by vociferous Independent Legislator **May Chin** (a former actress), whose mother was Atayal and who continues to be a controversial campaigner for indigenous rights. The Atayal are best known in Taiwan however, for their quality **weaving** and the tradition of **facial tattoos**, particularly on women: the practice was banned by the Japanese in 1913 and died out in the 1920s – the few remaining elders with tattoos live in the **Taian** area. Other important Atayal centres are **Fusing**, **Jienshih**, **Wulai**, **Baling** and **Wushe**.

Bunun

The **Bunun** occupy the central mountains of Taiwan, and are another widely dispersed tribe of around forty thousand, divided into six clans. High mountain dwellers with a reputation as formidable hunters and skilled guides, the Bunun were the last tribe to be suppressed by the Japanese. Their most important celebration is the **Ear-shooting Festival** held in April or May, traditionally a test of archery skills designed to mark the coming of age of men in the tribe, and to pray for a good millet harvest – years of traditionally hunted animals (usually deer) are used as target practice. In the last few years the Bunun have also been active players in the campaign for aboriginal rights: the **Bunun Culture and Education Foundation** was established in 1995 in **Yenping**, Taitung County, while in 1987 the destruction of ancient Bunun graves by a hotel contractor in **Dongpu** sparked the "Return Our Land" campaign – since the 1970s the village has also clashed with Yushan National Park over water and land rights. **Luona** in Sinyi Township (Nantou County) and **Haiduan** (Taitung County) are also large Bunun communities, but the village of **Hongye** is the best known in Taiwan: this was the home of a Little League baseball team whose defeat of a side from Wakayama (Japan) in 1968 thrilled the nation (though the Japanese team were not the world champions as is still sometimes claimed). As with many other tribes, one of the most visibly recognizable Bunun in Taiwan is a popular singer, **Wang Hong-en** (the tribe is famed for its eight-part harmonies), though another tribe member, **Topas Tamapima**, became a noted writer in the 1980s, his novel *The Last Hunter* highly acclaimed.

Kavalan

The two thousand **Kavalan** (or "people living in the plain") became Taiwan's eleventh indigenous tribe in 2002 (the first *pingpu* tribe to be given such status) after a ten-year campaign and the strong support of former premier Yu Shyi-kun. Originally from Yilan County, where legend has it they drove the Atayal into the mountains, most Kavalan migrated south along the east coast in the nineteenth century and developed cultural ties with the Ami. Today their largest settlement is **Sinshe** near Fongbin in Hualien County.

Paiwan

The sixty thousand **Paiwan**, inhabiting the far south of Taiwan in Pingdong and Taitung counties, have managed to retain a strong cultural and linguistic identity. The Paiwan call themselves the "descendants of the paipushe snake" and the snake, associated with their ancestors, is a common symbol amongst the tribe and eating it is banned. Major Paiwan settlements include **Sandimen**, **Taiwu** and **Mudan**, but their villages are also spread throughout the Hengchun Peninsula and Kenting National Park – many still use slate or **slab-stone houses**. The most important Paiwan **festival** is *Masarut*, which is an end-of year celebration rather than a harvest festival, taking place in individual villages between July and November. The Paiwan are renowned **woodcarvers** but have also produced some talented writers: Chen Ying-hsiung's collection of short stories *Traces of Dreams in Foreign Lands* (1971), is considered Taiwan's first piece of aboriginal literature, while blind poet **Monaneng** has been publishing since 1984. Writer **Sakinu Ahronglong,** whose *Mountain Pig, Flying Fox, Sakinu* was a big hit in Taiwan, also starred in a film adaptation of his book *The Sage Hunter* in 2005, which won plaudits in the US. He opened Taiwan's first traditional hunting school in November 2005. Other Paiwan celebrities include the rock band **Power Station**, famous Asia-wide in the late 1990s, and female pop singer **Dai Ai-ling**.

Puyuma

Inhabiting the plains around Taitung city, the ten thousand **Puyuma** (known as **Beinan** in Chinese, after the district in which most of them live), are traditionally divided into two main subgroups with different origin myths: the **Nanwang** group are "born from bamboo" while the **Jhihben** group are "born from stone". The tribe is further divided into eight villages, traditionally independent and ruled by a chief – villages often fought amongst each other, the Puyuma developing a tradition for Spartan-like training of young men in community halls known as **Parakwan**. The tribe's most important festival, the **Mangamangaya**, or "Monkey Ritual" grew out of this warrior tradition, marking the coming of age of male teenagers and involving wrestling and hunting monkeys – today the monkeys are made of straw. Puyuma singer **A-mei** (Chang Hui-mei) has become one of the island's most successful pop stars, while **Samingad** is becoming equally famous for singing in Puyuma as well as Mandarin.

Rukai

The ten-thousand-strong **Rukai** tribe is loosely divided into three groups: **Taitung** (east), **Wutai** (west) and those inhabiting the **Maolin National Scenic Area**. The tribe, like the Paiwan, is noted for their striking slate houses in villages such as **Duona** – the Rukai also traditionally cook food on stone slabs. In the mid-1990s the Rukai became involved in the still ongoing campaign to stop the **Majia (Machia) Dam** being built, which would mean the destruction of two villages and five historic sites. In 1990, the **Return to Kochapongan Movement** was established to rebuild traditional stone houses in an abandoned mountain village, evolving into a symbol of the Rukai's determination to maintain their culture.

Saisiyat

The **Saisiyat** ("true people"), numbering around five thousand, are based in the **Lion's Head Mountain** region and comprise a Northern Branch (**Wufong**) and the Southern Branch (**Nanjhuang** and **Shihtan** in Miaoli), each with its own dialect. Given the size of the tribe and their proximity to larger Atayal and Hakka populations, the struggle to maintain Saisiyat culture is particularly hard. The "**Ritual of the Short Black People**", held by both clans every ten years, with a smaller version every two, has become their most powerful expression of identity. The ceremony commemorates a legendary tribe of black pygmies, called *taai*, or "short people", that once lived in harmony with the Saisiyat. Things changed after some of the *taai* had sexually molested Saisiyat women – the whole tribe was exterminated. The ritual is meant to appease their spirits, many anthropologists suggesting the story might be based on true events, and that the *taai* may represent peoples that inhabited Taiwan before the aborigines.

Tao

The three thousand **Tao** or **Dawu** (previously known as the Yami) retain the strongest identity of any tribe in Taiwan, mainly because of their relative isolation. The only seagoing tribe, they inhabit **Lanyu** (Orchid Island) off the southeast coast, their language more closely related to those of the Philippines than to the aboriginal languages of mainland Taiwan. The most iconic expression of that identity is the Tao wooden canoe, hand-carved and richly decorated but serving a mostly ceremonial purpose today. The Tao's traditional dress is also very distinctive, the men wearing loincloths and striking steel helmets, generally worn now only at celebrations like the **Flying Fish Festival** in March/April. The Tao's traditional underground houses, protection against the fierce Pacific weather, are also becoming rare.

It's not as tranquil as it seems on Orchid Island however; in 1982 the state-owned Taiwan Power Company (Taipower) duped the Tao into building a **nuclear waste storage site** on Lanyu in return for more jobs. The Tao have campaigned long, and so far unsuccessfully, to have the waste removed: some fear the containers are leaking. Taipower plans to transport them off the island by 2010, and is desperately seeking an alternative dump overseas – North Korea appears the most likely destination.

Thao

Sun Moon Lake is the ancestral home of the Thao (pronounced "Shao", meaning "people"), **Taiwan's smallest aboriginal tribe**, with around 540 members. One of the most important Thao legends holds that a chief known as Paidabo stumbled upon Sun Moon Lake after an exhausting chase of a large **white deer** – Paidabo was so impressed he ordered that the whole tribe, originally located near Alishan, to move here, and today you'll see symbols of the white deer everywhere. When the Japanese flooded the lake in 1934, the last traditional Thao community clinging to the slopes of Lalu Island was destroyed, and the inhabitants forced to move to the village of Bujishe, known as Dehuashe after 1945 – the name means "moral teaching". Although the village was renamed Itashao ("we are the Thao") in 2001, it's still an unofficial segregated community. Many fear the Thao will become completely assimilated by the Chinese, with only seventeen "pure" Thao still living and even fewer fluent in the Thao language. However, the destruction wrought by the 921 Earthquake led to a re-examination of government policy and a greater focus on preserving Thao culture: in 2000 Lalu Island was renamed to reflect Thao tradition, and its sacred shores protected (only Thao are allowed on the island), while in 2001 the Thao became Taiwan's tenth official aboriginal tribe (previously they had been regarded as subgroup of the Tsou).

The most popular Thao festival is the **Harvest** or **Moon Festival** held Lunar August 1–15, marking the start of the Thao New Year. On the last day of Lunar July, Itashao villagers pound huge wooden pestles on stone mortars to call the tribe together – the thumping sound created, or **pestle music**, is one of the festival's chief attractions.

Truku

In 2004, after an eight-year campaign, the 23,000 Taroko or **Truku** were officially recognized as the twelfth indigenous ethnic group in Taiwan, though not without controversy. The Truku were formerly part of the Sedeq subgroup of the Atayal tribe, and the seven thousand Sedeq from Nantou that remain are unhappy at what they feel is an unnecessary split. As the name suggests, the tribe once inhabited the area around **Taroko Gorge**, (Taroko means "lookout on a hillside") though the largest settlements today lie outside the national park at Sioulin, Wanrong and Jhousi in Hualien County. The tribe is most noted for suffering one of the worst abuses of **land rights** in Taiwan; between 1973 and 1995 **Asia Cement** leased land from the tribe, but when the lease expired, it said it had documents proving all claim to it had been surrendered. The tribe denies this, and feeling the company has done little for the community, wants it removed. Even after a court found in favour of the Truku, Asia Cement refused to budge and nothing has been done by the government since – the local Land Reclamation Committee continues its protests. The case has larger implications for traditional land rights across the island, and raised the disturbing possibility that a major Taiwanese company forged important documents (vociferously denied by Asia Cement).

Tsou

The word Tsou essentially means "people", though elders often claim that its meaning is far more subtle, equating to something like "life at the moment of conception". The Tsou are usually divided into a northern group, centred on the **Alishan National Scenic Area**, and a southern tribe found in **Kaohsiung County**, with around 7500 people claiming Tsou ancestry altogether. There are only two Tsou **hosas** (also called *dashe*), which means "major village": Dabang and Tefuye, both in Alishan. Each *hosa* has an hereditary chief or *peogsi* who still has limited authority over the villagers. Only these villages contain a **kuba**, the traditional, male-only meeting houses which lie at the centre of all Tsou festivals and rituals. Other villages have smaller structures known as **hufu** which have similar functions but are less important.

By far the most interesting Tsou festival to watch, the **Mayasvi Festival** is hosted annually in rotation by Tefuye and Dabang villages in February: traditionally a celebration of warriors returning from battle, the rituals give thanks to the God of War and God of Heaven.

Religion in Taiwan

Religious belief is apparent everywhere you look in Taiwan: in addition to literally thousands of temples, almost every home and store has a shrine, taxi drivers hang icons inside their cars, and small altars laden with offerings or braziers burning "ghost money" stand on pavements outside shops and offices. Popular religious practice, often described as "**folk religion**", is usually lumped together with **Taoism** (the label is particularly applied to temples) to distinguish it from the clearly identifiable **Buddhist** and **Confucian** traditions, and whilst it's true that Taoist concepts are important, popular "folk religion" is really a blend of ancient animist beliefs with all three traditions. As a result, Taiwan has a broad pantheon of gods and goddesses that include Buddhist and Taoist deities, as well as famous historical figures. Although this reflects the situation in China before the 1949 Communist Revolution, Taiwan has developed several idiosyncrasies of its own.

The beliefs outlined below are subscribed to by the vast majority of Taiwanese, but there are many other faiths practised on the island. Since the 1950s there has been a **Buddhist revival** in Taiwan, with several monasteries advancing a purer form of teaching and practice, and strict adherents (there are around 3.67 million) dismissing the Buddhist deities in older folk temples as childish superstition. **Christianity** is next most popular, with over one million believers (mostly Protestants), followed by **I-kuan Tao** with 845,000 followers, a mixture of various religions, but with a fundamentally Chinese character and roots in Qing dynasty China. It's now primarily a Taiwanese faith after suppression on the mainland. There are also around fifty thousand Taiwanese **Muslims**. The indigenous tribes of Taiwan once practised a system of animist beliefs, but after a century of intense missionary work little of these remain: 95 percent of aboriginal people are Christian today.

Core beliefs

Ancestor worship lies at the heart of Taiwanese (and traditional Chinese) belief, based on the hazy boundary between the human and spirit worlds. Everyone is said to become a **ghost** after death; then, after passing through a series of courts in the afterlife (where a period in hell might be prescribed for wrongdoing), these spirits become either **ancestors**, or "**hungry ghosts**", uncared for by their families and destined to haunt the living (these are the unfortunates appeased in "Ghost Month"). Worship of ancestors, by offering incense, food or spirit money at family or clan shrines is therefore imperative. If worshipping certain individuals over the years proves particularly efficacious, they eventually become elevated to the status of **god** (Mazu and Guan Di are the best examples), joining the vast pantheon of folk and Taoist deities that emerged from a blend of Chinese myth and ancient nature worship. Gods live in an alternative reality, with an administration modelled on the old imperial bureaucracy, with their own courts and a strict system of hierarchy. The supreme deity is the **Jade Emperor** or the Lord of Heaven. Worship of **gods** is slightly different from that of ancestors as the latter (and ghosts) are spirits that must be appeased or looked after, while gods are worshipped in exchange for protection, specific types of help or general good fortune (usually in the form of wealth). Note that although almost all Taiwanese subscribe to the concept of ghostly afterlife, people describing themselves as Buddhists will normally believe in reincarnation.

The three teachings

The three teachings of Confucianism, Taoism and Buddhism have been a foundation for Chinese religious belief for centuries.

Confucianism

More philosophy than religion, **Confucianism** is associated with **Kong Zi** (551–479 BC), known as "Confucius" in the West, a scholar and teacher who lived during the Warring States period in modern Shandong, China. Confucius taught that if people behaved according to a strict code of moral and social values, society would be transformed and happiness achieved – discussion of gods and spiritualism is unimportant, though Confucian temples were created later in order to commemorate the great sage and perform important rituals. His sayings, collected in the *Analects*, along with the five ancient Confucian Classics, became the basis for Chinese imperial examinations until the end of the Qing dynasty, and the emphasis on virtuous rulers, strict hierarchy and education has influenced Chinese thought ever since. Confucianism, along with its temples, was completely abandoned in mainland China after 1949, but thrives in Taiwan, and the official 77th descendant of Confucius, K'ung Te-ch'eng (Kong Decheng) lives in Taipei.

Taoism

Taoism (pronounced "Daoism"), stems from the philosophy laid out in the *Tao Te Ching*, attributed to quasi-historical monk **Lao Zi** (a contemporary of Confucius), and the later teachings of **Zhuang Zi**. "Tao" means "the way", and in contrast to the humanistic ethos of Confucianism, Taoism emphasizes man's need to connect with the natural universe in order to lead a fulfilling life, replacing greed with harmony in nature.

Contemplative, spiritual and abstruse, **philosophical Taoism** is often differentiated from the more superstitious **religious Taoism**: the latter is closer to the "folk religion" practised in most of Taiwan, with its vast pantheon of gods and goddesses, and the more mystical teachings of **Zhang Dao-ling** who lived around the second century AD. Taoist thought is closely linked to practices such as *feng shui*, and the concepts of *yin* and *yang*, as well as many common daily rituals.

Buddhism

Buddhism is essentially a way of life, based on the teachings of Indian prince Siddhartha Gautama (563–483 BC), who attained enlightenment in 528 BC and was thereafter known as the Buddha or "enlightened one". The **Four Noble Truths** stand at the core of his teachings: the truth about *duhkha* (usually translated as "suffering"); the truth of how suffering in life arises; the truth that giving up desire will eliminate suffering; and that the eightfold path is a practical way to achieve this goal. **Enlightenment** (or *nirvana*) means to escape the endless cycle of rebirth (Buddhists built on the Hindu concept of reincarnation) and therefore suffering. A few hundred years after Buddha's death, his followers divided into two schools: **Theravada** (which thrives in Sri Lanka and Southeast Asia) and **Mahayana**, the interpretation most prevalent in Northeast Asia and Taiwan today. Mahayana Buddhism, and particularly the form that developed in China (where it mixed with Taoist and Confucian thought), differs primarily in its belief that there are multiple Buddhas (that the historical Buddha, known as **Sakyamuni**, is just one of a series of past and future enlightened ones); and that there are **bodhisattvas**, enlightened beings that have chosen continued rebirth in order to end the suffering of others (**Guanyin** is the most common in Taiwan – see p.528).

Buddhism in Taiwan

Taiwan is one of the world's great strongholds of Buddhism. The two main forms practised today are **Pure Land** and the meditative **Chan** (or Zen), though most Buddhist organizations on the island tend to blend aspects of the two. Buddhist **monasteries** developed in Taiwan during the Japanese occupation, and since the 1960s have blossomed, giving the island one of the highest monastic populations in Asia. As Taiwan has grown richer, it's become a pioneer for what's known as **Humanistic Buddhism** and its attempt to accommodate modern capitalism: accepting that becoming a monk isn't practical for most people, the emphasis is on blending daily life with Buddhist tenets, and particularly on performing charity and good works. The four main organizations in Taiwan are **Chung Tai** (based near Puli, p.273), **Dharma Drum Mountain** (on the north coast, p.168), **Foguangshan** (near Kaohsiung, p.354) and the **Tzu Chi Foundation** (based in Hualien, p.392). Other than Sakyamuni, the most common Buddhas represented in Taiwan are **Amitabha** (the Buddha of Boundless Light, who oversees the "Pure Land", a paradise attainable by prayer recitation), and the **Medicine Buddha** (known formally as Bhaisajyaguru or *Yaoshifo* in Chinese), a past Buddha famed for his healing abilities and usually portrayed holding a medicine ball or pagoda. The three are often arranged together in temples as a trinity, with Sakyamuni in the middle. The **Maitreya Buddha**, known as *Milefo* in Chinese, is portrayed as a fat, happy monk with a bag at his feet, an image which commemorates a past incarnation as a quasi-historical Chinese monk. Though he's still technically a bodhisattva, Milefo is expected to return as the next future Buddha, and is worshipped as such. The **World Maitreya Great Tao Organization**, based near Emei Lake (p.209), is dedicated to Milefo.

The Taoist pantheon

Most Taiwanese worship a mixture of Taoist and Buddhist **deities**, though this blurring of faiths would be considered wholly Taoist or "folk religion" by strict Buddhists today. The following is an introduction to the most common gods, though there are literally hundreds, often within the same temple. See Basics p.50 for the relevant festival days (usually described as "birthdays") for each one.

Mazu

Mazu, also known as *Tianhou* or Queen of Heaven, is the most important deity in Taiwan with almost a thousand temples devoted to her, and the largest religious festival on the island. Regarded as the **Goddess of the Sea**, it's not hard to work out why she became so important in Taiwan, an island nation, in large part dependent on fishing and immigration by sea in its early history. Like many deities in Taiwan, Mazu has historical roots in Fujian province, the ancestral home of most Taiwanese, but as the island developed into an agricultural community she also became associated with bringing the rains, a good example of the "Taiwanization" of many deities. Her popularity can also be explained by her perceived ability to grant the wishes of her believers, most evident in the tremendous wealth of Mazu temples, and their attraction of celebrities, politicians and huge donations. The historical Mazu was a woman called **Lin Moniang**, who was born around 960 AD on Meizhou Island off the Fujian coast. As a teenager she's said to have been taught the mysteries of the Tao by a priest, and thereafter began a life of selfless charity, guiding ships into harbour and saving seafarers from drowning. This culminated in the dramatic rescue of her father or brothers whilst in a trance (some stories say her father was lost after Lin was disturbed mid-trance). She died at the age of 28, and was later deified, being awarded the title "Queen of Heaven" in the Qing dynasty.

Statues of Mazu are usually identifiable by her mortarboard-like headdress, fronted with beads. Black-faced images (though often another colour darkened by incense smoke) symbolise her appearance when saving people, a red face is meant to represent how she looks in daily life, while a gold face symbolizes her understanding of the Tao. Mazu is usually flanked by statues of **"Ears That Hear on the Wind"** and **"Thousand-Mile Eyes"**, two demons that fell in love with her (she never married), and whom she converted to the Tao, now serving as trusted assistants with obvious special powers.

Mazu's birthday is one of the country's most exuberant and intense festivals, while the **Dajia Mazu Pilgrimage** (see p.250), which takes places before the birthday, has its roots in the practice of "spirit division". This is essentially a system of hierarchy, where "mother" temples, containing ancient or revered Mazu deities, provide new statues or relics to smaller "branch" temples (the system also applies to other deities, but in the case of Mazu, it's far more developed). Traditionally these subsidiary temples return their deities to the mother temple every year at the time of Mazu's birthday, to enhance their spiritual power. The highest ranking temple is undoubtedly the shrine on **Meizhou Island** in Fujian, but the problems start when trying to identify Taiwan's most senior place of worship: almost every major temple claims it's the "first" or "oldest" and many hold precious deities from Meizhou. Rivalries are fierce and disputes can become very heated. Today, the most popular contenders are in Beigang (p.289), Dajia (p.249), Singang and the Tainan area (pp.327–328).

Guanyin

Though a Buddhist bodhisattva, **Guanyin** is worshipped in Taoist temples throughout Taiwan (Mazu temples usually have a separate shrine to Guanyin), and even where she's the main deity in a nominally Buddhist temple, practice tends to follow popular Taoism rather than orthodox Buddhism. Guanyin was originally worshipped as a male Indian bodhisattva called Avalokitesvara, who represented the ideal of compassion, able to relieve suffering and grant children: the deity began to be depicted as a female during the twelfth century in China, and she's now known as the **"Goddess of Mercy"**. The reasons for the sexchange are still debated, though as a bodhisattva Guanyin can in theory be represented in numerous ways and in Buddhist terms it's not that important. She's normally depicted as an elegant lady, robed in white, and being associated with **vegetarianism**, her image also adorns many vegetarian restaurants.

Wang Ye

Wang Ye gods are incredibly popular throughout Taiwan, but particularly in the southern counties where they equal Mazu in importance. The name Wang Ye, or "pestilence gods", is an umbrella term for around 360 different deities: there are reckoned to be around 106 to 132 individual family names for each (Chih, Chu, Fan, Li, Su, Wen and Wu are the most common), and they are thought to have originally been diseased spirits, now honoured in an attempt to ward off plague and disease. The tradition migrated to Taiwan from Fujian and is linked to the practice of burning "spirit ships", or *wang chuan*: model boats loaded with Wang Ye gods, set alight, and launched into the ocean in an attempt to expel disease. There are numerous legends as to the origin of the Wang Ye, though most portray them as highly respected scholars or musicians from ancient China who died unnatural deaths, thus leaving potentially baleful spirits – once placated, they become useful deities. Taiwan's chief Wang Ye temple is in **Nan-kunshen** (p.333), north of Tainan. Note that these pestilence gods have come to be confused in Taiwan with local protective deities, that for various reasons were also accorded the title "Wang Ye". These local gods are usually based on historical figures, such as Koxinga, but because of the similar name, get treated in part as pestilence gods – genuine pestilence gods rarely appear in temples on their own, and are usually represented in groups of three, five or seven.

Guan Di

Red-faced **Guan Di** (or *Guanggong*) is one of the most admired deities in Taiwan, with over three hundred temples and numerous shrines in homes and shops. He's usually described as the **God of War**, but this is misleading. He was originally more like a patron of chivalrous warriors, and is today worshipped by executives, police, restaurant owners, rebels and criminal gangs, as well as being revered as a god of wealth and literature by the public in general. His appeal derives from being one of the most respected characters in the Chinese classic the *Romance of the Three Kingdoms*, loosely based on the historical events of the Three Kingdoms period (206-220 AD). Known then as **Guan Yu**, the general was one of the **three oath brothers** (the main characters in the saga), and noted for his extreme bravery and loyalty. Apart from the red face, he's usually depicted with a long, flowing beard and a Chinese halberd in his hands. Buddhists claim Guan Di was taught Buddhism by a great master on the night of his death, and as a result swore to protect the *dharma* (Buddhist teachings) – he's often seen in Buddhist temples where he's known as *Qielan*.

Earth God

The **Earth God**, known as *Tudi Gong* or *Fude* in Chinese, is traditionally one of the most important in the Chinese pantheon, though as Taiwan has modernized his popularity has waned. His main task in the Jade Emperor's administration is to keep a register of births and deaths and govern the local area in his charge, usually a village or parts of a town (towns traditionally had five Earth God shrines for north, south, east, west and central districts), though he's more associated with agriculture and probably evolved from ancient harvest rituals. In his secondary role as a god of wealth, shopkeepers erect temporary altars on the roadside to make offerings to him twice a month. Earth God shrines are usually very small but ubiquitous, found literally all over the island. He's normally represented by a statue of a cheerful old man, dressed in yellow robes with a long white beard and stick in his right hand. Tucked away under his altar is usually an effigy of the **Tiger God**, thought to be his servant and ridden by the Earth God on his spiritual "inspection tours" of the locale.

City God

Every major city in Taiwan has a **City God**, or *Chenghuang* (literally "Lord of Walls and Moats") which protects the inhabitants and like the Earth God, acts as a registrar of all births and deaths in the area. He also keeps account of the citizens' moral behaviour, and it's his report after death which will determine punishment in the courts of the underworld – it's usual to find a giant abacus somewhere in his temple, as well as graphic images of hell. Though the City God tradition is thought to have evolved from nature worship, and his role is the same in every city, each deity tends to double as an incarnation of a famous local figure, meaning his birthday is celebrated on different days. In Taiwan, many City God temples are branches of mainland counterparts, usually in Fujian.

In temples the City God usually appears flanked by a large entourage of smaller statues, representing officials in his administration; there are military and civilian branches, the latter with six departments. The most famous officials, and prominent at festivals, are **General Xie** (*Ba Ye*) and **General Fan** (*Chi Ye*), charged with capturing evil spirits.

Wenchang Dijun

Known as the **God of Literature** or Culture, the origin of **Wenchang Dijun** is thought to date back to the ancient worship of a constellation of six stars near the Big Dipper. He's portrayed today as a particularly honest court official; legend has it that the Jade Emperor made him head of all officials on earth, including all appointments through examinations. With the imperial system long gone, today he's popular with students (and their parents) preparing for school and university exams. Wenchang Dijun is one of **five culture gods** or *Wu Wenchang*: Kui Dou Xingjun, Zhuyi Fuzi, Guan Di and Fuyou Dijun (also know as Lu Dongbin, one of the Eight Immortals).

Qingshui Zushi

A quasi-historical figure, popular in North Taiwan, **Qingshui Zushi** is another deity that originated in Fujian. There are several legends concerning his life: some portray him as a Fujianese monk, while others claim he was Chen Zhao-ying, born in Kaifeng during the Song Dynasty (960–1128). Awarded a local government post in recognition of his wisdom and munificence, he later established a shrine at Qingshui rock near Anxi in Fujian where he spent his retirement – after his death people began to worship him as the "Divine Progenitor of Qingshui" and he became one of the guardian gods of the county ("Zushi" is an honorific title meaning "ancestor and teacher of the people"). His most famous temple is in Sansia (p.155), outside Taipei.

Baosheng Dadi

Baosheng Dadi or the "Great Emperor who Preserves Life" is known as a god of medicine or healing, and another well-liked deity based on an historical figure. Wu Tao was born in Tongan (in Fujian) in 979 AD, and led a selfless life helping and curing sick people. Villagers began to worship Wu after his death in 1037, claiming that this was very efficacious in times of epidemic, and he soon became part of a popular Fujianese cult that was brought to Taiwan in the seventeenth century – his formal title was awarded by an emperor in the Ming dynasty. Today there are over two hundred temples dedicated to him island-wide – Ciji Temple in Syuejia (p.333), Tainan County, is the oldest, but there are important shrines in Taipei and Taichung.

Jade Emperor

The **Jade Emperor** (*Tiangong* or *Yu Huang Da Di* in Chinese) is the chief Taoist deity, and the head of the celestial government that was thought to mirror that of Imperial China. Numerous myths concern his origins, often linked to the creation of the world, and most famously, the Chinese zodiac (with its twelve animals). Traditionally, he could only be worshipped by the living emperor and was symbolized by a tablet rather than an image (as in Tainan, p.322). In Taiwan today he's been absorbed into the pantheon of folk deities, with important temples in Dasi and Taichung. Usually depicted sitting on a throne, his face obscured by strings of pearls hanging from his hat (a bit like Mazu), he usually holds a piece of jade in his hands as a symbol of authority.

Queen Mother of the West

The highest ranking female deity, often portrayed as the **Jade Emperor's wife**, this goddess is known by a confusing number of alternate names in Chinese: *Xi Wang Mu, Wangmu Niangniang, Jinmu* and *Laomu*. She's said to live in the Kunlun Mountains in China's far west, and guards the "Peaches of Immortality" which only ripen every 3600 years – eating at the banquet she holds in honour of this event confers immortality. She's regarded as a particularly liberated female figure in the male-dominated pantheon, and subsequently popular with women; she's also a protector against epidemics and a symbol of longevity. Hualien is the centre of her cult in Taiwan (see p.391).

Supreme Emperor of the Dark Heaven

Known as *Xuantian Shangdi* in Chinese, this deity is thought to have developed from the tradition of worshipping the Pole Star. A powerful god, able to control the elements and particularly fire, the Supreme Emperor is usually depicted with long black hair and holding a sword in his right hand, symbolising his use of the seven stars of the Northern Dipper constellation to subdue demons. Statues usually show him stepping on a tortoise and a snake (once monster kings, now subdued). There are around four hundred temples dedicated to him in Taiwan.

Birth Goddess

The **Birth Goddess**, or *Zhusheng Niangniang* in Chinese, is a popular sub-sidiary deity in many temples, worshipped primarily by pregnant women, or those hoping to get pregnant. She's also thought to be able to determine the sex of a child, protect mothers during pregnancy and the birth itself, as well as being a guardian of children up to the age of sixteen. At many shrines she is flanked by the **Twelve Maternal Ancestors**, lesser deities that are thought to help the Birth Goddess deliver children, one for each month of the year. Legend suggests she's based on a historical figure from the Tang dynasty, but there's little evidence to back this up. In many respects she's similar to the goddess **Qi Niang Ma** and deity **Lady Linshui**, also guardians of children and childbirth.

Matchmaker

The Old Man Under the Moon (*Yue Xia Laoren*), better known as the **Matchmaker**, is the Chinese version of Cupid and one of the more fashionable of the minor deities in Taiwan today. Like a modern dating agency, he uses a list supplied by Lady Linshui to match ideal partners at birth, tying them together by an invisible red thread. Fate ought to bring these couples together later in life, but just to make sure, offerings are made to the Matchmaker (he's usually represented by an old man with a long white beard); single men and women buy "matrimonial thread" from the temple, keeping it close to them until their predetermined partner is found.

Dizang Wang

Dizang Wang (the bodhisattva Ksitigarbha), is misleadingly known as the **King of Hell** in English. Though portrayed as a monk in Chinese tradition, legend has it that Dizang Wang was originally a girl, heartbroken at the death of her mother who had been disrespectful of Buddhist teachings and had gone to hell. Through intense prayer and meditation, her daughter managed to assume enough merit to ensure her mother's release, but in the process glimpsed all the suffering in the underworld and vowed to empty hell before becoming a Buddha. Though from the Buddhist pantheon, Dizang Wang is now portrayed as a man and worshipped in many Taoist temples (see Chiayi, p.287).

Temples

No one really knows how many **temples** exist in Taiwan, though the number keeps growing and is probably close to twenty thousand (some estimates go as high as eighty thousand). Though each is unique, all temples contain the same basic design elements, and will be visited by worshippers practising the same kind of rituals: the guide below is an introduction to what you might see. Apart from admiring the stunning craftsmanship inside, temples are the best place to get a glimpse of Taiwan's everyday religious practice. With the exception of some Confucian temples, entrance is always free.

Architecture and art

Most folk or **Taoist temples** (*miao* or *gong*) in Taiwan feature South Fujianese architecture dating from the Qing dynasty, which is when most of them were established. Such temples are always built according to the principles of **feng shui**, a geomantic practice concerned with the balancing of *qi*, or cosmic energy, in the natural world. Note that the temple establishment date rarely refers to the building you'll see today: early shrines were built solely from wood, and in addition to damage caused by Taiwan's harsh typhoon and earthquake-prone environment, it's typical for temple followers to rebuild them every few generations. As a simple rule, the more paintings or visual decoration inside the temple, as opposed to calligraphy, the older it is: Qing dynasty Taiwan was mostly illiterate. Note that in this guide, directions (right and left), are provided assuming the reader is facing the temple: in Chinese it's normal to describe the sides of the temple as if looking outwards, from the point of view of god or goddess inside.

Exterior

Taiwanese temples tend to have similar gable and hip style **roof** structures, often with double eaves, and usually decorated with colourful dragons and *jian-nian* figures (literally "cut and paste"), made from pieces of coloured glass. Traditionally you could tell how important a temple was by finding the small decorative pagoda on the roof and counting how many storeys it had: the highest was nine, in theory only applying to temples frequented by the emperor or Confucian temples, while seven levels were more common. In modern Taiwan however, these rules are rarely followed and most temples now feature seven or nine-storey pagodas. Odd numbers are considered *yang* (or male) in Chinese cosmology, associated with heaven or sun and in opposition to *yin* and the underworld, and therefore favoured for shrines to the dead. Older temples usually have *koji* figures outside and inside the temple: these are hand-sculpted pottery figurines, usually making up vivid tableaux from Chinese legends – the craft is traditionally Chiayi based (see p.287).

Stone lions guard the temple entrance: the left is female, the right male, primarily decorative symbols of nobility and royalty. Always **enter** at the side entrance to the right of the main gate, and exit on the other side. The right side is more important in *feng shui* terms, and is usually adorned with paintings or images of **dragons** (yang), while **tigers** (yin) appear on the opposite side. Dragons are immensely powerful creatures in Chinese mythology, emblems of the emperor and symbols of fertility.

Interior

Chinese temples tend to be south-facing, though in Taiwan there are plenty of exceptions, and Mazu temples often face west, towards the Taiwan Strait and Fujian. Most are laid out as a series of halls and courtyards: the main gate, or **entrance hall**, leads to a **front hall** or a small courtyard facing the **main hall** in which the chief deity is enshrined. There is sometimes a **rear hall** beyond this, and often numerous shrines tucked away all over the site.

Every temple has at least two **Door Gods** painted on the main doors, usually selected from a group of around twenty different historical figures. The most common are Tang dynasty generals Qin Shu-bao and Yu-chi Jing-de, whose protection of the emperor against an evil dragon spirit was so effective even their painted images seemed to scare it away. The ceilings above the entrance hall are usually incredibly elaborate. Known as **algal wells**, they are supposed to trick demons into thinking the temple is underwater, and therefore impermeable to fire. Paintings inside were not just decoration, since everything had a meaning – temple walls are loaded with practical advice ranging from what to wear inside and how to pray, to when to have children.

The chief deity is worshipped at the main **altar**, usually represented by several statues (in some temples there are numerous images of the same god). Different **statues** can represent different incarnations of the god, and can have different uses: the oldest, most venerated effigy rarely leaves the protected casing of the altar, but others will be used for festivals and inspection tours (when the god "inspects" the local area as part of a boisterous parade). Hanging from the beams above the main altar, plaques and tablets from emperors and modern political leaders usually praise the main deity. Towards the back or sides of the temple you're likely to see towers of tiny lights, known as *guangming*: believers pay the temple to have their name inscribed under one of these lights for a set period, in the hope their generosity will be rewarded by the chief deity.

Traditional **Buddhist temples** (*si*) are similarly designed, but usually feature statues of the **Four Guardian Kings of the Four Directions** at the entrance, protecting the main images of Buddha inside and depictions of the eighteen *arhats* or *lohans* along the walls: these are Buddhist saints respected for their great wisdom and power. Newer Buddhist temples in Taiwan tend to be less gaudy than Taoist or popular shrines, and often form a part of monasteries or nunneries. **Confucian Temples** (*kong miao*) have a fairly standardized layout of halls and courtyards, the most notable difference being the absence of deities – Confucius is commemorated with a **tablet** (see p.109 for the best example of a Confucian temple).

Temple rituals

The most common form of *bai-bai* (worship) in temples is to make a series of bows before the image of the deity, hands together before the chest – usually **incense sticks** (*xiang*) will be held, the smoke symbolizing prayers floating to heaven. Believers ask for the deity's help for a specific problem, or just general good fortune, and it's also normal to give thanks to the deity for previous help. You'll often see people buying bundles of incense at the temple entrance, before making a circuit of all the main shrines and deities inside. Once *bai-bai* is complete, incense is placed in the large **censer**, usually facing the main hall. In addition, the tables in front of the main altars are often covered in **offerings**, usually food (especially types of fruit, which often have symbolic meaning), incense and **joss money** or "gold paper" (*jin zhi*), all intended to help convey the sincerity and loyalty of the worshipper. In order to pass into the spiritual realm, the money must be burnt – you'll see people throwing piles of it into the large chimney-like furnaces that stand in courtyards or outside the temple.

Various forms of **divination** or fortune-telling are practised in traditional Taiwanese folk religion, and you're likely to see several versions of this in temples. The most common is the use of *zhi jiao* (pronounced *bua-buei* in Taiwanese) or **throwing blocks**, also known as "moon blocks" on account of their crescent shape. Worshippers use these to ascertain the gods' answer to a specific question. If one lands flat-side up and the other the opposite, this is taken to be positive, or the "sacred" response – this needs to happen three times in a row for the believer to be sure the deity is in agreement. Any other combination requires a restart: if both blocks fall round side up, this is taken as a negative, while both landing round side down is the "laughing" response, meaning that you must rephrase the question.

Drawing lots (*chou qian*) is also popular. These are the thin bamboo strips lodged into a cylindrical container, each marked with a number. This corresponds to a piece of paper (usually contained in numbered drawers nearby) which contains an obscure saying or poem, a piece of ancient wisdom that usually requires an expert to interpret. Occasionally you might see a *jiaozi* (*gio-a* in Taiwanese), or **divination chair** being used: this looks like a small toddler's chair. Two men hold the chair in front of the altar, in order for the relevant deity to occupy it (the chair is bounced around by his or her presence). The deity is supposed to force the chair to trace characters on a nearby table – the interpretation of these characters is taken to be the answer to the worshipper's question.

Temples are also the best place to see **spirit mediums** or *jitong* (*tang ki* in Taiwanese), men who become possessed by a deity while in a trance (they usually specialize in just one), and thus can deliver far more effective oracles or responses to practitioners' queries. These men usually work in temples (see Tainan, p.322), but are not attached to them, being independent and free to work wherever they choose.

Arts and culture

Taiwanese **culture** is rooted in millennia of Chinese tradition, art and philosophy, and much of what is considered "Taiwanese" today emerged relatively recently, during the Japanese occupation. The Taiwanese contemporary arts scene is a dynamic blend of Western, Japanese, indigenous, Fujianese and northern Chinese influences, much of it tied to the search for a separate identity, at its most intense since the 1980s.

Visual arts

Generally recognized as the "father of modern Taiwanese art", **Kinichiro Ishikawa** (1871–1945) was one of many Japanese painters that came to Taiwan to paint and teach, arriving in 1910. In the 1920s and 1930s, artists such as **Chen Cheng-po** (1895–1947), Li Shih-ciao, Li Mei-shu, and **Yang San-lang** (1907–1995), who had all been pupils of Ishikawa and studied European oil painting in Japan, particularly French Impressionism, created the first **Nativist** movement, characterized by the depiction of typically Taiwanese images and scenes. Chen grew up in Chiayi, and his work captures the essence of rural south Taiwan and its languid street life: the oil painting *Streets of Chiayi* (1926) was the first by a Taiwanese painter to be exhibited at the Imperial Art Expo in Japan. Yang's contrast of light and colour is heavily reminiscent of Monet, his natural landscapes and scenes containing a nostalgic, plaintive quality.

After World War II, there was renewed interest in traditional Chinese painting, but by the 1960s disillusionment with conservative styles had precipitated a move towards abstract Western art; **Lee Chun-shan** (1911–1984) and **Liu Kuo-sung** (b.1932) were the most important and innovative painters of the period. Lee was an avant-garde pioneer, maintaining a reclusive existence in Changhua.

In the 1970s, **Nativism** (or "Native Soil Movement") was revived, partly as a rejection of the Western-inspired art of the 1960s. **Hung Tung** (1920–87) became one its most celebrated exponents, noted for his use of vivid colours and imaginative interpretation of Buddhist themes, Chinese myth and traditional historical drama. The movement also incorporated sculptors such as **Ju Ming** (see p.168) and his teacher **Yu Yu Yang**, who had studied in Japan, and is most famous for his dynamic stainless-steel sculptures, heavily influenced by Buddhism (see p.101).

The 1980s was a transitional period in art terms, mirroring the political upheavals which led to the ending of martial law in 1987. The most significant figures were **Yang Mao-lin** and **Wu Tien-chang**, both of whom dealt with social and political issues in their work. Wu became famous for his *Portraits of the Emperors* (completed in 1990), large caricatures of Mao Zedong, Deng Xiaoping, Chiang Kai-shek and Chiang Ching-kuo, but turned to photography in the 1990s and now uses digital imagery to blend flat and 3D graphics. Yang's *Made in Taiwan* series is a more subtle approach to Taiwanese history, blending a diversity of images such as aboriginal peoples, references to the Dutch period and domestic fruits and vegetables.

In the 1990s, influenced by Postmodernism and the growth in art galleries and museums, art in Taiwan blossomed in several different directions: the Nativist movement continued to evolve, and multimedia, particularly photography, video and installation art became more mainstream. **Lee Ming-sheng** is one of the most influential proponents of a mixed media approach, while **Chen Chieh-jen's** its has been exhibited all over the world, best known for its shocking photographic images such as *A Way Going to an Insane City* (1999) to explore the brutal side of colonisation, religion and the impact of globalization.

Taiwan also has a strong tradition of **art photography**: Chang Tsai, Deng Nan-guang and Lee Ming-diao are known as the "Three Swordsmen of Taiwanese Photography", their work documenting the island's development in the postwar period – Tsai is particularly lauded for his portraits of folk festivals and aboriginal people.

Music

Traditional Chinese music was brought to Taiwan with immigrants from the mainland, most audibly in the form of **folk music** played at celebrations, festivals and temples, but in recent years there has been a revival of the more complex traditions of Chinese **classical music**, particularly *nanguan*. **Contemporary music** is an important element of modern Taiwanese identity, with pop, rock and hip-hop offering an artistic outlet to the island's youth in much the same way as in other parts of the developed world.

Traditional music

Traditional Chinese music comes in many different styles, but in Taiwan it's usual to divide the whole field into two groups: *beiguan* ("northern music"), a fast-tempo music that commonly accompanies operas and traditional puppet shows, and *nanguan*, which originated in Fujian, and has a more delicate and soothing sound, traditionally far more popular in Taiwan. *Nanguan* often incorporates a female singer accompanied by Chinese lutes and flutes, the ballads usually tragic love stories. The **Han–Tang Yuefu Music Ensemble** (☏02/27252008, ⊛www.hantang.com.tw) is a Taiwanese cultural icon, founded

---

U-Theatre

Laoquan Mountain, shrouded in lush vegetation south of Taipei, is the home of esoteric drum and performance troupe **U-Theatre** (☏02/29388188, ⊛www.utheatre .org.tw), one of Taiwan's most famous and reclusive. Not a conventional theatre troupe the group is lauded internationally for its traditional **drumming** performances, often combined with powerful movement and dance, as well as traditional gongs and singing. Established in 1988 by Taiwan's most famous actress at the time, **Liu Ruo-yu**, U-Theatre comprises a group of ascetic performers that take their training very seriously. Its most celebrated achievement to date was a tour of Taiwan in 1996: a six-hundred-kilometre hike on foot took them to hundreds of tiny isolated villages and temples. They spend up to two years creating new performances, often with a premiere at their outdoor mountain theatre, where the performers meet each day to practise *tai-chi*, martial arts, drumming and meditation. A U-Theatre production can be an incredibly powerful, hypnotic experience: *Sound of the Ocean* has been performed many times since its creation in 1996 and is divided into five parts, each featuring a different arrangement of drumming, gongs, singing and movement.

in 1983 by famous performer Chen Mei-o to preserve *nanguan*. She later founded the **Liyuan Dance Studio**, which was inspired by "The Musical Theatre of the Pear Orchard", a form of dance that flourished during the Song and Yuan dynasties, usually combined with *nanguan* music.

In addition, there are four main professional Chinese music orchestras in Taiwan: the **Chinese Orchestra of the Broadcasting Corporation of China** (also known by the English moniker "The Power of 15"; ⓔchinesemusic@ mail.bcc.com.tw), the **Kaohsiung City Chinese Orchestra** (ⓦwww.kcco .org.tw/main1a.htm), the **National Chinese Orchestra** (based at the National Theater in Taipei; ⓦ192.192.14.59) and the **Taipei Chinese Orchestra** (based at Zhongshan Hall in Taipei; ⓦwww.tco.gov.tw).

Contemporary music

Taiwan is home to some of the biggest **Mandopop** (Mandarin Chinese pop music) stars in the world, though the music industry has suffered in recent years from pirated CDs – sales are down sixty percent since 1998. The undisputed queen of Chinese pop was (and some would say still is), **Teresa Teng** (or Deng Lijun) whose tragic early death in 1995 was mourned throughout Asia. Often compared to Karen Carpenter (perhaps simplistically), she influenced a generation of singers, and dominated pop music in the region throughout the 1970s and 1980s (see p.169). Since 2000 the Mandopop genre has begun to move away from syrupy love ballads and into the world of R&B and hip-hop. **Jay Chou** has been the undisputed king of Taiwan and Chinese pop since 2001 (even gracing the cover of *Time* magazine) while Chang Hui-mei, aka **A-Mei**, remains one of Taiwan's favourite female singers. There's plenty of other stars however, as the island produces a seemingly endless production line of singers/models/actresses, epitomized by cutesy Jolin Tsai, the "little queen of pop".

Though pop certainly dominates, Taiwan also has a vibrant **rock** scene, and a growing **hip-hop** culture (see box below). Rocker Wu Bai, "the father of Taiwan Rock", and his band China Blue have been performing dynamic live sets since the early 1990s, Power Station remains influential and death metal band Chthonic has fans Asia-wide. A small but well-attended network of live venues support an eclectic **alternative music** scene, with Tizzy Bac a leading player and plenty of groups like punk outfit LTK and Brit-pop inspired 1976 adding to the mix. In 2006, veteran folksinger Hu De-fu, better known as "Kimbo", achieved mainstream recognition after a thirty-year career. **Rock festivals** have become an important part of the scene in recent years: the largest are Ho Hai

Dog G

Hip-hop has become extremely popular in Taiwan, with some decent home-grown talent such as **Machi** (with **Jeff Huang**) and **MC Hotdog** challenging the globally established artists. Tainan-native Tseng Kuan-jung, alias **Dog G**, is one of the few that's chosen to rap predominantly in Taiwanese, and by addressing the thorny issue of Taiwan's identity has ensured fame or notoriety, depending on your point of view. His first solo album was *Lotus from the Tongue* (2002), which was claimed to be the world's first rap album in a Chinese language, but he's best known for the local hit *Taiwan Song* which includes the lyrics "Act Taiwanese, speak Taiwanese, stand up and declare you are Taiwanese", and "those who have no fear of losing are the true spirit of Taiwan; those who disagree, get out."

Yan in Fulong (p.184), Spring Scream in Kenting (p.371), and the Formoz Festival in Taipei (p.134), while the Hoping For Hoping Peace Festival (⊛www .hopingforhoping.com) in May features a varied programme of mostly local bands from punk to reggae, and the Taiwan Rock Alliance organizes the annual Say Yes to Taiwan rock festival to bolster national identity (held in Taipei and Kaohsiung in February or March). The Golden Melody Awards are Taiwan's version of the Grammies, held in May or June every year.

Dance

Taiwan's **modern dance** groups are world class, noted for their creative fusion of Western and Chinese traditions. **Liu Feng-shueh** is credited with bringing modern dance to Taiwan in the 1960s, creating the **Neoclassical Dance Company** (⊜neo@neo.org.tw) in 1976, and still choreographing shows today. The best-known group internationally is **Cloud Gate Dance Theatre** (☎02/27122102, ⊛www.cloudgate.org.tw), another Taiwanese cultural treasure. Established in 1973 by **Lin Hwai-min**, who studied in New York under Martha Graham, one of America's most famous dancers, the troupe fuses classical Asian traditions such as *taichi* with modern dance – the result is hauntingly beautiful. One of the best known of the newer companies is the **Taipei Dance Circle** (☎02/89720061, ⊛www.taipei-dance-circle .com.tw), established in 1984 by Liu Shao-lu (a Cloud Gate founder) and Yang Wan-rung.

Opera

Traditional Chinese opera is thriving in Taiwan. The most famous form is **Beijing Opera** (performed in Mandarin), though **Taiwanese Opera** (performed in Hoklo or Taiwanese) is more popular on the island. Opera is actually a mix of acrobatics, music, singing, stylized movements and dialogue, still performed on outdoor stages at festivals or in front of temples, as well as in formal indoor theatres. In either case you won't need to understand Chinese to appreciate what's going on, since most operas are visually stunning, elaborately costumed affairs.

History

Chinese opera has roots in the Song dynasty (960–1279), when teahouses hosted performances by travelling players. **Beijing Opera** evolved from a blend of several regional varieties, and takes its formal establishment from the performance in 1790 of an opera by four Anhui-based opera troupes for Emperor Qianlong. This led to opera becoming an acceptable form of entertainment for China's Qing dynasty nobles, and during the nineteenth century it continued to merge with other forms such as Hubei, becoming known as Beijing Opera by the end of the century. **Taiwanese Opera** developed in the late nineteenth century as a more down-to-earth blend of Beijing and Fujianese styles, initially performed at temples or on special occasions, and emerged formally in Yilan around a hundred years ago. In the 1920s, Japanese restrictions meant that operas were limited to theatres, but in the 1950s the art form flourished, with over five hundred troupes on the island. Competition from television and cinema caused a temporary decline in the 1960s, but by the 1970s several troupes had adapted to the new medium, many singers becoming TV stars. Today around two hundred troupes perform Taiwanese Opera in theatres all over Taiwan. **Hakka Opera**, which is based on traditional tea-farming folk songs and originally developed in China's Jiangxi province, has made a comeback in Taiwan in recent years, while the more obscure **Kun Opera** (from Jiangsu province), best known for the mammoth *Peony Pavilion*, and **Beiguan Opera** styles are also performed on the island.

Opera basics

The following primarily applies to Beijing Opera, though Taiwanese Opera follows more or less the same principles. Traditionally, operas have four types of lead characters. The *sheng* (male lead), who can be old (*laosheng*), young (*xiaosheng*) or a soldier (*wusheng*); the *dan* (female), who can be *qingyi*, or a virtuous, kindly middle-aged woman, a *huadan* or young woman, a *wudan* (militaristic or kung fu type character), *laodan* (old) or *choudan* (comical or crafty); the *jing* or *hualian* will usually have a painted face; and the *chou* (clown), also known as *xiaohualian*. Each painted face has a meaning: **red** symbolizes loyalty, **black** signifies bravery or determination; **white** means treacherous or sly; and **blue** or **green** signifies a violent temper. Clothing is similarly colour coded: **yellow robes** are worn by the imperial family, red by high officials, black by the short-tempered, brown by the elderly and green by the virtuous.

Sets are very basic: the same table and chairs are normally used throughout, operas relying on the ability of the actors and a strong imagination. **Props** are also used simply and symbolically (a single oar can represent a boat). Live **music** is an important part of any production, the action complemented by traditional instruments such as the *sansian*, a three-stringed banjo, the *pipa*, a four-stringed lute, the *dongsiao*, a flute, and the *shaona*, a trumpet-shaped horn.

Plots were traditionally based on Chinese myths, legends and historic dramas, set exclusively in classical China. Today however, Taiwanese Opera is often adapted to focus on contemporary issues such as Taiwan's relationship with China and national identity: *Taiwan, My Mother* (2000) and *Flower on the Other Side of the Bank* (2001) are good examples.

Opera companies

The **National Guoguang Opera Company** (☎02/2938-3567, ⊛www.kk.gov.tw) is the foremost exponent of Beijing Opera in Taiwan and regularly performs in Taipei, though they often tour smaller villages or suburbs during festivals and holidays. Tainan-based **Ming Hwa Yuan Taiwanese Opera Company** (☎02/27729398, ⊜mhy@mail2000.com.tw) was established in 1929 by opera star Chen Ming-chi, and is now the most respected name in Taiwanese Opera, still run by the Chen family. The **Ho Lo Taiwanese Opera Troupe** (☎02/25813029, ⊜holonet1@ms7.hinet.net) is primarily known in Taiwan for its acclaimed work on television, but it also performs on stage all over the world. The **Hsin-chuan Taiwanese Opera Troupe** (☎02/25854994, ⊜hsin.chuan80@msa.hinet.net) is celebrated for its founder and former leading lady, **Liao Chiung-chih**, known as the "queen of criers" for her tragic tear-drenched performances (she received a Living Heritage award in 1988). The **Rom-shing Hakka Teapicker Opera Troupe**

(℡037/725099, ✉hakka.fans@msa.hinet.net) is one of the best Hakka Opera companies, usually performing outdoors.

Film

Taiwan has a strong tradition of **film-making** dating back to the Japanese occupation, but these days the local movie industry knocks out little more than a dozen popular and high-quality art-house films per year; revenues are miniscule (just two percent of the domestic box office) compared to output from nearby Hong Kong, and light years away from the far more popular Hollywood-produced blockbusters. Taiwanese movie stars often double as pop singers, frequently working on both sides of the Taiwan Strait. Their profile beyond the Chinese-speaking world is limited, though respected actress **Sylvia Chang** has appeared in films such as *Red Violin* and **Shu Qi** appeared in Hollywood action flick *The Transporter* in 2002. Taiwanese **directors** are generally better known internationally, **Ang Lee** being the most famous.

The **Golden Horse Film Awards**, held annually in November or December, is Taiwan's version of the Oscars, honouring film throughout the Chinese-speaking world, but often dominated by Hong Kong movies and actors.

The New Taiwanese Cinema

Between the 1950s and early 1980s, Taiwan's domestic film industry was dominated by romantic melodramas and martial arts epics. In 1982, the movie *In Our Time* broke with tradition by depicting gritty social change in Taiwan over three generations, and is generally regarded as the birth of the **New Wave Movement**. **Hou Hsiao-hsien** and **Edward Yang** (both born in mainland China) are the best known of what is sometimes called the first generation of directors. Hou was one of three directors of the ground-breaking *Sandwich Man* (1983), a dramatization of three short stories written by Huang Chun-ming, examining the disintegration of Taiwanese rural life in the 1950s and 1960s; this theme, with particular focus on adolescent male characters, dominated Hou's subsequent movies. His most famous film is *City of Sadness* (1989), which was the first to allude to the 2-28 Incident (see p.513). *The Puppet Master* (1993), which followed the life of Li Tien-lu, a master puppeteer, and *Café Lumiere* (2003), a tribute to Japanese film-maker Ozu Yasujiro, were both well received by critics. His last movie, *Three Times* (2005), which blends three stories set in three different time periods and sees a return to familiar Hou themes, was nominated for the *Palme d'Or* at Cannes. His latest movie is a French production called *Ballon rouge* starring Juliette Binoche and due to be released in 2007.

In contrast, Yang tends to focus on female characters, the newly emerging middle class, and urban society. Yang is best known for his *Taipei Story* (1985) and especially *Yi Yi* (2000), a three-hour epic depicting a troubled year in the life of a Taipei family. In a radical change of pace, his next movie is expected to be a big-budget animated feature with Jackie Chan, *The Wind* (2007).

The Second New Wave

The most famous of the "**second generation**" of New Taiwanese cinema directors is undoubtedly **Ang Lee**, Oscar-winning director of *Crouching Tiger, Hidden Dragon* (2000) and *Brokeback Mountain* (2005). He's respected locally for his immensely entertaining *Wedding Banquet* (1993), which highlighted the dilemmas facing gay Chinese men, and *Eat Drink Man Woman* (1994) set in contemporary Taipei.

Often considered part of the New Taiwanese film movement, despite being born and raised in Kuching, Malaysia, **Tsai Ming-liang** settled in Taipei in 1977 and has become one of the country's most acclaimed directors. A successful TV film-maker, Tsai made his jump to the big screen in 1992 with *Rebels of the Neon God*, the story of a high-school dropout who becomes involved with organized crime. Tsai's films are highly stylized and thought-provoking, though the lack of dialogue, confusing plots and focus on dysfunctional families, inebriation and delinquency make them hard to watch and strictly art house material. *Vive l'Amour* (1994) won the Golden Lion, while the more recent *Goodbye, Dragon Inn* (2003) and the sexually explicit *Wayward Cloud* (2005) have been received less kindly by critics.

Chiayi-born **Sylvia Chang** is sometimes regarded as part of this group (though she's been acting for over thirty years), and is one of Taiwan's few female Chinese directors. Her *20, 30, 40* (2004) is an entertaining portrayal of the lives of three women in modern Taipei, and she's also the star of the cross-cultural comedy *American Fusion* (2005).

The Seventh Graders

The New Wave directors, whilst critically acclaimed overseas, were gradually seen as elitist and obscure in Taiwan, turning audiences away from even mainstream domestic movies. The hopes of Taiwan's film industry now rest with the island's younger directors. Referred to as the "**seventh-grade generation**" (a reference to the 1980s, the seventh decade after the 1911 Revolution), many were still university students when they started making movies. **DJ Chen** scored a big hit in 2004 with *Formula 17*, a frank and humorous exploration of gay life in Taipei, while **Leon Dai**'s *Twenty-Something Taipei* (2002) also focused on youth, sex and modern Taipei. **Alex Yang** is one of the most talented members of the group, his *Taipei 21* (2003) and 2005 romantic campus comedy *My Fair Laddy* receiving much international acclaim despite being shot on a shoestring and having limited release domestically. **Yee Chih-Yen** received international praise for *Blue Gate Crossing* (2003) as did **Leste Chen** for *Uninhibited* (2004), which follows the live of three youngsters through yet more sex, drugs and assorted street culture.

Books

aiwan has a rich literary tradition that goes back over a century, and a dynamic contemporary scene which is a fusion of all the island's multi-cultural elements. The problem is that very little of this is translated into English, in part a reflection of Taiwan's low profile on the international stage. Seminal figures such as **Lai He** (regarded as the father of Taiwanese literature), and Hakka pioneer **Chung Li-ho,** as well as modern writers such as **Li Ang** (one of Taiwan's top female authors), are rarely translated.

In other areas, apart from a fairly dry ensemble of books analyzing Taiwan's economic success, there's a dearth of material on the island, though you'll find plenty on Chinese culture in general. Expats have started writing guides to fill the gaps, usually published by local houses, and those interested in **Buddhism** will find a voluminous amount of English-language material knocked out by the island's premier monasteries. Books marked with 🏃 are particularly recommended.

Fiction

🏃 **Chang Ta-chun** *Wild Kids* (Columbia University Press). Two novellas from the 1990s popular literature icon, exposing the frustrations of Taiwanese youth and the darker side of Taipei in the 1980s. Chang's unpretentious style, with dashes of black humour, works well in translation.

Cheng Ch'ing-wen *Three-Legged Horse* (Columbia University Press). Collection of twelve simply written tales from one of Taiwan's most respected Nativist writers, restrained but lyrical portraits of the fast-changing island through a wide variety of characters.

Chu T'ien-wen *Notes of a Desolate Man* (Columbia University Press). A thoughtful study of a Taiwanese gay man reflecting on his life and loves as his friend lies dying of AIDS in the 1990s, by turns erotic, morose and humorous. Chu is one of Taiwan's best contemporary female writers.

Hsiao Li-hung *A Thousand Moons on a Thousand Rivers* (Columbia University Press). A captivating tale of love, betrayal and complex family relationships in a traditional south Taiwan town in the 1970s, from one of Taiwan's pre-eminent female writers.

Huang Chun-ming *The Taste of Apples* (Columbia University Press). Collection of nine compelling short stories, portraying the poverty and disintegration of traditional Taiwanese rural life in the face of rampant modernization. Penned by the doyen of the Nativist movement in the 1970s.

Li Ang *The Butcher's Wife and Other Stories* (Columbia University Press). This short novel from Taiwan's best-known female writer shocked the island in 1983 with its powerful critique of traditional Chinese society, and fearless portrayal of superstition, violence, and abuse of women.

Li Qiao *Wintry Night* (Columbia University Press). Vivid historical saga, following the lives of the Peng family from the 1890s to the end of World War II, Hakka settlers battling the elements, corrupt officials, aboriginal tribes and the Japanese.

Pai Hsien-yung *Crystal Boys* (Gay Sunshine Press, US) and *Taipei People* (China University Press, HK). *Crystal Boys* is still regarded as a groundbreaking classic, a tragic love story and evocative depiction of Taiwan's gay community in the repressive 1960s and 1970s. *Taipei People* is a fascinating collection of short stories, examining life in the post-1949 capital.

Wang Chen-ho *Rose, Rose I Love You* (Columbia University Press). One of Taiwan's most outrageous comic novels, this irreverent satire follows the citizens of Hualien as they prepare for a boatload of US soldiers on R&R. The result is hilarious, though Wang's subtle word plays are difficult to appreciate in translation.

🏃 **Wang Wen-hsing** *Family Catastrophe* (University of Hawaii Press). Publication of this Modernist classic caused a sensation in 1972, with its subtle but powerful depiction of the unraveling of a traditional Chinese family.

Wu Zhuoliu *Asia's Orphan* (Columbia University Press). Wu was one of Taiwan's leading literary figures in the 1940s and 1950s, this masterpiece spanning the entire period of Japanese occupation, an allegory of colonial rule and Taiwan's disillusion with Chinese nationalism.

Indigenous Writers of Taiwan *An Anthology of Stories, Essays and Poems* (Columbia University Press). First collection of indigenous literature in English, with contributions from writers such Topas Tamapima (*The Last Hunter*), Sakinu (*Wind Walker*) and Moaneng (*Five Poems*) providing an enlightening perspective on the state of aboriginal culture in modern Taiwan.

History and politics

Ian Buruma *Bad Elements* (Phoenix). One of Asia's most incisive Western journalists includes an insightful and entertaining chapter on Taiwan in this book highlighting Chinese rebels around the world.

Richard C. Bush *Untying the Knot: Making Peace in the Taiwan Strait* (Brookings Institution Press). One of the latest attempts to unravel the complexities of cross-strait relations; Bush does a pretty good job of explaining Taiwan's relationship with China: their similarities, economic ties and the difficulties that lie ahead.

Macabe Keliher *Out of China* and *Small Sea Travel Diaries* (SMC Publishing, Taipei). This Taipei-based writer has knocked out a decent translation of Chinese official Yu Yonghe's diary of his trip to Taiwan in 1697, a fascinating account of the island at the time. *Out of China* is an easy-to-read companion volume, enhancing the journal with history, anecdote and useful background.

April Lin and Jerome Keating *Island in the Stream* (SMC Publishing, Taipei). Another locally published book, this time a short and easily digested history of the island with a slight but discernible pro-independence bias.

George Mackay *From Far Formosa* (SMC Publishing, Taipei). Part autobiography, part history of the island, Mackay's original work of 1896 has been republished in Taipei. The Canadian missionary's observations are a fascinating insight into 1880s Taiwan, as well as the often chauvinistic attitudes dominant in the West at that time.

Jonathan Manthorpe *Forbidden Nation: A History of Taiwan* (Palgrave Macmillan). A well-written and comprehensive new history of the island.

🏃 **Denny Roy** *Taiwan A Political History* (Cornell University Press). Roy's crisp history of Taiwan is a good introduction, though its primary focus is political events post-1949.

Jay Taylor *The Generalissimo's Son: Chiang Ching-kuo and the Revolutions in China and Taiwan* (Harvard University Press). Long-overdue study of Chiang Kai-shek's son and successor, one of Taiwan's most complex figures who oversaw its transition from martial law to nascent democracy.

Shih-shan Henry Tsai *Lee Teng-hui and Taiwan's Quest for Identity* (Palgrave Macmillan). Biography of former President Lee Teng-hui, the primary figure in the island's political transformation over the past two decades.

Religion

🏃 **Mark Caltonhill** *Private Prayers and Public Parades* (Taipei Dept of Information). Accessible introduction to Taiwan's eclectic religious practices, especially focusing on its Taoist and folk traditions and customs. The author is an English long-time resident of Taiwan.

Dharma Master Cheng Yen *Still Thoughts I & II* (U-Wen Printing Co). These books contain a series of thought-provoking quotations derived from the numerous speeches and talks of Taiwan's senior female Buddhist master, the founder of Tzu Chi Foundation.

Confucius *The Analects* (Penguin). Modern translation of this classic collection of Confucius's sayings, compiled by his pupils after his death in 479 BC and now one of the most important texts in Chinese philosophy.

🏃 **Venerable Master Hsing Yun** *Humanistic Buddhism: A Blueprint for Life* (Buddha's Light Publishing). The founder of Foguangshan Monastery is one of Taiwan's most prolific Buddhist writers and teachers of Chan Buddhism. This book outlines the principles of Humanistic Buddhism and how it can be applied to daily life.

Lao Zi *Tao Te Ching* (Penguin). The collection of laconic, esoteric sayings that provides the philosophical basis for Taoism, attributed to the sixth century BC Chinese mystic.

Chan Master Sheng Yen *Zen Wisdom* (North Atlantic Books) and *Hoofprint of the Ox* (Oxford University Press). The founder of Dharma Drum Mountain monastery has written numerous books on Chan (or Zen) Buddhism and these two works are the best introductions. *Zen Wisdom* is structured as a series of questions and answers, while *Hoofprint* follows a more traditional essay type structure.

Miscellaneous

🏃 **Richard Saunders** *Taipei Day Trips 1 & 2.* (Community Services Center, Taipei). Written by another long-term English expat, these two books are handy for anyone contemplating an extended stay in the Taipei area, especially for those interested in hiking. Usually on sale in local bookshops.

Yeh Yueh-yu and Darrell Davis *Taiwan Film Directors: A Treasure Island* (Columbia University Press).

Insightful study of Taiwan's New Cinema via four of its most famous directors: Hou Hsiao-hsien, Ang Lee, Edward Yang and Tsai Ming-liang.

Christopher Logan and Teresa Hsu *Culture Taipei* (SMC Publishing, Taipei). This locally produced guide to Taipei is still excellent reading material for those spending more time in the capital, and especially strong on traditional arts and crafts, despite needing a bit of an update.

Language

Language

Language

T he official language of Taiwan is the same as China, **Mandarin Chinese**, commonly referred to as *guoyu* ("national language") on the island and *putonghua* ("common speech") across the Taiwan Strait. Though there are some differences in word use, pronunciation and slang, Chinese spoken on the mainland is indistinguishable from that used in Taiwan. The major divergence comes with **written Chinese**: Taiwan (like Hong Kong) uses **traditional characters**, while China follows the simplified system devised in the 1950s.

Mandarin Chinese is a relative newcomer to the island however: before 1945 very few people ever spoke the language in Taiwan. Although everyone learns Mandarin these days, **Taiwanese** (*taiyu*) was once the dominant tongue, and is still widely spoken as a first language. In much of south Taiwan you'll hear nothing else, though even here everyone but the very elderly will be able to understand Mandarin (though they'll try, optimistically, to converse with you in Taiwanese if they can). Taiwanese is a form of **Fujianese** (*minnan hua*), which originated in southern Fujian province in China and is similar to the Hokkien spoken by other Fujianese communities in Southeast Asia. Part of the same Sino-Tibetan family and usually described as a dialect of Chinese on the mainland, Taiwanese is in fact a totally different language, with its own dialects, seven tones, unique vocabulary and distinct philology. In the nineteeth century, missionaries developed a written form of Taiwanese known as *péh-ōe-jī*, using Roman letters, but otherwise Taiwanese can be written with the same Chinese characters as Mandarin. **Hakka** (*kejiahua*) is still spoken in Taiwan (see p.204), though along with numerous **aboriginal languages** on the island, faces an uphill struggle for survival. Given Taiwan's history and current economic and cultural ties with the country, it's no surprise many Taiwanese can speak **Japanese** quite well and, in the cities, you might find yourself in the odd situation of being addressed in Japanese rather than English.

Pronunciation and *pinyin*

The main distinguishing characteristic of Chinese languages is that they are **tonal**: each word must be pronounced not only with the right sound, but also the right tone. Mandarin has four tones, and in order to be understood it's vital to get these as accurate as possible. The **pinyin system**, a way of writing Chinese using the Roman alphabet, is the best way to learn the correct tones, represented by **accents** above each syllable. The first tone is usually described as "high", or a flat, level tone; the second is a rising tone, as when expressing surprise; the third is "falling-rising"; and the fourth is a falling tone. In practice however, you'll need to take some lessons (or at least listen to a native speaker) if you're serious about coming to grips with spoken Chinese.

In China, where *pinyin* is taught in schools, the system is widely used, but most Taiwanese have never seen or used pinyin. Schools on the island still use *zhuyin* or **bopomofo** to teach children pronunciation, a system of symbols that looks much the same as characters. As a result, Chinese characters on street signs, buildings or in restaurants are rarely translated. Where *pinyin* is used, Taiwan's notorious penchant for using a hodgepodge of different systems often adds to the confusion. Mainland China uses **Hanyu Pinyin**, favoured throughout most of the world by Chinese speakers and students. However, in Taiwan, Hanyu is only used extensively in Taipei, and partially in Taichung and Hsinchu. The KMT mayors of these cities favour the system, even though this is in opposition to Taiwan's DPP government which has made **Tongyong Pinyin**, created in Taiwan in 1998, the official *pinyin* for all highway signs, national parks, government publications and national scenic areas. These two systems have now largely replaced nineteenth-century **Wade-Giles** and **MPS2** (another Taiwanese script used in the 1980s), though you might still see vestiges of these in places – the names of Taiwan's major cities retain their basic Wade-Giles forms (for example "Kaohsiung" would be "Gaoxiong" in Hanyu Pinyin). The Chinese terms in this section (and Chinese boxes throughout the book) have been given in both characters and Hanyu Pinyin, to reflect the predominant global trend. In the main body text however, the approach has been to use the system most visible in each locale: Tongyong is considered the default, in line with government policy. Note however, everything could change again if the KMT win the presidency in 2008.

Hanyu v Tongyong

Though Hanyu and Tongyong *pinyin* are very similar, there are 83 syllables spelled differently. The most noticeable are the Hanyu *zh* becoming *jh* in Tongyong, and the lack of *x* and *q* in the latter, replaced by *s* and *c* respectively. The major differences are as follows:

Tongyong	Hanyu		
ci	qi	jhih/chih/shih/rih	zhi/chi/shi/ri
si	xi	cih/rih/sih/zih	ci/ri/si/zi
jh	zh	jyu/cyu/syu	ju/qu/xu
uei	ui	lyu/nyu	lü/nü
iou	iu	wun	wen
fong	feng	wong	weng
jyong/cyong/syong	jiong/qiong/xiong		

Useful words and expressions

All the words below are in common usage in Taiwan, the only exception being *zai jian*: these days "bye-bye" has become the universal way of saying farewell (as in Hong Kong and parts of China). Hong Kong-style Chinglish (Chinese littered with English words and mixtures of the two) has yet to make inroads into Taiwan, but you'll hear words like "OK" slipped into Chinese sentences, especially in the cities.

Basics

Hello	你好	nǐ hǎo
Thank you	謝謝	xièxie
You're welcome	不客氣	búkèqi

Sorry	對不起	*duìbùqǐ*
No problem	沒關係	*méi guānxi*
Goodbye	再見	*zài jiàn*
I	我	*wǒ*
You	你	*nǐ*
He	他	*tā*
She	她	*tā*
We	我們	*wǒ mén*
You (plural)	你們	*nǐ mén*
They	他們	*tā mén*
I want	我要	*wǒ yào*
I don't want	我不要	*wǒ bú yào*
Have	有	*yǒu*
Have not	沒有	*méiyou*
Mr	先生	*xiānshēng*
Mrs	太太	*tàitài*
Miss	小姐	*xiǎojiě*
I don't speak Chinese	我不會說中文	*wǒ bú huì shūo zhōngwén*
Can you speak English?	你會說英語嗎?	*nǐ huì shūo yīngyǔ ma?*
Please speak slowly	請慢慢說	*qǐng màn màn shūo*
I understand	我聽得懂	*wǒ tīngdedǒng*
I don't understand	我聽不懂	*wǒ tīngbùdǒng*
What does this mean?	這是甚麼意思?	*zhè shì shénme yisi?*

Countries

What country are you from?	你是哪國家的人?	*nǐ shì nǎ guó jiā de rén?*
Australia	澳洲	*àozhōu*
Canada	加拿大	*jiānádà*
England	英國	*yīngguó*
Ireland	愛爾蘭	*ài ěrlán*
New Zealand	紐西蘭	*niǔ xīlán*
Scotland	蘇格蘭	*sǔ gélán*
South Africa	南非	*nánfēi*
Taiwan	台灣	*táiwān*
United States	美國	*měiguó*
Wales	威爾士	*wei ěr shì*

Getting around

North	北	*běi*
South	南	*nán*
East	東	*dōng*
West	西	*xī*
Airport	飛機場	*fēi jī chǎng*
Dock/pier	碼頭	*mǎ tóu*
Left luggage office	寄存處	*jìcúnchù*
Ticket office	售票處	*shòupiào chù*

Ticket	票	*piào*
I want to go to ...	我要去...	*wǒ yào qù*
When does it leave?	幾點開車?	*jǐ diǎn kāi chē?*
When does it arrive?	幾點到?	*jǐ diǎn dào?*
How long does the journey take?	旅途需要多久?	*lǔtú xū yào duōjiǔ?*
Train	火車	*huǒchē*
Train station	火車站	*huǒchē zhàn*
Bus	公車	*gōngchē*
Bus station	公車站	*gōngchē zhàn*
Regional bus station	客運站	*kèyùn zhàn*
Express train (Tze-Chiang)	自強	*zìqiáng*
Chu-Kuang/Fu-Hsing/EMU trains	莒光/復興/電車	*jǔguāng/ fùxīng/diànchē*
Taiwan High Speed Rail	台灣高速鐵路	*táiwān gāosù tiělù*
Platform	站台	*zhàntái*
Map	地圖	*dìtú*
Where is...?	... 在那裡?	*... zài nàlǐ?*
Go straight on	直走	*zhízǒu*
Turn right	轉右	*zhuǎn yòu*
Turn left	轉左	*zhuǎn zuǒ*
Taxi	計程車	*jì chéng chē*
Car	汽車	*qìchē*
Underground/subway	捷運	*jiéyùn*
Bicycle	腳踏車	*jiǎotàchē*
Motor scooter	摩托車	*mótuōchē*
I want to rent...	我想租	*wǒ xiǎng zū*
How much is it per hour/day?	一小時/一天 多少錢?	*yí xiǎoshí/yí tiān, duō shǎo qián?*
When is the next bus?	下一班車幾點開?	*xià yí bān chē jǐ diǎn kāi?*
Does this bus go to...?	這輛車到...嗎?	*zhè liàng chē dào...ma?*
Please tell me where to get off	請告訴我在哪裡下車	*qǐng gàosu wǒ zài nàlǐ xià chē*
Museum	博物館	*bówùguǎn*
Temple	廟	*miào*
Toilet (men)	男廁所	*nán cèsuǒ*
Toilet (women)	女廁所	*nǚ cèsuǒ*
Road	路	*lù*
Street	街	*jiē*
Section	段	*dùan*
Number 12	十二號	*shí èr hào*
Lane	巷	*xiàng*
Alley	弄	*nòng*

Accommodation

Hotel	飯店/旅館	*fàndiàn/ lǔguǎn*
Youth hostel	年會館	*qīngniánhuì guǎn*
Homestay	民宿	*mínsù*
How much for a room?	一晚多少?	*yí wǎn duō shǎo?*

Can I have a look at the room?	能不能看一下?	*néng bù néng kàn yí xià?*
Single room	單人房	*dānrénfáng*
Twin room	雙人房	*shuāngrénfáng*
Passport	護照	*hùzhào*
Key	鑰匙	*yàoshi*

Numbers

Zero	零	*líng*
One	一	*yī*
Two	二/兩	*èr/liǎng*
Three	三	*sān*
Four	四	*sì*
Five	五	*wǔ*
Six	六	*liù*
Seven	七	*qī*
Eight	八	*bā*
Nine	九	*jiǔ*
Ten	十	*shí*
Eleven	十一	*shíyī*
Twelve	十二	*shíèr*
Twenty	二十	*èrshí*
Twenty-one	二十一	*èrshíyī*
One hundred	一百	*yībǎi*
Two hundred	二百	*èrbǎi*
One thousand	一千	*yīqiān*
Ten thousand	一萬	*yīwàn*
One hundred thousand	十萬	*shíwàn*
One million	一百萬	*yībǎiwàn*
One hundred million	一意	*yīyì*
One billion	十意	*shíyì*

Time

Now	現在	*xiànzài*
Today	今天	*jīntiān*
Morning	早上	*zǎoshàng*
Afternoon	下午	*xiàwǔ*
Evening	晚上	*wǎnshàng*
Tomorrow	明天	*míngtiān*
Day after tomorrow	後天	*hòutiān*
Yesterday	昨天	*zuótiān*
Week/month/year	星期/月/年	*xīngqī/yuè/nián*
Monday	星期一	*xīngqī yī*
Tuesday	星期二	*xīngqī èr*
Wednesday	星期三	*xīngqī sān*
Thursday	星期四	*xīngqī sì*

Friday	星期五	*xīngqī wǔ*
Saturday	星期六	*xīngqī liù*
Sunday	星期天	*xīngqī tiān*
What's the time?	幾點了?	*jǐ diǎn le?*
6 o'clock	六點	*liù diǎn*
6.20	六點二十	*liù diǎn èrshí*
6.30	六點半	*liù diǎn bàn*

Shopping and money

How much is it?	多少錢?	*duōshǎo qián?*
It's too expensive	太貴了	*tài guì le*
Do you accept credit cards?	可不可以用信用卡?	*kě bù kěyǐ yòng xìnyòngkǎ?*
NT$1	一塊	*yí kuài*
US$1	一塊美金	*yí kuài měijīn*
£1	一個英磅	*yí gè yīngbàng*
Change money	換錢	*huàn qián*
Chinatrust Commercial Bank	中國信託銀行	*zhōngguó xìntuō yín háng*
Traveller's cheques	旅行支票	*lǚxíngzhīpiào*
Bank	銀行	*yínháng*
ATM	提款機	*dīkuǎn jī*

Communications

Post office	郵局	*yóujú*
Envelope	信封	*xìnfēng*
Stamp	郵票	*yóupiào*
Airmail	航空信	*hángkōng xìn*
Poste restante	郵件候領處	*yóujiàn hòulǐngchù*
Telephone	電話	*diànhuà*
Reverse charges/collect call	對方付錢電話	*duìfāngfùqián diànhuà*
Fax	傳真	*chuánzhēn*
Telephone card	電話卡	*diànhuàkǎ*
Internet café	網吧	*wǎngbā*

Health

Hospital	醫院	*yīyuàn*
Pharmacy	藥店	*yàodiàn*
Medicine	藥	*yào*
Chinese medicine	中藥	*zhōng yào*
Diarrhoea	腹瀉	*fùxiè*
Vomit	嘔吐	*ǒutù*
Fever	發燒	*fāshāo*
I'm ill	我生病了	*wǒ shēngbìng le*
I've got flu	我感冒了	*wǒ gǎnmào le*

I'm (not) allergic to …	我(不)對…過敏	*wǒ (bù) duì… guòmǐn*
Antibiotics	抗生素	*kàngshēngsù*
Condom	避孕套	*bìyùntào*
Mosquito coil	蚊香	*wénxiāng*

Food and drink

General

Beerhouse	啤酒屋	*píjiǔ wū*
Bill/cheque	埋單	*máidān*
Chopsticks	筷子	*kuàizi*
Ice	冰	*bīng*
Lunchbox	便當	*biàndàng*
Knife and fork	刀叉	*dāochā*
Market	市場	*shìchǎng*
Menu	菜單	*càidān*
Night market	夜市	*yèshì*
Restaurant	餐廳	*cāntīng*
Snacks ("little eats")	小吃	*xiǎochī*
Spoon	匙子	*sháozǐ*
Supermarket	超級市場	*chāo jíshì chǎng*
Taiwan buffet/self-service caféteria	自助餐	*zìzhù cān*
Take-away	帶走	*dàizǒu*
Teahouse	茶館	*cháguǎn*
How much is that?	多少錢?	*duōshǎo qián?*
I'm a vegetarian	我是吃素的	*wǒ shì chī sù de*
I don't eat (meat)	我不吃 (肉)	*wǒ bù chī (ròu)*
I would like	我想要	*wǒ xiǎng yào*
Not spicy	不辣	*bùlà*

Drinks

Aiyu jelly drink	愛玉凍飲	*àiyù dòngyǐn*
Beer	啤酒	*píjiǔ*
Coffee	咖啡	*kāfēi*
Fruit juice	果汁	*guǒ zhī*
Gaoliang	高梁酒	*gāoliáng jiǔ*
Milk	牛奶	*niúnǎi*
Papaya milk	木瓜牛奶	*mùguā niúnǎi*
Red wine	紅酒	*hóng jiǔ*
Rice wine	米酒	*mǐjiǔ*
Shaohsing wine	紹興酒	*shàoxīng jiǔ*
Starfruit juice	楊桃汁	*yángtáozhī*
Sugar cane juice	甘蔗汁	*gānzhèzhī*
Taiwan Beer	台灣啤酒	*táiwān píjiǔ*
White wine	白酒	*bái jiǔ*
Wine	酒	*jiǔ*

Yoghurt	酸奶	*suānnǎi*
Tea	茶	*chá*
Baozhong tea	包種茶	*bāozhǒng chá*
Black tea	紅茶	*hóng chá*
Bubble tea	泡沫紅茶	*pàomò hóng chá*
Dongding oolong	凍頂烏龍	*dòngdǐng wūlóng*
Fruit tea	水果茶	*shuǐguǒ chá*
Green tea	綠茶	*lǜ chá*
Iron Guanyin tea	鐵觀音茶	*tiěguānyīn chá*
Jasmine tea	茉莉花茶	*mòlìhuā chá*
Oolong tea	烏龍茶	*wūlóng chá*
Oriental Beauty tea	東方美人茶	*dōngfāng měirén chá*
Pearl milk tea	珍珠奶茶	*zhēnzhū nǎi chá*

Staple foods, meat and vegetables

Beef	牛肉	*niúròu*
Bread	麵包	*miànbāo*
Chicken	雞	*jī*
Chilli	辣椒	*làjiāo*
Crab	螃蟹	*pángxiè*
Duck	鴨子	*yāzi*
Eel	鰻魚	*mán yú*
Egg	雞蛋	*jīdàn*
Fish	魚	*yú*
Garlic	蒜	*suàn*
Ginger	姜	*jiāng*
Green bean	綠豆	*lǜdòu*
Lamb	羊肉	*yángròu*
MSG	味精	*wèijīng*
Mushroom	香菇	*xiānggū*
Noodle	麵	*miàn*
Oyster	蠔	*háo*
Pork	豬肉	*zhūròu*
Red bean	紅豆	*hóngdòu*
Rice (uncooked)	米	*mǐ*
Rice (steamed)	白飯	*báifàn*
Rice (fried)	炒飯	*chǎofàn*
Salt	鹽	*yán*
Prawn/shrimp	蝦	*xiā*
Soup	湯	*tāng*
Soy sauce	醬油	*jiàngyóu*
Squid	魷魚	*yóuyú*
Sugar	糖	*táng*
Taiwanese basil	九層塔	*jiǔcéngtǎ*
Tofu	豆腐	*dòufu*
Vegetables	菜	*cài*

Fruit

Fruit	水果	*shuǐguǒ*
Apple	蘋果	*píng guǒ*
Banana	香蕉	*xiāng jiāo*
Cherry	櫻桃	*yīngtáo*
Coconut	椰子	*yēzi*
Durian	榴蓮	*liúlián*
Grape	葡萄	*pútáo*
Guava	芭樂	*bālè*
Honeydew melon	哈密瓜	*hāmì guā*
Kiwi fruit	奇異果	*qíyìguǒ*
Longyan	龍眼	*lóngyǎn*
Lychee	荔枝	*lìzhī*
Mango	芒果	*mángguǒ*
Orange (tangerine)	橘子	*júzi*
Papaya	木瓜	*mùguā*
Peach	桃子	*táozi*
Pear	梨子	*lízi*
Persimmon	柿子	*shìzi*
Pineapple	鳳梨	*fènglí*
Plum	李子	*lǐzi*
Pomelo	柚子	*yòuzi*
Watermelon	西瓜	*xīguā*

Breakfast

Clay oven roll	燒餅	*shāobǐng*
Congee	稀飯	*xīfàn*
Dough fritter	油條	*yóutiáo*
Egg pancake	蛋餅	*dànbǐng*
Soybean milk	豆漿	*dòujiāng*
Spring onion pancake	蔥油餅	*cōngyóu bǐng*
Steamed bread	饅頭	*mántóu*
Steamed bun	包子	*bāozi*

Everyday dishes/snacks

Baked sweet potatoes	烤蕃薯	*kǎo fānshǔ*
Beef noodles	牛肉麵	*niúròu miàn*
Boiled dumplings	水餃	*shuǐjiǎo*
Braised pork rice	滷肉飯	*lǔròufàn*
Fishballs	魚丸	*yúwán*
Fried dumplings	鍋貼	*guōtiē*
Fuzhou beef pepper pies	福州牛肉胡椒餅	*fúzhōu niúròu húijiāo bǐng*
Hot and sour soup	酸辣湯	*suānlàtāng*
Knife-cut noodles	刀削麵	*dāoxiāo miàn*
Lu wei	蘆薈	*lú huì*

Oyster omelette	蚵仔煎	é a jiān
Rice dumplings	粽子	zòngzi
Rice noodles	米粉	mǐfěn
Sanbei	三杯	sānbēi
Sesame paste noodles	麻醬麵	májiàng miàn
Shaved ice (dessert)	刨冰 (礤冰)	bào bīng (tsua bing in Taiwanese)
Spring roll	潤餅	rùnbǐng
Soybean pudding	豆花	dòuhuā
Steamed dumplings	小籠包	xiǎolóng bāo
Steamed meat buns	肉包子	ròubāozi
Steamed vegetable buns	素菜包子	sùcài bāozi
Stinky tofu	臭豆腐	chòu dòufu
Tea eggs	茶葉蛋	cháyè dàn

Local specialties

Bluefin tuna (Donggang)	黑鮪魚	hēiwěiyú
Brown-sugar cake (Penghu)	黑糖糕	hēitánggāo
Coffin bread (Tainan)	棺材板	guāncáibǎn
Dajia crispy cakes	奶油酥餅	nǎiyóu sūbǐng
Danzi noodles (Tainan)	擔仔麵	dān zǎi mián
Deep-fried meat cakes (Hsinchu)	竹塹餅	zhúqiàn bǐng
Dumplings in soup (Hualien)	扁食	biǎnshí
Green bean cakes (Keelung)	綠豆沙餅	lǜdòushā bǐng
"Little pastry wrapped in big pastry" (Taipei)	大餅包小餅	dà bǐng bāo xiǎo bǐng
Mashu (Hualien)	麻薯	máshǔ
Meatballs (Changhua/Hsinchu)	貢丸	gòngwán
Milkfish (south Taiwan)	虱目魚	sad vag hy (Taiwanese)
Ox-tongue cake (Lugang)	牛舌餅	niúshé bǐng
Phoenix-eye cakes (Lugang)	鳳眼糕	fèngyǎngāo
Rice dumplings (Shihmen)	肉粽	ròuzòng
Rice powder tea (Lugang)	麵茶	miàn chá
Sheng Chao Wu Wei (Lugang)	生炒五味	shēng chǎo wǔ wèi
Shrimp monkeys (Lugang)	蝦猴	xiāhóu
Shrimp rolls (Tainan)	蝦捲	xiājuǎn
Square cookies (Chiayi)	方塊酥	fāngkuàisū
Suncakes (Taichung)	太陽餅	tàiyáng bǐng
Taro balls (Jiufen)	芋丸	yùwán
Taro pudding (Hsinchu)	芋泥	yù ní
Turkey rice (Chiayi)	火雞肉飯	huǒjīròu fàn
Wah gwei (Tainan)	碗粿	wah gwei (Taiwanese)

Hakka specialties

Ban tiao	板條	bǎn tiáo
Bamboo shoots	竹筍	zhúsǔn
Braised stuffed tofu	釀豆腐	niàng dóufù

Fried pork intestines with ginger	生薑炒豬腸	*shēngjiāng chǎozhūcháng*
Kejia mashu	客家蔴薯	*kèjiāmáshǔ*
Kejia xiaofong	客家小封	*kèjiā xiǎofēng*
Lei cha (cereal tea)	擂茶	*léichá*
Wild lotus	蓮	*lián*

Aboriginal specialities

Bamboo rice	竹筒飯	*zhù tóng fàn*
Betel nut Chicken	檳榔雞	*bīnlángjī*
Millet wine	小米酒	*xiǎomǐjiǔ*
Mountain pig (boar)	山豬	*shān zhū*

Regional Chinese cuisine

Beijing duck	北京烤鴨	*běijīng kǎoyā*
Buddha jumps over the wall (Fujianese)	佛跳牆	*fótiàoqiáng*
Chicken with peanuts (Sichuan)	宮保雞丁	*gōngbǎojīdīng*
Dim sum (Cantonese)	點心	*diǎnxīn*
Drunken chicken (Shanghai)	醉雞	*zuìjī*
Hotpot (Sichuan)	火鍋	*huǒguō*
Mapo doufu (Shanghai)	麻婆豆腐	*mápó dòufù*
Songren yumi (Shanghai)	鬆軟玉米	*sōngrén yùmǐ*
Yellow croaker (Shanghai)	黃魚	*huángyú*

Japanese cuisine

Japanese curry rice	日本咖哩飯	*rìběn gālǐfàn*
Ramen	拉麵	*lāmiàn*
Sashimi	生魚片	*shēngyúpiàn*
Shabu shabu	涮涮鍋	*shuànshuàn guō*
Sushi	壽司	*shòusī*
Teppanyaki	鐵板燒	*tiěbǎnshāo*

Glossary

Amitofu Greeting used by Buddhist monks, a reference to Buddha.

Arhat Buddhist saint.

Aborigines Common English name for Taiwan's indigenous population.

ARC Alien Resident Certificate.

Austronesian Cultural and linguistic family which stretches across the Asia-Pacific region, and includes Taiwan's indigenous population.

Betel nut Seed of the Betel Palm, also known as areca nut, and used extensively in Taiwan as a stimulant, chewed but not swallowed.

Biandang Lunchbox (literally means "convenient"). Common take-away meal option, usually comprising chicken or a meat dish, rice and vegetables.

Binlang xishi Betel nut beauty, used to describe the scantily dressed young women that sell Betel nut from glass booths along roadsides island-wide. *Xishi* was a legendary beauty in ancient China.

Black Gold Term used to describe the KMT's links with local mafia and endemic corruption during the martial law period.

Bodhisattva Buddhist that has attained enlightenment, but who has chosen not to leave the cycle of birth and death (*samsara*) until all other beings are enlightened. Worshipped as a god or goddess.

Camphor Tree containing camphor crystals that produce aromatic oil. Used for its scent, as an embalming fluid and in medicines, especially in the nineteenth century.

Chaguan Teahouse (*cha* means tea).

Dalu Common term for mainland China, formally known as *zhongguo*.

Daizi Bag. Supermarkets and convenience stores will ask if you want to buy one (you don't get them for free in environmentally-friendly Taiwan).

Dao Island.

Democratic Progressive Party (DPP) Taiwan's first opposition party when it was established in 1986, winning the presidency under Chen Shui-bian in 2000 and 2004.

Dong Cave.

Executive Yuan The prime minister's cabinet.

Fandian Hotel (also *dafandian*).

Fo Buddha.

Formosa Name given to Taiwan by Portuguese sailors in the sixteenth century, and used in the West to describe the island until the 1950s.

Fujian Southeastern province in China, ancestral home of seventy percent of Taiwan's population.

Gang Harbour or port.

Gong Palace. Often forms part of the formal name for a Taoist temple. Can also mean duke, or lord (this is a different Chinese character), used as an honorific title for gods.

Gongli Kilometre.

Gongyuan Park.

Hakka Chinese ethnic group and language, known as *kejia* in Chinese.

Han Chinese Used to describe all the Chinese ethnic groups (including Taiwanese, Hakka and mainlanders), as distinct from Taiwan's Austronesian indigenous population.

Hanyu Pinyin System of transliterating Chinese script into Roman characters favoured by mainland China and a few cities in Taiwan such as Taipei.

Heping Peace.

Hoklo See "Taiwanese".

Homestay Private hotel, usually supplying bed and breakfast and often located in a family home. *Minsu* in Chinese.

KTV Karaoke TV. Usually refers to lavish karaoke centres with private rooms, drinks and food.

Kuai Money. New Taiwan Dollars (NT$) are known as *xintaibi* in Chinese.

Kuomintang (KMT) Chinese Nationalist Party established in 1912 in China, and led by Chiang Kai-shek from the 1920s. Defeated by Mao Zedong's Communist Party in China's civil war, and based in Taiwan from 1949 where it held power until 2000.

Legislative Yuan Taiwan's parliament.

Maidan Cantonese word for restaurant bill/cheque, but now widely used throughout Taiwan (and China).

Mainlanders Term used to describe the Chinese who fled to Taiwan from the mainland in the wake of the Communist victory in 1949.

Mandarin Chinese English name for the official language of China and Taiwan, where it's called *putonghua* ("common speech") and *guoyu* ("national language") respectively. Originally based on the Beijing dialect (spoken by "mandarins", or imperial government officials).

Mandopop Slang for Mandarin Chinese pop music. Cantopop refers to music from Hong Kong (Cantonese language).

Meiguoren American, but often applied to all foreigners in Taiwan.

Miao General name applied to Taoist or Confucian temples.

Ming dynasty Imperial family that overthrew the Mongolian Yuan dynasty and ruled China from 1368 to 1644, when China was seized by the Manchurian Qing dynasty.

Mingpien Business card.

Minquan Second of Sun Yat-sen's "Three Principles of the People", meaning "people power" or democracy. Common street name.

Minsheng Third of Sun Yat-sen's "Three Principles of the People", meaning "the people's welfare" or "government for the people", and equated with Socialism in China. Common street name.

Minzu First of Sun Yat-sen's "Three Principles of the People", loosely translated as Nationalism, or freedom from imperial domination. Common street name.

Oolong Type of semi-fermented tea, as opposed to black tea (fully fermented) and green tea (unfermented).

Pijiuwu Beerhouse/local pub.

Pingpu Umbrella term used to describe the indigenous peoples that traditionally lived on the plains rather than the mountains.

PRC People's Republic of China. Official name for mainland China.

Pubu Waterfall.

Qing dynasty Last imperial family to rule China (1644–1911), a Manchurian dynasty that overthrew the Ming and was in turn replaced by Sun Yat-sen's Nationalist Party.

Republic of China (ROC) Taiwan's official name.

Sakyamuni Name given to the historical Buddha.

Shan Mountain.

Shi City or municipality.

Shophouse Chinese-style house, long and narrow, with a store in the front and living quarters at the back.

Si Buddhist temple.

Stele Freestanding stone tablet carved with Chinese characters.

Sutra Sacred Buddhist text.

Taiwanese Commonly used to describe the ethnically Fujianese Chinese in Taiwan, and the language they speak. The term "Hoklo" is preferred officially, as technically all citizens on the island are Taiwanese.

Takasago Former Japanese colonial name for Taiwan, meaning "the country of high mountains".

Tian Heaven or the sky.

Tongyong Pinyin System of transliterating Chinese script into roman characters favoured by Taiwan's DPP government, devised by a Taiwanese professor in 1998.

Tsua bing Shaved ice. Popular Taiwanese snack.

Wade Giles Antiquated system of transliterating Chinese script into Roman characters, formerly used in Taiwan and still the preferred method of writing names for many of its citizens.

Waiguoren Foreigner.

Waishengren Mainlander. Resented by younger generations who feel the term suggests they are less Taiwanese.

Wang King or lord.

Wenquan Hot spring.

Yuanzhumin Official Chinese name for Taiwan's indigenous tribes, meaning "original inhabitants".

Zhongshan Chinese name for Sun Yat-sen. Common street name.

Zhongzheng Chinese name for Chiang Kai-shek. Common street name.

Travel store

ROUGH GUIDES Complete Listing

For more information go to www.roughguides.com

ROUGH
GUIDES

Small print and

Index

A Rough Guide to Rough Guides

Published in 1982, the first Rough Guide – to Greece – was a student scheme that became a publishing phenomenon. Mark Ellingham, a recent graduate in English from Bristol University, had been travelling in Greece the previous summer and couldn't find the right guidebook. With a small group of friends he wrote his own guide, combining a highly contemporary, journalistic style with a thoroughly practical approach to travellers' needs.

The immediate success of the book spawned a series that rapidly covered dozens of destinations. And, in addition to impecunious backpackers, Rough Guides soon acquired a much broader and older readership that relished the guides' wit and inquisitiveness as much as their enthusiastic, critical approach and value-for-money ethos.

SMALL PRINT

These days, Rough Guides include recommendations from shoestring to luxury and cover more than 200 destinations around the globe, including almost every country in the Americas and Europe, more than half of Africa and most of Asia and Australasia. Our ever-growing team of authors and photographers is spread all over the world, particularly in Europe, the USA and Australia.

In the early 1990s, Rough Guides branched out of travel, with the publication of Rough Guides to World Music, Classical Music and the Internet. All three have become benchmark titles in their fields, spearheading the publication of a wide range of books under the Rough Guide name.

Including the travel series, Rough Guides now number more than 350 titles, covering: phrasebooks, waterproof maps, music guides from Opera to Heavy Metal, reference works as diverse as Conspiracy Theories and Shakespeare, and popular culture books from iPods to Poker. Rough Guides also produce a series of more than 120 World Music CDs in partnership with World Music Network.

Visit www.roughguides.com to see our latest publications.

Rough Guide travel images are available for commercial licensing at www.roughguidespictures.com

Rough Guide credits

Text editor: Andy Turner
Layout: Ajay Verma
Cartography: Ashutosh Bharti
Picture editor: Mark Thomas
Production: Katherine Owers
Proofreader: Martin Moore
Cover design: Chloë Roberts
Photographer: Brice Minnigh
Editorial: London Kate Berens, Claire Saunders, Ruth Blackmore, Polly Thomas, Richard Lim, Alison Murchie, Karoline Densley, Keith Drew, Edward Aves, Nikki Birrell, Alice Park, Sarah Eno, Lucy White, Jo Kirby, James Smart, Natasha Foges, Roisin Cameron, Joe Staines, Duncan Clark, Peter Buckley, Matthew Milton, Tracy Hopkins, Ruth Tidball; New York Andrew Rosenberg, Steven Horak, AnneLise Sorensen, Amy Hegarty, April Isaacs, Ella Steim, Anna Owens, Joseph Petta, Sean Mahoney
Design & Pictures: London Scott Stickland, Dan May, Diana Jarvis, Jj Luck, Harriet Mills, Chloë Roberts, Nicole Newman; Delhi Umesh Aggarwal, Jessica Subramanian, Ankur Guha, Pradeep Thapliyal, Sachin Tanwar, Anita Singh,

Madhavi Singh, Karen d'Souza
Production: Aimee Hampson
Cartography: London Maxine Repath, Ed Wright, Katie Lloyd-Jones; Delhi Jai Prakash Mishra, Rajesh Chhibber, Rajesh Mishra, Animesh Pathak, Jasbir Sandhu, Karobi Gogoi, Amod Singh, Alakananda Bhattacharya, Athokpam Jotinkumar
Online: New York Jennifer Gold, Kristin Mingrone; Delhi Manik Chauhan, Narender Kumar, Rakesh Kumar, Amit Kumar, Amit Verma, Rahul Kumar, Ganesh Sharma, Debojit Borah
Marketing & Publicity: London Liz Statham, Niki Hanmer, Louise Maher, Jess Carter, Vanessa Godden, Anna Paynton, Rachel Sprackett; New York Geoff Colquitt, Megan Kennedy, Katy Ball; Delhi Reem Khokhar
Special Projects Editor: Philippa Hopkins
Manager India: Punita Singh
Series Editor: Mark Ellingham
Reference Director: Andrew Lockett
Publishing Coordinator: Megan McIntyre
Publishing Director: Martin Dunford

Publishing information

This first edition published April 2007 by Rough Guides Ltd,
80 Strand, London WC2R 0RL
345 Hudson St, 4th Floor,
New York, NY 10014, USA
14 Local Shopping Centre, Panchsheel Park,
New Delhi 110017, India
Distributed by the Penguin Group
Penguin Books Ltd,
80 Strand, London WC2R 0RL
Penguin Putnam, Inc.
375 Hudson Street, NY 10014, USA
Penguin Group (Australia)
250 Camberwell Road, Camberwell,
Victoria 3124, Australia
Penguin Books Canada Ltd,
10 Alcorn Avenue, Toronto, Ontario,
Canada M4V 1E4
Penguin Group (NZ)
67 Apollo Drive, Mairangi Bay, Auckland 1310,
New Zealand
Cover concept by Peter Dyer.

Typeset in Bembo and Helvetica to an original design by Henry Iles.
Printed in Italy bt LegoPrint S.p.A
© Rough Guides 2007

No part of this book may be reproduced in any form without permission from the publisher except for the quotation of brief passages in reviews.

584pp includes index

A catalogue record for this book is available from the British Library

ISBN: 9-78184-353-527-0

The publishers and authors have done their best to ensure the accuracy and currency of all the information in The Rough Guide to Taiwan, however, they can accept no responsibility for any loss, injury, or inconvenience sustained by any traveller as a result of information or advice contained in the guide.

1 3 5 7 9 8 6 4 2

Help us update

We've gone to a lot of effort to ensure that the first edition of The Rough Guide to Taiwan is accurate and up-to-date. However, things change – places get "discovered", opening hours are notoriously fickle, restaurants and rooms raise prices or lower standards. If you feel we've got it wrong or left something out, we'd like to know, and if you can remember the address, the price, the time, the phone number, so much the better. We'll credit all contributions, and send a copy of the next edition (or any other Rough Guide if you prefer) for the best letters. Everyone who writes to us and isn't already a subscriber will receive a copy of our full-colour thrice-yearly newsletter. Please mark letters: "Rough Guide Taiwan Update" and send to: Rough Guides, 80 Strand, London WC2R 0RL, or Rough Guides, 4th Floor, 345 Hudson St, New York, NY 10014. Or send an email to mail@roughguides.com
Have your questions answered and tell others about your trip at
www.roughguides.atinfopop.com

SMALL PRINT

Acknowledgements

Stephen: thanks to Christine Lai, Ting Li Li and Jeff Wu at the Taiwan Tourism Bureau, Chen Yu Gui, Cheng Li Chen for her insights into Chinese religion, Guu Yung-yuan at Lion's Head Mountain, Gary Ho in Meinong, Tim Hsu Ting-fa for all his help in Puli and Sun Moon Lake, Charlie Huang for his time and expertise in Lugang, Enzo Huang on the southwest coast, Goran Kuo for everything (including the scooter), Lee Chyen Yee for the extra research, Lin Chan-hui, Lin Cheng-huang, Chelle Liu and Christine Tai in Alishan, Mimi Liu for her hospitality in Taichung, Elisa Lu in Tainan, Lu Jian Cheng, Muk Na Na M'o for his invaluable insights into Tsou culture, Shih Chao-hul and Louis Chang on the north coast, Keith Tsai in Kaohsiung, Karen Tsao in Taichung, Melissa Su in Taipei, Sylvia Sun at the National Palace Musuem, Shozo Tateishi and Eiji Yoshikawa for a Japanese perspective, Keith Tsai in Kaohsiung, Anne Wang, Constancia Wu, Yang Ching-yun for being so generous in Keelung, Ya Ting in Kaohsiung, Yvonne Yao in Taichung, Jade Yeh for all her help in the south and lastly Tiffany Wu, without whose support this book would not have been possible.

Brice: thanks to Christine Lai and Ting Li Li at the Taiwan Tourism Bureau for help with paperwork and visas; Alex Hsu of the Taiwan Visitors Association's Hong Kong office for sourcing missing photos; Chelle Liu, Jovial Shen, Keng-Ku Lu and especially Christine Tai of the Alishan National Scenic Area for all the logistical support; Andy Chang for the hospitality and exhaustive tour of Ershuei; Tim Hsu Ting-fa and Robert Yu Chiu-po for information and updates on Sun Moon Lake; Jeff Sun in Dasi for advice on seasonal surf breaks; Mao-Hsung Peng, Allen Hsu and especially Yi-Ling Sung of Shei-Pa National Park for keeping me updated on trail conditions and issuing climbing permits on short notice; Shun-Hsing Yang and Uie-Liang Liou of Yushan National Park for prompt assistance with climbing permits; Sandra Yu of Taroko National Park for trail updates; Lily Lee for the lowdown on Taitung and the southeast coast; Seven Chan for the Penghu culture lecture; Julie Larson and the Taichung crew for the support and good times; Susana Tsui for helping provide emergency refuge; Michael Lawes for climbing some of the highest mountains with me; Action Asia Editor-in-Chief Steve White for his continued advocacy of Taiwan as an adventure-travel destination; Nichole Chan for invaluable assistance with Chinese-language boxes and insights into the vagaries of various Chinese dialects; Micah Stover for her patience and understanding; and to the hundreds of unnamed Taiwanese who gave directions, explanations and free rides to a weather-beaten travel writer in need.

Photo credits

Index

Map entries are in colour.

I

INDEX

I

INDEX

579

Map symbols

maps are listed in the full index using coloured text

– – – –	International boundary		⌂	Mountain refuge/lodge
– – –	Chapter division boundary		✦	Place of interest
═══	Highway		@	Internet access
══	Major road		ⓘ	Information office
──	Minor road		✉	Post office
──	Pedestrianized street		ℂ	Phone office
──	Unpaved road		⊞	Hospital
▬▬	Railway line		T	Toilets
-----	Path		🛢	Fuel station
– –	Ferry route		♦	Museum
──	River/coast		🏛	Monument
▬▬▬	Wall		∴	Ruin
–Ⓜ–	Metro station & line		⁜	Gardens
– Ⓜ –	Metro station & line (under construction)		🏛	Stately home/palace
●----●	Cable car & station		⍟	Lighthouse
⅏	Cliff		⍚	Fortress
⅍	Rocks		■	Tower
⌇	Crater		⊙	Statue
⌖	Mountain range		⌂	Observatory
▲	Peak		✂	Battlefield
⚓	Viewpoint		⊼	Picnic area
⌂	Cave		⍟	Beach
⌇	Waterfall		⤚	Snorkelling/diving area
⌇	Surf area		⌇	Whisky distillery
⌇	Spring		⌂	Monastery
☾	Sand dune		⌇	Chinese temple
⌇	Banyan tree		⌇	Hindu temple
–⁄–	Dam		⍤	Mosque
⌣	Bridge		⌂	Buddhist temple
⊠	Gate		⌇	Pagoda
⌒	Arch		⊓	Shrine
⚓	River boat/ferry		⊞	Church
★	Bus stop		■	Building
ℙ	Parking		▭	Market
✈	Airport		◯	Stadium
✗	Airport-domestic		⊞	Christian cemetery
◉	Accommodation		▨	Park
▣	Restaurant/bar		▨	Beach
⚕	Campsite			

WHEREVER YOU ARE,

WHEREVER YOU'RE GOING

WE'VE GOT YOU COVERED!

Rough Guides Travel Insurance

Visit our website at www.roughguides.com/insurance or call:

- UK: 0800 083 9507
- Spain: 900 997 149
- Australia: 1300 669 999
- New Zealand: 0800 55 99 11
- Worldwide: +44 870 890 2843
- USA, call toll free on: 1 800 749 4922

Please quote our ref: *Rough Guides books*

Cover for over 46 different nationalities and available in 4 different languages.

Travel Insurance

ROUGH
GUIDES